RESPONDING TO THE SCREEN
Reception and Reaction Processes

COMMUNICATION

A series of volumes edited by
Dolf Zillmann and Jennings Bryant

RESPONDING TO THE SCREEN
Reception and Reaction Processes

Edited by
Jennings Bryant
Dolf Zillmann
University of Alabama

LEA LAWRENCE ERLBAUM ASSOCIATES, PUBLISHERS
1991 Hillsdale, New Jersey   Hove and London

Lawrence Erlbaum Associates, Inc., Publishers
365 Broadway
Hillsdale, New Jersey 07642

Library of Congress Cataloging-in-Publication Data

Responding to the screen: reception and reaction processes / edited
    by Jennings Bryant, Dolf Zillmann.
        p.   cm. – (Communication)
    Includes bibliographical references and indexes.
    ISBN 0-8058-0033-6, ISBN 0-8058-1044-7 (p)
    1. Mass media–Psychological aspects. I. Bryant, Jennings.
II. Zillmann, Dolf. III. Series: Communication (Hillsdale, N.J.)
P96.P75R4   1991
    302.23–dc20   90-46695
Printed in the United States of America   CIP
10 9 8 7 6 5 4 3 2 1

Contents

Contributors

Daniel R. Anderson, Department of Psychology, University of Massachusetts-Amherst, Amherst, MA 01003

Jennings Bryant, College of Communication, University of Alabama, Tuscaloosa, AL 35487

John Burns, Department of Psychology, University of Massachusetts-Amherst, Amherst, MA 01003

Joanne Cantor, Center for Communication Research, University of Wisconsin-Madison, Madison, WI 53706

Peter B. Crabb, Department of Psychology, Westchester University, Westchester, PA 19383

Laurence W. Etling, College of Journalism and Mass Communication, University of Georgia, Athens, GA 30602

Russell H. Fazio, Department of Psychology, Indiana University, Bloomington, IN 47405

Diane E. Field, Department of Psychology, University of Massachusetts-Amherst, Amherst, MA 01003

Jeffrey H. Goldstein, Department of Psychology, Temple University, Philadelphia, PA 19122

Barrie Gunter, Independent Broadcasting Authority, 70 Brompton Road, London SW3 1EY England

Cynthia Hoffner, Department of Communication, Illinois State University, Normal, IL 61761

Maurya MacNeil, Department of Psychology, Ohio State University, Columbus, OH 43204

Edward L. Palmer, Department of Psychology, Davidson College, Davidson, NC 28036

Steven C. Rockwell, College of Communication, University of Alabama, Tuscaloosa, AL 35487

David M. Sanbonmatsu, Department of Psychology, University of Utah, Salt Lake City, UT 84112

Barry L. Sherman, Department of Telecommunication, University of Georgia, Athens, GA 30602

Ron Tamborini, Department of Communication, Michigan State University, East Lansing, MI 48824

James Weaver, Department of Communication, Auburn University, Auburn, AL 36849

Dolf Zillmann, College of Communication, University of Alabama, Tuscaloosa, AL 35487

Preface

During the 1980s, the contributions of several disparate disciplines concerned with human behavior began to fuse in productive ways. One domain that has benefited greatly from such synthesis has been the study of the psychological processes involved in communicating via the mass media. This area of inquiry has been blessed with substantial attention from cognitive psychologists and sociologists, social psychologists, linguists, communicologists, and computer scientists. Moreover, special attention has been devoted of late to the study of the *processes* involved in consuming media messages—that is, in viewing those ubiquitous stimuli whose abundance so characterizes life in our Information Age.

Historically, much of the research on mass communication has created a tradition that has been concerned primarily with media effects—that is, investigations into the psychological and social impact of consuming media messages on later behavior. More recently, however, research attention has shifted to examining media message consumption per se. Such attentional shifts spawned investigations into what messages are selected under different emotional and situational conditions,[1] polls of audience members in attempts to determine why they have selected the fare they have chosen to watch,[2] among other things.

It would seem that a natural next step in this evolution from effects to process-

---

[1]See for example, Kubey, R., & Csikszentmihalyi, M. (1990). *Television and the quality of life: How viewing shapes everyday experience*. Hillsdale, NJ: Lawrence Erlbaum Associates and Zillmann, D., & Bryant, J. (1985). *Selective exposure to communication*. Hillsdale, NJ: Lawrence Erlbaum Associates.

[2]See for example, Rosengren, K. E., Wenner, L. A., & Palmgreen, P. (Eds.). (1985). *Media gratifications research: Current perspectives*. Beverly Hills, CA: Sage.

es is a more detailed and microanalytical analysis of the psychological processes involved in receiving and reacting to electronic media messages. This domain would include investigations into those psychological processes that fall temporally between the process of selecting media messages for consumption and assessments of whatever processes mediate the long-term impact such message consumption may have on consumers' subsequent behavior. Fortunately, several investigators have been focusing considerable research attention on just these dimensions of "responding to the screen," and it is their pioneering work that this volume addresses.

The chapters in this book have been organized into two sections. Part I contains descriptions and explications of some of the critical psychological processes involved in viewing and responding to electronic media messages. Chapters in this section address attention processes, comprehension processes, construct accessibility, character perception, physiological arousal, empathy, fright reactions, online versus offline assessment methods, and more macroanalytic cognitive models of these processes.

The first chapter in this section, by Daniel Anderson and John Burns, begins with one of the early stages of information processing, "Paying Attention to Television." In this chapter, attention to television is first defined; then visual, auditory, and intensive aspects of attention to television are considered; and, finally, a discussion of theoretical orientations and lingering research problems is offered.

In chapter 2, "Children's Comprehension Processes: From Piaget to Public Policy," Edward Palmer and Maurya MacNeil take a developmental perspective on the issue of understanding television. A distinctive feature of this chapter is its comparison of Piagetian with information-processing approaches to the study of comprehension.

Media consumers' interpretations of the messages of film or television appear to be greatly influenced by the constructs stored in memory, which users call forth to help them interpret media content. In chapter 3, David Sanbonmatsu and Russell Fazio indicate the determinants and consequences of construct accessibility and their implications for processing media fare.

In "Perceiving and Responding to Mass Media Characters" (chapter 4), Cynthia Hoffner and Joanne Cantor examine the ways viewers form impressions of media characters and respond to characters' experiences as depicted on television and film. Included in this chapter is a section in which the ways specific viewer characteristics mediate perceptions of media characters are discussed.

Dolf Zillmann's chapter on "Television Viewing and Physiological Arousal" (chapter 5) presents various conceptualizations of arousal, then discusses the measurement of arousal, and finally considers how various theoretical models and available research evidence indicate how we must integrate arousal, emotion, and affect into our theoretical models if we are to more fully understand and assess media effects.

In chapter 6, on "Empathy: Affect from Bearing Witness to the Emotions of

Others," Dolf Zillmann tackles one of the most misunderstood and abused constructs in mass media research. A highlight of this chapter is the presentation and discussion of a new theoretical model of empathy.

During recent years, considerable research effort has gone into determining the prevalence and intensity with which anxiety is experienced as a result of exposure to media drama; and much theoretical speculation has been offered to explain why audiences should enjoy seeing frightening media fare. In "Fright Responses to Mass Media Productions" (chapter 7), Joanne Cantor examines this active research domain.

Chapter 8 provides somewhat of a change of pace. Daniel Anderson and Diane Field review and critique methodological aspects of laboratory and field research into reception and reaction processes in "Online and Offline Assessments of the Television Audience."

The final chapter of this section offers a more macroanalytic look at trends in information-processing research in mass communication. Jennings Bryant and Steven Rockwell examine some of the assumptions and contributions of the cognitive sciences in chapter 9, "Evolving Cognitive Models in Mass Communication Reception Processes."

Part II contains what might be considered the more "applied" chapters of this volume, although much theory construction is offered in these pages as well. In these chapters, the basic research findings regarding reception and reaction processes are applied to considerations of the viewing of several relatively distinct program genres. Also included are examinations of the processes involved in producing the social and psychological effects such viewing purportedly yields. The types of programming considered include the following: news and public affairs, comedy, suspense, mystery, horror, erotica, sports, and music television.

Chapter 10, by Barrie Gunter, "Responding to News and Public Affairs," considers responses to a variety of types of informational programming. A distinctive feature of this chapter is its integration of industry with academic and laboratory with survey research.

Comedy elicits complicated reactions from media consumers, and understanding its uses and effects requires the integration of cognitive and affective process models to explain the appeal of and reactions to its highly formatted messages. In chapter 11, Dolf Zillmann and Jennings Bryant present longitudinal normative data on audiences' receptivity to comedy and then offer theoretical rationales and research evidence to explain its persistent popularity on television and in films.

In "The Logic of Suspense and Mystery" (chapter 12), Dolf Zillmann offers systematic conceptualizations of both types of dramatic media fare. Then theory and research evidence are integrated into novel information theory-based models that are offered to explain audience members' enjoyment of, and complex reactions to, programs and films containing elements of suspense and mystery.

The horror film and the increasingly popular horror television program genre have come under much scholarly scrutiny during the past decade. In chapter 13,

"Responding to Horror: Determinants of Exposure and Appeal," Ron Tamborini reviews this research evidence and offers a synthesis of the findings.

Most scholarly considerations of erotic media messages focus on the social and psychological impact of consuming such fare. Although James Weaver reviews theory and research in this tradition in chapter 14, "Responding to Erotica: Perceptional Processing and Dispositional Implications," he also offers a fresh "processes" as well as the more traditional "effects" perspective to the topic.

In "The Social Psychology of Watching Sports: From Iluim to Living Room," Peter Crabb and Jeffrey Goldstein (chapter 15) first provide an historical overview of sports spectatorship from ancient Greece and Rome to the present. They then systematically examine the reception processes and cognitive and behavioral effects that have been identified by investigations into the consumption of this reality-based genre of entertainment media fare.

Examinations of the final genre being considered have typically generated more heat than light. Barry Sherman and Laurence Etling (chapter 16) provide a refreshingly balanced treatment of the topic in "Perceiving and Processing Music Television."

We hope that readers of this volume will recognize the rapid "maturing" process that has been experienced of late in the various disciplines represented by the authors of these chapters. A scant decade ago, very little was known about the subject matter of many of these chapters. Today, we know a great deal about the reception and reaction processes that occupy so much of our leisure time in modern society. At the very least we can say that we are beginning to understand some of the very basic processes that undergird the ways by which citizens of modern society gain entertainment and information.

And yet, so much remains to be explored. If the Information Age is to be characterized in part by a "Sovereign Consumer" of electronic media messages, it is imperative that we better understand reception and reaction processes. We seem to be underway, and the journey promises to be exciting and rewarding.

Jennings Bryant
Dolf Zillmann

PART

I

Reception and
Reaction Processes

CHAPTER

1

Paying Attention to Television

Daniel R. Anderson
John Burns
University of Massachusetts

It is surprising that there has been so little investigation into the nature of attention to television. Of the many thousands of empirical studies of television viewing and its effects, only a few dozen have included attention as a central focus, and a relatively few others have included attention as a subsidiary consideration. The lack of research is surprising for several reasons: (a) Television's great effectiveness as a medium of mass communication is often attributed to its power of eliciting and maintaining attention; words such as "mesmerizing" are commonly used to describe this power. (b) Attention is often assumed to play a role in television's impact. Most directly, TV is frequently declared as affecting attentional abilities, such as reducing children's "attention spans." (c) Most of television's presumed impact, of course, is due to the content retained by the viewers. It is obvious, however, that content is not uniformly absorbed by viewers; rather, there are numerous levels of selection that go on as part of television use. Selective attention is surely an aspect of this process, and is therefore a potentially crucial intervening factor in the effects of content. (d) Finally, from the practical point of view of the television producer or sponsor, eliciting and maintaining attention is an essential ingredient in gaining an audience.

Despite a lack of widespread research effort, several research groups have systematically examined attention to television since the mid-1970s, and other researchers have provided additional information. The dozen years of research have provided consistent descriptive data on some aspects of attention to television and a great deal has been learned. This chapter provides a summary of the major findings. After some definitional considerations we examine visual, auditory, and intensive aspects of attention to television. We conclude with a brief mention of theoretical approaches to the problem and then indicate major areas in which research is needed.

Defining Attention to Television

Any general definition of attention will be somewhat unsatisfactory until a scientific consensus has been established on the fundamental nature of human information processing. Without such a consensus, definitions must be provisional. For our purposes here, we consider attention to be a set of overt and covert perceptual and orienting processes by means of which information becomes available to central information-processing activities. Attention thus serves to channel some information to be processed by central cognitive functions, whereas other information is excluded. The issue of how attention is controlled and directed provides a fundamental problem for psychology long associated with the difficult issues of will and consciousness (e.g., James, 1890; Pillsbury, 1908), problems with which psychology has not always been prepared to cope (cf. Johnston & Dark, 1986; Neisser, 1967).

Mainstream Research on Attention

In contrast to recent optimism expressed by Reeves, Thorson, and Schleuder (1986) to the effect that general research on attention can help cast light on attention to television, we find that such research has had relatively little to offer. Unfortunately, most research and theory on attention concerns stimuli and settings that are not particularly relevant to the television viewing situation. Stimuli are usually simple, repetitive, unimodal, and not particularly meaningful to the experimental subjects; time courses of stimulation often involve durations of milliseconds to a few seconds; and the context usually involves repetitive, boring, speeded tasks in laboratory settings (see Johnston & Dark, 1986; Parasuraman & Davies, 1984, for reviews).

Television viewing, in contrast, involves complex multimodal and meaningful stimulation experienced over a time period of minutes to hours. Television is usually experienced in a familiar, comfortable, and comforting environment (i.e., the viewer's home) and rarely does the viewer have a specific externally assigned goal in viewing. With a few exceptions, then, principles of attention derived from nontelevision investigations, as interesting as they may be in their own right, do not have obvious face value for understanding the nature of attention to television. As such, researchers studying attention to television have largely been on their own, developing methodologies and theoretical concepts appropriate to television viewing. The difficulties of such methodological development probably account for the relatively small amount of research on attention to television.

comes increasingly engaged; or (b) attentional state is constant within a look but varies between looks—in this case the increasing conditional survival probability curves described by Anderson et al. (1979) are statistical artifacts produced by aggregating data from these varying states (Mendelson, 1983). Situation B is unlikely because the lognormal distribution cannot be created by such an aggregation of exponential distributions in which the conditional probability of survival does not change (Proschan, 1963). The major implication of this fact is that a dynamic process changes during the time course of a look and presumably underlies the maintenance of looks. We further consider this issue in the section on intensity of attention.

Individual Differences in Looking at Television. There are consistent individual differences in looking at television. Anderson et al. (1979) noted that there were session-to-session correlations of about .50 for percent looking and average look length for preschool children who viewed a variety of children's programs and commercials. Three individual difference variables—intelligence, age, and gender—have been implicated.

In laboratory studies brighter children tend to have higher levels of looking at television although the correlations are not large (e.g., Field & Anderson, 1985). From our work observing TV viewing in homes (Anderson, Field, Collins, Lorch, & Nathan, 1985), we found a correlation of .26 between percent looking at TV and IQ among the 5-year-olds who were the focus of our research (unpublished analysis based on 99 children each observed over 10-day periods). Aletha Huston and John Wright at the University of Kansas also found positive correlations of IQ and looking in their investigations with children (Huston, personal communication, April 24, 1987). More extreme IQ differences are also reflected in different levels of looking at television: Grieve and Williamson (1977) found that mentally retarded individuals looked less at TV than normals, and that, among the mentally retarded subjects, the lower functioning individuals looked less than the higher functioning individuals.

Age contributes to individual differences in looking, especially during early childhood. Numerous laboratory investigations have found a great increase in looking at television from infancy to 5 years of age (see Anderson & Smith, 1984), and this increase has been verified in observations of home TV viewing (Anderson, Lorch, Field, Collins, & Nathan, 1986). Looking at TV levels off at between 60% and 70% during the school-age years and significantly declines among adults (Anderson et al., 1986).

We suggest that the age and IQ findings reflect the same general phenomenon: Up to a certain point, looking at television increases with increasing comprehensibility of the TV program (a hypothesis with empirical support, as described later). Among young children and the mentally retarded, brighter individuals find the programming more comprehensible as do older children. Beyond some further point, however, virtually all TV is comprehensible, as among adults. We would therefore expect no relationship of IQ and visual attention to TV among adults. To our knowledge, no such analysis has been reported.

Anderson et al. (1986) found that although there were no gender differences in looking at television among children observed at home, adult men looked at the TV a greater percentage of the time than did women. Bechtel, Achelpohl, and Akers (1972), without providing details, observed a similar effect. Although laboratory studies with children often find no gender differences in levels of looking, where such differences are found they are in the direction of boys looking more than girls (Alvarez, Huston, Wright, & Kerkman, 1988). It is possible, therefore, that there is some general tendency for males to look at television more than females. At this writing, however, the appropriate meta-analyses investigating this hypothesis have yet to be reported.

In addition to these standard individual difference variables, pathological states may also influence levels of visual attention to television. Lorch et al. (1987) found that school-aged children diagnosed with Attention Deficit Disorder (ADD) looked at an educational TV program about half as much as normal controls. The ADD children looked at the TV as frequently as the normals, but their looks averaged only half the duration. To our knowledge, other pathologies that involve attentional disorders (e.g., schizophrenia) have not been studied relative to looking at TV (see Sprafkin, Gadow, & Grayson, 1984, for a review).

Influence of the Local Environment on Looking.   It is obvious that viewing context influences looking at TV; one would expect, for example, looking to be less in a noisy singles bar than in a quiet home environment. Indeed, looking by children is reduced in a social context (Anderson, Lorch, Smith, Bradford, & Levin, 1981) and looking is especially reduced by the availability of alternative activities such as toys with which to play (Lorch, Anderson, & Levin, 1979; Pezdek & Hartman, 1983). The social environment also provides an attentional synergy: Anderson et al. (1981) found that a child's looks at TV lead nonlooking peers to initiate looking, and similarly, a child who terminates a look at the TV induces other children to terminate their looks.

Task demands can influence looking: Children who are told they will be tested on their knowledge of the TV program increase their looking during those parts of the program without informative audio tracks (Field & Anderson, 1985). During the evening, perhaps because there are fewer demands on people at home to engage in chores and other activities, Allen (1965) reported that looking at TV tends to increase. Preliminary analyses of our home observations (Anderson, 1987) support this notion insofar as adults stay in the viewing room for longer periods of time as the day wanes so the opportunity for extended looking increases.

Program Content

It is not surprising that looking varies with TV program content. Allen (1965) noted that viewers at home looked less at commercials than other fare, and Bechtel et al. (1972) found that adults looked most at movies and least at commercials.

Children looked most at children's programs and least at sports. Boundaries between major units of content produce changes in looking: If a viewer is not looking at the time of a content change, he or she is likely to start looking. Conversely, if a viewer is looking at the time of the content change, he or she is likely to stop looking (Alwitt, Anderson, Lorch, & Levin, 1980). Beyond such broad demonstrations that looking varies with content, a number of investigations have been directed at determining in more detail the characteristics of TV programming that elicit and maintain looking. These investigations have examined humor, program comprehensibility, and a group of television attributes called *formal features*. All this work has been done with children.

Humor.   Only one investigation has examined the influence of humor on looking. Zillmann, Williams, Bryant, Boynton, and Wolf (1980) experimentally provided humorous inserts in educational messages. These inserts increased 5- and 6-year-olds' looking and also their acquisition of information from the educational messages, even though the inserts were not related to the messages.

Comprehensibility.   The interest in comprehensibility began when Lorch et al. (1979) observed that experimentally halving 5-year-olds' looking at "Sesame Street" (by allowing them to play with toys during the program) did not reduce their comprehension. They also noted that comprehension was correlated with looking; that is, children tended to correctly answer comprehension questions if they were looking at the TV at the time the information necessary to answer the question was presented. This effect held even for purely auditory information. Arguing that for young children comprehensibility is an important determinant of attention, Lorch et al. suggested that the children allowed to play with toys distributed their looking throughout the program strategically; that is, they selectively looked at those parts of the program most readily comprehended. Lorch et al. further argued that the strategy involved monitoring the audio for cues to comprehensible content. When such cues were detected, the child would then pay full attention to the TV program. Because auditory comprehension was correlated with looking, Lorch et al. suggested that, when not looking, the child tended not to listen at a level of full linguistic comprehension.

The notion that young children strategically deploy their attention in order to selectively view comprehensible content did not correspond well with the popular idea that children passively attend to television. The simple notion of passive attention is that looking is controlled by visual features of the TV program such as movement and scene changes (cf. Emery & Emery, 1976; Lesser, 1977; Mander, 1978; Moody, 1980; Singer, 1980; Winn, 1977). The discrepancy between the popular ideas and the strategic deployment hypothesis of Lorch et al. (1979) led to an additional series of investigations. Pezdek and Hartman (1983) replicated the essential findings of Lorch et al. (1979), indicating that the ability of children to effectively divide their looking between toy play and TV viewing is reasonably robust.

Anderson, Lorch, Field, and Sanders (1981) compared looking by preschoolers during "immediate" dialogue (in which the referent of the dialogue is concretely present) to looking during "nonimmediate" dialogue (in which the referent is abstract or displaced in time and space). They predicted that nonimmediate dialogue should be less comprehensible to preschoolers and that attention should therefore be lower. The results confirmed this prediction.

In a second study, Anderson et al. (1981) distorted the comprehensibility of "Sesame Street" segments while maintaining the visual and auditory appearance of the segments. They did this by randomly rearranging scenes, using backward dialogue (original voices), or by using foreign dialogue (professionally dubbed). They predicted that if preschoolers preferentially look at comprehensible content, that they should look more during normal segments than during distorted segments. This should occur despite the fact that the distortions did not affect features such as movement, animation, scene changes, and others that have been hypothesized as primary determinants of young children's passive attention. The results confirmed the prediction at ages 2 and 3.5 years, and for dialogue distortions at all ages. At 5 years the randomly rearranged scenes had only a marginal effect on looking. This study was subsequently repeated by Pingree (1986) who observed 3.5, 5, and 6.5-year-olds. The results were replicated except that no effect of random rearrangement of scenes was found in the two older groups. Lorch and Castle (in press) also repeated the study using 5-year-olds; again the results were replicated except that there was no effect of randomly rearranging scenes. The results from three experiments, then, are quite consistent: dialogue distortions reduced looking at all ages. Randomly rearranging scenes, however, reduced looking only in children under 5 years. It is not yet clear why older children are more likely to persist in attending under conditions of reordered and somewhat illogical scene sequences. It is possible that older children are more confident in their abilities to infer a logical structure in what is apparently familiar and ordinarily comprehensible material ("Sesame Street") and are therefore more persistent. Language distortions, however, are easily recognized as incomprehensible and so the children simply terminate looking.

Recently, Campbell, Wright, and Huston (1987) systematically varied the comprehensibility of a set of nutritional public service announcements (PSAs). They employed several levels of sentence complexity, abstractness, and amount of message redundancy. The easily comprehended segments were 90 seconds in length, the intermediate segments were 60 seconds, and the difficult segments were 30 seconds. Campbell et al. (1987) found only a small and nonsignificant effect of comprehensibility on looking by 5- and 6-year-olds, thus seemingly providing conflicting findings with the foregoing studies. Given the confounding of segment length with comprehensibility in the Campbell et al. (1987) experiment, it is quite possible that the difficulty of comprehension in the 30-second segments was not fully recognized by the children until the segments were almost over, thus producing a very small or null effect. It is also possible of course, that the Campbell et al. (1987) children were persistent in looking at difficult material in the same way as children 5 years and older with rearranged scenes.

Taken together, the studies indicate that young children are sensitive to the comprehensibility of television content and preferentially look at material that is more easily understood. Children 5 years of age and older, however, are more tolerant of content that is somewhat difficult to understand and may persist longer in looking at somewhat less comprehensible programming.

Formal Features. The term *formal features* was coined in the mid-1970s by Aletha Huston and John Wright of the University of Kansas. It refers to program characteristics that "can be defined independently from the content of a television program. That is, they are program attributes that result from production and editing techniques, and they are applicable to many types of content" (Huston & Wright, 1983, p. 36). Huston and Wright have pointed out that, in principle, formal features can play numerous roles in the cognitive processing of television including influencing looking at TV. Such influences could come about by eliciting primitive orienting reactions (formal features such as visual movement or visual novelty), by marking important content (e.g., "sneaking up on you" music), by helping the viewer parse the content (e.g., techniques of montage that indicate continuity or discontinuity in content), and by marking comprehensible content (e.g., children's voices would tend to indicate the content is "for kids").

A number of studies have shown that children's looking is indeed influenced by formal features. Looking increases or decreases in the presence of a variety of features, and the direction of the effects has been quite consistent across investigations (e.g., Alwitt et al., 1980; Anderson & Levin, 1976; Calvert, Huston, Watkins, & Wright, 1982; Campbell et al., 1987; Susman, 1978). Although some visual features maintain looking (e.g., movement), others terminate looking (e.g., long zooms). Overall, however, auditory features appear to be the most influential, probably because they can be perceived regardless of whether the viewer is visually attentive (Alwitt et al., 1980). The most powerful of the auditory features include auditory changes (from one sound source to another, e.g., man's voice to music), sound effects (positive), male voices (negative), children's voices (positive), and peculiar voices (positive). The influence of music is inconsistent and appears to depend considerably on tempo and other factors (Alwitt et al., 1980; Anderson & Levin, 1976; Wakshlag, Reitz, & Zillmann, 1982).

It has often been supposed that the pacing of formal features also affects looking at TV and that young children would be especially attracted to rapid pacing. Evidence of this, however, has been surprisingly difficult to obtain. Unfortunately, because investigators used varied definitions of pace, inconsistent results are not surprising, and comparisons between studies are hazardous.

Anderson, Levin, and Lorch (1977) created two versions of "Sesame Street" by editing together the most rapidly paced segments or the most slowly paced segments taken from four different programs. No difference in visual attention by 5-year-olds was found. Nathanson (1977) showed retarded teenagers rapid or slowly paced versions of a cartoon. Pacing did not influence looking. Gadberry and Brown (1981) varied the frequency of cuts in specially prepared videotapes concerning social skills. Pacing did not influence looking by mentally retarded adults. Wright et al. (1984) defined pace as rate of scene change and character change in programs with a story format or as rate of segment change in magazine format TV programs. The two types of programs represented a second dimension they referred to as continuity with stories representing high continuity programs and magazine formats ("Sesame Street") representing low continuity programs. Wright et al. (1984) examined visual attention in two age groups (Grades K-1 and 3-4) and found only one condition in which pacing approached significance in affecting attention: for the younger children when watching magazine format programs. In summary, pacing has not been consistently found to influence looking.

Given that some formal features do exert consistent influences on children's looking, the question arises as to how these effects come about. The major competing hypotheses are that the formal features access primitive attentional mechanisms such as the orienting reflex (cf. Reeves et al., 1986; Singer, 1980) or that children learn to look or suppress looking as a consequence of their exposure to television (cf. Anderson & Lorch, 1983; Huston & Wright, 1983).

The learning hypothesis suggests that, through many hours of exposure to television, children would come to associate particular features with general classes of content. Male voices, for example, would be associated with adult-oriented content that, for a variety of reasons, is less comprehensible and less interesting to children. Strategic deployment of attention by children presumably would include looking at those times when content is comprehensible and interesting, and suppressing looking when features predict incomprehensible and uninteresting content.

There is evidence in favor of both hypotheses, indicating that both are at least partially correct. In support of the primitive mechanism hypothesis is the observation by Reeves et al. (1985) that scene changes and movement can produce some aspects of the orienting response (particularly blocking of EEG alpha) in adult viewers. In support of the learning hypothesis, inspection of age trends in the effects of formal features indicates that few formal features have significant relationships to looking at television until after 30 months of age, the age at which children tend to become consistent TV viewers (Levin & Anderson, 1976). Alwitt et al. (1980) argued that if the effects were due to primitive orienting mechanisms, they should be apparent in children under 30 months because the orienting response is well established long before then.

Regardless of the mechanism by which formal features exert their influence over looking, it is clear that appropriate constellations of formal features can enhance learning from television, probably through their influence on attention. Calvert et al. (1982) reported that those children who most differentiated their looking on the basis of formal features also retained the most information. Bryant, Zillmann, and Brown (1983) found that experimentally inserting visual special effects in an educational TV show increased children's looking and also acquisition of information. Campbell et al. (1987) experimentally manipulated formal features in PSAs. The segments produced with features shown in previous work to be effective in increasing looking not only did in fact produce higher levels of looking but also produced greater comprehension.

Because the formal features experimentally manipulated by Bryant et al. (1983) and by Campbell et al. (1987) did not by themselves provide information necessary for comprehension, it can be reasonably suggested that the features increased comprehension because they increased the children's attention. These findings stand in contrast to the Lorch et al. (1979) and Pezdek and Hartman (1983) experiments that halved looking at TV by providing toys. This environmental manipulation did not influence comprehension. It is apparent that manipulations of looking that are internal to the TV program do affect comprehension, whereas manipulations of looking by factors external to the TV program do not necessarily affect comprehension. There appears to be something special about within-program formal features and humor that increase cognitive processing of content and that go beyond looking, per se. We further discuss this issue in the section on intensity of attention to television.

Eye Movements and Fixations

There has, to our knowledge, been no normative research concerning the frequency and extent of eye movements during television viewing. Such normative research would require viewing at normal distances and viewing angles, which in turn vary with the age of the viewer (cf. Nathan, Anderson, Field, & Collins, 1985). The viewer should also be free to turn his or her head away from the TV screen as occurs commonly during normal viewing. The research on eye movements that has been done has fixed the viewer's head with a chin rest or bite bar and required viewing from unusually close distances to the TV screen (Flagg, 1978; Sheena & Flagg, 1978). Slightly less constraining methods have been described by d'Ydewalle, Vanden Abeele, Van Rensbergen, and Coucke (1986), but detailed findings have yet to be published.

Flagg's (1978) and research by others was primarily concerned with children's eye movements during segments from educational programs that teach reading concepts ("Sesame Street" and "Electric Company"). By means of such research, Flagg was able to determine whether children tended to fixate the relevant portions of the screen at critical moments in the segments. She was able to show, for example, that with repetition of program segments, children's fixation times increase and they move their eyes less. By and large, however, the reports from this research are qualitative and do not easily lend themselves to generalizations beyond the specific segments studied.

It is not clear to us that eye movements are particularly relevant to understanding attention to television except in cases where TV programs present script to be read by the viewer. It is our impression that under normal conditions of American television viewing that eye movements are relatively infrequent, and that when they do occur, the fixation moves to a central information point usually planned by the producer or inherent in the action. The eye movements are infrequent, we believe, because television images are usually designed to be uncluttered and easily apprehensible in a single glance. When the fixation point changes, the reason is usually apparent, as when the image changes from one speaker's face to another in the course of a dialogue. If each speaker's face is slightly offset in different directions from the center of the screen, the viewer will change his or her fixation point appropriately. In other cases, fixations obviously follow the focus points of ongoing movements, as in following the ball carrier in a football game. Nevertheless, a normative investigation of eye movements during unconstrained ordinary TV viewing is clearly needed.

AUDITORY ATTENTION

Television is frequently described as a "visual" medium, but as we have already seen, average viewers do not look at television about one third of the time they are in its presence. Viewers could, in principle, listen to the TV all the time it is on. We are not the first, moreover, to note that much of the meaning of television content is conveyed by the audio track. The question of auditory attention to television is therefore of prime importance in understanding the nature of attention to television in general. Given the methodological difficulty of assessing auditory attention, however, it is not surprising that the research is sparse, and like other areas, is limited to children.

Several investigations indicate that young children are sensitive to audiovisual congruence. Hollenbeck and Slaby (1979) reported that 6-month-old infants looked more at programming with normal audiovisual congruence than at programming with a mismatched audio track. Hayes and Birnbaum (1980) found that when preschoolers were presented mismatched modalities, they remembered visual but not auditory information, a finding also reported by Pezdek and Stevens (1984). These results suggest that children may not always listen to (or at least remember) the audio. A question raised by these findings is whether the visual information in normal television actually interferes with listening by young children. This seems unlikely as Pezdek and Stevens (1984) found no difference in 5-year-olds in memory for audio from "Sesame Street" alone as compared to audio with the picture, although there was a trend for better recognition of audio with the picture, a trend opposite to that expected from interference. Gibbons, Anderson,

Smith, Field, and Fischer (1986), moreover, by carefully controlling the complexity of the audio and video content, showed that memory by 4-year-olds for spoken dialogue was actually superior if presented with video. This effect did not hold for 7-year-olds, indicating a possible age trend in the supporting effect of a visual framework for audio content. Nevertheless, the limited evidence indicates that television is a superior medium for preschool children's listening.

Listening to television apparently occurs with different levels of depth depending on whether or not the viewer is looking at the TV. When not looking, children clearly listen at the level of detecting sound qualities because features such as children's voices reliably elicit looking (Alwitt et al., 1980). Lorch et al. (1979), however, found that in 5-year-olds, cued recall of auditory material was better if the child was looking at the TV at the time the auditory material was presented. Field and Anderson (1985) replicated this result in both 5- and 9-year-olds but also found that the effect was weaker in 9-year-olds; that is, based on free and cued recall, 9-year-olds appeared to listen at the level of sentence comprehension more than younger children when they were not looking at the TV. One may speculate that looking and listening is also correlated even among adults, but that the linkage is weaker than that in children.

In summary, there appear to be several developmental trends in listening to television. Young children look at television with congruent audio and video tracks in preference to mismatched tracks. They listen at a level of semantic analysis more when they look at the TV than when not looking, but this linkage becomes weaker with age. When not looking, they listen at the level of sound quality that they use to provide cues to comprehensible and interesting content worthy of full attention. Taken together, the findings indicate that looking and listening are strongly linked in young children, but with age, listening is more likely to be deployed independently of the focus of visual attention.

INTENSITY OF ATTENTION

Theorists have long suggested that attention can be deployed with different levels of intensity. Terms applied in various contexts include *depth of processing, capacity utilization, engagement, involvement, mindfulness, mindlessness,* and others. With respect to television viewing, writers for the popular media have frequently proposed that viewers, especially children, attend to television with little intensity or depth (e.g., Emery & Emery, 1976; Mander, 1978; Winn, 1977). This notion has also been suggested by Singer (1980) and is one of the tenets underlying the idea of TV viewing as passive. In this section we examine research that has attempted to conceptualize the level of attentional engagement during TV viewing. This research has used physiological measures as well as behavioral measures.

Before considering this research, however, we briefly note that there exists body of research we do not examine here that deals with the question of how difficult or engaging TV viewing is in general or relative to other activities such as reading or working (cf. Csikszentmihalyi & Kubey, 1982; Kubey, 1984, 1985; Salomon, 1981, 1983a, 1983b; Salomon & Leigh, 1984). This research, which employs self-rating procedures, has usually characterized TV viewing as less involving than some other activities such as reading. Here we are concerned with variations in attentional engagement within the TV viewing situation. The existing research indicates that there are such variations and that children's TV viewing cannot be simplistically characterized as having little intensity or depth.

At this point, there is no general theory underlying research on the strength of engagement during TV viewing. It is clear, however, that engagement is greatly reduced when a viewer is not looking at the TV that can be a large proportion of the time a viewer is with TV (cf. Field & Anderson, 1985; Lorch et al., 1979; Lorch & Castle, 1986). The question of major concern here is variation of engagement while a viewer is looking. Extant research examines whether the viewer's involvement with the TV changes as a function of comprehensibility of the content, formal features of the medium (e.g., movement), centrality of the idea units within a narrative, and the time a look is maintained (attentional inertia).

Brain Electrical Activity

Much of the investigation of brain electrical activity during TV viewing is based on the canon that alpha varies inversely with mental arousal. When a research subject is asked to engage in a cognitive activity such as imaging or mental arithmetic, or is presented an unexpected stimulus, alpha ceases, a phenomenon known as *alpha blocking*. With regard to television viewing then, the hypothesis is that the strength of mental engagement can be indexed by varying levels of alpha recorded online. In support of this hypothesis, Appel and Weinstein (1979) reported that television commercials that produced greater amounts of brain activity (as indicated by increased beta wave levels and decreased alpha wave levels) also produced higher levels of recall. Several investigations (reviewed by Rothschild, Thorson, Reeves, Hirsch, & Goldstein, 1986) indicate that alpha and alpha blocking are common during TV viewing. The unsurprising implication is that intensity of processing of TV is variable.

Formal Features

An interesting and relatively sophisticated approach employing EEG is found in a recent report by Reeves and his colleagues (1985). The central question in this research is whether certain formal features increase the intensity of attention in adult viewers. Reeves et al. (1985) recorded central and occipital EEG alpha of adult subjects during presentation of nine 30-second commercials embedded within a half-hour situation comedy. In order to assess the effect of movement and scene changes on alpha, alpha series from each subject were regressed on these structural components. Reeves et al. reported strong effects of these components as indicated by decreases in alpha time-locked to movement and scene changes. Reeves et al. also reported an inverse relationship between aggregate levels of alpha (within subjects) and performance on recall and recognition tasks in both immediate and delayed conditions. These latter results help validate the notion that alpha blocking reflects increased intensity of information processing. Together, the results verify the Bryant et al. (1983) finding that formal features can directly increase attention and information acquisition.

An important consideration in evaluating the EEG research is the ecological validity of the methodology. In order to minimize electrical noise from muscle artifacts subjects were seated in the same position in an undistracting situation throughout the viewing session. Visual orientation to the screen was presumably close to complete. This constraint results in a viewing context that is quite unlike normal viewing (Allen, 1965; Anderson & Field, chapter 8, this volume; Bechtel et al., 1972). Because the situation would likely produce drowsiness and high levels of alpha, the Reeves et al. findings of alpha blocking produced by formal features may be of limited generality.

Keeping this caveat in mind, the work of Reeves et al. (1985) provides valuable insight into the relationship between formal features and attention. In discussing their findings, Reeves et al. suggested that the decrease in alpha following movement and scene changes support a dual process model of attention. External events such as movement and edits may invoke an increased intensity of attention while sustained attention may depend on internal processes or mechanisms. These internal processes presumably involve cognitive engagement with program content.

Thorson, Reeves, and Schleuder (1985) took a different approach to assessing the degree of cognitive involvement. Using the secondary reaction time procedure commonly employed in mainstream research on attention, they required adult viewers of commercials to respond as rapidly as possible to an auditory or visual signal (which was not part of the commercials). The general assumption underlying this technique is that the more a viewer is cognitively engaged in processing the TV program, the less "capacity" he or she has available to devote to the reaction time task, slowing the response. A slow response, then, indicates engagement with the TV program.

Thorson et al. (1985) examined commercials that were produced with a complex and frequent use of visual formal features as compared to commercials that were relatively visually simple. The results indicated greater general engagement during the simple commercials. Reeves and Thorson (1986) pointed out, however, that there was brief "local" engagement following the appearance of a formal feature such as a cut. In toto the Thorson et al. (1985) results are consistent with the EEG and other research suggesting brief periods of arousal produced by some formal features. It should be pointed out, however, that alternative interpretations are possible. Interpreting a cut, for example, may require inferential activities (see Smith, Anderson, & Fischer, 1985) that require attentional capacity and might produce alpha blocking.

Importance and Comprehensibility of Content. Meadowcroft and Reeves (1989) examined the role of content importance in a study with 5- through 8-year-old children. In this study, children were shown a cartoon that contained scenes central to understanding the story as well as scenes incidental to story comprehension. Using reaction time to a secondary task as an index of attentional engagement, Meadowcroft and Reeves reported significantly longer reaction times when the children were viewing central as opposed to incidental content. The children were presumably more intensely engaged with central content than with incidental content.

Using the secondary task procedure, Lorch and Castle (in press) showed 5-year-olds a specially constructed version of "Sesame Street" in which there were normal segments, randomly edited segments, and language distorted segments (the stimuli constituted a subset of those used by Anderson et al., 1981). The randomly edited segments were locally comprehensible (each individual scene could be understood), whereas the language distorted segments (foreign language or backward speech) were rendered largely incomprehensible. Lorch and Castle found that reaction times during normal segments were much longer than during language distorted segments (there was no difference between normal and randomly edited segments). These results indicate that not only does comprehensible content produce greater levels of looking at TV (as described earlier), but, given looking, it produces more intense engagement. Additional evidence indicates that engagement may increase as a look is maintained.

Attentional Inertia. Recall that looks have an increasing probability of survival the longer they have been maintained, and that the fact that looks are lognormally distributed implies an underlying process that changes as a look continues. The question here is whether there is a functional change in the intensity of processing as a look is maintained. Anderson and Lorch (1983) showed that attentional inertia served to maintain looks by young children across content boundaries during "Sesame Street." That is, the longer a child continuously looked prior to the content boundary, the longer the child would continuously look after the content boundary. This finding indicates that attentional inertia is not maintained by particular content, but reflects a general tendency to maintain looking regardless of content. We have since replicated this result in adult viewing of prime-time television. Anderson and Lorch (1983) suggested that attentional inertia may involve a progressive increase in attentional engagement as a look at television is maintained. They argued that a look is maintained by comprehensible and important content, but that after about 15 seconds of continuous looking, engagement becomes generalized to the source of the content, that is, to the medium itself. Once this generalization of engagement occurs, looking becomes relatively resistant to disruption.

There are, therefore, several hypotheses to be tested about attentional inertia. One hypothesis, that engagement becomes generalized, is supported by the Anderson and Lorch (1983) observation that looks are driven across content boundaries. A second hypothesis, that looking becomes resistant to external disruption, was tested by Anderson, Choi, and Lorch (1987). Anderson et al. examined distractibility in preschoolers while viewing "Sesame Street." In this procedure, the child was shown the program in a room that was also equipped with a rear slide projector. At random intervals a slide, accompanied by a beep, would be shown on the screen to the side of the TV. Videotape analysis of headturns toward the distractor revealed that children were much less likely to be distracted if a look at the TV had been in progress for 15 seconds or longer. If a head turn to the distractor occurred, furthermore, the reaction time of the head turn was greater if a look had been in progress for 15 seconds or longer. These results indicate that engagement becomes more intense and less disruptible after 15 seconds of continuous looking.

Lorch and Castle (1986) found that reaction time to a secondary task was slower if a look was maintained for 15 seconds or more. Interestingly, however, this effect held only for normally comprehensible segments, not for distorted segments.

In summarizing work on intensity, there is substantial evidence that the intensity of attention varies during looking at TV. Formal features, comprehensibility, and importance all play roles in increasing intensity, and intensity appears to increase as a look is maintained.

THEORETICAL CONSIDERATIONS AND FUTURE DIRECTIONS

Despite the lack of widespread research on attention to television, the work reviewed here indicates that we have learned much since the late 1970s. With regard to conceptions of television viewing as active or passive (cf. Anderson & Lorch, 1983; Huston & Wright, 1983; Salomon, 1983a; Singer, 1980), the evidence suggests that neither characterization is fully adequate; attention to TV is a combination of active and passive components.

Passive components of attention to television are revealed when an attentional response occurs more or less automatically without regard to the *meaning* of the content to the viewer. Several studies now suggest that certain formal features, especially cuts and movement, play a role in momentarily increasing the intensity of processing the content. Active components of attention to television are manifested when attentional processes are directed by meaningful aspects of the content (e.g., awareness that a particular character's next utterance is crucial to resolution of the plot). They are also directed by learned strategies that maximize exposure to certain important or meaningful elements of content and that minimize exposure to unimportant or meaningless elements. A number of investigations find such active direction of attention. It is clear that theoretical characterizations of attention to TV must go beyond simple descriptors such as "active" or "passive."

There appear to be four classes of attentional processes that have been revealed through television research. These classes can be tentatively labeled *attention getting, attention holding, attention suppressing,* and *attentional inertia.*

The attention-getting processes include those that direct visual orientation and listening toward the particular source of stimulation (the TV set). Component processes include learned auditory monitoring strategies such that orientation occurs when certain cues (e.g., children's voices) are detected that are indicative of relevant, comprehensible, and/or entertaining content. Also included are reflex-like orientations elicited by movement in peripheral vision, and the like.

Attention-holding processes are likely the most complex and varied. They include not only relatively automatic increases in intensity of processing produced by certain formal features, but also the processes involved in full cognitive processing of the content. The latter processes include semantic evaluation, accessing memories and schemas as part of comprehension, accessing schemas to provide anticipations of future content, and the like. It is primarily through these processes that judgments of comprehensibility, importance, and entertainment value are made.

We know little about attention-suppression processes except that they likely occur. Mainstream research on attention indicates that habituation of attention occurs readily, and that people can suppress attention to irrelevant stimulation in task situations (e.g., Lorch, Anderson, & Well, 1984). Children appear to suppress looking at TV in the presence of adult male voices (Alwitt et al., 1980). Presumably, looking at and listening to TV can be suppressed in the face of competing task demands.

Attentional inertia appears to go beyond involvement with particular content. The longer attention is maintained to a particular source of stimulation, there is an increasing generalized tendency to further maintain attention to that source, regardless of content. Although this is an attention-holding process, it appears to be somewhat different in kind than those just described, perhaps a form of sensitization of attention (cf. Bashinski, Werner, & Rudy, 1985; Groves & Thompson, 1970).

We believe that theoretical efforts to account for attention to television should take into consideration these four classes of processes. Ideally, such a theory would describe the temporal ordering of component processes in relation to ongoing stimulation from the TV set. The theory should also account for known quantitative and qualitative aspects of attention to television (e.g., lognormal distribution of look lengths) and predict new aspects. From our point of view, the prospects for such a theory are credible.

Although serious theoretical development is reasonable, there remain numerous areas that beg for empirical research:

1. There is strikingly little information concerning adult attention to television.

2. Much needs to be learned about auditory attention. Promising methodologies, however, are being explored including procedures that require the viewer to restore the audio following distortion (Rollandelli, Wright, & Huston, 1982), and auditory evoked responses to clicks while TV viewing (Herbert Krugman, personal communication, October 9, 1987).

3. Although a number of ingenious techniques have been developed that characterize the structure of narratives in linguistic or causal terms (e.g., coherence analyses, causal structures, story grammars, and the like), as yet no investigations have related these structures to attention.

4. More work needs to be done relating notions of entertainment, emotions, and attention.

5. The nature and generality of attentional inertia must be explored.

6. The relationship between attention to television and the development of attentional skills in other domains should be carefully examined. In particular, the hypothesis that television viewing affects attentional abilities should be thoroughly explored. A scattering of studies, reviewed by Anderson (1985), indicate that there may some effects, both positive and negative.

ACKNOWLEDGMENTS

This chapter was written while the authors were supported in part by a research grant from the National Institute of Mental Health. We appreciate Hyewon Choi's work in providing background information concerning properties of the lognormal distribution. Some unpublished research described in this chapter was supported by a research grant from the National Science Foundation and by an equipment grant from the John and Mary Markle Foundation.

REFERENCES

Allen, C. (1965). Photographing the TV audience. *Journal of Advertising Research, 14,* 2-8.

Alwitt, L. F., Anderson, D. R., Lorch, E. P., & Levin, S. R. (1980). Preschool children's visual attention to television. *Human Communication Research, 7,* 52-67.

Alvarez, M. M., Huston, A. C., Wright, J. C., & Kerkman, D. D. (1988). Gender differences in visual attention to television form and content. *Journal of Applied Developmental Psychology, 9,* 459-475.

Anderson, D. R. (1985). *The influence of television on children's attentional abilities.* New York: Childrens' Television Workshop.

Anderson, D. R. (1987). *Analysis of lengths of TV sessions.* Paper presented at the annual meeting of the Association for Consumer Research, Boston, MA.

Anderson, D. R., Alwitt, L. F., Lorch, E. P., & Levin, S. R. (1979). Watching children watch television. In G. Hale & M. Lewis (Eds.), *Attention and cognitive development* (pp. 331-361). New York: Plenum Press.

Anderson, D. R., Choi, H., & Lorch, E. P. (1987). Attentional inertia reduces distractibility during young children's television viewing. *Child Development, 58,* 798-806.

Anderson, D. R., & Field, D. E. (1983). Children's attention to television: Implications for production. In M. Meyer (Ed.), *Children and the formal features of television* (pp. 56-96). Munich, Germany: K. G. Saur.

Anderson, D. R., Field, D. E., Collins, P. A., Lorch, E. P., & Nathan, J. G. (1985). Estimates of young children's time with television: A methodological comparison of parent reports with time-lapse video home observation. *Child Development, 56*(5), 1345-1357.

Anderson, D. R., & Levin, S. R. (1976). Young children's attention to Sesame Street. *Child Development, 47,* 806-811.

Anderson, D. R., Levin, S. R., & Lorch, E. P. (1977). The effects of TV program pacing on the behavior of preschool children. *AV Communication Review, 25,* 159-166.

Anderson, D. R., & Lorch, E. P. (1983). Looking at television: Action or reaction? In J. Bryant & D. R. Anderson (Eds.), *Children's understanding of television: Research on attention and comprehension* (pp. 1-34). New York: Academic Press.

Anderson, D. R., Lorch, E. P., Field, D. E., Collins, P. A., & Nathan, J. G. (1986). Television viewing at home: Age trends in visual attention and time with television. *Child Development, 57,* 1024-1033.

Anderson, D. R., Lorch, E. P., Field, D. E., & Sanders, J. (1981). The effects of TV program comprehensibility on preschool children's visual attention to television. *Child Development, 52,* 151-157.

Anderson, D. R., Lorch, E. P., Smith, R., Bradford, R., & Levin, S. R. (1981). Effects of peer presence on preschool children's television viewing behavior. *Developmental Psychology, 17,* 446-453.

Anderson, D. R., & Smith, R. (1984). Young children's TV viewing: The problem of cognitive continuity. In F. J. Morrison, C. Lord, & D. F. Keating (Eds.), *Advances in applied developmental psychology* (Vol. 1, pp. 115-163). New York: Academic Press.

Appel, V. S., & Weinstein, C. (1979). Brain activity and recall of TV advertising. *Journal of Advertising Research, 19,* 7-15.

Atchinson, J., & Brown, J. A. C. (1963). *The lognormal distribution.* Cambridge, Great Britain: The University Press.

Bashinski, H. S., Werner, J. S., & Rudy, J. W. (1985). Determinants of visual fixation: Evidence for a two-process theory. *Journal of Experimental Child Psychology, 39,* 580-598.

Bechtel, R. B., Achelpohl, C., & Akers, R. (1972). Correlates between observed behavior and questionnaire responses on television viewing. In E. A. Rubinstein, G. A. Comstock, & J. P. Murray (Eds.), *Television and social behavior: Vol. 4. Television in day to day life: Patterns of use* (pp. 274-344). Washington, DC: U.S. Government Printing Office.

Bryant, J., Zillmann, D., & Brown, D. F. (1983). Entertainment features in children's educational television: Effects on attention and information acquisition. In J. Bryant & D. R. Anderson (Eds.), *Children's understanding of television: Research on attention and comprehension.* New York: Academic Press.

Calvert, S. L., Huston, A. C., Watkins, B. A., & Wright, J. C. (1982). The effects of selective attention to television forms on children's comprehension of content. *Child Development, 53,* 601-610.

Campbell, T. A., Wright, J. C., & Huston, A. C. (1987). Form cues and content difficulty as determinants of children's cognitive processing of televised educational messages. *Journal of Experimental Child Psychology, 43,* 311-327.

Choi, H. P. (1988), *Attentional patterns in 5-year-olds' toy play: Test of attentional inertia in toy play.* Unpublished doctoral dissertation, University of Massachusetts at Amherst, MA.

Csikszentmihalyi, M., & Kubey, R. (1982). Television and the rest of life: A systematic comparison of subjective experience. In D. C. Whitney & E. Wartella (Eds.), *Mass communication review yearbook* (Vol. 3, pp. 317-328). Beverly Hills, CA: Sage.

d'Ydewalle, G., Vanden Abeele, P., Van Rensbergen, J., & Coucke, P. (1986). *Incidental processing of advertisements while watching soccer games*. Unpublished manuscript.

Emery, F., & Emery, M. (1976). *A choice of futures*. Leiden: Martinus Nijhoff Social Sciences Division.

Field, D. E., & Anderson, D. R. (1985). Instruction and modality effects on children's television attention and comprehension. *Journal of Educational Psychology*, 77, 91-100.

Flagg, B. (1978). Children and television: Effects of stimulus repetition on eye activity. In J. W. Senders, D. F. Fisher, & R. A. Monty (Eds.), *Eye movements and the higher psychological functions* (pp. 279-292). Hillsdale, NJ: Lawrence Erlbaum Associates.

Gadberry, S., & Brown, W. (1981). Effects of camera cuts and music on selective attention and verbal and motor imitation by mentally retarded adults. *American Journal of Mental Deficiency*, 86, 309-316.

Gibbons, J., Anderson, D. R., Smith, R., Field, D. E., & Fischer, C. (1986). Young children's recall and reconstruction of audio and audiovisual narratives. *Child Development*, 57, 1014-1023.

Grieve, R., & Williamson, K. (1977). Aspects of auditory and visual attention to narrative material in normal and mentally handicapped children. *Journal of Child Psychology and Psychiatry*, 18, 251-262.

Groves, P., & Thompson, R. (1970). Habituation: A dual-process theory. *Psychological Review*, 77, 419-450.

Hayes, D., & Birnbaum, D. (1980). Preschoolers' retention of televised events: Is a picture worth a thousand words? *Developmental Psychology*, 16, 410-416.

Hollenbeck, A. R., & Slaby, R. G. (1979). Infant visual responses to television. *Child Development*, 50, 41-45.

Huston, A. C., & Wright, J. C. (1983). Children's processing of television: The informative functions of formal features. In J. Bryant & D. R. Anderson (Eds.), *Children's understanding of television: Research on attention and comprehension* (pp. 35-68). New York: Academic Press.

James, W. (1890). *The principles of psychology*. New York: Holt.

Johnston, W., & Dark, V. (1986). Selective attention. In M. Rosenzweig & L. Porter (Eds.), *Annual review of psychology* (pp. 43-75). Palo Alto, CA: Annual Reviews.

Kubey, R. W. (1984, April). *Television as escape: Subjective experience*. Paper presented to the 34th annual conference of the International Communication Association, San Francisco, CA.

Kubey, R. W. (1985, August). *Concentration and alertness during reading and television viewing*. Paper presented at 93rd Annual Convention of the American Psychological Association, Los Angeles.

Lee, E. T. (1980). *Statistical methods for survival data analysis*. Belmont, CA: Lifetime Learning.

Lesser, H. (1977). *Television and the preschool child*. New York: Academic Press.

Levin, S. R., & Anderson, D. R. (1976). The development of attention. *Journal of Communication*, 26, 126-135.

Lorch. E. P., Anderson, D. R., & Levin, S. R. (1979). The relationship of visual attention to children's comprehension of television. *Child Development*, 50, 722-727.

Lorch, E. P., Anderson, D. R., & Well, A. (1984). The effects of irrelevant information on speeded classification tasks: Interference is reduced by habituation. *Journal of Experimental Psychology: Human Perception and Performance*, 10, 850-864.

Lorch, E. P., & Castle, V. (in press). Preschool children's attention to television: Visual attention and probe response times. *Journal of Experimental Child Psychology*.

Lorch, E. P., Milich, R., Welsh, R., Yocum, M., Bluhm, C., & Klein, M. (1987, April). *A comparison of the television viewing and comprehension of attention deficit disordered and normal boys*. Paper presented at the meeting of the Society for Research in Child Development, Baltimore, MD.

Mander, J. (1978). *Four arguments for the elimination of television.* New York: William Morrow.

Meadowcroft, J., & Reeves, B. (1989). The influence of story schema development on children's attention to television. *Communication Research, 16,* 352-374.

Mendelson, M. J. (1983). Attentional inertia at 4 and 7 months? *Child Development, 54,* 677-685.

Moody, K. (1980). *Growing up on television: The TV effect.* New York: Times Books.

Nathan J. G., Anderson, D. R., Field, D. E., & Collins, P. A. (1985). Television viewing at home: Distances and visual angles of children and adults. *Human Factors, 27*(4), 467-476.

Nathanson, D. E. (1977). Designing instructional media for severely retarded adolescents: A theoretical approach to trait- treatment interaction research. *American Journal of Mental Deficiency, 82,* 26-32.

Neisser, U. (1967). *Cognitive psychology.* New York: Appelton-Century-Croft.

Parasuraman, R., & Davies, D. R. (Eds.). (1984). *Varieties of attention.* Orlando, FL: Academic Press.

Pezdek, K., & Hartman, E. (1983). Children's television viewing: Attention and comprehension of auditory versus visual information. *Child Development, 54,* 1015-1023.

Pezdek, K., & Stevens, E. (1984). Children's memory for auditory and visual information on television. *Developmental Psychology, 20,* 212-218.

Pillsbury, W. B. (1908). *Attention.* London: Swan Sonnerschein.

Pingree, S. (1986). Children's activity and television comprehensibility. *Communication Research, 13,* 239-256.

Proschan, F. (1963). Theoretical explanation of observed failure rate. *Technometrics, 5,* 375-383.

Reeves, B., & Thorson, E. (1986). Experiments in the viewing process. *Communication Research, 13,* 343-361.

Reeves, B., Thorson, E., Rothschild, M. L., McDonald, D., Hirsch, J., & Goldstein, R. (1985). Attention to television: Instrastimulus effects of movement and scene changes on a;'lpha variation over time. *International Journal of Neuroscience, 27,* 242-255.

Reeves, B., Thorson, E., & Schleuder, J. (1986). Attention to television: Psychological theories and chronometric measures. In J. Bryant & D. Zillmann (Eds.), *Perspectives on media effects* (pp. 251-279). Hillsdale, NJ: Lawrence Erlbaum Associates.

Rothschild, M. L., Thorson, E., Reeves, B., Hirsch, J. E., & Goldstein, R. (1986). EEG activity and the processing of television commercials. *Communication Research, 13*(2), 182-220.

Salomon, G. (1981). *Communication and education: Social and psychological interactions.* Beverly Hills, CA: Sage.

Salomon, G. (1983a). Television watching and mental effort: A social psychological view. In J. Bryant & D. R. Anderson (Eds.), *Children's understanding of television: Research on attention and comprehension* (pp. 181-198). New York: Academic Press.

Salomon, G. (1983b). Television literacy and television vs. literacy. In R. W. Bailey & R. M. Melanie (Eds.), *Literacy for life* (pp. 67-78). New York: Modern Language Association of America.

Salomon, G., & Leigh, T. (1984). Predispositions about learning from print and television. *Journal of Communication, 34,* 119-135.

Sheena, D., & Flagg, B. (1978). Semiautomatic eye movement data analysis techniques for experiments with varying scene. In J. W. Senders, D. F. Fisher, & R. A. Monty (Eds.), *Eye movements and the higher psychological functions* (pp. 65-76). Hillsdale, NJ: Lawrence Erlbaum Associates.

Singer, J. L. (1980). The power and limitations of television: A cognitive affective analysis. In P. H. Tannenbaum & R. Abeles (Eds.), *The entertainment functions of television* (pp. 31-65). Hillsdale, NJ: Lawrence Erlbaum Associates.

Smith, R., Anderson, D. R., & Fischer, C. R. (1985). Young children's comprehension of montage. *Child Development, 56*(4), 962-971.

Sprafkin, J. N., Gadow, K. D., & Grayson, P. (1984). Television and the emotionally disturbed, learning disabled, and mentally retarded child. In *Advances in learning and behavioral disabilities* (pp. 151-213). Bridgeport, CT: JAI Press.

Susman, E. J. (1978). Visual and verbal attributes of television and selective attention in preschool children. *Developmental Psychology, 14,* 447-461.

Thorson, E., Reeves, B., & Schleuder, J. (1985). Message complexity and attention to television. *Communication Research, 12,* 427–454.

Wakshlag, J., Reitz, R., & Zillmann, D. (1982). Selective exposure to and acquisition of information for educational television programs as a function of appeal and tempo of background music. *Journal of Educational Psychology, 74,* 666–667.

Winn, M. (1977). *The plug-in drug.* New York: Viking Press.

Wright, J. C., Huston, A. C., Ross, R. P., Calvert, S. L., Rolandelli, D., Weeks, L. A., Raessi, P., & Potts, R. (1984). Pace and continuity of television programs: Effects on children's attention and comprehension. *Developmental Psychology, 20,* 653–666.

Zillmann, D., Williams, B., Bryant, J., Boynton, K., & Wolf, M. (1980). Acquisition of information from educational television programs as a function of differently paced humorous inserts. *Journal of Educational Psychology, 72,* 170–180.

CHAPTER

2

Children's Comprehension Processes: From Piaget to Public Policy

Edward L. Palmer
Davidson College
Maurya MacNeil
Ohio State University

A kindergarten child and her sixth-grade brother watch televised nuclear holocaust in America's heartland ("The Day After" on ABC Theater, November 20, 1983). The sixth grader is disturbed by the program, whereas his kindergarten sister is not. Why? The very same program stimuli were there for each to see and to hear, and each had comparable neural pathways for sensory input to the brain. Yet their experiences from viewing are very different. It is natural for us to explain this phenomenon by saying their comprehension levels differed—that the sixth grader came to the program with a much greater capacity to assimilate contextual elements and to understand motivations and consequences. It is less natural to examine the basic models and assumptions on which our explanation is based and to determine their implications for children's comprehension processes and for the television viewing experience. Within this chapter we examine basic comprehension models and assumptions, the ways in which they have affected our perception of children's comprehension processes and the corresponding television-related questions that have been formulated and researched within the field.

COMPREHENSION ASSUMPTIONS: THEORETICAL BASES

Age/Stage Theories

Several "stage" theories have addressed the comprehension capabilities of the child at different levels of development. Bruner, Olver, and Greenfield (1966) characterized this development in terms of the enactive, iconic, and symbolic thought

27

processes. Kohlberg (1963, 1978) outlined stages in moral development, and Selman (1971) spoke of stages in role-taking ability. Each suggested a more sophisticated level of comprehension as the child progressed from one stage to the next. Kohlberg (1963, 1978) and others have been cognizant of the implications that underlie a stage-theory approach. By their very nature, stages suggest a qualitative difference in child comprehension and performance as one proceeds from a given stage to the next. Like walking a set of steps, the stages are seen as discrete events or plateaus rather than as a continuous, flowing progression. A second characteristic of stages is that their sequence is invariant. One does not reach the top step without having sequentially traveled all those in between. The rate at which one travels from one step to the next may be affected by hereditary and environmental factors, but the sequence itself does not change. As a third characteristic of stages, the activities characterizing them become related as a coherent whole. The bricks in each step are held together by a strong, cohesive mortar. The fourth major characteristic of stages is their hierarchical nature. Just as steps build into an integrative whole, so do stages. While the higher stages make increasing differentiations, they also integrate the lower stages into this new level of organization (Wartella, 1979).

Like any schemata or conceptualization, stage theories have their distinct advantages and equally distinct disadvantages. Although they provide a useful framework for incorporating comprehension data, they at the same time configure the data in a "framework way." It is the price we pay for any conceptualization, and one we must be ever alert to in comprehension research. As Kelly (1955) once suggested, the world is not beholden to any individual's interpretation of it. Neither are children beholden to our interpretations of their comprehension processes. Within our conceptualizations we must be continually alert to the "nonfits" and their vital messages for our existing conceptualizations. Within the organizational and communication advantages of stage theories, our need for research vigilance is an equally essential one.

The most pervasive set of stage-theory assumptions in the comprehension research literature has been that of Piaget. *Language and Thought in the Child* (1923) and *Judgment and Reasoning in the Child* (1924) were both published in English translation in 1926, bringing to England and the United States the child-oriented concepts that would dominate an era of research in cognitive development. Within this era, researchers and educators would develop their basic assumptions about the "cognitive equipment" a child has access to at different ages and how this equipment enables the child to comprehend environmental stimuli. Like the steps in a stage theory itself, these assumptions suggest levels of readiness—a child's readiness to comprehend a given set of stimuli in one way at an early age and in quite another way at a later age. The set of stimuli would be the same in each instance. It would be the readiness that would change both the boundaries and the nature of comprehension.

Piaget's work encompasses the two basic methods central to studying children's comprehension processes—observation and experiment. His early writings drew from the systematic and painstaking observations he had done with his own three children (Piaget, 1951, 1952, 1954). His later work brought his process approach more formally into the experimental laboratory (Piaget & Inhelder, 1973). This combination of methods provides a basic Piagetian perspective on the nature of children's comprehension processes as a function of age and stage.

In-depth treatment of Piaget's stages can be found in several works (Brainerd, 1978; Flavell, 1963; Furth, 1969; Ginsburg & Opper, 1979) and there are lucid, well-formulated accounts that skillfully distill the theory's complexities and give clear, meaningful expression (Ault, 1983). Here we introduce key Piagetian concepts as they relate to an examination of stages, moving from the concepts to the stages themselves and their implications for a child's comprehension of the many elements within the television stimulus.

Piaget speaks of structures and functions. The structures—organization and adaptation—have a biological basis and neither can be directly observed. They must be inferred. The term *organization* would suggest that isolated, discrete elements become clustered, and it here means the clustering of behaviors or thoughts into systems. Where the infant performs a given behavior such as grasping, sucking, or looking, the behavior is isolated and discrete. Some combination of looking, grasping, and sucking has not yet occurred, and when it does an organization will have occurred—isolated behaviors will at that point have clustered into a higher order, functioning unit. *Adaptation* encompasses the complementary processes of assimilation and accommodation. Expressing these processes in Piaget's own biological context of digestion, food is assimilated as it is processed and changed into a form the body can use. The body, on the other hand, has to accommodate to the food's entry into the internal environment with muscular contractions, glandular secretions, and so forth. Placed in the context of comprehension, a stimulus or event is assimilated differently at the individual stages of cognitive development. Where the young child may treat a broom as though it were a bird, the child has assimilated the broom as an object but has comprehended none of its functional characteristics. At a later age the child may comprehend the sweeping function of a broom and accommodate to that function by grasping and using the broom as a sweeping tool. As a stimulus is assimilated—in effect, changed into a form the child can mentally process—major elements of the stimulus object are not being perceived. As a stimulus is accommodated, the child's mental processing has changed to encompass additional aspects of the stimulus. In assimilation the change-pressure is on the stimulus. In accommodation the change-pressure is on the child. The latter moves the child to a more advanced level of comprehension.

As the child interacts with the environment, knowledge systems or *structures* develop. These structures take two forms—*schemes* and *operations*. Schemes can be thought of as habits. They are organized patterns of behavior or actions a person repeats within daily routine. The actions will not be identical, but they will be distinctly similar; and when old, established habits or schemes are applied to new events, assimilation is occurring. Operations are mental representations that have reversibility. They do not have a straightforward behavioral representation comparable to schemes and consequently have to be inferred from the approaches children make to solving a given set of problems. Operations will be more clearly demonstrated as we examine Piaget's four periods in cognitive development.

Piaget's four periods have had a profound impact throughout child-oriented research in both the general and the television context. Even when they are not explicitly stated, these periods are generally assumed, and with these assumptions comes an image of the child's comprehension capabilities. To examine these assumed capabilities we follow the mythical child "Piper" as she moves through the different stages. From birth to 18 or 24 months, Piper will be in Piaget's *sensorimotor period.* Begun with only innate, reflexive capabilities, Piper will end the period with a capacity to form primitive symbolic representations of behavior. The ball that once had vanished from existence when it vanished from sight will now have a continued existence when not in view. Far from the "aha" phenomenon, that object permanence will have progressed through several substages of search behavior beginning with partially covered object search at 4-8 months and culminating in the search for displaced, hidden objects at 18-24 months. With the onset of symbolic representation capability, Piper moves to Piaget's *preoperational period* (2-7 years). Her very concrete early representations such as toy hammer for real hammer or broom for bird will gradually move toward more abstract levels of sophistication—the word H-A-M-M-E-R to represent the object or class of objects. Symbolic functioning in this period begins with object permanence and continues with delayed imitation, symbolic play, and language. Piper sees a young girl throw a tantrum and sometime later will imitate the tantrum behavior—just as Piaget (1951) reported his own daughter having done—and symbolic play brings those moments when an object becomes something else. Piper's wagon becomes a car, her finger becomes a gun, and so on. Language brings with it not only a capacity for communication but a means to control one's own behavior. Piper may talk to herself, repeating some of the parent-delivered "do's" and "don'ts" in her daily experience. She also will use this language capacity for classifying objects, but she will be unable to classify on more than one dimension simultaneously (centration). She also will be limited by egocentrism—her inability to see an event from any perspective beyond her own—and by irreversibility. The latter makes it impossible for her to see water poured from a tall, thin glass into a short, wide glass and conclude that it is the same amount of water. She is only capable of seeing the end state of an event rather than the transformations that have occurred. Instead of deductive or inductive reasoning, Piper's reasoning is transductive. It proceeds from particular to particular in such a manner that if A causes B, Piper will also say that B causes A. Incapable of forming an hierarchy of categories, the relationships she forms between objects are not stable.

In Piaget's *concrete operational period* (7-11 years) the inabilities of the preoperational period will now become abilities. Irreversibility will now be replaced by reversibility as Piper develops the capacity to transform a mental action or thought. With reversibility by inversion she can now apply two operations successively to regain an original identity (as in addition or subtraction). With reversibility by compensation she can now successively apply two operations to reach an equivalent state (as in doubling or halving two numbers and recognizing their relationship equivalence). It is these capacities that enable her to solve conservation tasks—conservation of number at first, then continuous quantity, mass, length, area, weight, and finally volume. She can now see a situation or event from another person's perspective, as egocentrism fades, facilitating communication and cooperation. And centrism fades as she demonstrates her abilities to focus on more than one aspect of an event or object simultaneously. As she moves from the concrete operational period to the *formal operational* period (11-15 years), she will demonstrate a reversibility and mental representational ability in both. But there will be a notable difference. Although her concrete operations were actual representations, she will now be able to think in "what if" terms—entertaining and working with hypotheses and ideas that are not there to be seen and may be contrary-to-fact. No longer the "mental child," Piper will now have the capacity to generate multiple hypotheses, systematically check out all possible solutions, and operate on operations (invoking algebraic rules, for instance). What was concrete and transductive just a few years earlier, will now be abstract and deductive reasoning. In Piaget's terms, Piper's cognitive abilities and her comprehension capacities will have reached their maturity.

Information Processing

Where Piaget's approach began in the field and later moved toward more formal research verification, information processing had its beginnings and roots in the formal research tradition. Because it is not the genesis of one man observing his own children, its lens is broader and its connective links, perhaps a bit less unifying at times. Comprehension in this context relates to three thought-related processes— perception, memory, and hypothesis generation/testing. *Perception* brings a person's experience and existing cognitive categories to bear upon incoming sensory data. *Memory* involves the process of encoding data, storing it, and subsequently retrieving it. And *hypothesis testing* relates to proposing and evaluating possible solutions to a problem. Unlike the Piagetian model, information processing does not propose stages. Rather than discrete steps, information processing would be more like a ramp on which perception, memory, and hypothesis generation/ testing would be occurring to greater or lesser degrees at all points along the way.

Four thought units are basic to information processing—schemata, symbols, concepts, and rules. *Schemata* are conceptual organizations or classifications of prior sensory events. It is not essential that these conceptualizations be either pictorial or tied to language. Ault (1983) considered them like blueprints of distinguishing features. Because they are closely associated with direct sensory impressions, they are predominantly used by infants and very young children. Because symbols, concepts, and rules are more abstract mental representations, they are accessible to older children and adults. Language is one of our most prevalent symbol systems. The word "truck" does not resemble at all the item it represents. It simply stands for the object in a very arbitrary way. Concepts form abstractions of the elements common to a group of schemata or symbols. The more prototypical the concept, the better it represents a group. Consequently, a robin is a better conceptual representative of birds than is a crane.

Although not seen as distinct stages, there are four developmental changes in children's concepts. *Validity* is judged by the degree to which a child's concept has attained adult meaning. For a child who has not yet attained Piaget's conservation-of-number concept, there may be a concept of number that is based on a dimension such as shape or length. The child's number concept will become more valid as it approaches the adult concept of number. How precisely a concept is used—its *status*—also shows developmental change. Where a 3-year-old and a 10-year-old may both know that a parent's "in 2 hours" comment means a point in the future, the 3-year-old may be back in 10 minutes thinking the 2 hours have passed. The 10-year-old will use the concept with much greater exactness. *Accessibility* refers to a child's ease in using and communicating with others about a concept. In a game of Twenty Questions where a 6-year-old is asked to guess what the experimenter is hiding behind her back, the questions asked are likely to be specific-item ones—"Is it a ball?" "Is it a balloon?" Less likely will be conceptual questions such as "Is it blue?" "Is it a toy?" Conceptual accessibility has not yet been attained. The *relative* quality of concepts expresses a child's ability to move beyond absolutes. A child who is older than another may also be seen as younger than a third. For the child perceiving absolutes, red is red. For the child having mastered the relative conceptual quality, red may be maroon or pink, and so on. *Rules* specify relationships between concepts. Formal rules—such as multiplication tables—are always true. Informal rules—such as daddy being nice—may be violated on occasion. Children find some of their greatest rule challenges occurring within language acquisition where their newly acquired rule quickly encounters a verb tense that is idiosyncratic. Through overextending the rule the child learns the irregular verb form.

Like most conceptual phenomena, information-processing's thought units do not operate in convenient and comfortable isolation. Perception, memory, and hypothesis testing/generation are intricately interwoven. Memory of similar objects or events will affect one's perception of a current stimulus, and two theories—enrichment and differentiation—address the nature of relationship between information and sensory stimulus reception. *Enrichment theory* gives prior experiences and expectations the major role in interpreting current sensory input. The input itself is considered information deficient. Each experience with a stimulus adds information to the existing schema (Bruner, 1957; Vernon, 1955), giving older children access to more elaborate schemata for interpreting a current stimulus. *Differentiation theory,* on the other hand, perceives the sensory stimulus as information-rich. The process becomes one of extracting distinctive features (Gibson, 1969; Gibson & Levin, 1975). With repeated exposures to an object the child becomes more efficient in focusing on the distinctive. This capacity relates directly to developmental aspects of attention.

Within information processing, attention progresses from being stimulus-controlled in early infancy to being more voluntarily controlled (Allik & Valsiner, 1980). Size and movement are especially effective in getting the young infant's attention, whereas pattern complexity and familiarity prove effective in holding it. Novelty that is not too discrepant from the infant's existing schemata proves effective in attention-getting. With a greater voluntary-attention component in the older infant, selective attention becomes prominent. In that virtually limitless world of potential stimulus inputs, some inputs will be selectively attended to, whereas others will be ignored. This capacity for selective attention increases with age, enabling older children to eliminate distractions and ignore the irrelevant far more effectively than younger children (Santostefano & Paley, 1964; Shepp, Burns, & McDonough, 1980; Stroop, 1935). Whether finding distinctive features precedes schema development (differentiation theory; Lewis & Brooks, 1975) or schema precedes and is refined by adding distinctive features (enrichment theory; Cohen & Salomon, 1979), it is clear that perception and memory functions are very intricately interwoven.

Speaking in terms of Atkinson and Shiffrin's (1971, 1977) multiprocess view of human memory, age differences surface in short- and long-term memory while comparability across ages seems evident in sensory memory. The latter lends credence to the notion of a visual iconic memory system in which the image/representation is very similar to the original stimulus. Neisser (1967, 1976) proposed a comparable echoic memory system for auditory stimulation, and there well may be others in the remaining senses. As encoding strategies become essential to the memory process, younger children perform more poorly than older children. Although young children have access to rehearsal within short-term memory, they will not have the chunking and recoding sophistication of the older child or the adult. Neither by intent nor in fact can we give in-depth treatment to the topic of memory, but its basic perspectives are essential to a consideration of the information-processing model. (For greater depth in this area, see Atkinson & Shiffrin, 1971, 1977; Neisser, 1967, 1976; and related works.)

Comparison of Piaget and Information-Processing Approaches

The two approaches share notable common ground. Both perceive the child as active rather than passive. Although the progression within each moves from passive beginnings, the child as active participant soon takes prominence. This is especially true in the areas of attention and memory. What begins as stimulus-controlled attention later becomes more actively selective. A second area of agreement relates to novelty. Both approaches see the moderately different stimulus

as the most effective in getting attention. Piagetian theory would characterize it
as maximizing the potential for assimilation and accommodation, whereas
information-processing theory would see it as avoiding the two attention-losing
extremes—habituation, if familiar, and schematic divergence if too novel. Their
major point of difference is the steplike (Piaget) versus continuous (information-
processing) perspective, and even here the perspectives frequently appear more
complementary than divergent.

TELEVISION RESEARCH PERSPECTIVES
AND THEORY LINKAGES

Television is not something a child can play with and manipulate in the typical,
active sense. It lacks the opportunity of hypothesis testing with an environmental
stimulus in the characteristic Piagetian sense, and this difference has led many
researchers to pursue an assumption uncharacteristic of either Piaget or information processing. It is the assumption of the passive child viewer, coming to television as a young, impressionable tablet to be written by a television stimulus
with virtually total control. The Piagetian contribution to this assumption is generally that of supplying information about the comprehension readiness a child brings
to the set. It is a question of what can the child know and when can he or she
know it? Many developmental, age-related studies follow this approach by focusing
what the child brings to the set.

Age-Related Issues

Aggression and Imitability.   Aggression and imitability has been one of
the most heavily researched issues among children, and many of those studies
have had age as an independent variable. Leifer and Roberts (1972), for example, found that television's aggressive displays—whatever their motivation or
consequences—became increasingly effective in producing aggressive behavior
as children matured from preschool to early adolescence, and decreased from
early adolescence on. Although Grade 9 and 12 subjects understood most of the
motivations for violent acts and the immediate and final consequences to characters, kindergarten children understood very little about motivation and consequences for violence. But whether a child will imitate an aggressive act is not
dependent on the child understanding the act's consequences. In fact, it is the
latter—imitability without understanding—that has created the greatest general
and social concern. Extensive research in observational learning (Flanders, 1968)
has indicated that the kindergarten child is quite capable of imitability, and the
act may be a novel or unfamiliar one. Bandura (1965) and Hicks (1965) found
that the preschool child can imitate novel screen-mediated depictions of hitting,
kicking, and verbal abuse with a remarkable degree of fidelity, and the acts will
be demonstrated without any request to show what has been learned (Liebert &

Baron, 1972). Some of the most thought-provoking research outcomes relate to aggression against a bystander human. Preschool boys exposed to a brief, aggressive film clip were later placed in a room with a mallet, toy gun, and a Bobo doll clown or that identical setting with a human clown. Whereas the control (no film viewing) group did not demonstrate aggression against the human victim, the film-viewing children distinctly did (Hawratty, Liebert, Morris, & Fernandez, 1969). The human-aggression effect has been replicated with both boys and girls, across a wide age range of human-victim models and urban/rural settings (Savitsky, Rogers, Izard, & Liebert, 1971).

Program Plot and Character Judgments. It would be impossible to understand why Luke had been jumped from behind as he walked into an office if you did not relate this incident to an earlier program scene where Luke had seen a man stealing money. Collins and Westby (1981) used this type of program to study children's comprehension of program information and cause and effect. Where the children's program is a series of disconnected episodes, the dramatic program has a plot or narrative in which the scenes are subordinated. In this sense, television program comprehension becomes an "ill-structured problem" requiring inference from the viewer (Simon, 1976). Age differences are apparent in both content retention and inference. The second-grade child asked about an item of program content seen only moments earlier will perform much more poorly than the fifth or eighth grader (Collins & Westby, 1981; Purdie, Collins, & Westby, 1979). Similar age differences are found in content retention of children's programming (e.g., "Sesame Street"; Friedlander, Wetstone, & Scott, 1974). There is an equally apparent age difference in how the second grader and his or her older counterparts will retell the television story. The second grader mentions primarily common knowledge content. These are knowledge elements the child brought to the program (e.g., that police wear uniforms, that people go to the store to buy groceries, etc.). With fifth and eighth graders, the retelling becomes much more program-specific (e.g., that certain out-of-uniform characters were police, that groceries were bought to cash forged checks, etc.). Just as older viewers are more likely to move beyond their general knowledge to program-specific responses, they also are more likely to notice the event that deviates from expectation. Correspondingly, their response errors relate to facts-confusion experienced within the program itself, whereas younger viewers fill in with stereotypical responses based on their general knowledge and expectations (Collins, Wellman, Keniston, & Westby, 1978).

The fill-in tendency of younger children creates difficulties for them in comprehending the relative "goodness" or "badness" of given program characters. A friendly, nice character who turns out to be a villain will be detected and "found out" by the fifth grader quite early, whereas a second grader may not make the true character judgment even by the end of the program. Using a four-interruption procedure during program viewing, Collins and Westby (1981) found that only

46% of the second-grade children had changed their character assessment to negative by the fourth interruption, and only 25% of the second graders were negative by the third interruption (compared with an overwhelmingly negative 83% of fifth graders). Beyond the age differences themselves, what distinguished changers from nonchangers was not specific scene retention but rather, an understanding of relationships. And although changers were at first noncommittal, nonchangers made initially definite and stereotypical responses (Collins & Westby, 1981). Collins suggested that the nonchangers' initially positive perceptions may affect retention of critical plot events in much the same way that social prototypes or schemata can bias a person's processing of social information (Hastie, 1981; Nisbett & Ross, 1980; Schneider, Hastorf, & Ellsworth, 1980). Social expectations and the biases of the young child's more primitive schemata tend to interfere with the recognition of negative consequences.

Stimulus Factors, Video Sophistication, and Filmic Codes. *Stimulus factors* take on a central significance for the young, preschool viewer, and major efforts are devoted to giving these factors a perceptual salience or potency that will assure the child's attention. The role of attention in comprehension is a controversial one (e.g., Anderson, 1979; Anderson & Collins, 1956), but for purposes of our discussion in this context we assume what Anderson termed a *reactive theory approach*—that the television stimulus is the primary controlling factor for young preschoolers. Saturday morning becomes an excellent demonstration laboratory for observing the stimulus factors considered perceptually salient. These generally animated programs feature rapid action (characters in swift physical movement), rapid pace (frequent scene and character changes), novel and unexpected events, and intense/upbeat soundtracks. Music and special effects set the tone, and the mood is usually humorous (Rice, Huston, & Wright, 1982). Selective use of salient features can be especially helpful to comprehension in the preschool child. Information processing considers this child to be in an exploratory rather than a search mode, which means there is no sophistication nor capability for seeking out and selecting the vital stimulus elements. Like Piaget's assimilation concept, the pressure here is on the stimulus to become salient, vital, and attended to. It is this goal that constitutes the driving force in preschool television programming.

As children grow and mature, their television proficiency also develops strength and *sophistication*. Information processing would consider it a shift from exploratory to search mode, whereas the Piagetian view would find strong evidence of accommodation. Not only does the child gain skill in selecting relevant, central content, but a comparable skill develops for interpreting the formal features of television—those specific to given programs as well as those generally characteristic of the medium. Although the preschooler has only the barest glimmerings of a viewing technique vocabulary, the older child has a more sophisticated, elaborate viewing style (Krull & Husson, 1980; Ward, Levinson, & Wackman,

1972). This style gives older children a greater flexibility in viewing. Although the younger child will be more consistently program-attentive, the older child will demonstrate greater selective attention—responding to stimuli that accompany or announce central content. The older child has mastered the filmic codes—the language of the medium itself (Salomon, 1979).

Filmic codes are not explicitly taught. They are acquired through frequent contact with the television medium. The sophisticated child viewer perceives not only the dramatic plot of a program, but the video plot of the medium as well. He or she learns the significance of zooms, cuts, pans, a given music background, or a set of familiar cues associated with a given program. No longer are television's content events perceived as discrete and disconnected. Now the language of the medium itself provides a structure through which the content can be perceived and interpreted. It is a function of both child readiness and television exposure—a combination of factors vital to the acquisition of television literacy.

Advertising and Selling Intent.   Just as preschool children cannot comprehend dramatic plot, motivations, and consequences, those same children cannot comprehend the selling purpose of advertising (e.g., Adler et al., 1980; Roberts, 1979; Ward, Wackman, & Wartella, 1977). In a pattern very similar to that of dramatic plot, the majority of third-grade children reflect a grasp of the commercial's purpose. For most researchers—and for public policy petitions and formulations—the third grader has been the demarcation line. From a comprehension standpoint, the younger child is considered vulnerable, and this perspective has been the generating force within requests for special protection (Federal Trade Commission, 1978).

Because commercials are designed to obtain a seller-desired behavior, comprehension questions and issues of vulnerability take on central relevance with young children. These issues span a range from the question of advertising itself to those of time, product types, techniques, and appeals within children's advertising. We examine some of these issues in more depth as we examine policy implications.

Child Viewer Perception Issue

Active Versus Passive.   There are two mental pictures of the child in front of the television set. The passive picture is that of the child as a motionless sponge, absorbing and ingesting the television stimulus indiscriminately. The active picture finds the child interacting with television—attending, comprehending, and responding in a selective manner. In one sense, the two pictures blend together in that the passivity of an early point in development later evolves into the active, selective child. This blend is quite consistent with both theoretical models outlined earlier. In another sense, the two pictures have been separate and distinct—especially within general research approaches and issues. The research question becomes one of direction of influence. Is the direction of influence primarily from television to child viewer or is the direction of influence from child viewer to television? Acknowledging that the question itself is inherently arbitrary and over-simplified, it nonetheless carries significant research implications. Historically, the research questions have been heavily weighted toward television to child viewer. The vast majority of violence-oriented research has been effects-related. Gerbner's Violence Index (1972) exemplifies this basic focus on the television stimulus, cata-loguing the frequency of violent incidents, the role characteristics of aggressors and victims, and the potentially cumulative effects of child viewing (Gerbner & Gross, 1976; Gerbner, Gross, Jackson-Beeck, Jeffries-Fox, & Signorielli, 1978). Effects questions also have been studied longitudinally (e.g., Lefkowitz, Eron, Walder, & Huesmann, 1977) and cross-culturally (Granzberg & Steinbring, 1980), and major independent variables have included age (e.g., Palmer, Hockett, & Dean, 1983), race (e.g., Berry, 1979), and gender (e.g., Huesmann et al., 1978).

The child viewer to television perspective has been taken by several recent re-search efforts. Although researchers bring their individual variations to this per-spective, they hold in common the view that the child interacts with the television stimulus on the basis of prior knowledge and schemata. The young viewer in this context is seen not simply as a responder but as a potential determiner of the television experience—one who brings to the television stimulus differential back-grounds, culturally shared perceptions, and so forth. It is a view that encompasses the vast range of attribution-research findings and their implications. One specif-ic attribution researched by Salomon (1981) has been the amount of invested mental effort (AIME) a young viewer expects to make in the television activity com-pared to the activity of reading a book, for example. Children consistently antici-pate investing far less AIME in the television viewing experience than in other media. Salomon (1984) termed it "mindlessness" and pointed out that what the child processes in the television setting heavily depends on this initial perception of the medium. In something of a "Catch-22" type situation, it also seems clear that the more one knows about television, the less one attends to it with active, conscious processing (Langer, 1982). Although on the one hand this can be seen as evidence of selectivity (e.g., Anderson & Lorch, 1983), it also can be viewed as the prelude to mindlessness (Salomon, 1981; Salomon & Shavit, 1986). This research area encompasses a vast expanse of fertile research soil yet to be tilled.

CHILDREN'S COMPREHENSION
AND PUBLIC POLICY ISSUES

Children's comprehension issues have formed the core of public policy concerns. From the very dawn of commercial television, parents and educators have voiced concerns about television effects on the child viewer. The perception of limited comprehension capacities has been expressed through several public initiatives oriented toward protection and selective viewing. We examine the roots and the ramifications of each set of initiatives as they relate to young children.

Protection

When a pill bottle sits on the bathroom counter, natural questions arise about protecting young children. Whose responsibility is it: the pill manufacturer, the container creator, or the purchasing parent? The answers are not readily clear, nor are the television risks to children as clear-cut as the pill bottle analogy. With young children generally considered at risk, the realm of potential protectors has included federal agencies, congressional committees, network/advertiser self-regulation, and citizen action. Our purpose in discussing a given initiative here is to examine the nature of the protection concerns, and to see within them the comprehension-level assumptions expressed. Many of these concerns and assumptions are comparable within both violent programming and advertising, and we examine the *FTC Staff Report on Television Advertising to Children* (1978) as a "laboratory demonstration."

For several years prior to the ruling, citizen action groups (e.g., Action for Children's Television and the Council on Children, Media and Merchandising) had voiced concerns about television advertising and children's limited comprehension level. Concerns ranged from advertising itself to the commercial time available in children's programs, the products being advertised, and the selling techniques/appeals and value lessons being communicated. The comprehension-level issues underlying this range of concerns perceived the young child as vulnerable to advertising—its products, techniques, appeals, and value lessons. The child's inability to distinguish programs from commercials further deepened concern and this public awareness—coupled with general vulnerability—spurred Action for Children's Television (ACT) to undertake initiatives that led to an FCC ban on host selling in children's programming and a requirement that networks insert a buffer between children's programs and commercials. The details of these initiatives can be found in several works (e.g., Cole & Oettinger, 1978; Palmer & Dorr, 1980), but it is important here to note the degree to which children's comprehension levels and perceived vulnerability underscored them. That perception became all the more immediate when the network buffers themselves proved ineffective in facilitating a child's program/commercial distinction (Palmer & McDowell, 1979). The comprehension limitations among young children seemed both striking and clear.

The *FTC Staff Report on Television Advertising to Children* (1978) served to clarify the age distinctions associated with children's comprehension limitations. The issue in this instance was televised candy advertising and advertising for between-meal snacks. An ACT petition sought a ban on candy advertising prior to late evening and in any advertising appealing directly to children. A petition from Center for Science in the Public Interest (CSPI) sought a ban on between-meal snack foods with significant sugar content and corresponding health and dental risks. The FTC staff undertook its own investigation of these and related issues, and proposed a rulemaking that would ban all televised advertising to children too young to understand the selling purpose of advertising, would ban sugared product advertising to older children, and would require any sugared product advertising to older children not included in the ban to be balanced by nutritional or health disclosures funded by advertisers. There are key elements to observe in this proposed rulemaking. Older children were defined as those in the 8–11 age group. It was believed that they could understand and assimilate the required health-disclosure information. Younger children were defined as those in the younger-than-8 age range. These children were seen as distinctly at risk to advertising itself and unable to process the visual and audio messages with any effectiveness and sophistication. The age distinctions were far from arbitrary. This rulemaking had been based on one of the most widespread, in-depth inquiries ever undertaken by a governmental policymaking body. Testimony was requested and given by a vast array of the most active and renown researchers in the children's television field. And as we look at the final distillation of their testimony within the rulemaking itself we can see that Piaget did indeed come into policymaking. So, too, did information processing. And both highlighted the child's developmental limitations in comprehension prior to 8 years of age. In our own glimpse of the research base and its theoretical assumptions earlier in this chapter, the rulemaking age differentiations—although necessarily arbitrary—appeared to be valid.

Informed Viewing and Literacy

The unsuccessful outcome of the FTC rulemaking made it clear that little protection was likely to be forthcoming from the public or network sector. This brought questions of discriminating viewing and literacy to the fore. Dorr, Graves, and Phelps (1980) were among the early leaders in advocating a television literacy approach—one in which children were trained to be more critical evaluators of television program content. Using entertainment programming as their base, critical evaluation skills were identified, integrated into curricula that were then taught to children. The curriculum contained an industry and a process component. In the industry component children were taught basic facts about television production and broadcast economics. The process component conveyed reasoning about the fantasy and reality aspects of entertainment programming. They demonstrated that children as young as kindergarten and second grade could learn some basic facts about television and how to evaluate it. Their study did not give clear indication that their newly acquired knowledge led them to be more selective television viewers. They concluded that any curricula efforts in the future would experience enormous practical problems in reaching an entire nation of young children and that a major responsibility would necessarily rest with parents to exercise more viewing control. Like the comprehension limitations themselves, there were limitations to the effectiveness of a television literacy approach. These limitations suggested the importance of adult or parental guidance in television viewing — a guidance both in making conscious program-selection decisions and in viewing itself. Lesser and Flagg (1978) were among those who outlined vital steps in this process. The intent of both television literacy and discriminating viewing was to help children become selective viewers who — in Lesser's words — no longer watched "an awful lot of television . . . consequently . . . a lot of awful television" (p. 4). One could say that each of these approaches both acknowledged vulnerability and sought to maximize the concept of children as active and interactive viewers.

CONCLUSION

A kindergarten child and her sixth-grade brother watch televised nuclear holocaust in America's heartland ("The Day After" on ABC Theater, November 20, 1983). The sixth grader is disturbed by the program, whereas his kindergarten sister is not (Palmer, 1986). The models and their assumptions, the age/stage differences found within research, and their policy implications provide a renewed appreciation of this reality in children's comprehension. As we look to the future of research in this field, it is important to remain closely attentive to the outcomes that do not fit either our models or our assumptions, for it may well be these outcomes that hold the key to further breakthrough and understanding of this vital world in the developing child.

REFERENCES

Adler, R. P., Friedlander, B. Z., Lesser, G. S., Meringoff, L., Robertson, T. S., Rossiter, J. R., & Ward, S. (1980). *Research on the effects of television advertising on children* (rev. ed.). Lexington, MA: Lexington Books.

Allik, J., & Valsiner, J. (1980). Visual development in ontogenesis: Some reevaluations. In H. W. Reese & L. P. Lipsitt (Eds.), *Advances in child development and behavior* (Vol. 15). New York: Academic Press.

Anderson, D. R. (1979, August). *Active and passive processes in children's television viewing.* Paper presented at the annual meeting of the American Psychological Association, New York.

Anderson, D. R., & Collins, P. A. (1986, November) *The impact on children's education: Television's influence on cognitive development.* Paper presented at a conference sponsored by the United States Department of Education, Washington, DC.

Anderson, D. R., & Lorch, E. P. (1983). Looking at television: Action or reaction? In J. Bryant & D. R. Anderson (Eds.), *Children's understanding of television: Research on attention and comprehension* (pp. 1-34). New York: Academic Press.

Atkinson, R. C., & Shiffrin, R. M. (1971). The control of short-term memory. *Scientific American, 224,* 82-90.

Purdie, S., Collins, W. A., & Westby, S. (1979). *Children's processing of motive information in a televised portrayal.* Unpublished manuscript, University of Minnesota, Institute of Child Development, Minneapolis, MN.

Rice, M. L., Huston, A. C., & Wright, J. C. (1982). The forms and codes of television: Effects on children's attention, comprehension, and social behavior. In D. Pearl, L. Bouthilet, & J. Lazar (Eds.), *Television and behavior: Ten years of scientific progress and implications for the eighties* (pp. 24-38). Washington, DC: U.S. Government Printing Office.

Roberts, D. (1979, January). Testimony before the Federal Trade Commission's rulemaking on children and TV advertising, San Francisco, CA.

Salomon, G. (1970). *Interaction of media, cognition and learning.* San Francisco: Jossey-Bass.

Salomon, G. (1981). *Communication and education: Social and psychological interactions.* Beverly Hills, CA: Sage.

Salomon, G. (1984). Television is "easy" and print is "tough": The differential investment of mental effort in learning as a function of perceptions and attributions. *Journal of Educational Psychology, 76,* 647-658.

Salomon, G., & Shavit, R. (1986). *The role of mindfulness in televiewing and reading: A case of bi-directional causality.* Unpublished manuscript.

Santostefano, S., & Paley, E. (1964). Development of cognitive controls in children. *Child Development, 35,* 939-949.

Savitsky, J. C., Rogers, R. W., Izard, C. E., & Liebert, R. M. (1971). The role of frustration and anger in the imitation of filmed aggression against a human victim. *Psychological Reports, 29,* 807-810.

Schneider, D., Hastorf, A., & Ellsworth, P. (1980). *Person perception* (2nd ed.). Reading, MA: Addison-Wesley.

Selman, R. (1971). Taking another perspective: Role-taking development in early childhood. *Child Development, 42,* 439-453.

Shepp, B. E., Burns, B., & McDonough, D. (1980). The relation of stimulus structure to perceptual and cognitive development: Further tests of a separability hypothesis. In F. Wilkening, J. Becker, & T. Trabasso (Eds.), *Information integration by children.* Hillsdale, NJ: Lawrence Erlbaum Associates.

Simon, H. (1976). Cognition and social behavior. In J. Carroll & J. Payne (Eds.), *Cognition and social behavior.* Hillsdale, NJ: Lawrence Erlbaum Associates.

Stroop, J. R. (1935). Studies of interference in serial verbal reactions. *Journal of Experimental Psychology, 18,* 643-662.

Vernon, M. D. (1955). The functions of schemata in perceiving. *Psychological Review, 62,* 180-192.

Ward, S., Levinson, D., & Wackman, D. (1972). Children's attention to television advertising. In E. A. Rubinstein, G. A. Comstock, & J. P. Murray (Eds.), *Television and social behavior: Vol. 4. Television in day-to-day life: Patterns of use* (pp. 491-512). Washington, DC: U.S. Government Printing Office.

Ward, S., Wackman, D., & Wartella, E. (1977). *How children learn to buy.* Beverly Hills, CA: Sage.

Wartella, E. (1979). The developmental perspective. In E. Wartella (Ed.), *Children communicating: Media and development of thought, speech and understanding* (pp. 7-19). Beverly Hills, CA: Sage.

CHAPTER
3

Construct Accessibility: Determinants, Consequences, and Implications for the Media

David M. Sanbonmatsu
University of Utah
Russell H. Fazio
Indiana University

A basketball coach complains vociferously in response to what he views as poor officiating. An observer might infer that the coach is a "competitor" with a powerful desire to win. A second observer might infer that the coach is simply a "poor sport." The different interpretations may stem, in part, from differences in *construct accessibility*. Bruner (1957), in his seminal work on perceptual readiness, suggested that constructs in memory differ in the likelihood that they will be used to interpret events. Although an individual may possess several relevant constructs in memory for interpreting an event, he or she will tend to rely on the construct that is the most highly accessible. The differences between the two observers in the perception of the coach's personality may result because the construct "competitor" was highly accessible for the first observer, whereas the construct "poor sport" was highly accessible for the second.

The primary focus of this chapter is the determinants and consequences of construct accessibility. We review very generally the processes underlying changes in construct accessibility, and the processes through which construct accessibility affects judgments and behavior. Although there have been some excellent discussions of construct accessibility previously (notably Higgins & King, 1981), our treatment of the topic is broader than prior efforts.

This chapter is divided into four sections. The first section provides some basic definitions and a conceptual framework for understanding construct accessibility. The second section examines the different means or procedures that affect the accessibility of a construct. The third section reviews studies that have examined the effects of construct accessibility on perception, judgments, and be-

45

havior. The final section of the chapter discusses the relevance of construct accessibility to communication and concerns about the media.

AN OVERVIEW OF BASIC CONCEPTS

Accessibility.   Accessibility refers to the readiness with which a construct in memory can be utilized in processing incoming information. Although the two terms have often been used interchangeably, *accessibility* should be distinguished from *availability*, which refers to: (a) whether or not a particular representation exists in memory (Higgins & King, 1981; Tulving & Pearlstone, 1966); or (b) a judgmental heuristic in which the perceived likelihood or frequency of some event is based on the ease with which an instance of the event can be retrieved from memory (Tversky & Kahneman, 1973).

Priming.   Priming is simply a procedure that increases the accessibility of a construct or response pattern in memory. A *priming effect* is an instance where an increase in the accessibility of a construct has an impact on subsequent perceptions or behavior.

Increases in construct accessibility are to be distinguished from other changes that may occur with experience, such as learning. First, priming is not a change in the association, or the strength of the association, between two stimuli. Second, priming is not a change in belief or attitude, or the formation of a new belief or attitude. In particular, it is not a change in belief about the frequency of events or the likelihood of events (Higgins & King, 1981). Finally, priming should be distinguished from the provision of an active expectancy or set to respond in a particular manner in a specific situation. The acquisition of an expectancy is essentially the formation of an association between a response and a particular stimulus situation. And again, priming is not a change in association.

In essence, priming is a performance affecting factor. Priming, of course, does not occur in a vacuum. Experiences that alter the accessibility of a construct may also induce learning or lead to changes in other performance affecting variables. Thus, it is not always easy to distinguish the effects of priming from the effects of other changes induced by experience (Smith & Branscombe, 1987).

Priming has two different meanings—one specific and the other broad. On the one hand, priming is a particular, unobtrusive technique for influencing the judgments, perceptions, and behavior of others. More generally, however, priming is a universal cognitive process that is continuously occurring. With every experience the accessibility of a subset of constructs in memory is increased momentarily. Moreover, as we see here, priming is a process that mediates the impact of many important psychological variables such as motivation, attitudes, and mood on perceptions, judgments, and behavior.

Constructs. Bruner focused on constructs or categories in his discussion of accessibility and perceptual readiness. A construct is simply a representation in memory consisting of coherent information about some entity (Higgins & King, 1981). Constructs may contain information about individuals or groups (e.g., Ronald Reagan, dentists), objects (e.g., apples, nuclear power plants), procedures or types of events (e.g., ordering dinner, a baseball game), attributes (e.g., tall, aggressive), plans (e.g., the intention to write a letter), or goals (e.g., obtaining tenure). Alternatively, a construct may be primarily evaluative (i.e., an attitude).

Priming, of course, is not limited to constructs. The accessibility of specific exemplars and episodes in memory can also be increased. In addition, response patterns — emotional responses, motor behaviors, and cognitive skills — can be primed. Discussion in this chapter focuses on *construct* accessibility. The reader should note, however, that the basic principles characterizing construct accessibility generally apply to the accessibility of other representations in memory such as behaviors and episodes.

THE DETERMINANTS OF CONSTRUCT ACCESSIBILITY

A wide range of experience can prime a construct in memory. This section reviews some of the different ways in which the accessibility of constructs is increased.

Recent and Frequent Activation. The activation of a construct temporarily increases the accessibility of that construct. Numerous studies have shown that the recent exposure to a construct label increases the accessibility of the construct and the likelihood of its use in later judgments and impressions (e.g., Bargh, Bond, Lombardi, & Tota, 1986; Bargh & Pietromonaco, 1982; Carver, Ganellen, Froming, & Chambers, 1983; Fazio, Powell, & Herr, 1983; Herr, 1986, 1987; Herr, Sherman, & Fazio, 1983; Higgins, Bargh, & Lombardi, 1985; Higgins & Chaires, 1980; Higgins, Rholes, & Jones, 1977; James, 1986; Rholes & Pryor, 1982; Smith & Branscombe, 1987; Wilson & Capitman, 1982; Wyer, Bodenhausen, & Gorman, 1985).

Other research has demonstrated that the more frequently a category is activated, the greater its accessibility (cf. Higgins et al., 1985; Wyer & Srull, 1981). Studies by Srull and Wyer (1979, 1980) indicate that the greater number of times a construct is primed, the greater the likelihood that the construct will be used in later judgments and impressions.

Variations in the recency and frequency of activation of a construct may explain a sizable portion of the within-subject variability in perception and behavior. An individual does not always respond to a situation in the same way. This variability may stem, in part, from changes in the accessibility of relevant constructs over time. In general, the more accessible a construct is in memory, the greater the likelihood that the construct will guide perceptions, judgments, and behavior.

The implication of this principle is that, although a relevant construct may be available or present in memory, it may have little impact on how an individual responds to a situation. However, if a construct is primed by recent exposure, the likelihood that the construct will affect subsequent judgments and behaviors increases.

Between-subject variability also may be related to differences in construct accessibility. Constructs that have been repeatedly activated over a long period of time are said to be chronically accessible (Higgins et al., 1985; Higgins & King, 1981; Higgins, King, & Mavin, 1982). Chronically accessible constructs are habitually used in perception and responding, whereas other less accessible constructs in memory may be rarely employed. There are considerable individual differences in the constructs and responses that people possess in memory (Kelly, 1955). In addition, there is considerable variability between individuals in the extent to which a given construct is chronically accessible (see, e.g., Higgins et al., 1982). Such differences in construct accessibility may be one of the major contributors to the between-subject variability in perception and behavior (Fazio, 1986; Higgins & King, 1981; Higgins et al., 1982; Mischel, 1973; Snyder, 1982). Research indicates that people often perceive and respond to the same events differently because of chronic differences in the accessibility of relevant constructs (Bargh et al., 1986; Bargh & Thein, 1985; Fazio & Williams, 1986; Higgins et al., 1982; Houston & Fazio, 1987).

Activation of Related Constructs. The accessibility of a representation in memory can be increased indirectly through the activation of constructs that are associated with the representation. That is, a given construct can be primed through the activation of a number of different types of associated constructs. The construct "dog," for example, can be primed by presenting an exemplar of the construct such as "poodle" (cf. Srull & Wyer, 1979, 1980), a superordinate category word such as "pet," or a parallel construct such as "cat" (cf. Loftus, 1973). Priming can be achieved by presenting words that are phonetically related (cf. Meyer, Schvanveldt, & Ruddy, 1975). Finally, a number of studies have demonstrated that a construct can be primed through the activation of an evaluatively congruent construct (Fazio, Sanbonmatsu, Powell, & Kardes, 1986; Greenwald, Liu, & Klinger, 1986; Sanbonmatsu, Osborne, & Fazio, 1986).

The importance of the activation of related constructs is readily apparent when one considers the influential role of context cues. The encoding of a stimulus is typically facilitated by the cues present in the immediate context (e.g., Biederman, 1972; Palmer, 1975). The identification of a spatula, for example, is facilitated by the presence of other kitchen implements such as stove and a frying pan. The context affects encoding largely via simple priming processes. The perception of contextual cues typically primes constructs pertinent to those cues, thereby facilitating the later identification of related stimuli.

Motivation, Emotion, and Mood. Priming is an important mediator of the effects of many psychological variables on perceptions and behavior. The experience of a mood, emotional or motivational state primes associated constructs in memory. The primed constructs in turn, affect subsequent perceptions, judgments, and behavior.

Numerous studies have demonstrated that a person's general positive or negative mood state can influence the accessibility of material in memory (Bower, 1981; Isen, Shalker, Clark, & Karp, 1978; Rholes, Riskind, & Lane, 1987; Riskind, 1983; Teasdale & Fogarty, 1979). Generally, studies have found that a mood state increases the accessibility of representations in memory that are evaluatively congruent with the mood state. For example, Isen et al. found that subjects in a positive mood state were more likely to recall positive stimulus words from a previous task than negative stimulus words.

Similarly, specific emotional states (e.g., fear, anger) may serve as a retrieval cue increasing the accessibility of associated material in memory (Bower, 1981; Laird, Wegener, Halal, & Szegda, 1982). For example, subjects in the Laird et al. study were exposed to sentences referring to expressions of fear, anger, or sadness. Later they were asked to recall the sentences while assuming sad, angry, or fearful facial expressions. Subjects who were sensitive to the facial expression cues (and thus who were presumably more likely to be experiencing an emotional state corresponding to the facial expression) tended to recall sentences whose emotional content was congruent with the assumed facial expression.

We are primed or sensitized toward events that are related to our current motivations and needs (Higgins & King, 1981; Klinger, 1975; Srull & Wyer, 1986). It is adaptive to be prepared to perceive events that are threatening or aversive, as well as those that are beneficial or reinforcing (Jones & Gerard, 1967). Thus, a person's needs, "current concerns" (Klinger, 1975), and/or "momentary intentions" (Kahneman, 1973) heighten the accessibility of constructs associated with those concerns. For example, studies have shown that moderate hunger increases the accessibility of food-related constructs (Levine, Chein, & Murphy, 1942; Wispe & Drambarean, 1953).

Several studies have demonstrated state-dependent learning effects involving emotional or mood states, where material in memory is more readily retrieved if the state at recall is similar to the state that the person was in during encoding (Bower, 1981; Bower, Monteiro, & Gilligan, 1978; Clark, 1983; Leight & Ellis, 1981). This suggests that emotion or mood may serve as a general cue increasing the accessibility of whatever information was stored during that state.

UNDERLYING MECHANISMS

One explanation of priming assumes that semantic memory is an interlinked network consisting of nodes that represent constructs, and links between the nodes that represent relations between constructs (Anderson, 1976; Collins & Loftus, 1975). When a node is activated during retrieval, the activation spreads instantaneously along the paths of the network to adjacent, semantically related nodes. The level of activation of related nodes decreases as the distance from the retrieved node increases (Anderson & Pirolli, 1984; Ratcliff & McKoon, 1981).

Higgins and his colleagues (Higgins et al., 1985; Higgins & King, 1981) explained priming effects by analogizing nodes to the synapses of vertebrates. The stimulation of a particular category node increases the category's "action potential" to a maximum level of activation that then slowly dissipates over time. Like a synapse, the rate at which the level of activation of a category dissipates or decays varies. The level of activation of categories that are frequently stimulated dissipates more slowly than that of less frequently primed categories. Higgins et al. (1985) demonstrated that the most recently activated category will be accessed for encoding a stimulus when the interval between priming and stimulus presentation is brief. However, as the interval between priming and stimulus presentation increases, the more frequently activated category will be more likely to be used for encoding.

An alternative model of memory that has been used to explain priming effects is Wyer and Srull's (1981, 1986) storage bin model. According to this model, long-term memory consists of a set of content specific bins. The constructs in each bin are stored on top of one another in the order in which they were previously primed. The most recently primed construct is placed on top of the storage bin and is thus accessed first in the subsequent processing of information to which it is relevant.

Although some important differences exist among these and other models, discussion of their relative merits is beyond the scope of this chapter (see Higgins et al., 1985; Wyer & Srull, 1986; Ratcliff & McKoon, 1981, for such discussions). The reader is invited to consider construct accessibility via whichever metaphor he or she finds most comfortable. What we wish to emphasize is a commonality that the models possess. All the models view priming as a passive, automatic process. An automatic process is one that leads to the activation of some concept or to some response "whenever a given set of external initiating stimuli are presented, regardless of a subject's attempt to ignore or bypass the distraction" (Shiffrin & Schneider, 1977, p. 117). Automatic processes are to be distinguished from controlled processes that require the active attention of the perceiver.

The most convincing evidence for the automatic nature of priming stems from demonstrations that priming effects can be obtained even in situations in which the subject is unaware of the prime. Several recent studies suggest that conscious awareness or recognition of a stimulus is not necessary for the priming of the construct in memory (e.g., Bargh & Pietromonaco, 1982; Gabrielcik & Fazio, 1984; Greenwald et al., 1986; Marcel, 1983). For example, subjects in the Bargh and Pietromonaco study unknowingly were exposed to words semantically related or unrelated to hostility during the course of a "vigilance task." The words were presented in a manner that was shown to preclude conscious recognition of the words. Subjects who were exposed to a large proportion (as opposed to a small proportion) of hostility-related words were subsequently more likely to interpret the ambiguous behaviors of a hypothetical target person as hostile. Thus, the hostility-related constructs were primed despite subjects' lack of awareness.

The automatic activation of concepts strongly associated with the primed construct also has been demonstrated. For example, Fazio and his colleagues (Fazio et al., 1986; Sanbonmatsu et al., 1986), have found that attitudes can be activated from memory upon the mere presentation of the attitude object. In the Fazio et al. experiments, a priming procedure was employed to examine the extent to which the presentation of an attitude object facilitated the speed with which subjects could identify the evaluative connotation of a subsequently presented adjective. Presentation of attitude objects characterized by a strong object-evaluation association facilitated responses to adjectives that were evaluatively congruent with the object. For example, a subject whose attitude toward "cockroach" involved a strongly associated negative evaluation was facilitated in indicating that the target adjective "disgusting" had a negative connotation by the presentation of "cockroach" as a prime. Such facilitation occurred even though subjects were at no time instructed to consider their attitudes toward the objects that served as the primes. From the subject's perspective, the prime was merely a "memory word" that the subject was to recite at the end of the trial. Despite the irrelevance of attitudes to the subject's immediate task concerns, the presentation of the attitude object appears to have automatically activated the affect associated with the attitude object.

THE CONSEQUENCES OF ACCESSIBLE CONSTRUCTS

This section focuses on the consequences of construct accessibility on perceptions, judgments, and behavior. It should become clear that the effects of construct accessibility are significant and wide ranging. The consequences discussed here may stem from the chronic accessibility of a construct or from the construct having been made acutely accessible. That is, a construct may be utilized because it is chronically accessible or because it was recently primed. Bargh et al. (1986) have found that the effects of chronic and acute sources of accessibility are additive. Thus, recent activation of a chronically accessible construct has stronger priming effects than either of the sources alone.

Attentional Selectivity. Perceivers cannot possibly attend to all of the stimuli to which they are exposed. The capacity limitations of the processing system make selectivity necessary.

Processing can be primed toward input of a specific sensory modality. Perceivers are more responsive to stimuli of the sensory modality on which attention was preengaged than stimuli of a different modality (Anthony & Graham, 1983). Thus, a person previously engaged in auditory perception will be more responsive to auditory stimuli than someone who was preengaged in visual perception. Some evidence suggests that priming of a sensory modality may inhibit responsiveness to stimuli of other modalities (Oatman, 1984).

Constructs or schemas are developed to assist people in the processing of the plethora of stimuli that is encountered. Neisser (1976) suggested that perceivers "pick up what they have schemas for and willy-nilly ignore the rest" (p. 80). In particular, people attend to stimuli that are related to the most highly accessible constructs (Bruner, 1957; Geller & Shaver, 1976; Higgins & King, 1981; Srull & Wyer, 1986; Warren, 1972). For example, if the construct "friendly" is primed, a person will be particularly likely to attend to the cues in a situation relating to friendliness.

Stimuli relating to an individual's goals or current concerns are particularly likely to receive attention. This is because constructs relating to current concerns tend to be highly accessible (Bruner, 1957). An individual who is in financial straits, for example, is likely to be particularly attentive to money related events, as financial constructs such as "loans," "taxes," and "bills" are likely to be highly accessible.

Encoding. Bruner (1958) recognized that in encoding a stimulus perceivers "go beyond" the information given (see also Alba & Hasher, 1983; Higgins & King, 1981; Taylor & Crocker, 1981). Perceivers "fill in the gaps," and embellish stimuli with features and attributes that were actually present. For example, in categorizing another as "outgoing" perceivers assign to that person a host of attributes and behavior patterns that may not have actually been in display in the immediate situation.

Basically, categorization or encoding involves an assessment of the match between the features of the target stimulus with those of the candidate construct. If there is an adequate match between the features of the target and the accessed construct, identification occurs. Constructs that are highly accessible from frequent or recent use will, of course, be accessed for matching first. Numerous studies have demonstrated that increasing the accessibility of a construct heightens the likelihood that a stimulus will be judged as an instance of that construct (Bargh & Pietromonaco, 1982; Carver et al., 1983; Higgins et al., 1985; Higgins et al., 1977; James, 1986; Srull & Wyer, 1979). In the study by Higgins et al. (1977), for example, subjects were exposed to trait terms during an alleged experiment on perception. In a second, purportedly unrelated experiment, they read a paragraph consisting of four ambiguous descriptions of a target's behavior that could be interpreted as desirable or undesirable (e.g., "By the way he acted one could readily guess that Donald was well aware of his ability to do many things well"). Subjects who were exposed to positive trait terms that were related to the description (e.g., self-confident) evaluated the target more positively than subjects who were exposed to negative, relevant trait terms (e.g., conceited). Presumably, exposure to the trait terms increased the accessibility of the corresponding constructs, thereby affecting the manner in which the ambiguous behaviors were encoded. Other studies have demonstrated that construct accessibility can affect the likelihood that a situation is interpreted as an emergency (James, 1986), and the degree to which an individual is perceived as behaving in a hostile manner (Carver et al., 1983).

Construct accessibility has an impact on categorization primarily when the stimulus to be encoded is ambiguous. When a stimulus is ambiguous there is considerable diversity in terms of the constructs that can be used for encoding (Bruner, 1957). The relevant or applicable construct that is accessed first for matching is likely to be used to identify the stimulus. Construct accessibility has little impact on encoding in instances where the stimulus is an unambiguous exemplar of a construct. In these instances, the stimulus tends to be categorized in terms of the corresponding construct regardless of the level of accessibility of that construct (Bargh & Thein, 1985).

Accessible Constructs as Standards of Comparison. The encoding of a stimulus as an instance of the category represented by an accessible construct can be viewed essentially as an assimilation effect (Sherif & Hovland, 1961). It also is possible for a primed construct to serve as a standard of comparison against which the target stimulus is judged (e.g., Herr, 1986; Herr et al., 1983; Higgins & Lurie, 1983; Martin, 1986). In such a case, a contrast effect may occur. When the primed construct is extremely discrepant from the target stimulus that is being judged, the features of the category and the target would not match sufficiently for the target to be viewed as an instance of the category. Yet, the primed anchor will influence judgments of the target—judgments that are displaced away from the anchor.

As an example, consider the task employed by Herr et al. (1983), judging the size of two fictitious animals—a jabo and a lemphor. In an ostensibly separate Stroop experiment, the subject was earlier exposed to four animal names. The animals were ones that pretesting had shown to be perceived as extremely large, moderately large, moderately small, or extremely small. Subjects primed with moderate categories displayed an assimilation effect. Apparently, the fictitious animals were viewed as instances of the primed category. Hence, those subjects for whom moderately large animals were highly accessible judged the target animals as larger than did those from whom moderately small animals were highly accessible. On the other hand, it appears that subjects viewed it unlikely that the target animals were instances of either of the extreme categories. However, if when attempting to judge the size of a "jabo," the subject was considering extremely large animals such as elephant and whale, then the jabo seemed small by comparison. If extremely small animals, such as snail and minnow, were highly accessible, the jabo seemed large by comparison. In other words, heightening the accessibility of extreme levels resulted in a contrast effect.

Herr (1986) replicated these findings in the context of a person-perception task.

Assimilation effects in judging an ambiguously described target person were apparent when the subject had been primed with the names of moderately hostile and moderately unhostile people. Contrast effects were obtained when the subject had been primed with the names of extremely hostile or extremely unhostile individuals. Furthermore, Herr found that these effects on the impressions that were formed of the target person, in turn, influenced behavior toward the target person in a social interaction setting. Thus, depending on their extremity, accessible constructs either influenced the encoding of the target person or served as standards of comparison that affected judgments of, and behavior toward, the target person.

Biased Processing as a Function of Attitude Accessibility. As indicated earlier, exposure to an object can prime constructs that are clearly associated with the object. For example, attitudes characterized by a strong association between the object and one's evaluation of the object can be activated automatically upon exposure to the object. Studies by Houston and Fazio (1987) and Wood (1982) indicate that the accessibility of attitudes or attitudinally relevant information can moderate the interpretation, and influence, of new information. Houston and Fazio demonstrated that attitudes high but not low in chronic accessibility biased the assimilation of attitudinally relevant information. Perceivers were much more likely to derogate attitude inconsistent evidence when their attitude was high as opposed to low in accessibility. Wood found that the accessibility of attitudinally relevant information in memory affected a person's susceptibility to influence by a persuasive message. Subjects with little access to issue-relevant beliefs and experiences were more likely to be affected by a counterattitudinal message than subjects who had ready access to such material in memory.

In a study that is particularly relevant to the media context, Fazio and Williams (1986) examined subjects' views of the outcome of the nationally televised debates between the presidential and the vice-presidential candidates during the 1984 election. Just as one would expect, attitudes toward the candidates strongly influenced judgments of which candidate had performed better in the debate. For example, the more positive the attitude toward Reagan, the more likely the respondent was to view Reagan as having performed better than Mondale. However, the extent of this relation was found to be moderated by the accessibility of the respondents' attitude. The greater the chronic accessibility of the attitude, the stronger the relation between attitudes and judgments of the outcome of the debate. Apparently, chronically accessible attitudes are activated upon mere observation of the attitude object and, once activated, serve as a "filter" through which attitudinally relevant information is interpreted.

Retrieval-Based Judgments. In many instances, individuals must rely on their recall of specific information in making a judgment or evaluation (Tversky & Kahneman, 1973). The information that is most readily accessible from memory, of course, tends to serve as the primary basis for the judgment. Judgments or evaluations can often be manipulated by priming a limited subset, as opposed to a representative sample, of the relevant information (Chaiken & Baldwin, 1981; Gabrielcik & Fazio, 1984; Salancik & Conway, 1975; Wyer et al., 1985). Gabrielcik and Fazio, for example, showed that subjects subliminally primed with words containing the letter "T" judged that the letter "T" occurs more frequently in the English language than did unprimed subjects. Salancik and Conway (1975) manipulated the accessibility of proreligious or antireligious behaviors of subjects. Subjects who were primed with religious behaviors judged themselves to be more religious than those who were primed with antireligious behaviors.

Causal Attributions. Studies suggest that the accessibility of potential causal agents or causal reasons can affect causal explanations of events (Rholes & Pryor, 1982; Salancik, 1974). In the study by Salancik, subjects completed sentences such as "I attend class because I . . ." that increased the accessibility of intrinsic reasons for attending class, or sentences such as "I attend class in order to . . ." that increased the accessibility of extrinsic, instrumental reasons for attending class. Subjects primed with intrinsic reasons were more likely to explain their behavior as being intrinsically motivated, whereas subjects primed with extrinsic reasons tended to explain their behavior as being caused more by situational constraints. In the study by Rholes and Pryor (1982) priming a particular person or object (e.g., a teacher) was found to increase the estimated causal influence of that target in later events in which the target was involved.

Problem Solving. The possible solutions or decision alternatives that a person considers will tend to be those that are readily accessible from memory. Similarly, the types of strategies or rules that an individual employs in problem solving and decision making will be those that are highly accessible.

Increasing the accessibility of a particular strategy or rule for dealing with a problem should increase the likelihood that the strategy or rule will be employed. Chertkoff and Sanbonmatsu (1987) suggested that the accessibility of alternative rules of distribution may affect how rewards are allocated. Frequently a reward or payoff must be divided among a number of participants and a wide variety of rules ranging from proportionality to winner-take-all to less conventional rules may guide the decision. The authors suggest that people may be prone to employing the most accessible rules in distributing a reward.

La Rue and Olejnik (1980) have demonstrated that different approaches for solving a problem can be primed. Subjects in their experiment engaged in a verbal seriation task requiring propositional reasoning, a math task requiring concrete logic but no propositional reasoning, or no task at all. Shortly afterward, subjects performed the Defining Issues Task (DIT), a measure of moral reasoning. Subjects who were required to perform the task requiring propositional reasoning later displayed a higher level of moral reasoning on the DIT than subjects who performed the simpler task, or no task at all.

Higgins and Chaires (1980) have shown that priming can even affect performance on creative problem-solving tasks. Subjects in their study attempted to
solve the well-known Duncker candle problem. In this problem a candle, a book
of matches, and a box filled with thumbtacks are provided to the subject. The
subjects' task is to use the given items to affix the candle to a cardboard wall
so that the candle burns properly without dripping on the floor. The solution involves attaching the thumbtack box to the wall and placing the candle on top of
the box. The difficulty is in thinking of the box as having a use other than as
a container for the thumbtacks. In an ostensibly separate experiment, Higgins
and Chaires primed some subjects to think of containers as distinct from objects
(e.g., carton and eggs), whereas others were primed to think of the containers
and objects as a unit (e.g., carton of eggs). When subjects were primed to think
of the container as distinct from the objects, they were more likely to solve the
problem.

Behavior.   A number of studies have demonstrated that construct accessibility can have an influence on behavior (Berkowitz & LePage, 1967; Carver,
et al., 1983; Fazio & Williams, 1986; Herr, 1986; Snyder & Swann, 1976; Wilson & Capitman, 1982). Wilson and Capitman, for example, primed subjects with
a "boy meets girl" encounter or a control story. Subjects reading about the encounter later acted friendlier toward a female confederate than subjects not exposed to the story. Similarly, Carver et al. found that subjects who were primed
with exemplars of hostility displayed more aggression in a subsequent learning
task than control subjects. Studies of attitudes have shown that an individual is
much more likely to behave in an attitude-consistent manner if the attitude is high
as opposed to low in accessibility (e.g., Fazio & Williams, 1986; Snyder & Swann,
1976).

There are two processes through which construct accessibility may affect behavior. First, construct accessibility may affect behavior indirectly by influencing a person's definition or assessment of a situation. As we discussed previously, priming a construct may affect the manner in which a situation is construed.
This, in turn may elicit a particular response. This process is essentially that
delineated by Fazio (1986) with respect to the manner in which attitudes guide
behavior. Alternatively, priming may affect behavior more directly by increasing the accessibility of scripts (Schank & Abelson, 1977) or behavioral patterns.
Priming may increase the likelihood (i.e., lower the threshold) that a behavior
pattern is activated upon the recognition of the appropriate eliciting conditions.

Carver et al. (1982) suggested that modeling may be explained, in part, by
priming. The observation of a particular behavior may increase the likelihood
of that behavior being performed by the observer by increasing the accessibility
of the "mental records specifying the behavior" (p. 416). Observation of an aggressive encounter, for example, may increase the likelihood of interpreting a
later ambiguous encounter as provoking or antagonistic, thereby increasing the

likelihood of subsequent aggressive, retaliatory behavior on the part of the observer. In addition, the observation of aggression may simply increase the script for aggressive behavior, and thereby increases the likelihood of its implementation in a subsequent context. Thus, although some instances of modeling may involve the learning of reinforcement contingencies, others may be mediated by simple priming process.

IMPLICATIONS FOR THE MEDIA

In this section we outline some general ways in which the research on construct accessibility may further our understanding of mass media influence as well as more basic communication processes.

Much of our discussion has focused on networks and associations in memory, and on the strength of those associations. Obviously, such associative learning can occur through experience and through social interaction. Unquestionably, however, the media play a critical role in what we learn about our social world. The media are instrumental in developing the constructs that are available in memory, and in determining which of those constructs are chronically accessible. Many of the basic constructs a person possesses for perceiving and interpreting the world are created or shaped by media portrayals. Similarly, the media influence a person's repertoire of responses as well as the chronic accessibility of those responses in memory.

In addition, the media shape what constructs and responses are currently accessible in memory. These media-primed constructs may have a subtle, yet powerful impact on subsequent perceptions and behavior. For example, a person who has recently seen a television program depicting a "bad cop" may be more likely to perceive a real-life policeman as at fault in a case of questionable conduct than a person who did not see the program.

The research on construct accessibility also has important implications concerning how media messages are perceived. The research suggests that the amount of attention given to a message, the perceptions of a communicator, the interpretation of a message, and the responses to the perceived message may all depend heavily on what constructs and responses are accessible in memory. For example, whether a left-leaning communicator is categorized as "a liberal" or "a radical" may depend on the relative accessibility of the two constructs. The accessibility of arguments and attitudes pertaining to the topic of a message will be particularly important determinants of how a person responds to a message. As we noted earlier, the study by Fazio and Williams (1986) on the presidential debates illustrates how accessibility can influence what a viewer perceives. Viewers with highly accessible attitudes toward Reagan, in effect, "saw" different debates as a function of whether their attitudes were positive or negative.

Finally, the prior and immediate contexts in which a message is embedded may be crucial determinants of the effectiveness of the communication, for these contexts are likely to have considerable impact on which constructs are accessible in memory as the audience member views the message. To optimize the impact of a message, communicators should make a special effort to select or establish a context that will prime preferred constructs. Television advertisers, for example, should select commercial slots that are preceded by programs that prime constructs that will facilitate attention being directed toward the ad as well as the sought-after interpretation of the ad. An insurance advertisement, for example, might receive greater attention if placed following a sober news broadcast as opposed to a sitcom that paints an innocuous picture of the world. Similarly, programs that activate undesirable constructs should be avoided. Advertisers may already be implicitly aware of this. Firms such as General Foods and Coca-Cola shun commercial slots following news programs as they fear the negative impact that the typical "bad news" may have on the perception of their products ("G.F., Coke tell why," 1980).

People frequently are strongly dissuaded by overt attempts of influence or manipulation. Priming is a subtle influence technique, one that is unlikely to elicit psychological reactance (Brehm, 1966). By manipulating the prior and immediate context, a communicator may be able to prime the desired constructs and responses and, thus, influence judgments and behavior with a minimal likelihood of repercussions.

In summary, the media play a critical role in determining both what is available and what is accessible in memory. As a result of this mediating influence on constructs in memory, the media indirectly affect interpretations of events within our daily lives. Of course, the flip side is also true. Our interpretations of events depicted in the media are influenced by construct accessibility. Consequently, the effectiveness of the media as an agent of social influence can be undermined or enhanced by the heightening of the accessibility of constructs relevant to the message.

ACKNOWLEDGMENT

Preparation of this chapter was supported by NIMH Grant MH 38832 and NIMH Research Scientist Development Award MH 00452 to Russell H. Fazio.

REFERENCES

Alba, J. W., & Hasher, L. (1983). Is memory schematic? *Psychological Bulletin, 93*, 203-231.
Anderson, J. R. (1976). *Language, memory, and thought.* Hillsdale, NJ: Lawrence Erlbaum Associates.
Anderson, J. R., & Pirolli, P. L. (1984). Spread of activation. *Journal of Experimental Psychology: Learning, Memory, and Cognition, 10*, 791-798.
Anthony, B. J., & Graham, F. K. (1983). Evidence for sensory selective set in young infants. *Science, 220*, 742-744.

Bargh, J. A., Bond, R. N., Lombardi, W. J., & Tota, M. E. (1986). The additive nature of chronic and temporary sources of construct accessibility. *Journal of Personality and Social Psychology*, *50*, 869-878.

Bargh, J. A., & Pietromonaco, P. (1982). Automatic information processing and social perception: the influence of trait information presented outside of conscious awareness on impression formation. *Journal of Personality and Social Psychology*, *43*, 437-449.

Bargh, J. A., & Thein, R. D. (1985). Individual construct accessibility, person memory, and the recall-judgment link: The case of information overload. *Journal of Personality and Social Psychology*, *49*, 1129-1146.

Berkowitz, L., & LePage, A. (1967). Weapons as aggression eliciting stimuli. *Journal of Personality and Social Psychology*, *7*, 202-207.

Biederman, I. (1972). Perceiving real-life scenes. *Science*, *177*, 77-80.

Bower, G. H. (1981). Mood and memory. *American Psychologist*, *36*, 129-148.

Bower, G. H., Monteiro, K. P., & Gilligan, S. G. (1978). Emotional mood as a context of learning and recall. *Journal of Verbal Learning and Verbal Behavior*, *17*, 573-585.

Brehm, J. W. (1966). *A theory of psychological reactance*. New York: Academic Press.

Bruner, J. S. (1957). On perceptual readiness. *Psychological Review*, *64*, 123-152.

Bruner, J. S. (1958). Social psychology and perception. In E. Maccoby, T. Newcomb, & E. Hartley (Eds.), *Readings in social psychology* (pp. 85-93). New York: Holt, Rinehart & Winston.

Carver, C. S., Ganellen, R. J., Froming, W. J., & Chambers, W. (1983). Modeling: An analysis in terms of category accessibility. *Journal of Experimental Social Psychology*, *19*, 403-421.

Chaiken, S., & Baldwin, M. N. (1981). Affective-cognitive consistency and the effect of salient behavioral information on the self-perception of attitudes. *Journal of Personality and Social Psychology*, *41*, 1-12.

Chertkoff, J., & Sanbonmatsu, D. M. (1987). *A decision-making model of fairness judgments*. Unpublished manuscript, Indiana University, Bloomington, IN.

Clark, M. S. (1983). Arousal cues arousal-related material in memory: Implications for understanding effects of mood on memory. *Journal of Verbal Learning and Verbal Behavior*, *22*, 633-649.

Collins, A. M., & Loftus, E. F. (1975). A spreading-activation theory of semantic processing. *Psychological Review*, *82*, 407-428.

Fazio, R. H. (1986). How do attitudes guide behavior? In R. E. Sorrentino and E. T. Higgins (Eds.), *The handbook of motivation and cognition: Foundations of social behavior* (pp. 204-243). New York: Guilford Press.

Fazio, R. H., Powell, M. C., & Herr, P. M. (1983). Toward a process model of the attitude-behavior relation: Accessing one's attitude upon mere observation of the attitude object. *Journal of Personality and Social Psychology*, *44*, 723-735.

Fazio, R. H., Sanbonmatsu, D. M., Powell, M. C., & Kardes, F. R. (1986). On the automatic activation of attitudes. *Journal of Personality and Social Psychology*, *50*, 229-238.

Fazio, R. H., & Williams, C. J. (1986). Attitude accessibility as a moderator of the attitude-perception and attitude-behavior relations: An investigation of the 1984 presidential election. *Journal of Personality and Social Psychology*, *3*, 504-514.

Gabrielcik, A., & Fazio, R. H. (1984). Priming and frequency estimation: A strict test of the availability heuristic. *Personality and Social Psychology Bulletin*, *10*, 85-89.

Geller, V., & Shaver, P. (1976). Cognitive consequences of self-awareness. *Journal of Experimental Social Psychology*, *12*, 99-108.

Greenwald, A. G., Liu, T. J., & Klinger, M. (1986). *Unconscious processing of word meaning*. Unpublished manuscript, Ohio State University, Columbus, OH.

G. F., Coke tell why they shun TV news. (1980, January). *Advertising Age*, p. 39.

Herr, P. M. (1986). Consequences of priming: Judgment and behavior. *Journal of Personality and Social Psychology*, *51*, 1106-1115.

Herr, P. M. (1987). *Price perception: Priming-induced context effects.* Unpublished manuscript, Indiana University, Bloomington, IN.

Herr, P. M., Sherman, S. J., & Fazio, R. H. (1983). On the consequences of priming: Assimilation and contrast effects. *Journal of Experimental Social Psychology, 19,* 323-340.

Higgins, E. T., Bargh, J. A., & Lombardi, W. (1985). The nature of priming effects on categorization. *Journal of Experimental Psychology: Learning, Memory, and Cognition, 11,* 59-69.

Higgins, E. T., & Chaires, W. M. (1980). Accessibility of interrelational constructs: Implications for stimulus encoding and creativity. *Journal of Experimental Social Psychology, 16,* 348-361.

Higgins, E. T., & King, G. (1981). Accessibility of social constructs: Information-processing consequences of individual and contextual variability. In N. Cantor & J. F. Kihlstrom (Eds.), *Personality, cognition, and social interaction* (pp. 69-121), Hillsdale, NJ: Lawrence Erlbaum Associates.

Higgins, E. T., King, G. A., & Mavin, G. H. (1982). Individual construct accessibility and subjective impressions and recall. *Journal of Personality and Social Psychology, 43,* 35-47.

Higgins, E. T., & Lurie, L. (1983). Context, categorization, and memory: The "change-of-standard" effect. *Cognitive Psychology, 15,* 525-547.

Higgins, E. T., Rholes, W. S., & Jones, C. R. (1977). Category accessibility and impression formation. *Journal of Experimental Social Psychology, 13,* 141-154.

Houston, D. A., & Fazio, R. H. (1987). *Biased processing as a function of attitude accessibility.* Paper presented at the annual meeting of the Midwestern Psychological Association, Chicago, IL.

Isen, A. M., Shalker, T. E., Clark, M. S., & Karp, L. (1978). Affect, accessibility of material in memory, and behavior: A cognitive loop? *Journal of Personality and Social Psychology, 36,* 1-12.

James, K. (1986). Priming and social categorizational factors: Impact on awareness of emergency situations. *Personality and Social Psychology Bulletin, 12,* 462-467.

Jones, E. E., & Gerard, H. B. (1967). *Foundations of social psychology.* New York: Wiley.

Kahneman, D. (1973). *Attention and effort.* Englewood Cliffs, NJ: Prentice-Hall.

Kelly, G. A. (1955). *The psychology of personal constructs.* New York: Norton.

Klinger, E. (1975). Consequences of, commitment to, and disengagement from incentives. *Psychological Review, 82,* 1-25.

Laird, J. D., Wegener, J. J., Halal, M., & Szegda, M. (1982). Remembering what you feel: Effects of emotion on memory. *Journal of Personality and Social Psychology, 4,* 646-657.

La Rue, A., & Olejnik, A. B. (1980). Cognitive "priming" of principled moral thought. *Personality and Social Psychology Bulletin, 6,* 413-416.

Leight, K. A., & Ellis, H. C. (1981). Emotional mood states, strategies, and state dependency in memory. *Journal of Verbal Learning and Verbal Behavior, 20,* 251-266.

Levine, R., Chein, I., & Murphy, G. (1942). The relation of the intensity of a need to the amount of perceptual distortion: A preliminary report. *Journal of Psychology, 13,* 283-292.

Loftus, E. F. (1973). Activation of semantic memory. *American Journal of Psychology, 86,* 331-337.

Marcel, A. J. (1983). Conscious and unconscious perception: Experiments on visual masking and word recognition. *Cognitive Psychology, 15,* 197-237.

Martin, L. L. (1986). Set/reset: Use and disuse of concepts in impression formation. *Journal of Personality and Social Psychology, 51,* 493-504.

Meyer, D. E., Schvaneveldt, R. W., & Ruddy, M. G. (1975). Loci of contextual effects on visual word-recognition. In P. M. A. Rabbit & S. Dornic (Eds.), *Attention and performance* (Vol. 5, pp. 98-118). London: Academic Press.

Mischel, W. (1973). Toward a cognitive social learning reconceptualization of personality. *Psychological Review, 80,* 252-283.

Neisser, U. (1976). *Cognition and reality: Principles and implications of cognitive psychology.* San Francisco: Freeman.

Oatman, L. C. (1984). *Auditory evoked potential amplitude during simultaneous visual stimulation.* Paper presented at the Annual Meeting of the Psychonomic Society, San Antonio, TX.

Palmer, S. E. (1975). The effects of contextual scenes on the identification of objects. *Memory and Cognition, 3,* 519-526.

Ratcliff, R., & McKoon, G. (1981). Does activation really spread? *Psychological Review, 88,* 454-462.

Rholes, W. S., & Pryor, J. B. (1982). Cognitive accessibility and causal attributions. *Personality and Social Psychology Bulletin, 8,* 719-727.

Rholes, W. S., Riskind, J. H., & Lane, J. W. (1987). Emotional states and memory biases: Effects of cognitive priming and mood. *Journal of Personality and Social Psychology, 52,* 91-99.

Riskind, J. H. (1983). Nonverbal expressions and the accessibility of life experience memories: A congruence hypothesis. *Social Cognition, 2,* 62-86.

Salancik, J. R. (1974). Inference of one's attitude from behavior recalled under linguistically manipulated cognitive sets. *Journal of Experimental Social Psychology, 10,* 415-427.

Salancik, J. R., & Conway, M. (1975). Attitude inference from salient and relevant cognitive content about behavior. *Journal of Personality and Social Psychology, 5,* 829-840.

Sanbonmatsu, D. M., Osborne, R. E., & Fazio, R. H. (1986). *The measurement of automatic attitude activation.* Paper presented at the annual meeting of the Midwestern Psychological Association, Chicago, IL.

Schank, R. C., & Abelson, R. P. (1977). *Scripts, plans, goals, and understanding.* Hillsdale, NJ: Lawrence Erlbaum Associates.

Sherif, M., & Hovland, C. I. (1961). *Social judgment: Assimilation and contrast effects in communication and attitude change.* New Haven, CT: Yale University Press.

Shiffrin, R. M., & Schneider, W. (1977). Controlled and automatic human information processing: II. Perceptual learning, automatic attending, and a general theory. *Psychological Review, 84,* 127-190.

Smith, E. R., & Branscombe, N. R. (1987). Procedurally mediated social inferences: The case of category accessibility effects. *Journal of Experimental Social Psychology, 23,* 361-382.

Snyder, M. (1982). When believing means doing: Creating links between attitudes and behavior. In M. P. Zanna, E. T. Higgins, & C. P. Herman (Eds.), *Consistency in social behavior: The Ontario Symposium,* (Vol. 2, pp. 105-130). Hillsdale, NJ: Lawrence Erlbaum Associates.

Snyder, M., & Swann, W. B., Jr. (1976). When actions reflect attitudes: The politics of impression management. *Journal of Personality and Social Psychology, 34,* 1034-1042.

Srull, T. K., & Wyer, R. S., Jr. (1979). The role of category accessibility in the interpretation of information about persons: Some determinants and implications. *Journal of Personality and Social Psychology, 37,* 1660-1672.

Srull, T. K., & Wyer, R. S., Jr. (1980). Category accessibility and social perception: Some implications for the study of person memory and interpersonal judgments. *Journal of Personality and Social Psychology, 38,* 841-856.

Srull, T. K., & Wyer, R. S., Jr. (1986). The role of chronic and temporary goals in social information processing. In R. E. Sorrentino & E. T. Higgins (Eds.), *The handbook of motivation and cognition: Foundations of social behavior* (pp. 503-549). New York: Guilford Press.

Taylor, S. E., & Crocker, J. (1981). Schematic bases of social information processing. In E. T. Higgins, C. P. Herman, & M. P. Zanna (Eds.), *Social cognition: The Ontario Symposium* (Vol. 1, pp. 89-134). Hillsdale, NJ: Lawrence Erlbaum Associates.

Teasdale, J. D., & Fogarty, S. J. (1979). Differential effects of induced mood on retrieval of pleasant and unpleasant events from episodic memory. *Journal of Abnormal Psychology, 88,* 248-257.

Tulving, E., & Pearlstone, Z. (1966). Availability versus accessibility of information in memory for words. *Journal of Verbal Learning and Verbal Behavior, 5,* 381-391.

Tversky, A., & Kahneman, D. (1973). Availability: A heuristic for judging frequency and probability. *Cognitive Psychology, 5,* 207-232.

Warren, R. E. (1972). Stimulus encoding and memory. *Journal of Experimental Psychology, 94,* 90-100.

Wilson, T. D., & Capitman, J. A. (1982). Effects of script availability on social behavior. *Personality and Social Psychology Bulletin, 8,* 11-19.

Wispe, L. G., & Drambarean, N. C. (1953). Physiological need, word frequency, and visual duration thresholds. *Journal of Experimental Psychology, 46,* 25-31.

Wood, W. (1982). Retrieval of attitude-relevant information from memory: Effects on susceptibility to persuasion and on intrinsic motivation. *Journal of Personality and Social Psychology, 42,* 798-810.

Wyer, R. S. Jr., Bodenhausen, G. V., & Gorman, T. F. (1985). Cognitive mediators of reactions to rape. *Journal of Personality and Social Psychology, 48,* 324-338.

Wyer, R. S. Jr., & Srull, T. K. (1981). Category accessibility: Some theoretical and empirical issues concerning the processing of social stimulus information. In E. T. Higgins, C. P. Herman, & M. P. Zanna (Eds.), *Social cognition: The Ontario Symposium* (Vol. 1, pp. 161-197). Hillsdale, NJ: Lawrence Erlbaum Associates.

Wyer, R. S. Jr., & Srull, T. K. (1986). Human cognition in its social context. *Psychological Review, 93,* 322-359.

CHAPTER

4

Perceiving and Responding to Mass Media Characters

Cynthia Hoffner
Illinois State University
Joanne Cantor
University of Wisconsin—Madison

When people think about their favorite movies and television series, they often think first of the characters who populate them. Producers of entertainment fare seem to appreciate the role of characters in generating and maintaining audiences. In fact, many television executives believe that the most important aspect of a good program is the presence of likeable, intriguing characters (Gitlin, 1983). Sequels and spinoffs are often based on the assumption that the audience for an existing character will want to witness that character in new situations. For example, "Rhoda," "Phyllis," and "Lou Grant" were all based on characters developed on the "Mary Tyler Moore Show." Moreover, several film and television series, such as the James Bond films, have commissioned a series of actors, in succession, to play a single character, apparently under the assumption that interest in a specific character would be maintained even when a new actor played the part.

The viewers of popular television series and films become quite familiar with the characters and often experience strong reactions to the things that they do and to the things that happen to them. Over the course of several episodes of a series, or even during the course of a single episode or film, viewers engage in the process of impression formation in getting to know television and film characters.

This chapter deals with the manner in which viewers form impressions of media characters and respond to characters' experiences. The terms *impression* and *perception* are used to refer to a viewer's overall conception of what a character is like. An impression may include information about a character's personality attributes, behavioral tendencies, personal goals, and ideals (cf. Park, 1986). Many studies of character perception, however, have focused on evaluative judgments about characters' personal attributes, often with regard to social desirability (e.g., good or bad, nice or mean). This approach seems to reflect the assumptions of implicit personality theory (see Schneider, Hastorf, & Ellsworth, 1979), which contends that the content of impressions is organized around a few underlying dimensions. In other words, a person who possesses one specific attribute is assumed to possess a variety of related characteristics as well. In fact, research has found that a general evaluative dimension (favorable–unfavorable) accounts for the largest amount of variance in impressions of others. Thus, in this chapter, evaluations or judgments of characters refer to the general content of viewers' impressions.

Perceptions of media characters are considered important because understanding how viewers form impressions of characters promotes an understanding of viewers' responses to entertainment fare in general. Impressions and evaluations of characters have implications for various components of attraction, such as liking, perceived similarity, and the desire to be like characters. These reactions, in turn, have been shown to influence viewers' tendencies to identify with or take the perspective of characters, and to attend to and imitate their behaviors. They have also been shown to mediate short- and long-term emotional reactions to depicted events and to characters themselves.

The chapter is divided into three parts. The first part deals with the major sources of information about media characters and how each type of information affects impressions. The second part deals with how specific viewer characteristics influence the way viewers utilize the available information about media protagonists. The final section discusses implications of character perceptions for viewers' responses to depicted characters and events.

Some differences can be noted between the processes of "character perception" and impression formation in an interpersonal context. First, the media situation differs from the interpersonal context in that viewers have no expectation of meeting and interacting with the characters they perceive. Research has shown that an observer's goals or objectives in forming an impression of another person influence the selection and interpretation of information about that person (Cohen, 1981). There is some evidence that anticipated interaction affects the quality of impressions formed by both children and adults (Feldman, 1979, cited in Feldman & Ruble, 1981; Srull & Brand, 1983).

A second difference between person perception and character perception derives from the fact that the information typically available in interpersonal and mass media contexts is somewhat different. The process of interaction can provide feedback (e.g., through responses to self-disclosures) that shapes impressions of another's personality and behavioral tendencies. Of course, viewers do not have the opportunity to personally interact with mass media characters (Perse & Rubin, 1989). Yet viewers usually are able to observe media characters more closely and in more private situations than they can most of the people they encounter in their daily lives. For example, interpersonal perceivers are not privy to the private thoughts of others; in contrast, media consumers sometimes hear verbalizations or see visual enactments of characters' thoughts, memories, and fantasies. As another example, people do not have the opportunity to observe how other people behave when they are entirely alone; nevertheless media consumers are sometimes exposed to such potentially revealing information.

Another difference derives from the fact that the information viewers receive about characters is scripted, designed specifically to produce a particular impression in a relatively efficient manner. Camera angles, close-ups, and editing techniques influence viewers' selection and interpretation of character-relevant information. Exposure to other people's behaviors in interpersonal settings is less planful and systematic. Moreover, the viewer of a media presentation often has much more complete information regarding the motivations and constraints underlying a character's behavior and the psychological context in which it occurs. For example, the viewer of a televised scene has often witnessed the prior interactions and events that motivate a character to respond in a specific way. In an interpersonal context, an observer rarely has first-hand knowledge of the potentially critical experiences the other has undergone immediately prior to an interaction.

Despite these differences in the nature of the information that is generally available about characters versus people, the cognitive processes involved in forming impressions of characters and real people appear to be highly similar (see Babrow, O'Keefe, Swanson, Meyers, & Murphy, 1988; Perse & Rubin, 1989; Reeves, 1979). Because there is much consensus regarding the processes and crucial variables involved in person perception in interpersonal and mass communication contexts, the theories and findings of one area can be used to amplify and complement those of the other (cf. Hawkins, Wiemann, & Pingree, 1988).

SOURCES OF INFORMATION
ABOUT MEDIA CHARACTERS

In forming impressions of others, people utilize a wide variety of observable information, including physical appearance, speech characteristics, behaviors, emotional reactions, and nonverbal expressions (Schneider et al., 1979). These sources of information are also available in media presentations, and undoubtedly contribute to viewers' impressions of media characters. There are also some unique aspects of media presentations (e.g., program structure) that may modify the use or interpretation of character information, and these are noted whenever they seem relevant.

Characters' Physical Appearance

A character's physical appearance has an enormous potential to affect impressions because it is generally the first attribute that comes to the viewer's attention and is visible whenever the character is on screen. In the interpersonal realm, physical characteristics, particularly attractiveness, exert an important influence on perceptions of other people (Hatfield & Sprecher, 1986; Patzer, 1985). Physique, hair color, and manner of dress are related to attractiveness, but may also convey independent information. Other aspects of individuals that are conveyed mainly through physically prominent characteristics are their gender and ethnicity. However, because the effects of these variables on character perceptions vary according to many aspects of perceivers, they are discussed in a later section.

Physical Attractiveness.   Research has shown that physically attractive people are perceived as possessing more socially desirable personality traits than unattractive individuals (see Hatfield & Sprecher, 1986; Patzer, 1985). Several studies have found that the same behavior is evaluated differently when it is performed by an attractive versus an unattractive person (e.g., Dion, 1972; Efran, 1974). For example, unattractive children who engaged in a transgression were seen by adults as more dishonest and unpleasant than attractive children who performed the same behavior. Furthermore, the act itself was seen as more undesirable when performed by an unattractive child (Dion, 1972).

Only a few investigations have examined the relationship between physical appearance and perceptions of media characters. A series of studies by Reeves and his colleagues (Reeves & Greenberg, 1977; Reeves & Lometti, 1979; Reeves & Miller, 1978) showed that physical attractiveness was a salient feature children used to distinguish among the leading characters from different television series. However, a study by Alexander (1980), using a different sample of characters (parents and children in three television families), did not find attractiveness to be an important dimension. Alexander argued that different dimensions are important in judging different types of characters. Apparently, physical attractiveness contributes more strongly to impressions of characters in some roles than others.

In a study of children's reactions to the adventure series "The Incredible Hulk," Sparks and Cantor (1986) observed that the attractive main character, David Banner, was rated as more "good," more "nice," and more inclined to help people than was his alter ego the monstrous Hulk. They argued that the characters' physical attributes were strongly influential in the children's ratings. This conclusion was supported by a subsequent study (Hoffner & Cantor, 1985), which manipulated the appearance and behavior of a character in an original videotaped story. Hoffner and Cantor (1985) found that the physical appearance of the character, who resembled either a kindly grandmother or a witch, affected children's judgments of her personality and her behavioral tendencies. Specifically, the woman who resembled a grandmother was judged to be nicer and more likely to behave kindly toward other characters in the program than was the woman who resembled a witch.

Physique.   Physique or body type is also related to personality judgments (e.g., Lerner, 1969; Wells & Siegel, 1961). For example, Wells and Siegel reported that, compared to people with other physiques, those with endomorphic (overweight) body builds were seen as lazier, more talkative, and more warm-hearted and generous; mesomorphs (muscular, athletic) were perceived as stronger, more self-reliant, and more likely to be leaders; and ectomorphs (tall, thin) were rated as more ambitious, more suspicious of others, more tense, nervous, and stubborn.

There does not appear to be any media research specifically dealing with the influence of physique on perceptions of characters. Meehan (1988), however, recently suggested that characters' body shapes (e.g., slim, bony, or plump) contribute to their characterizations. In addition, a content analysis of food and eating behaviors on popular television series revealed that overweight characters were less often associated with positive personal and social characteristics (e.g., intelligence, popularity, success) than were characters with thin or average body types (Kaufman, 1980). It seems likely that television producers consider body stereotypes when casting roles, in the hope that the actor's body build will reinforce (or at least not contradict) the intended image of the character (Turow, 1978).

Other Physical Characteristics. There is also evidence that people share assumptions about the personality traits associated with certain facial characteristics, such as muscle tone and the spacing of facial features, especially if these characteristics resemble facial expressions associated with particular emotions (Ekman, 1978). For example, someone whose eyebrows are low and close together may seem to be habitually angry, and may thus appear to be an unpleasant, hostile person. Presumably actors are cast in roles that are compatible with their facial features (e.g., the kindly looking doctor, the vicious-looking hitman).

Other physical characteristics, such as hair color and ethnic origin, have also been associated with personality judgments. For example, blonde women are frequently assumed to be lacking in intelligence (Hatfield & Sprecher, 1986). However, it is likely that the attributes associated with some physical characteristics change along with changes in society. Scherer (1971) found that Germans in the late 1960s evaluated blonde, blue-eyed television actors more positively than dark-haired, dark-eyed actors on a variety of personality attributes. For example, the dark actors were more often judged to be wicked, sly, and calculating. After exposure to films featuring dark actors as likeable heroes, subjects became more positive in their evaluations of dark actors. Scherer also found support for the notion that viewers' conceptions of the physical attributes of heroes and villains are affected by social changes. The stereotype of the blonde hero was stronger among middle-aged Germans than among college students, a finding that Scherer attributed to the older group's greater exposure to Nazi ideology. Presumably, changes in evaluations associated with certain physical features can also be influenced by the media, either because of the impact of a single, popular media presentation, or due to changes in the types of actors selected for various roles (e.g., heroes increasingly portrayed by Blacks or other ethnic minorities).

Manner of Dress.   What someone wears often indicates his or her social status or occupation (e.g., wealthy socialite, police officer), and may also communicate information about the personality of the wearer. Aspects of dress that have been related to personality attributes include clothing, makeup, and eye glasses (e.g., Hamid, 1972; Rosenfeld & Plax, 1977). Argyle and McHenry (1971), for example, found that individuals who wore glasses were considered to be more intelligent and industrious than those who did not wear glasses, particularly when observers saw them for only a brief period of time.

Himmelweit, Oppenheim, and Vince (1958) reported that the physical appearance of television characters was frequently cited by adolescents as a way of distinguishing the "good guys" from the "bad guys." The heroes were typically described as clean and well-dressed, whereas the villains were reported to be dirty and scruffy looking. Apparently the characters' manner of dress was used as a means of identifying their respective roles within the programs.

Neumann, Cassata, and Skill (1983) reported that costume designers on soap operas choose attire that reflects characters' personalities and occupations. Informal observation confirms that clothing and other aspects of dress contribute to characterizations. For example, the title character in the television series "Mary Hartman, Mary Hartman" was described in the following way by Craft (1982): "Mary's eccentric, *jeune fille* appearance is the first clue to her character, this mother of a thirteen-year-old dressing in a younger manner than her daughter" (p. 153). In the *Superman* films, Clark Kent's transformation into Superman (and his corresponding change in personality and physical capabilities) is paralleled by an obvious alteration in his wardrobe, and the disappearance of his glasses.

Characters' Speech Characteristics

The way characters speak—their vocal qualities, accent, and language use—may also contribute to viewers' character impressions. Research on interpersonal perception has shown that a variety of nonverbal vocal characteristics influence listeners' impressions of speakers' personalities. Characteristics such as speech rate, pausing, pitch variation, and loudness have been related to a variety of personality traits, including dominance, assertiveness, politeness, competence, and benevolence (see Ray, 1986; Siegman, 1987). Ray argued that impression formation is guided by culturally shared prototypes for the vocal characteristics associated with specific personality traits (e.g., a competent person talks loudly and rapidly). Accents and dialects have also been shown to influence personality judgments, as well as attributions of status (see Siegman, 1987). These findings seem to reflect the influence of stereotypes associated with the ethnic or social groups to which speakers apparently belong (on the basis of their speech patterns). Some media observers have noted that vocal qualities contribute to television characterizations (e.g., a feminine character who speaks with a "little girl voice"; Meehan, 1988), but no empirical research appears to have examined the role of vocal cues in viewers' character perceptions. Nonetheless, there can be little doubt that vocal qualities and accents help convey information about characteristics such as personality, social class, and educational level.

A variety of language characteristics can also influence person perceptions. One line of research has documented male–female language differences that influence evaluations of speakers' personal and social characteristics (see Mulac, Incontro, & James, 1985). In an extension of this research, Mulac, Bradac, and Mann (1985) examined the effect of language characteristics on perceptions of characters appearing on children's television programs. The investigators found that male and female characters were distinguished by a variety of linguistic variables, such as sentence length, use of polite words and phrases, justifications for behavior, and grammatical errors. In addition, ratings of male and female characters based on dialogue transcripts were consistent with gender stereotypes. This research demonstrates that language use can contribute to impressions of characters, independent of other personal characteristics such as physical appearance.

Characters' Behaviors

Another important source of information about a television character is his or her behavior. In the mass media, as in real life, behaviors are ongoing and constantly changing, and occur in particular contexts in response to a wide variety of stimuli and situations. A viewer must extract and interpret behavioral information from an ongoing stream of program events. Research in the area of social cognition has shown that the behaviors an actor performs lead observers to make inferences about the actor's personality traits, abilities, and behavioral tendencies (see, e.g., Wyer & Srull, 1989).

Research indicates that viewers attend to and remember many of the behaviors performed by media characters, and that behavior is an important aspect of the impressions viewers form of characters. Wartella and Alexander (1977) asked children and adolescents to describe television characters, and found that the majority of character descriptions focused on the actions the characters performed. There is also evidence that viewers use behaviors and physical abilities to distinguish between real and fantastic characters (Dorr, 1983; Fernie, 1981). Several studies (Alexander, 1980; Reeves & Greenberg, 1977; Reeves & Lometti, 1979) reported that activity, strength, and humor were important attributes children used to differentiate television characters. It seems likely that these traits were derived from the behavior of the characters in the samples. Similarly, Livingstone (1987, 1989) suggested that the dimensions she found to be important in adults' representations of soap opera characters (e.g., morality, power) were based on their interpretations of the characters' behaviors and interactions within the narrative.

It would be virtually impossible to devise a complete taxonomy of behaviors and the types of attributions they lead to. In addition to the fact that there is no limit to the variety of different behaviors that people can perform, a given behavior may be interpreted differently, depending on characteristics of the observer and the context in which the behavior occurs (Higgins & King, 1981). Nonetheless, mass media researchers have attempted to classify specific categories of behavior for the purpose of content analyzing media presentations. Studies have examined media portrayals of a variety of different behaviors, including physical and verbal aggression (e.g., Greenberg, Edison, Korzenny, Fernandez-Collado, & Atkin, 1980; Harvey, Sprafkin, & Rubinstein, 1979), prosocial behavior (e.g., Greenberg et al., 1980; Harvey et al., 1979), intimacy and sexual behavior (e.g., Lowry, Love, & Kirby, 1981; Sprafkin & Silverman, 1981), methods of problem solving (e.g., Dominick, Richman, & Wurtzel, 1979), compliance-gaining strategies (Haefner & Comstock, 1990), giving and receiving emotional support (Henderson, Greenberg, & Atkin, 1980), giving and receiving orders and advice (Henderson et al., 1980; Turow, 1974), and alcohol and drug use (Breed & De Foe, 1980; Greenberg, Fernandez-Collardo, Graff, Korzenny, & Atkin, 1980).

In mass media research, aggressive and prosocial behaviors have received by far the greatest amount of attention. Studies of responses to videotaped portrayals have shown that even preschool children assign positive evaluations to actors who engage in prosocial behaviors such as generosity, and negative evaluations to actors who cause harm to another person through aggressive behavior (Berndt & Berndt, 1975; Bryan & Walbek, 1970). Similarly, investigations involving televised narratives have shown that preschoolers, as well as older viewers, assign more positive ratings to characters who engage in kind, helpful behavior than to those who behave cruelly or unkindly toward another character (Hoffner & Cantor, 1985; Wilson, Cantor, Gordon, & Zillmann, 1986; Zillmann & Cantor, 1977). Observing a character's behavior also leads viewers to expect similar behavior from the character in the future (Hoffner & Cantor, 1985).

Studies show that viewers, even those as young as kindergarten age, are able to distinguish the heroes from the villains in media presentations on the basis of the characters' behavior (Himmelweit et al., 1958; Liss, Reinhardt, & Fredriksen, 1983). Liss et al. found that nearly all the children who viewed a prosocial, nonaggressive cartoon cited the heroes' helpful behaviors as a reason for identifying them as the "good guys." When adolescents were asked by Himmelweit et al. to describe how they distinguished between the heroes and villains in Westerns, the behaviors and activities of the characters were mentioned more than any other criterion. Heroes were said to be polite and to engage in helpful, positive behaviors; their skill with guns was also mentioned. The villains were described as engaging in socially unacceptable behaviors such as gambling, drinking in bars, starting fights, and robbing banks. Aggressive behavior per se was not cited as a way of distinguishing the heroes from the villains, probably because both types of characters in westerns typically performed numerous violent acts (as a content analysis by the authors revealed).

Mass media research has examined the influence of only a few other behaviors (in addition to aggressive and prosocial acts) on character impressions. These behaviors include failing or succeeding (Albert, 1957; Fernie, 1981) and engaging in gender-stereotyped or counter-stereotyped activities (Williams, LaRose, & Frost, 1981). A wide variety of behaviors, of course, contribute to impressions of real people. There is commonality among observers regarding the traits implied by specific behaviors, and it seems reasonable to expect that the behaviors of media characters would be perceived similarly. In a study involving verbal descriptions of individuals, for example, someone who "attended the symphony concert" was seen as intelligent, whereas someone who "made the same mistake three times" was seen as unintelligent (Hastie & Kumar, 1979).

Greenberg (1982) noted that because people generally follow the characters in specific programs for many episodes, researchers should look at the behaviors of principal characters over time. However, research on the influence of behaviors on character impressions has not considered behavioral features such as the duration, frequency, or consistency of the behavior (cf. Ebbesen, 1981). Some of these aspects are undoubtedly important in forming impressions. For example, if a character slams a door following an argument, this action alone does not necessarily convey much information about the character's personality. However, if the character repeatedly behaves in this manner, he or she might be considered volatile or hot-tempered (Kelley, 1967).

Although behaviors can independently convey information about the characteristics of people who perform them, it is obvious that many additional aspects of a media presentation may affect viewers' interpretations of a behavior. These modifying factors include the motives and intentions of the actor, and the consequences of the behavior for the actor (e.g., punishment) and the recipient (if there is one, e.g., injury). In addition, viewers' behavior-based character impressions undoubtedly depend to some degree on the personal characteristics of the actor (e.g., age, occupation, social role) and the context in which the behavior occurs.

Motivations and Consequences.   Much mass media research has focused on the motives, intentions, and consequences related to aggressive behaviors. Although prosocial behaviors have also been investigated, there has been less concern with factors modifying the interpretation of such behaviors.

The motives or reasons underlying characters' behaviors constitute one set of factors that can modify impressions. For example, although aggression typically leads to negative evaluations, certain motives such as self-defense tend to justify aggressive actions (Hoyt, 1970), and should therefore lead to less negative judgments of an aggressor. Leifer and Roberts (1972) reported that, although "bad" motives for violent acts were associated with negative character evaluations, "good" motives were associated with positive evaluations, at least among adolescent and adult viewers. There is also evidence that intentionality (doing something accidentally vs. on purpose) affects evaluations of characters. In general, characters who cause harm intentionally and/or for socially unacceptable reasons (e.g., in the course of a robbery) are evaluated more negatively than characters who perform the same action accidentally and/or for socially acceptable reasons (e.g., in the course of capturing a criminal; Berndt & Berndt, 1975; Collins, Berndt, & Hess, 1974; see also Collins, 1983).

The consequences of a behavior for the actor may also influence viewers' evaluations (Collins et al., 1974). A given behavior may be successful and result in rewards or other positive consequences for the actor, or it may be unsuccessful and yield negative consequences, such as punishment or social rejection. Albert (1957) found that an aggressive hero was admired more when his behavior was depicted as successful than when it was unsuccessful. In another study (Bandura, Ross, & Ross, 1963), children tended to verbally derogate the loser in an aggressive interaction, and rejected him as a role model. Apparently, success tends to enhance the social status of a model, and punishment or failure tends to reduce the model's status (Bandura, 1977).

The outcome of the behavior for the recipient of the action may also affect impressions of the actor. Studies have shown that people assign greater responsibility to actors when the negative consequences of their actions are severe rather than mild (Harvey, Harris, & Barnes, 1975). In a study of viewers' perceptions of television violence, Gunter (1985) found that aggressive actions that resulted in harm to a victim were judged to be more violent than similar acts that produced no observable harm, although the study did not assess evaluations of the aggressor. In another study, viewers of an aggressive film considered a rapist more responsible for an assault when the victim expressed pain and distress than when she expressed pleasure (Donnerstein & Berkowitz, 1981).

Often, all aspects of a behavioral episode are consistent, such as when a villain intentionally harms someone and is punished for his or her behavior. However, sometimes portrayals are inconsistent: Characters may express both positive and negative motives or may perform two contradictory actions (Collins & Zimmermann, 1975; Gollin, 1958; see also Hoffner, Cantor, & Thorson, 1989). Villains may be successful, or heroes may behave in ways that contradict their rhetoric, such as using aggression while espousing a prosocial goal (Albert, 1957; Liss et al., 1983). In forming an evaluation of a character, particularly when the portrayal is inconsistent, certain pieces of information may be disregarded or considered less important by viewers. Media research indicates that mature viewers tend to rely more heavily on motives or intentions in evaluating actors than on the consequences of their acts (Collins et al., 1974). This finding is generally consistent with research on the attribution of responsibility (Fincham & Jaspars, 1980). Nonmedia research also suggests that several factors may modify viewers' use of motive, intention, and consequence information, including whether the actions affect another person, as opposed to property or material goods (Elkind & Dabek, 1977), and whether the action produces positive or negative consequences, such as praise or blame (Costanzo, Coie, Grumet, & Farnill, 1973).

Research suggests that negative information is more influential than positive information in forming impressions and evaluations of others (Skowronski & Carlston, 1989). Thus, a character who performs one cruel action may be evaluated negatively, regardless of how many kind actions he or she also performs.

Personal Characteristics of the Actor. The types of behaviors observers expect or consider acceptable vary according to characteristics of the actor (Jones & McGillis, 1976). As Gunter (1985) has argued, the same act performed by different types of media characters may be evaluated differently. The age and gender of a character, and his or her occupation or social role, are probably the most important characteristics in this regard.

Behavior-based evaluations should partly depend on the age of the person, because age is one factor that influences the perceived typicality and appropriateness of certain behaviors (Green, 1981). Crockett, Press, and Osterkamp (1979), for example, found that older individuals whose behavior deviated from negative stereotyped expectations about the elderly (e.g., a woman shown as actively involved in her community) were viewed more positively than their younger counterparts who engaged in the same activities. Behaviors that are seen as inappropriate for older individuals, however, may lead to negative evaluations. Kubey (1980) contended that older television characters who are sexually active or who engage in strenuous physical activity (e.g., riding a motorcycle) are often seen as comical rather than as healthy and energetic—which is how similar behaviors by a younger person would be viewed (see also Davis & Kubey, 1982). Age-related behavioral norms undoubtedly influence perceptions of media characters of all ages (cf. Nardi, 1973).

With regard to gender-based expectations, there are prevailing cultural beliefs about the traits and behaviors that are characteristic of males and females (Huston, 1983). The degree to which an actor's behavior conforms to such expectations affects observers' ratings of the actor's personality (Deaux & Lewis, 1984). Several studies suggest that gender-role beliefs are reflected in viewers' evaluations of media portrayals (see Gunter, 1986; Williams et al., 1981).

People also have expectations about the way people in certain occupations or roles behave, and the obligations associated with particular social roles (Hamilton, 1978; Jones & McGillis, 1976). Behavior that is in accordance with role-based expectations or obligations provides little information about the actor, beyond that which could be inferred from knowledge of the actor's role. In contrast, behavior that disconfirms expectations or represents a failure to fulfill an obligation, leads observers to make judgments about the actor's underlying personality or disposition (Jones, Davis, & Gergen, 1961). Based on this analysis, a character who ignored an accident victim would probably be judged more harshly if he or she were portrayed as a doctor or police officer (roles that entail an obligation to help) than if he or she were an ordinary citizen (see Messaris & Gross, 1977). Furthermore, as Gunter (1985) has argued, social roles may make certain actions seem more or less justified (e.g., violence committed by police vs. criminals) and thus may mediate impressions of characters who engage in those actions.

Context. Character impressions derived from behavior also may be influenced by the context in which the behavior occurs. In nonmedia research, context has been used to refer to the physical and interpersonal aspects of a behavioral episode (Forgas, 1982). Specific situations or settings (e.g., a football game, an elevator) have a limited range of behaviors that are considered appropriate (Price, 1974), and the relationship between the actor and others in the situation also affects the constraints on behavior (Nascimento-Schulze, 1981). Impressions of an actor, therefore, should partly depend on the context within which his or her behavior occurs (Price & Bouffard, 1974). To illustrate, someone who stands on a table and tells a joke at a party may be considered a fun-loving extrovert; someone who behaves the same way before a judge in a court of law would undoubtedly be evaluated quite differently.

It seems that media research has not addressed the influence of situational or interpersonal constraints on behavior-based character impressions. However, in a related study, Gunter (1985) found that acts of aggression were judged to be more violent when they occurred indoors rather than outdoors, possibly because aggression was considered more inappropriate in an indoor setting. Despite the lack of media research, it seems that the situations and the interpersonal context within which characters' actions are depicted should contribute to the impressions viewers form of the characters (cf. Potter & Ware, 1987, 1989).

The tone or format of a media presentation may also serve as a context for interpreting program events. A humorous context, in particular, may alter the meaning of certain behaviors, or may suggest that viewers do not need to take the characters' actions seriously (Dorr, Doubleday, & Kovaric, 1983; Himmelweit et al., 1958). For example, outrageous or potentially harmful behavior (e.g., pushing someone out of a window) may be discounted or taken lightly if performed in a comedy or cartoon program, or otherwise presented as humorous. Consistent with this view, there is evidence that aggressive acts are seen as less violent and disturbing when they occur in cartoons than when they occur in contemporary dramas (Gunter, 1985; Howitt & Cumberbatch, 1974).

Characters' Emotional States and Nonverbal Behaviors

Characters' emotional states also provide information that is useful in understanding mass media presentations (Dorr et al., 1983; Meringhoff et al., 1983), and ultimately in judging the characters themselves. The emotions of media characters may be conveyed verbally, through the characters' own statements or the responses of others, and nonverbally, through facial expressions, vocal tone, gestures, and overt behaviors. In addition, emotions may be inferred from situations or narrative events (Dorr et al., 1983; Meringhoff et al., 1983). Moreover, understanding of the emotional expressions in media presentations partly depends on the context established by preceding events (Goldberg, 1951).

Emotions expressed by or attributed to media characters may help explain the behaviors and reactions of participants in interactions (e.g., she ignored him because she was angry; he joked with her because she was sad; Flapan, 1968; Jaglom & Gardner, 1981), and may also influence other attributions about characters, such as guilt or responsibility (Donnerstein & Berkowitz, 1981). A character's emotional responses can also convey information about the character's personality or disposition (e.g., cheerful, hostile), particularly if he or she consistently responds in the same way, with little situational justification for doing so. For example, the Cowardly Lion in *The Wizard of Oz,* who repeatedly expresses fear in relatively nonthreatening situations, would undoubtedly be viewed as a coward by the audience, even if his emotional behavior were not commented on by other characters.

Although the verbal, nonverbal, and situational cues to emotion are usually consistent in mass media portrayals, this is not always the case (Dorr et al., 1983). Nonmedia research suggests that inconsistent cues may arise as the result of a character's idiosyncratic reaction to a situation (e.g., due to an emotional disturbance), an attempt to deceive other characters, the deliberate use of inconsistent cues, as in sarcasm, or the use of cultural display rules (Ekman & Friesen, 1969; Mehrabian, 1972; Zuckerman, DePaulo, & Rosenthal, 1981). The judged reasons for inconsistencies among emotional cues should have an influence on the impressions viewers form of characters (e.g., neurotic, dishonest, sarcastic, polite).

In addition to indicating emotional states, nonverbal behaviors such as facial expression and gesture can directly influence personality judgments. People share a common understanding of the meaning of many nonverbal behaviors. For example, Clore, Wiggins, and Itkin (1975) found that subjects showed high agreement in judging the positivity or negativity of a series of more than 100 nonverbal behaviors. Typically positive behaviors included looking, nodding, smiling, and using expressive hand gestures. Typically negative behaviors included looking away, staring coldly, frowning, and sneering. The affective meaning conveyed nonverbally during interpersonal interactions has been found to influence judgments about participants' personal characteristics, such as warmth, friendliness, or consideration of others (Bayes, 1974; Bugental, 1974).

Although there does not appear to be any research on the nonverbal behaviors (other than emotional expressions) displayed by media characters, it seems reasonable to assume that viewers would evaluate characters' nonverbal messages in much the same way they evaluate those conveyed interpersonally. In fact, formal aspects of television and film productions may enhance the salience of certain nonverbal behaviors. Close-ups of a character's nervous gestures, for example, may be used to ensure that viewers "pick up" subtle cues that are essential to understanding the character.

CHARACTERISTICS OF VIEWERS
THAT AFFECT PERCEPTIONS

Impressions of characters are not formed in the same way by all viewers. Rather, the knowledge, predispositions, and cognitive abilities people bring to the viewing situation mediate the effects of specific depictions.

Prior Knowledge and Experience

There is much evidence that the cognitive representations of perceivers affect the way they process information about other people (Taylor & Crocker, 1981; see also Wyer & Srull, 1989). There are at lest two types of prior knowledge that seem especially relevant to forming impressions of media characters. First, viewers' general familiarity with the situations depicted, and with the relevant social norms and conventions should influence perceptions of characters. A second potential influence on perceptions is viewers' prior experience with specific characters and settings, such as when viewing a weekly television series.

General Knowledge.   Numerous researchers have emphasized the role of knowledge in understanding and organizing new information (see Brown, Bransford, Ferrara, & Campione, 1983). With regard to media presentations, real-life experience with or knowledge about the types of people and situations depicted should help viewers to understand the motives, behaviors, and psychological states of the characters. Several studies indicate that familiarity with the roles, events, and situations depicted in mass media presentations affects viewers' comprehension of media portrayals (see Collins, 1984). In one study, Collins and Wellman (1982) found that common social knowledge about police, specific crimes, and the law facilitated children's understanding of characters and events in a police drama: The more varied and detailed viewers' background knowledge, the more accurate their interpretations. The authors argued that viewers who rely on limited knowledge to interpret media portrayals may miss subtle indications that a portrayal deviates from common expectations (e.g., a police officer who violates the law; Collins & Zimmermann, 1975). Another study (Newcomb & Collins, 1979) examined the relationship between children's socioeconomic status and their understanding of middle-class and working-class characters in situation comedies. The results showed that similarity between the viewers' own experience and that of the media characters facilitated second-graders' understanding of the characters' behaviors and emotions. This effect did not emerge among older viewers, presumably because the older children had more varied background knowledge, and better general comprehension skills. However, many media presentations are more complex than situation comedies, and involve characters and situations that may be unfamiliar to adults as well as to children. Under such circumstances, it seems likely that relevant background knowledge would facilitate even adults' understanding of media characters.

Familiarity With Specific Characters.   Regular viewers of television series gradually form detailed, complex impressions of characters' personalities, desires, goals, and interpersonal relationships. Studies in the area of social cognition have shown that impressions of another's personality affect interpretations and judgments of that person's subsequent behaviors (see Wyer & Srull, 1989). In addition, research on narrative comprehension indicates that knowledge of a character's goals or motives affects how a reader interprets the character's actions during the course of the story (e.g., Owens, Bower, & Black, 1979). Owens et al. called this the "soap opera effect," undoubtedly because regular viewers of television soap operas (and weekly television series as well) generally have a great deal of background knowledge about the characters that helps them to understand and evaluate characters' behaviors. Livingstone (1987, 1989) contended that soap opera viewers' knowledge of characters' personalities and histories adds meaning to seemingly simple actions or events. A character's angry outburst, for example, may be interpreted differently, depending on whether the viewer is familiar with the character's usual behavior and past experiences.

Other program-specific knowledge, such as the characters' roles and relationships with others, may also help viewers interpret the characters' motivations and behaviors (Collins & Wellman, 1982; Livingstone, 1987, 1989). Regular viewers of television series are presumably more familiar with this type of information, particularly regarding the characters' interpersonal relationships, which usually develop over a period of time. In general, then, the character evaluations of regular viewers would be expected to differ from those of first-time or occasional viewers due to differing levels of knowledge about the characters.

Assumptions About the Characteristics of Other People

Viewers' perceptions of media characters should also be affected by their prior expectations and beliefs about what specific types of individuals or groups are like. Studies in the area of person perception have repeatedly shown that people tend to "type" others, or classify them according to salient, concrete features such as gender, ethnicity, religion, and occupation (Hamilton & Trolier, 1986). In addition, person categories may be based on more abstract features, such as personality traits and political or social beliefs (e.g., extrovert, liberal, bigot; Cantor & Mischel, 1979). These types of classification schemes have been referred to as stereotypes or person prototypes, and are characterized by beliefs or expectations about the traits and behaviors of members of particular groups or social categories. These representations guide perceptions of new individuals who appear to exemplify a certain type of person or belong to a particular social group

(Cantor & Mischel, 1979). Although stereotypes and prototypes simplify the processing of person information, they also frequently lead to inaccurate perceptions of others.

The mass media research on person categorization has focused on stereotyping based on overt characteristics such as gender and ethnicity. Although the term *stereotype* has often been used to characterize limited and/or unfavorable media portrayals of certain groups, the term is used here to refer simply to the preconceptions people bring to the viewing situation. A number of studies have shown that the stereotypes people hold regarding various groups affect the way they perceive characters in media presentations. Most of this research has involved gender and ethnic stereotypes, but presumably the influence of other stereotypes or person prototypes would operate in similar ways.

Several studies suggest that preexisting sex-role stereotypes affect the way viewers perceive characters in television programs. Cordua, McGraw, and Drabman (1979) found that kindergartners who viewed an atypical portrayal involving a female doctor and a male nurse tended to reverse the gender of the doctor and nurse on a memory test. Similar findings were obtained in another study with preschool and elementary school children (Drabman et al., 1981). List, Collins, and Westby (1983) measured children's gender-role attitudes before exposing them to television programs involving women in traditional and nontraditional roles (wife and mother, army doctor). Children classified as having strong or moderate gender stereotypes tended to remember relatively more sex-role-relevant than sex-role-irrelevant information, whereas no differences in memory for the two types of content were observed among low-stereotype children. The authors contend that this finding is consistent with the view that stereotypes structure the types of information viewers extract from television programs. Although none of these studies assessed children's impressions of the characters, it seems likely that viewers' recognition of characters' occupations and their processing of sex-role related information would influence judgments such as the characters' competence and level of knowledge. A study by Messaris and Gross (1977), for example, suggests that even very young children have acquired assumptions about the inherent "goodness" of medical doctors.

A study by Durkin (1984) provides evidence that gender-role stereotypes affect interpretations as well as memory for character-relevant content. In his study, 4- to 9-year-olds were interviewed about their reactions to short television programs depicting women in stereotyped roles (e.g., caregiver, helpless victim). Children as young as 4 years perceived media portrayals in sex-stereotyped ways; that is, they justified various behaviors by citing gender roles. The findings also indicated that sex-role stereotypes influenced children's inferences about characters' emotions and motives (e.g., in explaining why Lois Lane was frightened in a particular scene, but Superman was not).

Several studies have shown that racial attitudes are related to viewers' evaluations of television characters (Brigham & Giesbrecht, 1976; Dates, 1980; Vidmar & Rokeach, 1974). In a study involving White adolescents and adults, Vidmar and Rokeach reported that highly prejudiced viewers of the television series "All in the Family" were more likely than less prejudiced viewers to perceive that the "lovable bigot" Archie Bunker tended to win arguments with his liberal son-in-law Mike, and to think that Archie generally made better sense than Mike. This outcome occurred despite the fact that the program was intended by the producer to ridicule racist attitudes. Generally, the research suggests that viewers' racial attitudes affect their interpretations of program content and their impressions of media characters.

Nonmedia research has shown that adults have prototypes for a wide range of "person types" (e.g., radicals, intellectuals, loners), and that these prototypes include information about the appearance, personality traits, and behaviors of the typical group member (Forgas, 1985). With regard to media presentations, an analysis by Turow (1980) of character descriptions used in casting television dramas revealed that program creators apparently have distinct views on the personality traits typically associated with certain character types (e.g., criminal, law-enforcement agent, blue-collar worker). There is also evidence that actors are often cast for roles because their appearance is consistent with common "clichés" or stereotypes associated with the roles (Turow, 1978). In other words, characters' physical appearance, clothing, and other observable characteristics are often used as a "short hand" approach to character development. Apparently media producers assume that viewers will attribute a variety of personality attributes to characters who appear to be exemplars of certain person prototypes.

Developmental Level

Developmental differences have been observed in the ways in which children form perceptions of television characters. Due to differences in information-processing tendencies, younger children utilize information about media characters in a different manner than older children and adults.

Importance of Physical Appearance.   Generally, very young children are more responsive to physical appearance than are older children or adults, at least when other relevant information about a person (e.g., behavior) is available. Studies of young children's perceptions of real people have shown that their descriptions of people tend to focus on overt physical characteristics; references to physical appearance decrease after age 7, and are increasingly replaced by references to personality traits and internal states (Brierly, 1966; Livesley & Bromley, 1973). Media research has also documented the early importance of physical attributes in children's responses to media characters. A detailed, 3-year study of three preschoolers' discussions about television found that the appearance of television characters was the first character attribute children referred to spontaneously, at age 2 (Jaglom & Gardner, 1981). In studying children's descriptions of television characters, Wartella and Alexander (1977) found a decrease with age in the use of physical characteristics that parallels the findings for descriptions of real people.

Sparks and Cantor (1986) observed that preschool children's evaluations of the television character the Incredible Hulk were less positive than those of older children. They attributed this difference, at least in part, to the younger children's overresponse to the grotesque appearance of the Hulk. In an experiment described earlier, Hoffner and Cantor (1985) manipulated a character's appearance and behavior, and found that preschoolers gave appearance cues more weight than did older children in forming impressions of the character. Specifically, when children evaluated the character's personality and predicted her future behavior, the effect of the character's appearance (grandmotherly vs. witchlike) was strongest for the youngest children, and decreased with age. In contrast, the effect of the character's behavior (kind vs. cruel) increased with age. Nonetheless, when children received no information about the character's behavior, the perceptions and predictions of children at all age levels were strongly affected by her appearance. These findings indicate that children at all age levels are responsive to physical appearance cues, but weight the cues differently when they occur in conjunction with other types of information.

Understanding and Evaluating Characters' Behaviors. As noted earlier, the behaviors relevant to understanding media characters are imbedded in a continuous stream of events and interactions that comprise media narratives. Some research has indicated that children's tendency to infer stable characteristics about other people on the basis of their behavior increases with age (e.g., Gnepp & Chilamkurti, 1988; Rholes & Ruble, 1984). Rholes and Ruble argued that young children are less able to extract relevant behavioral information from ongoing events, and thus may fail to notice consistencies in people's behavior over time. It therefore seems that young viewers may be less likely than older viewers to form behavior-based impressions of media characters. Consistent with this view is Hoffner and Cantor's (1985) finding that the influence of behavior on children's judgments of a character's personality and future actions increased with age.

There is also some evidence that the ability to interpret characters' inconsistent behaviors improves with age (cf. Blanck & Rosenthal, 1982). Gollin (1959) found an age-related increase in children's attempts to account for the discrepant behavior of a film character, who behaved prosocially and antisocially toward other characters in successive scenes. Young children should also have difficulty understanding a portrayal when cues to a character's true nature are revealed only after an alternative impression of the character has been conveyed. Research has shown that adults usually revise their impressions of others as new information becomes available (Crocker, Hannah, & Weber, 1983; Park, 1986). Among children, there is some evidence of an age-related increase in the tendency to reinterpret a story after receiving new information (Schmidt, Schmidt, & Tomalis, 1984).

Consistent with these findings, Collins (1983; Collins & Zimmermann, 1975) has argued that young viewers are less likely than older viewers to revise their impressions of a character who initially appears benevolent, but who is later revealed to be malevolent instead.

Much research has documented developmental changes in children's comprehension and use of a variety of factors that may modify interpretations of characters' behaviors. It was reported earlier that mature viewers consider both the motivations and consequences of behaviors when evaluating media characters. Numerous studies have shown that very young children are less likely than older children to mention characters' motives in retelling a television program's plot, and are less likely to understand the relationships among motives, behaviors, and consequences (Collins et al., 1974; Flapan, 1968; Gollin, 1958; Leifer & Roberts, 1972; Wartella & Alexander, 1977). Age differences have also been observed in the influence of motives and consequences on children's evaluations of media characters. Collins et al. (1974), for example, reported that kindergartners and second graders tended to evaluate characters solely on the basis of the consequences of their actions, whereas older children were more likely to take the characters' motives into account as well. Research on children's understanding of stories shows similar age differences in the effects of motives and consequences on impressions of story characters (e.g., Surber, 1982).

Young children's difficulties in understanding the motives of media characters may be due, in part, to the complex structure of many programs, and the unrelated scenes that frequently intervene between characters' motivations and the behaviors they lead to (Collins, 1983). Purdie et al. (1979, cited in Collins, 1983) showed second and fifth graders a police drama in which the main character's negative motives and his aggression were presented either in adjacent scenes or in scenes several minutes apart. Showing the scenes in immediate sequence facilitated second graders' understanding of the relationships between motives and aggression, but fifth graders understood both versions of the program equally well. Comprehension of the motive-aggression relationship was associated with more negative evaluations of the aggressor. In a related study, Collins and Westby (1981, cited in Collins, 1983) interrupted children at different points during the same police drama and asked them to evaluate the aggressive character. They found that second graders tended to evaluate the character negatively only after he had experienced adverse consequences for his actions, whereas fifth graders evaluated him negatively earlier in the program, after witnessing his motives and aggressive behavior. As in the earlier study, second graders' difficulties appeared to result from their failure to understand the relationship between the motives and the aggression.

Recognizing and Responding to Emotional and Nonverbal Cues.
Many studies have shown that there is a developmental improvement in the ability to recognize and interpret emotional and nonverbal information (Blanck & Rosenthal, 1982; Masters & Carlson, 1984). Dorr et al. (1983) reviewed much

of this research as it relates to children's understanding of emotions on television. Briefly, there is an increase with age in the ability to recognize emotions from facial and vocal cues, and to identify the emotions likely to arise in specific situations, although even young children's judgments are fairly accurate. Several additional developmental differences seem relevant to interpreting the emotional states of media characters. As children become better able to coordinate several sources of information simultaneously, there is an improvement in their ability to take into account both the expressed emotion and the emotional implications of the situation (Gnepp, 1983; Hoffner & Badzinski, 1989), and to consider the influence of prior experiences on a person's emotional reaction (Gnepp & Gould, 1985). In addition, as children grow older, they become more aware that people can modify or control their emotional expressions (Harris, Donnelly, Guz, & Pitt-Watson, 1986; Saarni, 1982). At the same time, they become better able to interpret inconsistent emotional cues (Blanck & Rosenthal, 1982).

A number of studies have shown an improvement with age in children's ability to recognize or infer the emotions experienced by mass media characters (Flapan, 1968; Leifer et al., 1971; Newcomb & Collins, 1979; Wilson & Cantor, 1985). Flapan, for example, performed a detailed analysis of 6-, 9-, and 12-year-olds' interpretations of sequences from a dramatic, family-oriented feature film. Children's descriptions of the events in the film revealed a developmental shift from recognizing simple, explicitly presented emotions, to inferring more complex emotions on the basis of the characters' own expectations or interpretations of a situation. Flapan also reported an increase with age in children's use of characters' feelings to explain their actions or the responses of other characters.

These studies did not examine how children's differential understanding of characters' emotional experience was related to their evaluations or impressions of the characters. However, as argued earlier, characters' emotional states and nonverbal behaviors can convey important information about the causes and consequences of behaviors, the personal attributes of characters, and their reactions to other characters. Thus, to the degree that emotional or nonverbal aspects of portrayals are important components of a media presentation, it seems likely that children of different ages will form different impressions of the characters.

Utilizing Information. Younger children undoubtedly have less general knowledge than older children about the types of people, events, and social situations depicted in media presentations, and are less familiar with the structure of narratives and with certain media characters. As reported earlier, Newcomb and Collins (1979) found that familiarity with the content of a television program facilitated younger children's comprehension of the characters' emotions and behaviors. They suggested that age differences in children's moral judgments of media characters may be due, in part, to their unfamiliarity with the depicted situations and events.

In addition, there is evidence that younger children are less flexible in utilizing the knowledge they possess to facilitate their comprehension of a media presentation (Collins, 1984). Several studies indicate that young children often fail to use relevant information in forming impressions of characters. In the study discussed earlier, Collins and Westby (1981, cited in Collins, 1983) demonstrated that second graders were less likely than older children to change their evaluations of a character as new information about him was presented. In another study, Collins and Wellman (1982) reported evidence that younger children's poorer comprehension of television plots is due, in part, to their reliance on stereotyped expectations about plot events. The authors argued that older viewers' more varied social knowledge enables them to better understand atypical characters and nonstandard events. Similar findings were reported by Messaris and Gross (1977) in a study of viewers' interpretations of a photographic narrative. In the story, a doctor behaves angrily toward his secretary and later fails to help an accident victim he encounters on his way home from work. The authors found that second graders, in contrast to older children and adults, evaluated the doctor positively and mistakenly reported that he had actually helped the victim. This finding was attributed by the authors to young children's reliance on a stereotyped conception of "the good doctor." In other words, the youngest subjects relied on prior beliefs instead of making use of the information that was presented in the story.

VIEWERS' RESPONSES TO MEDIA CHARACTERS

Components of Attraction to Characters

Interpersonal attraction is one of the most basic responses to other people. As a function of forming impressions of characters, viewers can be said to be attracted to the characters to varying degrees. Attraction to media characters has been investigated predominantly in terms of three interrelated reactions: liking, perceived similarity, and the desire to be like a character.

Liking. People generally develop feelings of liking or disliking for others as a function of forming impressions of them, and this seems to be true of their impressions of characters as well. The process of impression formation involves both inferring an individual's characteristics and extracting evaluative meaning from the information available. The evaluative component of impressions is thought to underlie liking responses (Wyer & Gordon, 1984). Liking for another individual is strongly related to the desirability of the personal characteristics attributed to that individual. Individuals who are judged to possess evaluatively positive attributes are generally liked more than those who are seen to possess negative attributes. Furthermore, individuals who display positive nonverbal and social behaviors are liked better than those who do not (see Berscheid, 1985, for review).

Despite the common observation that people develop strong feelings for characters in films and televisions series, little research seems to have directly examined viewers' liking for media characters. The few studies that have done so confirm that characters whose personal attributes and behaviors are perceived favorably are generally liked more. Zillmann and Cantor (1977) manipulated a character's behavior and found that, in general, the nicer the character was judged to be, the more he was liked. Several studies reported that viewers tended to like characters who were helpful or fair in their treatment of other characters, and to dislike characters who behaved unkindly or unfairly toward others (Wilson et al., 1986; Zillmann & Bryant, 1975; Zillmann & Cantor, 1977). In another study, liking for characters was enhanced by the characters' success in coping with a threat, especially when the threat was severe (Zillmann, Hay, & Bryant, 1975). Presumably, the successful characters were perceived as competent and resourceful.

Research on interpersonal attraction shows that, in addition to liking those who possess positive attributes, people tend to like others who are similar to themselves in important ways. Another person who shares some important characteristic may be assumed to have other desirable attributes as well. Similar others may also be liked because they tend to provide confirmation of one's opinions and beliefs. In contrast, dissimilar others are likely to be associated with negative outcomes, such as conflict or rejection (Berscheid, 1985). Research on responses to "All in the Family" showed that viewers liked the character (Archie or Mike) who shared their social beliefs more than they liked the character whose beliefs differed from their own (Brigham & Giesbrecht, 1976; Vidmar & Rokeach, 1974).

Perceived Similarity to Characters. Perception of similarity to a media character may be facilitated by shared characteristics such as gender, ethnicity, social class, and age (von Feilitzen & Linne, 1975; Maccoby & Wilson, 1957; Reeves & Miller, 1978; Sprafkin & Liebert, 1978). Perceived similarity may also be influenced by other aspects of a viewer's impression of a character, such as the character's personality attributes, behavioral tendencies, experiences, or life situation (von Feilitzen & Linne, 1975; Fernie, 1981). For example, a shy individual may feel an affinity for a character who appears to be shy. Similarly, von Feilitzen and Linne argued that children respond strongly to animal characters in the mass media, such as Lassie, because they perceive these animals in dependent roles that are analogous to children's roles in relation to adults. There is some evidence that the attributes on which similarity judgments are based change developmentally. Preschoolers tend to rely on physical characteristics, such as strength or possessions, whereas older children are more likely to consider psychological and moral aspects of another's personality. In addition, gender-based similarity judgments are less likely among preschoolers than among older children (Lickona, 1974).

Viewers seem to enjoy watching television and film characters whom they see as similar to themselves. Similar characters have the potential to confirm the validity of the viewer's own beliefs and concerns, as suggested by the previously discussed data on liking for "All in the Family" characters (Brigham & Giesbrecht, 1976; Vidmar & Rokeach, 1974). In addition, witnessing similar characters allows the viewer to observe a variety of events and outcomes that may be potentially relevant to his or her own life. Numerous theorists have proposed that viewers tend to "identify" with similar characters, or view media presentations from their perspective (von Feilitzen & Linne, 1975; Maccoby & Wilson, 1957; Tannenbaum & Gaer, 1965).

Consistent with the proposal that viewers tend to adopt the viewpoint of similar characters, perceived similarity can have a significant impact on the processing of character-relevant information in a media presentation. Several studies have shown that viewers attend more closely to the actions of same-sex characters, and remember more content concerning those characters (Maccoby & Wilson, 1957; Maccoby, Wilson, & Burton, 1958; Sprafkin & Liebert, 1978). Viewers may assume that the behaviors of similar characters are important indicators of appropriate or effective ways of behaving (Bandura, 1969; Bussey & Perry, 1976). One of the reasons given for watching soap operas and television series is that the characters' experiences suggest useful approaches for dealing with the viewer's own problems (e.g., Greenberg, Neuendorf, Buerkel-Rothfuss, & Henderson, 1982; Lichty, 1965). This type of viewing outcome may be part of the motivation behind media presentations that depict "average" characters successfully confronting serious personal difficulties, such as drug dependence or a life-threatening illness.

Desire to be Like Characters. Media characters are frequently depicted in ways that would not be expected to promote feelings of similarity, however. Characters who are extremely good looking, have prestigious or exciting occupations, or are highly successful in their endeavors are undoubtedly dissimilar in important ways to the majority of audience members. Furthermore, fantasy characters, such as Superman, possess unique abilities that are attractive but are clearly not shared by audience members (e.g., superhuman strength). Viewers are attracted to such characters, but rather than feeling similar, they often view them as individuals whom they want to be like. As with perceived similarity, the desire to be like a character is thought to promote the viewer's tendency to take the character's perspective while viewing; this process of perspective-taking has been referred to as *wishful identification* (von Feilitzen & Linne, 1975). Noble (1975), for example, found that children who wanted to be like one of the leading characters in a film found it easier to imagine themselves in the role, and felt more comfortable doing so, than did children who did not want to be like one of the characters.

The mass media seem especially well suited to promoting wishful identification with characters. Although the desire to be like an admired individual is typical of young children, who look to parents, teachers, and others as behavioral models (Bandura, 1977), media presentations provide even adults with a wide array of attractive models. Furthermore, some of the factors that underlie the interpersonal preference to associate with others who are similar, rather than more successful or attractive (e.g., less likelihood of rejection), are not operative in media viewing situations because there is virtually no possibility that viewers could actually interact with fictional characters.

Not surprisingly, the characters whom viewers report wanting to be like possess a variety of desirable attributes. Children in one study overwhelmingly aspired to be like the hero or heroine in a film rather than the villain, whom they explicitly rejected as a role model (Albert, 1957). Similar findings were reported by Noble (1975). Boys in a study by Fernie (1981) cited admired physical and social abilities (e.g., the ability to fly, success with girls) as reasons they wanted to be like media characters. The more fantastic or unrealistic the characters, the more the boys wanted to be like them. Many studies have found that the strength and activity of characters are important determinants of boys' choices of role models, whereas the characters' physical attractiveness is especially important for girls (Miller & Reeves, 1976; Reeves & Greenberg, 1977; Reeves & Lometti, 1979; Williams et al., 1981). The success of a character's behavior is also important. In several studies, viewers expressed the desire to like a successful character, even if the character's behaviors conflicted with the viewer's personal values (Albert, 1957; Bandura et al., 1963; Zajonc, 1954). Finally, one study found that viewers wanted to be like characters who belonged to the social class to which they aspired (Maccoby & Wilson, 1957).

Although all of this research involved children, it seems likely that adult viewers are also attracted to characters who have resources, abilities, or physical attributes that they would like to have as well. It has been argued that one of the motivations for viewing fictional presentations is the possibility of imagining oneself in the interesting, glamorous, or successful roles of the characters (Elkin, 1955; McGuire, 1974). Adults, as well as children, presumably obtain gratification from such fantasy experiences. It may be, of course, that adults focus on and are attracted by different character attributes than those found to be important for children.

There is evidence that viewers of all ages attempt to emulate the appearance and behaviors of admired media characters. Numerous studies have shown that both children and adults sometimes adopt the behaviors of attractive or successful characters (Bandura, 1977). Several studies reported a strong relationship between the way children said they would behave in a variety of situations and the way they thought their favorite television characters would act (Donohue, 1975; Loughlin, Donohue, & Gudykunst, 1980; Meyer, 1973). The authors interpreted the findings as evidence that children use favorite characters as behavioral models. In an interview study of viewers' responses to films, Blumer (1933) reported that adolescents frequently imagined themselves as the heroes and heroines of movies, and attempted to imitate their appearance and behaviors. Finally, as

McGuire (1974) and others have noted, there is much anecdotal evidence that viewers often adopt the clothing styles, mannerisms, and activities of popular film and television characters (e.g, Carlson, 1990; Langway & Reed, 1983). The prime-time serial "Dynasty," for example, inspired a successful line of clothing that features fashions worn by characters on the program.

Other things equal, some degree of similarity to media characters seems to promote a desire to be like them, possibly because certain similarities signal that it is both possible and appropriate for the viewer to become like the character in additional ways. Greenberg (1972) found that the majority of both Black and White viewers named a same-race character as one they most wanted to be like. Similar findings have been reported more recently as well (Dates, 1980; Greenberg & Atkin, 1982; see also Greenberg, 1986). There is also much evidence that viewers are more likely to want to be like characters of their own gender than characters of the other gender. This finding has been observed both when children were asked to select a character from a specific program shown during the course of a study (Albert, 1957; Maccoby & Wilson, 1957; Sprafkin & Liebert, 1978), and when children were asked about characters with whom they were already familiar (Howitt & Cumberbatch, 1976; Miller & Reeves, 1976). Several of these studies (Albert, 1957; Howitt & Cumberbatch, 1976; Miller & Reeves, 1976) found that male characters were chosen as role models by girls more often than female characters were chosen by boys. This finding was probably due, at least in part, to the fact that male characters were more plentiful and appeared in more exciting, interesting roles than did female characters (Miller & Reeves, 1976). In addition, it is more socially acceptable for females than for males to behave in ways traditionally associated with the other gender (Huston, 1983).

In general, the research shows that viewers are positively disposed toward characters who are seen to possess desirable attributes, and who are perceived as similar to themselves. These components of attraction promote the desire to be like characters, to attend more closely to character-relevant behaviors and events, and to imitate their appearance and behaviors.

Emotional Responses to Characters' Experiences

It has repeatedly been observed that viewers feel concern for the welfare of liked characters, and tend to feel emotions similar to the ones such characters experience (Zillmann, 1980). For example, in a study by Comisky and Bryant (1982), viewers' liking for a film character was manipulated by presenting a prologue that depicted him in a neutral, mildly positive, or strongly positive manner. During a subsequent sequence in which the character attempted to escape a firing squad, the degree of suspense reported by viewers was positively related to their liking for the character.

Empathy is one mechanism that has been proposed to account for the tendency to feel emotions similar to those experienced by characters. The term *empa-*

thy is used here to mean sharing another person's expressed or presumed emotion by mentally putting oneself in that person's place, or taking his or her perspective (Feshbach, 1982). As noted in the previous section, media researchers have frequently argued that viewers identify with characters who are similar to themselves, or who possess especially desirable attributes. In other words, through identification, viewers experience media events from these characters' perspectives and share their responses to program events. If a character reacts emotionally, the viewer should empathize, or experience the same emotion (Emery, 1959; Maccoby & Wilson, 1957; Tannenbaum & Gaer, 1965; Wilson & Cantor, 1985). Consistent with the hypothesis that perspective-taking mediates empathic responses, Wilson and Cantor found that the ability to role-take, or adopt the perspective of a threatened character, was related to children's empathy with the character's expression of fear.

There is some evidence that perceived similarity promotes empathy with characters. Feshbach and Roe (1968) showed young children slides of story characters experiencing different emotions. They found that the children empathized more with the emotions of same-sex characters than with the emotions of characters of the other gender. In a study with adults, Tannenbaum and Gaer (1965) found that the greater the similarity between viewers' perceptions of themselves and their perceptions of a media character, the stronger their empathic responses were to emotional scenes involving that character. Liking for a character has also been found to promote empathic distress (Bryant, 1978, cited in Zillmann, 1980).

There are times, however, when a viewer's emotional responses are not consistent with those experienced by a liked character. This may occur when the viewer has information not available to the character (Zillmann, 1980). For example, the viewer may have knowledge of an impending disaster before the protagonist learns of the threat. In accounting for emotional responses to such suspenseful scenes, Zillmann suggested that a viewer typically reacts as a "concerned third party," rather than by identifying with, or sharing the perspective of, the endangered character. In contrast to the unsuspecting character's lack of emotion, the viewer would be expected to feel suspense, concern, or fear. In other words, the viewer would feel for rather than with the character. Consistent with this view, Hoffner and Cantor (1990) recently reported that viewers of a suspenseful program typically began to worry about an endangered character before he was aware of any immediate threat.

The observation that some emotional responses cannot be accounted for by the notion of identification or perspective sharing should not be taken as evidence that viewers do not identify with characters whom they admire or perceive as similar to themselves. As noted earlier, media viewers sometimes claim to imagine themselves in the roles of characters. In fact, film and television presentations seem to promote identification by providing much more information about a character than one typically has about even a close friend. Furthermore, viewers are sometimes exposed to a character's visual perspective or private thoughts and fantasies—information that is usually available only about oneself. It seems likely that the degree to which a viewer shares the perspective of a character may change during a program, as the type and range of character-relevant information varies, and as the narrative focuses alternately on the concerns of different characters (cf. Emery, 1959; Maccoby & Wilson, 1957).

Thus, although it is clear that empathy cannot account entirely for the way a viewer responds emotionally to the experiences of liked characters, it seems that, to some degree, viewers do identify with and share the feelings of characters they like and admire. Emotional reactions to the experiences of disliked characters, however, cannot be explained by any form of empathy or emotional sharing.

Typically, viewers' emotional responses contrast with those experienced by disliked characters (Zillmann, 1980). Zillmann contended that viewers' affective dispositions toward characters (i.e., degree of liking or disliking) mediate emotional responses to characters, thus accounting for viewers' differential responses to the experiences of "good" and "bad" protagonists. In one study, Zillmann and Cantor (1977) manipulated children's liking for a character by varying his initial behavior (prosocial, neutral, antisocial) in different versions of a videotaped story. In the final scene of the program, viewers felt for the protagonist who was liked: They were happy when they saw him receive a new bike, and they were sad when they observed him fall off his bike and hurt himself. The disliked protagonist produced the opposite reactions: Viewers were happy when he fell off his bike and sad when he received the bike as a present. However, viewers' concepts of "deservingness" apparently limit the amount of suffering viewers enjoy seeing even disliked characters experience (Zillmann & Bryant, 1975).

A partial replication of Zillmann and Cantor's (1977) study, with retarded children of approximately the same age, found that these children's emotional responses were not mediated by their evaluations of the protagonist: The retarded children's emotions matched those of the protagonist regardless of how nice or bad they felt his prior behavior had been (Wilson et al., 1986). These results suggest that children's level of cognitive development is an important determinant of the degree to which evaluations or affective dispositions mediate emotional responses to characters.

To summarize, the research indicates that character impressions, particularly evaluative judgments and feelings of liking or similarity, influence viewers' emotional responses to the experiences of characters. Viewers' emotions tend to be similar to those felt by liked characters or characters with whom viewers identify, and to contrast with the emotions felt by disliked characters. Further research needs to clarify the relative importance of various underlying processes (e.g., empathy, dispositional mediation) in different circumstances.

Long-Term Emotional Involvement With Characters

In addition to mediating emotional responses while viewing, affective dispositions toward characters seem to be related to the formation of long-term emotional bonds with characters in continuing series. While viewing a media presentation, viewers often feel as though they are involved in the events, and they respond in some ways as if they were witnessing or participating in real interactions with people they know. The importance of characters to viewers frequently extends beyond the viewing situation, particularly when the characters are featured in recurring film or television roles. After watching a series regularly for a period of time, or several sequels to a film, viewers become familiar with the personalities, preferences, and habits of characters, and may come to feel that they know the characters as well as friends or neighbors (Dorr, 1982; Gitlin, 1983; Mayerle, 1987; Noble, 1975; Perse & Rubin, 1989). Himmelweit et al. (1958) argued that one of the major appeals of television is the presentation of personalities on intimate, everyday terms, so that viewers feel as though they know the individuals personally. This type of response, in which the viewer has the sense of a personal relationship with a character, was described by Horton and Wohl (1956) as parasocial interaction. Clearly, the degree to which viewers are attracted to characters should mediate the development of long-term concern about the characters, and feelings of involvement in the characters' "lives." In some cases, intense negative affect (e.g., toward J. R. Ewing on "Dallas") seems to promote enduring involvement as well (Corliss, 1980).

Research on viewers' responses to media presentations and their reasons for viewing supports the contention that people become emotionally involved with media characters. Noble (1975) reported that children who felt as though they knew film characters were more likely than other children to worry about the characters and to feel as though the characters had communicated with them during the show. Just as people are concerned about events in the lives of their friends, viewers claim to worry about characters whom they watch regularly (McQuail, Blumler, & Brown, 1972). Regular viewers of television serials report that they become involved in the problems and concerns of the characters, and cite their involvement as one of the gratifications of viewing (Carveth & Alexander, 1985; Greenberg et al., 1982; McQuail et al., 1972; Rubin & Perse, 1987).

Children only gradually come to understand that characters are portrayed by people who pretend to be the characters (Dorr, 1983; Fernie, 1981; Singer, Zuckerman, & Singer, 1980). Although older viewers are generally able to separate their knowledge of characters from their knowledge of the actors who play the roles, even adults sometimes appear to have difficulty remembering the fictional nature of media characters. Observers of popular culture have noted that viewers readily accept and sometimes even solicit medical advice from actors who portray doctors on television (Newcomb, 1974; Real, 1977). Perhaps more striking are instances in which viewers respond as though characters were real people, and actors were the characters they portray. For example, producers and cast members of soap operas report that viewers have sent gifts when a character has had a baby, have called to relay information regarding the whereabouts of a kidnapped character, and have physically assaulted actors who play villains on serials (Winsey, 1979). Tim Piggot-Smith, in an interview about his role as Ronald

Merrick in Masterpiece Theatre's "Jewel in the Crown" series, noted that the American public associated him so strongly with the despicable character he played that he felt obligated to grow a beard when traveling in the United States, in order to avoid hostile encounters with members of the audience there (Moreno & Atwood, 1985).

Of course, these types of reactions are extreme and are not typical of the way most people respond. Yet long-term involvement with media characters could be said to involve some type of extended "suspension of disbelief" in which viewers disregard or overlook the characters' fictional status. There is much evidence, both anecdotal and empirical, that children and adults form strong affective attachments to mass media characters and personalities (e.g., Carlson, 1990; Howitt & Cumberbatch, 1976; McQuail et al., 1972; Sturm, 1975; Waters & Huck, 1983). Sturm argued that viewers become so emotionally tied to characters in television series that the disappearance of these characters—either through the plot of the program, or because the series ends—may be emotionally upsetting to viewers. Public reaction to the deaths of characters suggests that this is so. The unexpected death of Colonel Henry Blake on "M*A*S*H" greatly disturbed viewers, and motivated many to write letters of protest to CBS. According to one of the producers of the series, "by killing a cherished character, you can approximate the feeling of losing someone you love" (Waters & Huck, 1983, p. 49). The notion that audience members develop emotional ties with media characters is also illustrated by public reaction to the termination of long-running series. The final episode of "M*A*S*H," for example, produced an overwhelming public response, including telegrams from President Reagan and ex-president Ford, welcoming the series characters home from Korea (Waters & Huck, 1983). McGuire (1974) cited a similar reaction in Britain to the ending of a radio serial.

SUMMARY AND CONCLUSIONS

This chapter has reviewed the literature on the sources of information about media characters, and the manner in which different characteristics of viewers affect their impressions of characters. Because few studies had perceptions of film or television characters as their major focus, relevant findings have been drawn from diverse areas of media research that do not share a unifying theoretical perspective. The literature dealing with impressions of real people has been utilized to provide a framework within which to consider how viewers perceive media characters, and to inform interpretations of the relevant media research.

Consistent with the nonmedia literature, evidence has been cited regarding the contribution of characters' appearance, behaviors, and emotional states to viewers' impressions of characters. The proposed mediators of the process of impression formation include general knowledge, familiarity with specific characters, and prior expectations, as well as developmental differences in viewers' utilization of the various sources of information. The relationship between viewers' impressions and their attraction to characters has also been discussed. Specifically, character evaluations have been linked to feelings of liking, perceived similarity, and the desire to be like characters. These responses, in turn, have been shown to have implications for both short- and long-term emotional responses to media productions.

Suggestions for Future Research

It is apparent that much research remains to be done. For one thing, although there is a wide range of potential sources of information about characters, the influence of many of these variables has not been examined systematically. Most of the studies that have focused on character perceptions have dealt with existing impressions of familiar characters. Such research provides valuable information about how impressions of characters are represented in memory, but cannot identify the specific aspects of characters (e.g., behaviors, style of dress) that contributed to those representations. Studies that involve controlled manipulations are necessary to determine the contribution of specific character attributes (cf. Hoffner & Cantor, 1985). Furthermore, it is important for researchers to examine how viewers weight and combine various sources of information in forming impressions of characters. Very little is known about how information is selected, interpreted, and combined during the process of impression formation, or how this integration process changes developmentally.

Surprisingly, only a few studies have examined adults' impressions of characters, or the character attributes that contribute to their liking for and identification with characters. This information would be useful, not only in understanding viewing preference and the selection of role models, but also in predicting emotional responses to media presentations. Although it may be safe to generalize some of the findings obtained with children to adults, there are numerous reasons to expect that adults' perceptions and responses will differ from those of children.

The literature on impression formation in interpersonal situations has provided many insights into how people perceive characters. However, although perceptions of real people and media characters are undoubtedly similar in many ways, the unique contributions of the medium to viewers' impressions need to be considered more closely. The ways in which media presentations structure information about characters should have important implications for the way characters are perceived. Some programs seem designed to simplify character impressions by making a few aspects of characters particularly salient (e.g., humor, morality); other programs devote much screen time to "character development" and include sequences designed to reveal personal information about characters that is unavailable in an interpersonal context (e.g., a character's thoughts or fantasies). In addition, it would be valuable to examine how impressions are affected by the knowledge that interaction with fictional characters is impossible. Although the research suggests that this should lead to more superficial impressions (Feldman & Ruble, 1981), it may be that the involving nature of media presentations is as strong a motivating factor as anticipated interaction.

The development of character impressions over the long term is another area that needs to be explored. Many characters who seem to be important to viewers are featured in regular television series, and are shown in new situations in each episode of the program. The content and organization of impressions undoubtedly evolve over time, as viewers learn more about the characters. As argued earlier, familiarity with a character should alter viewers' interpretations of new information about that character. Furthermore, certain categories of information may decline in importance as impressions develop. An interesting research strategy would be to examine viewers' perceptions of characters at different points in their acquaintance with the characters. For example, a naturalistic approach could assess impressions following weekly episodes of a new series (cf. Park, 1986). A more controlled approach might involve selecting a number of short "character-focused" scenes from a series unfamiliar to viewers. Impressions of the characters could then be measured following each scene, or the impressions of different groups of viewers could be measured at different points in the sequence (cf. Collins, 1983). The type and order of character-relevant information included in the scenes could be varied. Studies of the development of character impressions may illuminate the process by which viewers form affective attachments to characters, and may also contribute to our understanding of impressions of real people.

REFERENCES

Albert, R. S. (1957). The role of mass media and the effect of aggressive film content upon children's aggressive responses and identification choices. *Genetic Psychology Monographs, 55*, 221-285.

Alexander, A. (1980, May). *Children's perceptions of television characters: Validity in the multidimensional scaling approach.* Paper presented at the meeting of the International Communication Association, Acapulco, Mexico.

Argyle, M., & McHenry, R. (1971). Do spectacles really affect judgments of intelligence? *British Journal of Social and Clinical Psychology, 10*, 27-29.

Babrow, A. S., O'Keefe, B. J., Swanson, D. L., Meyers, R. A., & Murphy, M. A. (1988). Person perception and children's impressions of television and real peers. *Communication Research, 15*, 680-698.

Bandura, A. (1969). Social learning theory of identificatory processes. In D. A. Goslin (Ed.), *Handbook of socialization theory and research* (pp. 213-262). Chicago: Rand McNally.

Bandura, A. (1977). *Social learning theory.* Englewood Cliffs, NJ: Prentice-Hall.

Bandura, A., Ross, D., & Ross, S. A. (1963). Vicarious reinforcement and imitative learning. *Journal of Abnormal and Social Psychology, 67*, 601-607.

Bayes, M. A. (1974). Behavioral cues of interpersonal warmth. *Journal of Consulting and Clinical Psychology, 39*, 333-339.

Berndt, T. J., & Berndt, E. G. (1975). Children's use of motives and intentionality in person percep-tion and moral judgment. *Child Development, 46,* 904-912.

Berscheid, E. (1985). Interpersonal attraction. In G. Lindzey & E. Aronson (Eds.), *The handbook of social psychology* (Vol. 2, pp. 413-484). New York: Random House.

Blanck, P. D., & Rosenthal, R. (1982). Developing strategies for decoding "leaky" messages: On learning how and when to decode discrepant and consistent social communications. In R. S. Feldman (Ed.), *Development of nonverbal behavior in children* (pp. 203-229). New York: Springer-Verlag.

Blumer, H. (1933). *Movies and conduct.* New York: Macmillan.

Breed, W., & De Foe, J. R. (1980). The portrayal of the drinking process on prime-time television. *Journal of Communication, 31*(1), 58-67.

Brierly, D. W. (1966). Children's use of personality constructs. *Bulletin of the British Psychological Society, 19,* 197-207.

Brigham, J. C., & Giesbrecht, L. W. (1976). "All in the Family": Racial attitudes. *Journal of Com-munication, 26*(4), 69-74.

Brown, A. L., Bransford, J. D., Ferrara, R. A., & Campione, J. C. (1983). Learning, remember-ing, and understanding. In J. H. Flavell & E. M. Markman (Eds), *Handbook of child psychology* (Vol. 3, pp. 77-166). New York: Wiley.

Bryan, J. H., & Walbek, N. H. (1970). Preaching and practicing generosity: Children's actions and reactions. *Child Development, 41,* 329-353.

Bugental, D. E. (1974). Interpretations of naturally occurring discrepancies between words and into-nation. *Journal of Personality and Social Psychology, 30,* 125-133.

Bussey, K., & Perry, D. G. (1976). Sharing reinforcement contingencies with a model: A social-learning analysis of similarity effects in imitation research. *Journal of Personality and Social Psy-chology, 34,* 1168-1176.

Cantor, N., & Mischel, W. (1979). Prototypicality and personality: Effects on free recall and perso-nality impressions. *Journal of Research in Personality, 13,* 187-205.

Carlson, T. (1990, January 13). "Beauty and the Beast": The show that wouldn't die...and the fans who wouldn't let it. *TV Guide,* pp. 2-6.

Carveth, R., & Alexander, A. (1985). Soap opera viewing motivations and the cultivation process. *Journal of Broadcasting & Electronic Media, 29,* 259-273.

Clore, G. L., Wiggins, N. H., & Itkin, S. (1975). Judging attraction from nonverbal behavior: The gain phenomenon. *Journal of Consulting and Clinical Psychology, 43,* 491-497.

Cohen, C. E. (1981). Goals and schemata in person perception: Making sense from the stream of behavior. In N. Cantor & J. F. Kihlstrom (Eds.), *Personality, cognition, and social interaction* (pp. 45-68). Hillsdale, NJ: Lawrence Erlbaum Associates.

Collins, W. A. (1983). Interpretation and inference in children's television viewing. In J. Bryant & D. R. Anderson (Eds.), *Children's understanding of television: Research on attention and com-prehension* (pp. 125-150). New York: Academic Press.

Collins, W. A. (1984). Inferences about the actions of others: Developmental and individual differ-ences in using social knowledge. In J. C. Masters & K. Yarkin-Levin (Eds.), *Boundary areas in social and developmental psychology* (pp. 221-239). New York: Academic Press.

Collins, W. A., Berndt, T. J., & Hess, V. L. (1974). Observational learning of motives and conse-quences for television aggression: A developmental study. *Child Development, 45,* 799-802.

Collins, W. A., & Wellman, H. M. (1982). Social scripts and developmental patterns in comprehen-sion of televised narratives. *Communication Research, 9,* 380-398.

Collins, W. A., & Zimmermann, S. A. (1975). Convergent and divergent social cues: Effects of televised aggression on children. *Communication Research, 2,* 331-346.

Comisky, P., & Bryant, J. (1982). Factors involved in generating suspense. *Human Communication Research, 9,* 49-58.

Cordua, G. D., McGraw, K. O., & Drabman, R. S. (1979). Doctor or nurse: Children's perceptions of sex typed occupations. *Child Development, 50,* 590-593.

Corliss, R. (1980, August 11). TV's "Dallas": Whodunit? *Time*, pp. 60-66.

Costanzo, P. R., Coie, J. D., Grumet, J. F., & Farnill, D. (1973). A reexamination of the effects of intent and consequences on children's moral judgments. *Child Development, 44*, 154-161.

Craft, R. (1982). Elegy for Mary Hartman. In H. Newcomb (Ed.), *Television: The critical view* (3rd. ed., pp. 148-157, New York: Oxford University Press.

Crocker, J., Hannah, D. B., & Weber, R. (1983). Person memory and causal attribution. *Journal of Personality and Social Psychology, 44*, 55-66.

Crockett, W. H., Press, A. N., & Osterkamp, M. (1979). The effect of deviations from stereotyped expectations upon attitudes toward older persons. *Journal of Gerontology, 34*, 368-374.

Davis, R. H., & Kubey, R. W. (1982). Growing old on television and with television. In D. Pearl, L. Bouthilet, & J. Lazar (Eds.), *Television and behavior: Ten years of scientific progress and implications for the eighties* (Vol. 2, pp. 201-208). Washington, DC: U. S. Government Printing Office.

Dates, J. (1980). Race, racial attitudes, and adolescent perceptions of black television characters. *Journal of Broadcasting, 24*, 549-560.

Deaux, K., & Lewis, L. L. (1984). Structure of gender stereotypes: Interrelationships among components and gender label. *Journal of Personality and Social Psychology, 46*, 991-1004.

Dion, K. K. (1972). Physical attractiveness and evaluation of children's transgressions. *Journal of Personality and Social Psychology, 24*, 207-213.

Dominick, J. R., Richman, S., & Wurtzel, A. (1979). Problem-solving in TV shows popular with children: Assertion vs. aggression. *Journalism Quarterly, 56*, 455-463.

Donnerstein, E., & Berkowitz, L. (1981). Victim reactions in aggressive erotic films as a factor in violence against women. *Journal of Personality and Social Psychology, 41*, 710-724.

Donohue, T. R. (1975). Black children's perceptions of favorite TV characters. *Journal of Broadcasting, 19*, 153-167.

Dorr, A. (1982). Television and affective development and functioning. In D. Pearl, L. Bouthilet, & J. Lazar (Eds.), *Television and behavior: Ten years of scientific progress and implications for the eighties* (Vol. 2, pp. 68-77). Washington, DC: U. S. Government Printing Office.

Dorr, A. (1983). No shortcuts to judging reality. In J. Bryant & D. R. Anderson (Eds.), *Children's understanding of television: Research on attention and comprehension* (pp. 199-220). New York: Academic Press.

Dorr, A., Doubleday, C., & Kovaric, P. (1983). Emotions depicted on and stimulated by television programs. In M. Meyer (Ed.), *Children and the formal features of television* (pp. 97-143). New York: K. G. Saur.

Drabman, R. S., Robertson, S. J., Patterson, J. N., Jarvie, G. J., Hammer, D., & Cordua, G. (1981). Children's perceptions of media-portrayed sex roles. *Sex Roles, 7*, 379-389.

Durkin, K. (1984). Children's accounts of sex-role stereotypes in television. *Communication Research, 11*, 341-362.

Ebbesen, E. B. (1981). Cognitive processes in inferences about a person's personality. In E. T. Higgins, C. P. Herman, & M. P. Zanna (Eds.), *Social cognition: The Ontario symposium* (Vol. 1, pp. 247-276). Hillsdale, NJ: Lawrence Erlbaum Associates.

Efran, M. G. (1974). The effect of physical appearance on the judgment of guilt, interpersonal attraction, and severity of recommended punishment in a simulated jury task. *Journal of Research in Personality, 8*, 45-54.

Ekman, P. (1978). Facial signs: Facts, fantasies, and possibilities. In T. Sebeok (Ed.), *Sight, sound, and sense* (pp. 124-156). Bloomington, IN: Indiana University Press.

Ekman, P., & Friesen, W. V. (1969). The repertoire of nonverbal behavior: Categories, origins, usage, and coding. *Semiotica, 1*(1), 49-98.

Elkin, F. (1955). Popular hero symbols and audience gratifications. *The Journal of Educational Sociology, 29*, 97-107.

Elkind, D., & Dabek, R. F. (1977). Personal injury and property damage in the moral judgments of children. *Child Development, 48*, 518-522.

Emery, F. E. (1959). Psychological effects of the western film: A study in television viewing. *Human Relations, 12*, 195-213.

von Feilitzen, C., & Linne, O. (1975). Identifying with television characters. *Journal of Communication, 25*(4), 51-55.

Feldman, N. S., & Ruble, D. N. (1981). The development of person perception: Cognitive and social factors. In S. S. Brehm, S. M. Kassin, & F. X. Gibbons (Eds.), *Developmental social psychology*. New York: Oxford University Press.

Fernie, D. E. (1981). Ordinary and extraordinary people: Children's understanding of television and real life models. In H. Kelly & H. Gardner (Eds.), *Viewing children through television* (pp. 47-58). San Francisco: Jossey-Bass.

Feshbach, N. D. (1982). Sex differences in empathy and social behavior in children. In N. Eisenberg (Ed.), *The development of prosocial behavior* (pp. 315-338). New York: Academic Press.

Feshbach, N. D., & Roe, K. (1968). Empathy in six and seven year olds. *Child Development, 39*, 133-145.

Fincham, F. D., & Jaspers, J. M. (1980). Attribution of responsibility: From man the scientist to man as lawyer. In L. Berkowitz (Ed.), *Advances in experimental social psychology* (Vol. 13, pp. 81-138). New York: Academic Press.

Flapan, D. (1968). *Children's understanding of social interaction*. New York: Teachers College Press.

Forgas, J. P. (1982). Episode cognition: Internal representations of interaction routines. In L. Berkowitz (Ed.), *Advances in experimental social psychology* (Vol. 15, pp. 59-101). New York: Academic Press.

Forgas, J. P. (1985). Person prototypes and cultural salience: The role of cognitive and cultural factors in impression formation. *British Journal of Social Psychology, 24*, 3-17.

Gitlin, T. (1983). *Inside prime time*. New York: Pantheon.

Gnepp, J. (1983). Children's social sensitivity: Inferring emotions from conflicting cues. *Developmental Psychology, 19*, 805-814.

Gnepp, J., & Chilamkurti, C. (1988). Children's use of personality attributions to predict other people's emotional and behavioral reactions. *Child Development, 59*, 743-754.

Gnepp, J., & Gould, M. E. (1985). The development of personalized inferences: Understanding of other people's emotional reactions in light of their prior experience. *Child Development, 56*, 1455-1464.

Goldberg, H. D. (1951). The role of "cutting" in the perception of the motion picture. *Journal of Applied Psychology, 35*, 70-71.

Gollin, E. S. (1958). Organizational characteristics of social judgment: A developmental investigation. *Journal of Personality, 26*, 139-154.

Green, S. K. (1981). Attitudes and perceptions about the elderly: Current and future perspectives. *International Journal of Aging and Human Development, 13*, 99-119.

Greenberg, B. S. (1972). Children's reactions to TV blacks. *Journalism Quarterly, 49*, 5-14.

Greenberg, B. S. (1982). Television and role socialization: An overview. In D. Pearl, L. Bouthilet, & J. Lazar (Eds.), *Television and behavior: Ten years of scientific progress and implications for the eighties* (Vol. 2, pp. 179-190). Washington, DC: U. S. Government Printing Office.

Greenberg, B. S. (1986). Minorities and the mass media. In J. Bryant & D. Zillmann (Eds.), *Perspectives on media effects* (pp. 165-188). Hillsdale, NJ: Lawrence Erlbaum Associates.

Greenberg, B. S., & Atkin, C. (1982). Learning about minorities from television: A research agenda. In G. Berry & C. Mitchell-Kernan (Eds.), *Television and the socialization of the minority child* (pp. 215-243). New York: Academic Press.

Greenberg, B. S., Edison, N., Korzenny, F., Fernandez-Collado, C., & Atkin, C. K. (1980). Antisocial and prosocial behaviors on television. In B. S. Greenberg (Ed.), *Life on television* (pp. 99-128). Norwood, NJ: Ablex.

Greenberg, B. S., Fernandez-Collardo, C., Graff, D., Korzenny, F., & Atkin, C. K. (1980). Trends in use of alcohol and other substances on television. In B. S. Greenberg (Ed.), *Life on television* (pp. 137-146). Norwood, NJ: Ablex

Greenberg, B. S., Neuendorf, K., Buerkel-Rothfuss, N., & Henderson, L. (1982). The soaps: What's on and who cares? *Journal of Broadcasting, 26,* 519-536.

Gunter, B. (1985). *Dimensions of television violence.* New York: St. Martin's Press.

Gunter, B. (1986). *Television and sex role stereotyping.* London: Libbey.

Haefner, M. J., & Comstock, J. (1990). Compliance gaining on prime time family programs. *The Southern Communication Journal, 55,* 402-420.

Hamid, P. N. (1972). Some effects of dress cues on observational accuracy, a perceptual estimate, and impression formation. *The Journal of Social Psychology, 86,* 279-289.

Hamilton, D. L., & Trolier, J. K. (1986). Stereotypes and stereotyping: An overview of the cognitive approach. In J. F. Dovido & S. L. Gaertner (Eds.), *Prejudice, discrimination, and racism* (pp. 127-163). New York: Academic Press.

Hamilton, V. L. (1978). Who is responsible? Toward a social psychology of responsibility attribution. *Social Psychology, 41,* 316-328

Harris, P. L., Donnelly, K., Guz, G. R., & Pitt-Watson, R. (1986). Children's understanding of the distinction between real and apparent emotion. *Child Development, 57,* 895-909.

Harvey, J. H., Harris, B., & Barnes, R. D. (1975). Actor-observer differences in the perceptions of responsibility and freedom. *Journal of Personality and Social Psychology, 32,* 22-28.

Harvey, S. E., Sprafkin, J. N., & Rubinstein, E. (1979). Prime time television: A profile of aggressive and prosocial behaviors. *Journal of Broadcasting, 23,* 179-189.

Hastie, R., & Kumar, P. A. (1979). Person memory: Personality traits as organizing principles in memory for behaviors. *Journal of Personality and Social Psychology, 37,* 25-38.

Hatfield, E., & Sprecher, S. (1986). *Mirror, mirror . . . The importance of looks in everyday life.* Albany, NY: State University of New York Press.

Hawkins, R., Wiemann, J., & Pingree, S. (Eds.). (1988). *Advancing communication science: Merging mass and interpersonal processes.* Newbury Park, CA: Sage.

Henderson, L., Greenberg, B. S., & Atkin, C. K. (1980). Sex differences in giving orders, making plans, and needing support on television. In B. S. Greenberg (Ed.), *Life on television* (pp. 49-63). Norwood, NJ: Ablex.

Higgins, E. T., & King, G. (1981). Accessibility of social constructs: Information-processing consequences of individual and contextual variability. In N. Cantor & J. F. Kihlstrom (Eds.), *Personality, cognition, and social interaction* (pp. 69-121). Hillsdale NJ: Lawrence Erlbaum Associates.

Himmelweit, H. T., Oppenheim, A. N., & Vince, P. (1958). *Television and the child.* New York: Oxford University Press.

Hoffner, C., & Badzinski, D. M. (1989). Children's integration of facial and situational cues to emotion. *Child Development, 60,* 411-422.

Hoffner, C., & Cantor, J. (1985). Developmental differences in responses to a television character's appearance and behavior. *Developmental Psychology, 21,* 1065-1074.

Hoffner, C., & Cantor, J. (1990). Forewarning of a threat and prior knowledge of outcome: Effects on children's emotional responses to a film sequence. *Human Communication Research, 16,* 323-354.

Hoffner, C., Cantor, J. & Thorson, E. (1989). Children's responses to conflicting auditory and visual features of a televised narrative. *Human Communication Research, 16,* 256-278.

Horton, D., & Wohl, R. R. (1956). Mass communication and para-social interaction. *Psychiatry, 19,* 215-229.

Howitt, D., & Cumberbatch, G. (1974). Audience perceptions of violent television content. *Communication Research, 1,* 204-223.

Howitt, D., & Cumberbatch, G. (1976). The parameters of attraction to mass media figures. In R. Brown (Ed.), *Children and television* (pp. 167-183). Beverly Hills, CA: Sage.

Hoyt, J. L. (1970). Effect of media violence "justification" on aggression. *Journal of Broadcasting, 14,* 455-464.

Huston, A. C. (1983). Sex-typing. In E. M. Hetherington (Ed.), *Handbook of child psychology* (Vol. 4, pp. 387-468.). New York: Wiley.

Jaglom, L. M., & Gardner, H. (1981). The preschool television viewer as anthropologist. In H. Kelly & H. Gardner (Eds.), *Viewing children through television* (pp. 9–30). San Francisco: Jossey-Bass.

Jones, E. E., Davis, K. E., & Gergen, K. J. (1961). Role playing variations and their informational value for person perception. *Journal of Abnormal and Social Psychology*, *63*, 302–310.

Jones, E. E., & McGillis, D. (1976). Correspondent inferences and the attribution cube: A comparative reappraisal. In J. H. Harvey, W. J. Ickes, & R. F. Kidd (Eds.), *New directions in attribution research* (Vol. 1, pp. 389–420). Hillsdale, NJ: Lawrence Erlbaum Associates.

Kaufman, L. (1980). Prime-time nutrition. *Journal of Communication*, *30*(3), 37–46.

Kelley, H. H. (1967). Attribution theory in social psychology. In D. Levine (Ed.), *Nebraska symposium on motivation* (Vol. 15, pp. 192–238). Lincoln: University of Nebraska Press.

Kubey, R. (1980). Television and aging: Past, present, and future. *Gerontologist*, *20*, 16–35.

Langway, L., & Reed, J. (1983, July 4). Flashdance, flashfashion. *Newsweek*, p. 55.

Leifer, A. D., Collins, W. A., Gross, B. M., Taylor, P. H., Andrews, L., & Blackmer, E. R. (1971). Developmental aspects of variables relevant to observational learning. *Child Development*, *42*, 1509–1516.

Leifer, A. D. & Roberts, D. F. (1972). Children's responses to television violence. In J. P. Murray, E. A. Rubinstein, & G. A. Comstock.(Eds.), *Television and social behavior* (Vol. 2, pp. 43–180). Washington, DC: U. S. Government Printing Office.

Lerner, R. M. (1969). The development of stereotyped expectancies of body build-behavior relations. *Child Development*, *40*, 137–141.

Lichty, L. W. (1965). "The Real McCoys" and its audience: A functional analysis. *Journal of Broadcasting*, *9*, 157–166.

Lickona, T. (1974). A cognitive developmental approach to interpersonal attraction. In T. L. Huston (Ed.), *Foundations of interpersonal attraction* (pp. 31–59). New York: Academic Press.

Liss, M. B. Reinhardt, L. C., & Fredriksen, S. (1983). TV heroes: The impact of rhetoric and deeds. *Journal of Applied Developmental Psychology*, *4*, 175–187.

List, J. A., Collins, W. A., & Westby, S. D. (1983). Comprehension and inference from traditional and nontraditional sex-role portrayals on television. *Child Development*, *54*, 1579–1587.

Livesley, W. J., & Bromley, D. B. (1973). *Person perception in childhood and adolescence*. London: Wiley.

Livingstone, S. M. (1987). The implicit representation of characters in "Dallas": A multidimensional scaling approach. *Human Communication Research*, *13*, 399–420.

Livingstone, S. M. (1989). Interpretive viewers and structured programs. *Communication Research*, *16*, 25–57.

Loughlin, M., Donohue, T. R., & Gudykunst, W. B. (1980). Puerto Rican children's perceptions of favorite television characters as behavioral models. *Journal of Broadcasting*, *24*, 159–171.

Lowry, D. T., Love, G., & Kirby, M. (1981). Sex on the soap operas: Patterns of intimacy. *Journal of Communication*, *31*(3), 90–96.

McGuire, W. (1974). Psychological motives and communication gratification. In J. G. Blumler & E. Katz (Eds.), *The uses of mass communications: Current perspectives on gratifications research* (pp. 167–196). Beverly Hills, CA: Sage.

McQuail, D., Blumler, J. G., & Brown, J. R. (1972). The television audience: A revised perspective. In D. McQuail (Ed.), *Sociology of mass communications* (pp. 135–165). Middlesex, England: Penguin.

Maccoby, E. E., & Wilson, W. C. (1957). Identification and observational learning from films. *Journal of Abnormal and Social Psychology*, *55*, 76–87.

Maccoby, E. E., Wilson, W. C., & Burton, R. V. (1958). Differential movie-viewing behavior of male and female viewers. *Journal of Personality*, *26*, 259–267.

Masters, J. C., & Carlson, C. R. (1984). Children's and adults' understanding of the causes and consequences of emotional states. In C. E. Izard, J. Kagan, & R. B. Zajonc (Eds.), *Emotions, cognition, and behavior* (pp. 438–463). New York: Cambridge University Press.

Mayerle, J. (1987). Character shaping genre in "Cagney and Lacey." *Journal of Broadcasting & Electronic Media, 31,* 133-151.

Meehan, D. M. (1988). The strong-soft woman: Manifestations of the androgyne in popular media. In S. Oskamp (Ed.), *Television as a social issue* (pp. 103-112). Newbury Park, CA: Sage.

Mehrabian, A. (1972). *Nonverbal communication.* New York: Aldine-Atherton.

Meringhoff, L. K., Vibbert, M. M., Char, C. A., Fernie, D. E., Banker, G. S., & Gardner, H. (1983). How is children's learning from television distinctive? Exploiting the medium methodologically. In J. Bryant & D. R. Anderson (Eds.), *Children's understanding of television: Research on attention and comprehension* (pp. 151-179). New York: Academic Press.

Messaris, P., & Gross, L. (1977). Interpretations of a photographic narrative by viewers in four age groups. *Studies in the Anthropology of Visual Communication, 4,* 99-111.

Meyer, T. P. (1973). Children's perceptions of favorite television characters as behavioral models. *Educational Broadcasting Review, 7,* 25-33.

Miller, M., & Reeves, B. (1976). Dramatic TV content and children's sex-role stereotypes. *Journal of Broadcasting, 20,* 35-50.

Moreno, A. (Producer), & Atwood, D. (Director). (1985). *The Jewel in the Crown" Salute* [Television program]. Washington, DC: Public Broadcasting System.

Mulac, A., Bradac, J. J., & Mann, S. K. (1985). Male/female language differences and attributional consequences in children's television. *Human Communication Research, 11,* 481-506.

Mulac, A., Incontro, C. R., & James, M. R. (1985). A comparison of the gender-linked language effect and sex-role stereotypes. *Journal of Personality and Social Psychology, 49,* 1098-1109.

Nardi, A. (1973). Person-perception research and perception of life-span development. In P. Baltes & K. Schaie (Eds.), *Life-span developmental psychology: Personality and socialization.* New York: Academic Press.

Nascimento-Schulze, C. M. (1981). Toward situational classification. *European Journal of Social Psychology, 11,* 149-159.

Neumann, D. A., Cassata, M., & Skill, T. (1983). Setting the mood: Soap opera settings and fashions. In M. Cassata & T. Skill (Eds.), *Life on daytime television: Tuning-in American serial drama* (pp. 125-135). Norwood, NJ: Ablex.

Newcomb, A. F., & Collins, W. A. (1979). Children's comprehension of family role portrayals in televised dramas: Effects of socioeconomic status, ethnicity, and age. *Developmental Psychology, 15,* 417-423.

Newcomb, H. (1974). *TV: The most popular art.* Garden City, NY: Anchor Press.

Noble, G. (1975). *Children in front of the small screen.* Beverly Hills, CA: Sage.

Owens, J., Bower, G. H., & Black, J. B. (1979). The "soap opera" effect in story recall. *Memory and Cognition, 7,* 185-191.

Park, B. (1986). A method for studying the development of impressions of real people. *Journal of Personality and Social Psychology, 51,* 907-917.

Patzer, G. L. (1985). *The physical attractiveness phenomena.* New York: Plenum Press.

Perse, E. M., & Rubin, R. B. (1989). Attribution in social and parasocial relationships. *Communication Research, 16,* 59-77.

Potter, W. J., & Ware, W. (1987). An analysis of the contexts of antisocial acts on prime-time television. *Communication Research, 14,* 664-686.

Potter, W. J., & Ware, W. (1989). The frequency and context of prosocial acts on prime time TV. *Journalism Quarterly, 66,* 359-366, 529.

Price, R. H. (1974). The taxonomic classification of behaviors and situations and the problem of behavior-environment congruence. *Human Relations, 27,* 567-585.

Price, R. H. & Bouffard, D. L. (1974). Behavioral appropriateness and situational constraint as dimensions of social behavior. *Journal of Personality and Social Psychology, 30,* 579-586.

Ray, G. B. (1986). Vocally cued personality prototypes: An implicit personality theory approach. *Communication Monographs, 53,* 266-276.

Real, M. R. (1977). *Mass-mediated culture*. Englewood Cliffs, NJ: Prentice-Hall.

Reeves, B. (1979). Children's understanding of television people. In E. Wartella (Ed.), *Children communicating: Media and development of thought, speech, understanding* (pp. 115-155). Beverly Hills, CA: Sage.

Reeves, B., & Greenberg, B. S. (1977). Children's perceptions of television characters. *Human Communication Research, 3*, 113-127.

Reeves, B., & Lometti, G. (1979). The dimensional structure of children's perceptions of television characters: A replication. *Human Communication Research, 5*, 247-256.

Reeves, B., & Miller, M. M. (1978). A multidimensional measure of children's identification with television characters. *Journal of Broadcasting, 22*, 71-86.

Rholes, W. S., & Ruble, D. N. (1984). Children's understanding of dispositional characteristics of others. *Child Development, 55*, 550-560.

Rosenfeld, L. B., & Plax, T. G. (1977). Clothing as communication. *Journal of Communication, 27*(2), 24-31.

Rubin, A. M., & Perse, E. M. (1987). Audience activity and soap opera involvement: A uses and effects investigation. *Human Communication Research, 14*, 246-268.

Saarni, C. (1982). Social and affective functions of nonverbal behavior: Developmental concerns. In R. S. Feldman (Ed.), *Development of nonverbal behavior in children* (pp. 123-147). New York: Springer-Verlag.

Scherer, K. R. (1971). Stereotype change following exposure to counter-stereotypical media heroes. *Journal of Broadcasting, 15*, 91-100.

Schmidt, C. R., Schmidt, S. R., & Tomalis, S. M. (1984). Children's constructive processing and monitoring of stories containing anomalous information. *Child Development, 55*, 2056-2071.

Schneider, D. J., Hastorf, A. H., & Ellsworth, P. C. (1979). *Person perception* (2nd ed.). Reading, MA: Addison-Wesley.

Siegman, A. W. (1987). The telltale voice: Nonverbal messages of verbal communication. In A. W. Siegman & S. Feldstein (Eds.), *Nonverbal behavior and communication* (pp. 351-434). Hillsdale, NJ: Lawrence Erlbaum Associates.

Singer, D. G., Zuckerman, D. M., & Singer, J. L. (1980). Helping elementary children learn about TV. *Journal of Communication, 30*(3), 84-93.

Skowronski, J. J., & Carlston, D. E. (1989). Negativity and extremity biases in impression formation: A review of explanations. *Psychological Bulletin, 105*, 131-142.

Sparks, G. G., & Cantor, J. (1986). Developmental differences in fright responses to a television program depicting a character transformation. *Journal of Broadcasting & Electronic Media, 30*, 309-323.

Sprafkin, J. N., & Liebert, R. M. (1978). Sex-typing and children's television preferences. In G. Tuchman, A. K. Daniels, & J. Benet (Eds.), *Hearth and home: Images of women in the mass media* (pp. 228-239). New York: Oxford University Press.

Sprafkin, J. N., & Silverman, L. T. (1981). Update: Physically intimate and sexual behavior on primetime television, 1978-79. *Journal of Communication, 31*(1), 34-40.

Srull, T. K., & Brand, J. F. (1983). Memory for information about persons: The effect of encoding operations on subsequent retrieval. *Journal of Verbal Learning and Verbal Behavior, 22*, 219-230.

Sturm, H. (1975). The research activities of the Internationales Zentralinstitut fur das Jugend-und-Bildungsfernsehen. *Fernsehen und Bildung* (special English issue), *9*, 158-162.

Surber, C. F. (1982). Separable effects of motives, consequences, and presentation order on children's moral judgments. *Developmental Psychology, 18*, 257-266.

Tannenbaum, P. H., & Gaer, E. P. (1965). Mood change as a function of stress of protagonist and degree of identification in a film-viewing situation. *Journal of Personality and Social Psychology, 2*, 612-616.

Taylor, S. E., & Crocker, J. (1981). Schematic bases of social information processing. In E. T. Higgins, C. P. Herman, & M. P. Zanna (Eds.), *Social cognition: The Ontario symposium* (Vol. 1, pp. 89-134). Hillsdale, NJ: Lawrence Erlbaum Associates.

Turow, J. (1974). Advising and ordering: Daytime, prime time. *Journal of Communication, 24*(2), 138-141.

Turow, J. (1978). Casting for TV parts: The anatomy of social typing. *Journal of Communication, 28*(4), 18-24.

Turow, J. (1980). Occupation and personality in television dramas: An industry view. *Communication Research, 7,* 295-318.

Vidmar, N., & Rokeach, M. (1974). Archie Bunker's bigotry: A study in selective perception and exposure. *Journal of Communication, 24*(1), 36-47.

Wartella, E., & Alexander, A. (1977, April). *Children's organization of impressions of television characters.* Paper presented to the International Communication Association, Chicago.

Waters, H. F., & Huck, J. (1983, February 28). Farewell to the "M*A*S*H" gang. *Newsweek,* pp. 44-50.

Wells, W. D., & Siegel, B. (1961). Stereotyped somatotypes. *Psychological Reports, 8,* 77-78.

Williams, F., LaRose, R., & Frost, F. (1981). *Children, television, and sex-role stereotyping.* New York: Praeger.

Wilson, B. J., & Cantor, J. (1985). Developmental differences in empathy with a television protagonist's fear. *Journal of Experimental Child Psychology, 39,* 284-299.

Wilson, B. J., Cantor, J., Gordon, L., & Zillmann, D. (1986). Affective responses of nonretarded and retarded children to the emotions of a protagonist. *Child Study Journal, 16,* 77-93.

Winsey, V. (1979). How soaps help you cope. *Family Health, 11*(4), 30-33.

Wyer, R. S., & Gordon, S. E. (1984). The cognitive representation of social information. In R. S. Wyer, Jr. & T. K. Srull (Eds.) *Handbook of social cognition* (Vol. 2, pp. 73-150). Hillsdale, NJ: Lawerence Erlbaum Associates.

Wyer, R. S., Jr., & Srull, T. K. (1989). *Memory and cognition in its social context.* Hillsdale, NJ: Lawrence Erlbaum Associates.

Zajonc, R. B. (1954). Some effects of the "space" serials. *Public Opinion Quarterly, 18,* 367-374.

Zillmann, D. (1980). Anatomy of suspense. In P. H. Tannenbaum (Ed.), *The entertainment functions of television* (pp. 133-163). Hillsdale, NJ: Lawrence Erlbaum Associates.

Zillmann, D., & Bryant, J. (1975). Viewer's moral sanction of retribution in the appreciation of dramatic presentations. *Journal of Experimental Social Psychology, 11,* 572-582.

Zillmann, D., & Cantor, J. (1977). Affective responses to the emotions of a protagonist. *Journal of Experimental Social Psychology, 13,* 155-165.

Zillmann, D., Hay, T. A., & Bryant, J. (1975). The effect of suspense and its resolution on the appreciation of dramatic presentations. *Journal of Research in Personality, 9,* 307-323.

Zuckerman, M., DePaulo, B. M., & Rosenthal, R. (1981). Verbal and nonverbal communication of deception. In L. Berkowitz (Ed.), *Advances in experimental social psychology* (Vol. 14, pp. 2-59). New York: Academic Press.

CHAPTER
5

Television Viewing and Physiological Arousal

Dolf Zillmann
University of Alabama

American television has often been characterized as the nation's favorite unwinder. Indeed, surveys probing viewers' motives for watching television (Atkin, 1985; Bower, 1973; Rosengren, Wenner, & Palmgreen, 1985; Rubin, 1986) tend to confirm that consumption of television entertainment is primarily ascribed to a need for relaxation. Apparently, many viewers feel that television's entertainment fare can help them to calm down after the stressful activities of daily life. Television, then, is being viewed as an antidote to the rousing "fight for survival" in society. But the surveys also reveal that the consumption of televised entertainment is often attributed to an urge for excitement. Many viewers, it seems, seek to overcome an uneventful, dull, and boring state of affairs by exposing themselves to television's diversionary stimulation in hopes of being aroused.

There is, of course, no contradiction in the claim that the utility of television — television entertainment, in particular — may be twofold as far as states of excitement are concerned. Some people may use television predominantly to reduce unpleasant states of excitement; others may use it to generate or increase pleasant states of excitement. Moreover, the same people, although at different times, may use television in either one of the two principal ways, depending on prevailing experiential conditions of excitedness. Regardless of the particular effect on a state of excitement, however, it is apparently held, by viewers and media analysts alike, that television can profoundly influence the viewer's arousal state and, hence, affective and emotional behavior.

Notwithstanding such speculations about the function of arousal by media analysts, and despite numerous studies of viewers' introspective accounts (insightful and suggestive as these accounts may be), research on the actual effects of exposure to television fare on arousal, and on the consequences of these effects on subsequent behavior, has been conducted only recently. Only recently have new conceptualizations of arousal and theories based on these new conceptualizations become available. And only recently have the techniques for measuring bodily arousal states been simplified to a point where these techniques can be widely used. Moreover, the degree of reliability of the measurements in question has been improved significantly. These developments have given impetus to original research on the function of arousal, especially on the function of arousal produced by exposure to communication. The specific effects of exposure to television fare on excitatory reactions and on the consequences of these reactions are finally ascertained empirically; and aspects of arousal reactions are theoretically integrated and better understood. The resulting discoveries have sometimes confirmed earlier speculations. On other occasions they have contradicted them.

Because the new theoretical approaches to arousal, affect, and emotion are critical in understanding the progress in research on the role of excitatory phenomena in television's effects, we briefly introduce the conceptualization and measurement of arousal. Thereafter, we discuss theoretical models of the function of arousal in the context of television and discuss the research evidence pertaining to them.

CONCEPTIONALIZATIONS OF AROUSAL

In behavior theory (Brown, 1961; Hull, 1952; Spence, 1956), in activation theory (Duffy, 1962; Lindsley, 1951), and in emotion theory (Schachter, 1964; Zillmann, 1983), arousal has been conceived of as a unitary force that energizes or intensifies behavior that receives direction by independent means. Hebb (1955) succinctly expressed this conceptualization: Arousal (or drive) "is an energizer, but not a guide; an engine but not a steering gear" (p. 249). Behavior theory, in particular, has been most influential in promoting the view that arousal energizes the behavior that is prepotent in the habit structure; or expressed in more practical terms, that arousal energizes any and every behavior a person comes to perform for whatever reason (Tannenbaum, 1972). However, in view of pertinent research findings (e.g., Bryant & Zillmann, 1979; Cantor, Zillmann, & Bryant, 1975; Zillmann & Bryant, 1974), the assumption of a universal one-to-one correspondence between arousal and behavior intensity had to be abandoned eventually, and limiting conditions had to be specified (Zillmann, 1978, 1983, 1984). Nonetheless, within certain confines, arousal has continued to be viewed as a unitary force that intensifies motivated behavior under most circumstances.

Granted that there has been comparatively little disagreement on the energizing function of arousal, arousal itself has been conceived of quite differently in the various theoretical approaches. In behavior theory, arousal was synonymous with drive (Brown, 1961); and drive, as a universal energizer, was a hypothetical construct and an intervening variable (Hull, 1952). Activation theory focused on activities in the brainstem reticular formation. States ranging from coma through deep sleep, light sleep, drowsiness, relaxed wakefulness, and alert attentiveness to strong, excited emotions became measurable in characteristic wave patterns and rhythms in the encephalogram (Lindsley, 1951). The so-called peripheral theories of emotion (James, 1884; Lange, 1887) promoted an interest in the assessment of all conceivable bodily manifestations of arousal, especially visceral changes (Dunbar, 1939). Oddly enough, the criticism of these theories by Cannon (1927, 1929) brought much clarity to the conceptualization of arousal—in both peripheral and central theories (Bard, 1934; MacLean, 1949; Papez, 1937). In his well-known fight-or-flight paradigm, Cannon implicated sympathetic dominance in the autonomic nervous system with the function of providing energy for the vigorous, energy-consuming actions associated with attack and escape. Such energization is a critical concomitant of most emotional behaviors and is readily measurable in numerous peripheral manifestations. Recent theories of affect and emotion (Izard, 1977; Leventhal, 1974; Schachter, 1964; Zillmann, 1978) follow Cannon in conceiving of arousal mainly in terms of sympathetic activity in the organism.

It should be clear, then, that in the different approaches to arousal in which arousal is actually being measured, arousal has been operationalized in substantially different ways. Activation theory concentrated on assessing the excitatory consequences of the diffuse projection from the reticular formation to the cortex (Moruzzi & Magoun, 1949), whereas theories of emotion focused on activity in the autonomic nervous system throughout the body, selecting a great many manifestations of excitatory processes for assessment (Grings & Dawson, 1978).

Usually there is a high degree of correlation in the activity in the reticular formation and the autonomic nervous system. The function of arousal in these structures, however, can be viewed as markedly different. In fact, some theories have treated the two systems as being relatively autonomous. This is mainly because of functional differences and despite many acknowledged interdependencies. Routtenberg (1968, 1971), for instance, distinguished between two arousal systems: System I is the reticular activating system; this structure is viewed as the primary apparatus for producing cortical arousal and for controlling sensory gating and response organization. System II, in contrast, subsumes activity in various limbic structures and is held responsible for basic vegetative processes, including all vital emotions.

Routtenberg's distinction between *cortical* and *limbic* arousal, which—because of the high degree of correspondence between *limbic* and *autonomic* arousal— we refer to as a distinction between *cortical* and *autonomic* arousal, appears to be a most useful one. It separates arousal processes that serve attention, perception, and response preparation from those associated with affective and emotional reactions, and it thereby helps prevent much confusion. Although certain critical interdependencies must be recognized at all times, it appears to be advantageous to explore the implications of cortical and autonomic arousal independently in the study of behavior — in the study of reactions to events shown on television, in particular. For television research, the realm of cortical arousal is attention, alertness, and vigilance, on the one hand, and information processing, information acquisition, and information retrieval, on the other. The realm of autonomic arousal, in contrast, is constituted by affective and emotional reactions that are instigated, modified, or neutralized by exposure or that come about shortly thereafter.

MEASUREMENTS OF AROUSAL

Cortical arousal is commonly measured in alpha-wave blocking as recorded in the electroencephalogram. In research on television effects, however, this measurement technique does not have a tradition; and for all practical purposes, cortical arousal is treated as a hypothetical construct.

In contrast, autonomic arousal has been measured in numerous peripheral manifestations. Commonly used indices are systolic and diastolic blood pressure, heart rate, blood pulse volume, vasoconstriction (usually measured in skin-temperature decrease), and skin conductance (Buck, 1976). Of these measures, heart rate has produced the least reliable results (Zillmann, 1979), presumably because of its "paradoxical" involvement in the orienting response (Grings & Dawson, 1978). Assessment of activity in the sympathetic-adrenal medullary system has also been employed, but comparatively rarely so. When such activity was recorded, it was measured in the secretion of the catecholamines epinephrine and norepinephrine from urine samples (Frankenhaeuser, 1979).

TELEVISION AS THE UNWINDER

It is well documented (Cox, 1978; Levi, 1972; Selye, 1956) — in fact, it can be considered a cliche — that everyday life, especially the competitive work in most job situations, is highly stressful. A large portion of society's adult population should consequently be motivated to seek relief from labor-associated stress as the typical workday draws to a close. As workers return to their homes, the need for diversionary stimulation that could bring relief should be at a maximum; and as the peak consumption in this "prime time" indicates (Bower, 1973), television is certainly a major leisure activity to which people turn at this critical time. But is it because television offers relief from stress?

In terms of arousal considerations, the prediction of relief that can be obtained from exposure to television fare is straightforward. The person who returns from a day of labor uptight, if not upset, maintains an inappropriately high level of arousal. Endocrinological research (Levi, 1964, 1967) leaves no doubt about that. Also, there can be little doubt that the condition most conducive to maintaining arousal at a high level is a psychological one: It is the continued cognitive preoccupation with the events responsible for the experience of stress. The disruption of this rumination (Bandura, 1965, 1973) or rehearsal process (Zillmann, 1979), potentially through any form of distracting stimulation, should have the beneficial effect of reducing arousal, thereby providing the experience of relief (Novaco, 1979).

Watching television is of course not the only means of disrupting stress-maintaining rehearsal processes. Gardening, needlepoint, or puzzles (Konecni, 1975) can also reduce feelings of tension and annoyance. However, watching television appears to be a most potent means of providing relief from stress. Watching television, because of the wealth of diversionary stimuli offered, is likely to involve and absorb the ruminating person more effectively than many alternative activities.

Lacking acceptable research evidence, a meaningful comparison between the stress-alleviating effect of watching television and that of alternative leisure activities cannot be made. But the evidence at hand is sufficient to project the enormous potential for stress alleviation from exposure to various types of television content—from exposure to entertainment fare, in particular.

The available evidence unambiguously supports a simple theoretical model. This model originated in media-violence research (Zillmann & Johnson, 1973). It presents the effect of an annoyed individual's exposure to communication on level of arousal, the experience of annoyance, and hostile behavior as a function of the communication's *intervention potential*. The intervention potential is the communication's capacity to involve a person and thereby disrupt the maintenance of arousal through the rehearsal of grievances and related thoughts of coping and retaliating. As a point of departure from earlier positions, which simply concentrated on a communication's interest value, the capacity to intervene in ongoing cognitive processes is viewed as deriving from two factors: (a) the communication's potential to absorb the respondent regardless of particular experimental states, and (b) the communication's relationship to salient aspects of the respondent's state of stress or distress. It is suggested that "*contents that relate to the individual's acute emotional state potentially reiterate arousal-maintaining cognitions*" (Zillmann, 1979, p. 321) and that, therefore, such messages, which may under different circumstances prove highly absorbing, will do little to calm the individual. Applied to provocation and retaliation, this reasoning leads to the prediction that the acutely annoyed person's exposure to messages that feature the provocation and torment of others is unlikely to take that person's mind off the circumstances of his or her own annoyance, making it unlikely, in turn, that levels of arousal associated with the annoyance will be effectively reduced. Materials that do not relate to provocation and/or retaliation, in contrast, should readily cut into the rehearsal process, initiate the decay of arousal, and bring on the experience of relief.

The initial test of this reasoning (Zillmann & Johnson, 1973) produced supportive data. Annoyed adults' exposure to violent fare failed to reduce level of arousal and, hence, aggressive behavior, whereas exposure to nonviolent, neutral fare effectively lowered both level of arousal and aggressiveness. These findings show that, compared with a no-exposure control treatment, exposure to media violence tends to perpetuate — but not to heighten — an existing propensity for aggression. They also show that, compared with this control, it is the so-called "neutral" treatment that, because it accomplishes the diminution of arousal, reduces motivated aggressive behavior. The findings, then, show it to be inappropriate to interpret the finding of relatively higher aggressiveness after exposure to violent fare than after exposure to neutral fare as the result of aggression-facilitating powers of media violence. Rather, exposure to absorbing fare, unrelated to the viewer's affective state, proves to have the beneficial effect of soothing the irritated person, thereby helping to control antisocial reactions.

Bryant and Zillmann (1977) carried further the search for communication conditions with such beneficial effects. Specifically, these investigators tested the proposal that, among stimuli that are equally unrelated to the individual's affective state, the diminution of arousal from preexposure stimulation should be proportional to the communication's capacity to involve and absorb; that is, to intervene in arousal-maintaining cognitions. In their investigation, the intervention potential of numerous stimuli was determined through pretesting. The potential was behaviorally measured (a) in the frequency of errors made on a simple tactile task during exposure (with the greater number of errors indicating greater involvement with the message) and (b) in the recall of materials presented prior to exposure (with the poorer performance indicating greater involvement with the message). One violence-laden program was included. The pretest showed that the communications' intervention potential varied substantially from extremely low to very high. In the main experiment, adult subjects were provoked, exposed to one of the messages, and then provided with an opportunity to retaliate against their annoyer. Arousal was measured at various times, including immediately prior to and immediately after exposure to communication.

The findings, displayed in Fig. 5.1, give strong support to the proposal that the dissipation of annoyance-associated arousal — and along with it, the diminution of the propensity for antisocial behavior — is proportional to the intervention potential of messages, as long as these messages are unrelated to annoyance. But the findings show just as strongly that this relationship does not hold true when the contents of a message relate to the individual's affective state. The violence-laden program, although highly absorbing to unprovoked persons, clearly failed to effect a reduction in arousal and, hence, a reduction in aggressiveness. Its effect on arousal and aggressiveness was comparable to that of an entirely uninvolving, monotonous stimulus.

Concentrating on the consequences of communication exposure on arousal, and treating the experience of annoyance produced by provocation as representa-

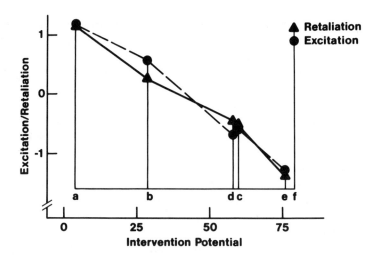

FIG. 5.1. Level of excitation and retaliatory behavior as a function of the intervention potential of communications. The greater the capacity of nonhostile contents to absorb the respondent (points connected by gradients), the greater the recovery from annoyance-produced excitation (circles) and the less severe the postexposure retaliation against the annoyer (triangles). Contents featuring hostilities were absorbing to nonannoyed subjects, but failed to prompt efficient recovery from excitation and lower the level of retaliatory behavior in annoyed subjects (isolated points on coordinate f). The communications were a: (a) monotonous stimulus, (b) nature film, (c) comedy show, (d) program featuring nonaggressive sport, (e) quiz show, and (f) program featuring contact sport entailing aggressive actions beyond the legitimate sports activity. Excitation and retaliation are expressed in z scores for ease of comparison (from Zillmann, 1979).

tive of annoyance generally, even of relatively unfocused feelings of tension, the available research evidence permits the following generalizations:

1. Exposure to communication, especially to entertainment fare, is likely to disrupt rehearsal processes that would perpetuate states of elevated arousal associated with negative affective experiences. Exposure is thus likely to produce feelings of relief.
2. The capacity of a message to effect a diminution of arousal associated with negative affect and to bring on the experience of relief is proportional to the capacity of that message to involve and absorb the individual, as long as the affinity between the individual's affective state and the events featured is minimal.
3. Contents likely to reinstate a negative affective experience tend to prevent the dissipation of arousal, thus perpetuating an aversive experience.

The findings of various recent investigations, summarized elsewhere (Zillmann, 1988a, 1988b; Zillmann & Bryant, 1985), lend further support to these generalizations.

It should be added to the third proposition that, for reasons yet to be detailed, exposure to highly arousing materials (e.g., erotica, thrillers, athletic contests, disturbing news reports) is also unlikely to initiate the decay of arousal and bring feelings of relief. On the other hand, some investigations have shown that particularly pleasant stimuli, relatively independent of how absorbing they may or may not be, can effectively reduce initially elevated arousal (Baron, 1977; Donnerstein, Donnerstein, & Evans, 1975; Ramirez, Bryant, & Zillmann, 1982).

It can be argued, of course, that the function of television as an unwinder is largely compromised by the fact that television offers highly exciting materials alongside programs that may seem capable of soothing a person in a state of acute stress. It would appear that persons in need of unwinding are as likely to be exposed to arousing as to calming fare. Recent research on selective exposure and mood management (Zillmann, 1988a, 1988b; Zillmann & Bryant, 1985) suggests, however, that acutely annoyed persons avoid exposure to materials likely to perpetuate their state of annoyance. It has been observed (O'Neal & Taylor, in press), for instance, that provoked persons who were unable to retaliate against their tormentor minimized their exposure to media entertainment featuring aggressive action. Being reminded of motivated but unfeasible or inadvisable actions apparently produces a noxious state that is to be avoided. Provoked persons who could take retaliatory action, in contrast, did not shun aggressive materials. In fact, when interacting with a person of low status against whom aggression could be expressed, exposure to media entertainment featuring aggressive action appeared to be particularly attractive and was maximized. Interestingly, subjects who were provoked but unable or inhibited to retaliate exhibited a preference for comedy. They behaved as if they knew that exposure to aggressive action could only intensify the experience of annoyance from which they could not find relief through the performance of such action, and that comedy could improve their state for lack of association with violence.

An investigation exploring more directly the control of arousal through communication choices has been conducted by Bryant and Zillmann (1984). Subjects were placed into a state of acute boredom or acute stress and then allowed to watch television in privacy. They could freely choose among six available programs. In a pretest with subjects who were neither bored nor under stress, three of these programs had been judged to be exciting, and three had been judged to be relaxing. Unbeknownst to the subjects, the six programs were received from playbacks in an adjacent room. This room also contained the apparatus that unobtrusively measured the subjects' consumption of entertainment. Choice of channel and time of exposure to each channel were recorded for the entire test period.

It was expected that stressed subjects would choose exposure to relaxing materials over exposure to exciting ones, and that bored subjects would exhibit the opposite preference. These are the choices that would serve excitatory homeostasis and, to the extent that the normalization of arousal levels is experientially desirable, would constitute effective mood management. The findings fully confirmed these expectations. Most subjects exposed themselves to material that seemed "excitationally right" for them.

The investigation actually included an assessment of the excitatory consequences of selective exposure. The subjects' heart rate was monitored telemetrically. Figure 5.2 shows the changes resulting from the consumption of entertainment. As can be seen, the understimulated and hypoaroused, bored subjects who elected to watch calming fare remained hypoaroused. It should be kept in mind that only a few subjects made this "inappropriate" message choice. The characteristic choice of hypoaroused, bored subjects was to consume exciting materials, and exposure to these materials effectively corrected the excitatory deficiency. Interestingly, the particular program choices proved inconsequential for overstimulated and hyperaroused, stressed subjects. Exposure to exciting television fare turned out to be as calming as exposure to calming fare. Both choices accomplished the normalization of arousal. The likely reason for this is that, compared to the stress produced by tormenting subjects with GRE and SAT exams, the "exciting" programs were not all that exciting. The subjects could only come down from the excitatory heights they experienced, and the comparatively exciting programs may have facilitated excitatory recovery because of their relatively great intervention potential (Bryant & Zillmann, 1977). The fact that quite a few stressed subjects had elected to expose themselves to exciting fare therefore does not challenge the theory, but is consistent with it. Only very few bored subjects selected stimulation that perpetuated their arousal state. All other subjects, whether stressed or bored, made choices that normalized levels of excitation.

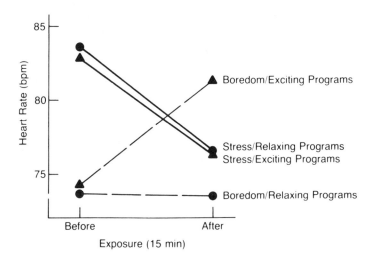

FIG. 5.2.   Heart rate associated with experiences of stress and boredom and after selective exposure to calming and exciting television programs (from Zillmann & Bryant, 1985).

In light of these findings, television indeed holds great promise as the nation's primary unwinder. Under the assumption that many viewers experience high levels of stress and are in acute need of relaxation, and that genuinely arousing programming is the exception rather than the rule, viewers are likely to pick and choose from the multitude of diversionary stimulation that television offers those materials that will effectively diminish their noxious states of hyperarousal.

TELEVISION FOR EXCITEMENT

There can be little doubt that, on occasion, exposure to television can be highly arousing. Intense autonomic activity may be instigated and foster affective reactions of considerable magnitude. Numerous investigations have shown that entertainment fare can greatly elevate viewers' levels of sympathetic excitation. It has been demonstrated, for instance, that suspenseful drama produces intense excitatory reactions in adults and children alike (Zillmann, 1980). Depictions of more or less all forms of interpersonal violence tend to liberate strong arousal reactions, especially when the kind of violence featured poses a threat to the respondents themselves (Frost & Stauffer, 1987). Although "innocuous" genres such as comedy need not be arousing and may actually be sedative under certain circumstances, comedy that creates true hilarity in adult audiences was found to be highly arousing (Tannenbaum, 1972). In fact, endocrinological research by Levi (1965) and Carruthers and Taggart (1973) leads to the conclusion that the excitatory reactions produced by exposure to extremely amusing films are very similar to those produced by exposure to suspenseful, violence-laden films. Televised athletic contests have also been shown to be capable of elevating arousal levels substantially (Bryant & Zillmann, 1977). If there is a stimulus category or genre that lacks the capacity to arouse, it is the stereotypical nature film. It has been shown consistently that this type of film not only fails to arouse, but actually lowers levels of arousal—at times markedly so (Levi, 1965; Wadeson, Mason, Hamburg, & Handlon, 1963). On the other hand, the stimulus category or genre that has the distinction of consistently producing the strongest excitatory reactions in both adult men and women is pornography (i.e., the explicit portrayal of sexual activities among humans). In addition to evoking genital reactions (e.g., Reifler, Howard, Lipton, Liptzin, & Widmann, 1971), erotica that graphically feature precoital and coital behavior have been found to produce extreme elevations in sympathetic arousal (e.g., Cantor, Zillmann, & Einsiedel, 1978; Donnerstein & Hallam, 1978; Levi, 1969; Zillmann, 1971; Zillmann & Bryant, 1984).

Outside the area of entertainment, little is known about the excitatory impact of television presentations. News reports on wars, natural disasters, tragic events such as plane crashes, or "bad news" about political happenings and the state of the economy might be expected to foster reactions associated with substantial increases in arousal. Such expectations may seem conservative and prudent, but have received little empirical support. Research on the reality–fiction dichotomy in communications (Geen, 1975; Geen & Rakosky, 1973) has shown that harm-inflicting actions believed to have actually happened tend to be more arousing (or tend to perpetuate initially elevated levels of arousal for longer periods of time) than the same actions believed to be fictional. This would appear to suggest that events in the news or in documentaries will produce more arousal than similar events in fiction. However, a recent study (Mundorf, 1987) in which excitatory reactions to tragic events featured in the local news (the drowning of two boys along with attempts to revive them and the mother's reaction) were ascertained failed to support such generalizations. Excitatory reactions were unexpectedly weak. An explanation for this might be the tendency to sanitize news accounts of tragic events. It is therefore conceivable that, on the whole, fiction produces stronger excitatory reactions than nonfiction because fictional portrayals are not subject to sanitization pressures and, in fact, seem designed to produce the strongest possible emotional impact.

In accord with the so-called law of initial values, which proclaims that the magnitude of an excitatory reaction decreases as the level of initial arousal increases (Sternbach, 1966; Wilder, 1957), it must be expected that arousal reactions are particularly strong in viewers who are initially relaxed or who are experiencing arousal near normal levels. Viewers who are already experiencing elevated levels of arousal are likely to experience a weaker excitatory reaction in response to the same stimuli, and viewers whose initial arousal is at a maximum obviously cannot be further aroused. Television's capacity to generate notable increments in autonomic arousal thus favors the relatively unaroused person. Viewers who are exhausted from repetitive daily work or who are simply bored with whatever they have been doing (but not those who are tense and inclined to relax) are likely to find the diversionary stimulation that television offers particularly exciting. Because of their repeated past experience of relief from humdrum and of getting excited, these viewers should seek out television programming that holds the greatest promise for excitement (Zillmann, 1988a, 1988b).

The view that moderate increases in arousal (and television usually provides just those) are pleasurable, whereas extreme increases are aversive, has been entertained in one form or another for some time. Bain (1875/1859) and Wundt (1893) were among the first to promote it. In more recent years, Berlyne (1971) was its chief promoter. A variation of this view, whose main advocate has been McClelland (McClelland, Atkinson, Clark, & Lowell, 1953), posits that both increases and decreases in arousal are pleasurable when their magnitude is moderate, and both are aversive when it is extreme. Common to all these views is the assumption that either the level of arousal or a change in arousal can, by itself, determine the hedonic quality of a reaction (Tannenbaum, 1980). Up to a point, an experience, of which a certain level of arousal or a certain change in arousal is a concomitant, is said to be one of pleasure; and beyond this point (which usually is entirely hypothetical), the experience, regardless of other circumstances, converts into one of aversion.

The neglect of those other circumstances limits the usefulness of this approach. It is not the proposition that extreme excitatory conditions can be aversive that needs to be challenged. Any truly extreme bodily condition constitutes an emergency which, presumably, constitutes a noxious experience. Rather, it is the fact that moderate changes in excitation that occur at intermediate levels of arousal can as readily be associated with noxious as with pleasant experiences (Buck, 1976; Schachter, 1964; Zillmann, 1978) that destroys the utility of the sole consideration of arousal levels and arousal changes. Although it may be useful to propose that persons strive for an optimal level of arousal (Duffy, 1957) or seek to vary their experience (Fiske & Maddi, 1961), it remains to be explained why some nonextreme excitatory reactions are concomitants of pleasure and others of aversion.

The pioneering work of Schachter (1964) made it abundantly clear that, in order to explain the diversity of affective and emotional behaviors with any degree of precision, it is imperative to consider cognitive processes along with excitatory reactions. In his two-factor theory of emotion, he assumed that autonomic arousal is largely nonspecific and proposed that people attribute their excitatory reactions to the stimuli immediately present in their environment and that they use interoceptive feedback from these excitatory reactions as an index of the intensity of their emotional responses. Thus, the *kind of affect* is considered *cognitively determined*; the *intensity of affect*, on the other hand, is considered *determined by the magnitude of the excitatory reaction*.

In the initial research on this two-factor model of affect and emotion, Schachter and Singer (1962) demonstrated that the artificial creation of arousal (injection of epinephrine believed to be a placebo) intensified both feelings of euphoria and dysphoria. The same arousal changes were capable of producing hedonically opposite effects, depending on situational conditions and their interpretation. A simultaneously conducted study by Schachter and Wheeler (1962), which pertains to television more directly, showed that enjoyment of comedy could readily be manipulated by altering arousal considered to be evoked by it. Injection of an arousal-facilitator (epinephrine) intensified enjoyment; injection of an autonomic blocking agent (chlorpromazine) dampened it.

The two-factor approach appears to have great utility in explaining affective and emotional reactions to television's offerings. It readily accommodates any hedonic experience, and it covers all conceivable nuances of affect. Depending on the viewers' cognitive appraisal of the events on the screen, they will be annoyed, angry, furious, sad, apprehensive, fearful, scared, terrified, satisfied, jubilant, joyous, repulsed, disgusted, amused, and so on. Whatever the result of this appraisal (that is, whatever affect viewers arrived at cognitively), the intensity of any feeling state is determined by the viewers' feedback from their concomitant excitatory reaction. Equally intense excitatory reactions can thus fuel, for example, sadness or joy, amusement or disgust. And, barring intolerably intense excitatory reactions, the intensity of affective reactions should increase with the magnitude of associated arousal reactions. The function of autonomic arousal, then, is not the determination of specific affective experiences, but the intensification of independently determined affective experiences and behaviors.

Considering both the law of initial values and two-factor theory, the following suggestions are possible:

1. Persons who experience low levels of arousal (because of monotonous environmental conditions, repetitive nonstrenuous tasks, or similarly unstimulating circumstances) are likely to respond more intensely than others to affect-inducing stimuli. To the extent that exposure to television fare fosters enjoyment and the magnitude of evoked arousal fuels this enjoyment, persons who are initially rather unaroused can be expected to obtain comparatively great pleasure from watching television.

2. As the experience of comparatively great pleasure is repeated, a tendency to seek out this excitement should manifest itself through operant learning. Hypoaroused persons should be those most strongly drawn to television "for the excitement of it."

NONSPECIFICITY OF AROUSAL AND ITS CONSEQUENCES

Although the cognitive determination of affect, as stressed in two-factor theory, is crucial to understanding the diversity of affective reactions that exposure to television is capable of evoking, the utility of this theory is rather limited. First and foremost, as a theory of affect and emotion, two-factor theory is patently incomplete because it fails to account for the origination of the excitatory reaction that, once it has occurred, is said to foster a search for an explanation that results in comprehending and labeling the "affective" reaction. Recent theorizing on affect and emotion is more complete by accounting for the excitatory response (Leventhal, 1979; Zillmann, 1978). It also relies less on a presumed need to explain any excitatory reaction to oneself, which is a central part of the two-factor model. However, in looking at reactions to television fare specifically, the issue that must concern us more than the origination of excitatory responses per se is that of possible excitatory confusions. If the assumption of nonspecificity of autonomic arousal that is made in two-factor theory has merit, the association between arousal and affect is unlikely to be a perfect one.

Although there is evidence that some emotions may be associated with somewhat specific excitatory reactions (Grings & Dawson, 1978; Schwartz, 1986; Sternbach, 1966), the bulk of the evidence shows that more or less all emotions are fed by elevated sympathetic activity in the autonomic nervous system (Kety, 1970; Mandler, 1975; Schachter, 1964; Zillmann, 1984, 1986). Granted that the excitatory reactions associated with the various conceivable affective states may vary somewhat, a high degree of overlap in excitatory patterns cannot be denied. Additionally, minor differences in excitatory reactivity may be lost in the comparatively insensitive interoceptive structures, so that for all practical purposes any feedback of an arousal state is nonspecific and can index its intensity only.

Transfer of Excitation

The fact that autonomic arousal in the various emotions is largely nonspecific has significant behavioral consequences, especially when the time course of excitatory processes is considered and compared to that of cognitive adaptation to stimulus changes. A theoretical model in which this is done is the excitation-transfer paradigm (Zillmann, 1971, 1978, 1983). Figure 5.3 presents this paradigm in graph form. The paradigm projects that, because of the comparatively slow decay of autonomic arousal (owing to humoral processes involved) and the individual's capacity to recognize stimulus changes and to select an appropriate response quasi-instantaneously (owing to speedy neural transmission), residues of excitation from a preceding affective reaction will *combine* with excitation produced by subsequent affective stimulation and thereby cause an *overly intense* affective reaction to the subsequent stimulus. In simple terms, a person who is still aroused from something that happened a while ago, whatever it may have been, and who is now confronted with a situation that causes him or her to respond emotionally, should experience this emotion more intensely and also behave more

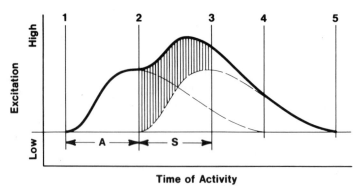

Time of Activity

FIG. 5.3.   A model of excitation transfer in which residual excitation from a preceding excitatory reaction combines additively with the excitatory reaction to current stimulation. An antecedent stimulus condition (A), persisting from Time 1 to Time 2, is assumed to produce excitatory activity that has entirely decayed only at Time 4. Similarly, a subsequent stimulus condition (S), persisting from Time 2 to Time 3, is assumed to produce excitatory activity that has entirely decayed only at Time 5. Residual excitation from Condition A and excitation specific to Condition S combine from Time 2 to Time 4. The extent to which the transfer of residues from Condition A increases the excitatory activity associated with Condition S is shown in the shaded area (from Zillmann, 1979).

intensely than he or she would without the presence of residual arousal from the earlier arousing experience. Residual arousal from anger, then, may intensify fear; residues from fear may intensify sexual behaviors; residual sexual arousal may intensify aggressive responses; and so forth. The only limiting condition is that persons cannot be cognizant of the fact that they are still aroused from an earlier experience (Cantor, Zillmann, & Bryant, 1975).

The validity of the transfer paradigm has been demonstrated for a wide range of emotional experiences. It has been shown, for example, that residues of excitation from physical exertion can intensify anger and aggressive behavior (Zillmann & Bryant, 1974; Zillmann, Katcher, & Milavsky, 1972), feelings of egotism (Gollwitzer, Earle, & Stephan, 1982), altruistic inclinations (Borden & Sloan, 1977; Sterling & Gaertner, 1984), and experiences of sexual excitement (Cantor, Zillmann, & Bryant, 1975). It also has been shown that residues of sexual arousal can potentiate aggression (Donnerstein & Hallam, 1978; Meyer, 1972; Ramirez, Bryant, & Zillmann, 1982; Zillmann, 1971; Zillmann, Bryant, Comisky, & Medoff, 1981), and that residues from sexual arousal or from feelings of annoyance can facilitate such diverse experiences as the enjoyment of music (Cantor & Zillmann, 1973; Zillmann & Mundorf, 1987), appreciation of humor (Cantor, Bryant, & Zillmann, 1974; Prerost & Brewer, 1974), and dysphoric empathy (Fry & Ogston, 1971; Zillmann, Mody, & Cantor, 1974).

Transfer Effects After Exposure to Communication

Most experimental research on the consequences of exposure to television fare has concentrated on effects immediately after exposure. Effects of exposure to violence-laden programs on aggressive behaviors, for example, have usually been assessed during the immediate postexposure period (Goranson, 1970; Geen, 1976). Effects of exposure on prosocial behavior (Rushton, 1979) and modeling effects generally (Bandura, 1965; Baron, 1977) have been ascertained analogously. Also, in most of this research, the observed effects have been attributed to particular characteristics of the content of messages, such as specific aggressive cues (Berkowitz, 1965) or the behavior of models (Bandura, 1965). The excitation-transfer paradigm makes it appear likely, however, that some of the effects reported in this type of research, especially in the research on media violence, are at least in part due to the excitatory effect of the messages.

In a first investigation designed to test this possibility (Zillmann, 1971), male adults were provoked, exposed to a neutral, an aggressive, or an erotic film and then provided with an opportunity to retaliate against their annoyer. It had been determined in a pretest that the neutral film was neither arousing nor aggressive, that the aggressive film was somewhat arousing, and that the erotic film was highly arousing yet entirely nonaggressive. Clearly, if aggressive cues are the critical mediators of exposure effects on motivated aggressive behavior, aggressiveness after exposure to the aggressive stimulus should be higher than after exposure to either one of the other stimuli. If, on the other hand, residual excitation from exposure to communication critically influences postexposure behavior, the intensity of aggressive reactions should be a simple function of the excitatory potential of the communications. The erotic film should thus produce more aggressiveness than the aggressive film, which in turn should produce more than the neutral one. The findings fully supported these theoretical expectations.

Subsequent investigations have corroborated the initial findings (Meyer, 1972; Zillmann, Hoyt, & Day, 1974). Additional research has extended them to females (Baron, 1979; Cantor, Zillmann, & Einsiedel, 1978) and to mixed-gender situations (Donnerstein & Barrett, 1978; Donnerstein & Hallam, 1978), has explored the effects on aggressiveness of various forms of pornography (White, 1979; Zillmann & Bryant, 1984; Zillmann, Bryant, & Carveth, 1981), has confirmed arousal effects on humor (Mueller & Donnerstein, 1977), and has sought to further implicate residual arousal as a promoter to help-giving (Mueller & Donnerstein, 1981; Mueller, Nelson, & Donnerstein, 1977). An investigation by Donnerstein, Donnerstein, and Barrett (1976) is noteworthy because it altered the typical sequence of events in the experimental procedure. Instead of interpolating exposure to communication between the instigation of a behavior and the opportunity to execute it, these investigators recorded transfer effects for aggression that was instigated after exposure to arousing materials (rather than beforehand).

Although the research on postexposure transfer is voluminous, it can readily be summarized:

1. It is well established that residual sympathetic excitation from exposure to communication can facilitate motivated affective behaviors.
2. Residual arousal potentially increases the likelihood and intensity of affective reactions. These reactions may be antisocial or prosocial (or nonsocial), depending on prevailing social circumstances and dispositions.
3. Stimuli capable of inducing excitatory reactions that are likely to exert some degree of influence on postexposure behavior come from numerous domains of communication content. Domains range from violence-laden programs to titillating sexual fare and hilarious comedy.
4. Because residual arousal is likely to dissipate within several minutes after exposure, transfer effects on postexposure behavior are comparatively short-lived (Day, 1976; Zillmann, Hoyt, & Day, 1974).

Although it is conceivable that excitation transfer from exposure to television is involved in many impulsive antisocial actions (e.g., aroused by the events on the screen, a parent might strike his or her child on minimal provocation or be overly punitive when corrective measures are indicated), it should be clear that such transfer does not favor hostile, aggressive, or violent reactions over other actions. Residual arousal is impartial to the kind of response it comes to intensify. If prosocial responses are motivated, it is likely to energize those responses (Mueller & Donnerstein, 1981). Analogously, if aggressive behavior has been instigated and aggressive dispositions exist, residual arousal from television exposure is likely to intensify the motivated asocial feelings and destructive actions (Zillmann, 1971; Zillmann, Katcher, & Milavsky, 1972). Consideration of the behavioral consequences of residues of communication-induced arousal, then, cannot possibly lead to the prediction of uniformly asocial effects.

Transfer Effects During Exposure to Communication

Although most communication research on excitation transfer has explored effects on overt behavior after exposure, several investigations have been conducted to establish that residual arousal from preexposure experiences also influences primarily covert affective reactions to communications. Enjoyment of rock music, for example, has been treated as an affective reaction, and it has been shown (Cantor & Zillmann, 1973) that, under the appropriate circumstances for transfer, residual excitation from prior hedonically positive or negative experiences intensifies such enjoyment. Similarly, both enjoyment of humor (Cantor, Bryant, & Zillmann, 1974) and empathetic distress, the latter occasioned by witnessing a liked protagonist suffer an unfortunate fate (Zillmann, Mody, & Cantor, 1974), have been found to be intensified by residual arousal, regardless of the hedonic valence of the arousal-producing prior experience.

Furthermore, the transfer paradigm has been applied to interdependencies among affective reactions that are elicited during exposure to entertaining communications. The phenomenon of suspense, in particular, has been investigated both in fiction (Zillmann, 1980) and in athletic contests (Zillmann, Bryant, & Sapolsky, 1989). Much attention has been given to the dispositional conditions responsible for the viewer's experience of empathetic distress during periods of acute suspense (i.e., the affective disturbance suffered while a liked protagonist is in peril or a favored competitor or team seems headed for defeat). However, of greater significance here is the "winning formula" for suspenseful drama that has emerged (Zillmann, 1980): If enjoyment of drama is to be more than a "cerebral" reaction — that is, if it is to be an intensely pleasant, emotional affair — it has to rely heavily on residual excitation from distress that precedes any satisfying resolution. The more intense the negative affective reaction during suspense, the more residual arousal will there be to intensify the experience of relief and enjoyment at the resolution of suspense. This theoretical position is well supported by the research evidence (Zillmann, 1980; Zillmann, Hay, & Bryant, 1975; Zillmann, chapter 12, this volume).

Enjoyment, then, can be greater than warranted by the excitationally appropriate affective response to the immediately present stimuli. It may be greatly enhanced by residual arousal from preceding stimulation. The recognition of such a dependency in the appreciation of dramatic fare has interesting consequences for television:

1. Television drama capable of moving the audience emotionally relies on, and benefits from, the involvement of stimuli that induce strong arousal reactions. It benefits from these arousal reactions, even if they derive from experiences of decidedly negative hedonic valence.

2. Images of sex and violence are proven arousal inducers (Tannenbaum & Zillmann, 1975). Arousal reactions to media violence appear to increase with the degree of reality in the portrayal of violence. This relationship seems to hold for adults (Geen, 1975, 1976) and for children (Osborn & Endsley, 1971). Depictions of sexual activities are particularly strong enhancers of potentially unrelated experiences of enjoyment (Hansen & Hansen, 1989; Zillmann & Mundorf, 1987). Without sex and violence as arousal inducers, television drama is likely to become unexciting and emotionally flat.

3. To the extent that the frequent employment of images of sex and violence as arousal inducers fosters exciting drama, and to the extent that only such drama attracts the large audiences upon which television commercially depends, it appears likely that any curtailment of the use of violent materials will result in an increased use of sexual materials, and vice versa.

THE HABITUATION ISSUE

It is common knowledge that in the 1970s the depiction of both aggressive and sexual behavior became increasingly explicit and graphic. It appears that stronger and stronger stimuli were called on to provide audiences with excitement and, more important here, that the use of more and more powerful material became necessary to get the job done. At the heart of this impression is the suspicion that audiences have become callous, mainly because their arousal reactions habituated. In other words, with repeated exposure to stimuli of a certain kind, initially strong excitatory reactions have become weak or have vanished entirely. Correspondingly, initially strong affective reactions have been blunted.

The possibility that excitatory reactions to aggressive and sexual fare readily habituate has interesting consequences. For one thing, it makes the search for increasingly stronger arousal inducers for greater and greater excitement seem pointless. But more significantly, it leads to the projection of socially undesirable side effects. If, for example, heavy exposure to violent behaviors that are featured in the media should cause aggressive callousness, viewers might become less disturbed when witnessing violence in real life and, hence, less inclined to intervene in, and attempt to stop, aggression among others. Similarly, it can be speculated that heavy exposure to sexual materials might foster callousness toward sex and sex-related issues in real life.

Some research evidence suggests that exposure to violent fare indeed creates aggressive callousness, making individuals more tolerant and accepting of violence among others. Drabman and Thomas (1974) and Thomas and Drabman

(1975), for instance, have shown that children (boys and girls, Grades 1 through 4) were more tolerant of hostile and aggressive behaviors among peers after exposure to a violent film than after seeing no film or after exposure to a non-aggressive film. However, these investigations did not involve any direct assessment of arousal reactions; and consequently, habituation of arousal cannot be considered implicated as a mediating mechanism. In a later study by Thomas, Horton, Lippincott, and Drabman (1977), arousal was assessed. But this study failed to yield unequivocal results. Both children (8- to 10-year-old boys and girls) and male and female adults were exposed to either violent fiction or nonaggressive sports. Thereafter they watched a film clip of real violence. It was found that, with the exception of female adults, subjects who had initially seen the aggressive film were less aroused by the scenes of real violence than subjects who had initially seen the control film. The findings on boys, girls, and male adults can be readily accepted as evidence that exposure to fictional violence creates a response set that tends to reduce the impact of exposure to actual violence (i.e., real violence may be trivialized by such preparatory treatment). But it is difficult to see how one-time exposure to fictional violence can simulate the presumed nontransitory habituation of excitatory reactions that frequently repeated exposure is expected to produce.

An investigation by Cline, Croft, and Courrier (1973) avoided the problems associated with one-time exposure. Boys (5- to 14-year-olds) with histories of comparatively little versus extensive exposure to violence-laden television drama were exposed to a violent movie. Heavy television viewers were found to be less responsive autonomically than light viewers, a finding that the investigators considered to support their proposal of desensitization from heavy exposure to violent fare. Thomas et al. (1977) employed a similar technique in a secondary analysis of their experimental data and found a corroborating negative relationship between the amount of television drama regularly consumed and the intensity of arousal reactions to violent contents.

These findings may well reflect a causal connection between consumption of violent fare and decreased reactivity, but they certainly do not establish such a connection. The correlational nature of the data does not permit causal inferences, and the findings are open to alternative causal explanations. For example, the findings are equally consistent with the proposal that autonomically hyporesponsive viewers, in order to be well entertained, seek out exposure to arousing, violent fare more often than do other viewers. This interpretational dilemma, it appears, can only be resolved by longitudinal experimental investigations.

Linz, Donnerstein, and Penrod (1984; see also Linz, 1985) conducted investigations that answer some of the questions raised. In a first study, male subjects were exposed to violent films featuring the victimization of women (films such as *The Texas Chainsaw Massacre*). Subjects watched one movie on five consecutive days. Immediately after the last showing, they participated in a rape trial. Subjects dealt with a case in which an encounter between strangers in a bar eventually led to the sexual assault. The first- and last-day films were counterbalanced to allow assessments of diminishing sensitivity to violence. Subjects evaluated numerous aspects of each film after exposure. The comparison of these evaluations shows that men came to report fewer emotional disturbances from the same films when shown last (i.e., after four similar others). Such habituation also manifested itself in the perception of lesser film violence. This perceptual shift was carried into the subsequent trial. Men who had consumed the series of violent films, compared to men without such exposure, came to judge the victim of violent assault and rape as having suffered less and as having been less injured.

In a second study, male subjects were exposed either to two or, as before, to five violence-laden films. Film ratings were again obtained immediately after exposure. However, the rape trial was delayed to the second day after exposure to the last film. For the perception of rape and its victims, this second study shows, as did the first, that the repeated consumption of violent material occasions a loss of compassion for the victims of sexual assaults. Following repeated consumption, any injury to the victims of violence was judged to be less severe.

Taken together, the investigations show that repeated exposure to media violence can trivialize violence in real life, especially the suffering that real violence inflicts on its victims. The findings suggest, moreover, that this effect is not transitory and may be of considerable duration. However, as excitatory reactions have not been monitored during exposure to communication, it remains unclear whether excitatory habituation occurred and, should it have occurred, whether it played a critical part in mediating the observed perceptional and judgmental changes.

The habituation of excitatory reactions to sexual materials has been demonstrated more directly. In a pioneering longitudinal study by Reifler, Howard, Lipton, and Liptzin (1971; see also Howard, Reifler, & Liptzin, 1971), access to pornography was manipulated over a period of 5 weeks. After the exposure treatment, male adults with heavy exposure to erotica were found to be less responsive autonomically (and sexually) to novel erotic materials than were control subjects. Similarly, Zillmann and Bryant (1982, 1984) created conditions of prolonged exposure to explicit erotica over a 6-week period and observed that excitatory reactions to such stimuli had undergone strong habituation. In addition to a no-erotica control, the investigation involved a condition in which exposure to erotica was at an intermediate level. Adult males' arousal reactions to erotica were found to be inversely proportional to the extent of prior exposure. Table 5.1 summarizes these findings. The evidence on excitatory reactions to pornography, then, seems to support projections of desensitization.

Such an interpretation is tempered, however, by the findings of "spontaneous recovery." Howard et al. (1971) observed that 8 weeks after pronounced excitatory habituation to pornography, responsiveness showed considerable recovery. Excitatory responsiveness moved back toward pretreatment levels, but failed to return fully to the initial strength.

TABLE 5.1
Excitatory Habituation to Explicit Erotica

	Habituating exposure		
Autonomic response	None	Intermediate	Prolonged
Acceleration of heart rate	20.6[c]	10.0[b]	0.4[a]
Increase in systolic blood pressure	24.8[c]	11.2[b]	0.8[a]

Note: The habituation treatment consisted of repeated exposure in weekly sessions over a 6-week period. Per session, subjects saw six erotic films (prolonged exposure), three erotic and three nonerotic films (intermediate exposure), or six nonerotic films (no exposure). The reported excitatory reactions to erotica were ascertained 1 week after the habituation treatment. Means having different superscripts differ at $p < 0.05$ by Newman-Keuls' test (from Zillmann & Bryant, 1984).

The demonstration of excitatory habituation to pornography should not be confused with a demonstration of desensitization in the sense that decreased responsiveness to erotic material carries with it a decreased sexual responsiveness in real life. At present, there is no acceptable evidence suggesting such generalization (Byrne & Byrne, 1977; Luria & Rose, 1979).

Returning to media violence, Gerbner and Gross (1976a, 1976b) proposed that heavy exposure to crime-laden television drama may cause concerns about personal safety in the viewer. If such possible apprehensions about becoming a victim of violent crime are treated as affective reactions, this proposal entails the suggestion that the affect-intensifying excitatory responses to fear-inducing stimuli become stronger with repeated exposure. It has been pointed out (Zillmann, 1980) that this projection is counter to a considerable amount of evidence that has been generated in behavior-modification research (Bandura, 1969). Repeated exposure to the risk-free, safe representation of those agents and events that induce fear "in real life" has been shown to prevent and ameliorate fear reactions with impressive consistency (e.g., Bandura & Barab, 1973; Bandura & Menlove, 1968; Hill et al., 1968; Weissbrod & Bryan, 1973). In fact, repeated exposure to safe representations of initially fear-inducing stimuli is the key element in the therapeutic treatment of phobias (Bandura, 1971). It thus would appear likely that repeated exposure to dramatic portrayals of violent crime reduces rather than increases affective reactions, especially fear reactions. Although frequent exposure may make crime salient and seemingly ever present, it also should trivialize it and diminish its emotional impact. The observed positive relationship between heavy consumption of television and apprehensions about personal safety (Gerbner & Gross, 1976a, 1976b) therefore does not by necessity reflect an effect of such consumption. It is conceivable that apprehensive persons are drawn to television (to crime drama, in particular) because repeated exposure is capable of alleviating their worries (Zillmann, 1980). Television drama dwells, after all, on the punishment of the perpetrators of violence and injustice. This ubiquitous theme should be music to the ears of crime-apprehensive individuals (see Zillmann & Wakshlag, 1985, for a more complete discussion of this issue).

Despite the demonstration of fear reduction from repeated exposure to so-called symbolic representations of the actual fear inducers, it remains unclear to what extent the habituation of excitatory reactions is involved in the mediation of these effects. The research on behavior modification has concentrated on the elimination of nonadaptive and maladaptive overt reactions. As a consequence, treatment effects were measured in behavioral terms. Arousal reactions, although assumed to play a critical part in the mediation of affective behaviors, have been neglected and were generally not assessed.

The available evidence on excitatory habituation can be summed up as follows:

1. Frequently repeated exposure to arousing stimuli can substantially diminish excitatory reactions to these stimuli.
2. Some degree of spontaneous recovery from reduced excitatory responsiveness is likely after the discontinuation of exposure.
3. The proposal that excitatory habituation of television stimuli generalizes to the respective stimuli in real life is without empirical support at present.
4. The research evidence on television's effect on excitatory habituation is scarce and rudimentary, rendering all conclusions tentative.

In the projection of television's impact on society, excitatory habituation appears to be a highly significant mechanism. Because both undesirable effects (i.e., impoverishment of adaptive social affect, callousness) and beneficial consequences (i.e., superior coping with maladaptive emotions) can be anticipated on the basis of this mechanism, impact projections are likely to be highly controversial. Given the significance of the mechanism, the role of excitatory habituation in television's societal impact is in dire need of further exploration.

TELEVISION AND CORTICAL AROUSAL

As has been stated earlier, cortical arousal has not been directly assessed in research on television effects. There are no investigations, then, that can be discussed. However, the concept of cortical arousal has been involved as a hypothetical construct. The construct has, in fact, become prominent in the controversy over educational television for children. Because of this, we briefly discuss the principal theoretical contentions and some investigations that bear directly on cortical arousal and vigilance.

Singer and Singer (1979; see also Singer, 1980) have taken issue with the fast pace of most educational programs for children, arguing that such rapid-fire expositions are likely to stunt the development of creative imagination. Indeed, children's television seems a continual bombardment of attention-controlling stimuli. Not only is there little time for the rehearsal of insights and for independent reflection on the information gained (circumstances that the Singers believe are detrimental to a desirable cognitive-affective development), but the control of attention seems to take the most primitive form possible: the continual exploitation of the orienting reflex (Lynn, 1966; Sokolov, 1960) and, to a lesser degree, the defensive response (Kimmel, van Olst, & Orlebeke, 1979). Children are confronted with incessant action. This translates into extreme stimulus changes in the visual field, extreme acoustical stimulus changes, and much unexpected vivid motion. Because the television set is stationary, orienting reactions are not particularly adaptive (i.e., spatial adjustments for superior stimulus control are not necessary). But this lack of adaptive value does not prevent execution of the responses. The arousal component of these responses should remain operative, even when the skeletal muscular part of the orienting reflex habituates. In this connection, the defensive response in perception (i.e., the reaction to stimuli such as rapidly approaching objects) must be considered especially resistant to habituation. The important consequence here is that both the orienting reflex and the defensive response are known to produce cortical arousal that serves attention. They are also capable of producing autonomic arousal. Autonomic arousal, in turn, can serve the maintenance of cortical arousal (Grings & Dawson, 1978).

Although there is little, if any, acceptable evidence of lasting undesirable effects of fast-paced programs (e.g., in terms of unfocused hyperactivity or antisocial actions; Anderson, Levin, & Lorch, 1977), there is some evidence that tends to corroborate the Singers' (1979) contention that arousing, action-packed materials are detrimental to imaginative play. Wright and Huston-Stein (1979), for instance, observed that preschool children's imaginative play after exposure to an action-packed program, compared to a slow-moving program, was greatly inhibited. What remains unclear is whether fast-paced programs disrupt individual and social creative play only temporarily, producing transitory and potentially trivial effects; or whether the effects of such disruptions accumulate and ultimately result in the impoverishment or loss of important skills.

The allegation that rapid-fire expositions shorten the attention span of children and interfere with the retention of new information (Singer & Singer, 1979) is similarly unsubstantiated. Longitudinal studies that demonstrate such effects have not been conducted. Additionally, and in contrast to the contention that information acquisition suffers from the fast pace of programs, recent investigations suggest that fast-paced programs foster superior attention and potentially superior learning. Zillmann, Williams, Bryant, Boynton, and Wolf (1980), for instance, observed that the fast-paced interspersion of humor in educational programs, compared to the slow-paced interspersion of the same materials, resulted in children's superior acquisition of educational information. These investigators speculated that this beneficial effect on information acquisition is mediated by the fast-paced version's greater impact on cortical arousal. Put simply, semi-attentive children in the audience may have been made alert by the inserted humorous tidbits, and this alertness may have carried over into exposure to the immediately subsequent educational material. The fast-paced program apparently produced this transitory alertness more often than the slow-paced program. The former program produced more vigilance overall than the latter program.

To rule out the possibility that the observed effects were specific to humor and its incentive value, Zillmann and Bryant (1983) conducted a subsequent investigation in which the humorous inserts were matched against the purest form of "fireworks" on educational television: color bursts and electronic sounds, exploding stars and swishing noises. These "synthetic" attention getters proved to facilitate information acquisition just as much as equally appealing and equally involving humor. Table 5.2 summarizes the findings in question. It thus appears that the so-called rapid-fire expositions that abound in educational television are capable of enhancing the educational process (see Zillmann & Bryant, 1983, for a more complete discussion of this issue).

The following tentative conclusions can be stated:

1. The creation of transient alertness, even by "primitive" means such as the frequent instigation of the orienting reflex, tends to facilitate information acquisition in audiences for which a high level of attentiveness cannot be expected.
2. The long-term consequences of exposure to fast-paced, information-rich programs, including the undesirable consequences of such exposure for the development of cognitive-affective and creative skills, remain to be determined.

In light of the enormity of the projected long-term consequences for society, it would seem imperative to investigate further the interrelationships between

TABLE 5.2

Information Acquisition From Educational Television Programs as a Function
of Vigilance Created by Interspersed Humorous Episodes
and Audiovisual Stimulus Bursts

	Attentional potential			
	Low		High	
	Hedonic quality		Hedonic quality	
Interspersed material	Low	High	Low	High
Humorous episodes	2.35	2.58	3.70*	4.10*
Stimulus bursts	2.32	2.50	3.80*	4.05*
Combined material	2.34	2.54	3.75*	4.08*

Note: A no-humor, no-bursts control condition yielded a mean score of 2.15. Means associated with asterisks differ significantly from the control-condition mean at $p < 0.05$ by Dunnet's test. The combination of all conditions featuring inserts of low attentional potential yielded $M = 2.44$. The combination of all conditions featuring inserts of high attentional potential yielded $M = 3.91$. These two means differ at $p < 0.001$ by F test (from Zillmann & Bryant, 1983).

prolonged massive stimulation by television exposure, cortical arousal, and the development of cognitive-affective abilities, along with possible motivational changes. Answers can be expected from longitudinal experimental studies. The exploration of the mediation of the hypothesized effects, furthermore, should greatly benefit from newly available technological means of ascertaining excitatory events in the central nervous system.

ACKNOWLEDGMENT

This chapter is a revised and updated version of a paper commissioned by the National Institute of Mental Health as a part of the 1982 report *Television and behavior: Ten years of scientific progress and implications for the eighties.*

REFERENCES

Anderson, D. R., Levin, S. R., & Lorch, E. P. (1977). The effects of TV program pacing on the behavior of preschool children. *AV Communication Review, 25,* 159-166.

Atkin, C. K. (1985). Informational utility and selective exposure to entertainment media. In D. Zillmann & J. Bryant (Eds.), *Selective exposure to communication* (pp. 63-91). Hillsdale, NJ: Lawrence Erlbaum Associates.

Bain, A. (1875). *The emotions and the will* (3rd ed.). London: Longmans, Green. (Original work published 1859)

Bandura, A. (1965). Vicarious processes: A case of no-trial learning. In L. Berkowitz (Ed.), *Advances in experimental social psychology* (Vol. 2, pp. 1-55). New York: Academic Press.

Bandura, A. (1969). *Principles of behavior modification.* New York: Holt, Rinehart & Winston.

Bandura, A. (1971). Analysis of modeling. In A. Bandura (Ed.), *Psychological modeling: Conflicting theories* (pp. 1-62). Chicago: Aldine-Atherton.

Bandura, A. (1973). *Aggression: A social learning analysis.* Englewood Cliffs, NJ: Prentice-Hall.

Bandura, A., & Barab, P. G. (1973). Processes governing disinhibitory effects through symbolic modeling. *Journal of Abnormal Psychology, 82,* 1-9.

Bandura, A., & Menlove, F. L. (1968). Factors determining vicarious extinction of avoidance behavior through symbolic modeling. *Journal of Personality and Social Psychology, 8,* 99-108.

Bard, P. (1934). The neuro-humoral basis of emotional reactions. In C. A. Murchison (Ed.), *A handbook of general experimental psychology* (pp. 264-311). Worcester, MA: Clark University Press.

Baron, R. A. (1977). *Human aggression.* New York: Plenum Press.

Baron, R. A. (1979). Heightened sexual arousal and physical aggression: An extension to females. *Journal of Research in Personality, 13,* 91-102.

Berkowitz, L. (1965). The concept of aggressive drive: Some additional considerations. In L. Berkowitz (Ed.), *Advances in experimental social psychology* (Vol. 2, pp. 301-329). New York: Academic Press.

Berlyne, D. E. (1971). *Aesthetics and psychobiology.* Englewood Cliffs, NJ: Prentice-Hall.

Borden, M. A., & Sloan, L. R. (1977, May). *Unjustified violence and physiological arousal increase the impact of altruistic appeals: Perhaps some televised sensationalism is good.* Paper presented at the meeting of the Midwestern Psychological Association, Chicago.

Bower, R. T. (1973). *Television and the public.* New York: Holt, Rinehart & Winston.

Brown, J. S. (1961). *The motivation of behavior.* New York: McGraw-Hill.

Bryant, J., & Zillmann, D. (1977). The mediating effect of the intervention potential of communications on displaced aggressiveness and retaliatory behavior. In B. D. Ruben (Ed.), *Communication yearbook 1* (pp. 291-306). New Brunswick, NJ: ICA-Transaction Press.

Bryant, J., & Zillmann, D. (1979). Effect of intensification of annoyance through unrelated residual excitation on substantially delayed hostile behavior. *Journal of Experimental Social Psychology, 15*, 470-480.

Bryant, J., & Zillmann, D. (1984). Using television to alleviate boredom and stress: Selective exposure as a function of induced excitational states. *Journal of Broadcasting, 28*(1), 1-20.

Buck, R. (1976). *Human motivation and emotion.* New York: Wiley.

Byrne, D., & Byrne, L. A. (Eds.). (1977). *Exploring human sexuality.* New York: Crowell.

Cannon, W. B. (1927). The James-Lange theory of emotions: A critical examination and an alternative theory. *American Journal of Psychology, 39*, 106-124.

Cannon, W. B. (1929). *Bodily changes in pain, hunger, fear and rage: An account of researches into the function of emotional excitement* (2nd ed.). New York: Appleton-Century-Crofts.

Cantor, J. R., Bryant, J., & Zillmann, D. (1974). Enhancement of humor appreciation by transferred excitation. *Journal of Personality and Social Psychology, 30*, 812-821.

Cantor, J. R., & Zillmann, D. (1973). The effect of affective state and emotional arousal on music appreciation. *Journal of General Psychology, 89*, 97-108.

Cantor, J. R., Zillmann, D., & Bryant, J. (1975). Enhancement of experienced sexual arousal in response to erotic stimuli through misattribution of unrelated residual excitation. *Journal of Personality and Social Psychology, 32*, 69-75.

Cantor, J. R., Zillmann, D., & Einsiedel, E. F. (1978). Female responses to provocation after exposure to aggressive and erotic films. *Communication Research, 5*, 395-411.

Carruthers, M., & Taggart, P. (1973). Vagotonicity of violence: Biochemical and cardiac responses to violent films and television programmes. *British Medical Journal, 3*, 384-389.

Cline, V. B., Croft, R. G., & Courrier, S. (1973). Desensitization of children to television violence. *Journal of Personality and Social Psychology, 27*, 360-365.

Cox, T. (1978). *Stress.* Baltimore, MD: University Park Press.

Day, K. D. (1976). Short-lived facilitation of aggressive behavior by violent communications. *Psychological Reports, 38*, 1068-1070.

Donnerstein, E., & Barrett, G. (1978). Effects of erotic stimuli on male aggression toward females. *Journal of Personality and Social Psychology, 36*, 180-188.

Donnerstein, E., Donnerstein, M., & Barrett, G. (1976). Where is the facilitation of media violence: The effects of nonexposure and placement of anger arousal. *Journal of Research in Personality, 10*, 386-398.

Donnerstein, E., Donnerstein, M., & Evans, R. (1975). Erotic stimuli and aggression: Facilitation or inhibition. *Journal of Personality and Social Psychology, 32*, 237-244.

Donnerstein, E., & Hallam, J. (1978). Facilitating effects of erotica on aggression against women. *Journal of Personality and Social Psychology, 36*, 1270-1277.

Drabman, R. S., Thomas, M. H. (1974). Does media violence increase children's toleration of real-life aggression? *Developmental Psychology, 10*, 418-421.

Duffy, E. (1957). The psychological significance of the concept of "arousal" or "activation." *Psychological Review, 64*, 265-275.

Duffy, E. (1962). *Activation and behavior.* New York: Wiley.

Dunbar, H. F. (1939). *Emotions and bodily changes: A survey of literature on psychosomatic interrelationships 1910-1933* (2nd ed.). New York: Columbia University Press.

Fiske, D. W., & Maddi, S. R. (1961). *Functions of varied experience.* Homewood, IL: Dorsey Press.

Frankenhaeuser, M. (1979). Psychoneuroendocrine approaches to the study of emotion as related to stress and coping. In R. A. Dienstbier (Ed.), *Nebraska Symposium on Motivation, 1978* (pp. 123-161). Lincoln: University of Nebraska Press.

Frost, R., & Stauffer, J. (1987). The effects of social class, gender, and personality on physiological responses to filmed violence. *Journal of Communication, 32*(2), 29-45.

Fry, P. S., & Ogston, D. G. (1971). Emotion as a function of the labeling of interruption-produced arousal. *Psychonomic Science, 24*(4), 153-154.

Geen, R. G. (1975). The meaning of observed violence: Real vs. fictional violence and consequent effects on aggression and emotional arousal. *Journal of Research in Personality, 9*, 270-281.

Geen, R. G. (1976). Observing violence in the mass media: Implications of basic research. In R. G. Geen & E. C. O'Neal (Eds.), *Perspectives on aggression* (pp. 193-234). New York: Academic Press.

Geen, R. G., & Rakosky, J. J. (1973). Interpretations of observed violence and their effects on GSR. *Journal of Experimental Research in Personality, 6*, 289-292.

Gerbner, G., & Gross, L. (1976a). Living with television: The violence profile. *Journal of Communication, 26*(2), 173-199.

Gerbner, G., & Gross, L. (1976b, April). The scary world of TV's heavy viewer. *Psychology Today*, pp. 41-45; 89.

Gollwitzer, P. M., Earle, W. B., & Stephan, W. G. (1982). Affect as a determinant of egotism: Residual excitation and performance attributions. *Journal of Personality and Social Psychology, 43*, 702-709.

Goranson, R. E. (1970). Media violence and aggressive behavior: A review of experimental research. In L. Berkowitz (Ed.), *Advances in experimental social psychology* (Vol. 5, pp. 1-31). New York: Academic Press.

Grings, W. W., & Dawson, M. E. (1978). *Emotions and bodily responses: A psychophysiological approach*. New York: Academic Press.

Hansen, C. H., & Hansen, R. D. (1989). *The influence of sex and violence on the appeal of rock music videos: How good is the conventional wisdom?* Unpublished manuscript, Oakland University, Rochester, MI.

Hebb, D. O. (1955). Drives and the C.N.S. (conceptual nervous system). *Psychological Review, 62*, 243-254.

Hill, J. A., Liebert, R. M., & Mott, D. E. W. (1968). Vicarious extinction of avoidance behavior through films: An initial test. *Psychological Reports, 22*, 192.

Howard, J. L., Reifler, C. B., & Liptzin, M. B. (1971). Effects of exposure to pornography. In *Technical Report of The Commission on Obscenity and Pornography* (Vol. 8, pp. 97-132). Washington, DC: U.S. Government Printing Office.

Hull, C. L. (1952). *A behavior system: An introduction to behavior theory concerning the individual organism*. New York: Wiley.

Izard, C. E. (1977). *Human emotions*. New York: Plenum Press.

James, W. (1884). What is emotion? *Mind, 9*, 188-204.

Kimmel, H. D., van Olst, E. H., & Orlebeke, J. F. (Eds.). (1979). *The orienting reflex in humans*. Hillsdale, NJ: Lawrence Erlbaum Associates.

Kety, S. S. (1970). Neurochemical aspects of emotional behavior. In P. Black (Ed.), *Physiological correlates of emotion* (pp. 61-71). New York: Academic Press.

Konecni, V. J. (1975). Annoyance, type and duration of postannoyance activity, and aggression: The "cathartic effect." *Journal of Experimental Psychology: General, 104*, 76-102.

Lange, C. (1887). *Über Gemütsbewegungen: Eine psycho-physiologische Studie* [On moods: A psychophysiological study]. Leipzig: Thomas.

Leventhal, H. (1974). Emotions: A basic problem for social psychology. In C. Nemeth (Ed.), *Social psychology: Classic and contemporary integrations* (pp. 1-51). Chicago: Rand McNally.

Leventhal, H. (1979). A perceptual-motor processing model of emotion. In P. Pliner, K. R. Blankstein, & I. M. Spigel (Eds.), *Advances in the study of communication and affect: Vol. 5. Perception of the emotion in self and others* (pp. 1-46). New York: Plenum.

Levi, L. (1964). The stress of everyday work as reflected in productiveness, subjective feelings and urinary output of adrenaline and noradrenaline under salaried and piece-work conditions. *Journal of Psychosomatic Research, 8*, 199-202.

Levi, L. (1965). The urinary output of adrenalin and noradrenalin during pleasant and unpleasant emotional states: A preliminary report. *Psychosomatic Medicine, 27,* 80-85.

Levi, L. (1967). *Stress: Sources, management, and prevention.* New York: Liveright.

Levi, L. (1969). Sympatho-adrenomedullary activity, diuresis, and emotional reactions during visual sexual stimulation in human females and males. *Psychosomatic Medicine, 31,* 251-268.

Levi, L. (Ed.). (1972). *Stress and distress in response to psychosocial stimuli.* Oxford: Pergamon Press.

Lindsley, D. B. (1951). Emotion. In S. S. Stevens (Ed.), *Handbook of experimental psychology* (pp. 473-516). New York: Wiley.

Linz, D. (1985). *Sexual violence in the media: Effects on male viewers and implications for society.* Unpublished doctoral dissertation, University of Wisconsin, Madison, WI.

Linz, D., Donnerstein, E., & Penrod, S. (1984). The effects of multiple exposures to filmed violence against women. *Journal of Communication, 34*(3), 130-147.

Luria, Z., & Rose, M. D. (1979). *Psychology of human sexuality.* New York: Wiley.

Lynn, R. (1966). *Attention, arousal and the orientation reaction.* Oxford: Pergamon Press.

MacLean, P. D. (1949). Psychosomatic disease and the "visceral brain": Recent developments bearing on the Papez theory of emotion. *Psychosomatic Medicine, 11,* 338-353.

Mandler, G. (1975). *Mind and emotion.* New York: Wiley.

McClelland, D. C., Atkinson, J. W., Clark, R. A., & Lowell, E. L. (1953). *The achievement motive.* New York: Appleton-Century-Crofts.

Meyer, T. P. (1972). The effects of sexually arousing and violent films on aggressive behavior. *Journal of Sex Research, 8,* 324-333.

Moruzzi, G., & Magoun, H. W. (1949). Brain stem reticular formation and activation of the EEG. *Electroencephalography and Clinical Neurophysiology, 1,* 455-473.

Mueller, C. W., & Donnerstein, E. (1977). The effects of humor-induced arousal upon aggressive behavior. *Journal of Research in Personality, 11,* 73-82.

Mueller, C., & Donnerstein, E. (1981). Film-facilitated arousal and prosocial behavior. *Journal of Experimental Social Psychology, 17,* 31-41.

Mueller, C., Nelson, R., & Donnerstein, E. (1977). Facilitative effects of media violence on helping. *Psychological Reports, 40,* 775-778.

Mundorf, N. (1987). *Affect bias in the response to news-story sequences.* Unpublished doctoral dissertation, Indiana University, Bloomington, IN.

Novaco, R. W. (1979). The cognitive regulation of anger and stress. In P. C. Kendall & S. D. Hollon (Eds.), *Cognitive-behavioral interventions: Theory, research, and procedures* (pp. 241-285). New York: Academic Press.

O'Neal, E. C., & Taylor, S. L. (in press). Status of the provoker, opportunity to retaliate, and interest in video violence. *Aggressive Behavior.*

Osborn, D. K., & Endsley, R. C. (1971). Emotional reactions of young children to TV violence. *Child Development, 42,* 321-331.

Papez, J. W. (1937). A proposed mechanism of emotion. *Archives of Neurology and Psychiatry, 38,* 725-743.

Prerost, F. J., & Brewer, R. E. (1974, August). *The common elements of sex and aggression as reflected in human preferences.* Paper presented at the Annual Meeting of the American Psychological Association, New Orleans, LA.

Ramirez, J., Bryant, J., & Zillmann, D. (1982). Effects of erotica on retaliatory behavior as a function of level of prior provocation. *Journal of Personality and Social Psychology, 43,* 971-978.

Reifler, C. B., Howard, J., Lipton, M. A., Liptzin, M. B., & Widmann, D. E. (1971). Pornography: An experimental study of effects. *American Journal of Psychiatry, 128,* 575-582.

Rosengren, K. E., Wenner, L. A., & Palmgreen, P. (Eds.). (1985). *Media gratifications research: Current perspectives.* Beverly Hills, CA: Sage.

Routtenberg, A. (1968). The two-arousal hypothesis: Reticular formation and limbic system. *Psychological Review, 75,* 51-80.

Routtenberg, A. (1971). Stimulus processing and response execution: A neurobehavioral theory. *Physiology and Behavior, 6,* 589-596.

Rubin, A. M. (1986). Uses, gratifications, and media effects research. In J. Bryant & D. Zillmann (Eds.), *Perspectives on media effects* (pp. 281-301). Hillsdale, NJ: Lawrence Erlbaum Associates.

Rushton, J. P. (1979). Effects of prosocial television and film material on the behavior of viewers. In L. Berkowitz (Ed.), *Advances in experimental social psychology* (Vol. 12, pp. 321-351). New York: Academic Press.

Schachter, S. (1964). The interaction of cognitive and physiological determinants of emotional state. In L. Berkowitz (Ed.), *Advances in experimental social psychology* (Vol. 1, pp. 49-80). New York: Academic Press.

Schachter, S., & Singer, J. (1962). Cognitive, social and physiological determinants of emotional state. *Psychological Review, 69,* 379-399.

Schachter, S., & Wheeler, L. (1962). Epinephrine, chlorpromazine, and amusement. *Journal of Abnormal and Social Psychology, 65,* 121-128.

Schwartz, G. E. (1986). Emotion and psychophysiological organization: A systems approach. In M. G. H. Coles, E. Donchin, & S. W. Porges (Eds.), *Psychophysiology: Systems, processes, and applications* (pp. 354-377). New York: Guilford Press.

Selye, H. (1956). *The stress of life.* New York: McGraw-Hill.

Singer, J. L. (1980). The power and limitations of television: A cognitive-affective analysis. In P. H. Tannenbaum (Ed.), *The entertainment functions of television* (pp. 31-65). Hillsdale, NJ: Lawrence Erlbaum Associates.

Singer, J. L., & Singer, D. G. (1979, March). Come back, Mister Rogers, come back. *Psychology Today,* pp. 56; 59-60.

Sokolov, E. N. (1960). Neuronal models and the orienting reflex. In M. A. Brazier (Ed.), *The central nervous system and behavior* (pp. 187-276). New York: Macy.

Spence, K. W. (1956). *Behavior theory and conditioning.* New Haven, CT: Yale University Press.

Sterling, B., & Gaertner, S. L. (1984). The attribution of arousal and emergency helping: A bidirectional process. *Journal of Experimental Social Psychology, 20,* 586-596.

Sternbach, R. A. (1966). *Principles of psychophysiology: An introductory text and readings.* New York: Academic Press.

Tannenbaum, P. H. (1972). Studies in film- and television-mediated arousal and aggression: A progress report. In G. A. Comstock, E. A. Rubinstein, & J. P. Murray (Eds.), *Television and social behavior: Vol. 5. Television's effects: Further explorations* (pp. 309-350). Washington, DC: U.S. Government Printing Office.

Tannenbaum, P. H. (1980). Entertainment as vicarious emotional experience. In P. H. Tannenbaum (Ed.), *The entertainment functions of television* (pp. 107-131). Hillsdale, NJ: Lawrence Erlbaum Associates.

Tannenbaum, P. H., & Zillmann, D. (1975). Emotional arousal in the facilitation of aggression through communication. In L. Berkowitz (Ed.), *Advances in experimental social psychology* (Vol. 8, pp. 149-192). New York: Academic Press.

Thomas, M. H., & Drabman, R. S. (1975). Toleration of real life aggression as a function of exposure to televised violence and age of subject. *Merrill-Palmer Quarterly, 21,* 227-232.

Thomas, M. H., Horton, R. W., Lippincott, E. C., & Drabman, R. S. (1977). Desensitization to portrayals of real-life aggression as a function of exposure to television violence. *Journal of Personality and Social Psychology, 35,* 450-458.

Wadeson, R. W., Mason, J. W., Hamburg, D. A., & Handlon, J. H. (1963). Plasma and urinary 17-OHCS responses to motion pictures. *Archives of General Psychiatry, 9,* 146-156.

Weissbrod, C. S., & Bryan, J. H. (1973). Filmed treatment as an effective fear-reducing technique. *Journal of Abnormal Child Psychology, 1,* 196-201.

White, L. A. (1979). Erotica and aggression: The influence of sexual arousal, positive affect, and negative affect on aggressive behavior. *Journal of Personality and Social Psychology, 37,* 591-601.

Wilder, J. (1957). The law of initial values in neurology and psychiatry: Facts and problems. *Journal of Nervous and Mental Disease, 125,* 73-86.

Wright, J. C., & Huston-Stein, A. (1979, March). *The influences of formal features in children's television on attention and social behavior.* Paper presented at the meeting of the Society for Research in Child Development, San Francisco, CA.

Wundt, W. M. (1893). *Grundzüge der physiologischen Psychologie* [Foundations of physiological psychology]. Leipzig: Engelmann.

Zillmann, D. (1971). Excitation transfer in communication-mediated aggressive behavior. *Journal of Experimental Social Psychology, 7,* 419-434.

Zillmann, D. (1978). Attribution and misattribution of excitatory reactions. In J. H. Harvey, W. J. Ickes, & R. F. Kidd (Eds.), *New directions in attribution research* (Vol. 2, pp. 335-368). Hillsdale, NJ: Lawrence Erlbaum Associates.

Zillmann, D. (1979). *Hostility and aggression.* Hillsdale, NJ: Lawrence Erlbaum Associates.

Zillmann, D. (1980). Anatomy of suspense. In P. H. Tannenbaum (Ed.), *The entertainment functions of television* (pp. 133-163). Hillsdale, NJ: Lawrence Erlbaum Associates.

Zillmann, D. (1983). Transfer of excitation in emotional behavior. In J. T. Cacioppo & R. E. Petty (Eds.), *Social psychophysiology: A sourcebook* (pp. 215-240). New York: Guilford Press.

Zillmann, D. (1984). *Connections between sex and aggression.* Hillsdale, NJ: Lawrence Erlbaum Associates.

Zillmann, D. (1986). Coition as emotion. In D. Byrne & K. Kelley (Eds.), *Alternative approaches to the study of sexual behavior* (pp. 173-199). Hillsdale, NJ: Lawrence Erlbaum Associates.

Zillmann, D. (1988a). Mood Management: Using entertainment to full advantage. In L. Donohew, H. E. Sypher, & E. T. Higgins (Eds.), *Communication, social cognition, and affect* (pp. 147-171). Hillsdale, NJ: Lawrence Erlbaum Associates.

Zillmann, D. (1988b). Mood management through communication choices. *American Behavioral Scientist, 31*(3), 327-340.

Zillmann, D., & Bryant, J. (1974). Effect of residual excitation on the emotional response to provocation and delayed aggressive behavior. *Journal of Personality and Social Psychology, 30,* 782-791.

Zillmann, D., & Bryant, J. (1982). Pornography, sexual callousness, and the trivialization of rape. *Journal of Communication, 32*(4), 10-21.

Zillmann, D., & Bryant, J. (1983). Uses and effects of humor in educational ventures. In P. E. McGhee & J. H. Goldstein (Eds.), *Handbook of humor research: Vol. 2. Applied studies* (pp. 173-193). New York: Springer-Verlag.

Zillmann, D., & Bryant, J. (1984). Effects of massive exposure to pornography. In N. M. Malamuth & E. Donnerstein (Eds.), *Pornography and sexual aggression* (pp. 115-138). Orlando, FL: Academic Press.

Zillmann, D., & Bryant, J. (1985). Affect, mood, and emotion as determinants of selective exposure. In D. Zillmann & J. Bryant (Eds.), *Selective exposure to communication* (pp. 157-190). Hillsdale, NJ: Lawrence Erlbaum Associates.

Zillmann, D., Bryant, J., & Carveth, R. A. (1981). The effect of erotica featuring sadomasochism and bestiality on motivated intermale aggression. *Personality and Social Psychology Bulletin, 7,* 153-159.

Zillmann, D., Bryant, J., Comisky, P. W., & Medoff, N. J. (1981). Excitation and hedonic valence in the effect of erotica on motivated intermale aggression. *European Journal of Social Psychology, 11,* 233-252.

Zillmann, D., Bryant, J., & Sapolsky, B. S. (1989). Enjoyment from sports spectatorship. In J. H. Goldstein (Ed.), *Sports, games, and play: Social and psychological viewpoints* (2nd ed., pp. 241-278). Hillsdale, NJ: Lawrence Erlbaum Associates.

Zillmann, D., Hay, T. A., & Bryant, J. (1975). The effect of suspense and its resolution on the appreciation of dramatic presentations. *Journal of Research in Personality, 9,* 307-323.

Zillmann, D., Hoyt, J. L., & Day, K. D. (1974). Strength and duration of the effect of aggressive, violent, and erotic communications on subsequent aggressive behavior. *Communication Research, 1,* 286-306.

Zillmann, D., & Johnson, R. C. (1973). Motivated aggressiveness perpetuated by exposure to aggressive films and reduced by exposure to nonaggressive films. *Journal of Research in Personality, 7*, 261-276.

Zillmann, D., Katcher, A. H., & Milavsky B. (1972). Excitation transfer from physical exercise to subsequent aggressive behavior. *Journal of Experimental Social Psychology, 8*, 247-259.

Zillmann, D., Mody, B., & Cantor, J. R. (1974). Empathetic perception of emotional displays in films as a function of hedonic and excitatory state prior to exposure. *Journal of Research in Personality, 8*, 335-349.

Zillmann, D., & Mundorf, N. (1987). Image effects in the appreciation of video rock. *Communication Research, 14*(3), 316-334.

Zillmann, D., & Wakshlag, J. (1985). Fear of victimization and the appeal of crime drama. In D. Zillmann & J. Bryant (Eds.), *Selective exposure to communication* (pp. 141-156). Hillsdale, NJ: Lawrence Erlbaum Associates.

Zillmann, D., Williams, B. R., Bryant, J., Boynton, K. R., & Wolf, M. A. (1980). Acquisition of information from educational television programs as a function of differently paced humorous inserts. *Journal of Educational Psychology, 72*, 170-180.

CHAPTER

6

Empathy: Affect From Bearing Witness to the Emotions of Others

Dolf Zillmann
University of Alabama

> *How selfish soever man may be supposed, there are evidently some principles in his nature, which interest him in the fortune of others, and render their happiness necessary to him, though he derives nothing from it except the pleasure of seeing it.*
>
> —Smith (1759/1971, p.1)

This chapter explores the merits of various conceptual approaches to the phenomenon of empathy. The principal theories of empathy are outlined, and their strengths, weaknesses, and limitations are discussed. A new theoretical model of empathy is then presented. This model incorporates and integrates much established theory. The presentation is followed by a discussion of pertinent research findings. Finally, the new model's implications for affective development are projected. Special consideration is given to the changing ecology of empathetic experience. Focus is on the new communication technology with its enormous capacity for replacing immediate, affect-producing social exchanges with sign events that abstract, simulate, and represent such exchanges.

CONCEPTUALIZATIONS OF EMPATHY

Empathy has meant different things to different scholars, both in philosophy (e.g., Scheler, 1913; Smith, 1759/1971, Stein, 1970) and in psychology (e.g., Berger, 1962; Hoffman, 1977; Stotland, 1969). It has been construed, for instance, as the ability to perceive accurately the emotions of others (e.g., Borke, 1971; Tagiuri, 1969), the proficiency of putting oneself into another person's lot (e.g., Dymond, 1949, 1950; Katz, 1963; Mead, 1934), the skill of understanding the affective experiences of others (e.g., Cline & Richards, 1960; Davis, Hull, Young, & Warren, 1987; Truax, 1961), the sharing of particular emotions with others (e.g., Aronfreed, 1968; Feshbach, 1978; Lipps, 1907), hedonic concordance of affect in a model and an observer (e.g., Berger, 1962; Stotland, 1969; Stotland, Mathews, Sherman, Hansson, & Richardson, 1978), affinity in the autonomic response patterns associated with the model's and observer's affective behavior (e.g., Berger, 1962; Hygge, 1976a, 1976b; Tomes, 1964), the conscious or unconscious assimilation of another ego through a process called *identification* (e.g., Fenichel, 1954; Freud, 1921/1950, 1933/1964), the mental entering into another person or thing that results in fused consciousness (e.g., Lipps, 1903, 1906; Worringer 1908/1959), instinct-like affect propagation and primitive action-inspiring emotional contagion (e.g., McDougall, 1908), and the instigation to act so as to relieve distress in others (e.g., Mehrabian & Epstein, 1972; Stotland et al., 1978).

This diversity in the specification of what is to be considered empathy may give the impression that different investigators have addressed different phenomena, and that the discrepant specifications are irreconcilable. Such an impression is overly pessimistic, however, as there is sufficient commonality in the definitional approaches to consider them delineations of one particular behavioral phenomenon.

The impression of incompatible specifications seems created by varying attention to individual facets of empathy. Some definitions have focused on specific mechanisms of empathetic behavior and/or on a limited set of manifestations of the behavior in question. Others have concentrated on behavioral implications, such as the motivation to render help to fellow beings. Yet others have emphasized the utility of presumed empathetic processes, such as diagnostic skills and interpersonal sensitivity. Nonetheless, with the exception of Lipps' and Worringer's proposals concerning aesthetic experience, all definitional approaches seem to address a process by which persons respond emotionally to the emotions of others, and do so with some degree of affinity between witnessed emotion and their emotional reaction to it.

For our purposes, this descriptive account of empathy is insufficient, however. It is too restrictive in that it limits the empathy concept to affective responses to the expression of emotions by others. Some time ago, Smith (1759/1971) observed that the anticipation of a model's emotional reaction alone could induce the affective response that actual witnessing of the reaction would produce. "When we see a stroke aimed and just ready to fall upon the leg or arm of another person," he wrote, "we naturally shrink and draw back our own leg or our own arm" (p. 3). Stotland (1969) reviewed research that corroborated the existence of such "anticipatory empathetic reactions" and felt compelled to include these responses under the empathy heading. He defined empathy as "an observer's reacting emotionally because he perceives that another is experiencing *or is about to experience an emotion*" (p. 272; italics added). Emotional expression being manifest or impending, the definition still limits empathy to others' expressions. This limitation is unacceptable because model-observer affect concordance is frequently in evidence when the observer is exposed to information that seemingly precipitates the model's facial and bodily expressions. Characteristically, the observer responds to both (a) the circumstances that produce the model's emotional reaction and (b) the expressive elements of that reaction. In recognition of this fact, Hoffman (1978) defined *empathy* as "a largely involuntary, vicarious response to affective cues from another person *or from his situation*" (p. 227; italics added). Aronfreed (1968), on the other hand, thought it necessary to keep the two potential sources of affect conceptually separated and suggested that the empathy construct should be restricted to affective reactions induced by exposure to others' emotional expressions. He further suggested that affect in response to witnessing the conditions that produce emotional reactions in others, or to learning about them indirectly, be termed *vicarious reactions*.

There seems to be merit in both approaches. First, it is most important to recognize the joint operation of information about (a) the apparent causes of a model's affect and (b) the model's expression of affect. This joint operation may be considered a "natural confounding"; that is, an ecologically undeniable and valid concurrence. The separation of the confounded elements appears to create a degree of ambiguity that prevents meaningful reactions. Or meaningful reactions occur only after the observer "infers" deleted events. For instance, the facial expression of discomfort, in and of itself, might well produce an appreciable impact on an observer. This might occur because of facial mimicry and afferent feedback thereof. It cannot be ruled out, however, that the respondent guesses a cause for the discomfort, and that an empathy-like affective reaction comes about only thereafter. It could be argued that respondents make sense of a model's expressions in terms of their own affective experiences with specific stimulus situations and then respond on the basis of these experiences. Exposure to facially expressed affect, then, via presumptions about their stimulation, might liberate readily accessible affective memories, and these memories might foster affect in the observer.

Regardless of particular mechanisms of emotional reactions to a model's expressions of affect, such expressions are frequently too vague to allow meaningful empathetic reactions to a fellow being's affect. For example, tears are shed on joyous occasions as well as on miserable ones, laughter can accompany despair as well as gaiety, and smiles do not necessarily signal a state of well-being. It is common observation, however, that empathy is rarely miselicited by "inappropriate" affective expressions. It should be the rare exception, for example, that people respond grievously upon seeing others cry at what they know to be a happy reunion—even if they should shed some tears themselves. This attests to the fact that information about the instigation of affect in displayers is of overriding significance in the determination of the observer's potentially empathetic experiential state. Consequently, information about a model's *affective responding* may be considered incomplete, in general; and the role of information about the *causal circumstances* of the model's affective responding will have to be acknowledged if an ecologically valid comprehension of empathy and its function in human affairs is to be achieved.

It should be clear that the argument is reversible. Causal circumstances may be ambiguous, leaving it unclear how particular persons might respond to them. If a person's response is not exhibited, an observer may well, accurately or erroneously, anticipate a specific reaction and its expressive manifestations. This anticipation may then greatly modify, even create, feelings of empathy.

Second, the conceptual separation of causal and expressive elements in a model's affect is nonetheless useful, if not imperative, because it assures attention to the relative contributions that these components make to empathetic reactions. It is conceivable that the contribution of the expression of affect is substantial at times and insignificant at others. The two components seem sequentially dependent, too. Prior knowledge of the causal circumstances of a model's display of affect should promote pronounced empathetic reactions. Exposure to similar displays whose causation is unclear during exposure should produce comparatively subdued reactions. But more importantly, the conceptual separation leads to focused attention on types of causal circumstances that precipitate a model's affect, as well as on the relationship between the model's and the observer's responsiveness to the causal condition.

Presentation and representation of causal conditions are extremely variable. Affect-inducing circumstances may be provided verbally. They can be reported in a roundabout or in a precise fashion, and they can be dramatically embellished to different degrees. In our daily lives, all emotional happenings that we did not witness directly are subject to the indicated variation. Novels, with their partiality to the display of emotions, are by definition limited to verbal accounts. In case of direct witness of emotional events, the causal circumstances tend to be audiovisually defined. They may be manifest in vivid action and, most importantly, in events that, in and of themselves, are capable of inducing emotional reactions in an onlooker. The same holds true for audiovisual representations of such events — events known to abound in movies and television programs of any kind.

With regard to the type of presentation, it seems likely that the affective impact on an observer increases with the veridicality of the portrayal of the circumstances that foster emotions in a model. A person's facial and bodily expression of fear and panic, for instance, may be the apparent result of his or her entrapment in a house on fire. Any affective reaction of a respondent who is exposed to the situation at large may in part derive from the exhibition of fear in the model. Also in part, however, it is likely to result from the verbal specification or the audiovisual properties, immediate or in representation, of the causal circumstances — that is, the inferno. One might be inclined to believe that the more closely any representation of such inferno mimics the actual stimulus conditions, the greater its affective impact. This reasoning suggests that audiovisual representations (or in semiotic terms, iconic representations) tend to generate more affect than alternative forms. It is nonetheless conceivable that verbal or other non-iconic representations are equally powerful in the elicitation of affect, because they entice the individual to imagine the circumstances in terms of experiences that proved arousing in the individual's past. This likely involvement of stimulus-bound affective experience applies, of course, to all modes of representation. For instance, individuals who experienced fire as a threat to personal welfare should respond more strongly than those lacking such experience with inferno-like situations. This should hold true whether fire is presented in vivid images or presented verbally, because affective memory should be revived in both cases.

Our account entails a formidable dilemma for the conceptualization of empathy. First of all, negative affect in response to witnessing a model confronted with life-endangering events is likely to come (in part, at least) from exposure to an affect-inducing stimulus, such as flames engulfing a home. Individuals are unlikely to know which part of their affective reaction is the result of this kind of exposure and which derives from responding to the model's despair. In fact, individuals are highly inefficient in separating contributions to affect, if they are at all capable of making such a separation (Zillmann, 1978, 1983b). Individuals will, as a rule, construe their reactions as resulting *in toto* from the most plausible, immediately present inducing conditions. Under empathy-evoking conditions, the model's obtrusive behavior is a likely candidate. If picked, individuals may erroneously construe reactions, that in large measure result from exposure to ulterior affect-inducing stimuli, as entirely empathetic. To complicate matters further, it is conceivable that the non-empathetic response component of empathy, such as negative affect liberated by a condition commonly posing a threat, ultimately enhances the empathetic reaction because it amplifies the model's endangerment. In the inferno example, affect triggered by the sight of a home ablaze should facilitate the perception of peril for the entrapped person and thereby intensify feelings of empathetic distress about his or her situation. The same considerations apply, of course, to positive affect in empathetic reactions. Observers might respond strongly to the rewards that a model attains and, in focusing on the model's expression of contentment and satisfaction, come to construe their responses as purely empathetic.

Finally, misreadings of contributions to affect in empathetic experiences are likely to arise in situations where the respondents truly share, to some degree, the model's satisfaction or endangerment. This is to say that a model's benefaction may also benefit the observer; and likewise, a model's endangerment may also constitute a threat to the observer. Parents, for instance, might construe their feelings in response to seeing their son or daughter rejoice upon receiving a college diploma as empathy, although much of their excitedness is likely to stem from self-gratification and the anticipation thereof (i.e., from celebrating their own accomplishment). Similarly, empathetic grief for a brother or sister who has been stricken by a hereditary disease is likely to be fueled by the fear that the disease might eventually victimize the respondents themselves.

Given these conceptual difficulties, and given that the specifiable types of stimuli and conditions that contribute to affective reactions elude measurement and probably will do so in the foreseeable future, it appears appropriate to conceive of empathy as an affective reaction that the reacting individual deems produced by happenings to another person and/or by this person's expressive and behavioral responses to them. Empathy is thus viewed as a feeling state that is thought to be brought on by the observation of a fellow being in a specific situation. The feeling state is particular, however, as not all affective reactions would and could be considered empathy. Clearly, affect that is hedonically opposite to that observed is unlikely to be construed as "feeling with" or "feeling for" somebody; that is, as empathetic. Only reactions that are hedonically compatible and concordant qualify. If someone's pain is an observer's joy, or someone's joy is an observer's pain, the construct of empathy as subjective experience does not apply. Efforts to retain it for these conditions (e.g., by labeling the discordant affective experience *negative empathy* or *counterempathy*) seem misplaced and confusing, because they can be construed as suggesting that counterempathy is a form of empathetic experience — where in fact it refers to the absence of such an experience, or to a response based on its absence. Experientially, then, counterempathy is not an empathetic reaction. However, the concept of counterempathy can be granted descriptive utility in that it unambiguously specifies an affective reaction opposite in hedonic valence to empathy.

The involvement of attributional processes in the conceptualization of empathy makes stipulations about hedonic concordance or affect affinity unnecessary. Unfortunately, it creates some problems in the process. The reliance on causal attribution, no matter how implicit and rudimentary this process is presumed to be, presupposes conceptual and linguistic skills that are lacking in linguistically immature children. As a result, the conceptualization seems wanting and useless for the assessment of empathy in such children. But the situation can be remedied. First, the empathetic response in preattributional children can be considered incomplete because the conscious component of the possible feeling state is absent. Second, the problem can be resolved at the operational level by having a third party establish (a) that the child intentionally focuses on events that come a model's way and/or on the model's expressive and behavioral response to them, and (b) that the resulting affect is hedonically concordant with that exhibited by the model. It would seem preferable, however, to consider such concordant affective reactions just that — rather than fulfledged empathetic experiences.

Before formalizing these considerations in a definition of empathy, some clarifications are in order.

First, in the cited definitions, and in the preceding conceptual efforts, it has been assumed that affect is a response that is associated with a notable increase in arousal. Those who have measured the arousal component of affect

(Cacioppo & Petty, 1983; Grings & Dawson, 1978; Wagner & Manstead, 1989) have invariably operationalized it as a sympathetic reaction; that is, as an increase of sympathetic excitation in the autonomic nervous system. We follow this tradition in conceptualizing affect as a reaction associated with an appreciable increase in sympathetic activity. However, we cannot commit ourselves to operational specification of what, exactly, would qualify as an appreciable increase.

Second, in our considerations of empathy and affect we have avoided the term *vicarious reaction*. Vicarious, if taken to mean "instead of" or "in place of," refers to a mechanism of empathy that entails the assumption of some sort of ego confusion in respondents. Confronted with a model's situation and behavior, observers are apparently viewed as imagining themselves in the model's place and then to feel and respond accordingly. As it cannot possibly be considered established that all affective reactions to the emotions of others or to their apparent causes are brought about by the respondents' placing themselves into others' stead, the use of the term *vicarious* seems careless and unfortunate. The definitional use of the term amounts to a foregone conclusion about the mechanics of empathy. In this connection, Aronfreed's (1968) suggestion to consider as vicarious any affect that is produced by exposure to the circumstances that eventually lead to a model's emotions seems particularly misleading. How can a response to affect-inducing circumstances (e.g., a house on fire) be vicarious? How can it be in someone's stead, especially when models are only scarcely defined or there are none?

Third, we have suggested that empathy be considered an experiential state in which observers attribute model-concordant affect to exposure to the model. It was recognized that this global attribution is likely to entail the misattribution of some elements of the affective reaction. The excitatory component of affect, in particular, may aggregate response elements from stimuli salient to self rather than to the model's welfare. Should an empathetic response contain such elements, or even be primarily composed of them, one might be inclined to label the affective reaction *pseudo-empathy*. This possible characterization is based in part on the conceptual distinction that Aronfreed (1968) introduced, and it thus maintains the distinction. The characterization seems of questionable value, however, because it is difficult to operationalize; in addition, and more importantly, because likely misconceptions about contributions to affect in observers' attributions do not detract from the experiential reality of their empathetic responses.

Empathy, then, may be defined as any experience that is a response (a) to information about circumstances presumed to cause acute emotions in another individual and/or (b) to the facial and bodily expression of emotional experiences of another individual and/or (c) to another individual's behaviors presumed to be precipitated by acute emotional experiences, that (d) is associated with an appreciable increase in excitation, and that (e) respondents construe as feeling with or feeling for another individual.

THEORIES OF EMPATHY

Theories of empathy can be grouped into three categories: (a) those that posit that the phenomenon is due to reflexive and innate processes, (b) those that posit that these processes are learned without the involvement of deliberate cognitive operations, and (c) those that focus on deliberate or habitual cognitive operations and consider them the crucial mediators.

Empathy As a Reflexive Response

Theories of the first type have been proposed by McDougall (1908) and Lipps (1907), among others. McDougall held that an innate response disposition, which he called "primitive passive sympathy," simply compels observers to experience the emotions of others. He feared, in fact, that individuals might get so caught up in empathizing with the joys and miseries of others, especially with the latter, that this innate disposition would prove maladaptive; and he developed theoretical amendments to show how debilitating empathy is prevented and sanity maintained (e.g., McDougall, 1922). Lipps' related proposal focused more strongly on the expressive elements of emotional experience. Specifically, he posited that observers, because of innate dispositions, mimic the observed party's postural and gestural expressions and that afferent feedback from this motor mimicry liberates empathetic affect, as it connects to the observer's affective experiences that are associated with the expressions in question. The self's experience of pain, for instance, is associated with afferent feedback of a specific facial expression, and the elicitation of this expression and its afferent feedback by way of motor mimicry is thought to produce or reproduce this experience to some degree. The second step of Lipps' theory of empathy (i.e., the assumed capacity of emotional expression, especially facial expression, to produce affective states) is an integral part of several more recent theories of emotion (e.g., Izard, 1977; Tomkins, 1962, 1963; Zajonc, 1980).

Evidence for motor and facial mimicry comes from studies with both children and adults. For instance, infants cry reflexively to the cries of other infants rather than to similarly noxious cries of another kind (e.g., Sagi & Hoffman, 1976; Simner, 1971). In the so-called smiling response, they smile at smiling faces (e.g., Spitz & Wolf, 1946; Washburn, 1929). Children mimic a variety of facial expressions (e.g., Hamilton, 1972). Adults show increased lip movement and a higher frequency of eye blinking upon observing stuttering or a high eye-blink rate, respectively, in others (e.g., Berger & Hadley, 1975; Bernal & Berger, 1976). Even the frequency of individuals' yawning is known to vary with that of yawning models (Cialdini & McPeek, 1974). The proposal that afferent feedback from the facial muscles fosters expression-specific affect has received some support from research in which subjects were made to express emotions that were either consistent or inconsistent with concurrent external stimulation (Laird, 1974).

The supportive findings could not be replicated, however (Tourangeau & Ellsworth, 1979). In related research, the suppression of the expressive component of affect was found to reduce both the intensity of felt affect and the excitatory concomitant of that affect (Lanzetta, Cartwright-Smith, & Kleck, 1976). Exaggeration of facial expression, on the other hand, amplified affect-linked excitatory reactions (Vaughan & Lanzetta, 1980). Such findings suggest that afferent feedback from affect expression is capable of modifying affective experience. But they also make it clear that the power of feedback in controlling affect is far more limited than suggested by the proposal under consideration (cf. Buck, 1980).

Empathy As an Acquired Response

Theories of the second type, meaning proposals that project empathetic reactions as acquired in a more or less mechanical fashion, have been implied in the reasoning of many investigators. The presumed mechanics of the acquisition process have been most clearly articulated by Aronfreed (1970) and Humphrey (1922).

Aronfreed suggested that empathetic reactions are acquired in socially parallel affective experiences. Specifically, in the concurrent, externally induced experience of pain or pleasure in a model and an observer, the model's expression of pain or pleasure becomes associated with these responses. With repeated experiences of this kind, the model's expression gradually assumes the power to elicit sensations akin to pain and pleasure. Two children, for instance, may be punished for a jointly committed misdeed and observe each other's expressions of distress during and after the ordeal. Upon witnessing similar expressions in others, they should come to feel a touch of their own distress reaction that is associated with these expressions. The behavioral conditions under which empathetic responses are acquired need not be entirely parallel, however. Many investigators have pointed to the mother–infant caretaker relationship as a most critical one in which empathy is likely to develop (e.g., Hoffman, 1973; Sullivan, 1940). The mother's expression of contentment is predominantly linked to the child's benefaction and the experience of well-being. Likewise, the mother's expression of distress is mostly connected with the child's experience of distress. A model's expression of negative and positive affect is thus consistently paired with an observer's affect of the same kind, despite the asymmetry in the behavioral situation.

Humphrey's theorizing proves more inclusive yet. He started on the premise that the elicitation of affect is mostly mediated by stimuli from so-called distance receptors and that, because of this, affect-inducing stimuli for self and for others are often very similar. For instance, the visual experience of cutting one's finger is essentially the same as that of seeing another person cutting his or her finger. Or a child's perception of his or her own crying is much the same as that of the crying of another child. Surely, the sensations associated with these expressions are private and subjective. But Humphrey insisted that visual, auditory, and olfactory access to self is principally no different than that to others. In making his point on distance reception he wrote: "my own body and that of my neighbour are on a par, not identical but similar" (1922, p. 115). Given such perceptual similarity between self and other, he then proposed that the individual, upon exposure to stimuli that are highly similar to those that were associated with positive or negative affective reactions in the past, will experience this affect again – to some degree, at least. Using the classical conditioning paradigm, Humphrey argued that stimuli that were consistently paired with or followed by affective reactions would assume the power to elicit these reactions. Empathy-like responses may thus be expected after a stimulus-sensation linkage has been established and the individual is exposed to the critical stimulus condition in the behavior, especially the expressive behavior, of others. Humphrey went beyond classical conditioning, however, when he proposed that empathetic reactions could be induced by exposure to events that, as percepts, have not been linked with affective reactions before. He suggested that in the absence of sufficient stimulus similarity, a *complex* integrating related percepts and sensations would be activated, and that this complex would be capable of mediating empathetic responses. For instance, a person may never have seen him- or herself stand on the edge of a precipice, especially not on one that is in the process of breaking off. But upon witnessing another stand there, confronted with disaster, the onlooker is bound to empathize – virtually sensing the model's loss of balance. According to Humphrey, the empathetic reaction is the result of stimulus components of a complex such as "soil slipping beneath" that is activated by the perception of the model's dilemma. Should the observer lack affective experience with slipping soil, the concept of "losing balance" could be invoked as the empathy mediator. Essentially, then, any percept is viewed as capable of activating experientially pertinent complexes. If complexes integrating immediately related experiences do not exist, those that integrate more remotely related experiences are called on. Because Humphrey did not focus attention solely on the expressive component of affect, his reasoning, especially his expansion of the conditioning paradigm, resulted in a model that is sensitive to causal circumstances and postexpressive behaviors as well. Perhaps most importantly, however, it created a model that is sensitive to affective experience and affective memory generally.

The proposal that initially neutral stimuli can, through conditioning, assume the power of eliciting empathetic reactions, especially their excitatory concomitants, has received considerable support (e.g., Berger, 1962; Craig & Lowery, 1969). In such acquisition of empathetic reactions, information about the experiential quality of the model's reaction (regardless of its immediately perceptible facial or bodily expression) appears to be more important than information about the experience-inducing conditions per se (e.g., Hygge, 1976a, 1976b). Most of the research done in this area has focused on the affect-eliciting properties of facial expression, however. Generally speaking, facial expressiveness, autonomic activity, and self-reported intensity of affect tend to be positively correlated (e.g., Zuckerman, Klorman, Larrance, & Spiegel, 1981). As the likely consequence of this state of affairs, conditioning of empathetic reactions to facial expressions proved to be comparatively easy under conditions of face-affect congruity and rather difficult under conditions of face-affect incongruity (e.g., Lanzetta & Orr, 1981; Orr & Lanzetta, 1980). The significance for empathy of a person's conditioning history concerning facial expressions was most impressively demonstrated in an investigation by Englis, Vaughan, and Lanzetta (1982). Symmetry between a model's facially expressed affect and an observer's contingent affective experience was found to produce particularly strong empathetic reactions to facially expressed affect after discontinuance of the contingent stimulus. Asymmetry, in contrast, produced anti-empathetic reactions (i.e., discordant affect) or indifference. It has further been shown that the excitatory component of empathetic reactions that were established under conditions of face-affect symmetry is more resistant to extinction than is that of reactions established under other circumstances (e.g., Öhman & Dimberg, 1978). Empathetic responding thus seems readily acquired and maintained under some conditions, but not under others. Learning is apparently partial to ecologically concurrent response components (cf. Seligman, 1970).

Empathy As a Cognitively Mediated Response

Finally, theories of the third type have been pioneered by Smith (1759/1971) and, among others, by Stotland (1969). In these theories, cognitions that accomplish, or seem to accomplish, the imaginary placement of an observer into the observed and his or her lot, whether deliberate or instigated by environmental stimuli, are assigned the key role in the elicitation of empathy.

Smith, in his classic theory of moral sentiments, anticipated much of contemporary cognitive psychology—or more accurately, its application to affect and empathy. "By the imagination," he wrote, "we place ourselves in his [i.e., the observed person's] situation, we conceive ourselves enduring all the same torments, we enter as it were into his body and become in some measure him, and thence form some idea of his sensations, and even feel something which, though weaker in degree, is not altogether unlike them" (pp. 2-3). Despite early criticism of this view as an overintellectualization of the empathy process (Humphrey, 1922), the suggested mechanism (i.e., empathy as more or less deliberate and conscious place-taking) is probably the one that is best known and most widely adopted (cf. Katz, 1963; Mead, 1934; Rogers, 1967).

The work of Stotland and his colleagues (e.g., Mathews & Stotland, 1973; Stotland, 1969; Stotland et al., 1978) can be considered to have firmly established that imagination indeed produces and enhances empathy, both the subjective experience and its physiological accompaniments. In particular, the instruction to imagine oneself in an affect-exhibiting person's place has been shown to foster empathetic reactions of greater intensity than observing this person without such instruction. Pronounced affective reactions were often observed to occur with considerable latency after the onset of exposure to others in distressing situations, and this circumstance has been interpreted as showing that empathy does not so much result from exposure to external stimuli, even when favorable perceptual conditions exist (i.e., an empathy-directed cognitive set), as from the cognitive operations involved in the observer's imagination of the observed person's experiential situation. It is conceivable that imaginative efforts that take off on the stimuli impinging on the observer revive related images from the observer's own past, and that these ideational stimuli trigger affective responses. If so, the enhancement of empathy is not directly the result of "putting oneself into the place of another." Instead, it would be the result of ideational stimuli that were activated by efforts at role-taking, a process that could be described as "sensing past pleasures or pains again feels like responding intensely to the model's apparent pleasures or pains." It should be noticed that the mechanics under consideration are very similar to those in Humphrey's proposals. Granted vast differences in terminology and conceptual specifics, the empathetic response is viewed as the result of generating ideational stimuli that reinstate related past experiences of self.

Toward the Integration of Theories

If we label empathetic or empathy-like reactions that are controlled by built-in dispositions *reflexive*, those that are acquired through some form of conditioning *learned*, and those that are mediated by purposeful, comparatively complex cognitive operations *deliberate*, it can be said that there is some supportive evidence for reflexive, learned, and deliberate empathy. At the same time it becomes clear, however, that none of the individual mechanisms can provide a satisfying explanation for all empathy phenomena. It also becomes clear that the basic mechanisms of empathy tend to be confounded in most empathetic experiences of interest. Reflexive empathetic reactions, for instance, make for an incomplete empathetic experience, unless some form of appraisal is involved (Hoffman, 1978). Any appraisal is likely to entail components of deliberate empathy, however, possibly of learned empathy. Similarly, learned empathy is likely to entail components of reflexive empathy and to foster an appraisal that may have a deliberate empathy-enhancing component. Deliberate empathy, finally, might exploit reflexive and learned reactions to ideational stimuli that are purposely produced.

   As far as the explanation of empathy phenomena is concerned, the limitations of individual mechanisms are obtrusively evident. It is difficult to see, for instance, how facial mimicry could be explained as the result of time-consuming, deliberate cognitive operations. It is equally difficult to see how any reference to complex, deliberate cognitive action could explain the elicitation of learned excitatory reactions that accompany empathy and that critically influence the depth of the experience. On the other hand, reflexive and learned mechanics, as long as stimulation is restricted to immediately present environment stimuli, are at a loss in explaining empathy that is brought on deliberately through imaginative processes.

We now turn to formulating a model of empathy that integrates the basic paradigms in order to account more fully for empathy phenomena. The model does not merely combine the principal mechanisms, however, but specifies modes of their interaction.

THREE-FACTOR THEORY OF EMPATHY

The theory to be specified is an application of the three-factor theory of emotion (Zillmann, 1978, 1979, 1983b, 1984) to empathy phenomena. Briefly, three-factor theory projects emotional behavior as the result of the interaction of three behavior-controlling forces: the dispositional, the excitatory, and the experiential component.

The *dispositional* component is conceived of as a response-guiding mechanism. Immediate motor reactions to emotion-inducing stimuli are assumed to be largely under stimulus and reinforcement control. In emotional behavior, then, initial skeletal-motor reactions are viewed as direct, unmitigated responses to stimuli; that is, as responses made without the substantial latency that is characteristic of complex cognitive mediation.

The *excitatory* component is conceived of as a response-energizing mechanism. Excitatory reactions, analogous to skeletal-motor reactions, are also assumed to be largely under stimulus and reinforcement control, again without the necessary involvement of complex cognitive mediation. Excitation is operationalized as heightened activity in the sympathetic nervous system, primarily, that prepares the organism for the temporary engagement in vigorous action such as needed for fight or flight. It is not assumed, however, that the preparedness for vigorous action has appetitive properties in the sense that it motivates specific goal-directed behaviors.

The *experiential* component, finally, is conceived of as the conscious experience of the skeletal-motor and/or the excitatory reaction to emotion-inducing stimuli. It is assumed that exteroceptive and/or interoceptive information about many facets of an immediate emotional reaction reaches awareness, and that this awareness fosters an appraisal of the response-eliciting circumstances. It is assumed that the individual continually monitors his or her emotional behavior; and furthermore, that he or she, by applying pertinent criteria to the monitoring process, determines the utility and appropriateness of emotional reactions and actions. Actions that are deemed inappropriate are discontinued; and unfolding reactions that are similarly appraised are inhibited and terminated—to the extent that this can be accomplished by deliberate intervention. On the other hand, immediate emotional reactions that are deemed appropriate are continued and may be redirected to better achieve desirable ends. The experiential component of emotion is thus viewed as a corrective capable of altering the course of emotional behavior and experience. It might be considered a cognitive means of control that can modify and override, to some degree, the operation of the more archaic mechanics stipulated in the dispositional and excitatory components of emotional behavior. Applied to empathy, the three components can be specified as follows.

1. Reflexive (i.e., unconditioned) and learned (i.e., conditioned) skeletal-motor reactions that are elicited by exposure to another person's manifest or impending emotional behavior constitute the *dispositional component of empathy*. Motor mimicry, especially mimicry involving the facial muscles, comprises a multitude of specific reflexive responses. Many facial and gross motor responses are likely to be learned, however. Especially in confrontation with acutely dangerous situations, individuals tend to acquire personally specific, immediate coping reactions.

Reflexive and learned skeletal-motor reactions elicited by exposure to representations of high iconicity (i.e., photography, cinematography) that exhibit another person's manifest or impending emotional behavior are also subsumed in the dispositional component of empathy. So are such reactions that are elicited by exposure to non-iconic representations (i.e., signs with arbitrarily defined stimulus-referent relationships; practically speaking, almost all linguistic signs and sign aggregates) that specify another person's manifest or impending emotional behavior. It is assumed that the control exerted by iconic and non-iconic representations over skeletal-motor reactions is different for reflexive responses, but similar for learned ones. Specifically, iconic representations are considered capable of eliciting reflexive reactions because of great stimulus similarity with the represented events. Non-iconic representations cannot have this capacity, as responses to arbitrarily established signs would have to be learned. Learning makes iconicity immaterial. Potentially all stimulus conditions can come to assume the power to elicit particular responses. Additionally, it is assumed that iconic and non-iconic elements of the representation of emotional events are interconnected in memory, forming complex networks that integrate pertinent percepts and operations (Kieras, 1978; Kintsch, 1974; Lang, 1979, 1984; Pylyshyn, 1973). External stimuli in one representational mode may thus activate stored representational information in another mode and thereby extend their impact.

2. Excitatory reactions resulting from exposure to another person's manifest or impending emotional behavior that are concomitant to reflexive and learned motor responses, or that are unconditioned or conditioned but independent of motor responses, constitute the *excitatory component of empathy*.

Unconditioned and conditioned excitatory reactions elicited by exposure to iconic or non-iconic representations that exhibit another person's manifest or impending emotional behavior are also subsumed in the excitatory component of empathy. All considerations concerning the semiotic modality of representation that were developed with regard to the dispositional component apply equally to the excitatory component.

3. In the *experiential component of empathy*, three subcomponents can be distinguished: processes that serve (a) the experience proper, (b) the correction and

redirection of affective reactions, and (c) the generation of affective reactions.

a. An affective reaction elicited by exposure to another person's manifest or impending emotional behavior or to any kind of representation thereof constitutes empathy only to the extent that the observer is cognizant of his or her reaction and appraises it as "feeling with" or "feeling for" the person observed. It is assumed that such appraisal presupposes hedonic parallelity in the observed and observing persons' responses; that is, an observer's affective reaction that is hedonically opposite to that apparent in the observed person is unlikely to be construed as an empathetic reaction.

An affective reaction that is elicited by exposure to the conditions specified above and that a third party perceives as being similar to and hedonically concordant with that displayed by the observed person can be considered a rudimentary empathetic reaction.

As an affective experience (or feeling state), a complete empathetic reaction is comprised of dispositional, excitatory, and experiential response elements.

b. An affective reaction elicited by exposure to another person's manifest or impending emotional behavior or to any kind of representation thereof is monitored for appropriateness. The respondent assesses his or her reaction in terms of social and moral judgment; that is, he or she employs his or her knowledge of the prevailing contingencies of social approval and reproach, as well as internalized moral standards of conduct, in determining the appropriateness of the reaction. If the reaction is deemed appropriate, it is allowed to unfold. If it is deemed inappropriate, it is inhibited and redirected so as to conform with (or, at least, so as to be less in violation of) accepted rules of social conduct and moral precepts.

It is assumed that, as a rule, affective reactions are initially comprised of unconditioned and conditioned response elements. Because of neural mediation, skeletal-motor responses, in particular responses in the facial muscles, follow the onset of stimulation quasi-instantaneously. Owing to the involvement of humoral processes, the excitatory reaction develops with appreciable latency. Cognizance of an affective reaction (i.e., of a response that has both a dispositional and an excitatory component) thus manifests itself also only after some latency. It is further assumed that skeletal-motor responses, including responses in the facial muscles, are mostly under volitional control; and that, in contrast, excitatory responses largely elude volition (Zillmann, 1979, 1983a, 1988).

Based on these assumptions, it is proposed that potentially empathetic reactions that the individual deems inappropriate take the following characteristic course: Upon stimulation, skeletal-motor responses, especially facial responses, materialize quasi-instantaneously. The excitatory response unfolds with some latency. The individual attains proprioceptive and, to some degree, exteroceptive information from both his or her muscular and excitatory responses. The reception of proprioceptive and exteroceptive feedback instigates appraisal processes. If these processes render the affective reaction inappropriate, the ongoing skeletal-motor behavior, including facial expression, is inhibited and redirected into an affective reaction that conforms with prevailing rules of conduct. As the inhibition of the elicited excitatory reaction cannot be accomplished, at least not immediately, excitation will enter into and influence the affect arrived at through cognitive control and correction (Zillmann, 1978, 1983b). The cognitive "override" of affective reactions is considered capable of converting the reactions' hedonic valence. If hedonic conversion occurs, the affective reaction loses its potentiality for being construed as empathy.

Affective dispositions toward persons observed undergoing emotional experiences create a preparedness for the cognitive sanctioning and overruling of affective reactions in response to these persons' experiences. Positive affective dispositions are conducive to empathy. Negative affective dispositions, in contrast, demand the hedonic conversion of affect; that is, any empathy-like response and its maintenance constitutes a noxious state to be terminated. Corrective readiness is likely to accelerate the inhibition of expressive elements of potentially empathetic reactions and terminate them in their incipient stages. Corrective readiness may also result from cognizance of display rules for affect (Saarni, 1982). Such cognizance is potentially independent of affective dispositions held toward persons involved.

c. Affective reactions that are construable as empathy can be deliberately elicited by the imagination of stimulus conditions that are related to those confronting an observed party and that have produced intense affective reactions in the observer's past. The process need not be deliberate, however. Imagination of this kind may be instigated by exposure to conditions conducive to the elicitation of empathetic reactions, and affect generated by ideational stimuli may complement and enhance affect in response to external stimulation.

It is assumed that the imagination of stimulus conditions to which motor and excitatory reactions have been conditioned is capable of eliciting these reactions (Lang, 1979, 1984). However, owing to proficient volitional control of motor responses, apparently inappropriate gestural, postural, and gross motor responses are, as a rule, effectively inhibited. Furthermore, owing to habituation (Grings & Dawson, 1978; Zillmann, 1984), excitatory responses are likely to be of diminished strength. These qualifications notwithstanding, ideational representations of stimulus conditions to which excitatory reactions have been conditioned are capable of eliciting these reactions to some degree (Schwartz, 1974, 1977). To the extent that these representations can be controlled volitionally, affect — or more accurately, its excitatory component — can be generated deliberately. Empathy through role-taking can thus be viewed as mediated through the partial revival of related past experiences or of some components thereof.

It should be recognized that the possibility of generating affective reactions and empathy through the ideational representation of potent stimuli has also implications for the inhibition of empathetic reactions. If empathy is deemed inappropriate, the individual can avoid ideation of affectively potent representations, or he or she can practice ideation of unrelated, nonpotent representations to accomplish the former.

Dispositional Override of Empathy

As part of the three-factor approach, the concept of dispositional override is the most significant point of departure from alternative models and seems in need of further explication. The concept projects, essentially, that an empathetic experience entails both archaic and, phylogenetically speaking, more recently developed elements. Comparatively primitive processes, such as motor mimicry and involuntary excitatory responses, are viewed as being superseded by complex cognitive processes, with these latter processes taking control of the experience in determining its final status. The concept is reminiscent of McDougall's (1908, 1922) position discussed earlier: Primitive passive sympathy, when producing suffering that the individual deems unwarranted, is expected to convert to mirth—in the interest of maintaining emotional health. The position taken here is far broader, however, and it is independent of considerations concerning adaptation and emotional adjustment. Regardless of the experiential quality of immediate affective reactions, cognitive monitoring should effect their inhibition or hedonic conversion if this brings the responses into better agreement with socially and/or individually sanctioned emotional behavior. This is to say that inappropriate initial affect, when positive, can become nil or negative; and, when negative, can become nil or positive.

Because of the proposed sequence of events, the three-factor model can make sense of mixed affective reactions that are left unexplained by alternative views. If, for example, a student witnesses from a private corner her oppressive, resented professor mount a bicycle, lose balance, fall to the ground, get up, and hobble around in apparent pain, she may well cringe upon seeing him fall, but quickly come to chuckle and grin, if not to laugh out loud. The dominant affective experience being one of delight, the student is unlikely to construe her response as empathy—despite the initial cringe. Had the student been in a public situation, chuckling and laughing would probably have been drowned in their incipient stages. The deliberate curtailment of expression should have been of little consequence for the experience of delight, however. This is because it is not feedback from the expression of affect, but the cognitive appraisal of the circumstances, that is expected to function as the primary determinant of affective experience. The example can readily be altered to illustrate dispositional preparedness. If the student did not merely feel resentment toward her professor, but acutely feared and hated him, virtually hoping for some misfortune to come his way, seeing the bike sway might foster expectations of delight. If so, witnessing the accident might not produce initial cringing, but unqualified euphoria from the beginning. On the other hand, even a lot of spite might not assure continued delight. Should it become apparent, for example, that the accident crippled the professor, it would be unlikely that the student goes on rejoicing. Appraisal would make continued delight an unacceptable response. To the extent that thoughts of pity are evoked, the experience might actually come to be construed as empathy. Such arrival at empathy would not preclude that the student had awareness of the fact that her initial reaction was of a different kind.

Clearly, the hedonically opposite sequence of events (i.e., the case not considered by McDougall) is equally conceivable. Students who tenaciously competed for a particular award, for example, may well facially exhibit a moment of joy as they respond to the winner's display of triumph and happiness. Such mimicry is likely to be overpowered, however, by expressive responses deriving from disappointment and envy, from feelings of having suffered an injustice, or from contempt for the winner and the system. The important point is that, although such complex and mixed affective reactions are likely to contain rudiments of empathy, the affective experience as a whole is not likely to be construed as empathy because of the dominance of cognitions alien to the concept of "feeling with" and "feeling for."

Development of Empathy and Dispositional Override

The adaptive significance of rudimentary empathy (i.e., concordant affect elicited by a model's response) has been stressed by many scholars (e.g., Darwin, 1872/1965; Lockard, 1980; MacLean, 1958, 1967). Quite obviously, the survival of a species is served well by immediate fight-or-flight reactions, especially the latter, to the distress expressions of endangered members of groups of particular species. The elicitation of concordant positive affect seems equally important, however, as it assures appeasement and aids the formation of social bonds among individuals in social aggregates (cf. Eibl-Eibesfeldt, 1970; Hinde, 1970). Motor mimicry thus emerges as a most archaic response form with considerable adaptive value. The limits of this adaptive quality are equally obvious, however. Motor mimicry would be quite maladaptive, for instance, if animals exhibited it in response to witnessing one of their kind falling ill and facing certain death through predation. At the human level, as McDougall has so aptly pointed out, such "primitive sympathy" would also be of questionable value. Cosuffering, in and of itself, has no utility. Only to the extent that it promotes behavior directed at lessening the model's misery does it become adaptive (Hoffman, 1978; Stotland et al., 1978). In order to accomplish the behavioral plasticity needed for adaptive intraspecific interaction, mechanisms more complex than those governing motor mimicry had to evolve. The mechanics of stimulus and reinforcement control can be viewed as the postreflexive stage that provided much needed plasticity. And the human capacity for the arbitrary handling of information—in particular, the greater independence from immediately present stimuli—can be viewed as having provided greater behavioral plasticity in turn. Phylogenetically, then, the progression of control in empathy-like behaviors is from reflexive through learning and, in humans, from learning through cognitive mediation.

This progression is also evident in individual development. Hoffman (1978) has reviewed the pertinent research on empathy and found it to be consistent with such a developmental ordering. Empathy-like responses are initially fixed. They then become varied but remain largely involuntary. Finally, cognitive modification of affect comes into being, and deliberate empathy becomes possible.

Although the developmental age at which the capacity for the dispositional overriding of empathetic reactions materializes has not been determined, it may be assumed that it is closely tied to the emergence of monitoring affect of self and of moral judgment in its basal forms. As soon as individuals recognize prevailing contingencies of reinforcement (in the sense of responding to them properly), they are likely to be disturbed at seeing these contingencies waived for others (Zillmann, 1979). Witnessing the benefaction of an undeserving party is annoying and perturbs moral sentiment. Witnessing the aversive treatment of a party considered deserving of such treatment, in contrast, is in line with basal morality; it may be applauded and enjoyed. At the very least, seeing those who attained gratifications by violating established rules of social conduct, or simply by brutalizing others, be duly punished for their transgressions does not call for empathetic cosuffering. Onlookers seem morally entitled to the callousness that is manifest in responding non-empathetically, even euphorically, to seeing aversive treatments applied to villainous parties and to seeing the impact of these treatments (Zillmann, 1980; Zillmann & Cantor, 1976).

It can only be speculated that, in the transition from reflexive and stimulus/reinforcement control of empathy to the predominantly cognitive mediation of affect, children experience considerable affective conflict: empathetic inclinations, on the one hand, and perceptions of envy (in case of undeserved benefaction) and moral sanction (in case of deserved punishment), on the other. Possibly ambivalent affect should soon give way, however, to unequivocal affective reactions that are mediated by considerations of appropriateness and justice. To the extent that such cognitively controlled affect produces anti-empathetic reactions, every reaction can be considered a learning trial in the formation of response dispositions for discordant affect. Specifically, discordant affect becomes associated with parties undeserving of good fortunes and deserving of misfortunes. Discordant affect, in short, is consistently linked to outcomes concerning the "bad guys" and villains; that is, to persons disliked, resented, or acutely despised by the respondent. A negative affective disposition toward a model, then, becomes predictive of anti-empathy. Disliking comes to signal that empathy is unnecessary and, in fact, inappropriate. Because discordant affect is consistently sanctioned under these dispositional circumstances, it should become the characteristic response mode. Negative affect should create a readiness for counterempathetic reactions; and the reactions, once initiated, should become mechanical in the sense that the individual need not engage in explicit judgmental deliberations concerning the circumstances.

Affective Experience and Empathy

As discordant affect can become a highly mechanical response (one that takes its cue from dislike and resentment that at first might be inspired by apprehension and fear, and that later grows on disapprobation and condemnation of the model's actions), so can empathy by role-taking. Although the initial stages of the mental exercise of placing oneself into another person's situation are entirely deliberate, affect is likely to be evoked by the recall of related affective experiences of self. Once such recall occurs and the deliberate empathizer senses responding in an excited fashion, the arousal state itself may function as a cue to recalling further emotional experiences (Clark, 1982; Leight & Ellis, 1981). It can be argued, in fact, that the initial "make-believe" effort in deliberate empathy is incapable of eliciting appreciable affect unless it hooks into related affective experiences of self (Scheler, 1913). Deliberate empathy, in this view, is akin to system acting—a procedure in which actors and actresses use volition to access affective memory in order to trigger the emotional experience they seek to display. Such reasoning makes it very clear that role-play empathy relies on affective memory in the observer, and that it cannot be more than mere pretense if the observer does not have related experiences that can be revived. This dependence of empathy on pertinent experience has been emphasized by many investigators (e.g., Allport, 1924; Murphy, 1937, 1983; Sapolsky & Zillmann, 1978). Scheler (1913) used it to show that empathy can never be a true sharing of feelings, but is at best a close approximation of affect in observer and observed—because observers are only capable of responding in terms of their own, private and unique affective experience.

Disapprobation, Disliking, and Discordant Affect

The proposed processes leading to discordant affect, along with the parallel processes leading to empathy, are summarized in Fig. 6.1. As can be seen, dis-

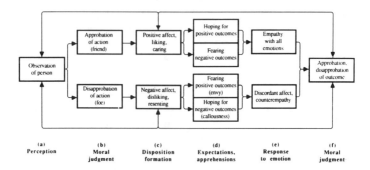

FIG. 6.1. A model of the dispositional mediation of concordant affect (empathy) and discordant affect (counterempathy). The principal processes assumed to operate at the various stages from (a) through (f) are indicated beneath the flow chart.

approbation of a model's action (or cues predictive of the likelihood of disapproved action) is considered to produce negative affect that, in turn, mediates callousness in preparing the observer to sanction aversive experiences and to deny positive ones for the model, this ready acceptance and unwillingness to accept expressing itself in discordant affect.

Zillmann and Cantor (1977) conducted an investigation with second- and third-grade boys and girls that strongly supports the proposed chain of events. Films were especially produced, and subjects' affective responses to them were assessed in facial expressions and in structured interviews. Perceptions of, and dispositions toward, the protagonist were also ascertained. The films featured a peer protagonist who was presented either as a most pleasant and helpful character or as an obnoxious and hostile one. The different character development was accomplished by depicting the protagonist as kind and supportive in interacting with his peers, pet, and younger brother versus as rude and mean in the same interactions. The findings showed that, in accord with the manipulation, the character was perceived either as benevolent or as malevolent. They showed, furthermore, that subjects came to like the "nice" protagonist and dislike the "bad" one. These findings corroborate the proposal that a person's behavior is judged in terms of approval and disapproval, and that affective dispositions toward a person are formed on the basis of this approval and disapproval. The films, finally, were given different endings. In a happy-ending version, the protagonist was seen receiving a new bicycle. He expressed euphoria in response to the gift, jumping for joy with a happy smile on his face. In the alternative ending, tragedy came about as the protagonist jumped on his old bike, and starting off down the street, lost balance and crashed. His dysphoria was bodily and facially evident as he cringed in pain. Affective responses to these concluding events, as measured through interview, showed empathy to both the euphoric and the dysphoric outcome only under conditions of positive affective dispositions toward the protagonist. Under conditions of negative affective dispositions, empathy was not only absent, but discordant affect was observed. The transverse interaction between affective disposition and affective response is displayed in Fig. 6.2 (graph at left). This data pattern applies to boys and girls equally.

Apparently, subjects did pass judgment concerning how deserving of a particular outcome the protagonist was. Such judgment made it inappropriate to enjoy witnessing the benefaction of the malevolent and, hence, undeserving character. It seems to have resulted in acute annoyance with the outcome that could only be perceived as utterly unfair and unjust. Such judgment made it very appropriate, however, to enjoy witnessing the suffering of the malevolent and, hence, deserving character.

The analysis of respondents' facial expressions, interestingly, failed to exhibit a close correspondence with verbally expressed empathy and discordant affect. This finding can be interpreted as evidence against the view that facial responses serve as the primary determinant of feeling states. The influence of cognitive oper-

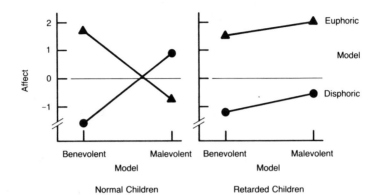

FIG. 6.2. Affective reactions of normally developed and retarded children to the
expression of euphoria or dysphoria by a model perceived to be good or bad. Normal children exhibited empathy only when the model was good and liked. Disapproval of action fostered disliking, and disliking produced discordant affect in
response to the bad model's emotions. Retarded children failed to develop dislike
for the bad model and, hence, the disposition to respond with discordant affect.
(Adapted from Zillmann & Cantor, 1977, and Wilson, Cantor, Gordon, & Zillmann,
1986.)

ations apparently dominated that of facial expressions in the production of concordant and discordant affect. The analysis leaves it unclear, however, to what
extent the low correlation between reported affect and facial expression may
have resulted from inconsistent and contradictory facial responses in the conditions producing discordant affect. It is conceivable that subjects, when exposed
to the malevolent character's bicycle accident, initially cringed reflexively, but
then quickly brought their face in line with their cognitive appraisal of the events
before them. It is also conceivable that such a correction was made in case of
the malevolent character's surprising benefaction. Subjects may have responded
positively at first, if only momentarily, and then corrected their reaction. Such
possible reversion of facially expressed affect is entirely consistent with the proposed three-factor model of empathy. According to this model, faces can follow
cognition as much as cognition can follow faces. The findings do not help resolve
this issue, however, as facial responses were assessed over the entire concluding
events only. When the need for a more detailed analysis became apparent, records
had been destroyed already to assure subject confidentiality.

   The moral-judgment mediation of empathy and, especially, of discordant affect is more clearly apparent in comparing the responses of children who have
developed equity judgment with responses from children who have not. Wilson,
Cantor, Gordon, and Zillmann (1986) used the stimuli employed by Zillmann
and Cantor (1977) in an investigation with retarded children who were thought
to be lacking equity judgment. Consistent with data from emotionally disturbed

children reported by Feldman, White, and Lobato (1982), the retarded children proved capable of perceiving the character correctly as "nice" or "bad" (although, similar to children at the lowest levels of moral development, their perception was partly a function of events for which the character could not be held accountable—e.g., the nice protagonist was perceived as being nicer when he received a gift than when he suffered a misfortune). The retarded children thus seem to have managed the approbation/disapprobation of a model's action, at least in the sense of correctly classifying and labeling persons in accord with social sanction/condemnation. However, these children gave no evidence of executing assessments of deservingness, nor of forming a disposition consistent with such assessments. They seemed not to hope for particular outcomes, nor fear others. In particular, they failed to arrive at disliking and its concomitants of envy and callousness. The absence of this moral mediation led them to respond empathetically, regardless of the particular circumstances. As can be seen from Fig. 6.2 (graph at right), they responded euphorically when the bad character was benefited, and they responded dysphorically when this character suffered a misfortune. These findings suggest strongly that discordant affect in response to witnessing a resented agent's euphoria or dysphoria or the conditions conducive of such reactions are indeed mediated by considerations of deservingness (i.e., by moral judgment).

The moral-judgment mediation of discordant affect has been further established in an investigation by Zillmann and Bryant (1975). An audiovisually presented fairy tale was manipulated to create different punitive treatments. A thoroughly good prince combated a thoroughly bad prince. In their struggle, the bad prince got the upper hand and condemned the good prince to exile in an undesirable part of the kingdom. The good prince eventually returned to power, however, and now was in a position to punish his tormentor. This punishment was either equitable (the good prince applying the punishment that the bad prince had planned for him), too mild (the good prince being forgiving), or too severe (the good prince being more brutal than the bad prince would have been). As punishment was justified, normal children were expected to enjoy its application (i.e., to approve of it and exhibit callousness in a discordant affective reaction). Dependent on the level of moral development, different approvals may be expected, however. Children matured to the level of equitable retribution (Kohlberg, 1964; Piaget, 1948) should approve of equitable punishment, but neither of under- nor over-retaliation. In these cases of inequitable retribution, their sense of justice should be left disturbed, and this disturbance should hamper and reduce the euphoric reaction to witnessing the application of punishment. Children at the level of expiatory retribution, in contrast, should freely enjoy witnessing any amount of punishment. In fact, as they tend to infer the magnitude of a transgression from the severity of punishment, it can be expected that enjoyment increases with the severity of punishment because a greater violation of unquestioned rules of conduct is believed to be corrected.

Figure 6.3 shows data that fully corroborate these predictions concerning the

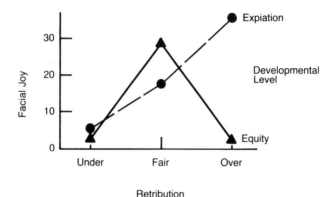

FIG. 6.3. Enjoyment of punitive action against a transgressor. For children at the developmental level of expiatory retribution, the enjoyment of punishment increased with its severity. Children at the developmental level of equitable retribution enjoyed equitable punishment more than inequitable punishment, regardless of the direction of inequity. (Adapted from Zillmann & Bryant, 1975.)

joy that is liberated by the infliction of aversion upon a party apparently deserving of such treatment. The findings are furthermore supportive of processes outlined in the schema presented in Fig. 6.1. The schema stipulates a post-affect approval or disapproval of an outcome that is capable of feeding back into affective dispositions toward observed persons. The assessment should be in moral terms and mediate liking and disliking of punished and punishing parties. This mediation was in fact observed. Most importantly, it conformed entirely with the respondent's system of moral judgment. Children at the level of equitable retribution exhibited intense dislike for the bad prince when he was not duly punished. When his punishment was overly severe, in contrast, disliking became negligible. It was as though they felt pity for him. These children liked the good prince only when he had been fair in applying punishment. His failure to be punitive, but especially his being "unnecessarily" brutal, prompted a considerable loss in liking. Children at the level of expiatory retribution responded very differently. They maintained a strong disliking for the bad prince. In fact, they disliked him the most when he had been brutalized. They also liked the good prince the most when he had been overly punitive. This bears out Piaget (1948) who commented that for this developmental level the severity of punishment correlates with the perception of justice: "The sterner it is, the juster" (p. 199).

These and other findings on discordant affect (cf. Zillmann, 1980) leave little doubt that moral considerations play a significant part in justifying, allowing, and motivating discordant affective reactions to the emotional experiences of others.

COMMUNICATION TECHNOLOGY AND AFFECT

The new communication technology—in particular, the capacity for recording, storing, recreating, and manipulating complex audiovisual events in a seemingly unrestricted fashion—has often been said to influence affect and affective development in critical ways. The specific processes thought to mediate presumed effects have remained rather unclear in these speculations. Research into the effects of the media has similarly neglected the specifics of hypothesized affect-enhancing and affect-diminishing processes. It has failed, furthermore, to establish that any effects on affect and affective development have socially significant consequences.

Clearly, communication technology has enormously altered the conditions for affect development and, perhaps more importantly, for affect maintenance. Compared with a child's or an adult's exposure to others' affects and emotions in a pretechnological situation, both children and adults in contemporary society are bombarded with portrayals of affects and emotions. In pretechnological society, exposure to emotions was limited to the immediate social environment and to story telling, the latter possibly embellished by the presenter's playacting. With the availability of printed materials, exposure probably became somewhat more pronounced. But portrayals remained limited to verbal form and still pictures. As far as the portrayal of affects and emotions is concerned, the invention of the motion picture constitutes a turning point. Uncounted characters exhibited a wealth of emotions to so-called mass audiences. The movies reached essentially all members of technological society. All members became more and more frequently exposed to emotions that were infrequent or nonexistent in the immediate environment. Adults who had never witnessed someone's exultation upon striking oil, the emotional aftermath of a brutal beating, the despair of a rape victim, or the rage of a killer could now see it—or more accurately, they could see what directors and actors made it appear to be. Analogously, children were now exposed to persons in fear, anger, rage, hatred, or joy about an enormity of conditions that usually do not materialize in the family and peer context. As entertainment thrives on the exhibition of human emotions (Tannenbaum, 1980; Zillmann, 1982), there can be no doubt that in modern society children and adults alike are massively exposed to others' affective experiences. News programs and documentaries are similarly partial to the exhibition of emotion-laden happenings and further exacerbate this situation.

Compared to pretechnological times, then, today's children and adults are far more frequently exposed to others' affective experiences. It is equally clear that both parties are exposed to a greater variety of affective experiences. A less obvious but potentially significant change lies in the portrayal of emotions itself. Whereas individuals in their own social environment tend to get only glimpses of someone else's affective responses, the media—nonfiction as well as fiction—present these reactions most graphically. Respondents are invited to take an extremely close look into the face, for example, of a mother as she learns that her son has drowned, a man who just hit a multi-million dollar jackpot, or a child suffering from terminal cancer. To the extent that the facial expression of emotion is critically involved in the elicitation of empathy and discordant affect, this "supernormal" portrayal of human emotions should prove to have important developmental consequences, indeed.

First, it is conceivable that at early developmental stages the supernormal facial exhibition of a model's emotion fosters facial mimicry of great fidelity. If so, the child's empathetic response to a variety of others' emotional experiences could be facilitated. Second, and regardless of whether or not facial mimicry plays a part in affective development, frequent exposure to extremely detailed portrayals of others' affective reactions, especially their facial manifestations, should further the acquisition of display rules (cf. Saarni, 1982); that is, of specifications concerning the social approval and disapproval of the expression of affect under particular circumstances. To the extent that portrayals accurately reflect prevailing rules, children (and adults) should become acquainted with a multitude of display rules and learn to enact them in novel situations—situations for which their limited social environment may not have prepared them. Whether competence regarding display rules influences concordant or discordant affect, when displayed or when inhibited, is another matter entirely, however.

Another principal difference between exposure to others' affect in pretechnological and technological societies concerns the semiotic modality of representations. Initially, representations were non-iconic. The poor stimulus relationship between sign and referent (i.e., between designating and designated stimuli) made empathetic or counterempathetic reactions in all probability dependent on generating ideational representations that, in turn, depended on experience by self with similar affect-inducing conditions. In short, to come from verbal reports of others' emotions, even when aided by some grimacing and gesticulating by the reporter, to intense concordant or discordant affect relied on considerable imaginative activity. Today's iconic representations, because of their extreme reproductive fidelity, seem to make such activity superfluous. Nothing is to be transformed or filled in. It remains quite unclear, however, whether the greater or the lesser reliance on imaginative processes fosters stronger empathetic or counterempathetic reactions. It is conceivable that the conversion of non-iconic signs to an iconic ideational representation of others' emotions, because it draws heavily from related experiences of self, is particularly conducive to liberating affect. But it is equally possible that high-fidelity iconic representations also activate related affective memory structures; furthermore, that these representations constitute most powerful affect inducers, because in the affect they elicit, they combine affect from memory revival with unmitigated affect to the iconic portrayal itself.

Yet another fundamental difference in the portrayal of others' emotions in pretechnological and technological societies concerns the pace of presentations. Whereas affect to the nonmediated perception of others' emotional experiences is usually not temporally curtailed (i.e., it is allowed to take its course), and verbal representations tend to be paced by the teller or are self-paced by a reader so as to permit the complete unfolding of affective responses, iconic representations in the mass media are characteristically fast paced. Specifically, the story moves on before affective reactions to the emotions of others can run their course.

In fast-paced, action-packed adventure films, for example, children have seen friendly, beloved parties get killed and their cohorts grieve about the loss of their friends. All that tends to happen in about 3 to 5 seconds. The story usually returns immediately to spectacular, amazing and amusing chases of the villains. Similarly, adults are exposed to news programs in which, for example, an interview with a wife who has just lost her husband to a mine disaster is followed, without delay, by a report on union demands in a strike of the auto workers, the revelation that trading on Wall Street reached an all-time high, or a commercial for a cologne. Newscasters aggregate their stories with little regard for emotional reactions in the audience—apparently without concerns about the time course of emotions that are elicited by their materials (Mundorf, Drew, & Zillmann, 1989). For children's entertaining fare, this situation is different in that the message makers seem deliberate in trying to minimize aversive reactions in their audiences. The victimization of liked characters, it seems, is practiced only to the extent that it is necessary to establish credibility for the villainous deeds, motives, and the potentiality for harmdoing.

But whatever the intentions behind message pacing may be, the pace that characterizes contemporary audiovisual storytelling and reporting is likely to produce affective confusion and shallowness in both children and adults. Consideration of excitatory activity as the intensity-determining component of affective reactions (Zillmann, 1978, 1984) leads to the projection that, owing to the latency of excitatory responses, many of these responses materialize too slowly and manifest themselves too late for the "affective" reactions to which they belong. More importantly, owing to the slow dissipation of excitatory activity, it leads to the projection that excitation elicited by a particular episode or report will come to intensify reactions to the subsequently presented episode or report (Scott & Goff, 1988). A temporally curtailed sadness reaction to the misfortunes of a liked character (i.e., empathetic distress), for instance, will produce increased amusement with subsequent humorous happenings (e.g., Cantor, Bryant, & Zillmann, 1974). And a temporally curtailed reaction of empathetic distress to nonfictitious events is likely to enhance the appeal of an advertised product (e.g., Mattes & Cantor, 1982), among other things.

The rapid pacing of affect-inducing events in modern media presentations, then, appears to minimize affective and, especially, empathetic reactions (a) by preventing the complete unfolding of the response because distracting, competing information is provided too soon after the elicitation of affect; and (b) by creating affective confusions through the intensification (by excitation transfer) of subsequent, potentially non-empathetic affect. Empathetic reactions, in short, are often deprived of their inherent intensity, while other reactions are often artificially intensified. (At times, of course, an empathetic response may be intensified by preceding excitatory happenings; see Zillmann, Mody, & Cantor, 1974.) To the extent that individuals' reflection on their own affective responding is critical in the development and maintenance of affective sensitivity (Singer, 1980), a further factor could be considered implicated in the creation of affective impoverishment through the fast-paced exposition of affect-inducing contents.

Finally, the research on affective dispositions and their implications for empathetic and counterempathetic reactions points to the need to feature characters in drama, especially in drama for children at the lower levels of moral development, whose actions unambiguously characterize them as good versus bad, loveable versus hateable, hero versus villain, or friend versus foe. Unqualified liking constitutes the optimal condition for the development of empathetic reactions; unqualified disliking for the development of callousness necessary for counterempathetic responses — a form of callousness whose development is essential for self-assertion. Indifference or ambivalence toward a person constitutes the condition under which concordant and discordant affect are likely to be minimal and negligible. This condition is consequently not conducive to the development of empathetic sensitivity in children. Melodrama emerges as a genre that is well suited for the teaching of such sensitivity. It might prove beneficial for the maintenance of empathetic and counterempathetic sensitivity in adults, too, because it avoids the involvement of bad heroes and good villains, of monsters with a heart, and of heroes with a tragic flaw. It avoids, in short, the dispositional circumstances that make the respondent not care one way or another, and that eventually may produce affective indifference and insensitivity.

The prevalence of violence in the entertainment media (Gerbner & Gross, 1976; Gerbner, Gross, Jackson-Beeck, Jeffries-Fox, & Signorielli, 1978) gives rise to further concern. Because displays of suffering and/or devious pleasures on the part of disliked personnel are more frequent than euphoric and/or dysphoric displays on the part of liked protagonists, it can be argued that these media are partial to teaching counterempathy — not empathy. Gratuitous violence tends to victimize parties who seem somehow deserving of the treatment that they receive. Empathy with their plight would be wasted sentiment. Counterempathetic euphoria is the "appropriate" response. The popularity of drama dwelling on such violence would seem to indicate that respondents have mastered the skill of responding counterempathetically to the minimally justified infliction of human suffering.

As has been indicated already, the frequent poor development of characters in fiction is bound to lead to affective indifference. The sheer massiveness of exposure to events that under ordinary circumstances produce affective reactions should cause a diminution of affect. Respondents often do not have time to develop affective dispositions that would make them care and empathize or despise and counterempathize. Affective indifference toward affect displayers then fosters conditions under which the habituation of affective reactions can flourish (cf. Zillmann, 1982, 1989). Weaker responding is likely to be combated with stronger stimulation (Zillmann & Bryant, 1986), creating an escalation that can only end in affective callousness (Anscombe, 1987).

Clearly, all these possibilities are derivations from theoretical proposals. The empirical exploration of the impact of the media on affective development in children, on affective sensitivity in adults, on the maintenance of affective sensitivity, and on habituation and affective callousness has just begun. The truism that "much remains to be done" applies to the study of media effects on affect much more than to any other aspect of media research.

REFERENCES

Allport, F. (1924). *Social psychology*. New York: Houghton Mifflin.

Anscombe, R. (1987, May 4). Stranger than fiction. *Newsweek*, pp. 8-9.

Aronfreed, J. (1968). *Conduct and conscience: The socialization of internalized control over behavior*. New York: Academic Press.

Aronfreed, J. (1970). The socialization of altruistic and sympathetic behavior: Some theoretical and experimental analyses. In J. Macaulay & L. Berkowitz (Eds.), *Altruism and helping behavior* (pp. 103-126). New York: Academic Press.

Berger, S. M. (1962). Conditioning through vicarious instigation. *Psychological Review*, 29, 450-466.

Berger, S. M., & Hadley, S. W. (1975). Some effects of a model's performance on observer electromyographic activity. *American Journal of Psychology*, 88, 263-276.

Bernal, G., & Berger, S. M. (1976). Vicarious eyelid conditioning. *Journal of Personality and Social Psychology*, 34, 62-68.

Borke, H. (1971). Interpersonal perception of young children: Egocentrism or empathy? *Developmental Psychology*, 5, 263-269.

Buck, R. (1980). Nonverbal behavior and the theory of emotion: The facial feedback hypothesis. *Journal of Personality and Social Psychology*, 38, 811-824.

Cacioppo, J. T., & Petty, R. E. (Eds.). (1983). *Social psychophysiology: A sourcebook*. New York: Guilford Press.

Cantor, J. R., Bryant, J., & Zillmann, D. (1974). Enhancement of humor appreciation by transferred excitation. *Journal of Personality and Social Psychology*, 30, 812-821.

Cialdini, R. B., & McPeek, R. W. (1974, May). *Yawning, yielding, and yearning to yawn*. Paper presented at the meeting of the Midwest Psychological Association, Chicago, IL.

Clark, M. S. (1982). A role for arousal in the link between feeling states, judgments, and behavior. In M. S. Clark & S. T. Fiske (Eds.), *Affect and cognition: The seventeenth annual Carnegie Symposium on Cognition* (pp. 263-289). Hillsdale, NJ: Lawrence Erlbaum Associates.

Cline, V. B., & Richards, J. M., Jr. (1960). Accuracy of interpersonal perception: A general trait? *Journal of Abnormal and Social Psychology*, 60, 20-30.

Craig, K. D., & Lowery, H. J. (1969). Heart-rate components of conditioned vicarious autonomic responses. *Journal of Personality and Social Psychology*, 11, 381-387.

Darwin, C. (1965). *The expression of emotions in man and animals*. London: Murray. (Original work published 1872)

Davis, M. H., Hull, J. G., Young, R. D., & Warren, G. G. (1987). Emotional reactions to dramatic film stimuli: The influence of cognitive and emotional empathy. *Journal of Personality and Social Psychology*, 52, 126-133.

Dymond, R. F. (1949). A scale for measurement of empathetic ability. *Journal of Consulting Psychology*, 14, 127-133.

Dymond, R. F. (1950). Personality and empathy. *Journal of Consulting Psychology*, 14, 343-350.

Eibl-Eibesfeldt, I. (1970). *Ethology: The biology of behavior*. New York: Holt, Rinehart & Winston.

Englis, B. G., Vaughan, K. B., & Lanzetta, J. T. (1982). Conditioning of counter-empathetic emotional responses. *Journal of Experimental Social Psychology, 18,* 375-391.

Feldman, R. S., White, J. B. & Lobato, D. (1982). Social skills and nonverbal behavior in children. In R. S. Feldman (Ed.), *Development of nonverbal behavior in children* (pp. 259-277). New York: Springer-Verlag.

Fenichel, O. (1954). *The psychoanalytic theory of neurosis.* New York: Norton.

Feshbach, N. D. (1978). Studies of empathetic behavior in children. In B. A. Maher (Ed.), *Progress in experimental personality research* (Vol. 8, pp. 1-47). New York: Academic Press.

Freud, S. (1950). *Group psychology and the analysis of the ego* (J. Strachey, Trans.). New York: Bantam Books. (Original work published 1921)

Freud, S. (1964). New introductory lectures on psycho-analysis. In J. Strachey (Ed. & Trans.), *The standard edition of the complete psychological works of Sigmund Freud* (Vol. 22, pp. 7-182). London: Hogarth Press. (Original work published 1933)

Gerbner, G., & Gross, L. (1976). Living with television: The violence profile. *Journal of Communication, 26*(2), 173-199.

Gerbner, G., Gross, L., Jackson-Beeck, M., Jeffries-Fox, S., & Signorielli, N. (1978). Cultural indicators: Violence profile no. 9. *Journal of Communication, 28*(3), 176-207.

Grings, W. W., & Dawson, M. E. (1978). *Emotions and bodily responses: A psychophysiological approach.* New York: Academic Press.

Hamilton, M. L. (1972). Imitation of facial expression of emotion. *Journal of Psychology, 80,* 345-350.

Hinde, R. A. (1970). *Animal behaviour: A synthesis of ethology and comparative psychology* (2nd ed.). New York: McGraw-Hill.

Hoffman, M. L. (1973). *Empathy, role-taking, guilt and the development of altruistic motives* (Developmental Psychology Report No. 30). Ann Arbor: University of Michigan.

Hoffman, M. L. (1977). Empathy, its development and prosocial implications. In H. E. Howe, Jr. (Ed.), *Nebraska Symposium on Motivation* (Vol. 25, pp. 169-217). Lincoln: University of Nebraska Press.

Hoffman, M. L. (1978). Toward a theory of empathetic arousal and development. In M. Lewis & L. A. Rosenblum (Eds.), *The development of affect* (pp. 227-256). New York: Plenum Press.

Humphrey, G. (1922). The conditioned reflex and the elementary social reaction. *Journal of Abnormal and Social Psychology, 17,* 113-119.

Hygge, S. (1976a). *Emotional and electrodermal reactions to the suffering of another: Vicarious instigation and vicarious classical conditioning* (Studia psychologica Upsaliensia 2). *Uppsala: Acta Universitatis Upsaliensis.*

Hygge, S. (1976b). Information about the model's unconditioned stimulus and response in vicarious classical conditioning. *Journal of Personality and Social Psychology, 33,* 764-771.

Izard, C. E. (1977). *Human emotions.* New York: Plenum Press.

Katz, R. L. (1963). *Empathy: Its nature and uses.* Glencoe, IL: The Free Press.

Kieras, D. (1978). Beyond pictures and words: Alternative information-processing models for imagery effects in verbal memory. *Psychological Bulletin, 85,* 532-554.

Kintsch, W. (1974). *The representation of meaning in memory.* Hillsdale, NJ: Lawrence Erlbaum Associates.

Kohlberg, L. (1964). Development of moral character and moral ideology. In M. L. Hoffman & L. W. Hoffman (Eds.), *Review of child development research* (Vol. 1, pp. 383-431). New York: Russell Sage Foundation.

Laird, J. D. (1974). Self-attribution of emotion: The effects of expressive behavior on the quality of emotional experience. *Journal of Personality and Social Psychology, 29,* 475-486.

Lang, P. J. (1979). A bio-informational theory of emotional imagery. *Psychophysiology, 16,* 495-512.

Lang, P. J. (1984). Cognition in emotion: Concept and action. In C. E. Izard, J. Kagan, & R. B. Zajonc (Eds.), *Emotions, cognition, and behavior* (pp. 192-226). Cambridge: Cambridge University Press.

Lanzetta, J. T., Cartwright-Smith, J., & Kleck, R. E. (1976). Effects of nonverbal dissimulation on emotional experience and autonomic arousal. *Journal of Personality and Social Psychology*, *33*, 354-370.

Lanzetta, J. T., & Orr, S. P. (1981). Stimulus properties of facial expressions and their influence on the classical conditioning of fear. *Motivation and Emotion*, *5*, 225-234.

Leight, K. A., & Ellis, H. C. (1981). Emotional mood states, strategies, and state-dependency in memory. *Journal of Verbal Learning and Verbal Behavior*, *20*, 251-266.

Lipps, T. (1903). *Ästhetik: Psychologie des Schönen und der Kunst: Vol. 1. Grundegung der Ästhetik* [Aesthetics: Psychology of beauty and art: Vol. 1. Foundations of aesthetics]. Hamburg: Voss.

Lipps, T. (1906). *Ästhetik: Psychologie des Schönen und der Kunst: Vol. 2. Die ästhetische Betrachtung und die bildende Kunst.* Hamburg: Voss. [Aesthetics: Psychology of beauty and art: Vol. 2. Aesthetic analysis and the creative arts].

Lipps, T. (1907). Das Wissen von fremden Ichen [Knowledge of foreign Is]. *Psychologische Untersuchungen*, *1*(4), 694-722.

Lockard, J. S. (Ed.). (1980). *The evolution of human social behavior.* New York: Elsevier.

MacLean, P. D. (1958). The limbic system with respect to self-preservation and the preservation of the species. *Journal of Nervous and Mental Disease*, *127*, 1-11.

MacLean, P. D. (1967). The brain in relation to empathy and medical education. *Journal of Nervous and Mental Disease*, *144*, 374-382.

Mathews, K., & Stotland, E. (1973). *Empathy and nursing students' contact with patients.* Mimeo, University of Washington, Spokane, WA.

Mattes, J., & Cantor, J. (1982). Enhancing responses to television advertisements via the transfer of residual arousal from prior programming. *Journal of Broadcasting*, *26*, 553-556.

McDougall, W. (1908). *An introduction to social psychology.* London: Methuen.

McDougall, W. (1922). A new theory of laughter. *Psyche*, *2*, 292-303.

Mead, G. H. (1934). *Mind, self and society.* Chicago: University of Chicago Press.

Mehrabian, A., & Epstein, N. (1972). A measure of emotional empathy. *Journal of Personality*, *40*, 525-543.

Mundorf, N., Drew, D., Zillmann, D. (1989, April). *Effects of disturbing news on recall of subsequently presented news.* Paper presented at the annual convention of the Broadcast Education Association, Las Vegas, NV.

Murphy, L. B. (1937). *Social behavior and child personality.* New York: Columbia University Press.

Murphy, L. B. (1983). Issues in the development of emotion in infancy. In R. Plutchik & H. Kellerman (Eds.), *Emotion: Theory, research, and experience: Vol. 2. Emotions in early development* (pp. 1-55). New York: Academic Press.

Öhman, A., & Dimberg, U. (1978). Facial expressions as conditioned stimuli for electrodermal responses: A case of "preparedness"? *Journal of Personality and Social Psychology*, *36*, 1251-1258.

Orr, S. P., & Lanzetta, J. T. (1980). Facial expressions of emotion as conditioned stimuli for human autonomic responses. *Journal of Personality and Social Psychology*, *38*, 278-282.

Piaget, J. (1948). *The moral judgment of the child.* Glencoe, IL: The Free Press.

Pylyshyn, Z. W. (1973). What the mind's eye tells the mind's brain: A critique of mental imagery. *Psychological Bulletin*, *80*, 1-24.

Rogers, C. R. (1967). *Person to person.* Lafayette, CA: Real People Press.

Saarni, C. (1982). Social and affective functions of nonverbal behavior: Developmental concerns. In R. S. Feldman (Ed.), *Development of nonverbal behavior in children* (pp. 123-147). New York: Springer Verlag.

Sagi, A., & Hoffman, M. L. (1976). Empathic distress in newborns. *Developmental Psychology*, *12*, 175-176.

Sapolsky, B. S., & Zillmann, D. (1978). Experience and empathy: Affective reactions to witnessing childbirth. *Journal of Social Psychology*, *105*, 131-144.

Scheler, M. (1913). *Zur Phänomenologie und Theorie der Sympathiegefühle und von Liebe und Hass.* (Mit einem Anhang über den Grund zur Annahme der Existenz des fremden ich). [On the phenomenology and theory of feelings of love and hate]. Hall a. S.: Niemeyer.

Schwartz, G. E. (1974). Toward a theory of voluntary control of response patterns in the cardiovascular system. In P. A. Obrist, A. H. Black, J. Brener, & L. V. DiCara (Eds.), *Cardiovascular psychophysiology: Current issues in response mechanisms, biofeedback, and methodology* (pp. 406–440). Chicago: Aldine.

Schwartz, G. E. (1977). Biofeedback and patterning of autonomic and central processes: CNS-cardiovascular interactions. In G. E. Schwartz & J. Beatty (Eds.), *Biofeedback: Theory and research* (pp. 183–219). New York: Academic Press.

Scott, R. K., & Goff, D. H. (1988). How excitation from prior programming affects television news recall. *Journalism Quarterly, 65*, 615–620.

Seligman, M. E. P. (1970). On the generality of the laws of learning. *Psychological Review, 77*, 406–418.

Simner, M. L. (1971). Newborn's reponse to the cry of another infant. *Developmental Psychology, 5*, 136–150.

Singer, J. L. (1980). The power and limitations of television: A cognitive-affective analysis. In P. H. Tannenbaum (Ed.), *The entertainment functions of television* (pp. 31–65). Hillsdale, NJ: Lawrence Erlbaum Associates.

Smith, A. (1971). *The theory of moral sentiments.* New York: Garland. (Original work published 1759)

Spitz, R. A., & Wolf, K. M. (1946). The smiling response: A contribution to the ontogenesis of social relations. *Genetic Psychology Monographs, 34*, 57–125.

Stein, E. (1970). *On the problem of empathy* (2nd ed.). The Hague: Nijhoff.

Stotland, E. (1969). Exploratory investigations of empathy. In L. Berkowitz (Ed.), *Advances in experimental social psychology* (Vol. 4, pp. 271–314). New York: Academic Press.

Stotland, E., Mathews, K. E., Jr., Sherman, S. E., Hansson, R. O., & Richardson, B. Z. (1978). *Empathy, fantasy, and helping.* Beverly Hills, CA: Sage.

Sullivan, H. S. (1940). *Conceptions of modern psychiatry.* London: Tavistock Press.

Tagiuri, R. (1969). Person perception. In G. Lindzey & E. Aronson (Eds.), *The handbook of social psychology: Vol. 3. The individual in a social context* (2nd ed., pp. 395–449). Reading, MA: Addison-Wesley.

Tannenbaum, P. H. (Ed.). (1980). *The entertainment functions of television.* Hillsdale, NJ: Lawrence Erlbaum Associates.

Tomes, H. (1964). The adaptation, acquisition, and extinction of empathetically mediated emotional responses. *Dissertation Abstracts, 24*, 3442–3443.

Tomkins, S. S. (1962). *Affect, imagery, consciousness: Vol. 1. The positive affects.* New York: Springer-Verlag.

Tomkins, S. S. (1963). *Affect, imagery, consciousness: Vol. 2. The negative affects.* New York: Springer-Verlag.

Tourangeau, R., & Ellsworth, P. C. (1979). The role of facial response in the experience of emotion. *Journal of Personality and Social Psychology, 37*, 1519–1531.

Truax, C. B. (1961). A scale for the measurement of accurate empathy. *Psychiatric Institute Bulletin 1*(12). Wisconsin Psychiatric Institute, University of Wisconsin.

Vaughan, K. B., & Lanzetta, J. T. (1980). Vicarious instigation and conditioning of facial expressive and autonomic responses to a model's expressive display of pain. *Journal of Personality and Social Psychology, 38*, 909–923.

Wagner, H., & Manstead, A. (Eds.). (1989). *Handbook of social psychophysiology.* New York: Wiley.

Washburn, R. W. (1929). A study of the smiling and laughing of infants in the first year of life. *Genetic Psychology Monographs, 6*, 398–537.

Wilson, B. J., Cantor, J., Gordon, L., & Zillmann, D. (1986). Affective response of nonretarded and retarded children to the emotions of a protagonist. *Child Study Journal, 16*(2), 77–93.

Worringer, W. (1959). *Abstraktion und Einfühlung: Ein Beitrag zur Stilpsychologie* [Abstraction and empathy: A contribution to the psychology of style]. München: Piper. (Original work published 1908)

Zajonc, R. B. (1980). Feeling and thinking: Preferences need no inferences. *American Psychologist*, *35*(2), 151-175.

Zillmann, D. (1978). Attribution and misattribution of excitatory reactions. In J. H. Harvey, W. J. Ickes, & R. F. Kidd (Eds.), *New directions in attribution research* (Vol. 2, pp. 335-368). Hillsdale, NJ: Lawrence Erlbaum Associates.

Zillmann, D. (1979). *Hostility and aggression*. Hillsdale, NJ: Lawrence Erlbaum Associates.

Zillmann, D. (1980). Anatomy of suspense. In P. H. Tannenbaum (Ed.), *The entertainment functions of television* (pp. 133-163). Hillsdale, NJ: Lawrence Erlbaum Associates.

Zillmann, D. (1982). Television viewing and arousal. In D. Pearl, L. Bouthilet, & J. Lazar (Eds.), *Television and behavior: Ten years of scientific progress and implications for the eighties: Vol. 2. Technical reviews* (pp. 53-67). U.S. Public Health Service Publication No. ADM 82-1196. Washington, DC: U.S. Government Printing Office.

Zillmann, D. (1983a). Arousal and aggression. In R. G. Geen & E. I. Donnerstein (Eds.), *Aggression: Theoretical and methodological issues* (pp. 75-101). New York: Academic Press.

Zillmann, D. (1983b). Transfer of excitation in emotional behavior. In J. T. Cacioppo & R. E. Petty (Eds.), *Social psychophysiology: A sourcebook* (pp. 215-240). New York: Guilford Press.

Zillman, D. (1984). *Connections between sex and aggression*. Hillsdale, NJ: Lawrence Erlbaum Associates.

Zillmann, D. (1988). Cognition-excitation interdependencies in aggressive behavior. *Aggressive Behavior*, *14*, 51-64.

Zillmann, D. (1989). Effects of prolonged consumption of pornography. In D. Zillmann & J. Bryant (Eds.), *Pornography: Research advances and policy considerations* (pp. 127-157). Hillsdale, NJ: Lawrence Erlbaum Associates.

Zillmann, D., & Bryant, J. (1975). Viewer's moral sanction of retribution in the appreciation of dramatic presentations. *Journal of Experimental Social Psychology*, *11*, 572-582.

Zillmann, D., & Bryant, J. (1986). Shifting preferences in pornography consumption. *Communication Research*, *13*, 560-578.

Zillmann, D., & Cantor, J. R. (1976). A disposition theory of humour and mirth. In A. J. Chapman & H. C. Foot (Eds.), *Humour and laughter: Theory, research and applications* (pp. 93-115). London: Wiley.

Zillmann, D. & Cantor, J. R. (1977). Affective responses to the emotions of a protagonist. *Journal of Experimental Social Psychology*, *13*, 155-165.

Zillmann, D., Mody, B., & Cantor, J. R. (1974). Empathetic perception of emotional displays in film as a function of hedonic and excitatory state prior to exposure. *Journal of Research in Personality*, *8*, 335-349.

Zuckerman, M., Klorman, R., Larrance, D. T., & Spiegel, N. H. (1981). Facial, autonomic, and subjective components of emotion: The facial feedback hypothesis versus the externalizer-internalizer distinction. *Journal of Personality and Social Psychology*, *41*, 929-944.

CHAPTER
7

Fright Responses to Mass Media Productions

Joanne Cantor
University of Wisconsin—Madison

This chapter investigates fright reactions produced by mass media presentations. First, research findings related to the prevalence and intensity with which feelings of anxiety are experienced as a result of exposure to media drama are reviewed, along with conjectures about the appeal of frightening media. Then the paradox that fright reactions to media drama occur at all is discussed, and an explanation is proposed based on principles of stimulus generalization. Other factors that are needed to account for observed effects are also explored, and research evidence on the emotional effects of both dramatic and documentary presentations is reviewed in conjunction with the proposed mechanisms of emotional effects.

FEELINGS OF FRIGHT IN REACTION TO THE SCREEN

Anyone who has ever been to a horror film or thriller appreciates the fact that exposure to television shows, films, and other mass media presentations depicting danger, injury, bizarre images, and terror-stricken protagonists can induce intense fright responses in an audience. Most of us seem to be able to remember at least one specific program or movie that terrified us when we were a child and that made us nervous, remained in our thoughts, and affected other aspects of our behavior for some time afterward. And this happened to us even after we were old enough to know that what we were witnessing was not actually happening at the time and that the depicted dangers could not leave the screen and attack us directly. These reactions can also occur when we know that what is being portrayed did not actually happen; at times we may have such reactions even when we understand that there is no chance that the depicted events could ever occur.

The predominant interest in this chapter is fright as an *immediate emotional response*, which is typically of relatively short duration, but that may endure, on occasion, for several hours or days, or even longer. The more long-lasting "cognitive" effects of media presentations on perceptions of the dangers involved in society are not explored here because they have been treated quite extensively elsewhere (see, e.g., Gerbner, Gross, Morgan, & Signorielli, 1986; Hawkins & Pingree, 1982), and are not likely to be mediated by the same mechanisms. Also excluded are fright reactions to telecommunicated presentations of live events or to reports of imminent danger that happen to be communicated via the mass media (such as tornado warnings or on-the-spot coverage of an attempt to recapture armed escapees from a local prison).

The research focus here is on emotional reactions involving components of anxiety, distress, and increased physiological arousal that are frequently engendered in viewers as a result of exposure to specific types of media productions. Although the major interest is in reactions of this type that are evoked by exposure to dramatic entertainment fare, there is a good deal of research on adults' reactions to "stressful" documentary films (e.g., by Lazarus and his associates) that is relevant to this issue. A review of the literature reveals that most studies of children's fright reactions deal with responses to fictional or fantasy entertainment programming, whereas most studies of adults deal with responses to extremely upsetting documentary material. This dichotomy undoubtedly has a great deal to do with ethical issues in the conduct of research. It seems, however, that these two bodies of research should be considered together because, as is discussed later, there is a great deal of overlap in important aspects of the stimuli presented, in the nature of the audience's reactions, and in the processes apparently underlying such reactions.

In this chapter, a clear-cut distinction is not being made between fear and anxiety. Although different theorists make a variety of distinctions between these two terms, many use the two terms largely interchangeably or consider anxiety to be a vague form of fear (see Hilgard, Atkinson, & Atkinson, 1971). Most experimental studies of adults' responses to stressful films use some form of "anxiety," or "state anxiety" as their major self-report variable (see Lazarus, Speisman, Mordkoff, & Davidson, 1962, for a comparison of effects on major self-report dimensions). Reports of emotional disturbance, tension, degree of upset, and emotional arousal are frequently used as supplementary measures. Physiological responses are also usually employed in studies of adults, the most typical of which include heart rate and a measure of palmar skin conductance (e.g., Falkowski & Steptoe, 1983; Koriat, Melkman, Averill, & Lazarus, 1972). Although there have been studies in which state anxiety was assessed in children (e.g., Kase, Sikes, & Spielberger, 1978), children's self-reports of their fright responses to drama are typically assessed in terms of the degree to which viewers feel scared, worried, or upset (e.g., Sparks & Cantor, 1986), the degree to which they perceive a program as scary (e.g., Osborn & Endsley, 1971), or whether or not their reactions are hedonically "negative" (Wilson & Cantor, 1985). The most prevalent physiological responses used with children have been heart rate and skin temperature (e.g., Wilson & Cantor, 1985; Zillmann, Hay, & Bryant, 1975). In addition, children's facial expressions of fear have been analyzed by some researchers (e.g., Wilson & Cantor, 1987; Zillmann et al., 1975).

Research interest in the phenomenon of fright reactions to mass media has been sporadic at best. Several investigators in the 1930s and 1940s focused primary concerns on fear reactions to mass media (Blumer, 1933; Cantril, 1940; Dysinger & Ruckmick, 1933; Eisenberg, 1936; Preston, 1941). In addition, some major volumes reporting research conducted in the 1950s addressed this issue seriously (Himmelweit, Oppenheim, & Vince, 1958; Schramm, Lyle, & Parker, 1961; Wertham, 1953). But fright responses to mass media were largely ignored in the 1960s and early 1970s. There were only passing references to fright in the Surgeon General's report (Comstock & Rubinstein, 1972), and in the Surgeon General's Update (Pearl, Bouthilet, & Lazar, 1982), fear was addressed in terms of the long-term effects of media exposure on perceptions of danger, but, for the most part, not in terms of the more transitory emotional effects produced by witnessing a particular program or film.

One reason for the resurgence of interest in fright responses may be that mass media content has become increasingly graphic and horror-filled (see Stein, 1982). As anecdotal reports of intense emotional responses to such popular films as *Jaws* and *The Exorcist* have proliferated in the press, public attention seems to have become more focused on the phenomenon. Although many adults have experienced such reactions, the major share of public concern has been over children's responses. The furor over children's reactions to especially intense scenes in *Indiana Jones and the Temple of Doom* and *Gremlins* prompted the Motion Picture Association of America to add "PG-13" to its rating system, in an attempt to caution parents that, for whatever reason, a film might be inappropriate for children under the age of 13 (see Zoglin, 1984). In addition, the widespread prior speculation about children's potential emotional responses to the broadcast of the nuclear holocaust film *The Day After* seems to have been unprecedented (see Schofield & Pavelchak, 1985). Finally, the rapid expansion in the number of cable channels has meant that most films produced for theatrical distribution, no matter how brutal or bizarre, eventually end up on television and thus become accessible to large numbers of children, often without their parents' knowledge.

Although some psychoanalytically oriented observers would seem to argue to the contrary (e.g., Bettelheim, 1975; Smetak, 1986), many researchers have speculated on the potential negative effects on children of exposure to frightening media fare. Blumer (1933) spoke of "emotional possession," during which ordinary control over one's feelings and perceptions is lost. Preston (1941) contended that "addiction" to mass media horrors has profound negative effects on children's general physical and psychological health. More recently, Singer (1975) argued that children exposed to frightening movies that are beyond their capacity to comprehend may be haunted *for years* by night terrors and bizarre and weird fantasies. Sarafino (1986) has placed a great deal of blame on scary television shows and films for inducing and exacerbating children's fears. His recent book, which uses research findings and case studies to help parents identify and reduce fearful states in children, contains countless anecdotes involving the media's negative impact and contends that exposure to "scary portrayals of animals, violence, and monsters on TV and in the movies can impair children's psychological development" (p. 56). Because of such concerns about the potential negative effects of exposure to frightening media on children, research on how to predict and prevent or reduce children's fears can be seen as having immediate practical value.

Research into potential negative effects on children has unique problems, however, in that it is not feasible, for ethical reasons, to demonstrate harmful effects in the experimental laboratory. Thus, what evidence there is for intense emotional disturbances in children comes from anecdotes, case studies, in-depth interviews, and survey research. In these studies, effects observed in the "real world" are reported, but control over variables is impossible, and causal conclusions remain highly tentative. The laboratory research that has been conducted on the issue of fright responses to mass media, in contrast, has not been designed to demonstrate negative effects, but rather to determine the variables that contribute to immediate and short-lived fright responses, and those that prevent or mitigate them.

Although the potential practical applications of research on mass media-induced fears seems to have been a major impetus to their study, the value of such research in advancing theory has not been ignored. Because children's fright reactions have been observed to vary as a function of differences in their cognitive processing of mass media stimuli, this research has been helpful in investigating relationships between cognitive development and emotional reactions to mass media, and relationships between cognition and emotion in general.

Prevalence and Intensity of Media-Induced Fright Reactions

Most researchers who have investigated the issue have found that a substantial proportion of the respondents questioned admitted having experienced fright while watching mass media productions, although the percentages vary greatly as a function of the sample selected and the nature of the question asked.[1] Blumer (1933)

---

[1]Some of the percentages noted here are approximate. For the sake of simplicity, the percentages reported for separate age groups have been combined without being weighted by subgroup size.

reported that 93% of the children in his sample said they had been frightened or horrified by a motion picture. Approximately 33% of a sample questioned by Himmelweit et al. (1958) reported having been frightened by something on television. Lyle and Hoffman (1972) reported that 48% of a sample of first graders said they were frightened "sometimes or often" by what they saw on TV. In a national survey conducted by Zill (1977), 25% of the children questioned said they were "afraid" of TV programs involving fighting and shooting. Although they did not ask their respondents to report on their own reactions, Groebel and Krebs (1983) found that 92% of a representative sample of youths believed that television could evoke fear. Most recently, about 75% of the respondents in two separate samples of preschool and elementary-school children said that they had been scared by something they had seen on television or in a movie (Wilson, Hoffner, & Cantor, 1987).

Other findings reflect the prevalence of more intense reactions, that last beyond the time of media exposure. Although von Feilitzen (1975), in summarizing the results of Danish research, concluded that few children have suffered severe effects in the form of anxiety, nightmares, or lost sleep, other researchers have reported that enduring and intense responses are more pervasive. Blumer (1933) stated that the fear induced by movies "very frequently" lasts beyond the time of viewing. Eisenberg (1936) found that approximately 43% of a sample of children had recently dreamed about things they had heard on the radio and that about 50% of these children said that their dreams had involved witches, murders, crimes, nightmares, and the like. Preston (1941) reported that among her respondents under the age of 12, sleep disturbances necessitating intervention by the mother were "common reactions" to movie horrors and radio crime. When Wall and Simson (1950) asked adolescents about the films they had seen in the preceding 2 weeks, one film, a thriller, was reported to have produced "lasting fright" in more than 33% of those who had seen it. Himmelweit et al. (1958) reported that approximately 18% of the children they questioned thought there were things on television that were bad for children, and the most typical reason given was that they cause fright and bad dreams. In a study by Hess and Goldman (1962), 75% of the parents interviewed agreed that children sometimes get nightmares from television programs; 63% agreed *strongly*. Cantor and Reilly (1982) reported that 26% of a group of adolescents said that they experienced enduring fright "sometimes or often" after watching television shows. Moreover, 22% said they sometimes or often *regretted* having seen a scary program because of how much it had upset them. Finally, about 50% of a sample of elementary-school children questioned by Palmer, Hockett, and Dean (1983) reported that they experienced enduring fright reactions to television programs "sometimes or frequently" and over 33% said that they sometimes or frequently were sorry they had seen such programs.

In a study designed to assess the severity of typical enduring fright reactions to mass media, Johnson (1980) asked a random sample of adults whether they had ever seen a motion picture that had disturbed them "a great deal." Forty percent replied in the affirmative, and the median length of the reported disturbance was 3 days. Respondents also reported on the type, intensity, and duration of symptoms such as nervousness, depression, fear of specific things, and recurring thoughts and images. Based on these reports, Johnson judged that 48% of these respondents (19% of the total sample) had experienced, for at least 2 days, a "significant stress reaction" of the type identified by Horowitz (1976) and Lazarus (1966) as constituting a "stress response syndrome." When Johnson replicated this survey, using randomly selected moviegoers standing in line outside of theaters, 61% of the sample said they had been greatly disturbed by a movie, and 43% of these respondents (26% of the total sample) were judged on the basis of their symptoms, to have had a severe stress reaction. Johnson argued that "it is one thing to walk away from a frightening or disturbing event with mild residue of the images and quite another thing to ruminate about it, feel anxious or depressed for days, and/or to avoid anything that might create the same unpleasant experience" (p. 786). On the basis of his data, he concluded that such reactions were more prevalent and more severe than had previously been assumed.

The most extreme reactions reported in the literature come from psychiatric case studies in which acute and disabling anxiety states enduring several days to several weeks or more are said to have been precipitated by the viewing of horror movies such as *The Exorcist* and *Invasion of the Body Snatchers* (Buzzuto, 1975; Mathai, 1983). Most of the patients in the cases reported had not had previously diagnosed psychiatric problems, but the viewing of the film was seen as occurring in conjunction with other stressors in the patients' lives.

Together, these studies suggest that transitory fright responses to dramatic mass media stimuli are quite typical, that enduring emotional disturbances occur in a substantial proportion of the audience, and that intense and debilitating reactions affect a small but appreciable minority of particularly susceptible viewers.

Parental Knowledge and Children's Exposure

Preston (1941) found that for the most part, the parents of her respondents either were unaware of their children's fright responses to mass media horrors, or minimized their significance. More recent findings are in accord with this generalization. Cantor and Reilly (1982) found that parents' estimates of the frequency of their children's media-induced fright reactions were significantly lower than their children's self-reports. They also found that, generally speaking, the parents' estimates were not even correlated with those of their children.

Cantor and Reilly (1982) further reported that parents' estimates of their children's exposure to frightening media were also significantly lower than children's self-reports. The difference between parents' and children's estimates of exposure is difficult to interpret because it may reflect either the parent's ignorance of what the child has seen or a difference between the parent's and the child's definition of scary programs. Data reported here demonstrate that children often experience fright reactions to programs that most parents would not expect to be scary. Nevertheless, there is evidence that children are widely exposed to televised stimuli that were originally intended for adults and that are considered frightening by a large proportion of adult moviegoers. Sparks (1986b), for example, reported that almost 50% of the 4- to 10-year-olds he interviewed had seen *Poltergeist* and *Jaws*, and substantial proportions of his sample had seen *Halloween* and *Friday the 13th*. Most of this viewing was done in the home, on cable television.

Relationship Between Fright Reactions and Enjoyment

Given the data just cited on the prevalence of immediate fright and other more enduring emotional disturbances produced by exposure to frightening productions, the question obviously arises as to why viewers subject themselves the risk of such "psychic trauma." Preston (1941) argued that children cannot avoid being exposed to such fare if their parents insist on consuming "thrilling" programs. She also maintained that children choose such fare for themselves so that they can talk about the "hair-raising details" with their friends at school. But in speaking of the habitual consumption of media horrors as "addiction," Preston implicitly endorsed the notion that such exposure produces intrinsic rewards as well. In fact, most researchers who have asked the question have discovered that many children enjoy frightening media presentations, in spite of the unwanted side-effects that sometimes occur, Blumer (1933) reported that in a third-grade class he interviewed, 86% of the children gave instances of being frightened, on occasion severely, by motion pictures; yet 82% of those who had been frightened said that they liked to be frightened by movies. Eighty percent of the adolescents interviewed by Cantor and Reilly (1982) and over 50% of the elementary-school children interviewed by Palmer et al. (1983) said they liked scary television and films "somewhat or a lot." Sparks (1986b) found that more than 33% of the elementary-school children he interviewed said they enjoyed scary programs, and another 25% of the children said they both enjoyed and disliked them. Finally, in a study reported by Wilson et al. (1987), almost 66% of the children in one sample responded in the affirmative when asked whether or not they liked scary programs; about 75% of the children in another sample stated that they liked them, with about 50% of the sample saying they liked them "a lot."

Blumer (1933) argued that many children enjoy being frightened while viewing scary presentations, but suffer unwanted effects afterward. Himmelweit et al. (1958) argued that the child "enjoys being frightened just a little, but not too much," and that the child "likes the suspense for the pleasure of the relief that follows it" (p. 210). Zillmann (1980) has provided evidence relevant to the latter mechanism underlying the appreciation of suspenseful presentations. He has argued that physiological arousal is produced by the anticipation of threatened negative outcomes and that, through the process of *excitation transfer* (e.g., Zillmann, 1971), this arousal intensifies enjoyment of the positive (or at least nonnegative) outcomes that such presentations usually provide. Furthermore, Zillmann has noted that the enjoyment of suspenseful presentations does not necessarily hinge upon the final outcome, but may occur throughout the presentation as various episodes within a plot induce and then reduce suspense (Zillmann et al., 1975).

Consistent with Zillmann's reasoning, Cantor and Reilly (1982) presented evidence that undergoing fright reactions to scary presentations does not necessarily reduce the enjoyment of such presentations, and that fright may even be positively associated with liking. In a sixth-grade sample, respondents who reported experiencing enduring fright reactions sometimes or often did not differ from their less reactive peers in their liking for scary media. Moreover, in a 10th-grade sample, highly reactive respondents tended to like scary programs more than less reactive respondents. Furthermore, respondents who were highly reactive did not differ from those who were less reactive in their reports of frequency of exposure to scary presentations.

An experimental study of adults' appreciation of horror (Zillmann, Weaver, Mundorf, & Aust, 1986) also supports the positive relationship between fright and appreciation. In this study, mean self-report ratings of reactions to *Friday the 13th, Part III*, on a "distress" factor were extremely highly correlated with mean ratings on a "delight" factor.

A STIMULUS GENERALIZATION APPROACH
TO UNDERSTANDING MEDIA-INDUCED FEAR

As can be seen from the literature summarized here, there is a good deal of evidence regarding viewers' subjective experiences of fear in response to mass media presentations. The next part of this chapter is devoted to speculations about why such fear reactions occur and the factors that promote or inhibit their occurrence. Data from controlled experiments as well as surveys, and studies that have employed physiological, expressive, and behavioral measures of fear as well as self-reports are cited where they are relevant to these speculations.

Fear is generally conceived of as an emotional response of negative hedonic tone related to avoidance or escape, due to the perception of real or imagined threat (e.g., Izard, 1977). A classic fear-arousing situation is one in which the individual senses that he or she is in physical danger, such as upon encountering a poisonous snake on a walk through the woods. Fear can be conceived of as a response involving cognitions, motor behavior, and excitatory reactions that, except under extreme conditions, prepare the individual to flee from the danger.

Using this definition of fear, it is not difficult to explain the public terror that was produced by perhaps the most infamous frightening media drama on record— the 1938 radio broadcast of H. G. Wells' *War of the Worlds*. Many people who tuned in late thought they were listening to a live news bulletin informing them that Martians were taking over the United States (Cantril, 1940). Thus, if they believed what they heard, they justifiably felt that their own lives and indeed the future of their society were in great peril.

But in typical situations in which people are exposed to mass media drama, the audience understands that what is being depicted is not actually happening; in many cases, they know that it never did happen; and in some cases, they know that it never could happen. Objectively speaking, then, the viewer is not in any immediate danger. Why then, does the fright reaction occur? Although an individual's fright response to a media presentation is undoubtedly the result of the complex interaction of a variety of processes, a preliminary explanation for this phenomenon might be proposed, based on the notion of stimulus generalization (see Pavlov, 1927; Razran, 1949). In conditioning terms, if a stimulus evokes either an unconditioned or conditioned emotional response, other stimuli that are similar to the eliciting stimulus will evoke similar, but less intense emotional responses. This principle implies that, because of similarities between the real and the mediated stimulus, a stimulus that would evoke a fright response if experienced first hand will evoke a similar, but less intense response when encountered via the mass media. In order to evaluate the implications of this explanation, it should be instructive, first, to identify major categories of stimuli and events depicted in the mass media that tend to induce fear in real-life situations, and, second, to delineate factors that should promote or reduce the viewer's tendency to respond emotionally to the mediated stimulus.

Stimuli and Events That Generally Produce Fear

Based on a review of the literature on the sources of real-world fears and on the effects of frightening media, three categories of stimuli and events that occur frequently in frightening presentations and that tend to produce fear in real-life situations are proposed. They are dangers and injuries, distortions of natural forms, and the experience of endangerment and fear by others. These categories are obviously not mutually exclusive; on the contrary, a frightening scene usually involves more than one of these categories.[2]

---

[2]These categories are also not considered exhaustive. Many theorists have proposed additional categories of stimuli that readily evoke fear, such as certain types of animals (especially snakes; see Jersild & Holmes, 1935; Yerkes & Yerkes, 1936) and loud noises, darkness, and stimuli related to loss of support (see Bowlby, 1973). These categories are not discussed separately here because it seems that in mass media productions, such stimuli tend to co-occur with danger or signal its imminence. For example, the snakes, bats, and spiders in horror films are usually depicted as poisonous as well as repulsive. Sudden loud noises and darkness are often used to intensify the perceived dangerousness of situations. Finally, visual stimuli associated with loss of support, such as those experienced when traveling uncontrollably through space in a roller coaster (see Tannenbaum, 1980), are typically presented in horror films to represent threats to a character's safety.

Dangers and Injuries.   Stimuli that are perceived as dangerous should, by definition, evoke fear. The depiction of events that either cause or threaten to cause great harm is the stock-in-trade of the frightening film. Natural disasters such as tornadoes, volcanoes, plagues, and earthquakes; violent encounters on an interpersonal, global or even intergalactic level; attacks by vicious animals, and large-scale industrial and nuclear accidents are typical events in frightening media fare. If any of these events were witnessed directly, the onlooker would be in danger, and fear would be the expected response. In addition, because danger is often present when injuries are witnessed, the perception of injuries should come to evoke fear as a conditioned response, even in the absence of the danger that produced the injuries. Through stimulus generalization, one might thus expect mediated depictions of danger or injury to produce fright reactions as well.

Many examples of fright produced by depictions of dangerous stimuli in media drama are reported in the survey literature. Blumer (1933) reported that scenes involving accidents and disasters, such as drownings, wrecks, collisions, fires, and floods, and dangerous animals such as gorillas, bears, and tigers were particularly powerful in inducing fright in his sample. Criminal activities and violence were mentioned as important by Blumer (1933), Eisenberg (1936), Groebel and Krebs (1983), and Himmelweit et al. (1958). Sparks (1986b) reported that a large portion of his sample said they were frightened by the violent films *Friday the 13th, Jaws,* and *Halloween.* Finally, Johnson (1980) reported that depicted brutality was one of the most frequently mentioned sources of film-induced emotional disturbances in adults.

In Dysinger and Ruckmick's (1933) laboratory investigations of emotional responses to motion pictures, scenes of danger were typically associated with increases in skin conductance and self-reports of excitement. In more recent laboratory investigations by Osborn and Endsley (1971) and Kase et al. (1978), children found violent presentations scarier or more anxiety-provoking than neutral scenes, although it must be acknowledged that the scenes compared differed in a variety of respects other than the presence or absence of violence. In a similar vein, Noble (1975) reported that children played "less creatively" and talked less after viewing a war documentary than after viewing a film involving puppets, and he argued that these effects were indicators that the violent film increased anxiety.

In a controlled experiment in which a videotaped adventure program was manipulated to produce three levels of depicted danger, Zillmann et al. (1975) found that children's fear, as measured in facial expressions and heart rate, was more intense the more dangerous the situation was depicted to be. In another experiment, Bryant (1978, cited in Zillmann, 1980) manipulated a Western drama to depict five levels of depicted threats and dangers, and found that viewers' mean heart-rate changes were proportional to the depicted levels of threat.

In addition to the aforementioned studies on the emotional impact of dangers and injuries in dramatic presentations, the many experiments involving documentary films on such topics as industrial accidents, autopsies, and aboriginal circumcision rituals (e.g., *It Didn't Have to Happen, Basic Autopsy Procedures, Subincision*) have demonstrated that filmed depictions of bodily injuries substantially increase adults' physiological arousal and self-reports of anxiety (Averill, Malmstrom, Koriat, & Lazarus, 1972; Boyle, 1984; Davidson & Hiebert, 1971; Falkowski & Steptoe, 1983; Girodo & Pellegrini, 1976; Horowitz, 1970; Kamen, 1971; Koriat et al., 1972; Lazarus & Alfert, 1964; Lazarus et al., 1962; Nomikos, Opton, Averill, & Lazarus, 1968; Pillard, Atkinson, & Fisher, 1967; Pillard, Carpenter, Atkinson, & Fisher, 1966; Speisman, Lazarus, Mordkoff, & Davidson, 1964; Thayer & Levenson, 1983).

Distortions of Natural Forms. In addition to dangerous stimuli and the outcomes of dangerous situations, a related set of stimuli that typically evoke fear might be referred to as deformities and distortions, or *familiar organisms in unfamiliar and unnatural forms.* Hebb (1946) observed fear responses to such "deviations from previously experienced patterns" in chimpanzees and argued that such responses are spontaneous, in that they do not require conditioning. Organisms that have been mutilated as a result of injury could be considered to fall into this category as well as the previous category. In addition, distortions that are not the result of injury are often encountered in thrillers in the form of realistic characters like dwarves, hunchbacks, and mutants. Moreover, monsters abound in thrillers. Monsters are unreal creatures that are similar to natural beings in many ways, but deviant from them in other ways, such as through distortions in size, shape, skin color, or facial configuration. In scary movies, monstrous and distorted characters are typically, but not universally depicted as evil and dangerous.

Lyle and Hoffman (1976) reported that young children overwhelmingly designated monsters as the things that frightened them most on television, and Blumer (1933), stated that movie characters in the form of spooks, ghosts, phantoms, and devils were frequently cited by children as causing fright. More recently, Leishman (1981) and Dorr, Doubleday, and Kovaric (1983) have reported anecdotal accounts of intense fright reactions produced by televised depictions of monsters, vampires, and mummies. The prevalence of fright produced by the monstrous characters in the TV show "The Incredible Hulk," the music video "Thriller," and the movies *The Wizard of Oz* and *Poltergeist* (Cantor & Sparks, 1984; Sparks, 1986b) has also been reported recently. Finally, in a controlled field experiment, Heisler (1975) observed that the viewing of the "supernatural-violent" film *The Exorcist* produced a significant increase in viewers' reported levels of state anxiety.

The Experience of Endangerment and Fear by Others. Although in some cases, viewers seem to respond directly to depictions of fear-evoking stimuli such as dangers, injuries, and distortions, in most dramatic presentations these stimuli are shown to affect the emotional responses and outcomes of depicted characters. In many cases, the viewer can be said to respond *indirectly* to the stimuli through the experiences of the characters. One mechanism underlying such responses is *empathy*. Although there is controversy over the origins of empathic processes (see Berger, 1962; Feshbach, 1982; Hoffman, 1978), it is clear that under some circumstances, people experience fear as a direct response to the fear expressed by others. Many frightening films seem to stress characters' expressions of fear in response to dangers more than the perceptual cues associated with the threat itself.

In a laboratory investigation, Wilson and Cantor (1985) provided evidence of the role of empathic processes in media-induced fright. They found that 9- to 11-year-old children who watched a scene depicting a character's expressions of fear experienced as much fear (assessed in self-reports, skin temperature, and electromyogram) as did those who watched a scene depicting the frightening stimulus that was responsible for the character's fear. In contrast, preschool children showed significantly less fear in response to the character's emotion than in response to the frightening stimulus, in spite of the fact that almost all of the children who were exposed to the character's emotion were aware of the nature of his feelings. The observed developmental difference is consistent with the notion that true empathy does not occur until the child acquires role-taking skills (see Feshbach, 1982; Selman & Byrne, 1978).

Another indirect mechanism that may be proposed to account for emotional responses to the experiences of others derives from the fact that witnessing other people risk danger can produce the "vicarious" experience of fear, even when the persons at risk do not express fear because they are either unaware of the danger or unafraid. As Zillmann (1980) has argued, much of the tension in suspenseful presentations arises from the fear that something horrible will happen to characters for whom we feel positive affect. The fear evoked may derive, in part, from the fear of imagined "separation" from these characters if they should meet their demise (see Bowlby, 1973). Also, because Zillmann and Cantor (1976) have argued that people respond with dysphoria to the misfortunes of persons for whom they have affection, or at least for whom they do not feel antipathy (Zillmann & Cantor, 1977), fear may be seen as deriving from anticipation of the viewer's own distress or from anticipation of empathy with the distress responses of liked characters.

Dysinger and Ruckmick (1933) observed that viewers often showed increased skin conductance and feelings of apprehension when they anticipated that something dangerous was about to happen to movie characters. Himmelweit et al. (1958) and Schramm et al. (1961) noted that children often experienced fright in response to the threat of harm to a character or animal, and that these responses were especially intense when the child had developed feelings of attachment toward the threatened character or animal (see also Leishman, 1981). Tannenbaum and Gaer (1965) reported that subjects who identified more with the hero of a Western reported more stress than did those who identified with him less, after viewing a scene in which the hero was about to be hanged. Bryant (1978, cited in Zillmann,

1980) demonstrated the importance of affect toward a threatened character, by creating a film in which the major character's personality characteristics (sympathetic vs. indifferent vs. obnoxious) and the level of threats she encountered (low vs. high) were manipulated. The findings revealed that when the protagonist had behaved indifferently or obnoxiously, excitatory reactions and self-reported distress levels were low and were unaffected by the level of depicted threat. In contrast, when the threatened character was depicted as sympathetic, self-reports of distress and levels of physiological arousal were higher, and under these conditions, responses were more intense under high than low threat.

Factors Affecting the Tendency to Respond Emotionally to Mediated Stimuli

Three factors are proposed to have an impact on viewers' tendencies to respond emotionally to mediated fear-evoking stimuli. They are the similarity of the depicted stimuli to real-life fear-evokers, viewers' motivations for media exposure, and factors affecting emotionality, generally.

Similarity of Depicted Stimuli to Real-Life Fear-Evokers. The notion of stimulus generalization implies that the greater the similarity between a conditioned or unconditioned stimulus and the substitute stimulus, the stronger the generalization response will be. *Perceptually* speaking, realistic depictions of threatening events are more similar to events occurring in the real world than are animated or stylized depictions of the same events. Thus, the stimulus generalization notion would predict more intense responses to live-action violence than to cartoon violence, for example. Consistent with this expectation, Gunter and Furnham (1984) reported that adult viewers rated episodes of violence portrayed by human characters as significantly more frightening than episodes of cartoon violence. Osborn and Endsley (1971) found that young children considered a program depicting human violence to be scarier than one depicting cartoon violence. In a more tightly controlled experiment, Surbeck (1975) observed that children tended to consider a program depicting human violence to be scarier than a program in which the same actions were portrayed by puppets.

The *similarity of depicted stimuli to those stimuli that provoke fear in a particular individual* should also enhance stimulus generalization. Himmelweit et al. (1958) argued that "whether an incident will disturb depends less on whether it is fictional or real than on whether it comes within the child's experience and is one with which he can identify himself" (p. 203). Thus, an individual's fears and prior experiences with stressful events should influence the effect that mediated stimuli and events will have. For example, Hare and Blevings (1975) observed that subjects with phobias of spiders had more extreme physiological reactions and higher levels of self-reported fear while viewing depictions of spiders than did nonphobics. As another example, Weiss, Katkin, and Rubin (1968) found that subjects scoring high on a Fear of Death and Illness scale experienced greater disruptions of task performance after viewing a film about fatal illness than did subjects scoring lower on this scale. Finally, Sapolsky and Zillmann (1978) showed that prior primary experience with an emotion-evoking event is associated with increased emotional responses to filmed depictions of similar events. In their study, subjects who had previously given birth had greater heart-rate increases and higher levels of self-reported arousal while watching a film of childbirth than did subjects who had not given birth.

Another aspect of similarity that should have an impact on the tendency to generalize from the real to the mediated stimulus has to do with the *perceived similarity between viewing the depicted event and undergoing the corresponding real-world event itself.* At one extreme is the response of the very young child who does not understand the difference between mediated depictions and reality and who thinks that the frightening stimuli are actually present in the living room or the theater (see Dorr, 1980). At the other extreme is the mature viewer who is well aware that what is being witnessed is only an image being reproduced via media technology. Based on this distinction, one would expect that young children would respond intensely to mediated depictions of things that frighten them because they would react as they would to real-life stimuli. This distinction would also lead to the expectation that, due to the process of *stimulus discrimination,* there would be a rapid diminishment of response intensity, with age and with repeated viewing trials, as the viewer would increasingly discriminate between the reinforcement contingencies associated with the live and the mediated stimulus.

Consistent with the notion of stimulus discrimination, there is some evidence for short-term habituation to stressful movie stimuli. Davidson and Hiebert (1971) reported that 10 repeated exposures to an industrial accident film reduced viewers' subjective anxiety (but not their skin conductance responses) while watching the film. In an experiment by Averill et al. (1972), 20 exposures to an isolated accident scene from this film reduced subjects' skin conductance and self-reported distress in response to that scene when it was viewed in the context of the entire movie. This habituation did not generalize to other accident scenes in the film, however. Generalization of habituation to similar but novel stimuli has been demonstrated in an experiment by Wilson and Cantor (1987). In this study, elementary-school children who were first shown a videotape of snakes tended to show less fear (as assessed in self-reports and heart rate) than did control subjects, while subsequently watching a dramatic movie scene depicting snakes. Pillard et al. (1967) also demonstrated the generalization of habituation to stressful film stimuli. In their study, subjects who had just seen a film about autopsies reported significantly less anxiety while viewing a film on aboriginal circumcision rituals than did subjects who had just witnessed a neutral film.

The notion of stimulus discrimination should be considered to be more relevant to the long-term effects of exposure to media than to short-term habituation, however, and in this context, the data are unsupportive of the stimulus generalization model. In contrast to the data on short-term desensitization, studies of long-term effects do not provide evidence of a diminution of emotional responses with repeated exposure to stressful films. Surveys by Himmelweit et al. (1958), von Feilitzen (1975), and Cantor and Reilly (1982) all reported that heavy viewing of frightening media was not associated with a lowering of reactivity to such fare. In addition, Sapolsky and Zillmann's (1978) experiment revealed that women who had previously watched a film depicting childbirth reported themselves to be more aroused while witnessing a childbirth film than did those who had never seen such a film.

Because research indicates that fear responses to mass media stimuli are quite common in adults (e.g., Johnson, 1980), and that heavy exposure to frightening media does not necessarily produce a lessening of fright responses, stimulus generalization alone is clearly not a sufficient explanation for fright responses to media stimuli.

Motivations for Media Exposure. One set of factors that the stimulus generalization notion does not take into account are the motivations for media exposure. As Zillmann (1982) has argued, mature viewers often seek out media programming for entertainment and arousal. In order to enhance the emotional impact of a drama they may, for example, adopt the "willing suspension of disbelief," by cognitively minimizing the effect of knowledge that the events are mediated. In addition, mature viewers may enhance their emotional responses by generating their own emotion-evoking visual images or by cognitively elaborating on the implications of the portrayed events.

Mature viewers who seek to avoid intense arousal may employ other appraisal processes (see Zillmann, 1978), to diminish fright reactions to media stimuli by using the "adult discount," for example (see Dysinger & Ruckmick, 1933), and concentrating on the fact that the stimuli are only mediated. Although such appraisal processes must be taken into account, they are by no means universally effective. A viewer wanting to enjoy an intense emotional response to a drama may be prevented from downplaying the fact that the events are mediated if, for example, the acting is poor or the special effects are inadequate. On the other hand, a viewer attempting to dampen his or her emotional reactions may nonetheless be "caught off guard" by a particularly arresting or realistic depiction.

Several studies by Lazarus and his co-workers have shown that adults can modify their emotional responses to stressful films by adopting different "cognitive sets." Koriat et al. (1972) reported that subjects who were instructed to "involve" themselves in a film on industrial accidents and to "let themselves go" reported more emotional arousal and had greater heart-rate increases than did subjects who were instructed to detach themselves emotionally from the film. Speisman et al. (1964) showed that a "trauma" soundtrack, playing up the threatening aspects of a film about aboriginal circumcision rituals, increased skin conductance responses significantly and increased ratings of tension, approaching significance. In addition, two "defensive" soundtracks, one focusing on denial and the other on intellectualization, significantly reduced skin conductance during portions of the film. Neither of these defensive soundtracks reduced self-reports of reactions related to anxiety or tension, however. In a subsequent study, Lazarus and Alfert (1964) demonstrated that denial instructions were more effective in dampening emotional reactions to the subincision film when they were provided prior to the film than when they accompanied the film in the form of narration. Heart rate was significantly reduced by the denial treatments (as was skin conductance, approaching significance). Although self-reports of tension and anxiety were unaffected by these treatments, the treatments reduced self-reports of depression.

In a related study, Cantor and Wilson (1984) showed that children in their later elementary-school years can cognitively modify their emotional responses to frightening films. In their experiment, 9- to 11-year-olds' self-reports of fear in response to a scene from *The Wizard of Oz* were reduced by instructions to remember that what was being seen was not real, and increased by instructions to imagine themselves in the threatened heroine's situation. The fear responses of 3- to 5-year-olds were largely unaffected by the same instructions, however, and this finding is consistent with the well-documented inability of children in this age group to willingly alter their thought processes (see Flavell, 1963).[3] Dorr et al. (1983) also noted that the tendency to successfully use the "viewer discount" increases with age.

In addition to seeking entertainment, viewers may expose themselves to media for purposes of acquiring information. If information gain is a goal, it would seem that the viewer would pay particular attention to whether or not the events portrayed are real or fictional. Because part of the emotional response to such stimuli might arise from viewers' *anticipations of future consequences to themselves,* depictions of real threats should evoke more fear than dramatic portrayals. Studies of adults have shown that presentations of violent actions that are perceived to have actually happened are far more arousing than depictions of the same actions that are believed to be fiction (Geen, 1975; Geen & Rakosky, 1973). In addition, in their almost exclusive reliance on documentaries as stimulus materials, most of the researchers studying adults' responses to stressful films seem implicitly to endorse the assumption that responses to real incidents will be more intense than responses to fictional events.

---

[3]The effects of cognitive sets on the intensity of emotional responses are discussed here, as they seem necessary to explain the fact that adults' fright reactions to dramatic stimuli do not necessarily extinguish over time. Long-term strategies for reducing emotional reactions to media stimuli, such as through relaxation training (e.g., Falkowski & Steptoe, 1983), or through critical viewing instructions (e.g., Cantor, Sparks, & Hoffner, 1988) are not discussed in this chapter. Research on intervention strategies that are effective for children of different ages is reported in an article by Cantor and Wilson (1988).

Children have also been reported to respond more intensely to real than to fictional events. von Feilitzen (1975) reported that older children were more frightened by documentaries and news programs than by detective stories and horror films. Groebel and Krebs (1983) noted that adolescents were much more frightened by a semidocumentary crime program than by the dramatic series "Kojak," and they attributed the difference to the viewer's knowledge that the events on "Kojak" were not real. There is evidence, however, that younger children are less responsive than older children and adults, to the distinction between real events and fictional portrayals. Himmelweit et al. (1958) remarked that children generally react to events similarly whether they are depicted as part of newsreels or in plays. Moreover, both Himmelweit et al. and Cantor and Sparks (1984) have noted children's relative lack of emotional responsiveness to news broadcasts and documentaries. Young children's general failure to discriminate between real and fictional events may be due to developmental differences in comprehension of the distinction between televised events and real-world happenings (see Hawkins, 1977). The related developmental changes in children's understanding of realistic versus fantastic dramatic content are discussed in a later section.

It might also be argued that because of viewers' concerns about their own future safety, depicted threatening agents that are considered to be proximate or imminent should evoke more fear than remote threats. Himmelweit et al. (1958) argued that one reason crime and detective stories were more frightening than Westerns was that the settings were much "nearer to home." Support for this notion comes from anecdotes regarding the especially intense reactions to *Jaws,* a movie about shark attacks, by people who saw the movie while attempting to enjoy their seaside vacations. Similarly, in a recent experiment (Cantor & Hoffner, 1990), children who thought that the threatening agent depicted in a movie existed in their environment were more frightened by the movie than were children who did not believe that the threat could be found in their local area.

Factors Affecting Emotionality Generally. It is clear from the research reported above that physiological arousal is an important component of viewers' reactions to frightening media. The theory of excitation transfer (e.g., Zillmann, 1971, 1972, 1978) holds that the interoception of excitatory reactions associated with various emotional states is generally nonspecific. It further states that the individual usually does not identify all factors that contribute to an experienced state of excitation, and tends to ascribe his or her entire excitatory reaction to one particular, inducing condition. Experiments testing the role of excitation transfer in responses to emotion-evoking films have demonstrated that excitatory residues from prior arousing experiences can combine with responses to unrelated, subsequently presented movie scenes and thereby intensify emotional reactions to the movie (Cantor, Zillmann, & Bryant, 1975; Zillmann, Mody, & Cantor, 1974). Excitation transfer theory also implies that if two unrelated arousal-inducing conditions occur simultaneously, the excitation produced by one source will tend to intensify emotional responses to the other, unless distraction or other factors prevent the misattribution of arousal (see Girodo & Pellegrini, 1976; Schachter & Singer, 1962).

This reasoning leads to the expectation that factors within a frightening presentation that tend to produce arousal may combine with the depiction of fear-evoking stimuli to increase the viewer's arousal and thus the intensity of the fear experienced while viewing. Producers of frightening movies seem to employ a variety of stylistic devices, in addition to plot elements, in attempting to intensify the audience's fright. Himmelweit et al. (1958) observed that sound effects, particularly music, were considered by children as frightening elements of scary presentations. Consistent with the effectiveness of such devices, Thayer and Levenson (1983) showed that the addition of different types of music to a stressful film could either intensify or reduce the emotional impact of the film, depending on the nature of the music. They found that the addition of "horror music," based on diminished seventh chords and harsh timbres, increased skin conductance reactions to a documentary on industrial accidents, relative to a no-music control; the addition of "documentary" music, composed of a mildly active chord progression based on major seventh chords, significantly reduced skin conductance levels. The addition of music had no significant impact on subjects' self-reports of anxiety, however.

Other studies have investigated the intensification of emotional responses to frightening events through the provision of forewarnings or foreshadowings that the events would occur. Nomikos et al. (1968) reported that skin conductance responses to a version of the industrial accident film in which the upcoming events were foreshadowed early on were more intense than responses to a version in which the events occurred as a surprise. Self-reports of anxiety were not significantly different in the groups that saw the two different versions, however. Cantor, Ziemke, and Sparks (1984) found that adults' emotional responses to disturbing events in a horror film were intensified by verbal forewarnings of the events to come. Subjects who heard an explicit forewarning rated themselves as significantly more frightened and more upset than did those who received no forewarning. The findings of both of these studies are consistent with the reasoning that the physiological arousal produced by the anticipation of the upsetting events intensified emotional responses to the events when they occurred. A recent study by Hoffner and Cantor (1990) confirmed that forewarning of upcoming threats in a film sequence increases anticipatory fear in children. It has also recently been demonstrated (Sparks, 1989), however, that the effects of forewarning may differ as a function of the viewer's preferred style of coping.

DEVELOPMENTAL DIFFERENCES IN FRIGHT RESPONSES TO MEDIA PRODUCTIONS

It should be recognized from the previous discussion that responses to the mediated depiction of frightening stimuli and events will depend to some extent on characteristics of the viewer. Some researchers have reported that specific personality characteristics, such as sensation seeking or the Machiavellian trait of "deceit" are positively associated with liking for scary media (e.g., Sparks, 1986a; Tamborini, Stiff, & Zillmann, 1987). Others have found that personality factors such as "trait anxiety," or preferred coping style are correlated with emotional responses to frightening media fare (e.g., Girodo & Pellegrini, 1976; Kamen, 1971; Sparks, 1989; Sparks & Spirek, 1988), although several studies have reported inconsistent relationships between personality variables and such responses (e.g., Koriat et al., 1972).

Over and above specific personality variables, chronological age is an extremely important viewer characteristic determining emotional reactions to frightening media. This is not to say that children at certain ages are more responsive to media stimuli in general, but that developmental differences are important determinants of the types of media stimuli and events that will produce fright.

The expectation of developmental differences is based on several factors. First, research shows that there are consistent developmental trends in the real-world stimuli and issues that evoke fear (e.g., Angelino, Dollins, & Mech, 1956; Maurer, 1965), and such differences should be reflected in responses to mediated depictions. Second, perceptions of danger will depend in some cases on world knowledge or experience. Although an attacking animal might be feared automatically because it provides what Bowlby (1973) referred to as "natural cues" to danger, such as rapid approach, sudden or strange movement, and loud noise, a certain degree of knowledge is necessary to fear such awesome threats as nuclear weapons or the disease AIDS.

A third reason to expect age differences derives from the fact that the perception of stimuli and the comprehension of event sequences are involved, in varying degrees, in the viewer's response. Therefore, developmental differences in information-processing tendencies related to media viewing (see Collins, 1983; Wartella, 1979) should affect the nature and intensity of fright responses to specific depictions. Finally, it was argued earlier that certain complex cognitive operations are involved in fright reactions to some types of media stimuli, and the ability to perform such operations is limited in very young viewers and improves throughout childhood. It was reported earlier, for example, that older elementary school children but not preschool children empathized with a protagonist's fear (Wilson & Cantor, 1985) and adopted cognitive sets that influenced the intensity of their fright responses (Cantor & Wilson, 1984).

Developmental differences in cognitive processing are thus expected to affect media-induced fright in a variety of ways. The remainder of this chapter discusses two aspects of cognitive development that have been shown to have important implications for children's fright reactions to mass media: (a) the comprehension of fantasy-reality distinctions, and (b) perceptual versus conceptual processing.

Developmental Differences Influencing Fright Reactions

Systematic differences have been observed in the predominant sources of fear in children of different ages. According to a variety of studies using diverse methodologies, children from approximately 3 to 8 years of age are frightened primarily by animals, the dark, supernatural beings, such as ghosts, monsters, and witches, and by anything that looks strange or moves suddenly. The fears of 9- to 12-year-olds are more often related to personal injury and physical destruction and the injury and death of relatives. Adolescents continue to fear personal injury and physical destruction, but school fears and social fears arise at this age, as do fears regarding political, economic, and global issues (see Cantor, Wilson, & Hoffner, 1986, for review).

Comprehension of Fantasy-Reality Distinction. The data on trends in children's fears suggest that very young children are more likely than older children and adolescents to fear things that are not real, in the sense that their occurrence in the real world is impossible (e.g., monsters). The development of more "mature" fears seems to presuppose the acquisition of knowledge regarding the objective dangers posed by different situations. One important component of this knowledge includes an understanding of the distinction between reality and fantasy. Much research has been conducted on the child's gradual acquisition of the various components of the fantasy–reality distinction (see Flavell, 1963; Kelly, 1981; Morison & Gardner, 1978). Until a child understands the distinction, he or she will be unable to understand that something that is not real cannot pose a threat, and thus, the reality or fantasy status of a media depiction should have little effect on the fear it evokes. As the child comes increasingly to understand this distinction and increasingly appreciates the implications of real-world threats, depictions of real dangers should gain in fear-evoking potential relative to depictions of fantasy dangers.

In an earlier section of this chapter, it was reported that younger children were less responsive than older children and adults to whether they were viewing real events or dramatic portrayals (Himmelweit et al., 1958; Cantor & Sparks, 1984). Research has also demonstrated that in responding to media drama, older children are more influenced than younger children by whether the depicted events are realistic vs. fantastic. In Cantor and Sparks' (1984) survey, parents of children in different age groups (preschool, first, and fourth grade) were asked to report on the mass media stimuli and events that had evoked the most intense fear responses in their children. As expected, the tendency to mention fantasy offerings, depicting events that could not possibly occur in the real world, decreased as the child's age increased, and the tendency to mention fictional offerings, depicting events that might possibly occur, increased with the child's age. Sparks (1986b) replicated this study, using children's self-reports rather than parents' observations, and reported similar findings. Both surveys included controls for possible differences in exposure patterns in the different age groups.

It seems that the only controlled study that compared children's and adults' fright responses to the same presentation is a survey of parents' perceptions of their own and their children's fright responses to the televised nuclear holocaust film *The Day After* (Cantor et al., 1986). Consistent with the notion that comprehension of the extent of the *real threat* posed by nuclear war increases with age and is not fully developed until adulthood, this survey found that the intensity of fright responses increased with the age of the child and was highest among the adults.

Perceptual Versus Conceptual Processing. As suggested earlier, visually grotesque stimuli form a major component of frightening films. Many people seem to find the unwelcome return of ghastly images to be a particularly enduring side-effect of exposure to this type of presentation (Horowitz, 1970). A consideration of developmental changes in children's fears and in children's information-processing tendencies leads to the expectation that grotesque media images should have the most intense effects on the youngest children.

A review of the trends in children's fears suggests that fears in young children derive largely from the direct or mediated experience of perceptually salient stimuli (e.g., animals, monsters). The fears of older elementary-school children are characterized by objectively dangerous events that have strong perceptual components when they occur (e.g., kidnapping, accidents, natural disasters), but the fears seem to derive from the anticipation that the events might occur, more often than from the experience of the dangers themselves. The fears of adolescents become even more abstract and diverse (exams, dating, war) and involve the threat of psychological as well as physical harm.

Research on cognitive development indicates that, in general, very young children react to stimuli predominantly in terms of their perceptible characteristics and that with increasing maturity, they respond more and more to the conceptual aspects of stimuli. Piaget referred to young children's tendency to react to things as they appear in immediate, egocentric perception as *concreteness* of thought (see Flavell, 1963); Bruner (1966) characterized the thought of preschool children as *perceptually dominated.* A variety of studies have shown that young children tend to sort, match, and remember items in terms of their perceptible attributes, and that around the age of 7 this tendency is increasingly replaced by the tendency to use functional or conceptual groupings (e.g., Birch & Bortner, 1966; Melkman, Tversky, & Baratz, 1981).

The notion of a developmental shift from perceptual to conceptual processing leads to the expectation that young children will be the most responsive to visually grotesque characters, such as monsters, and that the tendency to be frightened by such stimuli will decrease with age. There are several studies of media-induced fears that are consistent with this expectation. In the surveys by Cantor and Sparks (1984) and Sparks (1986b), the presentations that were mentioned as frightening younger children significantly more often than older children involved visually grotesque, fantastic creatures—the adventure series "The Incredible Hulk," the movie *The Wizard of Oz,* and the music video "Thriller."

Young children's intense fright reactions to "The Incredible Hulk" seem particularly relevant to the notion of perceptual dependence. Cantor and Sparks' (1984) survey produced the surprising finding that 40% of the parents of preschool-aged children spontaneously mentioned this series as a mass media presentation that had upset their child. This program was generally not considered frightening by parents, and to many of them, the intensity of the preschoolers' responses was puzzling.

The series involves a normal-looking hero who, when in danger, undergoes a physical transformation into a grotesque, green-faced monster with superhuman powers (the Hulk), who continues to be benevolently motivated in spite of his menacing appearance. Based on the notion that preschool children are perceptually dependent, Sparks and Cantor (1986) reasoned that the intense levels of fear among children of this age were produced in response to the presence of the grotesque Hulk character. Consistent with this reasoning, they observed that preschool children's self-reports of fear while watching this program were significantly higher after the hero was transformed into his monstrous state than before the transformation. Also as expected, older elementary-school children reported significantly more fear before the transformation, when the hero was in danger, than after it, when the Hulk was successfully averting the threat.

In an experiment designed to assess the impact of immediately perceptible cues more directly, Hoffner and Cantor (1985) produced four versions of a videotaped story about an old woman, by manipulating her appearance (attractive and grandmotherly vs. ugly and witchlike) and her behavior (kind vs. cruel). Children in three age groups (3–5, 6–7, and 9–10 years) were exposed to the different versions of the story and rated their perceptions of the old woman, their predictions of her future behavior, and their own fear responses. Based on considerations of perceptual dependence, it was predicted that the youngest children would be the most strongly affected by the character's appearance and that this effect would decrease as the age of the groups increased. It was further predicted that the youngest children would be the least affected by the protagonist's behavior, and that the effect of this variable would increase with age. The findings regarding fear were nonsignificant, apparently due to the fact that none of the versions were considered very frightening. However, subjects' ratings of how nice or mean the protagonist was, and their predictions of whether she would be generous or hostile to children who wandered into her home, were consistent with expectations. A second study, in which subjects were shown still photographs of the protagonist but given no information about her behavior, showed that children in the three age groups were equally responsive to her appearance in rating her personality and in predicting her future actions.

The two studies suggest that older children are as likely as younger children to engage in physical appearance stereotyping. However, older children attach relatively less weight to physical appearance when other, less perceptually salient but more objectively relevant information is presented at the same time.

The observed developmental differences in fright reactions to "The Day After" (Cantor et al., 1986), seem also to be relevant to developmental changes in perceptual versus conceptual processing. The general lack of responsiveness of young children to this movie may derive, in part, from the abstract and conceptual nature of the threat of nuclear annihilation. Relatively few visual displays of graphic destruction and injury are included in the movie. The major sources of fear seem to be based on shortages of food, radiation sickness, and, ultimately, the end of civilization as we know it, and these dangers are conveyed mainly through the dialog and emotional reactions of the characters.

The increase of fear reactions to "The Day After" with increasing age seems not to have been expected by organizations such as Educators for Social Responsibility, and many school systems, which urged that children under the age of 12 not be permitted to watch the movie (Schofield & Pavelchak, 1985). Blumer (1933) noted that adults often are unable to visualize how the child's mind and feelings may react to media depictions. The research cited here supports the contention that developmental issues in perception, comprehension, and interpretation must be taken into account in understanding and predicting children's media-induced fright reactions.

SUMMARY AND CONCLUSIONS

This chapter has summarized research indicating that adults and children often experience anxiety and distress while watching mass media productions and that these feelings, in varying intensities, sometimes linger on after exposure. Although these reactions tend to be of negative hedonic tone, the research shows that many people like frightening presentations and that the capacity of such fare to produce fear may be part of their appeal.

An explanation has been proposed to account for the fact that media productions often induce anxiety and fear when the viewer, objectively speaking, is in no immediate danger. It has been argued that through stimulus generalization, stimuli and events that would evoke fear if encountered live produce fear when depicted in the media. The major stimuli and events producing fear in media presentations have been categorized as dangers, injuries, distortions, and the endangerment and fear experienced by others. These categories of stimuli are prevalent in both fictional "horror" shows and in realistic "stressful" documentaries.

The notion of stimulus generalization has further been employed to predict that various types of similarity between real-life fear-evokers and media stimuli will enhance fright reactions to media depictions. But stimulus generalization alone has been found to be an inadequate explanation because it leads to the expectation that media-induced fear responses will extinguish over time. Viewers' various motivations for exposure, such as for entertainment and arousal or for information gain have been proposed as important modifying factors. Elements within a media presentation that affect emotionality generally have also been discussed as influential. Finally, it has been proposed that cognitive developmental factors are important in determining the intensity of fear evoked in children by media stimuli.

The findings of surveys and experiments regarding the effects of dramatic media productions as well as realistic documentaries have been discussed in support of these speculations.

A Note on Directions for Future Research

It is evident from this review of research that there are many gaps in our knowledge of media-induced fright reactions. A multitude of variations in media content and stylistic elements remain to be explored, as they interact with a variety of viewer characteristics. In addition, although many observers have speculated about the effects on fear of characteristics of the viewing situation, this area has not been examined in a systematic fashion.

One area that particularly warrants further inquiry regards the longer term implications of frightening presentations. Although it did not specifically involve long-term effects, a recent experiment (Cantor & Omdahl, in press) is suggestive of potential longer term influences. In this study, exposure to dramatized depictions of a deadly house fire or a drowning increased children's self-reports of worry about similar events in their own lives. In addition, these fictional depictions affected the children's preferences for normal, everyday activities: Children who had seen a movie depicting a drowning showed less willingness to go canoeing than other children; those who had seen the program about a house fire were less eager to build a fire in a fireplace.

Research on long-term effects may be especially valuable because some variables may have more pronounced long-term than short-term effects, and the observation of effects occurring with differential delays may provide important insights into the phenomenon of media-induced fear. Heisler (1975) observed, for example, that although state anxiety was elevated immediately after viewing *The Exorcist* and had returned to base level after 1 week, other effects such as increased fearfulness that an intruder would break into the home and enhanced sensitivity to strange noises around the house, were not observed until a week to a month after exposure. It may be, for example, that the degree to which a liked protagonist is threatened has a greater influence on immediate than on long-term reactions. In contrast, the perceived similarity between aspects of the depicted situation and one's own environment might be likely to influence the viewer at a later time rather than during exposure.

ACKNOWLEDGMENTS

Much of the research reported herein was supported by Grant MH 35320 from the National Institute of Mental Health and by grants from the Graduate School of the University of Wisconsin. My thanks to Cynthia Hoffner for her helpful input and comments.

REFERENCES

Angelino, H., Dollins, J., & Mech, E. V. (1956). Trends in the "fears and worries" of school children as related to socio-economic status and age. *Journal of Genetic Psychology, 89,* 263-276.

Averill, J. R., Malmstrom, E. J., Koriat, A., & Lazarus, R. S. (1972). Habituation to complex emotional stimuli. *Journal of Abnormal Psychology, 1,* 20-28.

Berger, S. M. (1962). Conditioning through vicarious instigation. *Psychological Review, 69*, 450-466.

Bettelheim, B. (1975). *The uses of enchantment: The meaning and importance of fairy tales.* New York: Vintage Books.

Birch, H. B., & Bortner, M. (1966). Stimulus competition and category usage in normal children. *Journal of Genetic Psychology, 109*, 195-204.

Blumer, H. (1933). *Movies and conduct.* New York: Macmillan.

Bowlby, J. (1973). *Separation: Anxiety and anger.* New York: Basic Books.

Boyle, G. J. (1984). Effects of viewing a road trauma film on emotional and motivational factors. *Accident Analysis and Prevention, 16*, 383-386.

Bruner, J. S. (1966). On cognitive growth I & II. In J. S. Bruner, R. R. Oliver, & P. M. Greenfield (Eds.), *Studies in cognitive growth* (pp. 1-67). New York: Wiley.

Buzzuto, J. C. (1975). Cinematic neurosis following *The Exorcist. Journal of Nervous and Mental Disease, 161*, 43-48.

Cantor, J., & Hoffner, C. (1990). Children's fear reactions to a televised film as a function of perceived immediacy of depicted threat. *Journal of Broadcasting and Electronic Media.*

Cantor, J., & Omdahl, B. (in press). Effects of dramatized depictions of realistic threats on children's emotional responses, expectations, worries, and liking for related activities. *Communication Monographs.*

Cantor, J., & Reilly, S. (1982). Adolescents' fright reactions to television and films. *Journal of Communication, 32*(1), 87-99.

Cantor, J., & Sparks, G. G. (1984). Children's fear responses to mass media: Testing some Piagetian predictions. *Journal of Communication, 34*(2), 90-103.

Cantor, J., Sparks, G. G., & Hoffner, C. (1988). Calming children's television fears: Mr. Rogers vs. the Incredible Hulk. *Journal of Broadcasting & Electronic Media, 32*, 271-288.

Cantor, J., & Wilson, B. J. (1984). Modifying fear responses to mass media in preschool and elementary school children. *Journal of Broadcasting, 28*, 431-443.

Cantor, J., & Wilson, B. J. (1988). Helping children cope with frightening media presentations. *Current Psychology: Research & Reviews, 7*, 58-75.

Cantor, J., Wilson, B. J., & Hoffner, C. (1986). Emotional responses to a televised nuclear holocaust film. *Communication Research, 13*, 257-277.

Cantor, J., Ziemke, D., & Sparks, G. G. (1984). Effect of forewarning on emotional responses to a horror film. *Journal of Broadcasting, 28*, 21-31.

Cantor, J., Zillmann, D., & Bryant, J. (1975). Enhancement of experienced sexual arousal in response to erotic stimuli through misattribution of unrelated residual excitation. *Journal of Personality and Social Psychology, 32*, 69-75.

Cantril, H. (1940). *The invasion from Mars: A study in the psychology of panic.* Princeton, NJ: Princeton University Press.

Collins, W. A. (1983). Interpretation and inference in children's television viewing. In J. Bryant & D. R. Anderson (Eds.), *Children's understanding of television* (pp, 125-150). New York: Academic Press.

Comstock, G. A., & Rubinstein, E. A. (Eds.). (1972). *Television and social behavior.* Washington, DC: U.S. Government Printing Office.

Davidson, P. O., & Hiebert, S. F. (1971). Relaxation training, relaxation instruction, and repeated exposure to a stressor film. *Journal of Abnormal Psychology, 78*, 154-159.

Dorr, A. (1980). When I was a child I thought as a child. In S. B. Withey & R. P. Abeles (Eds.). *Television and social behavior: Beyond violence and children* (pp. 191-230). Hillsdale, NJ: Lawrence Erlbaum Associates.

Dorr, A., Doubleday, C., & Kovaric, P. (1983). Emotions depicted on and stimulated by television programs. In M. Meyer (Ed.), *Children and the formal features of television* (pp. 97-143). New York: K. G. Saur.

Dysinger, W. S., & Ruckmick, C. A. (1933). *The emotional responses of children to the motion picture situation.* New York: Macmillan.

Eisenberg, A. L. (1936). *Children and radio programs*. New York: Columbia University Press.

Falkowski, J., & Steptoe, A. (1983). Biofeedback-assisted relaxation in the control of reactions to a challenging task and anxiety-provoking film. *Behavior Research and Therapy, 21,* 161-167.

Feilitzen, C., von (1975). Findings of Scandinavian research on child television in the process of socialization. *Fernsehen und Bildung, 9,* 54-84.

Feshbach, N. D. (1982). Sex differences in empathy and social behavior in children. In N. Eisenberg (Ed.), *The development of prosocial behavior* (pp. 315-338). New York: Academic Press.

Flavell, J. (1963). *The developmental psychology of Jean Piaget*. New York: Van Nostrand.

Geen, R. G. (1975). The meaning of observed violence: Real vs. fictional violence and consequent effects on aggression and emotional arousal. *Journal of Research in Personality, 9,* 270-281.

Geen, R. G., & Rakosky, J. J. (1973). Interpretations of observed violence and their effects on GSR. *Journal of Experimental Research in Personality, 6,* 289-292.

Gerbner, G., Gross, L., Morgan, M. & Signorielli, N. (1986). Living with television: The dynamics of the cultivation process. In J. Bryant & D. Zillmann (Eds.), *Perspectives on media effects* (pp. 17-40). Hillsdale, NJ: Lawrence Erlbaum Associates.

Girodo, M., & Pellegrini, W. (1976). Exercise-produced arousal, film-induced arousal and attribution of internal state. *Perceptual and Motor Skills, 42,* 931-935.

Groebel, J., & Krebs, D. (1983). A study of the effects of television on anxiety. In C. D. Spielberger & R. Diaz-Guerrero (Eds.), *Cross-cultural anxiety* (Vol. 2, pp. 89-98). New York: Hemisphere.

Gunter, B., & Furnham, A. (1984). Perceptions of television violence: Effects of programme genre and type of violence on viewers' judgements of violent portrayals. *British Journal of Social Psychology, 23,* 155-164.

Hare, R. D., & Blevings, G. (1975). Defensive responses to phobic stimuli. *Biological Psychology, 3,* 1-13.

Hawkins, R. P. (1977). The dimensional structure of children's perceptions of television reality. *Communication Research, 4,* 299-320.

Hawkins, R. P., & Pingree, S. (1982). Television's influence on social reality. In D. Pearl, L. Bouthilet, & J. Lazar (Eds.), *Television and behavior: Ten years of scientific progress and implications for the eighties* (Vol. 2, pp. 224-247). DHHS Publication No. ADM 82-1196. Washington, DC: US Government Printing Office.

Hebb, D. O. (1946). On the nature of fear. *Psychological Review, 53,* 259-276.

Heisler, G. H. (1975). The effects of vicariously experiencing supernational-violent events: A case study of *The Exorcist*'s impact. *Journal of Individual Psychology, 31,* 158-170.

Hess, R. D., & Goldman, H. (1962). Parents' views of the effects of television on their children. *Child Development, 33,* 411-426.

Hilgard, E. R., Atkinson, R. C., & Atkinson, R. L. (1971). *Introduction to psychology*. New York: Harcourt Brace Jovanovich.

Himmelweit, H. T., Oppenheim, A. N., & Vince, P. (1958). *Television and the child*. London: Oxford University Press.

Hoffman, M. L. (1978). Toward a theory of empathic arousal and development. In M. Lewis & L. A. Rosenblum (Eds.), *The development of affect* (pp. 227-256). New York: Plenum.

Hoffner, C., & Cantor, J. (1985). Developmental differences in responses to a television character's appearance and behavior. *Developmental Psychology, 21,* 1065-1074.

Hoffner, C., & Cantor, J. (1990). Forewarning of a threat and prior knowledge of outcome: Effects on children's emotional responses to a film sequence. *Human Communication Research, 16,* 323-354.

Horowitz, M. J. (1970). *Image formation and cognition*. London: Appleton-Century-Crofts.

Horowitz, M. J. (1976). *Stress response syndromes*. New York: Appleton-Century-Crofts.

Izard, C. E. (1977). *Human emotions*. New York: Plenum Press.

Jersild, A. T., & Holmes, F. B. (1935). Methods of overcoming children's fears. *Journal of Psychology, 1,* 75-104.

Johnson, B. R. (1980). General occurrence of stressful reactions to commercial motion pictures and elements in films subjectively identified as stressors. *Psychological Reports, 47,* 775-786.

Kamen, G. B. (1971). A second look at the effects of a stress-producing film on adult test performance. *Journal of Clinical Psychology, 27,* 465-467.

Kase, J., Sikes, S., & Spielberger, C. (1978). Emotional reactions to frightening and neutral scenes in story theatre. *Communication Monographs, 45,* 181-186.

Kelly, H. (1981). Reasoning about realities: Children's evaluations of television and books. In H. Kelly & H. Gardner (Eds.), *Viewing children through television* (pp. 59-71). San Francisco: Jossey-Bass.

Koriat, A., Melkman, R., Averill, J. R., & Lazarus, R. S. (1972). The self-control of emotional reactions to a stressful film. *Journal of Personality, 40,* 601-619.

Lazarus, R. S. (1966). *Psychological stress and the coping process.* New York: McGraw-Hill.

Lazarus, R. S., & Alfert, E. (1964). Short-circuiting of threat by experimentally altering cognitive appraisal. *Journal of Abnormal and Social Psychology, 69,* 195-205.

Lazarus, R. S., Speisman, J. C., Mordkoff, A. M., & Davidson, L. A. (1962). A laboratory study of psychological stress produced by a motion picture film. *Psychological Monographs: General and Applied, 76*(34), Whole No. 553.

Leishman, K. (1981, January 10). When is television too scary for children? *TV Guide,* pp. 5-6, 8.

Lyle, J., & Hoffman, H. R. (1972). Children's use of television and other media. In E. A. Rubinstein, G. A. Comstock, & J. P. Murray (Eds.), *Television and social behavior* (Vol. 4., pp. 129-256). Washington, DC: U.S. Government Printing Office.

Lyle, J., & Hoffman, H. R. (1976). Explorations in patterns of television viewing by preschool-age children. In R. Brown (Ed.), *Children and television* (pp. 45-61). Beverly Hills, CA: Sage.

Mathai, J. (1983). An acute anxiety state in an adolescent precipitated by viewing a horror movie. *Journal of Adolescence, 6,* 197-200.

Maurer, A. (1965). What children fear. *Journal of Genetic Psychology, 106,* 265-277.

Melkman, R., Tversky, B., & Baratz, D. (1981). Developmental trends in the use of perceptual and conceptual attributes in grouping, clustering and retrieval. *Journal of Experimental Child Psychology, 31,* 470-486.

Morison, P., & Gardner, H. (1978). Dragons and dinosaurs: The child's capacity to differentiate fantasy from reality. *Child Development, 49,* 642-648.

Noble, G. (1975). *Children in front of the small screen.* Beverly Hills, CA: Sage.

Nomikos, M., Opton, E., Averill, J., & Lazarus, R. (1968). Surprise versus suspense in the production of stress reaction. *Journal of Personality and Social Psychology, 8,* 204-208.

Osborn, D. K., & Endsley, R. C. (1971). Emotional reactions of young children to tv violence. *Child Development, 42,* 321-331.

Palmer, E. L., Hockett, A. B., & Dean, W. W. (1983). The television family and children's fright reactions. *Journal of Family Issues, 4,* 279-292.

Pavlov, I. P. (1927). *Conditioned reflexes* (G. V. Anrep, Trans.). London: Oxford University Press.

Pearl, D., Bouthilet, L., & Lazar, J. (Eds.). (1982). *Television and behavior: Ten years of scientific progress and implications for the eighties.* (DHHS Publication No. ADM 82-1196). Washington, DC: U.S. Government Printing Office.

Pillard, R. C., Atkinson, K. W., & Fisher, S. (1967). The effect of different preparations on film-induced anxiety. *Psychological Record, 17,* 35-41.

Pillard, R. C., Carpenter, J., Atkinson, K. W., & Fisher, S. (1966). Palmar sweat prints and self-ratings as measures of film-induced anxiety. *Perceptual and Motor Skills, 23,* 771-777.

Preston, M. I. (1941). Children's reactions to movie horrors and radio crime. *Journal of Pediatrics, 19,* 147-168.

Razran, G. (1949). Stimulus generalization of conditioned responses. *Psychological Bulletin, 46,* 337-365.

Sapolsky, B. S., & Zillmann, D. (1978). Experience and empathy: Affective reactions to witnessing childbirth. *Journal of Social Psychology, 105,* 131-144.

Sarafino, E. P. (1986). *The fears of childhood: A guide to recognizing and reducing fearful states in children.* New York: Human Sciences Press.

Schachter, S., & Singer, J. (1962). Cognitive, social, and physiological determinants of emotional state. *Psychological Review, 69,* 379-399.

Schofield, J., & Pavelchak, M. (1985). *The Day After:* The impact of a media event. *American Psychologist, 40,* 542-548.

Schramm, W., Lyle, J., & Parker, E. P. (1961). *Television in the lives of our children.* Stanford, CA: Stanford University Press.

Selman, R. L., & Byrne, D. (1978). A structural analysis of levels of role-taking in middle childhood. *Child Development, 45,* 803-807.

Singer, J. L. (1975). *Daydreaming and fantasy.* London: Allen & Unwin.

Smetak, J. R. (1986). Steven Spielberg: Gore, guts, and PG-13. *Journal of Popular Film and Television, 14*(1), 4-13.

Sparks, G. G. (1986a). Developing a scale to assess cognitive responses to frightening films. *Journal of Broadcasting and Electronic Media, 30,* 65-73.

Sparks, G. G. (1986b). Developmental differences in children's reports of fear induced by the mass media. *Child Study Journal, 16,* 55-66.

Sparks, G. G. (1989). Understanding emotional reactions to a suspenseful movie: The interaction between forewarning and preferred coping style. *Communication Monographs, 56,* 325-340.

Sparks, G. G., & Cantor, J. (1986). Developmental differences in fright responses to a television program depicting a character transformation. *Journal of Broadcasting and Electronic Media, 30,* 309-323.

Sparks, G. G., & Spirek, M. M. (1988). Individual differences in coping with stressful mass media: An activation-arousal view. *Human Communication Research, 15,* 195-216.

Speisman, J. C., Lazarus, R. S., Mordkoff, A., & Davidson, L. (1964). Experimental reduction of stress based on ego-defense theory. *Journal of Abnormal and Social Psychology, 68,* 367-380.

Stein, E. (1982, June 20). Have horror films gone too far? *New York Times,* Arts & Leisure sect., pp. 1, 21-22.

Surbeck, E. (1975). Young children's emotional reactions to T.V. violence: The effects of children's perceptions of reality. *Dissertation Abstracts International, 35,* 5139-A.

Tamborini, R., Stiff, J., & Zillmann, D. (1987). Preference for graphic horror featuring male versus female victimization: Personality and past film viewing experiences. *Human Communication Research, 13*(4), 529-552.

Tannenbaum, P. H. (1980). Entertainment as vicarious emotional experience. In P. H. Tannenbaum (Ed.), *The entertainment functions of television* (pp. 107-131). Hillsdale, NJ: Lawrence Erlbaum Associates.

Tannenbaum, P. H., & Gaer, E. P. (1965). Mood change as a function of stress of protagonist and degree of identification in a film-viewing situation. *Journal of Personality and Social Psychology, 2,* 612-616.

Thayer, J. F., & Levenson, R. W. (1983). Effects of music on psychophysiological responses to a stressful film. *Psychomusicology, 3,* 44-52.

Wall, W. D., & Simson, W. A. (1950). The emotional responses of adolescent groups to certain films. *British Journal of Educational Psychology, 20,* 153-163.

Wartella, E. (1979). The developmental perspective. In E. Wartella (Ed.), *Children communicating: Media and development of thought, speech, understanding* (pp. 1-19). Beverly Hills, CA: Sage.

Weiss, B. W., Katkin, E. S., & Rubin, B. M. (1968). Relationship between a factor analytically derived measure of a specific fear and performance after related fear induction. *Journal of Abnormal Psychology, 73,* 461-463.

Wertham, F. (1953). *Seduction of the innocent.* New York: Rinehart.

Wilson, B. J., & Cantor, J. (1985). Developmental differences in empathy with a television protagonist's fear. *Journal of Experimental Child Psychology, 39,* 284-299.

Wilson, B. J., & Cantor, J. (1987). Reducing children's fear reactions to mass media: Effects of visual exposure and verbal explanation. In M. McLaughlin, (Ed.), *Communication yearbook 10* (pp. 553-573). Beverly Hills, CA: Sage.

Wilson, B. J., Hoffner, C., & Cantor, J. (1987). Children's perceptions of the effectiveness of techniques to reduce fear from mass media. *Journal of Applied Developmental Psychology, 8,* 39-52.

Yerkes, R. M., & Yerkes, A. W. (1936). Nature and conditions of avoidance (fear) response in chimpanzee. *Journal of Comparative Psychology, 21,* 53-66.

Zill, N. (1977). *National survey of children: Summary of preliminary results.* New York: Foundation for Child Development.

Zillmann, D. (1971). Excitation transfer in communication-mediated aggressive behavior. *Journal of Experimental Social Psychology, 7,* 419-434.

Zillmann, D. (1972). The role of excitation in aggressive behavior. In *Proceedings of the Seventeenth International Congress of Applied Psychology, 1971.* Brussels: Editest.

Zillmann, D. (1978). Attribution and misattribution of excitatory reactions. In J. H. Harvey, W. Ickes, & R. F. Kidd (Eds.), *New directions in attribution research* (Vol. 2, pp. 335-368). Hillsdale, NJ: Lawrence Erlbaum Associates.

Zillmann, D. (1980). Anatomy of suspense. In P. H. Tannenbaum, (Ed.), *The entertainment functions of television* (pp. 133-163). Hillsdale, NJ: Lawrence Erlbaum Associates.

Zillmann, D. (1982). Television viewing and arousal. In D. Pearl, L. Bouthilet, & J. Lazar (Eds.), *Television and behavior: Ten years of scientific progress and implications for the eighties* (Vol 2, pp. 53-67). DHHS Publication No. ADM 82-1196. Washington, DC: U.S. Government Printing Office.

Zillmann, D., & Cantor, J. (1976). A disposition theory of humor and mirth. In A. J. Chapman & H. C. Foot (Eds.), *Humor and laughter: Theory, research, and applications* (pp. 93-115). London: Wiley.

Zillmann, D., & Cantor, J. (1977). Affective responses to the emotions of a protagonist. *Journal of Experimental Social Psychology, 13,* 155-165.

Zillmann, D., Hay, T. A., & Bryant, J. (1975). The effect of suspense and its resolution on the appreciation of dramatic presentations. *Journal of Research in Personality, 9,* 307-323.

Zillmann, D., Mody, B., & Cantor, J. (1974). Empathetic perception of emotional displays in films as a function of hedonic and excitatory state prior to exposure. *Journal of Research in Personality, 8,* 335-349.

Zillmann, D., Weaver, J. B., Mundorf, N., & Aust, C. F. (1986). Effects of an opposite-gender companion's affect to horror on distress, delight, and attraction. *Journal of Personality and Social Psychology, 51,* 586-594.

Zoglin, R. (1984, June 25). Gremlins in the rating system. *Time,* p. 78.

CHAPTER

8

Online and Offline Assessment of the Television Audience

Daniel R. Anderson
Diane E. Field
University of Massachusetts

Every day millions of Americans spend time at home with television. In a typical viewing session they enter a TV viewing area, turn on the TV if it is not already on, look at the television for some period of time, look away, and look back again. They may leave the viewing area and then return. They may engage in a variety of concurrent activities ranging from homework to housework to lovemaking to sleeping. They may change the channel, turn off the TV set, or exit the viewing area. Subsequently, TV viewers may remember some of the content and their economic, social, political, and intellectual behavior may be influenced.

This wide range of activity falls roughly under the rubric of "watching TV." Watching TV requires decision processes that lead a person to enter the viewing area and to be exposed to TV programming. Watching TV involves overt and covert attentional activities including accommodating to or ignoring a distracting viewing environment. Watching TV requires comprehension strategies of considerable complexity. Watching TV means choosing programming and eventually deciding to stop watching TV. Given that Americans spend a large portion of their lives in front of TV sets, a scientific understanding of "watching TV" is of considerable utility for a variety of economic and social policy concerns. In this chapter we describe field research with an emphasis on the dynamics of TV viewing as it actually occurs. We contrast that "online" approach to understanding TV viewing to the more usual "offline" approaches that gather information from a variety of sources outside the viewing situation. The online work reviewed in this chapter is field research that employs automated observation equipment. Other sources (e.g., Anderson & Burns, chapter 1, this volume; Anderson

199

& Lorch, 1983; Huston & Wright, 1983; Watt & Welch, 1983) review laboratory-based online research. We first contrast offline and online approaches to audience assessment.

OFFLINE RESEARCH ON TV VIEWING

The industries and institutions that produce television technology, programming, advertising, and instruction must daily make significant practical decisions based on considerations of the television audience. These decisions stem from anecdote, assumption, experience, intuition, and sometimes systematic empirical research about the composition of the audience and the ways they "watch TV." The decisions are not based on a well-structured general theory of TV viewing because such a theory does not exist.

When systematic research-based information is available, it is most frequently obtained offline. Viewers are queried at a time when they are not in the act of watching TV about viewing habits, attitudes, preferences, memories, expectations, and behaviors. In the case of children, parents are often the respondents. The instruments for offline research are questionnaires, comprehension tests, viewing diaries, telephone interviews, focus groups, and others. The results of offline research form much of the basis for evaluating the success of TV programs, for choosing advertising strategies, and for informing national debates about the effects of television on social behavior. Whole industries and professions have sprung up to collect and interpret offline data.

The success of offline research is undeniable. Without offline research, estimating the size and composition of the television audience would be mere guesswork and the very economic basis of commercial broadcast television would (until recently) be doubtful. Offline copy testing and product attitude testing provide major sources of information about the likely success of commercials, and are routinely employed in planning advertising campaigns. The research itself, furthermore, is relatively inexpensive to carry out and can optimally obtain data from a large number of respondents in a matter of days.

Offline research, however, has its problems. The central problem is that the validity of offline instruments is usually unknown. The viewing diary, as employed until very recently by the major TV rating services, is a straightforward example. The primary purpose of the diary is to determine the composition of the television audience at particular times. Viewers are asked to check off each 15-minute interval of each day that they watch TV. They are also asked to indicate to which channels their TVs are tuned and which programs they watched. There have been, however, relatively few systematic attempts to determine the accuracy of viewing diaries, or to determine what kinds of reporting biases are typical. There are claims that diaries may not be wholly accurate. In a study employing video cameras in homes, Bechtel, Achelpohl, and Akers (1972), for example, reported that viewing diaries overestimated actual viewing by about 30%.

We discuss this and other studies in more detail later, but the point is that attempts to validate even the most commonly used offline measure of TV viewing have raised serious questions about its accuracy.

A second problem with offline research is that it is best used to measure relatively enduring behaviors and traits of which the respondent has some conscious awareness. Memory for commercials, product attitudes, and preference for TV programs are typical examples. It is likely, however, that some behaviors or mental processes, such as amount of attention paid to the news, are not fully available to conscious introspection. A third and related problem is that questions employed in offline research instruments require active interpretation by the research subject. A given question may produce different interpretations by different subjects, whereas two questions that attempt to assess the same thing may produce two different interpretations by the same subject.

As examples of these problems, consider some offline research in which we asked parents about their preschool children's television viewing behaviors (Anderson, Alwitt, Lorch, & Levin, 1979). In one part of a questionnaire, we provided an extensive listing of current TV programs and asked the parents to indicate how many minutes per week their children watched each of those programs. In another part of the questionnaire we asked how many hours their children watched TV each morning, afternoon, and evening of each day of the week. The underlying question in both of these measures was the same: How much television did the children watch? Parents consistently estimated greater amounts of viewing by the children when the program list was used (32.7 hours per week) as compared to the other measure (24.3 hours per week). Thus, two different offline measures gave different estimates of behavior from the same respondents. We also asked the parents a number of questions about the age their child consistently started to watch television. Not only did the parents indicate different ages depending on the question, but also, the ages they gave depended on the current age of the child. Parents of older children gave greater ages than parents of younger children. The pattern of results indicated that parents of older children had different criteria for the onset of TV viewing than the parents of the younger children. They had, therefore, different interpretations of the same questions based on their different experiences.

Besides questions of validity and subjects' interpretations of research questions, there are some kinds of information about television viewing that simply cannot be reliably obtained offline. For example, it is doubtful that a person accurately estimates what percentage of time he or she actually looks at the TV screen. It is even more doubtful that the viewer could accurately estimate the frequency of looks at the TV or how long they last. People probably do not know how frequently they leave the viewing room during a night of TV viewing or how long they are gone before they return. Respondents probably do not know how much they listen to the TV or whether they listen more when looking as compared to not looking at the screen. Issues of this sort are best studied by online research techniques involving ongoing moment by moment observation of TV viewing.

ONLINE MEASURES OF TV VIEWING

There has long been a recognition that online measures of TV viewing are desirable and potentially useful. Online methodologies are either "active" insofar as they require some conscious response from the viewer, or "passive" insofar as they record some aspect of the viewing situation with no viewer action required. The most basic passive online technique, used by A.C. Nielsen and by Arbitron for years, is a device that simply records whether a TV set is on and to what channel it is tuned. This simple system has very recently been replaced by the "peoplemeter," a device with which the viewer actively identifies his or her presence in the viewing room by pressing keys.

More sophisticated approaches examine TV viewing itself. An early active measure, developed initially for radio, is the Lazarsfeld–Stanton technique in which people are presented programming and asked to push buttons corresponding to their liking or disliking of the material. The buttons are connected to a device that records when the button pushes occur. Temporal profiles of audience liking for the material are constructed and sometimes used by producers to revise the program material prior to broadcast (Levy, 1982). A similar technique has been used with school-age children by Children's Television Workshop, which employed specially designed portable microcomputers in schools as part of the process of doing formative research for "3-2-1 Contact." There have also been occasional uses of passive online physiological measures such as heartrate, galvanic skin response, voice stress analysis, and derivative measures from electroencephalographic recording. Also employed, especially with children, are ratings of visual orientation toward the television screen, a measure pioneered primarily by Children's Television Workshop (Palmer, 1972). Today, a number of advertising research firms offer services based on many of these online techniques. The general form of these services is to produce a profile of response over the timecourse of the program. Interpretation of the profiles is usually that the program (or commercial) is good (in terms of the measure used) when the response is high and the program is bad when the response is low. One examines the profile and attempts to determine what in the program causes any given peak or valley in the response.

Profiles of online response to programs and commercials assess audience behavior in ways beyond the reach of offline measures. Like many offline measures, however, the validity of these online techniques is usually based more on intuition than on research and established theory. A problem with most online measures is that they are employed in somewhat artificial laboratory settings in which a normal viewing environment is simulated. One cannot know with certainty that the behavior measured in these settings accurately reflects behavior that would occur in a field setting. A small set of online studies have attempted to circumvent this problem. These studies employ automated passive observation equipment in homes.

AUTOMATED ONLINE FIELD STUDIES

An obvious but frequently neglected first step in research is systematic detailed description of the phenomenon in question. There have been few such descriptions of TV viewing, perhaps because TV viewing appears to be such an obvious and transparent behavior. There also may be few such descriptions because truly systematic observation of TV viewing with a large and diverse sample of subjects is a difficult and expensive undertaking. There have been only four automated online field studies on a substantial scale that have attempted to describe home television viewing behavior. These four studies all have in common the installation of film or video equipment in homes, usually with one camera shooting the viewing area and another shooting the TV screen. In each of these studies the equipment would automatically begin recording when the TV set was turned on and stop recording when the TV set was turned off. The two early studies (Allen, 1965; Bechtel et al., 1972) were only briefly and sketchily reported. The third study, our work (Anderson, Field, Collins, Lorch, & Nathan, 1985; Anderson, Lorch, Field, Collins, & Nathan, 1986; Nathan, Anderson, Field, & Collins, 1985), is as yet only partially analyzed, and the fourth, by a British research group, has, at this writing been only informally described in newspaper and magazine articles and unpublished reports (Collett & Lamb, 1986, cited in Gunter & Svennevig, 1987). These studies provide a significant glimpse into the nature of television viewing. An impressive aspect of the studies is that although they were done in different geographic areas, over three decades, the observations from each prove to be very similar. Despite evolving receiver and video production technologies, and despite fads and enduring changes in TV program content, home television viewing behavior appears remarkably constant.

The Allen Study

Allen (1965) published only a brief report of his time-lapse filming of family TV viewing in Oklahoma and Kansas during the early 1960s. He noted that the viewing room contained no people 19% of the time the TV was on. Of the time that viewers were present, he found that individuals were frequently inattentive, with nobody in the room actually looking at the TV 21% of the time. The audience tended to be especially inattentive during the daytime and they engaged in a variety of concurrent activities during TV viewing 25% of the time they were with TV. Children were described as frequently "eating, drinking, dressing, sleeping, playing, and fighting. Often they pay no attention to the TV, and may leave the room for periods varying from one minute to a half hour. As the number of small children in a family increases so does total set-in-use time and 'no audience' time" (p. 5). Adults were also described as frequently inattentive: "Adults eat, drink, sleep, play, argue, fight, and occasionally make love in front of the TV set" (p. 6). Taken together, no audience or an inattentive audience were observed during 52% of set-in-use time in the morning, 47% in the afternoon, and 35% at night. During commercials, these figures were, respectively, 58%, 54%, and 43%.

The Bechtel, Achelpohl, and Akers Study

As part of the Surgeon General's investigation into the effects of television on social behavior in the early 1970s, a field observation study was commissioned. Bechtel et al. (1972) installed video cameras and microphones in the homes of 20 families in Kansas City, Missouri, for 6-day periods. Their sample, methodology, and results were reported in more detail than Allen's (1965) research. Limiting factors, however, included the small sample size and a frequent lack of statistical analysis. Because they reused the videotapes throughout the course of the research, their analyses of viewer behavior were also limited.

As we noted earlier, Bechtel et al. (1972) compared viewing diaries to observed viewing. Importantly, they defined "watching TV" as actually looking at the TV rather than simply being in the same room with a TV set in use. They found that the percent agreement between viewing diaries and observed visual attention ranged from 92% in the best case to 54% in the worst case, with the average agreement being 71.4%. They found underreporting of viewing time was rare (5.5%), whereas overreporting was relatively frequent (24.8%). Unfortunately, Bechtel et al. (1972) do not provide data sufficient to determine whether the underreporting is due to the family members defining "watching TV" as simply being present with a set in use. If so, the families may have accurately reported their presence but not their attention. This, of course, is an example of how research subjects may interpret an offline research instrument in a manner different from the investigator.

As found by Allen (1965), the viewers in the Bechtel et al. (1972) study did not look at the TV all the time it was on. Movies were the most watched programs, such that 76% of the time a movie was on at least one person was looking at it. In descending order, children's shows received the next most attention, 71%; followed by suspense series, 68%; religious programs, 67%; family series, 66%; game shows, 66%; talk shows, 64%, melodramas, 59%; sports events, 59%; news, 55%; and finally, commercials, 55%. These figures can be roughly compared to Allen (1965) who reported 65% for evening programs and 57% for evening commercials. Similar figures have been reported by Anderson et al. (1986), as are described later, and in newspaper reports of the British field studies. The consistency across studies is impressive.

Bechtel et al. (1972) divided their sample into three age groupings: children (1 to 10 years of age), adolescents (11 to 19 years), and adults (20 to 75 years). Overall, the children visually attended 52% of the time they were with TV, the adolescents attended at a level of 69%, and the adults attended at a level of 65%, suggesting to Bechtel et al. an inverted U relationship of attention and age. The investigators noted that women attended less than men. Again, as described later, we found essentially the same age and sex effects (Anderson et al., 1986). Bechtel et al. found that attention to different types of programs, reasonably, varied with the age of the viewer. Children attended most to children's programs (86%) and least to melodrama and sports (8%). Adolescents attended most to suspense programs (84%) and least to sports (43%). Adults looked most at movies (78%) and least at commercials (52%).

Like Allen (1965), Bechtel et al. (1972) observed a good deal of activity concurrent with TV viewing. They found families to be surprisingly sociable while watching TV, with talking the most common activity, followed by eating. They pointed out that viewers come and go while the TV set is on but provided no details on frequency. They also noted distinctive and regular styles of family TV viewing. Again, these observations are consistent with ours.

Bechtel et al. (1972) concluded the report of their observations with a sense similar to that of Allen (1965) of the dynamic complexity of TV viewing:

> The findings point to the fact that television viewing is a complex and various form of behavior intricately interwoven with many other kinds of behavior. It will not be a simple matter to sort out how . . . the interfering behaviors filter out the television stimulus. Clearly, watching television . . . is a mixture with many threads of which the viewer seems only partially aware. (p. 299)

The Anderson et al. Study

We installed time-lapse video cameras in the homes of 99 families from the Springfield, Massachusetts metropolitan area (Anderson et al., 1985). The families all had a child near the fifth birthday (who was the focus of the research effort and was designated the "focus" child) and were, by and large, White and middle class. The families consisted of 272 children ranging in age from infants to 17 years of age and 192 adults from 18 to 62 years of age. Equipment was placed in homes for 10 full days of time-lapse recording. One video frame was recorded each 1.2 seconds that the TV was on, or at a ratio of 1:36. The camera that shot the viewing area was equipped with a wide angle lens with auto-servo iris that allowed it to record in widely varying light levels encountered in homes. The equipment automatically began recording when the TV set was turned on and stopped recording when the TV set was turned off. Over a 20-month period about 4,600 hours of recordings were obtained. Details about the recording procedure may be found in Anderson et al. (1985).

The earlier online field investigations did not include any control groups to assess the effects of having observation equipment in their homes. Therefore, in addition to the families who had observation equipment installed in their homes, the study included three control groups of families who went through all the same procedures but did not get equipment installed homes. These control groups were used to assess the effects of the observation equipment on subject selection and viewing behavior as reported in viewing diaries.

The analyses from this study will be in progress for several years with the results published as a series of papers in research journals. To date, the analyses concern five issues: (a) the effects of the observational equipment itself on subject selection and viewer behavior, (b) accuracy of viewing diaries as compared with observed viewer presence and observed viewer visual attention, (c) viewer distances and visual angles relative to the TV set, (d) age trends in visual attention to TV, and (e) the length of time viewers stay in the room before leaving. Our findings from each of these areas are summarized.

The Effects of Observation Equipment on Subject Selection and Viewer Behavior.   There is a kind of Heisenberg principle inherent in much behavioral science research; the behavioral system being examined may be changed by the very fact that it is being studied. The problem is most extreme, of course, when subjects are aware of the behavior being studied. Research on television viewing would appear to be no exception to this problem. For home observation studies, the major question is whether the behavior observed is different from that which normally occurs without observation. Ultimately, the question is undecidable barring observation procedures which would violate research ethics. We have, nevertheless, some information on the issue. At this point we have compared the experimental families to the control families on a large number of demographic and other measures. We have also compared the viewing reported by the experimental families to viewing reported by the control families (Anderson et al., 1985; Choi, Anderson, Burns, Collins, & Field, 1988).

The results are encouraging. Although a lower percentage of families agreed to participate in the experimental group, the families that did participate were not significantly different from control families on a large number of demographic variables and other measures including attitudes toward television and family stress (Anderson et al., 1985). During the time the observation equipment was installed in the homes of the experimental group, there were no significant differences in reported viewing by the focus 5-year-olds as compared to the control groups (Anderson et al., 1985). For other family members, however, we found that the group with observation equipment reported slightly more viewing than did two of the three control groups. The experimental group also indicated slightly less uncertainty in filling out their diaries (Choi et al., 1988). Taken together, there appeared to be no effects of the observation procedure on subject selection and there were no reported viewing effects for children who were the focus of the research. For other family members, however, the equipment may have induced slightly more time with TV, and slightly more careful diary keeping.

Comparisons Between Viewing Diaries and Observed Viewing.   Our study included as a major goal the comparison of viewing diaries to videotaped observations of TV viewing. The major validation of viewing diaries has been based on coincidental telephone surveys (Beville, 1985). Families are interviewed over the telephone at a randomly selected point during the diary period in order to obtain a report of current TV use. These telephone reports are then compared to the diaries concurrently maintained by the same families. There are several obvious problems with this validation technique. First, there is no guarantee that the phone reports are themselves accurate; biases such as misreporting for prestige reasons are quite possible. Second, there is nothing to prevent respondents from filling in diaries so that they correspond to the telephone reports. Third, it is unlikely that the telephone calls were made late at night or early in the morning, so that diary accuracy during these periods is probably unassessed.

A passive automated observation validation procedure avoids these problems. Because the equipment records all viewing, there are no selective biases. As we have seen, however, the presence of the viewing equipment itself has slight effects on diary keeping (slightly more viewing reported, slightly less uncertainty). The marginal nature of these effects, however, leaves online automated observation the method of choice.

Given these considerations, the Bechtel et al. (1972) study provides some reason to question the validity of viewing diaries insofar as Bechtel et al. found overreporting of viewing. A problem, however, is that Bechtel et al. did not provide sufficient information to settle the question. They found only that families overestimated viewing when the criterion for TV viewing was eyes actually directed toward the TV screen. In particular, they did not determine whether the families may have accurately reported the presence of family members in the viewing room. The diaries may be accurate records of what most people consider to be "watching TV," namely presence in a room with a set in use.

Our viewing diaries were fashioned after those used by the major rating services; the families were asked to indicate during each 15-minute block whether the TV was on, what program was on, and who was present. There were also a number of questions about the viewing behavior of the focus 5-year-olds. We examined the diaries with respect to the focus children separately from the other family members because the parents may have been particularly diligent about maintaining the viewing diaries for these children.

Observers rated the videotapes on a time-sampling basis such that they stopped a tape after each 55 minutes of set-in-use time and noted who was in the room and whether or not each person in the room was looking at the TV. Interobserver agreement was quite high (see Anderson et al., 1985, for details). At this time our analyses compare diaries to the videotapes only in terms of total amount of time that each viewer was present and total amount of time each viewer looked at the TV. In later work we examine the accuracy of the diaries with respect to viewing of specific TV programs.

We found that parents were highly accurate in indicating the "focus" 5-year-olds' presence in the viewing room. On the average, the viewing diaries indicated that the focus children were with television 14.1 hours per week and our observations showed them present 13.4 hours per week. The difference is not significant. The correlation between time the child was present and the time indicated by the diaries was high (.88). Parents accurately maintained viewing diaries for young children when those children were the focus of the research effort. It was quite clear, however, that the parents did not fill out the viewing diaries in terms of whether or not the child was actually paying attention to the TV. The actual observed hours of visual attention by the 5-year-olds was 9.3; this figure was significantly different from the 14.2 hours reported in the diaries. If the criterion for TV viewing had been visual attention to the TV, then the diaries indeed overestimate TV viewing by 53%.

The correlation of total time looking with the diary time, while significant, was reduced (.67). The significant correlation is due to the obvious fact that the more time one spends in the presence of a set in use, the more time one will, in general, look at it. There is, however, no significant correlation between the time 5-year-olds spend with TV and the percent of that time spent visually attending to the TV (−.10). "Heavy" viewers are not more or less likely to look at the TV than "light" viewers, given that they are with TV.

The question remains whether the viewing diaries are accurate for other members of the family who are not the focus of the research effort. The accuracy of the diaries for these family members is probably more like the accuracy of the diaries analyzed by the major TV rating services, since no particular family members are the focus of the diaries. Our analyses indicated that the diary accuracy depended on the age of the family member. Using the age categories employed by the major rating services, we found that the correlations increased with age, with a low of .64 for nonfocus preschoolers to a high of .82 for adults (Choi et al., 1988), as summarized in Fig. 8.1. Again there was little relationship in any age group between percent visual attention and total time spent with TV.

Viewer Distances and Viewing Angles.   Information about viewing distances and viewing angles is relevant to a variety of enterprises including the design of new screen technologies, the design of characters and graphics for videotext displays, as well as for considerations of receiver radiation emissions on viewer health. There has, however, been no previous online study of viewer location. One offline study has been reported (National Center for Radiological Health, 1968). In that study, families in the Washington, DC area were interviewed as to how far viewers typically sat from their TV receivers.

We analyzed the viewing locations of each viewer in a subset of 78 families of our home viewing study (Nathan et al., 1985). Without going into the detailed findings here, we compared our data with those obtained by the National Center for Radiological Health some 14 years earlier. The average distance we found for viewers over 15 years of age (130 inches) was only about 12 inches further than the earlier research, and the average distance for viewers under 15 years (89 inches) was within 4 inches of that found by the earlier research. Again, where

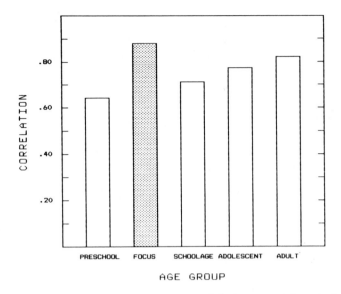

FIG. 8.1.   Correlation between total amount of viewing reported from viewing diaries and time-lapse observation.

a comparison is possible, there is impressive consistency in TV viewing behavior across decades and geographical regions. In this case, online research in the field corresponded well with earlier offline research.

There are two additional points to be made from our analysis of viewer location. The first is that children were much more variable in their viewing position than were adults. This is indirectly illustrated in Fig. 8.2, which shows the percentage of time that viewers of different age groups spend sitting or lying on a chair or couch. Not only do adults view from furniture nearly all the time, but they almost always watch television from exactly the same location. Children, on the other hand, place themselves on the floor about half the time.

The second point to be made from the analysis of viewer location concerns the issue of the visual angle subtended by the screen from the perspective of the viewer. The horizontal visual field is around 180 degrees, but most visual activity makes use of the middle area which consists of the region of parafoveal vision (about 10 degrees around the center horizontally) and the foveal region in the very center of the visual field (about 1.5 degrees horizontally). The parafoveal region allows detection of movement and moderately good resolution of detail and color whereas the foveal region allows extremely fine resolution of detail and color. Figure 8.3 plots the average visual angle subtended by the TV screen for viewers of different age groups. Note that only the children sit close enough to the TV so that part of the image falls outside the parafoveal region, and even they sit so that the screen nicely frames the parafoveal region. Consider an im-

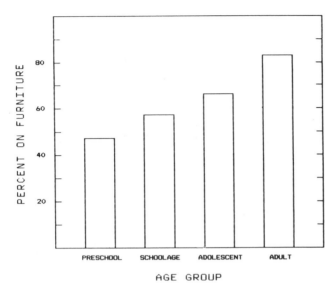

FIG. 8.2.   Percentage of time spent viewing television from furniture as a function of age.

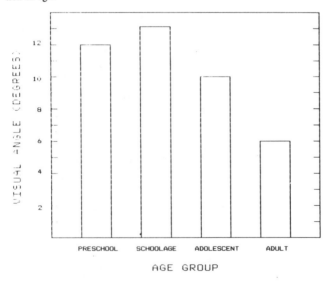

FIG. 8.3.   Average visual angle subtended by the television screen as a function of age.

plication of this observation: Viewers need few eye movements in order to perceive the television image. Indeed, perception research has indicated that picture identification is most rapidly and efficiently accomplished at a visual angle of about 11.5 degrees and under. Viewers place themselves so that they can readily and efficiently perceive the rapidly paced sequence of relatively simple images typical of contemporary broadcast television.

Age Trends in Visual Attention to TV. The Allen (1965) and Bechtel et al. (1972) studies provided some indication that there is an inverted U-shaped function of visual attention to television in relation to age. Specifically, attention may increase through childhood, peak in late childhood, and decline among adults.

A number of studies using preschool children as subjects have found that visual attention to television increases throughout the preschool years. These studies were based on observations of TV viewing of 1 to 3 hours of children's programming in the context of a research center viewing room (cf. Anderson & Smith, 1984). There is little laboratory evidence concerning age trends in older children and adults.

We analyzed our home TV viewing data of visual attention for age trends (Anderson et al., 1986). A summary of the results appear in Fig. 8.4, which presents average percent visual attention for each age group. Within the preschool age, visual attention increases dramatically from near zero in infants to near 70% in 5-year-old children. Over the school-age and adolescent years attention is high at 71%, dropping significantly to an average 60% among adults. Although there

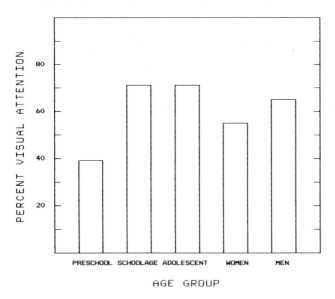

FIG. 8.4.   Percent visual attention to television as a function of age group.

was no significant age trend after 18 years, adult men paid significantly more attention (65%) to the TV than adult women (55%). These results are quite consistent with the laboratory studies of preschoolers, with the earlier automated on-line field studies, and with the scattered reports from the study done in the 1980s in Great Britain. Television viewing behavior has remained within constant parameters across three decades of observation.

Lengths of Viewing Sessions.   Overall, we found that there was no one in the viewing room about 15% of the time the TV was on. This is reasonably close to Allen's (1965) finding of 19%. We have examined a subset of our families (53) in terms of the lengths of time that each individual remained in the room with the TV before exiting (Anderson, 1987). These viewing session lengths are highly skewed such that median viewing sessions are extremely brief, on the order of 1 minute! Means of these skewed distributions, on the other hand, are on the order of 6 to 10 minutes, depending on age and gender.

The typical brevity of these "viewing sessions" is due to the fact that in most families with children, there is considerable activity and movement in and out of the viewing room. Individuals may enter the room, talk to someone who is watching TV, briefly look at TV themselves, and then step out. A mother watching TV, for example, may exit and re-enter the viewing room as she checks on something cooking, answers the phone, empties the dryer, deals with a child, or the like, all the while monitoring the TV "on the fly." This is not to say that long viewing sessions are necessarily uncommon; among adult men, for example, 58% of all time spent with TV was spent in sessions longer than 30 minutes.

Viewing session lengths depend on age, gender, time of day, and day of the week. For children, sessions were longest in the morning, shortest in the afternoon, and intermediate in the evening. Adults' sessions were shortest in the morning, intermediate in the afternoon, and longest in the evening. Preschool girls had longer sessions than boys, there was no gender difference among school-age children, and the difference was reversed among adults.

In principle, the "peoplemeter" technology, in which viewers press buttons on a remote device each time they enter or exit the viewing room, should provide rating services with up-to-date data on viewing sessions. From our observations and analyses, however, we are somewhat skeptical as to the results from this online technology. Because a substantial proportion (on the order of 15% to 20%) of exposure to television is in the form of brief viewing sessions (under 15 minutes), it is open to question whether these brief sessions are recorded by the viewers. Qualitatively, we also question whether children routinely record their presence on the meters. All too often, a child leaps up and runs out of the viewing room, or rolls out, or cartwheels out, or is carried out or pushed out by another child. Such spontaneous and exuberant behavior typical of children does not seem to us to be compatible with data entry responsibilities. In any case, it remains to be seen whether such online audience assessment techniques are better or worse than offline viewing diaries. As yet, no validation studies have been published.

Detailed Analyses. Online video recording of TV viewing behavior allows highly detailed analyses of moment-by-moment fluctuations in visual attention and concurrent activities. As yet, such analyses have only been reported from "laboratory" studies (see Anderson & Burns, chapter 1, this volume, for a review of online studies of attention). Preliminary to a full-scale effort, we have examined the visual attention of several adults and children from our home viewing study.

Consider our analyses of two adults. One of these viewers is a 32-year-old woman and the other is a 33-year-old man. We rated the woman's visual attention to TV from 95 viewing sessions; the man was rated from 56 sessions. The rating was accomplished by means of a computer controlled videocassette deck. Raters pressed a button when, in their judgment, the viewer initiated a look at the TV screen and released it when the look was terminated. Each button press and release caused the computer to store the video frame number that was current at the time of the press and release. The rater was able to reverse the deck and rerate any part of the videotape. In this manner, a continuous record of the temporal fluctuations of visual attention to the television was stored by the computer for further analysis.

We found that the man looked at the TV 67% of the time he was in the viewing room, and his looks at the TV lasted an average 27.5 seconds. Nonlooking "pauses" between looks lasted an average 13.8 seconds (for technical reasons, our minimum temporal resolution in this study was 1.2 seconds; these data do not therefore include very brief glances to or away from the TV). The woman looked at the TV 45% of the time she was in the viewing room; her looks lasted an average 17.9 seconds. Her nonlooking pauses lasted an average 22.2 seconds. Importantly, in both viewers, most looks at the TV were short, under 10 seconds in length. The relative frequency distributions of look length are plotted for the man in Figure 8.5 and for the woman in Figure 8.6. It should be clear that continuous episodes of visual attention as long as 60 seconds are relatively rare. Analyses of several children's visual attention produced very similar distributions. These relative frequency distributions are in fact typical of both child and adult TV viewers observed in laboratory studies (see Anderson and Burns, chapter 1, this volume, for further discussion of this issue).

FINAL COMMENT

We have described here only the beginnings of our online analyses of home TV viewing behavior. Many matters of description remain, including analyses of concurrent activities during TV viewing, accuracy of diaries in relation to the view-

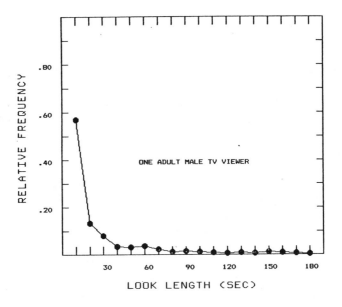

FIG. 8.5. Relative frequency of look lengths by a 32-year-old man.

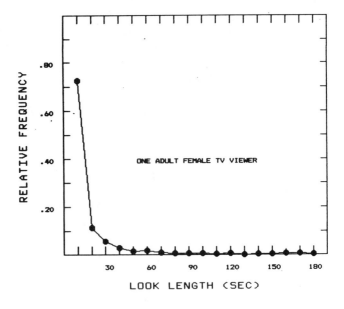

FIG. 8.6. Relative frequency of look lengths by a 33-year-old woman.

ing of specific programs, analyses of visual attention to commercials, and many others. In addition, we expect to see numerous analyses emerge from the field studies of the British research group (cf. Gunter & Svennevig, 1987). We would like to point out that our observations of thousands of hours of television viewing behavior have convinced us (along with Allen, 1965, and Bechtel et al., 1972) that families incorporate television into their lives in highly individual ways but ways that are remarkably consistent and stereotyped from day to day. Television becomes part of a complex family ecology and is frequently a central feature of family activity.

Despite this complexity, however, we believe that many aspects of TV viewing are common to virtually all viewers and subject to relatively straightforward research analysis. In many cases, however, ideal analyses require observation of viewing with experimentally produced television programming shown under controlled circumstances. Such online "laboratory" research allows detailed examination of patterns of attention and comprehension. A body of such research has now emerged—primarily with children—and it has produced the beginnings of systematic and detailed scientific theory. At this time, furthermore, no observations from online field studies have produced results contradictory with results from online laboratory studies, and the consistency of results across field studies is impressive.

Combined, field and laboratory online research is helping to validate and elaborate findings from offline research. Together, online and offline techniques are providing a body of data with consistency, breadth, and quantitative rigor. Such research, supplemented by qualitative studies, makes an observationally based scientific theory of television viewing as much more than a remote possibility.

ACKNOWLEDGMENTS

The research described here was supported by grants from the National Institute of Mental Health, the National Science Foundation, and the John and Mary Markle Foundation. We would like to thank Ilene Sussman, John Burns, and Patricia Collins for assistance with the preparation of this chapter.

REFERENCES

Allen, C. (1965). Photographing the TV audience. *Journal of Advertising Research, 14*, 2-8.

Anderson, D. (1987, November). *Analysis of lengths of TV viewing sessions.* Paper presented at annual meeting of the Association for Consumer Research, Boston, MA.

Anderson, D., Alwitt, L., Lorch, E., & Levin, S. (1979). Watching children watch television. In G. Hale & M. Lewis (Eds.), *Attention and cognitive development* (pp. 331-361). New York: Plenum.

Anderson, D., Field, D., Collins, P., Lorch, E., & Nathan, J. (1985). Estimates of young children's time with television: A methodological comparison of parent reports with time-lapse video home observation. *Child Development, 56*, 1345-1357.

Anderson, D., & Lorch, L. (1983). Looking at television: Action or reaction? In J. Bryant & D. R. Anderson (Eds.), *Children's understanding of television: Research on attention and comprehension* (pp. 1-34). New York: Academic Press.

Anderson, D., Lorch, E., Field, D., Collins, P., & Nathan, J. (1986). Television viewing at home: Age trends in visual attention and time with TV. *Child Development, 57,* 1024-1033.

Anderson, D., & Smith, R. (1984). Young children's TV viewing: The problem of cognitive continuity. In F. J. Morrison, C. Lord, & D. F. Keating (Eds.), *Advances in applied developmental psychology* (Vol. 1, pp. 115-163). New York: Academic Press.

Bechtel, R., Achelpohl, C., & Akers, R. (1972). Correlates between observed behavior and questionnaire responses on television viewing. In E. A. Rubinstein, G. A. Comstock, & J. P. Murray (Eds.) *Television and social behavior* (Vol. 4), *Television in day-to-day life: Patterns of use* (pp. 274-344). Washington, DC: U.S. Government Printing Office.

Beville, H. (1985). *Audience ratings.* Hillsdale, NJ: Lawrence Erlbaum Associates.

Choi, H., Anderson, D., Burns, J., Collins, P., & Field, D. (1988). *Time spent with television: A comparison of diary estimates with time-lapse video observation.* Unpublished manuscript, University of Massachusetts, Amherst, MA.

Gunter, B., & Svennevig, M. (1987). *Behind and in front of the screen: Television's involvement with family life.* London: John Libbey.

Huston, A., & Wright, J. (1983). Children's processing of television: The informative functions of formal features. In J. Bryant & D. Anderson (Eds.), *Children's understanding of television: Research on attention and comprehension* (pp. 35-68). New York: Academic Press.

Levy, M. R. (1982). The Lazarsfeld-Stanton program analyzer: An historical note. *Journal of Communication, 32,* 30-38.

Nathan, J., Anderson, D., Field, D., & Collins, P. (1985). Television viewing at home: Distances and visual angles adopted by children and adults. *Human Factors, 27,* 467-476.

National Center for Radiological Health. (1968). A summary of the Washington, DC metropolitan area survey of color television receivers. *Radiological Health Data and Reports, 9,* 531-538.

Palmer, E. (1972, March 23-25). *Formative research in the production of television for children.* Paper prepared for Panel III of the International Symposium on Communication: Technology, impact and policy, the Annenberg School of Communications, University of Pennsylvania, Philadelphia, P.A.

Watt, J., & Welch, A. (1983). Effects of static and dynamic complexity on children's attention and recall of televised instruction. In J. Bryant & D. Anderson (Eds.), *Children's understanding of television: Research on attention and comprehension* (pp. 69-102). New York: Academic Press.

CHAPTER
9

Evolving Cognitive Models in Mass Communication Reception Processes

Jennings Bryant
Steven C. Rockwell
University of Alabama

For many years, mass communication scholars viewed the mass communication consumption process in a somewhat linear and unidimensional manner—mediated stimuli were viewed, heard, or read; then, after being subjected to unknown processes within the consumer, they were perceived as causing some observable behavior. Instead of trying to determine why people selected certain media messages over others or what processes allowed for individual variations in responses among different audience members consuming the same messages, these early researchers were more interested in the behavioral norm of media effects, or the averaging of all observable response categories. In doing so, they sought to determine the most frequently observed response to a given media message, temporarily ignoring any mental processing that led to this behavior.

In recent years, however, a strong tradition has emerged in mass communication for studying what media messages people select (e.g., Zillmann & Bryant, 1985) and why they make the choices they do (e.g., Rosengren, Wenner, & Palmgren, 1985). Moreover, some of the research into the area of mass communication effects has begun to focus on the internal processes of the receiver. Anderson and Bryant (1983), for example, suggested that communication research must define and understand internal mental processes if the study of media effects was to advance. The model they posited did not attempt to accurately specify the internal processes involved in attending to and understanding media messages; however, it illustrated the place of the processes and indicated that they are inseparable from other more readily observable factors, such as that of the viewing environment. The more macroanalytic form of Anderson and Bryant's (1983)

217

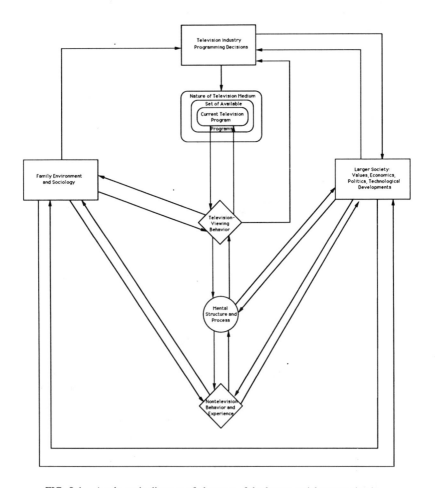

FIG. 9.1. A schematic diagram of elements of the larger social system that influence behavior in the television-viewing situation. The diamonds represent observed behavior; circles represent mental entities; rectangles are potentially observable aspects of the environment; and items in the ovals represent "television."
Reprinted with permission from Anderson and Bryant (1983, p. 333).

model is presented here for illustrative purposes (see Fig. 9.1), but the central
cognitive processing portion of the model is discussed more fully later.

Admonitions to include cognitive processes in mass communication models
may seem superfluous to many today; however, cognitive approaches in mass
communication research are relatively recent and are still perceived to be less
than orthodox in some circles. In fact, scholarly inquiry into the processes involved in cognition is limited to the latter half of the 20th century exclusively.
Although precursors to the cognitive sciences can be traced to researchers of the

late 19th century, especially Wundt and his work with perception, radical behaviorism, which did not allow for any internal processes, dominated the field until around World War II (Allport, 1980).

It is likely that the advent of the computer and the emergence of computer science as a discipline were the most critical catalysts in the development of cognitive psychology as a serious field of scholarly inquiry (Neisser, 1967). By basing cognitive models on the computing process, concepts such as information manipulation, storage, and retrieval, essential to much of the modern study of cognition, were established. Other critical components to the "cognitive revolution" were the ideas of psychologists like Herbert Simon and George Miller, the work of linguists like Noam Chomsky, and the theories of the cyberneticists like Norbert Wiener (Mendelsohn, 1990). Once these ideas began to be accepted, "essentially the focus of the new cognitive theorists turned to how the human organism acquired information and knowledge and what it did in processing the information so acquired in order to 'construct' meaning for taking action" (Mendelsohn, 1990, p. 43).

Because cognitive approaches offered new insight into the communication process, communication researchers were quick to explore and adopt the cognitive dimensions of communication. Soon research was being conducted to determine how people select, process, and remember, as well as how they are influenced by media messages. Areas receiving substantial scholarly interest from these perspectives include, but are not limited to, children's understanding of television (e.g., Anderson & Bryant, 1983), consumer information processing (e.g., Thorson, 1983), mood management through entertainment (e.g., Zillmann, 1988), and the processing and effects of political advertising (e.g., Biocca, in press; Kraus, 1990). This chapter reviews some of the key concepts in the cognitive research tradition, showing how they have been applied in mass communication research. Then it examines a couple of different mass communication models posited by this research tradition in order to assess trends in the evolution of theories and models of the cognitive processes underlying the consumption of media fare.

KEY CONCEPTS IN THE COGNITIVE RESEARCH TRADITION

Greene (1989) has offered a threefold division of the constructs of cognitive science: structures, content, and processes (cf. Littlejohn, 1989). In his model, the *structure* construct seeks to explain what form information takes or how information is organized while it is stored in the mind. Schema or script theory is one approach addressing this notion of structure. The information that forms these structures is referred to by Greene as cognitive *content* (i.e., attitudes, thoughts, dispositions, feelings, etc.). The cognitive *processes* construct addresses how the content is acquired, acted upon, and utilized. In order to better understand behavior resulting from a mediated message, an information-processing model of the communication process must at the very least be able to account for the structure the mediated messages take, the process or processes by which the message is acted upon and utilized, and the nature of the message content.

Schemas. One of the primary components of many cognitive models is the notion of *schema*. A schema is roughly defined as "a network of interrelated elements that defines a concept for some individual" (Crockett, 1988, p. 33). Schemas, then, are abstractions held in the mind about concrete reality that give new information a structure around which to be oriented. McQuail (1987) has applied this concept to the mass communication context in this way:

> Any newspaper reader or television viewer has an implicit theory in the sense of a set of ideas about the medium in question, what it is, what it is good for, how it fits into daily life, how it should be "read," what its connotations are and how it may relate to other aspects of social life. Most people will carry an elaborate set of associations and ideas of this kind which enable them to act consistently and satisfactorily in relation to the media. (p. 5)

Schemas are often considered to be hierarchical in nature, with more abstract schemas built up around a series of more specific information (subschemas) (Fiske & Taylor, 1984). Schemas are also thought to be horizontally ordered with varying degrees of relations among them (Crockett, 1988). Thus, the activation of one schema can cause associative links to other schemas closely associated to the initial one.

Schemas have been suggested as serving two primary functions: ordering new information, and allowing for inferences to be made from incomplete information (Taylor & Crocker, 1981). Because new information is clustered around similar, previously acquired information, any gaps in the new information can be filled with the information already existing in the schema. Thus, if a person misses a bit of information crucial to the formation of an inference, this bit of information is extracted from the schema and the inference is made. Whether or not the inference is correct depends on which schema was activated and, more importantly, whether or not the information held by the schema is accurate. Thus, the *process* of schema formation and activation takes primary importance in how reality is shaped for a given individual.

In the mass communication domain, most mature television viewers have well-established schemas that correspond to the so-called "formats" of different television genres. Therefore, if viewers miss any 5 minutes of the program, say a situation comedy, so long as the program does not violate orthodoxy, they will be able to call on their schema for sitcoms and quickly "fill in the gap" on any missing action or plot developments.

Conscious Versus Automatic Information Processing. A second key notion in cognitive approaches to mass communication inquiry has to do with the level of consciousness of information processing. Haskell (1987) has delineated three disparate areas in the development of the study of the process of cognition, which are differentiated in part by the levels of consciousness of the processing models posited. He criticized the first area, which he called the mainstream cognitive approach, as being too linear and narrow in focus. Based on the computer-based model of information processing, this approach deals with the linear flow of information from one phase of processing to the next. Because this approach is so mechanistic, Haskell argued, it allows little room for theory expansion and does not lend itself to the incorporation of competing approaches to the study of cognition, including those involving different levels of consciousness in information processing.

The second area of cognitive psychology outlined by Haskell assumes a more active role on the part of the individual. Based on Neisser's (1967, 1976) view that individuals *consciously* construct and order input, this approach, Haskell claimed, falls somewhere between the first and third approaches to cognition.

The third approach is described by Haskell as having *unconscious* parallels to the conscious cognitive operations outlined by the second area. Haskell suggested that it is this third area that needs to be focused on in order to increase understanding of the processes involved in cognition. This chapter utilizes this third approach in examining the aforementioned models.

In cognitive psychology's brief history, there has been a relative abundance of scholarly work in the area of the conscious processing of information. In the field of communication, the area of rules theory (e.g., Pearce & Cronen, 1980; Shimanoff, 1980), which is increasingly being applied in the mass communication context, exemplifies this line of inquiry. Rules theorists view individuals as acting purposively according to (or in defiance of) operators (i.e., rules) in attempting to achieve conscious goals. In the study of mass communication, these rules are conceived of as being *known* by the individual, and a given set of possible behavioral actions is *consciously* compared to the set of *known* rules in order to gauge or explain the appropriate response. The dominant cognitive process, then, serves simply to apply a set of established rules. Higher order cognitive processes come into play, for example, in many so-called "metacommunicative" or "metacognititve" situations, say when two potential movie goers are discussing their reasons for wanting to go to different movies that are expected to provide quite different sorts of gratifications.

It is unlikely that an individual is or even can be aware of all the cognitive processing occurring at any given time. Some processing must take place at a level of the unconscious or the person would surely suffer debilitating information overload. Imagine trying to sort through and control every bit of information received in a newsroom or at the stock exchange. It would be maddening. Selectivity, at both conscious and nonconscious levels, is essential in an Information Age society.

Regardless, however, of whether cognitive processing occurs in the conscious or the unconscious, at issue is whether or not the control of this process is intentional or unintentional. Bargh (1988) contended that some types of cognitive processing occur outside of the control of the individual. These automatic processes are unintentional and uncontrollable and are a function of the individual's environment and prior knowledge. In other words, these automatic processes occur along pre-established neural links that are formed by previous associations (Bargh, 1988). This frees up limited attentional capacity (Kahneman, 1973) so that more attention can be devoted to the intentional processing of information.

Although Bargh (1988) contended that automatic processing plays a larger role in the processing of *social information* (i.e., "the socially relevant features of a person's behavior, verbal or nonverbal, and the context in which they occur," p. 13), he did suggest that some elements of the mass media are subject to this automatic processing. Depending on the person's intention in selecting from the various, competing stimuli, Bargh suggested that certain attributes of the mass media are subject to automatic processing. These include: motion, color, contrast, contour, intensity, and change (James, 1890; Neisser, 1967).

Bargh (1988) has also suggested that since mass media consumption is goal-directed and intentional, little automatic processing occurs unless the individual is attempting to engage in a "mindless" activity. On the other hand, the individual could engage in automatic processing, thereby resting his or her intentional processing resources, if the media content being consumed contained elements such as those mentioned earlier that would sustain the automatic processing resource. Furthermore, if the content the medium is presenting is comprised of a story that is similar to the individual's past experiences or is in line with a well-established cognitive schema, automatic processing should also be operative (Bargh, 1988).

It has been suggested by other researchers that automatic processing might play a greater role in the processing of mediated messages than simply the pursuit of "mindless" activities. Biocca (in press) has argued that mediated messages, especially political advertisements, automatically activate previously held schemas. According to this view, the actual meaning of a political advertisement can differ depending on what schemas are activated or whether these activated schemas are altered by newly acquired information. Further, if a schema is primed prior to the exposure of the intended message, the message could be influenced by the activated schema.

Bargh (1988) has expressed a similar concept. He stated that a stimulus is automatically classified as positive or negative according to the evaluation of similar, previously experienced stimuli. Thus, this automatic value judgment could possibly influence the evaluation and subsequent behavior of an individual, and, because the individual is unaware of this process, correction for the bias becomes difficult.

Although Bargh's (1988) automatic evaluation mechanism does not appear to be as involved or complex a model of the mass communication process as does Biocca's (in press) model of the process of schema activation, both these processes exhibit similarities in that they can account for the evaluation of new stimuli. Taken together, these models would suggest that automatic processir ̤ does indeed play some role in the formation of meaning in the processing of mediated information and therefore must be included in any models attempting to accurately gauge the cognitive processes involved in meaning formation. If a cognitive model is to be an accurate depiction of the processes involved in processing information, then it must be able to account for all levels of information processing, not just ones that appear obvious and suited for a given phenomenon.

THE EVOLUTION OF COGNITIVE MODELS IN MASS COMMUNICATION

Two models are now presented that illustrate the rapid evolution of cognitive models in mass communication inquiry. The earlier model, shown in Fig. 9.1 and 9.2, is Anderson and Bryant's (1983) schematic portrayal of the process of televiewing; the later model, shown in Fig. 9.3, is Thorson's (1989) model of viewer responses to television commercials. Only a half decade separates the publication of the two models, both of which represented "the state of the art" of their respective areas at the time they were published. Even a cursory comparison of the centrality and elegance with which cognitive processes are represented will aptly illustrate the remarkably rapid development of the cognitive sciences during the decade of the 1980s.

Figure 9.1, which depicts the macoanalytic version of Anderson and Bryant's (1983) model, shows that "mental structure and process" was considered to be an essential element for understanding the television viewing process. This assertion was quite rare at the time. Figure 9.2 presents a closer look at what the authors consider to be "the central processes of television viewing" (Anderson & Bryant, 1983). As can readily be seen from the diagram, four "mental entities" are represented: (a) comprehension and viewing strategies; (b) memory for the program; (c) the viewer's conception of the attributes of television and its demands; and (d) the viewer's general knowledge structure, needs, values, and mental abilities. As can be seen from examining Fig. 9.1 and 9.2, the three aforementioned essential elements of a cognitive model of the mass communication process—structure, process, and content—are all present in this model, and some of the principle components of today's cognitive models are at least implicitly present (e.g., "the viewer's conception of the attributes of television and its demands" corresponds closely with our concept of "schema"); nonetheless, the model is rather primitive when considered in light of more recent models, and it certainly fails to consider elements such as the level of consciousness of the viewer during various portions of the televiewing process.

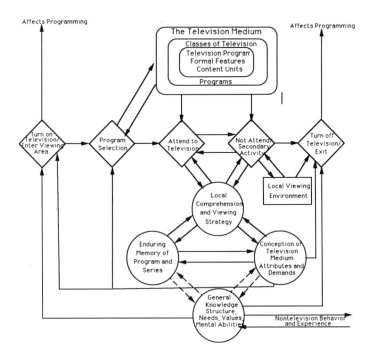

FIG. 9.2. A schematic diagram of the central processes of television viewing. The diamonds represent observed behavior; circles represent mental entities; rectangles are potentially observable aspects of the environment; and items in the ovals represent "television." Reprinted with permission from Anderson and Bryant (1983, p. 335).

In contrast, Thorson's (1989) processing model of viewer responses to commercials, depicted in Fig. 9.3, is in most ways a fully developed cognitive communication model. Not only are a number of primary and higher order cognitive processes represented in this model (see ovals; e.g., conscious attention, working memory), a number of structural cognitive storage areas are represented also (see rectangles; e.g., grammar analyzer, semantic dictionary). Moreover, this later model succinctly indicates two levels of awareness of processing on the part of the viewer and delineates "processes unavailable to consciousness" and "processes available to consciousness." Not only that, Thorson's textual elaboration of the model includes elements such as the place of emotion in the cognitive processing of commercials, the role of environmental and programmatic distraction, the role of program context, and other elements that had received almost no research attention at the time of the publication of Anderson and Bryant's (1983) model just half a decade earlier.

Although Thorson's (1989) model represents, almost ideally, the considerable development in cognitive theory and research that has taken place in the decade

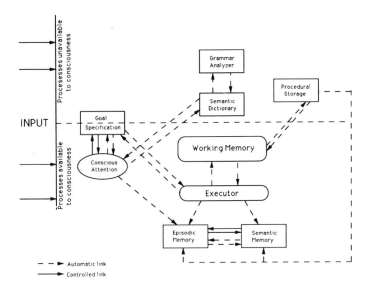

FIG. 9.3. A processing model of viewer response to commercials. The rectangles represent memory storage areas; the ovals represent processing mechanisms; the broken lines represent flow of information that occurs without conscious control of the viewer; the solid lines represent flow of information that requires conscious control of the viewer. Reprinted with permission from Thorson (1989, p. 401).

of the 1980s, it should be noted that a close reading of her chapter will indicate that the model is still more of a heuristic tool than a full-blown explanatory model. That is not meant to be a criticism of the model; it serves its (and our) purposes very well. It is just to say that we still have a long way to go in developing sophisticated explanatory and predictive models of cognitive mass communication reception processes.

In other words, as far as cognitive models of mass communication are concerned, we seem to have come a long way in a short time. The simultaneous convergence of several streams of the cognitive sciences on multidimensional problems and issues, made more readily accessible via new information technologies, has created rapidly evolving models of mass communication reception processes. Whether all of the structures and processes posited will ultimately prove to be valid and useful is quite another issue that will be resolved only via the patient probing of empirical evidence. In the meanwhile, it is an exciting time to be developing cognitively based mass communication theory.

REFERENCES

Allport, D. A. (1980). Patterns and actions: Cognitive mechanisms are content-specific. In G. Claxton (Ed.), *Cognitive psychology: New directions* (pp. 26–64). London: Routledge & Kegan Paul.
Anderson, D., & Bryant, J. (1983). Research on children's television viewing: The state of the art.

In J. Bryant & D. Anderson (Eds.), *Children's understanding of television: Research on attention and comprehension* (pp. 331-354). New York: Academic Press.

Bargh, J. A. (1988). Automatic information processing: Implications for communication and affect. In L. Donohew, H. Sypher, & E. T. Higgins (Eds.), *Communication, social cognition, and affect* (pp. 9-32). Hillsdale, NJ: Lawrence Erlbaum Associates.

Biocca, F. (in press). Viewers' mental models of political messages: Towards a theory of the semantic processing of television. In F. Biocca (Ed.), *Television and political advertising, Vol. 1: Psychological processes.* Hillsdale, NJ: Lawrence Erlbaum Associates.

Crockett, W. (1988). Schemas, affect, and communication. In L. Donohew, H. Sypher, & E. T. Higgins (Eds.), *Communication, social cognition, and affect* (pp. 33-52). Hillsdale, NJ: Lawrence Erlbaum Associates.

Fiske, S., & Taylor, S. (1984). *Social cognition.* Reading, MA: Addison-Wesley.

Greene, J. (1989). Action assembly theory. In B. Dervin, L. Grossberg, B. J. O'Keefe, & E. Wartella (Eds.), *Rethinking communication, Vol. 2: Paradigm exemplars* (pp. 117-128). Newbury Park, CA: Sage.

Haskell, R. E. (1987). Cognitive psychology and the problem of symbolic cognition. In R. Haskell (Ed.), *Cognition and symbolic structures: The psychology of metaphoric transformation* (pp. 85-102). Norwood, NJ: Ablex.

James, W. (1890). *Principles of psychology.* New York: Holt.

Kahneman, D. (1973). *Attention and effort.* Englewood Cliffs, NJ: Prentice-Hall.

Kraus, S. (Ed.). (1990). *Mass communication and political information processing.* Hillsdale, NJ: Lawrence Erlbaum Associates.

Littlejohn, S. W. (1989). *Theories of human communication* (3rd ed.). Belmont, CA: Wadsworth.

McQuail, D. (1987). *Mass communication theory* (2nd ed.). London & Newbury Park, CA: Sage.

Mendelsohn, H. (1990). Mind, affect, and action: Construction theory and the media effects dilectic. In S. Kraus (Ed.), *Mass communication and political information processing* (pp. 37-45). Hillsdale, NJ: Lawrence Erlbaum Associates.

Neisser, U. (1967). *Cognitive psychology.* New York: Appleton-Century-Crofts.

Neisser, U. (1976). *Cognition and reality.* San Fransisco, CA: Freeman.

Pearce, W. B., & Cronen, V. (1980). *Communication, action, and meaning.* New York: Praeger.

Rosengren, K. E., Wenner, L. A., & Palmgreen, P. (Eds.). (1985). *Media gratifications research.* Beverly Hills, CA: Sage.

Shimanoff, S. B. (1980). *Communication rules: Theory and research.* Beverly Hills: Sage.

Taylor, S., & Crocker, J. (1981). Schematic bases of social information processing. In E. T. Higgins, C. P. Herman, & M. P. Zanna (Eds.), *Social cognition: The Ontario symposium* (Vol. 1, pp. 89-134). Hillsdale, NJ: Lawrence Erlbaum Associates.

Thorson, E. (1989). Processing television commercials. In B. Dervin, L. Grossberg, B. J. O'Keefe, & E. Wartella (Eds.), *Rethinking communication, Vol. 2: Paradigm exemplars* (pp. 397-410). Newbury Park, CA: Sage.

Zillmann, D. (1988). Mood management: Using entertainment to full advantage. In L. Donohew, H. Sypher, & E. T. Higgins (Eds.), *Communication, social cognition, and affect* (pp. 147-172). Hillsdale, NJ: Lawrence Erlbaum Associates.

Zillmann, D., & Bryant, J. (Eds.). (1985). *Selective exposure to communication.* Hillsdale, NJ: Lawrence Erlbaum Associates.

PART II

Responding to Program Genres

10

Responding to News and Public Affairs

Barrie Gunter
Independent Broadcasting Authority

The News Function of Television

One of the main reasons people give for watching television is to obtain news information. Out of the many reasons people may volunteer as to why they watch television, learning about things happening in the world tends to finish near the top of the list. One investigator examined relationships between motives for watching television and preferences for particular types of programmes (Rubin, 1984). From a list of 14 reasons for watching television, the information and learning function was the most strongly endorsed. About 70% of the study's respondents from two mid-western U.S. communities said they watched television to learn about people and events. In the context of how motives related to patterns of viewing, it emerged that watching television to learn about events, to acquire topics for conversation and to seek behavioral guidance were the best motivational indicators of watching television news and other informational programming.

Motives for watching programs can themselves be quite varied, however. Even so, the most prominent reasons for tuning in to the news are usually related to perceived cognitive benefits. In a study of motives related to watching three television news interview programs, Levy (1978) found that nearly all viewers believed that these programs gave them food for thought and taught them about public issues. It was also evident, however, that viewers liked seeking how leading public figures performed under the pressure of being interviewed on television and gave them an opportunity to evaluate politicians' abilities.

Since the late 1950s television has evolved into the medium that most people have come to regard as their principal and most trusted source of public affairs information. In the United States, for example, two thirds of respondents questioned about it in a national survey claimed that television is their main source of national and international news (Roper, 1983). Similar results have emerged from the United Kingdom (IBA, 1985, 1986, 1990).

When in 1959, Roper first asked people in the United States where they get most of their information about what is going on in the world today, newspapers were ahead of television with radio in third place. By 1963, television and newspapers were even, and by 1967, television had moved ahead and has been there ever since.

The public's perceptions of the relative informativeness of television is not consistent across all types of news, however. Although commonly regarded as the main source for world news, on the local front, attitudes exhibit a different pattern. On a local or regional level, newspapers generally are still ranked by people ahead of television (IBA, 1982, 1985, 1990; Roper, 1983).

When pressed, people are capable of making even more refined judgments about which media are best for finding out about particular kinds of news. Bogart (1980) reported a 1966 survey in which respondents were presented with one-sentence distillations of 120 news stories and asked in each case which was the best way to find out about it. Newspapers were the most favored source of 59% of items, whereas television was thought to be best for just 29%. One reason for this perceived advantage of newspapers may be the fact that they do tend to cover a greater breadth and variety of news topics than does television and may therefore be seen as the best source of information for a much wider array of news.

Television, as a news source, is invested with a greater degree of trust than newspapers. Faced with conflicting television and newspaper reports about the same story, many more are inclined to believe the television version than the one they read in the newspaper (Lee, 1975; Roper, 1983)

Despite the research evidence that television news is highly regarded by the public as an accurate and trustworthy source of information about public affairs, just how effective is it as an informational medium? People may believe that they gain most of their information about the world from television, and that they can understand what television newscasters tell them, but to what extent are these beliefs verified in the more objective terms of actual knowledge gain?

Learning From Television News

That news is an important part of broadcasting on television attested to by formal policy statements of broadcasting institutions (BBC, 1976; IBA, 1981). Television newscasts have a certain goal—audience impact—and this can be measured in terms of how much a program is enjoyed or by how much information it imparts to the viewer. To the extent that informing the public is a fundamental aim of television news broadcasting, and one that is recognized by broadcasters and public alike, an important question is how successfully this aim is achieved.

If we accept the premise that one of the principle aims of television news is to convey information, it is rather disappointing to find that measured retention for program content among heterogeneous audiences often turns out to be poor, even when only a short time has passed since viewing. In one American survey, viewers questioned by telephone in their homes about a television news bulletin they had watched the same evening, were able spontaneously to recall little over 5% of the reported news topics (Neuman, 1976). Even following topic-related cues to aid recall, few gave details of more than 20% of the items. Indeed half of the respondents were unable to remember any items at all less than an hour after the program had been broadcast.

More recently, news recall was tested immediately after each newscast on several consecutive evenings in face-to-face interviews in people's homes and somewhat better overall memory performance was reported (Robinson, Davis, Sahin, & O'Toole, 1980). Tests of free recall of the 12 to 20 major news items typically presented per broadcast were followed by brief descriptive labels referring to the personalities or locations of news events that were provided to trigger respondents' further recall of the salient content of individual news stories. Viewers here recalled some elements of about half the bulletin items on average. However, this fairly creditable memory performance was offset by frequent distortion or misunderstanding of important details of news stories. One finding was that viewers sometimes confused the content from two stories, so that elements of one story became merged with elements from another — a phenomenon referred to by Robinson and his colleagues as "meltdown." This American evidence has been corroborated elsewhere by researchers in Sweden and the United Kingdom. Findahl and Hoijer (1975b) found that more than half a sample of Stockholm residents who took part in a laboratory study of memory for televised news, either failed to recall or misunderstood the content of nearly all the items of a 7 minute bulletin of 13 items. In the United Kingdom, laboratory research has demonstrated that packages of news stories about similar topics, such as politics, or foreign affairs, can generate considerable memory losses (Gunter, Clifford, & Berry, 1980).

Even when people believe, on a subjective level, that they have learned from information broadcasts, objective measurement of learning often reveals that they have not. One example of this is remembering weather forecast information. People say they value these broadcasts and find forecasts easy to follow and understand. And yet, audience research has revealed that comprehension of the meanings of the symbols shown on weather charts or of the terms used by weather forecasters is poor (Wober & Gunter, 1981). Furthermore, these highly valued forecasts, both on radio and television, are usually only poorly recalled (Wagenaar, 1978; Wagenaar & Visser, 1979).

Another area covered extensively by television news programs is the economy. The public's understanding about the way the economy works, however, tends to be poor. In Israel, Adoni and Cohen (1978) found that concepts such as balance of payments, gross national product, value added tax, and cost of living index were understood properly by one third of the population. And yet, regardless of how much they actually knew, many people tended to believe that television was helping them to understand.

There has accumulated consistent evidence of poor comprehension and retention to televised news from around the world (e.g., Neuman, 1976; Robinson et al., 1980, in the United States; Katz, Adoni, & Parness, 1977, in Israel; Findahl & Hoijer, 1975b, 1984, in Sweden; Gunter, 1987; Robinson & Sahin, 1984, in the United Kingdom) which indicates that television newscasts may not be as effective at communicating information to the public as the prevalence and popularity of television news might lead one to suppose. What reasons can be identified and offered as explanations as to why this happens?

AUDIENCE VARIABLES

Until recently, most research on news effectiveness focused on the mitigating influences of audience variables. Much work has been conducted within a sociology of mass communications research framework in which the acquisition of information from the mass media is linked to a complex set of determinants that exist among individuals and principally involve their "information needs." This perspective asks questions about the instrumental utility of media messages for the individual and whether they will provide useful input to guide responding to environmental demands or to defend personal beliefs and attitudes. It is assumed therefore that attention to the news may often be selective and driven by particular motivational forces. Hence, individuals will tend to learn messages that are intrinsically of interest or use to them. Interest may also be driven by noninstrumental factors, however, such as the perceived entertainment value of mass media material. Motivational and interest factors are commonly inter-related with sociodemographic characteristics of audience such as gender, age, social class, and level of education, which are recognized to act as mediators of tastes in and learning from different mass media materials.

There is no doubt that general knowledge levels about public affairs do vary across demographic subgroups in heterogeneous populations. Levels of awareness of recent news events, and in the extent to which different sources of news are consumed, vary likewise in relation to these population variables. But as we see here, these differences in knowledge levels are little more than descriptive and do not offer explanations as to why the informational impact of the media, and in particular television, is often so ineffective.

The significance of the educational level of individuals in learning from the media has been embodied in the knowledge-gap hypothesis (Tichenor, Donohue, & Olien, 1970). Research conducted within this framework observed that there is attendency for the already well-informed to become better informed relative to the already ill-informed. Hence, the gap between their respective levels of knowledge widens. It has been demonstrated that both educational level and occupational status are associated with knowledge of world affairs (Robinson, 1967). Those who have achieved higher levels of educational attainment and hold higher status occupations tend to be better informed. These early findings that were concerned more with learning from print than from television have been corroborated more recently for learning from television news however.

Gunter (1985) found that better educated people had higher levels of awareness than less well educated about personalities and events that had featured prominently in the news on television and in the press during the previous week. Robinson and Sahin (1984) also reported high knowledge levels for recent news stories among individuals with higher status occupations and higher level of educational attainment.

Connections have been found between information *recall* from news broadcasts and viewers' levels of education. Although differences associated with education in this context have not consistently been great. Neuman (1976) found only small differences in recall from single television newscasts as a function of education. College-educated respondents recalled more news topics spontaneously and more story details when probed than did noncollege educated respondents, but differences in depth recollection from stories was not great. In Israel, Katz et al. (1977) found small differences in item recall from a television bulletin seen earlier the same evening as a function of education. In a telephone survey in which recall was tested from a television newscast within 2 to 3 hours of transmission, Stauffer, Frost, and Rybolt (1983) reported that college-educated respondents recalled more items on average than did respondents who finished full-time education before college.

Laboratory research by Renckstorff (1980) reported that a significant amount of the variance in recall of television news bulletins made up in the styles of the two West German networks was attributable to educational differences between viewers. Recall scores were about 30% higher for subjects with the high school leaving qualification than for those without it.

Findahl and Hoijer (1975b) found that although education level to some extent predicted learning from the news, the relation between recall of a fictional news bulletin and viewers' education was complex. A good background knowledge of news events was related overall to learning and this was a necessary but not a sufficient condition for good recall. Knowledge scores accounted for 22% of the recall variance. Although the better educated formed a disproportionate number of the high knowledge group, those with only elementary education nevertheless constituted two thirds of the best-informed of a random sample.

Renckstorff's data also revealed a significant interaction between education level and item content. Better educated individuals did better on all items except for one about a trade union conference, but on the whole the differences were least pronounced for items treating routine domestic affairs. Such differences suggest that it is probably misguided to make blanket statements about the mitigating effects of education or other demographic factors on learning from broadcast news. Instead, attention needs to be given to the detailed type and structure of the knowledge acquired and to viewers' pre-existing knowledge.

Another area of interest has been motivational variables, which also tend to be treated in a global way. This perspective may shed more light on the role of audience variables in as much as viewers who say they watch television news to get information, recall significantly more than those who say they do so to be entertained (Neuman, 1976).

According to proponents of the uses-and-gratifications perspective, motivational factors can have a profound influence on information recall from television programs. Those individuals who actively seek information from the media will tend to learn more than those who approach the media for some other purpose such as entertainment. In a study of memory for television news conducted within this framework, Gantz (1979) carried out telephone interviews with over 500 people. Respondents were questioned about their reasons for watching the news and on their memory for a television newscast aired a short time before the interview. Gantz divided respondents into four motivational categories: information seekers, recreation-diversion seekers, information and recreation seekers, and casual viewers. Results showed that recall of news items from the newscast correlated significantly with both information-seeking a recreation-seeking motives, but with information seekers tending to remember slightly more than recreation seekers. The worst recall performance was recorded for individuals who sought information and recreation from watching the news. Thus, a single fairly precise reason for watching the news may be more advantageous to remembering the stories in news bulletins than mixed and possibly conflicting reasons.

A limitation to the findings of this research is the fact that many viewers appeared to have no specific motivation at all for watching the news. Neuman (1976) found that although respondents who watched the news to keep informed remembered more than did those who watched for entertainment, both together comprised only one third of the sample. The great majority of viewers consisted of individuals who "just happened to catch the news" and had no special reasons for doing so. Indeed, on close examination, motivational variables turn out to be fairly weak indicators of news retention. Neuman found that the combined effect of motivational and educational variables amounted to only 2% of the total variance in recall. Likewise in Gantz' study, more than one type of motivation was associated with enhanced recall, but at best motivational variables accounted for just 5.4% of total recall variance.

In summary, broad social and educational differences have not afforded an adequate general account of differences in information gains from television news programs and the main determinants of news recall seen to lie outside the domain of sociological research frameworks. Motivational differences have also not been very promising so far, perhaps because they need to be operationally defined as specific interests pertinent to memory for news items of particular content, rather than as global characteristics of viewers conceived to underlie global news retention.

NARRATIVE VARIABLES

Story Attributes and Themes

Under this heading, one idea is that audience learning and retention of news stories is affected by the attributes of "newsworthiness" used by news editors to guide their selection of news stories for their program. Hard news about politics or economic events tends to dominate television bulletins along with emotionally arousing stories involving crime, violence, or natural catastrophes. And then there are bizarre, humorous, touching, human interest stories.

There is no doubt that the public show varying degrees of interest in different news topics (Wober, 1978). In addition there is evidence that public levels of interest in particular events are good predictors of the extent to which information about them diffuses through society (Funkhouser & McCombs, 1971). The processes involved in this diffusion, however, can be subtle and complex, and may be related only weakly and inconsistently with levels of education and claimed interest in particular news items (Genova & Greenberg, 1979).

In a few studies of memory for broadcast news comparisons have been made of retention of different types of news story. There is some indication that news editors look for stories with particular characteristics (Galtung & Ruge, 1965). According to Galtung and Ruge, events are more likely to be reported if they concern short, dramatic happenings, have a clear interpretation, have meaning and familiarity for the audience, are relevant to the audience, are about things one expects to happen, or are highly unexpected. The news must also have a balance across stories. Thus, the more stories of a particular type that emerge at one time, the greater does the news value of any single item have to be if it is to be selected. Finally, the likelihood of an event becoming a news item is increased if it concerns elite nations, elite people, the more personalized it is, and the more negative its consequences. Story categories have been used to infer interest in items among certain members of the audience. Some research has indeed indicated that the newsworthiness attributes such as those described by Galtung and Ruge do correlate with audience interest in stories (Sparkes & Winter, 1980). At a cognitive level, several studies have indicated that the identification, recall, and understanding of news stories is sometimes related significantly to the news structures of Galtung and Ruge (e.g., Katz et al., 1977; Robinson & Sahin, 1984; Schulz, 1982). These findings, however, do not yet provide clearcut evidence of how much difference interest makes to audience learning from the news (Berry, 1983b).

Neuman (1976) examined viewers' memories for various types of news stories to find out if one category of news was better remembered than another. He found substantial variations in the salience and memory of different story types. Overall, best recall was recorded for weather items and human interest stories. But the most salient items, as indicated by unaided or spontaneous recall scores, were those about Vietnam—a particularly important news topic in the United States in the early 1970s when this study was carried out.

Katz et al. (1977) reported two studies of recall of broadcast news in Israel in which retention levels for different story categories were examined. Several schemes of news classification were investigated in connection with story recall. Relevance to Israeli interests emerged as one important attribute. Domestic items were recalled better than foreign items, although among the latter, those with implications for internal Israeli affairs were recalled better than those with no such implications. News items were also classified according to institutional content such as economic, cultural, political, and so on. Items dealing with defense policy were best recalled. Finally, Galtung and Ruge's (1965) scheme of news classification based on newsmen's implicit criteria of newsworthiness was used. Katz et al. found in one study that there was a direct relationship between the number of Galtung and Ruge criteria an item met and its rate of recall among television viewers. Their second study revealed that items with negative consequences were particularly well remembered.

An experimental study of memory for television news among children suggested that dramatic or emotionally arousing items, especially when supported by film material, are more likely to be spontaneously recalled than more neutral items (Cohen, Wigand, & Harrison, 1976). However, aided recall of story details was higher than unaided recall and also showed less inter-item variation. Detailed learning of neutral items, which would have provided a useful comparison condition, was not tested. Cohen et al. found no clearcut effects of type of critical item ("sad," "happy," or "violent") nor of relevance as manipulated by geographical proximity to the homes of their 11- and 12-year-old subjects. An unfortunate shortcoming of this experiment was the confounding of story attributes with serial position by using a single order of presentation, and with visual format, in that "emotionally arousing items" but not neutral items contained film footage. It is not certain therefore whether story attribute effects or presentation order and format effects produced differences in memory for items.

Story Structures

Another feature of news stories that carries important implications for news memory and comprehension is the way the stories themselves are told. Observational studies of the inner workings of television newsrooms have revealed that news editors tend to employ particular, stereotyped narrative structures with the intention of creating interest and increasing comprehension of news (see Golding

& Elliott, 1979). One popular style of storytelling has been referred to as the *inverted pyramid*. This style was developed by newspaper journalists but has been adopted by television journalists too. This style of reporting puts the major, attention-grabbing facts at the head of the story, secondary facts next, and finally background details at the base of the pyramid. However, to what extent are the routine methods of narrative construction used in broadcast news conducive to effective learning?

In research on learning texts, cognitive psychologists have found that the way information in extended narratives is organized can have a significant effect on how much is remembered. Various cognitive theorists have proposed different structural frameworks that embody specifications concerning how information in narratives can best be organized to enhance learning from them (see Kintsch, 1974; Thorndyke, 1979; van Dijk, 1980).

Several recent news comprehension studies have reported evidence that standard storytelling formats in news broadcasting may not provide the optimal conditions for learning and have offered alternative story frames that have been demonstrated as producing better learning from news broadcast materials under laboratory conditions than did original broadcast versions of the same stories (Berry & Clifford, 1987; Findahl & Hoijer, 1984, 1985; Larsen, 1981).

VISUAL FORMAT CONDITIONS AND NEWS RECALL

Broadcasters have traditionally thought of television as an essentially visual medium and many TV newsmen hold that the visual channel should always be utilized to its fullest extent. In particular, film material is highly favored because it conveys an impression of immediateness or "actuality" that is regarded by many producers as so important for impact on the audience (see Schlesinger, 1978). The studio-presenter, on the other hand, is regarded as very much the second best method of presentation, and is claimed by some producers to distract the viewer's attention from what is being reported, thus interfering with retention of program content (Whale, 1969). But how accurate are these naive psychological assumptions of TV newsmen? Do visuals such as film or stills enhance learning or does eagerness to use pictures at every opportunity result in distraction that inhibits information processing from the bulletin narrative?

The research literature offers widely varying estimations of the value of visual material in news reports. Jorgenson (1955) found no difference in information gain from televised presentations between newscaster-only format and the newscaster speaking over film, but did report that items containing still pictures fared somewhat worse. This pattern has not been replicated. Subsequently, Hazard (1963) also failed to find that film produced more information gain than did the newscaster seen alone.

Until very recently, inconclusive and contradictory evidence was the rule in research on television news recall. Katz et al. (1977) looked at the extent to which pictures enhanced topic recall among Israeli respondents and found in one study that radio listeners forgot more bulletin items than television viewers, but in second study that individuals who saw a television newscast performed no better on tests of news retention than others who had been asked to listen only to the same program. Unfortunately, these field studies failed to control adequately for a number of confounding variables, such as the length and number of items contained in test bulletins and the amount of attention paid to news broadcasts.

Laboratory studies of presentation style and news recall have produced conflicting results in recent years. Baggaley (1980) found no effect of visual accompaniment on memory for news narratives, whereas Gunter (1979, 1980a) reported substantial variations in spontaneous recall of brief news headlines differing in visual format characteristics. The different recall tasks employed in each case here probably accounted for the lack of consistency in findings as may the nature and length of the items presented. Baggaley (1980) compared recall from an extensive news narrative in newscaster-only versions (with the presenter facing camera, or in profile, or looking at notes) and in newscaster plus film versions. Following each version, subjects were administered a questionnaire containing 30 phrases taken from the item's text. Up to four words were omitted from each phrase and subjects were asked to fill these in. No differences in recall emerged as a function of treatments, although the effectiveness of this method of testing news recall must be questioned. No indications were given about the types of information tested and it is doubtful that viewers under natural viewing conditions would encode and store news texts in this rote fashion.

In the first of two studies by Gunter referred to earlier, free recall was tested of the verbal content of 15 brief newscast items recorded from national television newscasts several months before the study and edited so that no two successive items were of the same news category (Gunter, 1979). Subjects received the news items either via both auditory and visual channels as would normally be the case when viewing a television newscast (video mode) or in soundtrack only (audio mode). Within the video mode, five items contained film footage, five contained still pictures, and five consisted of the newscaster only. These items were edited together as five successive trials with fixed within-triad item order: film-item, still-item, and newscaster-only item across all triads. Overall spontaneous recall was better from the video mode than from the audio mode and within the video mode, items accompanied by moving film were better recalled than those accompanied by stills, and better in the latter case than for newscaster-only items. Although item content and visual format were confounded, these results cannot be attributed to the intrinsic properties of the news items because there were no differences in recall of items from different format categories to parallel those in the video treatment for those subjects who listened only to the materials in the audio condition. These findings were replicated in a similar study by Gunter (1980a), and appear to support broadcasters views on the value of visual accompaniments, at least when these are appropriate to the spoken text.

Several interpretations may be placed on these results. One possible explanation of picture enhancement effects is that greater attention is paid to items with visual accompaniment than to items presented in a plain studio setting resulting in the former being encoded better than the latter. Picture superiority in retrieval tasks has also been explained in terms of stimulus differentiation (Dominowski & Gadlin, 1968; Wicker, 1970; Wicker & Evertson, 1972). The discriminability hypothesis asserts that imagery increases the distinctiveness of items and reduces inter-item interference. Another explanation stems from the dual-coding hypothesis (Paivio, 1969, 1971) and suggests that picture items are more variably encoded than nonpictorial items. Picture items (e.g., news items with film or still accompaniment) may be stored in terms of two separate codes—a verbal code and a picture code—whereas items not accompanied by picture material would normally have only one available code a verbal one. During recall, it is the availability of an extra memory code that can serve as retrieval cues, which accounts for the superiority of picture items over those without pictures.

In a further study, Gunter (1980b) tested immediate recall among a college sample who had seen a sequence of full-length news items, each of around 1-minute duration. Three versions of each news item were prepared; newscaster-only presentation, newscaster presentation with still illustrations, and newscaster presentation with film footage. Results here were the reverse of the two previous studies (Gunter, 1979, 1980a). Recall was best from the newscaster-only condition.

In a further analysis of Gunter's (1980b) findings, however, Berry (1983a) found that film material did enhance learning, but from a particular part of the item rather than across the item as a whole. This re-analysis found an apparent impairing effect of visuals (still or film) upon audience recall of parallel narrative content. However, recall of the talking-head's lead-in narrative (presented prior to the onset of visual material) was enhanced in the conditions with visual illustrations. These results were consistent with others (Edwardson, Grooms, & Proudlove, 1981; Findahl, 1971; Renckstorff, 1977), all of whom reported better cued recall from visually enriched news stories than from extended "talking-head" presentations.

It needs to be said, however, that the studies discussed here employed a relatively simplistic manipulation of visual format. Research elsewhere has found that complex relationships can exist between visual features and narrative context that mediate the type of effect visuals have on audience reaction of news content (Brosius, 1989; Reese, 1984). Learning from television news can be enhanced where visuals and script are informationally redundant, although excessive redundancy can begin to impede learning (Reese, 1984). Whether or not supportive illustrations lead to impaired memory for news also depends on which particular story details are visually reinforced.

Cuing Properties of Visual Illustrations
and News Recall

In their review of educational media research, Chu and Schramm (1967) concluded that the use of visuals will improve learning from audiovisual messages
where it contributes to the information contained in the audiotrack; otherwise
visual images may actually impair learning through distraction. Severin (1967,
1968) hypothesized that presentation of irrelevant cues in either the visual or
audio channels will cause a loss of learning from the other channel, but when
additional and nonredundant cues are presented in either channel, greater overall
learning will take place. Applied to television news broadcasting, this "cue-
summation" theory predicts that newsfilm not conveying information consistent
with the story would prove distracting. Such distraction. Severin found, could
be particularly powerful when the information presented in one channel is only
partially irrelevant to information carried in the other channel.

In a direct test of the effects of nonredundant film accompaniment on detailed
recall of story content in television newscasts, Edwardson, Grooms and Pringle
(1976) showed subjects eight different news items that consisted of actual stories
written with some alteration of names and facts so that subjects would not remember the information from previous newscasts or newspaper reports. A male
newscaster was recorded on videotape reading the news stories in two versions.
In one treatment, four of the stories were accompanied by silent motion-picture
film; and in the second treatment, the remaining four stories were shown with
film. Content retention from each item was tested by a series of multiple-choice
questions. A pretest on a separate sample of subjects who saw the film from each
item without audio and were then tested for knowledge acquisition, indicated that
none of the film clips conveyed any of the information contained in the news items.

In the experiment proper, no substantial differences emerged between the number of correct responses to questions concerning news materials given with or
without film. It should be noted finally that the film used with these stories was
typical of film footage used in actual news bulletins and the observed learning
effects might therefore be expected to occur also in naturalistic viewing situations. There is no unequivocal answer to the question whether it is always best
to use film or stills or no visuals at all in television news production.

An important factor when visual accompaniment is presented is the degree
of correspondence between picture material and verbal material. Although film
has been regarded by news professionals as a natural means of portraying actuality in television bulletins (Altheide, 1976; Schlesinger, 1978), research has shown
that where effective communication is the ultimate goal, the impact of still pho-
tos, graphics, or schematic drawings can often be just as good (Findahl, 1971;
Findahl & Hoijer, 1976), although there is some evidence to support the thesis
that film is more appreciated by the audience than other visual modes of presentation (Reckenstorff, 1977). From a production standpoint, the use of still or graph-

ic material affords considerably more flexibility and control in the design of individual news items and indeed the bulletin as a whole than the use of film material. While film is often allowed to dominate production strategy, with the availability or nonavailability of appropriate footage an important factor determining that stories are selected for eventual presentation, stills, graphics, and schematic drawings can be tailored more precisely to fit in with specific news storylines that deserve selection on merit for their intrinsic interest quite apart from their visual potential. However, accompanying the greater flexibility afforded by visual stills is the need for considerable care in the way they are applied.

Research in Sweden has shown specific properties for pictures with respect to recall of different parts of the storyline of news items (Findhal, 1971; Findahl & Hoijer, 1976). By systematically varying which aspects of the story were illustrated, Findahl (1971) showed that recall was best where visual accompaniment clearly corresponded to the verbal information in the narrative and was poorest with no illustration. No difference was found between movie film illustrations and stills, although the relevant comparison here was made only for one news item.

Findahl and Hoijer (1976) produced fuller evidence that the correspondence between narrative content and visual content and the story aspects recalled is more important than the broad visualization category. Their research showed that viewers often retain only fragments of news events, isolated from their contexts particularly when only personalities or locations were illustrated. Emphasizing the causes and consequences of an event by suitable visual accompaniment to the verbal text, however, enhanced the recall of other content in addition to these aspects.

From an applied standpoint, balanced recall and proper understanding of news stories seems to depend heavily on careful and selective use of visual illustrations. These should be determined by the requirements of the story content rather than predominating over what is said, as is apparently so often the case, especially in the use of film (see Schlesinger, 1978). Indeed, the greater control afforded by using still-photographic and specially designed schematic or graphic material when matching visual to the story text suggests the more extensive the use of these kinds of visualization in the news.

ORGANIZATION AND FORMULATION
OF CONTENT AND NEWS RECALL

News Taxonomy and Item-Order Effects

Television news programs are characterized by a number of structural attributes that determine the way news is put together and that embody certain intuitive assumptions on the part of news editors about informing their audiences. These assumptions can be experimentally tested. Among the attributes of probable importance to news retention are serial-ordering and the grouping and placement of news reports according to story category.

Content research has shown that some types of story are more likely than others to occupy the first three positions in TV bulletins. Usually, early bulletin positions are occupied by political, foreign or industrial items, whereas the latter half of the program consisted more often of sports, science, and human interest items. There is also a tendency to cluster together items from a common taxonomic category, usually found with foreign and industrial items (Glasgow University Media Group, 1976). Thus, it is usual practice to have a round-up of foreign news consisting of a series of stories that have the common characteristic of being located outside the United Kingdom. Also, industrial news concerning pay claims or strikes is frequently clustered with stories on broader and often unconnected, although semantically quite similar, economic issues, with implied causal connection between them.

Producers apparently assume that this sequencing of bulletin content serves to package together isolated events into more meaningful combinations that can be more readily learned by the audience. If newscast profiles exhibit strong and consistent biases in their serial ordering and treatment of news topics, then these factors need to be examined for their effects on the kinds of news events that are predominantly learned and remembered by audiences. As evidence from psychological research presented in the following sections indicates, the attempt to arrive at clarity and simplicity of presentation by packaging the news according to taxonomy may in fact impair memory for bulletin content.

In an early study of story-placement effects, Tannenbaum (1954) found a clear pattern of differential recall from a radio bulletin as a function of item position, with items near the end recalled best of all. In a study of memory for a TV news sequence, Gunter (1979) found a distinct serial learning curve showing strong primacy and recency effects for item recall following video and audio-only presentation. However, within the video mode, serial position effects were much weaker for film and still items than for newscaster-only items.

Recently, more detailed investigation of sequence factors in news programs has been completed that focused on the effects of the production technique of clustering items from a common news category. This research was based on the release from proactive-interference (PI) paradigm described by Wickens (1970, 1972), who used the technique as an indicator of the attributes along which individuals encode linguistic materials. In the traditional paradigm, recall has been found to decline over successively presented taxonomically homogenous sequences of simple linguistic material such as word triads (Loess, 1967, 1968) and more recently with complex prose passages (Blumenthal & Robbins, 1977; Gunter, 1979). The analysis of PI effects with TV news represented a further natural and logical extension of the traditional paradigm of particular interest because it offers a potential index of how people categorize and perhaps differentially encode news items as well as an empirical test of the practical consequences of news clustering in TV bulletins.

Gunter et al. (1980) presented a series of four trials, each of which consisted of three short television news items videorecorded several months before from actual networked broadcasts. The items were selected to control for length and visual format differences as far as possible, and were shown on a small monochrome television monitor to subjects individually. Following each news triad, the subject worked on a distracter task (crossword puzzle) for 1 minute and then recalled all the items he or she could from that trial in any order by writing a short account of each item. The accuracy of recall was scored on each trial.

In each experiment, subjects were divided into two groups, a "no-shift" group for whom the news category of the items was held constant over all four trials, and a "shift" group, for whom the taxonomy was constant over the first three trials only and was switched to a different category on the fourth trial. Several different random sequences of the same items were used within this design to minimize idiosyncratic effects related to particular items. In one experiment, subjects were shown items about political events of items about sport. Half of the subjects in the no-shift condition received triads of political items over all trials, whereas half received only sports items. In the shift condition, half of the subjects were switched from political items over the first three trials, to sports items on the fourth trials, whereas half were switched in the opposite direction (Gunter et al., 1980, Experiment 1).

It was found that recall performance declined over successive triads of items from the same taxonomy, in the no-shift condition from over 80% of responses correct on the first trial to less than 45% correct on the fourth trial. Following a critical switch in news taxonomy, however, as occurred on the fourth trial in the shift condition, a substantial improvement in recall performance (over 70% correct) resulted. The PI build-up and release effects occurred for political and sports items, and in a study reported elsewhere (Gunter, Berry, & Clifford, 1981, Experiment 2) across foreign and industrial items too, hence it seems unlikely that they are specific to particular news categories. Wickens (1970, 1972) interpreted PI release as an indicator of the encoded attributes of linguistic materials. Consequently, the current findings may signify that viewers encode broad taxonomic features of news items along with more specific details of the story narrative.

Television news reports may often be quite detailed and so too, therefore, might be information gain from them. Gunter et al., (1980) tested only brief news headline recall that may have primed subjects' awareness of the taxonomic similarities and dissimilarities of news items, thus artificially inducing taxonomically based PI effects. To what extent do these same effects occur under conditions of detailed content retention were relatively superficial taxonomic labels might be much less salient?

To examine this question, Gunter et al. (1981, Experiment 2) attempted a replication of their first study on taxonomic encoding employing a detailed news-learning situation. With all items of constant visual format (newscaster-only presentation), they presented one news story per learning trial. Following a filler task (crossword puzzle) to minimize rehearsal, subjects received a series of four questions on details of the item. After four such trials, a final, delayed cue-recall test was given, consisting of eight new and eight repeated questions covering all items shown during the initial phase. Once again, recall declined across taxonomically similar items and improved on shifting to a new learning category. This pattern of responding carried over from the immediate recall phase to delayed recall and interestingly, although recall of information previously tested during the first phase was remembered much better during delayed testing than previously untested material, PI build-up and release patterns were strongly evident across both new and repeated delayed recall.

In summary, these results suggested that news information is forgotten because of taxonomically based interference over a sequence of items from the same story category. The main practical implication is that it may be unwise to cluster news items in television bulletins according to taxonomy. This point is important in view of the salient role of news taxonomy in the production of television, newscasts, especially in relation to the problem of clarity and comprehensibility of program content.

Visual Illustrations and News Clustering Effects

Some editors and producers may be reluctant to follow the recommendations to avoid taxonomic packaging of news in TV bulletins for one reason (aesthetic or historic professional) or another, so does experimental research with television news materials offer any other workable solutions? One alternative answer may lie in the use of visualizations within taxonomic packages.

In television, verbal news items are characterized by features other than taxonomic ones. News broadcasters place much emphasis on presenting a very "visual" news and changes in visual context are used to break up the program and make it more interesting, and in the case of film, to make its content seem more realistic. Research within the release-from-PI framework has shown that with simple linguistic materials, visual context features may also be encoded as salient attributes of to-be-remembered stimuli (Brodie & Lippmann, 1970; Turvey & Egan, 1969). It should be remembered that Gunter (1979, 1980a) showed that brief news items accompanied by film or by stills are better recalled than newscaster-only items. Do these visual format features of news materials also represent encodable dimensions of verbal news reports?

Gunter et al. (1980, Experiment 2) again employed a Wickens-type design, this time with taxonomic category held constant across all items for viewers in both shift and no-shift conditions. Items were differentiated instead according to their visual format characteristics. Two visual categories were used, newscaster-only items consisting of the presenter reading the news directly into camera, and visual-still items in which a still photograph relating to the news event was inserted over the newscaster for between 15% and 20% of the duration of the item. As in the taxonomic-shift experiments, the two categories of items were allocated equally to viewers in the no-shift condition and visual shifts from newscasters-only to newscaster-plus-still items or vice versa were balanced across viewers in the shift condition. Recall performance declined over taxonomically and visual-homogenous news triads and improved following a visual format shift.

However, this shift produced a substantial improvement in memory performance in one direction only (i.e., when changing from newscaster-only items to newscaster-plus-stills). The reverse shift resulted in only slight release from PI. According to Wickens (1970, 1972), a symmetrical release effect in both directions is necessary to infer differential encoding along the two critical categories (in this case, visual formats) of stimulus materials. These data suggest that viewers may not differentially categorize and encode news items along gross visual format features to the same degree that they do along taxonomic attributes. However, they also indicate that taxonomically generated interference can nevertheless be alleviated by changes in visual format. Thus, visual format variations may be effectively utilized to offset to some extent the information losses that occur in taxonomically homogeneous news packages. Although the experiments on news-clustering effects seem to point to important factors influencing the processing of news information, it has yet to be made clear how extensive these effects are. These experiments used demographically narrow subject samples and examined news recall in artificial laboratory settings. We need to know whether these effects occur for people in general and when they view TV news in more natural settings. There is some evidence to suggest, for example with PI effects and TV news, that not all individuals exhibit equal amounts of forgetting over certain categories of homogeneous news sequences (Gunter, 1980c).

Speed of Presentation Effects

Vast quantities of news information are generated in the world today and one of the major responsibilities of television news broadcasters is to sample widely from this flow of knowledge and to present as much of it as possible to their audiences. Television bulletins are, however, of limited duration and capacity and are therefore restricted in what and how much information they can show. One solution to this problem may be to compress knowledge and speed up the rate at which information is presented. But what effect will this have on comprehension and recall of bulletin content? To what extent can presenter news-delivery rate vary without detrimentally affecting either audience recall of message content? If delivery rate can be increased without concomitant negative effects, a greater amount of news information could be presented in a fixed-length program.

It is now possible to vary the speed of speech with an electronic technique called time compression. Normally, when the speed of a tape recording is increased, the speed of speech increases but sounds unnaturally high and strident in pitch. To eliminate this distortion, a computerized time-compression device is connected to the recording and restores the voice to normal regardless of the speed at which it is played. Using time compression, it is possible to vary the presentation rate of the audiotrack without distorting natural voice quality as long as the speed is not increased by more than 40% (MacLachlan & La Barbera, 1978).

Most experimental studies on delivery rate in spoken informational sequences have dealt with single-topic messages, but have rarely investigated multiple-topic material such as that typically found in television news bulletins. Fairbanks, Guttmann, and Miron (1957) found little difference in the comprehension of listening selections presented at 141, 201, and 282 words per minute. Thereafter, comprehension as indicated by percent of test questions correctly answered, declined from 58% correct at 282 words per minute to 26% at 470 words per minute. In a later study, Foulke (1978) reported no serious deterioration in listeners' comprehension of a passage as presentation rate was decreased from 125 words per minute to 250 words per minute, but it declined rapidly thereafter.

From these results, it appears that time is required to perceive and encode words properly, and that as word rate is increased beyond a certain point, the perception time available to the listener becomes inadequate and a rapid deterioration of listening comprehension commences. Using single-topic messages, researchers in speeded and compressed speech have generally reported that recall does not significantly decline until a delivery rate of around 300 words per minute is reached. In news broadcasts, however, a wide range of topics may be covered in rapid succession, and on television such changes occur not only in the audio narrative but also visually.

Does this additional complexity of newscast materials relative to single-topic audio-messages usually studied in compressed-speech experiments mean that the optimal delivery rate of broadcast news can be varied over only a fairly narrow range without damaging comprehension and memory of bulletin content? In an early directly relevant study, Nelson (1948) tested recall of multiple-topic radio news materials. Extending presentation rate from 125 to 225 words per minute produced a slight, although nonsignificant decline in recall of bulletin content at the upper end of this range.

More recently, Smith and McEwan (1974) compiled two 5- minute radio newscasts of exactly 800 words each. One newscast consisted of a detailed single topic message only, whereas the other contained 12 different and much briefer news items. A professional newscaster read each message at each of four presentation rates; 160, 190, 220, and 250 words per minute. Delivery rate was found to have a significant effect on recall and the point at which the onset of detrimental effects occurred depended on the complexity of the program. Recall began to decline at and above 220 words per minute for the single-topic newscast but at only 190 words per minute for the multiple-topic newscast. The results indicated that a newsreader could vary his or her rate of delivery from 160 to 190 words per minute in multiple-topic newscast situations, and from 160 to 220 words per minute in single-topic commentary-style situations without experiencing detrimental rate effects.

Clearly, audio delivery rates can have important effects on comprehension and recall of broadcast news material, but in the case of television in particular, presentation rate may vary visually as well as auditorily. How important is rapid visual change during a bulletin to memory for news content? Relevant research here has been carried out by Schlater (1970) who examined the maximum rate of presentation at which relevant visual information could be transmitted in a television newscast before recall was impeded. Simulated newscasts were prepared in which a 4½-minute narrative was accompanied by visual material under a number of rates of presentation.

Viewers were tested for comprehension and memory of pictorial information and verbal information from the news message. Memory for picture information in response to picture cues declined as rate of picture presentation increased, but picture information tested by verbal questions *increased* as rate of picture presentation was increased, and leveled off at about seven visuals per 30 seconds. One explanation for this difference in picture recall between test conditions is that verbal questions formulated about picture content provided additional information to aid memory performance that was not contained in pictorial recall cues. Increasing rate of picture presentation had no substantial effect on viewers' ability to comprehend and remember the audio-narrative of the television bulletin. However, this is not to say that visual presentation changes are unlikely to affect verbal recall from television newscasts. Schlater (1970) admitted that much of the picture content presented in this study was informationally redundant with respect to the verbal text of the message. Where this is not the case, as is likely in many live news broadcasts, the effects of rate of visual change on memory for story narrative might be more substantial. Further research is needed here before any clearcut statement can be made concerning the effects of presentation rate of information in one channel (e.g., visual) upon recall of information from the other major channel (e.g., audio) in television news programs.

All the studies on effects of presentation rate on memory for television messages reported above focused on accelerating materials in only one modality — either auditory or visual — but not in both simultaneously. However, if material is speeded up in one channel it may be necessary to increase presentation rate in the other channel to synchronize information flow in each modality. What is the effect of increasing speed of information flow in two channels simultaneously upon comprehension and memory for television content? As yet no evidence has been forthcoming with news material, but research with advertising content has implied that the effectiveness of television commercials, in a number of respects, may be increased through speeding them up using the time-compression technique (MacLachlan & La Barbera, 1978). With these audiovisual materials, increased rate of presentation was achieved in both channels simultaneously through use of a variable speed projector in conjunction with a computerized time-compression device. As the speed of the projector was increased, so too did the speed of the motion picture. At the same time the soundtrack was synchronized with the projected image and the pitch of the speeded sound was normalized by computer-controlled time compression.

To test the effectiveness of time compression with audiovisual advertising, MacLachlan and La Barbera (1978) showed six television commercials to viewers either at normal speed or 25% faster than normal and tested level of interest and recall afterwards for each commercial. For five of the six advertisements, interest level was higher for the speeded up version, and three of these differences were statistically significant. Unaided brand-name recall measured for these commercials 2 days after presentation showed no appreciable differences for normal or accelerated treatments. On three commercials, recall was better for the faster paced versions, in two cases it was higher for the normal speed versions. However, the fact that recall was not adversely affected by faster pacing led the authors to recommend use of time compression with television advertising because of the shorter time they require, thus cutting down on expensive air-time. With respect to advertising specifically, there is a need however to find out whether certain types of commercials or aspects of commercials can be time compressed with greater success than others, and whether certain aspects might suffer from being accelerated in this way. This last point has implication of time compression to other types of televised message such as those presented in news bulletins. For instance, will certain news topics benefit more than others from accelerated presentation, whether in the audio channel only, or in both audio and visual channels simultaneously?

Repetition and Reformulation Effects

In television bulletins, news information is presented in a steady stream over which viewers have no control. Unlike the case of reading a newspaper, they do not have the opportunity to go back over a news story again at their own pace to pick up further details from it which they missed first time around. One way to offset the information losses that might occur because of inadequate time to process bulletin content effectively on its first presentation is to repeat or reformulate portions of that content at some point in the program. Two important questions arise here. First, at what points in the program relative to the main reports should repetitions occur, and second, which aspect of the news report should be repeated or reformulated to best enhance learning overall?

Repetition of material can be "massed" or "distributed." The majority of studies have operationalized distributed practice as repetition or review of material interspersed within the body of a presentation and massed practice as a summary occurring at the end of the main body of to-be-learned material—much like the summary of main headlines occurring at the end of a television news bulletin. Within this framework, Maccoby and Sheffield (1961) found massed practice to be less effective than spaced practice for mastering a sequential learning task, whereas Ash and Jasper (1953) found spaced practice to be more effective than massed practice in learning military tasks. Further studies by Underwood and Ekstrand (1967) and Rothkopf (1968) have suggested that spaced practice is superior to massed practice in promoting the retention of verbal and motor skills.

Although the evidence on the effect of repetition on learning print material is far from conclusive, most producers of informational television programming hold firmly to the belief that repetition of material will enhance memory for it. But although massed summary treatment seems to be preferred style of reviewing information in television newscasts, is there any empirical evidence to show that this treatment is the most effective method of structuring a television program to enhance learning?

Coldevin (1975) examined the effects of various styles of information reformulation on learning from 20-minute program on forest fires among groups of 12- and 13-year-old children. In the three treatments, repetitions of information were distributed within the body of the program material (massed review), distributed with the addition of a pause between the review statement and the body of the text under review (spaced review), or finally, a simple summing-up of all repeated material at the end of the program (summary review). Recall scores were substantially greater for all repetition treatments than for the program without repetitions, indicating that reviewing material in a program strengthens information gain from it. There was some indication from an earlier study reported by Coldevin (1974) that the style of review treatment itself was important too, with superior learning recorded for the spaced review treatment over both massed and summary treatments. It is possible that the dominance here resulted from greater internationalization of content and covert practice between repetitions facilitated by pauses between reviews and the main body of material.

Perloff, Wartella, and Becker, (1982) designed an experiment in which repetition and speed of presentation of news were manipulated. Repetition was manipulated by the presence or absence of a brief recapping of the main points of the major items in the newscast at the end of the program. Pace of delivery of the items was also varied by length of pauses between stories. Results revealed a highly significant effect of recapping, whereby news recaps affected both immediate recall and delayed recall, 1 week later. There was no major effect of pause length on recall.

Repetition need not involve simply literal re-presentation of the content. Re-emphasizing the central, vital elements of the basic news message may prove much more effective at enhancing recall of the essential aspects of the reported issue or event. Findahl and Hoijer (1972) investigated the effects of reformulating news messages in this way. They presented respondents with items under several different conditions in which various portions of the content were repeated within each news report. A fictitious news bulletin was prepared consisting of thirteen items. Five of these were independently manipulated under four treatment conditions:

repetition of information about the participants or location of an event, repetition of cause information, repetition of consequences information, or repetition of all these aspects of story content. There was also a control condition consisting of the basic news message with no additional verbal information. Retention of story details was measured by means of short open-ended questions that could be answered in one or two words. Results showed that verbal reformulation of any part of an item enhanced retention for the same information relative to the basic message condition but did not necessarily improve overall memory for item content.

If verbal reformulation place additional emphasis on the location and participants of the news event, these facts were retained nearly twice as well as other more abstract elements of the story concerning cause and effect relationships. However, stressing the latter components not only improved knowledge of causes and consequences, but also effected a more general improvement in retention even for those elements (i.e., details of participants and results of course recurred in a subsequent study by the same researchers on the effects of additional *visual* information on news recall; Findahl & Hoijer, (1976). This study was discussed in an earlier section of this chapter.

Findahl and Hoijer (1976) also examined the effects on memory for television news of jointly reformulating news texts and manipulating visual accompaniment, and suggested ways in which one mode of additional input may or may not serve to balance the other so as to enhance learning. For example, visually illustrating the location of an event with a map preceded an imbalance in memory for item content because although recall of the illustrated portion of the item was enhanced other aspects of the story were less well remembered. Balance was successfully restored, however, when the non-illustrated relational aspects of the item (i.e., cause and consequence information) were verbally reformulated. But this counterbalancing relationship between additional visual input and verbal repetition does not apparently always lead to improved overall recall on item content. In another treatment, Findahl and Hoijer (1976) used schematic drawings to illustrate the causes and consequences of news events. This improved memory not only for illustrated features but also for other aspects of the story. When in addition to this, however, information about the location and people involved in the event were verbally reformulated within the text, repetition counterfaced the effect of the picture material detrimentally, and resulted in poorer recall for causes and consequences information. The most successful condition of all, however, was when the cause of the event was visually illustrated and verbally repeated. In this case, their respective effects were additive.

The Swedish findings reported here indicate that employing visual illustrations with verbal repetition of the narrative can enhance viewers' recall of item content, but that certain combinations of the two work better than others. Under some circumstances, pictures and repetition are mutually beneficial and under others they are not.

SCHEDULING EFFECTS

News program are broadcast throughout the day on television in the United States and United Kingdom Even a fairly casual glance reveals differences in styles of presentation and in the types of news stories presented in these broadcasts across the day. These stylistic and content differences reflect "professional" judgments of news editors about the character and mood of audiences at different times of day. It is assumed, for instance, that viewers will want a different, lighter style of news presentation to start the day. But from a learning point of view, to what extent and in what ways do cognitive information-processing capacities of individuals vary from one part of the day to the next? And what implications do such variations have for learning from the news and for the way in which it is presented?

It has long been known in experimental research on human learning that cognitive performance varies at different times of the day, reflecting cyclical changes in physiology and basic psychological processes throughout the day (Conroy & Mills, 1970; Folkard, 1980; Hockey & Colquhoun, 1972). Historically, the earliest evidence of time of day effects dates back to Ebbinghaus (1913/1964) who found that he was able to learn lists of nonsense syllables more quickly in the morning than in the evening. Then, during the early part of this century, educational researchers began to investigate this effect in more detail when considering how best to arrange school timetables to facilitate different kinds of learning (Gates, 1916; Winch, 1911, 1912, 1913). In more recent years, experimental psychologies have begun to treat time of day seriously as an independent variable that can significantly affect learning and memory for simple and complex verbal materials alike (Folkard, 1981; Folkard & Monk, 1978, 1980). From an applied standpoint, interest in time of day effects on cognitive performance was stimulated among broadcasting researchers following the introduction in Britain of early morning television, whose two new services focused on news and information features (BBC1's "Breakfast-time" and TV-am's "Good Morning Britain"). National opinion polls have for many years indicated a public perception that television is the most important source of news about the world (IBA, 1985; Roper, 1983). There is evidence too that people trust the news on television more than news from any other mass media source (Gunter, 1986; Lee, 1975). Given the promise by its producers that breakfast television would provide depth to news coverage and enhance viewers understanding of both domestic and world affairs, therefore, it became of interest to find out whether the achievement of this objective would be helped or hindered by the time when these programs are transmitted.

Prior to the inception of breakfast television, experiments carried out by psychologists in Britain using complex learning materials such as magazine articles, story narratives, and instructional films, had indicated that the time of day when presentation and learning occurs could have a significant effect on levels of information retention. In each case, the material was learned better earlier in the day than later on, when tests were conducted immediately after presentation (Folkard & Monk, 1980; Folkard, Monk, Bradbury, & Rosenthal, 1977).

Time of day effects were found to vary, however, depending on the type of memory performance being investigated. Although immediate memory for news material benefitted from early presentation, delayed memory was found to *improve* rather than *deteriorate* across the day (Folkard & Monk, 1980; Folkard et al., 1977). What happens in both cases when the test material is news?

Time of Day Effects and Memory for TV News

In general, the traditional findings are replicated. Gunter, Jarrett and Furnham (1983) tested time of day effects on immediate memory for televised news information. Three groups of randomly assigned subjects received the same sequence of television news items at 09.30, 13.30, or 17.30. The purpose of the experiment was disguised from subjects who were led to believe they were taking part in a TV programs evaluation study involving several categories of programs of which the news was one. Unexpected tests of free recall, cued recall, and recognition of news content were given immediately after presentation. Results showed significant decrements in memory performance on all tests across the day. Immediate memory for the news was best at 09.30 and worst at 17.30. Furthermore, there were variations in the extent to which memory performance declined for different aspects of news stories. Recall of meaningful information about the causes of events fell away more rapidly with time of day than did recall of concrete factual information about the people involved in or the locations of events. In a follow-up study, Gunter, Furnham, and Jarrett (1984) explored time of day effects on delayed memory for television news. Once again, three groups were run, at 09.30, 13.30, and 16.30. Unexpected tests of free recall, cued recall, and recognition followed about 2 hours after presentation. Time of day effects were not as powerful for delayed memory as they had been find to be for immediate memory, but they were in the expected direction. Memory performance improved slightly across the day on tests of recall circumstances where individuals have to actively retrieve news information that has been given time to consolidate in memory, time of presentation has only a slight effect on performance levels. But under conditions where viewers are required to recognize and correctly identify information from items and differentiate it from bogus information delayed performance benefits from presentation later in the day.

Since the publication of these two studies, the author with Adrian Furnham, has conducted another experiment that explores further time of day effects on immediate memory for the news (Furnham & Gunter, 1987). On this occasion, however, the focus has been not just on television news, but also on news presented via other media.

Because people read newspapers and listen to radio as well as watch television for their news information at different times of day, the question arises: Is one medium any more effective than another at a particular time? And to time of day effects has a more pronounced impact on learning via one medium than another? Put more explicitly, are time of day effects more pronounced when watching the news on television, listening to it on the radio, or reading about it in a newspaper? Or do time of day effects learning from each of these news media to the same degree?

Memory was best when the news was presented in print and was worst when presented audiovisually. Recall from print was significantly better than recall from audio-only presentation, and recall from the latter was significantly better in turn than recall from earlier experiments by the same authors (Furnham & Gunter, 1985; Gunter & Furnham, 1986).

Immediate recall of news also varied significantly as a function of the time of day. Once again reinforcing earlier findings, memory performance was best in the morning and worst in the evening—although for overall news recall only morning and evening sessions produced recall levels which were significantly different from each other (Gunter et al., 1983). With regard to types of news content, violent news was recalled better than nonviolent news in all media and at all times of day, thus also replicating earlier findings (Gunter et al., 1984; Gunter & Furnham, 1986).

In addition to these main effects, a number of interesting interactions between them occurred to exert further influences on immediate news recall. These in turn may indicate more about the psychological processes operating to affect memory performance under different presentation conditions. Recall of violent news presented either audiovisually or in soundtrack only deteriorated more from morning to afternoon than did nonviolent news recall. Recall of the latter from the two media was observed to decline more substantially across the second half of the day, whereas recall of violent story content presented audiovisually slowed down later in the day. The pattern of deterioration in memory performance with print was different. With violent news, recall dropped off more across the afternoon than across the morning, whereas memory performance for nonviolent news had hardly slipped at all by early afternoon, but then deteriorated much more by the early evening. How are these recall patterns to be explained?

Time of day effects have been accounted for previously in terms of changes in arousal throughout the day (see Eysenck, 1982), which in turn are hypothesized to affect cognitive information processing. As arousal increases across the day, as part of the normal diurnal cycle, the processing of new information is presumed to become less efficient as the optimal level of excitation is surpassed. This effect can be observed especially in immediate memory performance, during which new information is still being actively processed at the time memory for it is tested.

In the present experiment it may be presumed further that the medium of presentation and nature of the to-be-remembered content will also affect arousal level. The presence of moving pictures in the audiovisual medium and the violence in some news stories may all produce additional arousal in receiver over and above whatever his or her base level of arousal happened to be at the time of news presentation. In the morning when arousal levels are known still to be quite low the presence of exciting violent film footage may have produced additional arousal, but total arousal may not have pushed beyond optimal levels. By evening, however, when basal arousal levels are known to be higher, the additional excitement of violent film sequences may have reduced the efficiency of information interference, if indeed that is what occurred, seemed to spill over and have a more pronounced deleterious effect on recall of the non-violent items and the violent one.

Even though time of day effects appear on this evidence to influence information processing from all media, the results also suggest that where additional sources (such as film footage) are absent, such as in the print condition, memory performance does not deteriorate so much. Indeed, recall, both of violent and nonviolent news as better from print in the evening than from an audiovisual presentation in the morning.

At a practical level, the current findings, whose replication across several experiments is testament to their robustness, indicate the need for producers of television news especially to exercise caution in the way they utilize film footage offering "eyewitness" accounts of violent events. On the evidence of this experiment, greater care probably needs to be taken with evening news broadcasts on television than at any other time of day, because the arousal that may be produced by violent footage combined with enhanced personal arousal associated with natural diurnal cycles could exceed optimum levels of excitation conducive to effective information processing. This may not only affect memory for the narrative content accompanying film material, but may even more severely impede information uptake from adjacent story narratives.

FINAL REMARKS ON IMPLICATIONS OF EXPERIMENTAL RESEARCH

Although research with TV news programs is still in its infancy, a number of applied implications for broadcasting and future research in this field can be drawn from the evidence collated and discussed in this chapter. These implications apply also to the possible future testing and expansion of experimental psychology and its techniques to a new and more complex variety of stimulus material than it has hitherto examined—the visual and verbal presentation of television.

Methodological Problems

In assessing the practical value and implications of research in this field, it is important to address the issue of methodology. The validity of any research is underpinned by the soundness of the techniques and instruments employed. Some investigators have observed that the measures of recall frequently used in broadcast news research may be insufficient to provide a full assessment of information retention. Recognition of strong details or unaided recall of topics are only vague indicators of memory (Berry, 1983b). More sophisticated cued-recall questions can provide further important insights into how much information audience members retain from broadcast news bulletins.

Recently, another investigator has emphasized the need to address interactions between program variables and the use of different dependent measures (Brosius, 1989). Thus, although recognition measures may provide a comprehensive assessment of viewers' retention of certain aspects of a news broadcast, cued recall may prove to be more effective at eliciting memory for other program aspects. In drawing practical recommendations for news professionals from their findings, researchers must be confident that the procedures they have used are sufficiently sophisticated and sensitive to provide accurate and valid measures of memory performance.

Research Implications

From an applied perspective, psychological studies of memory for bulletin materials undertaken to date have implied that certain of the assumptions made by professional broadcasters about viewers' abilities to learn are often inaccurate, and that the content profiles and presentation styles shaped by these assumptions and the standardized production practices they embody may often inhibit as much as enhance learning from television.

This chapter has emphasized the practical implications of research into memory for television news programs. A cognitive-experimental approach appears on the evidence just cited to have proved more successful so far than the sociological paradigms that have traditionally dominated mass communications research at unearthing important program factors that have profound effects on information gain from TV news bulletins. As well as practical implications, there are no doubt important theoretical implications to emerge from this research and these are discussed elsewhere by the authors.

While televised news messages may fail to permeate mass audiences to some degree because large sections of the public show poor attention to receptivity to particular or all types of news content, the evidence discussed in this chapter has indicated a number of recurrent production variables in television news programming that also have significant effects on the abilities of viewers to encode, store, and retrieve news information. This is not to deny the importance of audience factors on information. This is not to deny the importance of audience factors on recall, particularly those that relate to the perceived function and credibility of television news stories and viewers' general appreciation or liking for a story, each of which variables have been shown by recent research to be significant indicators of information gain from news programs in addition to presentation context (Drew & Reeves, 1980). Explaining how program features operate, however, either independently or through interactions with audience factors on the public's knowledge acquisition from TV bulletins requires conceptualization in cognitive-psychological terms rather than just in sociological ones. A clear elucidation in this sense of the relationships between program attributes and cognitive reactions will be essential to a more complete understanding of the occurrence of extensive information losses from TV news broadcasts. This knowledge might also prove extremely useful in improving production techniques not only for television news but also for other kinds of audiovisual information (e.g., educational and instructional) programming.

REFERENCES

Adoni, A., & Cohen, A. (1978). Television economic news and the social constrictions of economic reality. *Journal of Communication, 28,* 61-70.

Altheide, D. L. (1976). *Creating reality: How TV news distorts events.* Beverly Hills, CA: Sage.

Ash, P., & Jasper, N. (1953). *The effects and interactions of rate of development, repetition, participation and room illumination on learning from a rear projected film* (Technical Report SFD 269-7-39). Fort Washington, NY: US Special Services Centre.

Baggaley, J. P. (1980). *The psychology of the TV image.* Aldershot, England: Saxon House.

BBC. (1976). *The book of broadcasting news* (Report of a study by the BBC General Advisory Council) London: British Broadcasting.

Berry, C. (1983a). A dual effect of pictorial enhancement in learning from television news: Gunter's data revised. *Journal of Educational Television, 9,* 171-174.

Berry, C. (1983b). Learning from television news: A critique of the research. *Journal of Broadcasting, 27,* 359-370.

Berry, C., & Clifford, B. (1987). *Learning from television news: Effects of perceptions factors and knowledge on comprehension and memory.* London: North East London Polytechnic and Independent Broadcasting Authority.

Blumenthal, G. B., & Robbins, D. (1977). Delayed release from proactive interference with meaningful material. How much do we remember after reading prose passages? *Journal of Experimental Psychology: Human Learning and Memory, 3,* 764-761.

Bogart, L. (1980). Television news as entertainment. In P. Tannenbaum (Ed.). *The entertainment functions of television* (pp. 209-249). Hillsdale, NJ: Lawrence Erlbaum Associates.

Brodie, D., & Lippmann, L. G. (1970). Symbolic and size shifts in short-term memory tasks. *Psychonomic Science, 20,* 361-362.

Brosius, H. B. (1989). Influence of presentation features and news content on learning from television news. *Journal of Broadcasting and Electronic Media, 33,* 1-14.

Chu, G., & Schramm, W. (1967). *Learning from television: What the research says.* Washington DC: National Association of Education Broadcasters.

Cohen, A. A., Wigand, R. T., & Harrison, R. P. (1976). The effects of type of event, proximity and repetition on children's attention to and learning from television news. *Communication Research, 3,* 30-36.

Coldevin, G. (1974, April). *The differential effects of voice-over, superimposition and combined review treatments as production strategies for ETV programming.* Paper presented at the International Conference for Education Technology, Liverpool, England.

Coldevin, G. (1975). Spaced massed and summary treatments as review strategies for ITV production. *AV Communication Review, 23,* 289-303.

Conroy, R. T., & Mills, J. N. (1970). *Human circadian rhythms.* London: Churchill.

Dominowski, R. L., & Gadlin, H. (1968). Imagery and paired associate learning. *Canadian Journal of Psychology, 22,* 336-348.

Drew, D., & Reeves, B. (1980). Learning from a television news story. *Communication Research, 7,* 121-135.

Ebbinghaus, H. (1964). *Uber das Gedachtnis: Untersuchugen zur experimentellan Psychologie* (H. A. Ruger & L. E. Bussenius, Trans.) (Original work published 1913). New York: Dover.

Edwardson, M., Grooms, D., & Pringle, P. (1976). Visualization and TV news information gain *Journal of Broadcasting, 20,* 373-380.

Edwardson, M., Grooms, D., & Proudlove, S. (1981). Television news information gain from interesting video vs. talking heads. *Journal of Broadcasting, 25,* 15-24.

Eysenck, M. W. (1982). *Attention and arousal: Cognition and performance,* Berlin: Springer-Verlag.

Fairbanks, G., Guttmann, N., & Miron, M. S. (1957). Auditory comprehension in relation to listening rate and selective verbal redundancy. *Journal of Speech and Hearing Disorders, 27,* 23-32.

Findahl, O. (1971). *The effects of visual illustrations upon perception and retention of news programmes.* Stockholm: Swedish Broadcasting Corporation, Audience and Programme Research Department.

Findahl, O., & Hoijer, B. (1972). *Man as a receiver of information: Repetitions and reformulations in a news programme.* Stockholm: Swedish Broadcasting Corporation, Audience and Programme Research Department.

Findahl, O., & Hoijer, B. (1975a). Effect of additional verbal information in retention of a radio news programme. *Journal Quarterly, 52,* 493-498.

Findahl, O., & Hoijer, B. (1975b). *Man as a receiver of information: On knowledge social privilege and the news.* Stockholm: Swedish Broadcasting Corporation, Audience and Programme Research Department.

Findahl, O., & Hoijer, B. (1976). *Fragments of reality: An experiment with news and TV visuals.* Stockholm: Swedish Broadcasting Corporation, Audience and Programme Research Department.

Findahl, O., & Hoijer, B. (1984). *Comprehension analysis: A review of the research and an application to radio and television news.* Lund: Studentlitteratur. (English summary available only).

Findahl, O., & Hoijer, B. (1985). *Some characteristics of news and memory and comprehension.* Unpublished manuscript.

Folkard, S. (1980). A note on time of day effects in school children's immediate and delayed recall of meaningful material—the influence of the importance of the information tested. *British Journal of Psychology, 71,* 95-97.

Folkard, S., & Monk, T. H. (1978). Time of day effects in immediate and delayed memory. In M. M. Grunenberg, P. E. Morris, & R. N. Sykes (Eds.), *Practical aspects of memory* (pp.). London: Academic Press.

Folkard, S., & Monk, T. H. (1980). Circadian rhythms in human memory. *British Journal of Psychology, 71,* 295-307.

Folkard, S., Monk, T. H., Bradbury, R., & Rosenthal, J. (1977). Time of day effects in school children's immediate delayed recall of meaningful material. *British Journal of Psychology, 68,* 45-50.

Foulke, E. (1968). Listening comprehension as a function of word rate. *Journal of Communication, 18,* 198-206.

Funkhouser, G., & McCombs, M. (1971). The rise and fall of news diffusion. *Public Opinion Quarterly, 35,* 107-113.

Furnham, A., & Gunter, B. (1985). Sex presentation mode and memory for violent and non-violent news. *Journal of Educational Television, 11,* 99-105.

Furnham, A., & Gunter, B. (1987). Effects of time of day and medium of presentation on recall of violent and non-violent news. *Applied Cognitive Psychology, 1,* 255-262.

Galtung, J., & Ruge, M. H. (1965). The structure of foreign news: The presentation of the Congo, Cuba and Cyprus crises in four foreign newspapers. *Journal of Peace Research, 2,* 64-91.

Gantz, W. (1979). How uses and gratifications affect recall of television news. *Journalism Quarterly, 56,* 115-123.

Gates, A. I. (1916). Diurnal variations in memory and association. *University of California Publications in Psychology, 1,* 323-344.

Genova, B. K., & Greenberg, B. J., (1979). Interests in the news and the knowledge gap. *Public Opinion Quarterly, 43,* 79-91.

Glasgow University Media Group. (1976). *Bad news,* London: Routlege & Kegan Paul.

Golding, P., & Elliott, P. (1979). *Making the news.* London: Longman.

Gunter, B. (1979). Recall of television news items: Effects of presentation mode, picture content and serial position. *Journal of Education Television, 5,* 57-61.

Gunter, B. (1980a). Remembering television news. Effects of picture content. *Journal of General Psychology, 102,* 127-133.

Gunter, B. (1980b). Remembering televised news: Effects of visual format in information gain. *Journal of Educational Television, 6,* 8-11.

Gunter, B. (1980c). Interpreting release from proactive interference for the individual subject. *Psychological Report, 46,* 1044-1046.

Gunter, B. (1985). News sources and news awareness. A British survey. *Journal of Broadcasting, 29*(4), 397-406.

Gunter, B. (1986). *The audience for TV-am* (special report). London: Independent Broadcasting Authority.

Gunter, B. (1987) *Poor reception: Misunderstanding and forgetting broadcast news.* Hillsdale, NJ: Lawrence Erlbaum Associates.

Gunter, G., Berry, C., & Clifford, B. (1981). Release from proactive interference with television news items: Further evidence. *Journal of Experimental Psychology: Human Learning and Memory, 7,* 480-487.

Gunter, B., Clifford, B., & Berry, C. (1980). Release from proactive interference with television news items: Evidence for encoding dimensions within televised news. *Journal of Experimental Psychology: Human Learning and Memory, 6,* 216-223.

Gunter, B., & Furnham, A. (1986). Sex and personality differences in recall of violent and non-violent news from three presentation modalities. *Personality and Individual Differences, 1,* 829-837.

Gunter, B., Furnham, A., & Jarrett, J. (1984). Personality, time of day and delayed memory for TV news. *Personality and Individual Differences, 5,* 35-39.

Gunter, B., Jarrett, J., & Furnham, A. (1983) Time of day effects on immediate memory for television news. *Human Learning, 2,* 1-7.

Hazard, W. R. (1963). On the impact of television's news. *Journal of Broadcasting, 7,* 43-51.

Hockey, G. R., & Colquhoun, W. P. (1972). Divisional variation in human performance: A review. In W. P. Colquhoun (Ed.), *Aspects of human efficiency diurnal rhythm and loss of sleep.* (pp.). London: English Universities Press.

IBA. (1981). *Television and radio 1981.* London: Author.

IBA. (1982). *Attitudes to broadcasting* (Research Department Special Report). London: Author.

IBA. (1985). *Attitudes to broadcasting* (Research Department Research Paper). London: Author.

IBA. (1986). *Attitudes to broadcasting in 1985.* London: Author.

IBA. (1990). *Attitudes to television in 1989.* London: Author.

Jorgenson, F. S. (1955). *The relative effectiveness of these methods of television newscasting.* Unpublished doctoral dissertation, University of Wisconsin.

Katz, E., Adoni, H., & Parness, P. (1977). Remembering the news: What the picture adds to recall. *Journalism Quarterly, 54,* 231-23.

Kintsch, W. (1974). *The representation of meaning in memory.* Hillsdale, NJ: Lawrence Erlbaum Associates.

Larsen, S. F. (1981). *Knowledge updating: Three papers on news memory, background knowledge and text processing.* Aarhus: University of Aarhus, Institute of Psychology.

Lee, R. (1975). Credibility of newspaper and TV news. *Journalism Quarterly, 55,* 282-287.
Levy, M. (1978). The audience experience with television news. *Journalism Monographs* (no. 55).
Loess, H. (1967). Short-term memory, word class and sequence of items. *Journal of Experimental Psychology, 74,* 556-561.
Loess, H. (1968). Short-term memory and item similarity. *Journal of Verbal Learning and Verbal Behavior, 1,* 87-91.
Maccoby, N., & Sheffield, F. D. (1961) Combining practice with demonstration in teaching complex sequences: Summary and interpretations. In A. A. Lumsdaine (Ed.) *Student response in programmed instruction: A symposium.* Washington, DC: National Academy of Sciences National Research Council.
MacLachlan, J., & La Barbera, P. (1978). Time compressed TV commercials. *Journal of Advertising Research, 18,* 11-15.
Nelson, H. E. (1948). The effect of variation of rate on the recall by radio listeners of "straight" newscasts. *Speech Monographs, 15,* 173-180.
Neuman, W. R. (1976). Patterns of recall among television news viewers. *Public Opinion Quarterly, 40,* 115-123.
Paivio, A. (1969). Mental imagery in associative learning and memory. *Psychological Review, 76,* 241-263.
Paivio, A. (1971). *Imagery and verbal processes.* New York: Holt.
Perloff, R., Wartella, E., & Becker, L. (1982). Increasing learning from TV news. *Journalism Quarterly, 59,* 83-86.
Renckstorff, K. (1977). Nachrichtensendungen im Fernsehen eine empirische Studie zur Wirkung unterschiedlicher Darstellung in Fernsehnachrichten. *Media Perspektiven, 1/77,* 27-42.
Renckstorff, K. (1980). *Nachrichtensendungen im Fernsehen (I): Zur Wirkung von Darstellungsforme in Fernsehnachrichten.* Berlin: Volker Spiess Verlag.
Reese, S. D. (1984). Visual-verbal redundancy affects on television news learning. *Journal of Broadcasting, 28,* 79-87.
Robinson, J. P. (1967). World affairs information and mass media exposure. *Journalism Quarterly, 44,* 23-40.
Robinson, J. P., Davis, D., Sahin, H., & O'Toole, T. (1980, August). *Comprehension of television news: How alert is the audience?* Paper presented to the Association for Education in Journalism, Boston, MA.
Robinson, J. P., & Levy, M. (1985). *The main source: Learning from television news.* Beverly Hills, CA: Sage.
Robinson, J. P., & Sahin, H. (1984). *Audience comprehension of television news: Results from some exploratory research.* London: British Broadcasting Corporation, Broadcasting Research Department.
Roper Organization, (1983). *Trends in attitudes towards television and other media: A twenty year review.* New York: Television Information Office.
Rothkopf, E. A. (1968). Textual constraint as a function of repeated inspection. *Journal of Educational Psychology, 1,* 20-25.
Rubin, A. (1984). Ritualized and instrumental television viewing. *Journal of Communication, 34,* 67-77.
Schlater, R. (1970). Effect of speed of presentation on recall of television messages. *Journal of Broadcasting, 14,* 207-214.
Schlesinger, P. (1978). *Putting "reality" together: BBC news.* London: Constable.
Schulz, W. (1982). News structure and people's awareness of political events. *Gazette, 30,* 139-153.
Severin, W. (1967). The effectiveness of relevant pictures in multiple-channel communications. *AV Communication Review, 15,* 386-401.
Severin, W. (1968). *Cue summonation in multiple-channel communication* (Tech. Rep. No. 37). University of Wisconsin, Madison, Wisconsin Research and Development Center for Cognitive Learning.
Smith, J. R., & McEwan, W. J. (1974). Effects of newscast delivery rate on recall and judgement of sources. *Journal of Broadcasting, 18,* 73-83.
Sparkes, V. M. & Winter, J. P. (1980). Public interest in foreign news. *Gazette, 20,* 149-170.

Stauffer, J., Frost, R., & Rybolt, W. (1983). The attention factor in recalling network television news. *Journal of Communication, 33,* 29-37.

Tannenbaum, P. H. (1954). Effect of serial position on recall of radio news stories. *Journalism Quarterly, 31,* 319-323.

Thorndyke, P. W. (1979). Knowledge acquisition from newspaper stories. *Discourse Processes,* 95-112.

Tichenor, P. J., Donohue, G. A., & Olien, C. N. (1970). Mass media flow and differential growth of knowledge. *Public Opinion Quarterly, 34,* 159-170.

Turvey, M. T., & Egan, J. (1969). Contextual change and release from proactive interference in short-term verbal memory. *Journal of Experimental Psychology, 81, 396-397.*

Underwood, B. J., & Ekstrand, B. R. (1967). Response term integration. *Journal of Verbal Learning and Verbal Behaviour, 6,* 432-438.

van Dijk, T. (1980). *Macrostructures: An interdisciplinary study of global structures in discourse interaction and cognition.* Hillsdale, NJ: Lawrence Erlbaum Associates.

Wagenaar, W. A. (1978). Recalling messages broadcast to the general public. In M. M. Gurneberg, P. E. Morris, & H. C. Foot (Eds.), *Practical aspects of memory.* (pp.). New York: Academic Press.

Wagenaar, W. A., & Visser, J. G. (1979). The weather forecast under the weather. *Erogonomics, 22,* 909-917.

Whale, J. (1969). *The half-shut eye: Television and politics in Britain and America. London: Macmillan.*

Wickens, D. D. (1970). Encoding categories of words: An empirical approach to memory. *Psychological Review, 77,* 1-15.

Wickens, D. D. (1972). Characteristics of work encoding. In A. W. Melton & E. Martin (Eds). *Coding processes in human memory.* (pp.). New York: Wiley.

Wicker, F. W. (1970). On the locus of picture-word differences in paired-associate learning. *Journal of Verbal Learning and Verbal Behaviour, 9,* 52-57.

Wicker, F. W., & Evertson, C. M. (1972). Prerecall and postrecall imagery ratings with pictorial and verbal stimuli in paired-associate learning. *Journal of Experimental Psychology, 92,* 75-82.

Winch, W. H. (1911). Mental fatigue during the school day as measured by arithmetical reasoning. *British Journal of Psychology, 4,* 315-341.

Winch, W. H. (1912). Mental fatigue in day school children as measured by immediate memory: Parts I and II: *Journal of Educational Psychology, 3,* 18-28, 75-82.

Winch, W. H. (1913). Mental adaptation during the school day as measured by arithmetical reasoning: Part I and II. *Journal of Educational Psychology, 4,* 17-28, 71-84.

Wober, J. M. (1978). *The need for news: Audience attitudes towards nine news topics.* London: Independent Broadcasting Authority Research Report.

Wober, J. M., & Gunter, B. (1981). *Recall of TV weather forecast information: An introductory experiment.* London: Independent Broadcasting Authority, Research Department Special Report.

CHAPTER

11

Responding to Comedy: The Sense and Nonsense in Humor

Dolf Zillmann
Jennings Bryant
University of Alabama

We grow tired of every thing but turning others into ridicule, and congratulating ourselves on their defects.
—Hazlitt (1826/1926, p. 239)

In this chapter, we describe the contemporary marketplace of comedy. We specify the characteristic contents of the so-called sitcom and trace its popularity. Thereafter, we briefly discuss theories that seek to explain what, in and about comedy, it is that stirs people to laugh, and why this genre is the giant that it is among the various genres of entertainment.

THE COMEDY MARKETPLACE

Postman (1985) has argued that the prevalence of entertainment forms and features in contemporary society has transmutated the very nature of public discourse in the United States. "Politics, religion, news, athletics, education and commerce have been transformed into congenial adjuncts of show business" (pp. 3-4), he asserted, with the result that "we are a people on the verge of amusing ourselves to death" (p. 4). Such stinging criticism of modern American culture provides an appropriate context from which to examine the comedy marketplace. Elements of humor and comedy seemingly have become ubiquitous in modern society.

Comedy in Film. The ubiquity of humor in film is by no means a recent development. Some of the earliest primitive motion pictures foreshadowed modern filmic comedies. An example is Louis Lumière's 1895 *L'Arroseur arrosé*, in which a boy steps on a garden hose thereby cutting off the water, then removes his foot, releasing the water so that it gushes into the face of the unsuspecting gardener who is inspecting the nozzle. Film historian Mast (1981) noted that "this little film contains many elements of a comic art that would one day mature" (p. 21).

Whether or not comedy films have "matured" beyond such "slapstickiness" is left to aesthetic judgment and may, consequently, vary freely. What is not in question is that comedy has become and remained an important film genre. As can be seen from an examination of Fig. 11.1, when the "Top 100" film rentals of all-time (Top 100 all-time film rental champs, 1990) are classified by genre (Wiener, 1989), 40 of them are comedies. Combining the two next most successful genres—drama and action adventure—results in only 36 entries in the Top 100, clearly indicating the dominance of comedy in attracting a large audience to the theater.

Many of the comedy entries in the list of all-time film rental champions are of recent vintage. For example, as of the beginning of 1990, *Ghostbusters* (the highest-ranking comedy at #6), which was released in 1984 by Columbia, had earned more than $130 million in total film rentals. *Beverly Hills Cop* (ranked #11) was released by Paramount, also in 1984, and as of January 1, 1990 had earned $108 million. *Three Men and a Baby* (ranked #20) and *Who Framed Roger Rabbit* (ranked #21), both distributed by Buena Vista, and released in 1987 and 1988 respectively, had both earned more than $80 million and will undoubtedly yield more film rental revenue, thereby moving up in the ranking. It is clear from examining Variety's list of "Top 100" that the recent era has been a particular boon for comedies. In fact, one has to go a long way down the list, to rank #69, to find a comedy that is more than 15 years old. It is Mel Brook's *Blazing Saddles,* which was released by Warner Brothers in 1974 and has earned nearly $48 million. If anything, the success of comedy films seems to be increasing.

Comedy in Television.   Comedy has been at least as successful in attracting an audience to the small screen as to the large. Figure 11.2 depicts the 100 highest rated television series of all time, sorted by genre. As can be seen, 46% of those are comedies. The next most popular genre, drama, accounts for only 23% of the Top 100 television series—half as much as comedy.

The persistent potency of television comedy in attracting an audience is perhaps more clearly revealed by employing a chronological examination. Figure 11.3 shows the percentage of Top 25-rated television series sorted by genre and presented decade by decade. As can be seen from an examination of this figure, the 1950s was the decade in which comedy made up the smallest proportion (33%) of top-rated programs. This seems somewhat surprising, because much if not most of early television programming was adapted from popular radio shows, and "for many years in succession during the period of radio's dominance, ten of the first fifteen programs in audience popularity were comedy programs" (Willis, 1967, p. 282). Obviously the lack of success of comedy in its early transition from radio to television failed to demonstrate the full potential this genre would achieve on the small screen.

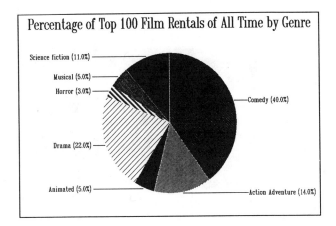

Fig. 11.1. The listing of films is from Variety magazine's "Top 100 All-Time Film Rental Champs" (1990). Assignment of films to a particular genre was according to Wiener (1989).

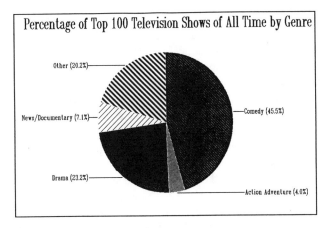

Fig. 11.2. The shows are all prime-time network television series. The list was from Brooks and Marsh (1988), updated by Nielsen Media Research (1990), and the assignment of a series to a particular genre was according to Brooks and Marsh (1988).

Many of the earliest successful television comedies featured discrete skits in which the show's featured stars played various comedic roles. "The Red Skelton Show" and "The Jack Benny Show" were early successful examples of this type of comedy. However, the 1950s also saw the emergence of the situation comedy as an audience favorite, with programs like "The Aldrich Family," "I Love Lucy", and "Amos 'n' Andy" achieving high ratings.

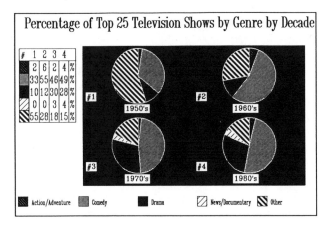

Fig. 11.3. The shows are all prime-time network television shows. The list of
shows from 1950 to 1979 is from Brooks and Marsh (1988). The list of shows
from 1980 to 1989 is courtesy of Nielsen Media Research (1990). Assignment of
series to a particular genre was according to Brooks and Marsh (1988).

By the 1960s, comedy had become the dominant drawing card on television.
As Fig. 11.3 indicates, 55% of the top 25 series of this decade were comedies.
Most, such as "The Beverly Hillbillies" (which made the "Top 12" list for seven
consecutive seasons), "The Andy Griffith Show," and "Gomer Pyle, U.S.M.C.,"
were situation comedies. But comedy-variety programs, such as "The Dean Martin
Show," "Rowan & Martin's Laugh-In," and "The Smothers Brothers Comedy Hour"
continued to add diversity to the comedy fare that Americans had come to love.

In the 1970s, comedy continued to dominate the list of highest rated programs.
However, the comedy landscape was to change somewhat during this period.
Comedy-variety shows, a mainstay of earlier decades, would practically disap-
pear from the small screen, and the vast majority of successful comedy programs
were to follow the situation comedy (sitcom) format of "funny characters in funny situations" (Willis, 1967, p. 293). The macro-structure of situation comedies
frequently has been described as CONFUSION–DILEMMA–UNTANGLING,
and, indeed, this has proven to be a perennially accurate shorthand description
of the thema for situation comedies.

Although the macro-structure might remain relatively constant, the nature of
the humorous interchanges between protagonists was to change dramatically in
this decade, especially during the early years. The primary catalyst for these
changes was Norman Lear, and his initial vehicle was "All in the Family." As
Lear himself described the pre-Archie Bunker era, "all the forerunners of "All
in the Family" dealt with lost skate keys and roasts that were ruined while the
boss was coming to dinner" (Wilde, 1976, p. 207). Lear opted instead to produce
what has frequently been called "reality" comedy, but what might just as well

be called "hostile" or "tendentious" comedy. In "All in the Family" (as well as in its many video progeny), insults, put-downs, racist remarks, and other forms of veiled viciousness ruled the day. "Ruled" is an appropriate word, for "All in the Family" was the top-rated series for 5 years, from 1971–1972 through 1975-1976, sometimes leading the rest of the pack by six rating points.

Beginning with the Fall of 1976, a new type of zanier, less hostile situation comedy moved into the forefront, where it remained for the remainder of the decade. That type of fantasy-based situation comedy, designed primarily to attract the youth audience, is perhaps best represented by "Happy Days" and "Laverne & Shirley." Also to become extremely popular during this decade were comedies featuring sexy stars and suggestive, titillating dialogue with the characters thrust in a variety of awkward situations. This type of sitcom is best represented by "Three's Company." Off-beat, slightly risque comedies, such as "Soap," also began to appear in the lists of top-rated programs as the 1970s ebbed. As Fig. 11.3 indicates, throughout this decade these several types of situation comedies accounted for 46% of the top 25 television series.

The character of situation comedies was to take still other turns during the 1980s; but whatever the prevalent form of the genre, it was to continue to account for the lion's share (49%) of the top 25 programs. The earliest portion of this decade saw the continued appeal of the "jiggle comedies," but a touch of seriousness, at least in setting or situation, was to temper the zaniness of some of the most successful comedies of the first half of the decade. "M*A*S*H," "One Day at a Time," and "Kate & Allie" are examples.

All situation comedies rely on more than "funny characters in funny situations" to elicit mirth from the viewing audience. They also have elements of drama.

> Being drama, in addition to making audiences laugh, they must be written to meet the criteria that apply to any type of drama. The writer must create characters and a plot, try to build suspense, enlist audience sympathy for his characters, make those characters believable insofar as he can within the confines of his comedy idea, construct a story that immediately engages the attention of his viewers, carry them forward on a rising plane of interest to a climax, and provide a sound and satisfying resolution. (Willis, 1967, pp. 293-294)

During the 1980s, producers began to introduce hybrid programs that emphasized drama somewhat more than comedy. Appropriately, many critics began calling these hybrid forms "dramedy." Although several of these programs, like "Hooperman," "Slap Maxwell," and "Frank's Place," received critical acclaim, none of them cracked the Top 25 barrier. By the end of the decade, most had disappeared from the airwaves, perhaps indicating that the television audience does not want to take its comedy too seriously.

Another hybrid comedy format that was to receive much airtime in the 1980s was the comedy-adventure program, typically presented in hour-long episodes.

Several of these programs, such as "The Dukes of Hazzard," "Greatest American Hero," "A-Team," and "Hart to Hart," did make the Top 25 list, even rising to the number one rank on occasion. However, the sources relied on for assigning programs to the particular categories from which the data presented in Fig. 11.2-11.4 are derived (Brooks & Marsh, 1988; Nielsen Media Research, 1990) typically classified these hybrid forms as belonging in the action adventure category, so they do not show up in the comedy ratings. This artificially deflates the proportion of comedies in the most recent decade, especially during the first half of the 1980s (see Fig. 11.4).

The last half of the 1980s was dominated by family comedies, exemplified by "The Cosby Show" and "Family Ties." Although more realistic than the family comedies of the 1950s and 1960s (e.g., "The Danny Thomas Show," "Father Knows Best"), these highly successful programs featured rather gentle, nontendentious forms of humorous interaction. As the 1980s drew to a close, however, the success of the raucous and sometimes vicious "Roseanne" seemed likely to spawn another cycle of imitators and launch yet another trend within situation comedies. Whatever the nature of these changes, if the past is any indication of the future, it may be considered certain that comedy, in general, and situation comedies, in particular, will play a dominant role in entertaining television audiences.

Figure 11.4 presents a more detailed look at the percentage of comedies in the Top 25 television series per year between 1950-1988. As can be seen from an examination of that figure, except for 1958, at least 20% of the Top 25 series have been comedies. In 5 years—1975, 1978, 1980, 1986, and 1988—comedies accounted for at least 60% of the Top 25 series. Moreover, it is apparent from this figure that the most consistent trend has been a relatively steady increase in the number of comedy programs that make it into the lists of most popular regularly scheduled television programming. This trend would be even more clear cut if the comedy-adventure successes of the early 1980s were included as comedies.

Humor on Television in Genres Other Than Comedy. Although the descriptions and discussion of the comedy marketplace to this point have focused on the comedy genre, it seems appropriate to heed Postman's (1985) warning about the ubiquitousness of entertainment and note that, indeed, humor does reach the screen in forms other than in comedy per se.

Cantor (1977) reported that humor can be found in virtually all television programming, including news, sports, soap operas, and religious programs. Moreover, approximately 15%-20% of television commercials were found to contain humor (Cantor, 1976), a proportion that is almost certain to be significantly higher in today's commercials.

A more recent detailed content analysis of local television newscasts found, as can be seen in Fig. 11.5, that only 23% of the time of local newscasts was

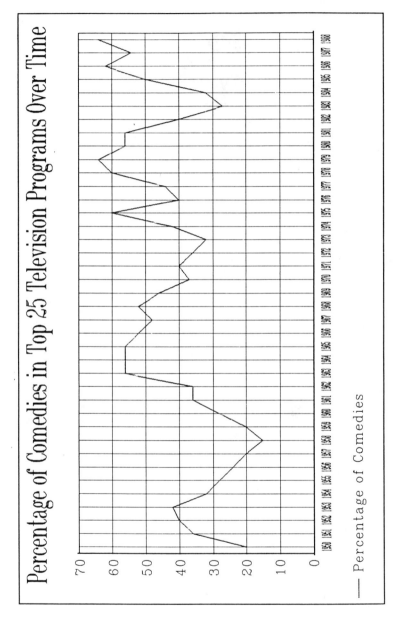

Percentage of Comedies in Top 25 Television Programs Over Time

— Percentage of Comedies

Fig. 11.4. The shows are all prime-time network television shows. The list of shows from 1950 to 1979 is from Brooks and Marsh (1988). The list of shows from 1980 to 1989 is courtesy of Nielsen Media Research (1990). Assignment of series to a particular genre was according to Brooks and Marsh (1988).

PERCENTAGE OF NEWS CONTENT AND
COMMMERCIALS DURING NONSWEEPS

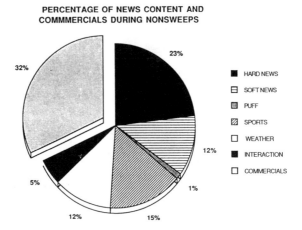

Fig. 11.5.   The data are from Bryant et al. (1990) and represent one full week
of local television newscasts from three network affiliated stations in the Birming-
ham and Tuscaloosa, AL, markets during March 1989. The 5 p.m., 6 p.m., and
10 p.m. CST newscasts were all included. Forty-five newscasts were analyzed on
a second-by-second basis.

devoted exclusively to "hard" news. Much of the remainder of the newscasts was
found to rely at least partially on elements of entertainment (Bryant et al., 1990).

Recent events concerning the suspension of Andy Rooney, the humorist who
has the final word on the CBS program "60 Minutes," suggest that even the most
ambitious news programs cannot do without the comic. The executive producer
of this program attributed a marked decline in the program's ratings to the removal
of Rooney (Gerard, 1990), who—in the interest of getting an audience for news
and despite protests by gays and Blacks whom he had offended—was promptly
reinstated.

As indicated earlier, the "selling of news" in humorous packages has drawn
sharp criticism (Postman, 1985). Comedy as such, however, continues to appeal
to massive film and television audiences around the world; and it appears to serve
a useful function in providing much needed relaxation and recreation (Brown &
Bryant, 1983) by facilitating the desirable changeover from so-so and bad moods
to more positive ones, if not to outright gaiety, in uncounted individuals (Zillmann,
1988; Zillmann & Bryant, 1985).

EXPLAINING COMEDY'S APPEAL

Humor seems to be a primordial phenomenon. It has been found in all recorded
human cultures; not in deficient quantity, but in conspicuous abundance. It should
not be a surprise, then, to find that wise men of note took the time to ponder

the issue of what it might be that makes people smile, giggle, chuckle, and burst out in incapacitating laughter.

Greek philosophers are usually credited with the creation of initial theories of humor and comedy (e.g., Feibleman, 1962; Lauter, 1964). Plato (*Philebus*), Aristotle (*Poetics*), and Cicero (*Oratore*) are typically lumped together (e.g., Olson, 1968) as promoters of the view that humor, as featured in comedy and occurring in actual social situations, dwells on the exhibition of baseness and deformities. Their writings did little to explain why such exhibition produces mirthful reactions. These thinkers concentrated, instead, on condemning reactions of this kind as inappropriate and immoral (Zillmann & Cantor, 1976). Much later, the British philosopher Hobbes (1651/1968) echoed this condemnation in his so-called superiority theory of humor. According to Hobbes, "those grimaces called laughter" express the passion of self-glorification, which is brought about "by the apprehension of some deformed thing in another, by comparison whereof they (the glorifiers) suddenly applaud themselves" (p. 125). And he condemned this passion as being "incident most to them, that are conscious of the fewest abilities in themselves; who are forced to keep themselves in their own favor, by observing the imperfections of other men" (p. 125). Needless to say, humor and comedy were deemed inapropos for the noble.

The German philosopher Kant (1788/1922) engaged in less castigation and offered a nonmoralizing formula instead. He posited that humor-induced laughter is "an affection arising from a strained expectation that is suddenly transformed into nothing" (p. 409, authors' translation). People were expected to respond in a mirthful fashion when what seemed to be problematic resolved itself, proving negligible or trivial. The British philosopher Spencer (1888) rephrased this formula, stating that laughter results when an effort suddenly encounters a void. This transition from problematic to laughable was termed *descending incongruity*. The notion was broadened eventually by another German philosopher, Schopenhauer (1891), who thought that any incongruity between concepts and percepts would trigger mirthful behavior.

Spencer is further recognized for suggesting a physiological theory of humor. He proposed that laughter, because of its semi-convulsive actions, depletes nervous energy and thus provides relief from any initial apprehension. In agreement with Kant's view, Spencer considered humor capable of diminishing unpleasant states. Kant (1788/1922) had evaluated this capability as a blessing. In contrast to views prevalent in ancient Greece, he furnished a positive verdict of humor. Having a sense of humor, or being humorous, was admired as "the talent of being able to put oneself at will into a certain frame of mind in which everything is judged in unusual (even opposite) ways, yet in accordance with particular principles of reason that characterize this frame of mind" (p. 412, authors' translation).

These early views on humor and its kin may seem crude, but proved to be pivotal in the development of psychological theories of humor, comedy, and laughter. Conceptions of humor as hostile, demeaning activity capable of creating feelings of superiority were eventually refined in reference group (La Fave, 1972; Wolff, Smith, & Murray, 1934) and disposition theories of humor (Zillmann, 1983; Zillmann & Cantor, 1976). Analogously, conceptions of congruity-inspired mirth were nurtured and improved on in so-called incongruity theories (e.g., Berlyne, 1969; Koestler, 1964; Nerhardt, 1976; Shultz, 1976; Suls, 1972). Efforts at integrating the views partial to tendentious and nontendentious humor, essentially a blending together of superiority and incongruity proposals, were also evident in the creation of psychological theories (Freud, 1905/1958; Suls, 1977; Zillmann, 1983; Zillmann & Bryant, 1980). Finally, the views of humor as a relief-provider and apprehension-trivializer have matured into formulations of mood management through humor (Zillmann, 1988; Zillmann & Bryant, 1985) and humor therapy (Levine, 1963; Robinson, 1983).

The enjoyment of situation comedies on television and elsewhere is probably best explained by the application of the disposition theory of humor (cf. Zillmann, 1983). Such situation comedies feature sequences of actions and transactions between persons and groups, and these actions and transactions tend to place some parties at a disadvantage and, by implication, yield benefits to others. It is no secret that comedy on television is highly tendentious in these terms, dwelling on hostile exchanges, in particular (Stocking, Sapolsky, & Zillmann, 1977). Much comedy, then, can be construed as an aggregation of miniature plots in which some persons or groups triumph over others, and in which these others are debased, demeaned, disparaged, ridiculed, humiliated, or otherwise subjected to undesirable experiences short of truly grievous harm.

Disposition theory addresses these "dramatic" exchanges in comedy. Specifically, it focuses on the affective dispositions that respondents hold toward disparaging and disparaged persons or things, and it projects enjoyment as a function of the dispositional constellation. Analogous to the enjoyment of drama (Zillmann, chapter 12, this volume, 1980), it should prove to be more fun witnessing a liked party stick it to a disliked one than seeing a disliked party triumph over a liked one. Bearing witness to the humiliation of a liked by a liked party, or to that of a disliked by a disliked party, should be a mixed blessing and yield intermediate results.

These expectations have been formalized in the following propositions:

1. The more intense the negative disposition toward the disparaged agent or entity, the greater the magnitude of mirth.
2. The more intense the positive disposition toward the disparaged agent or entity, the smaller the magnitude of mirth.
3. The more intense the negative disposition toward the disparaging agent or entity, the smaller the magnitude of mirth.
4. The more intense the positive disposition toward the disparaging agent or entity, the greater the magnitude of mirth.

The indicated relationships can be alternatively expressed in schematic form. Figure 11.6 shows the dispositional field for tendentious exchanges in comedy and indicates the regions for maximal, minimal, and intermediate mirth reactions. Classifications of comedy readily translate into this dispositional schema. Olson's (1968) categorization of plots of folly and plots of cleverness, for instance, specifies that for comedy to be enjoyable both the ill-intentioned fool and the ill-intentioned wit must come to harm, and both the well-intentioned fool and the well-intentioned wit must come to glory. Witnessing ill intentions and deplorable actions should prompt negative affective dispositions, and these dispositions should foster mirth upon the revelation of failures, mishaps, and setbacks for ill-intentioned parties, whether clumsy or clever. In contrast, witnessing good intentions and laudatory actions should prompt positive affective dispositions, and these dispositions would prevent mirth in response to misfortunes. To liberate mirth, well-intentioned, liked characters, clever or clumsy, must consequently "come out on top."

For comedy to be effective, then, it is imperative that characters not be met with affective indifference. Loveable and hateable characters must be developed, especially the latter kind. Pleasant, honest, and otherwise virtuous characters are mostly needed as targets for the abusive behavior of the "evil cast": those characters who display arrogance, snobbishness, vainglory, vanity, ignorance, bigotry, selfishness, egotism, contemptuousness, insensitivity, rudeness, brutality,

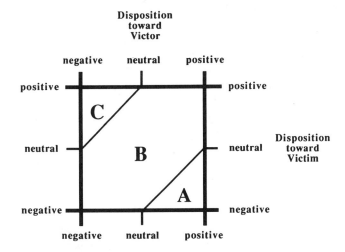

Fig. 11.6. Dispositional field for tendentious exchanges. Highly positive dispositions toward the victor together with highly negative dispositions toward the victim define the subfield of intense mirth reactions (Region A). Highly negative dispositions toward the victor together with highly positive dispositions toward the victim define the subfield of minimal mirth reactions (Region C). All other dispositional constellations define an area of intermediate mirth (Region B).

or other utterly despicable traits. Characters with these despicable traits are, of course, the butt of all belittlement and ridicule (Charney, 1978). They are obviously deserving of such treatment, and respondents are free to rejoice in smiles, laughter, and approving roars.

The disposition theory of humor has attracted considerable research support (cf. Zillmann, 1983). This support comes mainly from studies of jokes and cartoons, rather than from the investigation of comedy as such (e.g., Cantor & Zillmann, 1973; Love & Deckers, 1989; McGhee & Lloyd, 1981; Zillmann & Bryant, 1974; Zillmann & Cantor, 1972). Tendentious jokes and cartoons can be construed as the smallest of plots depicting social exchanges of the described kind. Character development is very limited, however, and jokes and cartoons usually rely on well-established affective dispositions by drawing upon stereotypes and prototypes. This is not to say that situation comedy avoids stereotypical portrayals. It is to make the point, instead, that comedy is less dependent on stereotypes and clichés.

Disposition theory proved useful in projecting enjoyment from entertaining happenings other than humor. In particular, it proved useful in predicting the enjoyment of drama (Zillmann, 1980) and sports events (Zillmann, Bryant, & Sapolsky, 1989). This generality makes it a broadly applicable theory of enjoyment, but not necessarily a complete theory of amusement and mirth (see Zillmann, 1983, for a discussion of this issue). To illustrate: Imagine an athletic contest in which your favorite team clobbers a team you despise. You probably find yourself rejoicing, possibly grinning and laughing. But would you consider your mirth-like reaction mirth? You obviously enjoyed the outcome. But would you consider your enjoyment amusement? Or would you consider the game a comedy? Probably not!

The conceptual differentiation of enjoyment and amusement is not as easy as it may seem. Intuitively, there is something lighthearted about comedy, but not about other forms of drama or dramatic human endeavors. This characteristic lightheartedness proved elusive definitionally.

Olson's (1968) approach may seem to resolve the dilemma. He pointed to the "contrariety to the serious" (p. 13) in comedy and in the audience reaction to comedy. The audience, he suggested, must approach events in a particular frame of mind. Respondents must be free from acute desires and "inclined to take nothing seriously and to be gay about everything" (p. 25). All concerns should be relaxed, and respondents should be confident and carefree.

Such stipulations may seem to put the carriage before the horse. A carefree, relaxed state of mind is usually considered the result of exposure to comedy, not a precondition. Olson's point is well taken, however. It is common observation, after all, that those in acute grief over tragic happenings are unable to leave their state at will and respond to lighthearted fare as others do. A readiness to amuse oneself—in the sense of a willingness to relax serious concerns about the so-called real world, if only temporarily—may indeed, as was proposed, constitute a necessary condition for the enjoyment of comedy.

Research on mood management through entertainment choices (Zillmann, 1988; Zillmann & Bryant, 1985) supports the proposal that comedy requires appropriate prior states. It has been observed (Zillmann, Hezel, & Medoff, 1980), for instance, that aggressively instigated, angry persons avoid comedy and seek exposure to alternative genres of entertainment, usually less lighthearted fare, instead. The rejection of comedy was found to be particularly strong in men (Medoff, 1979), who behaved as if anger was too serious an issue to be swept away by frolic and hilarity. Acute anger was apparently no laughing matter to them; and the prospect of seeing such a somber experience diminished by reactions to comedy, rather than come to fruition in retaliatory action, seems to have been unacceptable. Similarly serious, security-threatening experiences, such as intense grief, presumably create a similar reluctance to enter into lighthearted gaiety—at least for some time.

There are, on the other hand, circumstances that are conducive to seeking out and "jumping into" the merry world of comedy. Bad moods generally, especially when they cannot be removed or lessened by actions against their origin, constitute such circumstances.

The mood changes associated with the menstrual cycle make this point very nicely. According to much research (e.g., Hamburg, 1966; Melgres & Hamburg, 1976), the rapid withdrawal of progesterone and estrogen with their anesthetizing properties create the so-called premenstrual syndrome, a syndrome characterized by depressive moods and irritable dispositions. Many women, although by no means all, are trapped in these moods. Medication may offer some degree of relief. Nonetheless, premenstrual women should be left with enough blah feelings and a stronger motivation than at other times (i.e., during other cycle phases) to seek relief. To the extent that humor and comedy are recognized as potent relief providers, premenstrual women should take a particularly strong interest in comedy and prefer it, more than at other times, over alternative genres.

This proposal has actually been tested (Meadowcroft & Zillmann, 1987). Women were given the choice between comedy, serious drama, and game shows. Consistent with expectations, premenstrual and menstruating women showed a significant preference for comedy. They experienced the greatest need to be cheered up, and they chose comedy in the apparent belief that this genre does a better job of it than available alternatives. Women midway through the cycle showed the least interest in comedy and, comparatively speaking, were ready for serious drama.

These observations have been extended to pregnancy (Helregel & Weaver, 1989). It was found that hormonally determined and subjectively experienced bad-mood periods during pregnancy corresponded closely with an increased appetite for comedy. But in more general terms, all nagging negative mood states, all strains and stresses, whose perpetuation serves no purpose, should define preconditions for the acceptance of stimulation capable of inducing merriment—humor and comedy being cases in point.

There should be no shortage, then, of dispositions that favor the abandonment of an unproductive serious frame of mind and the self-indulgence in the merry, nonthreatening world of comedy.

This raises the question as to what it is that characterizes the unique world of comedy? What is it that signals that the happenings presented in this genre are not to be taken too seriously? Numerous answers have been offered. Most frequently, contrarieties with, and exaggerations of, the respondent's concepts of reality have been pointed out (e.g., Berlyne, 1969; Flugel, 1954; Olson, 1968). Sheer absurdity and arbitrariness (as contrarieties) are the exception, however; and there usually is some "logic to the madness."

Freud (1905/1958) has been most influential with his listing of procedures and maneuvers of *Witzarbeit* (joke work) that not only signal the play context of humor and comedy, but also make matters laughable. To illustrate: It is unlikely to be very funny to learn that a prostitute, suffering from the flu, is asking a fellow prostitute for $100 to be repaid once she is having an income again. The situation is different, if the story is told such that the prostitute is asking her peer: "Can you lend me a hundred bucks until I am back on my back?" "Back on my feet" would not have done the trick—as the chuckle hinges on the very violation of an established concept, along with the invited imagination of on-the-back labor. Or picture a totally dehydrated Martian creature on its knees in the middle of the desert, whispering "Amonia, amonia!" The contrariety with clichés of the real world are apparently sufficient for an amusement reaction. So are uncounted exploitations of ambiguities. The joke "Doctor, doctor! I broke my arm in three places." "Well, stay away from them in the future!" makes this point. The discourse starts at a particular level and is continued at another. This sudden shift between incompatible contexts (Koestler, 1964) should initially produce bewilderment, if not confusion. However, the very recognition of this deliberately created confusion identifies humor, and the accomplishment of following the switch from one level of discourse to another—of getting the point of the playful venture—apparently generates an aha! experience of the laughable kind.

Take the children's joke "How does a bee sound when it flies backwards?" "Zzub . . . zzub!" It exemplifies Kant's (1788/1922) suggestion that mirth derives from strained expectations that suddenly evaporate into nothing. The question can be viewed as the creator of puzzlement. Getting the point in spotting the backward concept in the spelling leaves no doubt about the nonserious nature of the problem. A "problem" vanished into nothingness.

Plays on words and images are, of course, the same in comedy. Think of the comic newscaster who, in a business report, reveals that boomerangs are coming back. Or think of a sitcom in which a man complains about his lover's apparent absentmindedness during sex, with her quipping: "Well, would you like it better if I was thinking of *you* while sleeping with Robert Redford?" All these situations require transforms and inferences. But it is this unraveling of odd ambiguities and this spotting of hidden meanings that signals humor and produces some degree of amusement.

Freud (1905/1958) distinguished between nontendentious and tendentious humor. Nontendentious humor thrives on joke work (innocuous plays on words, etc.) and does not victimize, humiliate, or disparage anybody. Tendentious humor, in contrast, features the victimization of one party by another. This humor is, by definition, hostile. It is demeaning to some, the butts; and it shows others, mostly people, coming out on top—usually, but not necessarily. It is the kind of humor that produces victors and victims, winners and losers, disparagers and disparagees.

It can be said that, since the theorizing and moralizing by Hobbes (1651/1968), most humor theorists have focused their attention on the innocuous, nontendentious forms of humorous material. Freud is the notable exception. He recognized that much word and image play embellishes and camouflages tendentious elements, mostly hostility and taboo behavior such as sex. He further recognized that innocuous, nontendentious forms of humor rarely cause intense mirth. Not too many people will roll on the floor when they learn that boomerangs are coming back or backward-flying bees go "zzub." Belly laughter may be expected, however, when sexual revelations are involved and deserving parties get their just deserts by demeaning and frequently brutal treatments. Although there is little joke work involved, those who find Jews less than cleanly will get a kick out of the following joke related by Freud: In the old days when bathrooms consisted of a toilet and a sink, two German Jews meet in front of a public bath house, look each other over, with one saying "Gosh, another year went by!" Or imagine demeaning sexual humor. Imagine a cartoon showing a middle-aged nude woman kneeling before a middle-aged nude man. He looks down on her, apparently expecting to be fellated. The caption has him say "No, I don't think Richard Simmons would be upset if you took in a few extra calories."

It was Freud's (1905/1958) contention that the mirth reaction liberated by such tendentious humor is disproportional to the joke work involved. He argued, in fact, that people do not know exactly what it is that they laugh about. Because of this, he suggested, they find themselves laughing about taboo information, while possibly believing to laugh at the innocuous joke work accompanying it.

These contentions eventually led to the formulation of a misattribution theory of humor (Zillmann, 1983; Zillmann & Bryant, 1980). Following Freud, the theory distinguishes between nontendentious elements within humor and comedy.It stipulates that the nontendentious elements (joke work such as plays on words or obvious exaggerations) are necessary to make the tendentious elements humorous and enjoyable. Take the fellatio cartoon. The reference to diet guru Simmons, which invites an inference about the woman's concern with obesity, seems necessary, as it allows respondents to perceive their reaction as resulting from this joke work. The respondents may well enjoy the reluctant woman's humiliation. But they are, thanks to the joke work, absolved from ever thinking that they did.

The experimental evidence supports the various projections from the misattribution theory of humor. In an investigation by Zillmann and Bryant (1980), a comic situation containing both nontendentious and tendentious elements was manipulated in order to separate these elements. In one condition, only the nontendentious elements were shown (i.e., innocuous "funny" happenings). In another, only the tendentious ones were presented (i.e., a mishap, victimizing a person). In a third condition, these events were combined (i.e., the victimizing mishap was now associated with joke work). Additionally, affective dispositions toward the victim were manipulated. Respondents were either resentful or indifferent toward the victim.

The findings are summarized in Fig. 11.7. Indifferent respondents showed little appreciation of the nontendentious elements and minimal appreciation of the dispositionally inappropriate tendentious ones. Appreciation combined additively in the combination of these elements. The situation was dramatically different for resentful respondents. Whereas their appreciation of the nontendentious elements did not appreciably differ, their enjoyment of the dispositionally appropriate victimization produced considerable enjoyment. Most importantly, however, the combination of this dispositionally appropriate victimization with the innocuous joke work generated mirth that significantly exceeded the sum of its contributing parts. In agreement with theoretical expectations, the respondents be-

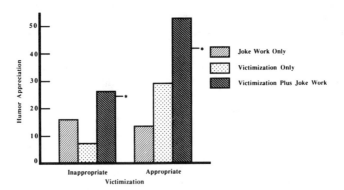

Fig. 11.7. Mirth in response to tendentious humor and its components. Reactions to the nontendentious portion alone (joke work) were moderate and independent of motives to enjoy the victimization. Reactions to the tendentious portion alone (victimization) were minimal in respondents to whom it appeared inappropriate, and pronounced in respondents motivated to enjoy it. The combination of the nontendentious and tendentious portions (joke work plus victimization) produced mirth that, for respondents not motivated to enjoy the featured victimization, was the sum of the independent portions; and that, for respondents who were motivated to enjoy the featured victimization, exceeded this sum. The summing of mirth components is indicated by the mark associated with an asterisk.

haved as if the presence of the joke work had set them free to uninhibitedly enjoy the debasement, humiliation, and ridicule of a resented person. If Freud's speculations and this research are any indication, tendentious situation comedy can be expected to have a great future. Joke work is obviously needed—although at times it seems sufficient to define humor by the cartoon format or comedy by canned laughter. It would appear, however, that the comedy mainstay must concentrate and rely on the belittlement, debasement, and humiliation of those who seem to deserve such treatment.

REFERENCES

Berlyne, D. E. (1969). Laughter, humor, and play. In G. Kindzey & E. Aronson (Eds.), *The handbook of social psychology: Vol. 3. The individual in a social context* (2nd ed., pp. 795-852). Reading, MA: Addison-Wesley.

Brooks, T., & Marsh, E. (1988). *The complete directory to prime time network TV shows, 1946-Present.* New York: Ballantine.

Brown, D., & Bryant, J. (1983). Humor in the mass media. In P. E. McGhee & J. H. Goldstein (Eds.), *Handbook of humor research. Vol. 2. Applied studies* (pp. 143-172). New York: Springer-Verlag.

Bryant, J., Rockwell, S. C., Scott, L. E., Davenport, S., Rawlins, B., Elliott, D., McKissack, S., Seigler, P., & Mei-Chiung, S. (1990). *The use of humor in local television newscasts.* Unpublished manuscript, University of Alabama, Tuscaloosa, AL.

Cantor, J. R. (1976). Humor on television: A content analysis. *Journal of Broadcasting, 20,* 501-510.

Cantor, J. R. (1977). Tendentious humour in the mass media. In A. J. Chapman & H. C. Foot (Eds.), *It's a funny thing, humour* (pp. 303-310). Oxford: Pergamon.

Cantor, J. R., & Zillmann, D. (1973). Resentment toward victimized protagonists and severity of misfortunes they suffer as factors in humor appreciation. *Journal of Experimental Research in Personality, 6,* 321-329.

Charney, M. (1978). *Comedy high and low: An introduction to the experience of comedy.* New York: Oxford University Press.

Feibleman, J. (1962). *In praise of comedy: A study in its theory and practice.* New York: Russell & Russell.

Flugel, J. C. (1954). Humor and laughter. In G. Lindzey (Ed.), *'Handbook of social psychology: Vol. 2. Special fields and applications* (pp. 709-734). Reading, MA: Addison-Wesley.

Freud, S. (1958). *Der Witz und seine Beziehung zum Unbewussten* [Jokes and their relation to the unconscious]. Frankfurt: Fischer Bücherei. (Original work published 1905)

Gerard, J. (1990, March 2). *Andy Rooney may return to "60 Minutes."* N.Y. Times News Service.

Hamburg, D. A. (1966). Effects of progesterone on behavior. In Association for Research in Nervous and Mental Disease, *Research Publications: Vol. 43. Endocrines and the central nervous system* (pp. 251-265). Baltimore, MD: Williams & Wilkins.

Hazlitt, W. (1926). On the pleasure of hating. In *Essays* (pp. 235-247). New York: Macmillan. (Original work published 1826)

Helregel, B. K., & Weaver, J. B. (1989). Mood-management during pregnancy through selective exposure to television. *Journal of Broadcasting & Electronic Media, 33*(1), 15-33.

Hobbes, T. (1968). *Leviathan.* Harmondsworth: Penguin. (Original work published 1651)

Kant, I. (1922). Kritik der praktischen Vernunft: Zweites Buch. Analytik des Erhabenen. [Critique of practical reason: Second book. Analysis of the revered]. In E. Cassirer (Ed.), *Immanuel Kants Werke* (Vol. 5, pp. 315-412). Berlin: B. Cassirer. (Original work published 1788)

Koestler, A. (1964). *The act of creation.* London: Hutchinson.

Lauter, P. (1964). *Theories of comedy*. Garden City, NY: Doubleday.

La Fave, L. (1972). Humor judgments as a function of reference groups and identification classes. In J. H. Goldstein & P. E. McGhee (Eds.), *The psychology of humor: Theoretical perspectives and empirical issues* (pp. 195-210). New York: Academic Press.

Levine, J. (1963). Humor and mental health. In A. Deutsch & H. Fishman (Eds.), *Encyclopedia of mental health* (Vol. 3, pp. 786-799). New York: F. Watts.

Love, A. M., & Deckers, L. H. (1989). Humor appreciation as a function of sexual, aggressive, and sexist content. *Sex Roles, 20*, 649-654.

Mast, G. (1981). *A short history of the movies* (3rd ed.). Indianapolis: Bobbs-Merrill.

McGhee, P. E., & Lloyd, S. A. (1981). A developmental test of the disposition theory of humor. *Child Development, 52*, 925-931.

Meadowcroft, J. M., & Zillmann, D. (1987). Women's comedy preferences during the menstrual cycle. *Communication Research, 14*, 204-218.

Medoff, N. J. (1979). *The avoidance of comedy by persons in a negative affective state: A further study in selective exposure*. Unpublished doctoral dissertation, Indiana University, Bloomington, IN.

Melgres, F. T., & Hamburg, D. A. (1976). Psychological effects of hormonal changes in women. In F. A. Beach (Ed.), *Human sexuality in four perspectives* (pp. 269-295). Baltimore, MD: Johns Hopkins University Press.

Nerhardt, G. (1976). Incongruity and funniness: Towards a new descriptive model. In A. J. Chapman & H. C. Foot (Eds.), *Humour and laughter: Theory, research and applications* (pp. 55-91). London: Wiley.

Nielsen Media Research. (1990, February 15). [Top-25 prime time programs of the 1980s by year.] Unpublished data.

Olson, E. (1968). *The theory of comedy*. Bloomington: Indiana University Press.

Postman, N. (1985). *Amusing ourselves to death: Public discourse in the age of show business*. New York: Penguin.

Robinson, V. M. (1983). Humor and health. In P. E. McGhee & J. H. Goldstein (Eds.), *Handbook of humor research: Vol. II. Applied studies* (pp. 109-128). New York: Springer-Verlag.

Schopenhauer, A. (1891). Erstes Buch: Der Welt als Vorstellung [First book: To the world for consideration]. In J. Frauenstadt (Ed.), *Arthur Schopenhauer's sämtliche Werke* (Vol. 2, pp. 3-109). Leipzig: F. A. Brockhaus.

Schultz, T. R. (1976). A cognitive-developmental analysis of humour. In A. J. Chapman & H. C. Foot (Eds.), *Humour and laughter: Theory, research and applications* (pp. 11-36). London: Wiley.

Spencer, H. (1888). The physiology of laughter. In *Illustrations of universal progress: A series of discussions* (pp. 194-209). New York: D. Appleton.

Stocking, S. H., Sapolsky, B. S., & Zillmann, D. (1977). Sex discrimination in prime time humor. *Journal of Broadcasting, 21*, 447-457.

Suls, J. M. (1972). A two-stage model for the appreciation of jokes and cartoons: An information-processing analysis. In J. H. Goldstein & P. E. McGhee (Eds.). *The psychology of humor: Theoretical perspectives and empirical issues* (pp. 81-100). New York: Academic Press.

Suls, J. M. (1977). Cognitive and disparagement theories of humour: A theoretical and empirical synthesis. In A. J. Chapman & H. C. Foot (Eds.), *It's a funny thing, humour* (pp. 41-45). Oxford: Pergamon Press.

Top 100 all-time film rental champs. (1990, January 24). *Variety*, p. 46.

Wiener, T. (1989). *The book of video lists*. Lanham, MD: Madison Books.

Wilde, L. (1976). *How the great comedy writers create laughter*. Chicago: Nelson-Hall.

Willis, E. (1967). *Writing television and radio programs*. New York: Holt, Rinehart & Winston.

Wolff, H. A., Smith, C. E., & Murray, H. A. (1934). The psychology of humor: I. A study of responses to race-disparagement jokes. *Journal of Abnormal and Social Psychology, 28*, 341-365.

Zillmann, D. (1980). Anatomy of suspense. In P. H. Tannenbaum (Ed.), *The entertainment functions of television* (pp. 133-163). Hillsdale, NJ: Lawrence Erlbaum Associates.

Zillmann, D. (1983). Disparagement humor. In P. E. McGhee & J. H. Goldstein (Eds.), *Handbook of humor research: Vol. 1. Basic issues* (pp. 85-107). New York: Springer-Verlag.

Zillmann, D. (1988). Mood management: Using entertainment to full advantage. In L. Donohew, H. E. Sypher, & E. T. Higgins (Eds.), *Communication, social cognition, and affect* (pp. 147-171). Hillsdale, NJ: Lawrence Erlbaum Associates.

Zillmann, D., & Bryant, J. (1974). Retaliatory equity as a factor in humor appreciation. *Journal of Experimental Social Psychology, 10,* 480-488.

Zillmann, D., & Bryant, J. (1980). Misattribution theory of tendentious humor. *Journal of Experimental Social Psychology, 16,* 146-160.

Zillmann, D., & Bryant, J. (1985). Affect, mood, and emotion as determinants of selective exposure. In D. Zillmann & J. Bryant (Eds.), *Selective exposure to communication* (pp. 157-190). Hillsdale, NJ: Lawrence Erlbaum Associates.

Zillmann, D., Bryant, J., & Sapolsky, B. S. (1989). Enjoyment from sports spectatorship. In J. H. Goldstein (Ed.), *Sports, games, and play: Social and psychological viewpoints* (2nd ed., pp. 241-278). Hillsdale, NJ: Lawrence Erlbaum Associates.

Zillmann, D., & Cantor, J. R. (1972). Directionality of transitory dominance as a communication variable affecting humor appreciation. *Journal of Personality and Social Psychology, 24,* 191-198.

Zillmann, D., & Cantor, J. R. (1976). A disposition theory of humour and mirth. In A. J. Chapman & H. C. Foot (Eds.), *Humour and laughter: Theory, research, and applications* (pp. 93-115). London: Wiley.

Zillmann, D., Hezel, R. T., & Medoff, N.J. (1980). The effect of affective states on selective exposure to televised entertainment fare. *Journal of Applied Social Psychology, 10,* 323-339.

CHAPTER

12

The Logic of Suspense and Mystery

Dolf Zillmann
University of Alabama

In this chapter, we explore the informational structures of suspenseful drama and mystery, and we examine the cognitive and affective reactions to the information flow in these popular genres of entertainment. We analyze both suspense and mystery in conceptual terms, specify unique characteristics, and indicate pure forms and common admixtures. Focus is on the different strategies of cognitive and affective manipulation and on the diverse combinations of cognitive and affective enjoyment that results from such manipulation. Theories projecting the enjoyment of both suspense and mystery are presented. Finally, the theories are evaluated in the light of the available research evidence.

CONCEPTUALIZATION OF SUSPENSE

According to dictionary definitions, the concept *suspense* has at least three shades of meaning. Suspense is said to be a state of (a) uncertainty in the sense of doubtfulness and indecision, (b) anxiety-like uncertainty, and (c) pleasant excitement about an expected event. Essentially, then, suspense is seen as an experience of uncertainty whose hedonic properties can vary from noxious to pleasant. Furthermore, the uncertainty in question apparently applies not only to decisional dilemmas, but also to any social event or environmental happening deemed capable of upsetting or gratifying respondents.

The usefulness of such general definitions for the consideration of enjoyment from drama is very limited. To obtain a workable definition, it would seem desirable to exclude the experience of ambivalence about entirely certain outcomes and to restrict the concept to *apprehensions about future events*. If, for example, a young man finds himself in a dilemma over which of two equally excellent cars he should buy, it is only confusing to regard him to be in a state of suspense about the choice. But more importantly, the view that uncertainty can assume any conceivable hedonic valence is troublesome. Uncertainty about a future event is obviously the more pronounced, the closer the subjective probability of the event's occurrence is to that of its nonoccurrence. Uncertainty is thus at a maximum when the odds for a desired or a feared outcome are 50:50. In the face of such even odds, the experience of uncertainty about a desired outcome should prove noxious because of the relatively high perceived likelihood that the outcome will not materialize. By the same token, the experience of such uncertainty about a feared outcome should prove noxious because of the relatively high perceived likelihood that the feared event will occur. In short, uncertainty at high levels is unlikely to be hedonically neutral or positive. It tends to produce decidedly noxious states (Berlyne, 1960).

The fact that the experience of suspense has been considered *pleasant* excitement indicates that, in the conceptualization of suspense, uncertainty often has been assigned an entirely secondary role. It would appear that pleasant excitement can result only from the anticipation of desired outcomes when this anticipation is not tempered by a substantial likelihood of alternative, undesirable outcomes. In other words, uncertainty about favorable happenings is likely to be pleasantly experienced only when it is negligible! Uncertainty, especially high levels of uncertainty, may altogether be less critical to the experience of suspense than has been commonly assumed. We return to this issue.

Suspense in Drama

Considering drama, the conceptualization of suspense must be more specific to be useful. First of all, it should be recognized that respondents are *witnesses* to dramatic events involving others, and that they are consequently neither directly threatened nor directly benefited by these events. Whatever the particular mechanism mediating the respondents' affective reaction is presumed to be, suspense can manifest itself only through the *perceived likelihood of outcomes* that either endanger or benefit others (i.e., protagonists and other members of the cast) and/or through the respondents' reactions to the events producing these outcomes. But the experience of suspense in drama is subject to further unique and seemingly universal restrictions: (a) drama must preoccupy itself with negative outcomes, (b) liked protagonists must be selected as targets for negative outcomes so as to make these outcomes feared and dreaded, and (c) for the occurrence of outcomes that threaten liked protagonists, high degrees of subjective certainty (not uncertainty!) must be created.

Focus on Negative Outcomes. It is generally accepted that *conflict*, especially human conflict, constitutes the very essence of drama (Marx, 1940; Smiley, 1971). The clash of two or more antagonistic forces is viewed as a basic, necessary condition for drama. Any and every dramatic situation is said to arise from such conflict, and it is explicated or implied that drama cannot exist without the display of conflicts and crises in one form or another. Suspense in drama, in turn, is viewed as the experience of apprehension about the resolution of conflicts and crises. More specifically, suspense is conceptualized as the experience of uncertainty regarding the outcome of a potentially hostile confrontation.

This experience of uncertainty can derive, in principle, from (a) the fear that a favored outcome may not be forthcoming, (b) the fear that a deplorable outcome may be forthcoming, (c) the hope that a favored outcome will be forthcoming, (d) the hope that a deplorable outcome will not be forthcoming, and (e) any possible combination of these hopes and fears. It has been shown that the fears and hopes in question are largely a function of respondents' affective dispositions toward the antagonistic parties (Zillmann, 1983a; Zillmann, Bryant, & Sapolsky, 1989; Zillmann & Cantor, 1976). Disposition-theoretical considerations lead to the expectation that (a) respondents will hope for outcomes that are both favorable for liked and deserving protagonists and deplorable for disliked and undeserving ones; and that (b) respondents will fear outcomes that are both deplorable for liked and deserving protagonists and favorable for disliked and undeserving ones. With hopes and fears thus confounded, the question arises as to whether suspenseful drama thrives on hopes or on fears.

The issue can be construed in two ways. First, favorable and deplorable outcomes can be thought of as entirely interdependent. A sympathetic protagonist may be up against a hostile environment, for example, and respondents are placed in suspense by watching her face a thousand dangers as she struggles through savage swamps toward safety. The respondents' affective reactions to these events could be regarded mediated by the fear that the protagonist will be injured or killed. But they could equally well be considered to result from the hope for the protagonist's welfare. It could be argued that, if respondents had no such hopes, they would not have the fear that things might go wrong—that is, the very fear that produces the gripping experience of suspense. This reasoning suggests that hopes and fears are inseparably intertwined in the apprehensions that produce suspense. In fact, the conceptual separation of hopes and fears would seem to be pointless because the two concepts appear to constitute two alternative ways of describing the same phenomenon of apprehension about an outcome.

Second, and in contrast, outcomes can be thought of as events that cause experiences that are hedonically classifiable as either negative or positive. Outcomes can be noxious or pleasant to protagonists, and they can assume the one or the other hedonic valence to different degrees. Death, mutilation, torture, injury, and social debasement can be categorized as negative outcomes, whereas gain of money, glory, and privileges can be classified as positive ones. Essentially, the distinction is between outcomes that constitute *annoyances* and outcomes that constitute *incentives*.

If outcomes are conceptualized in these terms, it becomes clear that suspense in drama is predominantly created through the suggestion of negative outcomes. As in the woman-versus-swamps example, protagonists often fight for dear life. Although some glory may be attached to sheer survival and the avoidance of injury, the provision of incentives is obviously not a necessary condition for suspense to take. Generally speaking, the attainment of incentives in suspenseful drama is secondary to the creation of apprehensions about deplorable, dreaded outcomes. Suspenseful drama features events such as bombs about to explode, dams about to burst, ceilings about to cave in, ocean liners about to sink, and fires about to rage. It features people about to be jumped and stabbed; about to walk into an ambush and get shot; and about to be bitten by snakes, tarantulas, and mad dogs. The common denominator in all of this is the likely suffering of the protagonists. It is impending disaster manifest in anticipated agony, pain, injury, and death. Suspenseful drama, then, appears to thrive on uneasiness and distress about anticipated negative outcomes. Slightly overstated, it thrives on fear.

This is not to say that suspense cannot be built on the anticipation of good fortunes. As the popular television game shows attest, people can be thrilled with uncertainty about grand prizes hidden behind curtains and in chests. This "treasure-hunt" type of suspense appears to derive to a large extent from the expectation of great rewards. The contestants in such games are obviously not placed at risk. The only "misfortune" that can befall them is the lack of good fortune. Oddly, it is conceivable that the very possibility of losing (i.e., the fear of not winning) is what produces the experience of suspense in these respondents. Be this as it may, a close look at suspenseful drama should convince anyone that suspense is characteristically generated through the creation of apprehensions about bad fortunes rather than good ones. In order to be truly suspenseful, drama must show more than the respondents' likely failure to gain incentives. Something more than not winning must be at stake. A car race, for example, devoid of threats and dangers, without risks to the liked protagonist, and with prizes and glory for all, not only would be uncharacteristic of suspenseful drama, it also would fail to induce suspense reactions of appreciable magnitude. The successful creation of the gripping experience of suspense apparently depends on the display of credible endangerments. The audience must think it likely, for example, that the protagonist's car will skid on the oil slick, that a wheel will come off, that the motor will catch on fire, or that he will fly out of the curve and tumble down the mountain.

In summary, suspenseful drama relies heavily on the exhibition of threats and dangers to protagonists. It is designed, primarily, to evoke apprehensions about decidedly noxious experiences that the protagonists are about to undergo. Although suspense can be generated through the anticipation of favorable, pleasing outcomes, this technique of suspense induction is uncharacteristic, even alien, to suspenseful drama as such. It should be recognized, however, that in suspenseful drama the primary technique of suspense induction, namely the creation of apprehensions about deplorable outcomes, is often confounded with the creation of the anticipation of favorable outcomes as a secondary technique (Zillmann, Johnson, & Hanrahan, 1973).

Affective Dispositions Toward Endangered Characters. It has been stated already that the respondents' hopes and fears regarding likely events that would affect the welfare of protagonists are dispositionally mediated. Research evidence (Zillmann & Cantor, 1977; see also the chapter on empathy by Zillmann, this volume) indicates that (a) a positive outcome is enjoyed when the protagonist whom it benefits is liked or, at least, not disliked. In sharp contrast, (b) a positive outcome that benefits a disliked protagonist is deplored. The inverse applies to negative outcomes: (c) a negative outcome is deplored when the protagonist whom it victimizes is liked or, at least, not disliked; and (d) a negative outcome that victimizes a disliked protagonist, again in sharp contrast, is enjoyed. (Note that what we refer to as *disliked protagonist* is commonly referred to as *antagonist*.) If it is assumed that these affective reactions are precipitated by hopes for and fears about certain outcomes, it follows that the hopes and fears regarding the same events will be totally different for liked and disliked protagonists. Whereas liked protagonists are considered deserving of positive outcomes, the very possibility of disliked protagonists' benefaction becomes deplorable and distressing. Even more important for suspenseful drama, whereas liked protagonists are regarded undeserving of negative outcomes, the impending victimization of disliked protagonists is usually not only not deplored, but very much enjoyed. After all, disliked protagonists—typically, mean, obnoxious, and evil antagonists who demean and torment others—are merely getting their just deserts (Zillmann & Bryant, 1975).

Obvious as the dispositional mediation of suspense may seem, it is not generally recognized. Smiley (1971), for instance, insisted that "suspense *automatically* occurs during all crises" (p. 68, italics added). Expressed in dramaturgical nomenclature, he proposed that any "hint" that (a) two identified, opposing forces will fight, and that (b) the one or the other party will win, produces the experience of suspense in the "wait" (i.e., the period of time in which the fighting is about to erupt or is in progress) for the "climax" that comes with the resolution of the conflict.

Smiley's automatic suspense reaction is not only at variance with what is known about the dispositional mediation of affective reactions, but is noncompelling intuitively. In the case where two intensely disliked parties fight to the finish, for example, onlookers are likely to be utterly indifferent about, rather than fearful of, any particular outcome. And in the case where a resented agent is about to walk into an ambush set by liked protagonists, the only source of suspense appears to be the possibility that something could go wrong with the hoped-for destruction of the villain (which might place the "good guys" at risk). Not surprisingly, then, suspense in drama favors the projection of negative, feared outcomes for beloved protagonists – not the projection of such outcomes for just any member of the cast.

Subjective Certainty About Outcomes.   This delineation of the characteristic and presumably most effective conditions for the creation of suspense in drama should make it clear that maximal uncertainty associated with a feared outcome does not necessarily constitute the point of maximal suspense. In fact, it seems quite unlikely that degree of uncertainty and intensity of suspense vary proportionally. One would expect, for instance, that witnessing the endangerment of an intensely liked protagonist produces less fearful apprehensions, and thus less suspense, when the odds for her safety are perceived to the 50:50 rather than, say, 25:75. It would appear that suspense will be more intensely experienced the greater the respondents' subjective *certainty* that the liked protagonist will succumb – this time – to the destructive forces against which she is struggling. However, although even odds (i.e., maximum uncertainty) may indeed constitute a condition of rather moderate endangerment, total subjective certainty about the liked protagonist's forthcoming victimization does not, in all probability, produce maximal suspense. It may be argued that as soon as respondents are confident that a feared outcome is indeed forthcoming, they are no longer in suspense. The respondents may, at this point, start to experience disappointment and sadness. There is reason to believe that certainty about a forthcoming deplorable event will serve a preparatory appraisal function, which protects against overly intense noxious arousal in response to the depiction of the event once it materializes (Lazarus, 1966; Leventhal, 1979). Subjective certainty about a deplorable outcome not only seems to terminate the experience of suspense, it also may be expected to minimize the emotional impact of tragic happenings. According to these considerations, then, uncertainty is a necessary condition for suspense, but the experience of suspense will be more intense the greater the onlookers' subjective certainty that a deplorable outcome will indeed befall a liked protagonist. However, as extreme levels of certainty are reached and the outcome is no longer in doubt, the experience of suspense vanishes and gives way to more definite dysphoric reactions.

Consideration of the other extreme of the uncertainty scale (i.e., certainty that the liked protagonist will not come to harm) suggests that most dramatic fare will produce suspense at near-zero levels. In television drama series, with recurrent characters and formats, it is clear from the outset that the main protagonists will survive all conflicts in which they are engaged. The situation is not all that different for the movies. Usually there are cues that permit respondents to infer, with considerable certainty, which parties will be victorious in the end. Fearful apprehensions about deplorable outcomes may seem groundless under these circumstances.

The *macrostructure* of drama, the overall plot or "theme" (Marx, 1940) that terminates in the ultimate resolution of a dramatic presentation, may indeed contribute little, if anything, to suspense. However, in the course of a single play, the experience of suspense can be produced many times over. In the *microstructure* of drama, specific plots can show the liked protagonists credibly endangered. Although loss of life may not be a viable threat, loss of limb may have considerable credibility; and the possibility of being beaten, stabbed, shot, or otherwise subjected to painful, agonizing, and humiliating treatment certainly can have great credibility. Respondents thus need not fear for the heroine's life, for example, but there can be ample cause for worrying about her being hit, raped, strangled, or severely injured.

Ultimate Outcomes. Clearly, drama that has unpredictable themes lends itself more than predictable fare to the creation of high levels of suspense. Unpredictable plots may well generate heightened suspense, but they do not, in and of themselves, produce superior appreciation. The enjoyment of suspenseful drama apparently depends, in large measure, on the respondents' sanction of ultimate outcomes (Zillmann & Bryant, 1975; Zillmann, Hay, & Bryant, 1975). It presumably also depends on the degree to which respondents tolerate affective disturbances. It is possible that drama that produces extremely high levels of suspense is too disturbing to be enjoyable (Berlyne, 1971). Furthermore, it is conceivable that drama with a rather predictable macrostructure or theme, and with numerous unpredictable plots of suspenseful actions, creates optimal conditions for enjoyment.

The latter format is obtrusive in children's fare. Liked protagonists are often nearly omnipotent. They handle any predicament with ease. Apprehensions and empathetic distress on the children's part seem misplaced sentiments. The format is also manifest in melodrama—that is, in plays in which the good and the evil forces are sharply contrasted and in which the ultimate outcome of the conflict between them is never in doubt. The popularity of melodrama makes it clear that high levels of suspense cannot be equated with great enjoyment of drama.

Affect in Response to Drama

Before entering into a discussion of likely and unlikely mechanisms of the enjoyment of suspenseful drama, a summarizing statement seems in order.

In accordance with all considerations to this point, we define the *experience of suspense* that is brought on by exposure to dramatic presentations as an affective reaction that characteristically derives from the respondents' acute, fearful apprehension about deplorable events that threaten liked protagonists, this apprehension being mediated by high but not complete subjective certainty about the occurrence of the anticipated deplorable events. Furthermore, we define *suspenseful drama* as drama that features sympathetic protagonists in peril, thus having the capacity to instigate experiences of suspense.

Feeling With Versus Feeling For. It is a widely held belief that those exposed to drama featuring sympathetic, liked protagonists "identify" with these protagonists and "vicariously" experience whatever these protagonists experience. This view is exceedingly popular and treated as a secure and unquestionable key element of our understanding of enlightenment from drama. However, attempts at explaining the enjoyment of suspenseful drama primarily on the basis of some form of empathetic coexperience result in bewilderment only.

Suspenseful drama, as has been suggested, thrives on the projection of deplorable happenings. Those exposed to such drama, as they witness sympathetic characters in fear and danger, should frequently find themselves in a state of empathetic dysphoria. Distressing events are not only very frequent in suspenseful drama, they also take up longer periods of time than scenes depicting the benefaction and happiness of liked protagonists. Opportunities for sharing misery are simply more abundant than are opportunities for sharing happiness. Accordingly, respondents should experience more empathetic dysphoria than empathetic euphoria in the course of a play.

The dominance of empathetic distress over positively toned empathetic reactions is difficult to reconcile with the apparent enjoyment of suspenseful drama that is characterized by such dominance. Reconciliation is particularly difficult on the basis of considerations of vicarious affect and experiential sharing. If vicarious responses were a crucial mediator of enjoyment, drama should be more enjoyable (a) the less distress-inducing happenings are featured and (b) the more emphasis is given to the depiction of good fortunes and the liked protagonists' contentment and joy. The assumption that vicarious affective responding is what fosters enlightenment from drama leads ultimately to the proposal that enjoyment of suspenseful drama can best be accomplished by reducing the frequency and duration of suspenseful parts.

This assessment is not appreciably altered when empathetic distress is not conceived of as a vicarious reaction. Suspense-induced empathetic distress may be viewed as feeling "for someone" rather than as feeling "with someone" (i.e., feeling "instead of someone," which means "vicariously"). In recent theoretical treatments of the empathetic process (e.g., Berger, 1962; Stotland, 1969), *empathy* is defined as an affective reaction to the witnessed display of emotion by another person, or to the anticipation of such a display. At times, the empathy concept is restricted to instances of affective concordance (between the emotion witnessed or anticipated in another and that in response to it). On occasion, however, all affective reactions to the stipulated stimulus conditions (discordant as well as concordant) are considered empathetic. Either conception of empathy is broad enough to encompass both mediating possibilities—namely, that an affective reaction is a response along with a person, or that it is a response to the observed or anticipated expression of emotion in another person.

The indicated ambiguity in the empathy concept is nicely illustrated by the ambush cliché of suspenseful presentations. Imagine youngsters watching a

Western hero ride unexpectingly into a trap, with plenty of bad guys hiding on rooftops, their rifles ready for action. Such an exhibition of impending disaster may well cause distress in the onlookers. But is it because they "identify" with the endangered protagonist? Is it because they *feel with* him? Or could it be that they are disturbed because they *feel for* him—simply because they like him and care about him? Could it be that the children also respond to the signs of danger, regardless of the protagonist's coping with his endangerment?

The characteristic reaction of small children to suspenseful situations of this sort is common knowledge and most revealing. Children tend to talk to their screen heroes, mostly to alert them to hidden dangers—dangers of which the heroes, in accordance with textbook suspense prescriptions, are patently unaware (Hitchcock, 1959). Such attempts at beneficial intervention cast doubt on the truism-like belief that respondents, especially children, *identify* with liked protagonists. If children did identify with the hero witnessed in the described predicament— that is, if the children's affective reactions were determined by some sort of ego confusion with the hero—their affective behavior should be controlled by the hero's expression of calmness and self-confidence. The consideration of vicarious reactivity thus not only fails to explain distress in response to most scenes of entrapment and peril, but actually projects an absence of distress, unless or until the hero is seen in fear and agony.

The Illusion of Being There.   As indicated, suspense can be built and enhanced by liked protagonists' apparent unawareness of acute danger, a condition that renders them especially vulnerable. It seems that onlookers, regardless of the protagonists' potentially limited comprehension of the circumstances of endangerment, utilize all the information available, make an appraisal, and respond in accordance with this appraisal. If a protagonist is liked and deemed undeserving of a particular deplorable treatment, the imminence of that treatment should prove disturbing. Onlookers even should be inclined to intervene and prevent the deplorable outcome that they are unable to sanction and accept (Zillmann & Bryant, 1975). The mature drama enthusiast has learned, of course, to inhibit any attempt at intervention. Little children, in contrast, can become so engulfed in the dramatic happenings that they lose sight of the fact that intervention is pointless, and they yell their warnings anyway. If such behavior entails an illusion, it is not identity confusion with the esteemed protagonist, nor is it an experience "instead of" the protagonist. Rather, the illusion lies in the fact that respondents behave as if they were there—as if they witnessed actual happenings. Such behavior demands that suspense-induced empathetic distress, in children and adults alike, must be treated as affective reactions of concerned "third parties" who vehemently deplore impending outcomes. Assumptions about vicarious activities and about identification processes are not necessary. No matter how plausible they may seem, they are erroneous and misleading.

Empathetic Distress and Euphoria.   Given that suspenseful drama produces empathetic distress for considerable periods of time, and given that such drama is nonetheless capable of generating great enjoyment, two related issues demand clarification. First, it is to be determined exactly what, within suspenseful drama, fosters enjoyment. (It is stipulated, of course, that the stimuli that induce empathetic distress, at least for the period of time during which they have this effect, do not per se constitute enjoyment-evoking stimuli.) Second, it is to be determined whether or not the experience of distress can influence and enhance enjoyment.

The first issue is readily clarified. Generally speaking, it is the benefaction of good and liked protagonists and the just, punitive treatment of their transgressive and resented opponents, the antagonists, that evoke joyful reactions (Zillmann & Bryant, 1975; Zillmann & Cantor, 1976, 1977; see also the chapter on empathy by Zillmann, this volume).

It has also been suggested, however, that the mere reduction or termination of the experience of empathetic distress, accomplished by the end of the distressing episode, is a sufficient condition for enjoyment (Berlyne, 1960). As sympathetic protagonists avert acute danger, onlookers can "breathe a sigh of relief." It is this experience of relief that has been said to constitute the minimal condition for joyful reactivity.

The consideration of *relief* brings us to the second issue. If relief from distress is pleasantly experienced, and if relief is brought about by the effective resolution of suspense, a peculiar connection between distress and relief becomes apparent: The intensity of empathetic distress seems to determine the intensity of the euphoric reaction to its resolution. The intensity of joy seems to vary proportionally with that of the antecedent state of dysphoria. According to this view, little suspense creates little distress; and in turn, little distress creates little relief and not much enjoyment. Great suspense, in contrast, produces severe distress, which in turn produces great relief and great enjoyment. Provided that suspense is promptly resolved, it thus appears possible that suspense-induced empathetic distress, or something thereof, can be converted into enjoyment.

In a model that has come to be known as the arousal jag, Berlyne (1960) concentrated on the physiological concomitants of aversion and relief. He proposed, essentially, that distress is arousing, that this arousal is noxious, that relief manifests itself in a sharp drop of noxious arousal, and that this arousal drop, analogous to drive reduction, is pleasantly experienced and rewarding.

At first glance, Berlyne's proposal does appear to unravel the mystery of the enjoyment of suspense-induced distress. New research findings made it clear, however, that arousal reduction is not necessarily rewarding. Worse yet, they established that arousal increments can be rewarding. In view of these findings, Berlyne (1967, 1971) modified his original model, allowing for the possibility that both arousal drops and arousal boosts may be rewarding and pleasantly experienced (see Zillmann, 1980, for a detailed discussion of Berlyne's proposals).

Unfortunately, the modified model no longer explains the distress–euphoria conversion. It fails, in fact, to explain distress as a noxious experience. The arousal boosts associated with distress (Grings & Dawson, 1978) are obviously not pleasantly experienced. Additionally, the arousal-jag reasoning suffered from imprecision in the conceptualization of arousal. What kind of arousal is supposed to be jagging? Studies in which autonomic arousal (the kind critically involved in affective reactions) has been measured have failed to show a sharp drop in arousal upon suspense resolution (Zillmann et al., 1975). In the face of these and other difficulties with the jag model (Zillmann, 1980), the distress–euphoria conversion in suspenseful drama calls for an alternative approach.

A THEORY OF SUSPENSE ENJOYMENT

We now develop a theory that projects the affective intensity of the enjoyment of suspenseful drama as a function of the magnitude of empathetic distress from suspense. The theory also focuses on suspense-induced arousal. More precisely, it focuses on the autonomic manifestations and consequences of such arousal. However, in contrast to Berlyne's arousal-jag model, the rather slowly changing levels of excitatory activity are considered crucial — not rapid arousal drops, nor quick boosts. In addition, the hedonic valence of reactions to drama is not thought to be determined by changes in arousal levels. This valence is considered to be the result of cognitive operations, instead. More specifically, the hedonic valence of experiential states is seen to be determined by the respondents' appraisal of the environmental stimulus conditions to which they find themselves reacting (Lazarus, 1966; Schachter, 1964; Zillmann, 1978).

We explain the enjoyment of suspenseful drama mainly in terms of the excitation-transfer paradigm (Zillmann, 1978). This paradigm has been detailed elsewhere (Zillmann, 1983b, 1984). Suffice it here to present only those of its features that are essential to the explanation of the enjoyment of suspenseful drama.

It is proposed that individuals who anticipate or witness the victimization of agents toward which they are favorably disposed (a) experience an elevation of sympathetic excitation and (b) appraise their reactions as dysphoric. The intensity of these dysphoric reactions, which we define as *empathetic distress*, is determined by prevailing levels of sympathetic activity. (The dispositional part of this proposition derives from disposition theory; Zillmann, 1983a; Zillmann et al., 1989; Zillmann & Cantor, 1976, 1977.)

It is further proposed that, because of humoral mediation of excitatory processes, elevated sympathetic activity decays comparatively slowly. Portions of it persist for some time after the termination of the arousing stimulus condition. Such residual excitation tends to go unrecognized, mainly because of poor interoception. It is, therefore, capable of combining inseparably with the excitatory activity that is produced by subsequent stimuli.

Finally, it is proposed that the experiential status of subsequent affective reactions is determined by the respondents' appraisal of the environmental circumstances that produce the reactions. The intensity of these affective reactions, however, is determined by the union of (a) excitation specifically produced by the subsequent stimulus condition and (b) residual excitation from preceding stimulation.

In general, then, the experiential status of any affective reaction is viewed as being cognitively determined. The intensity of affect, in contrast, is viewed as being determined by the prevailing level of sympathetic activity. To the extent that an affective reaction is associated with sympathetic activity that derives in part from earlier stimulation, the intensity of affect will be higher than it should be on the basis of present stimuli alone.

This projection of an affective "overreaction" to subsequent stimuli is the key element in our approach to suspense. We conceptualize suspense and its resolution as a sequence of affective reactions in which residues of excitation from the antecedent condition intensify the reaction to the subsequent condition. The experience of empathetic distress during the suspense period may well be acutely negative, hedonically speaking. Regarding excitatory residues from distress that enter the resolution period, the consideration of hedonic valence is not relevant, however. Residues from negative states are expected to intensify positive or negative subsequent states just as much as residues from positive states. Residues of sympathetic excitation are simply impartial to the hedonic quality of the experiences they come to intensify.

It should be clear at this point that the transfer paradigm predicts the intensification of euphoria after empathetic distress only if euphoria is cognitively achieved. Only if there is a "happy turn of events" in the resolution of suspense can this be expected. In line with earlier considerations, the mere removal of the threat that produced empathetic distress may be regarded a minimal stimulus condition for the cognitive switch from dysphoria to euphoria. But satisfying, happy endings usually offer more than relief alone. They tend to confound relief with a wealth of gratifications that await the protagonists who have faced danger (Zillmann et al., 1973). Characteristically, suspense resolutions provide ample cause for the hedonic turnabout from distress to positively toned affect.

Once the resolution of suspense accomplishes the discussed adjustment, the resultant feelings of euphoria should be enhanced by residual excitation from the distress response to suspense. The euphoric reaction to a satisfying resolution of suspense should be more intensely experienced the greater the excitatory residues from the precipitating suspense-induced distress. Whether the macro- or microstructure of suspenseful drama (theme vs. plot) is considered, the more such drama initially distresses, the more it is ultimately enjoyed. The better a suspense treatment takes effect, the more enjoyment will be liberated by its satisfying resolution. By the same token, the same satisfying resolution, when not precipitated by arousing events, can only produce flat drama—drama incapable of generating intensely felt enjoyment.

It should be recognized that predictions for the appreciation of tragic events are quite different. A sad turn of events in drama is likely to produce dysphoric feelings. Analogous to our proposal regarding satisfying resolutions, it is now to be expected that dysphoric reactions to dissatisfying resolutions of suspense will be more intensely experienced the greater the excitatory residues from the preceding suspense-induced distress. The more empathetic distress is activated by the events preceding the resolutions, the sadder the tragic resolutions (Zillmann, Mody, & Cantor, 1974); and to the extent that the ultimate outcome is tragic, the sadder the tragedy. Consequently, if the creation of profound, deep feelings of sadness is accepted as the central objective of tragedy, distress from suspense (or more accurately, residual excitation from such distress) offers itself as a potent facilitator.

As suggested earlier, the two principal forms of truly satisfying resolutions (i.e., resolutions that accomplish more than mere stress relief) are the benefaction of good and liked protagonists and the just, punitive treatment of their transgressive and resented opponents. Drama usually features a combination of both. The contribution of these "gratifiers" to the enjoyment of drama should not be underestimated. It must be acknowledged, in fact, that the display of gratifying happenings may foster excitatory reactions of nontrivial magnitude. Pronounced excitatory reactions are certainly not restricted to aversions, and they may well accompany joyous responses to hoped-for outcomes.

The possibility of appreciable to strong excitatory reactions to satisfying suspense resolutions is readily integrated into our theoretical model. We simply propose that enjoyment of suspenseful drama that features satisfying resolutions in plots and themes will be greater (a) the more residual excitation from suspense treatments persists during the satisfying resolutions of these treatments, (b) the longer the excitatory residues in question persist, and (c) the more excitation the resolutions themselves contribute.

CONCEPTUALIZATION OF MYSTERY

In contrast to the conceptualization of suspense, dictionary definitions of *mystery* as a genre of entertainment are to the point and useful. Mystery is said to be fiction that usually deals with the solution of mysterious crimes. Something "mysterious," in turn, is said to excite wonder, curiosity, or surprise while baffling efforts at comprehension. The only trouble spot is the parallel, possibly intruding definition of mystery as a mostly religious truth that can be known only by revelation and that cannot be fully understood. Such mystery may have a place in Gothic horror and science fiction. In these genres, incomprehensible happenings often remain incomprehensible; events do not necessarily abide by the commonly accepted laws of physics, and "resolutions" may entail more magic and foster more bewilderment than earlier occurrences. In the classic format of mystery, in contrast, bewilderment from mysterious happenings is terminal. The mystery is resolved, usually by logical inference and in strict adherence to prevailing conceptions of physical and social reality. Some aberrations (such as unresolved or insoluble mystery) may exist, of course (Grossvogel, 1979).

Mystery relates to suspense in the sense that respondents are considered to be "in suspense about" the resolution; that is, in the sense of eagerly and impatiently awaiting an acceptable, plausible explanation for what initially proved to be puzzling and possibly appeared insoluble. Obviously, this kind of suspense has nothing to do with empathetic distress from high subjective certainty that liked protagonists will suffer misfortunes. It is, instead, the kind equatable with uncertainty about the veridicality of circumstances. The circumstances in question are usually of little, if any, affective consequence to respondents. The issue is not fear of, or hopes for, particular resolutions, but the correctness or incorrectness of solutions. Uncertainty concerns the rightness or falsehood of circumstances as solutions to unexplained, bewildering events. Such uncertainty should, of course, be at a maximum when subjective probabilities for "it is" versus "it is not" meet at 50:50.

The point that mystery, in its pure form, does not thrive on apprehensions about negative outcomes for protagonists is made most clearly by the fact that the negative outcome of central importance is a given. In one form or another, a transgression—usually a criminal transgression such as murder—has occurred already. Victimization is a thing of the past. It is not to be feared. It is, instead, to be explained. The "Who-done-it?" characterization, although too narrow, is essentially appropriate. The immediate questions raised by the acknowledged victimization of particular parties are: Who is responsible? Who did this? And why was it done? The means by which the victimization was accomplished are often equally important: Exactly how was it done? Uncertainty about the who, why, and how of criminal transgressions is what mystery thrives on. Individually or, more characteristically, in combination, these elements of uncertainty are used to create the puzzlement and bewilderment that is to be resolved. Once such bewilderment about the specifics of a crime has been accomplished, the play features an agent who, through inquisitiveness and by deduction, eliminates erroneous whos, whys, and hows and eventually arrives at a veridical assessment of all circumstances that caused the investigated victimization. This agent, then, literally puts an end to "the mystery" by enlightening respondents about the etiology of the case.

One might characterize suspenseful drama as drama that plays on respondents' emotions. Mystery, in contrast, may be characterized as drama that offers cerebral titilation. It can be construed as an invitation to solve, along with the play's agent, an intriguing crime (Bennett, 1979).

Responses to mystery, compared with those to suspense, are similarly different. Whereas the enjoyment of resolved suspense is largely an emotional affair, with enjoyment being a function of prevailing sympathetic arousal, resolved bewilderment from mystery amounts to enlightenment. Such enlightenment, in and of itself, gives little cause for euphoria or other affects. The removal of uncertainties about circumstances may well provide some degree of relief (Berlyne, 1954, 1960) and the associated "aha!" experience may prove rewarding. However, as the circumstances in question are affectively inconsequential for respondents, expectations of strong relief reactions would seem unwarranted. The pleasant glow of the experience of enlightenment appears to be the gratifier of central importance. But in view of the popularity that mystery enjoys, one is inclined to believe that other factors may contribute to and facilitate enjoyment.

One such factor could be the respondents' admiration of the clever operations of the problem-solving agents. Because of this admiration, respondents might grow fond of these problem-solving agents and then respond euphorically to their success in breaking the mystery—much like they would respond to the victorious action of protagonists in suspenseful drama.

The possibility that respondents scrutinize the puzzling circumstances and correctly infer the who, why, and how of criminal transgressions constitutes another factor (Bennett, 1979). That is to say that respondents may conduct their own problem solving—on the basis of the so-called clues that are provided in a play—and then, upon revelation of the etiology of the crime, obtain pleasure from having been right. The existence of television mystery programs that invite respondents to infer or guess the who-done-it before the specifics of the transgression are revealed would seem to support the proposal that viewers celebrate their own brilliance in correctly resolving mysteries. However, support of this kind is not compelling. It is compromised by the fact that the etiology of a crime must be kept transparent enough to ensure that most viewers can infer it correctly. Transparency is necessary to prevent that a majority of viewers "guesses wrong" and experiences failure—failure suspect of being detrimental to enjoyment. But transparency is what intriguing mystery may not have. It is virtually the antidote to mystery.

A THEORY OF MYSTERY ENJOYMENT

Mystery, in its pure form, presents puzzling transgressions and then proceeds to introduce and develop characters who might be responsible for these transgressions. Investigative agents scrutinize the circumstances and eventually break "the mystery" of the transgressions in question by compellingly implicating those who did it, why they did it, and how they did it.

Clearly, the elements involved in the revelation of the etiology of crimes are highly interdependent. Motives and means regarding transgressions are commonly used to implicate persons. Although mystery occasionally focuses on the means employed in the commission of unexplained crimes, it characteristically focuses on people; that is, it focuses on motives, on criminal propensities, on opportunities, and on the destructive means of persons who might have committed the crimes under investigation. This focus manifests itself in the flow of information: The presentation of unexplained crimes is followed by the *development of a cast of suspects*. Characteristically, a small number of persons who had some relationship or business with, or are related to, the victimized party is introduced in a way that gives all persons motive, opportunity, and means for the commission of the unexplained crime. It is the exceedingly rare exception that all suspects will turn out to be involved in the commission of criminal transgressions. The rule is that some suspects will be vindicated. In fact, the number of vindicated suspects tends to exceed the number of those who are ultimately implicated with the commission of the crimes. Typically, just one person is found to be the perpetrator. There may be an accomplice or two, however.

On the basis of the assumption that enjoyment of mystery increases with the magnitude of preresolution bewilderment which, in turn, increases with the magnitude of uncertainty about the correctness of a resolution, this analysis of information flow in mystery leads to the following hypotheses.

H1: In the unlikely case of one suspect in a play, the enjoyment of mystery is greatest when the respondents' subjective probability for that suspect's criminal involvement is 0.5 (or 50:50 for involvement vs. noninvolvement).

H2: In the more common case of multiple suspects, the rationale concerning the respondents' subjective probability applies to all suspects. Accordingly, enjoyment of mystery is at a maximum when, other things equal, the respondents' subjective probability for considering a suspect implicated with a crime is at 0.5 for all suspects.

The corollary is that enjoyment is greater the more closely a situation approximates the specified equiprobability of criminal implication versus vindication for all suspects.

H3: Enjoyment of mystery increases with the number of suspects considered equally implicated.

The amount of uncertainty – uncertainty that upon the presentation of the resolution of mystery is expected to convert into enjoyment – is readily quantified. Information theory (Hartley, 1928; Shannon & Weaver, 1949) offers a possible algorithm:

$$\mathrm{H}_n = -\sum_{i=1}^{n} p_i \log_2 p_i.$$

In this formula, n is the number of supects, and p_i is the subjective certainty of a suspect's criminal involvement.

However, as this algorithm stipulates that all probabilities sum to unity, its immediate application is limited to mystery that features one perpetrator only. Although this would not impair the analysis of most plays, it would seem desirable to construct an algorithm that can handle all suspect/perpetrator constellations. The formula presented next has this capability. It has the additional advantage of being modifiable to accommodate alternative enjoyment models that are yet to be presented.

$$U = \sum_{i=1}^{n} 1 - 4 \, (p_i - 0.5)^2 \text{ or } n - 4 \sum_{i=1}^{n} (p_i - 0.5)^2,$$

where, as before, n is the number of suspects and p_i the subjective certainty of a suspect's criminal involvement. As can be seen, $U_{min} = 0$ and $U_{max} = n$.

There are obvious restrictions of, and alternatives to, this basic theoretical model. Possible elaborations are apparent as well.

First, the number of suspects cannot be increased beyond respondents' capability or willingness to process all pertinent information. The involvement of too many suspects, all featured in intricate situations, is likely to overwhelm respondents. Many may not care to invest labor-like effort and lose interest as a result.

Second, and conceptually more important, it may be argued that the resolution of maximal bewilderment does not constitute an optimal condition for enjoyment. It is conceivable that it is high erroneous certainty, instead of high uncertainty, that fosters great surprise; and that greater surprise, in turn, fosters greater enjoyment. (Note that this conceptualization of "surprise" differs from that of information theory, where surprise or "surprisal" is often equated with uncertainty.) The consideration of maximal surprise, not maximal uncertainty, thus projects greatest enjoyment for resolution patterns that totally thwart expectations.

H4: Enjoyment of mystery is at a maximum when, other things equal, the respondents' subjective probability for considering suspects criminally implicated is zero for perpetrators and unity for vindicated persons.

The corollary is that enjoyment is greater the more closely a situation approximates the specified distribution of subjective probabilities.

H5: Enjoyment of mystery increases with the number of suspects considered implicated.

The algorithm offered for the computation of uncertainty, now applied to the computation of surprise, becomes:

$$S = \sum_{i=1}^{n} (p_i - v_i)^2,$$

where n is the number of suspects, p_i is the subjective certainty of a suspect's criminal involvement, and v_i is the veridical or actual criminal-involvement status of a suspect (0 vs. 1). Obviously, if the guesses concerning involvement are correct for all suspects in a play, surprise upon resolution is at a minimum ($S = 0$). If all guesses are in error, surprise is at a maximum ($S = n$).

Third, the surprise scheme may be reversed to accommodate the possibility that respondents take pleasure from guessing along and being right.

H6: Enjoyment of mystery is at a maximum when, other things equal, the respondents' subjective probability for considering suspects criminally implicated is unity for perpetrators and zero for vindicated persons.

The corollary is as before: Enjoyment is greater the more closely a situation approximates the specified distribution of subjective probabilities.

H7: As stated in H5, enjoyment of mystery increases with the number of suspects considered implicated.

The value of estimate confirmation is, of course, the inverse of surprise value:

$$C = \sum_{i=1}^{n} 1 - (p_i - v_i)^2 \text{ or } n - \sum_{i=1}^{n} (p_i - v_i)^2 \text{ or simply } n - S.$$

Thus, if $S = O$, $C = n$, and if $S = n$, $C = O$.

It has been suggested (Grossvogel, 1979) "that only an infinitesimally small number" (p. 41) of mystery enthusiasts ever undertakes to resolve mysteries ahead of the resolving agents, and that most enthusiasts simply expect and await a clever, grand resolution. If so, the resolution of maximally opaque, uncertainty-laden, bewildering situations would seem to constitute the condition for greatest enjoyment. Because it is presumed that respondents do not attempt to resolve the puzzling circumstances themselves, there would be no expectations that could be faulted or confirmed. If it is assumed, however, that respondents entertain notions concerning the guilt or innocence of suspects, the surprise model (H4, H5) should prove superior to the uncertainty model (H1, H2, H3) in predicting the enjoyment of respondents who can accept failure in guessing and who take pleasure from witnessing the exhibition of cleverness, if not brilliance, by others. By the same token, the confirmation model (H6, H7) should prove superior to the uncertainty model in predicting the enjoyment of respondents who seek reassurance about their problem-solving skills and who have difficulty accepting failure.

To the extent that most, if not all, respondents derive more pleasure from seeing their expectations confirmed rather than thwarted, confirmation may be considered a factor that contributes, in a general way and for all people, to the enjoyment of mystery. It must be recognized, however, that this can only be expected for mysteries whose resolution poses an appreciable degree of difficulty for respondents. Under no circumstances may mysteries appear "easy" (to resolve, that is). They obviously must be transparent enough to be soluble, but they must be so without ever appearing to be transparent.

In this connection it also must be acknowledged that enjoyment can readily be spoiled by resolutions that are inconsistent with earlier presented clues. Revelations that do not accord with these clues tend to be upsetting. Respondents may well be surprised by "mystical revelations" that do not square with earlier clues, but their surprise rightly converts to feelings of having been cheated. In these terms, the not infrequent practice of providing critical clues only "in the last minute" just prior to or even during resolution, thereby plausibly "resolving" essentially insoluble mysteries, is deplorable and amounts to poor and deceptive writing.

The discussed alternative models need not be treated as competing predictive systems that project enjoyment of mystery for all people in all situations. The likelihood of individual differences has been pointed out already. It is conceivable that traits exist that make the one or the other model more applicable to particular subpopulations. Roughly speaking, there may exist uncertainty-seekers, surprise-seekers, and confirmation-seekers. The uncertainty model, for instance, might best explain the behavior of thrill- or sensation-seekers (Zuckerman, 1979) who value confronting problems more than they value solving them—as solutions terminate the thrill of puzzlement. In contrast, the behavior of those who enjoy trying their luck at the game of mystery-solving should be better explained by the other models. The confirmation model should best project the reactions of persons of relatively low self-esteem. The surprise model, on the other hand, should best forecast the enjoyment of persons who love to take on a challenge and who are not disturbed when they find themselves outwitted. Essentially, then, the models are not mutually exclusive in the sense that only one of them can be valid. They all might have validity that is limited to specifiable conditions. A given model might best explain the behavior of people characterized by particular traits. Analogously, the models may be specific to different states experienced by persons exhibiting particular traits. It is conceivable that persons at times are relaxed and in a "problem-solving mood," making the surprise model applicable. At other times they may be exhausted, unable or unwilling to comprehend complex circumstances in order to infer outcomes, and be appreciative of others' efforts at resolving the mystery; this would make the uncertainty model applicable. The models thus may be viewed as being truly complementary.

Up to this point, we have implied that subjective probabilities are formed in the course of a play, and that their distribution across suspects just prior to resolution is crucial. Such a conceptualization is not entirely satisfactory, however, because it ignores changes over time. It must be recognized that the probabilities in question are subject to continual manipulation. Respondents may be relatively certain, at a given time, that some suspects are guilty and that others are innocent. As additional information becomes available, they may alter their assessment, becoming less certain about earlier indictments and/or more certain about the guilt of others. They might, in fact, change their assessment repeatedly, causing frequent shifts in the attribution of guilt and innocence to suspects.

This fluctuation of subjective probabilities during the course of a play must be assumed to influence the experience of bewilderment and, ultimately, that of enjoyment. It would appear that mystery that accomplishes the indicated shifting to a large degree is more bewildering and enjoyable upon resolution than, other things equal, mystery producing relatively time-stable suspicions only.

The consequences of uncertainty manifest in the specified fluctuations may be projected as follows.

H8, extending H1, H2, and H3: The enjoyment-enhancing experience of bewilderment increases with changes in uncertainty about suspects' guilt or innocence during the course of a play. Specifically, it increases (a) with the amount of variance over time for any given suspect and (b) with the number of suspects exhibiting such variance.

The distribution of uncertainty over time is readily integrated with the various models under consideration. Variation might be estimated in conventional ways. For instance, the variance (s^2) per suspect could be summed across all suspects. In uncertainty models, the resulting total could then be combined, additively or multiplicatively, with the estimates defined by the formulae provided earlier. The weight that the summed variance should receive for this combination would have to be empirically determined, however (through the exploration of the relationship between the various sources of uncertainty and enjoyment). Such variance estimates could be used analogously to amplify enjoyment projected from the surprise and confirmation models.

The indicated variance estimates depend, of course, on multiple assessment of subjective probabilities. These successive assessments lend themselves to uncertainty comparisons for given times. Such comparisons are capable of differentiating between mystery that builds toward an uncertainty climax just prior to resolution and mystery that sustains uncertainty levels or that occasionally offers partial resolutions (akin to miniplots in suspenseful drama), thereby relieving uncertainty at times. Incremental mystery (U at t_1 < U at t_2 < U at t_3 < . . . < U at t_k) would seem to combine well with the surprise model and may be expected to enhance surprise-based enjoyment. Decremental mystery (U at t_1 > U at t_2 > U at t_3 > . . . > U at t_k), in contrast, appears to combine more readily with the confirmation model and — because it amounts to a scheme that gives respondents an early taste of success in demystifying matters and thus feeds the expectation of ultimate success — may be expected to enhance confirmation-based enjoyment.

ADMIXTURES

Although, as we have seen, the information flow in, and the type of reaction to, suspense and mystery are strikingly different, the two schemes may be liberally combined in the creation of eventful, captivating, and thrilling drama. There is no contradiction in drama that seeks to engage both our analytic abilities and our emotions.

Combination appears difficult for overall dramatic themes (i.e., plots or "masterplots" that span entire plays). The reasons for this are obvious. For instance, in order to create suspense effectively, suspenseful drama needs to develop and feature dangerous agents who imperil liked protagonists. There is little room for mystery in that the identity of these agents can not be concealed for any length of time—certainly not until the conclusion of plays. Analogously, the search for the perpetrators of fiendish crimes in mysteries is difficult to exploit for one-plot suspense because respondents are, to the end, uncertain about the identity of the dangerous agents.

In contrast, the combination of suspense and mystery poses no problems at the microplot or "miniplot" level. Elements of suspense are readily incorporated in mystery. Subjective probabilities may be manipulated early in a play, for instance, such that respondents feel quite certain that particular suspects are perpetrators who pose grave dangers to others who are not, or not yet, suspected of wrongdoing. These conditions can not be maintained, however, as the mystery would suffer from the respondents' premature convictions of having identified the transgressors. Further manipulation thus has to alter the subjective certainties in question. The indicated alterations terminate, of course, the conditions necessary for the effective creation of suspense.

Elements of mystery are as readily incorporated in suspense. Although the dangerous perpetrators may be identified and known, their ways of operation may be highly uncertainty-laden, puzzling, and mysterious. Mystery, in this context, does not so much concern the who and/or why, but pertains to the how and also the when of criminal transgressions.

Quite obviously, the information flow in mystery and suspense differs with regard to the respondents' knowledge of the transgressors. In mystery, the identity of these transgressors is obscured. In suspense, their identity tends to be exceedingly well established. On the basis of these characteristics it may be proposed that, in combining elements of suspense and mystery, the sequence mystery-suspense holds greater promise for great drama than the sequence suspense-mystery. In the former sequence, transgressions occurred and their perpetrators are to be identified; once they are identified, their criminal propensity persists; eventually, they are brought to justice. These conditions offer every opportunity for developing both mystery and suspense to the fullest. In contrast, the latter sequence, suspense-mystery, seems counterproductive. Unless the cast of characters is heavily supplemented or totally exchanged, suspenseful episodes, by revealing the identity of transgressors, would destroy the basis for subsequent mysterious episodes. The emerging combination formula thus calls for (a) the early involvement of elements of mystery in suspenseful drama and (b) the late involvement of elements of suspense in mystery.

THE STATE OF THE RESEARCH EVIDENCE

Suspense theory has inspired a considerable amount of research, mostly experimental investigations. This work has been reviewed elsewhere (Zillmann, 1980). Here we only summarize the most pertinent demonstrations.

It has been found that, as proposed, the experience of suspense is a function of the subjective certainty that imperiled liked protagonists will come to harm; it has not been found to be a function of uncertainty about this outcome (Comisky, 1978).

Also as proposed, it has been found that greater endangerment of liked protagonists produces greater distress associated with greater sympathetic activity; and that greater residual sympathetic activity during satisfying suspense resolutions fosters greater enjoyment (Bergman, 1978, cited in Zillmann, 1980; Zillmann, 1980; Zillmann et al., 1975).

Additionally, and again as proposed, it has been observed that greater endangerment of liked protagonists, although producing greater distress associated with greater sympathetic activity, does not foster greater enjoyment when the resolution of suspense is unsatisfying; and that it tends to reduce enjoyment when the resolution is dissatisfying (Bergman, 1978, cited in Zillmann, 1980; Zillmann, 1980).

The research findings, then, are highly supportive of the proposed theory of suspense enjoyment.

In stark contrast, mystery theory is presently without empirical substantiation. The role of psychology and psychologists in mysteries has received some attention (Krasner, 1983). Regarding the psychology of mystery and mystery enjoyment, however, the only thing that can be found is an abundance of presumptions. Pertinent research demonstrations simply do not exist. Hopefully, this deplorable state of affairs will soon be corrected.

REFERENCES

Bennett, D. (1979). The detective story: Towards a definition of genre. *PTL: A Journal for Descriptive Poetics and Theory of Literature*, *4*, 233-266.

Berger, S. M. (1962). Conditioning through vicarious instigation. *Psychological Review*, *29*, 450-466.

Berlyne, D. E. (1954). A theory of human curiosity. *British Journal of Psychology*, *45*, 180-191.

Berlyne, D. E. (1960). *Conflict, arousal and curiosity*. New York: McGraw-Hill.

Berlyne, D. E. (1967). Arousal and reinforcement. In D. Levine (Ed.), *Nebraska Symposium on Motivation* (Vol. 15, pp. 1-110). Lincoln: University of Nebraska Press.

Berlyne, D. E. (1971). *Aesthetics and psychobiology*. New York: Appleton-Century-Crofts.

Grings, W. W., & Dawson, M. E. (1978). *Emotions and bodily responses: A psychophysiological approach*. New York: Academic Press.

Grossvogel, D. I. (1979). *Mystery and its fictions: From Oedipus to Agatha Christie*. Baltimore: Johns Hopkins University Press.

Hartley, R. V. L. (1928). Transmission of information. *Bell System Technical Journal, 7*, 535-563.

Hitchcock, A. (1959, July 13). Interview by H. Brean. *Life*, p. 72.

Krasner, L. (1983, May). The psychology of mystery. *American Psychologist*, 578-582.

Lazarus, R. S. (1966). *Psychological stress and the coping process*. New York: McGraw-Hill.

Leventhal, H. (1979). A perceptual-motor processing model of emotion. In P. Pliner, K. R. Blankstein, & I. M. Spigel (Eds.), *Advances in the study of communication and affect: Vol. 5. Perception of the emotion in self and others* (pp. 1-46). New York: Plenum.

Marx, M. (1940). *The enjoyment of drama*. New York: F. S. Crofts.

Schachter, S. (1964). The interaction of cognitive and physiological determinants of emotional state. In L. Berkowitz (Ed.), *Advances in experimental social psychology* (Vol. 1, pp. 49-80). New York: Academic Press.

Shannon, C. E., & Weaver, W. (1949). *The mathematical theory of communication*. Urbana, IL: University of Illinois Press.

Smiley, S. (1971). *Playwriting: The structure of action*. Englewood Cliffs, NJ: Prentice-Hall.

Stotland, E. (1969). Exploratory investigations of empathy. In L. Berkowitz (Ed.), *Advances in experimental social psychology* (Vol. 4, pp. 271-314). New York: Academic Press.

Zillmann, D. (1978). Attribution and misattribution of excitatory reactions. In J. H. Harvey, W. J. Ickes, & R. F. Kidd (Eds.), *New directions in attribution research* (Vol. 2, pp. 335-368). Hillsdale, NJ: Lawrence Erlbaum Associates.

Zillmann, D. (1980). Anatomy of suspense. In P. H. Tannenbaum (Ed.), *The entertainment functions of television* (pp. 133-163). Hillsdale, NJ: Lawrence Erlbaum Associates.

Zillmann, D. (1983a). Disparagement humor. In P. E. McGhee & J. H. Goldstein (Eds.), *Handbook of humor research: Vol. 1. Basic issues* (pp. 85-107). New York: Springer-Verlag.

Zillmann, D. (1983b). Transfer of excitation in emotional behavior. In J. T. Cacioppo & R. E. Petty (Eds.), *Social psychophysiology: A sourcebook* (pp. 215-240). New York: Guilford Press.

Zillmann, D. (1984). *Connections between sex and aggression*. Hillsdale, NJ: Lawrence Erlbaum Associates.

Zillmann, D., & Bryant, J. (1975). Viewer's moral sanction of retribution in the appreciation of dramatic presentations. *Journal of Experimental Social Psychology, 11*, 572-582.

Zillmann, D., Bryant, J., & Sapolsky, B. S. (1989). Enjoyment from sports spectatorship. In J. H. Goldstein (Ed.), *Sports, games, and play: Social and psychological viewpoints* (2nd ed., pp. 241-278). Hillsdale, NJ: Lawrence Erlbaum Associates.

Zillmann, D., & Cantor, J. R. (1976). A disposition theory of humour and mirth. In A. J. Chapman & H. C. Foot (Eds.), *Humour and laughter: Theory, research, and applications* (pp. 93-115). London: Wiley.

Zillmann, D., & Cantor, J. R. (1977). Affective responses to the emotions of a protagonist. *Journal of Experimental Social Psychology, 13*, 155-165.

Zillmann, D., Hay, T. A., & Bryant, J. (1975). The effect of suspense and its resolution on the appreciation of dramatic presentations. *Journal of Research in Personality, 9*, 307-323.

Zillmann, D., Johnson, R. C., & Hanrahan, J. (1973). Pacifying effect of happy ending of communications involving aggression. *Psychological Reports, 32*, 967-970.

Zillmann, D., Mody, B., & Cantor, J. R. (1974). Empathetic perception of emotional displays in films as a function of hedonic and excitatory state prior to exposure. *Journal of Research in Personality, 8*, 335-349.

Zuckerman, M. (1979). *Sensation seeking: Beyond the optimal level of arousal*. Hillsdale, NJ: Lawrence Erlbaum Associates.

CHAPTER

13

Responding to Horror: Determinants of Exposure and Appeal

Ron Tamborini
Michigan State University

When the lights went out, everything that was comforting and familiar suddenly became threatening and strange. The film was about to begin, and the horror would not be long in coming. What would become of us now?

One wonders whether or not it is really any fun to watch scary movies. If you are a genuine fan of horror films you might find great pleasure safely hidden in your seat at the theater as some hideous creature stalks its next victim. You might even laugh after the shock of a sudden surprise attack causes you to send popcorn flying in all directions. But not everybody responds to graphic horror in quite the same way. In fact, it is probably easier to explain why some people hate horror films so intensely than to explain why others seem to enjoy them so much. Few of us would question another's dislike for movies that contain the type of graphic violence or induce the kind of fright and disgust produced by many of today's horror films. This type of reaction would be considered a normal response to events that are distasteful. On the contrary, the hard part is finding a reasonable explanation for the great popularity of these films. How could any rational person enjoy watching the very realistic portrayal of a young man's head exploding in a film like *Scanners*? Why would any sane person pay money to see a movie when they know it will scare them senseless? Yet, because millions of people watch and enjoy these films year after year, it is reasonable to assume that sane individuals find something very rewarding in this type of experience.

Questions concerning the impact and appeal of horror as a genre of entertainment have taken scholars in many different directions. Some consider the desire to watch frightening films as having social origins (e.g., Zillmann, Weaver, Mundorf, & Aust, 1986). Others have looked at horror's influence in relation to individual differences (e.g., Edwards, 1984; Sparks, 1986; Tamborini, Stiff, & Zillmann, 1987). Most writers agree, however, that factors controlling a viewer's emotional response to horror are important variables in accounting for the popularity of this genre, and they look at these factors in an attempt to understand both reasons for selective exposure to horror and the reactions it creates in individuals.

In this chapter we attempt to provide some insight on horror's attraction and the circumstances that can result in exposure being a pleasurable experience. Instead of accepting the traditional wisdom that an individual who seeks out unpleasant situations is sadistic or abnormal, we discuss conditions that would lead many rational people to find these films quite appealing, while causing others to dread the thought of watching them. To do this, we concentrate on factors associated with the social benefits that might be derived from exposure to horror, individual differences in the way they are experienced, the content commonly depicted in these feature films, and the sensations of arousal that result.

SOCIAL FACTORS AND REACTIONS TO HORROR

Although many scholars have commented on the sociology of exposure to horror, surprisingly little empirical work has attempted to investigate related issues. Several rationales have attempted to explain the appeal of graphic horror by focusing on the social factors dealt with in the content of these films. Instead of focusing on specific content, other explanations have looked at both exposure and responses to horror in terms of the genre's ability to satisfy needs associated with gender-role socialization. Extensions of these rationales can also be used to explain appeal in terms of the integrative needs served by the social contact associated with exposure.

Social Factors in Horror's Content

The popularity of horror films has often been associated with periods of social anxiety. Several writers have asserted that at times of social tension, *attendance* at horror films is extremely high (e.g., Daniels, 1975; Dickstein, 1980). They suggest that feelings of apprehension created by social stress build to a point where some manner of dealing with this anxiety is necessary. One manner of doing this would be to symbolically confront these issues in film. For example the popularity of *The Stepford Wives* has been interpreted as a reaction to the tensions created by the women's movement of the 1970s (King, 1979). Other writers have claimed that the *production* of these materials is greatly influenced by the social climate (e.g., Clark & Motto, 1980). Dickstein (1980) has suggested that horror films flourished during times of low-level social anxiety such as the Depression. Daniels (1975) has noted the decreased production of horror films during periods of high-level anxiety such as World War II. According to Twitchell (1989) during the two world wars, popular culture of all types was free of graphic violence since real violence was so prevalent. Edwards (1984) suggested that horror films can be viewed in this manner as a type of socio-ecolological barometer of problems in our natural and social environment.

Similar to these attempts to explain the conduct of horror in relation to social anxiety, the appeal of horror has also been looked at as a function of content that provides a reaffirmation of social norms. King (1981a) claimed that the message contained in many modern horror films is a warning that states that "terrible things happen to those who venture beyond societal boundaries into the taboo" (p. 87). Good triumphs over evil. Violation of the norm can lead to disaster, and those who violate the norm will be punished. This interpretation suggests that the content of these films serves to provide society with the assurance that its norms and beliefs are appropriate. According to Edwards (1984), recent trends in horror containing resolutions that show evil triumphant indicate a move away from this social function. However, the trend could also be interpreted as an even stronger warning of the dangers associated with violating society's norms. These films tell you to watch out! If you don't, all will be lost in the end.

Such interpretations by critical scholars may provide us with some insight on the *production* of materials dealing with horror and graphic violence. Clearly, when you have time to read and think about the critical interpretations of certain films, it is not hard to understand the types of symbolic confrontations intended by the director of a film. Unfortunately, it is much more difficult to imagine that viewers understand this symbolism. Campbell (1984) made a good argument for the sociologically motivated explorations of modern sexual mores in the films of David Cronenberg. However, it seems unlikely that viewers benefit from the symbolic confrontation of these issues when watching *Scanners*. Sharrett (1984) asserted that *The Texas Chainsaw Massacre* reflects an apocalyptic perspective on the moral schizophrenia of the Watergate era. But do viewers see this as anything but another slasher film? If they don't, then it may be more beneficial to look at social factors from a different perspective when attempting to understand responses to graphic horror.

Responding to Horror and Gender-Role Socialization

In addition to investigations of the sociological processes associated with symbolic messages presented in the content of many current horror films, the determinants of emotional reactions to horror have also been investigated in relation to the functions served by social factors associated with exposure. Some scholars (e.g., Mundorf, Weaver, & Zillmann, 1989; Zillmann et al., 1986) have looked at horror's appeal in terms of the genre's relationship to functions associated with learned gender roles.

Zillmann et al. have attempted to explain the need or desire for exposure to horror based on the *socialization* functions that are served by films of this genre. This reasoning suggests that the exposure setting provided by graphic horror films is unique in that it offers a socially approved context in which young men and women can engage in gender-specific behaviors that are denied to them in most circumstances. Adolescent males have the opportunity to show their manhood by acting fearless when being confronted by atrocities on screen. At the same time, young female viewers can "display the appropriate fear response, obtain protection from men, and admire them for their heroics" (Mundorf et al., 1989, p. 5). The rationale for this is based on the assumption that young men and women are strongly influenced by cultural norms concerning gender roles and typically "come to perceive, evaluate, and regulate both their own behavior and the behavior of others in accordance with cultural definitions of gender appropriateness" (Bem, 1976, 1985). Included in these gender role-determined behaviors are norms associated with the expression of affect. Apparently, the opportunity to engage in these gender-appropriate behaviors is rewarding in itself.

According to Zillmann et al., delight and distress resulting from exposure to horror films can be explained in the context of excitation transfer theory (Zillmann, 1984) and the social factors associated with gender-role expectations. When viewing graphic violence in opposite-gender constellations, affective responses of males and females can be expected to differ. Both men and women should experience elevated levels of distress during exposure to films in which pain is graphically portrayed and their companion appears to suffer. However, as a result of the socialized tendency to display mastery, men would be expected to show no fear in a female's company. They might even be expected to demonstrate their mastery by laughing and expressing amusement. At the end of the film, perhaps even as a response to the exteroceptive feedback resulting from their expressed amusement, males should move easily from any distress experience during exposure to feelings of pleasure. In fact, residual excitation from distress experienced during exposure should serve to intensify feelings of pleasure following the film's conclusion. In contrast, women would not be expected to have the same affective response. Having been socialized to express great fear, females should find it much more difficult to feel pleasure as a result of the viewing experience. Because there is no positive exteroceptive feedback associated with exposure, it might be expected that the intensity of the distress resulting from the atrocities in the film would be associated with the displeasure experienced after exposure. It may be, however, that the social pleasure of the male's companionship interferes with experience of distress created by the actions in the film and results in a somewhat confused affective state following exposure.

Research on opposite-gender companion viewing by Zillmann et al. (1986) supports this reasoning. The research demonstrates that although levels of reported distress during exposure were correlated with levels of reported enjoyment following exposure for males, no such relation was found for females. Research by Sparks (1989) replicates this pattern of results with different stimuli and demonstrates that results from physiological responses lend support for the excitation transfer rationale provided for the findings.

Exposure to Horror and Gender-Role Socialization

Similar to the manner in which horror's *appeal* has been explained in terms of social determinants, the *need* or *desire* to view horror has been looked at as resulting from the functions served by social factors associated with viewing. If, as suggested earlier, young men and women in our society are socialized to exhibit gender-specific expressions of affect according to traditional cultural gender roles, there must be some manner of teaching these norms to adolescents. In *Beyond the Pleasure Principle*, Freud (1959) discussed the manner in which children learn to subdue their fears and to gain control over threatening situations by making a game centered around the things that are feared the most. According to Dickstein (1980), horror films are a safe, routinized way of playing with these fears. Watching horror films allows children to confront their anxieties. The sense of relief that comes with the film's end is said to provide a catharsis that neutralizes fear, and this catharsis is thought to be important in learning to overcome anxiety.

The notion that exposure to horror provides a form of catharsis enabling us to learn to deal with our fears is supported by several writers (e.g., Brosnan, 1976; Clarens, 1967; Douglas, 1966). Although taking issue with the catharsis explanation, Zillmann et al. (1986) discussed similar processes in relation to exposure and gender-role socialization.

Zillmann et al. asserted that societies have instituted rites to encourage the control of fear. Historically, this mastery was necessary for hunters and others who were likely to encounter life-threatening situations. In order to prepare for these situations, adolescent males were often taught to overcome their fears by being exposed to iconic and/or symbolic representations of threatening objects and rewarded for showing no fear in response to them. Although the evolution of civilization may have altered this need, these dispositions have endured and are still part of our culture. Today, there is great pressure on adolescent males to show no fear when confronted with danger. The same expectation does not apply to females, however. It might even be argued that female adolescents are not only free to express their fear, but are actually encouraged to do so in much the same manner of women from earlier ages who relied on the protection provided by men. In most parts of our society, it is no longer common for an adolescent male to find himself in a perilous situation. Instead, the opportunity to confront life-threatening conditions can be found at the movie theater. Going to a horror film enables an adolescent male to test his courage and prove his fearlessness. In fact, frequent exposure to films of this genre should enable him to grow so callous that most of the graphic violence portrayed in the films will no longer be disturbing.

Horror and Social Contact

The manner in which social factors determine responses to horror films is closely associated with characteristics found in the exposure context. In the social structure of the setting, adolescents might be expected to experience pleasure from the comforts provided by the presence of protectors during times of great distress, pride that comes from the opportunity to demonstrate triumph over difficult challenges, or joy associated with being part of a group experience that provides great exhilaration. Each of these experiences is likely to influence the viewer's general reaction to exposure.

The comfort of protectors is an important consideration in understanding the appeal of exposure for those who have not learned to master their fears. The reasoning provided by Zillmann et al. to explain the manner in which children learn to subdue their fears suggests that excitatory habituation allows male adolescents to grow so callous that they are not disturbed by scenes showing the most preposterous forms of violence. However, this explanation says little concerning female reactions, nor does it explain young boys' initial ability to confront their fears. If the content presented in horror films is frightening and the boy has not yet learned to cope with this fear, initial exposure may be so distressing that it should be avoided at all costs. What makes the horror film a safe, routinized way of playing with these fears? Although the threat in film is not real, it seems unlikely that this would be very comforting to a young boy who has not learned mastery. Instead, protection from the threats on screen as well as enjoyment from the exposure experience are likely to come from the comfort provided by the presence of an adult, perhaps more often than not a male. In a similar manner, the pleasure experienced by a young woman who has not been socialized to master her fear is likely to be influenced by the comfort provided by the presence of another. In traditional settings this could come from the company of an adult or a young man who has already learned to master his fear.

A somewhat different experience can be expected for young men who have learned to master their fears. According to Zillmann et al. (1986), the horror film provides the opportunity for these adolescents to demonstrate how fearless they are to those around them. By appearing to be bored or even amused by the mayhem on screen, an adolescent can show his peers that he is truly a brave man. His male friends will be impressed by his courage, and the young woman he is trying to impress should find comfort in his mastery of the threat. In fact, it can be assumed that the fearless young man's provision of comfort and protection to the distressed young woman is the gender-role function served by going to horror movies. In addition, the pleasure that comes from the opportunity to defend his companion should intensify the enjoyment he attributes to the film.

It may not always be the case that those needing comfort are in the company of others who have learned to master their fears. In most cases, this is likely to lead to avoidance behavior. Occasionally, however, some will dare to expose themselves to horror films in the company of frightened others. Fortunately for them, because everyone else is scared to death, there should be less shame in showing fear. Still, when considering traditional gender-role socialization, female adolescents might feel more free to place themselves in situations where they are likely to show great fear. For these girls, sharing fear along with other members of the group can provide an avenue for desired of social integration and result in great pleasure from being part of the group. In fact, once again we might expect that residual excitation from the horrors of the film and the screams of one's companions should intensify the rewards experienced from acceptance in the group.

Explanations of this type provide us with some insight into the social benefits gained from graphic horror and the group dynamics associated with exposure. However, it is unlikely that these are the only dynamics at work. It is clear that people are not always influenced by groups, and are not always exposed in groups. Although it may not seem to be the best idea when dealing with exposure to horror, what happens if you are viewing alone?

INDIVIDUAL DIFFERENCES
AND REACTIONS TO HORROR

Several individual difference rationales have been advanced to explain the appeal of horror to audience members. Psychotherapists have attempted to trace the genre appeal to functions associated with an individual's subconscious and the film's ability to provide psychic relief from internal conflicts by allowing the displacement of anxieties onto story materials (Goldsmith, 1975). Film critics have alternately suggested that the viewing public likes horror because it provides an escape from what is a boring reality for many (Ansen, Kasindorf, & Ames, 1979); because it provides a test of strength for the viewer who dares the film to "scare me" (Werner, 1980); or because watching a terrifying scene gives us a thrill that makes us feel alive (Rickey, 1982). Research in this area by social scientists, however, has concentrated on a variety of personality traits and their relationship to certain content characteristics typically found in graphic horror.

Empathy and Responding to Horror

An important factor in any discussion of emotional reactions to frightening film is the concept of empathy. Individual differences on various dimensions of empathy have been shown to influence emotional responses in a variety of distressing contexts (Coke, Batson, & McDavis, 1978; Hoffmann, 1977; Stotland, Mathews, Sherman, Hansson, & Richardson, 1978). According to Zillmann (see chapter on empathy, this volume; and 1990), the media's capacity for graphically portraying human emotions can be critical in the elicitation of these empathic reactions.

Although there are nearly as many definitions of empathy as there are individuals attempting to study it, in a simple sense, *empathy* refers to the reactions of one individual to the observed experiences of another (Davis, 1983). Dating back to the work of Smith (1759/1971), it has commonly been thought of as a process by which we place ourselves in another person's situation, and through our imagination "we conceive ourselves enduring all the same torments, we enter as it were into his body and become in some measure him, and thence form some idea of his sensations, and even feel something which, though to a weaker degree, is not altogether unlike them" (pp. 2-3). Of course, empathic reactions need not always occur as a result of individuals imagining themselves in the place of a model, but can also be thought of as reactions to the circumstances alone (cf. Stotland, 1969). In the case of graphic horror, an example might be the feeling of distress resulting from simply knowing that a sadistic killer is preparing to torture an undetermined victim.

The definition of *empathy* as a somewhat deliberate and conscious perspective-taking process limits the type of reactions considered empathic to those that are concordant to the observed experience, and expressly excludes reactions that are discordant. For example, an individual watching a film showing the face of a young woman writhing in pain from the wounds inflicted by a hatchet-wielding killer would not be considered to have an empathic reaction if that reaction was one of comfort and pleasure. Instead, the expected empathic response would be more one of distress and anguish. According to Zillmann's (this volume) model of empathic delight and distress, we might expect an empathic reaction to occur as follows. First, due to the high iconicity of film, exposure to the scene results in a somewhat reflexive reaction of distress to the pain and suffering of the young woman. Next, the feelings of distress create an excitatory reaction intensifying the emotional experience of the viewer. Finally, quasi-instantaneously the viewer appraises his or her reaction as feeling concordant to that of the character, deems this reaction proper, and generates the appropriate affective reaction by imagining similar situations from the viewer's own past that have produced intense negative affect.

The high iconicity of film and its ability to focus attention on facially expressed emotion is an important consideration in the discussion of empathic reactions to graphic horror. Unlike most real-life situations in which individuals usually see only a glimpse of someone else's emotional expression, film presentations provide us with a detailed look of a person's facial expressions throughout their emotional experience. To the extent that the facial expression of emotion is an integral part in the creation of empathy, these close-up pictures of human emotions will strengthen empathic reactions (Zillmann, this volume). Add to this the film's ability to present a highly dramatic audio and visual presentation of the circumstances and events causing the emotional condition, and you are left with a powerful emotion-inducing medium. When taking into account the circumstances and emotions contained in graphic horror films, it might be expected that empathic processes would be strong determinants of an individual's reaction to these films.

Research by Tamborini, Stiff, and Heidel (1990) suggests that individual differences in empathy play an important role in determining graphic horror's appeal. Based on the work of several scholars who consider empathy to be a multidimensional construct (cf. Davis, 1980, 1983; Dillard, 1982; Johnson, Cheek, & Smither, 1983; Mehrabian & Epstein, 1972), Tamborini et al. demonstrated that several dimensions of empathy are important in determining this appeal. According to their research, non-empathic individuals find horror more appealing. Low levels of wandering imagination (a tendency to fantasize and daydream about unreal situations in an undirected manner), fictional involvement (the ability to imaginatively transpose oneself into the feelings and actions of fictitious characters in books and movies), and emotional contagion (a susceptibility to the emotions of those around you) are good predictors of horror's appeal.

The explanation offered for their findings on appeal is based on the expected response for non-empathic viewers. The fact that some individuals are not empathic can be seen to inhibit the highly noxious reaction normally expected. It is conceivable that individuals who do not daydream or who do not let their imagination wander never forget that what they are watching is *only a movie*, and thus do not get upset by these events. Those who lack the ability to imaginatively sense the feelings of the character being victimized would be unsusceptible to experiencing that pain and suffering themselves. In situations where this noxious experience does not occur, the reaction of a viewer to the film would be determined by a number of other factors. If these factors result in a positive reaction, the elevated levels of arousal created by exposure to the film should intensify pleasure experienced by the viewer.

Sensation Seeking and Exposure to Horror

The personality variable that has been researched most often in association with exposure to horror films is sensation seeking, the desire to seek out environmental stimuli that produce "sensation" and arousal. It has been suggested that much of the appeal found in frightening films lies in the thrill and sensation created by the shock of horror. According to Berlyne (1960), one can see this appeal when looking at the posters used to advertise horror films that "graphically depict the allurements of being scared out of one's wits" (p. 198). This reasoning can be used to suggest that the thrill created by the fear that horror films induce can be experienced by some individuals as pleasure (cf. Tannenbaum, 1980), and that those who experience this type of thrill as rewarding would learn to seek out horror films for these gratifications. The type of person who would react in this manner might be considered a sensation seeker. The Sensation-Seeking scale

(Zuckerman, 1979) has been used successfully as a measure of a personality trait associated with the extent to which an individual is motivated to seek out environmental stimuli that produce "sensation" and arousal. Included in this scale are four unique dimensions of sensation seeking identified by Zuckerman: thrill and adventure seeking, experience seeking, disinhibition, and boredom susceptibility.

Several studies have attempted to investigate the relationship between the attraction to horror films and sensation seeking. The first attempt to look at this issue was reported by Sparks (1984), who correlated his own 20-item scale measuring Enjoyment of Frightening Films with the Sensation Seeking scale, and found an overall positive correlation between the two for both males and females. A second study (Tamborini & Stiff, 1987) also found an association between the liking of horror films and a measure of sensation seeking computed from the combination of disinhibition, experience-seeking, and thrill and adventure-seeking scores. Finally, Edwards (1984) found a strong correlation for interest in horror movies with the entire Sensation Seeking scale as well as with each subdimension.

The three studies taken together clearly suggest that sensation seeking is associated with the attraction to horror films. What is not clear from these studies is the strength of this association, or how strong a *predictor* sensation seeking is for the attraction to horror films.

The results of other investigations question the strength of sensation seeking as a strong predictor of selective exposure to graphic horror (Mundorf et al., 1989; Tamborini et al., 1987). Using regression analysis, Tamborini et al. (1987) found that the dimensions of sensation seeking were not very good indicators of a desire for graphic horror. The one exception to this was boredom susceptibility, where some support was found for Edwards' suggestion that this dimension was a good predictor of selective exposure to horror.

These results seem surprising in light of prior research. Mundorf et al. (1989) suggested that it is possible to recast previous findings in terms of gender-role socialization considerations. Tamborini et al. explained these findings by suggesting that a close look at the individual subscales might lead us to different expectations. The fact that these variables drop out in regression analysis suggests that their association with preference for graphic horror is moderated by some other set of variables. More recent evidence from research on physiological reaction, however, suggests that sensation seeking can be an important predictor of reactions while viewing (Tamborini, Miller, Stiff, & Heidel, 1988).

Machiavellianism and Exposure to Horror

Another personality trait studied in association with the attraction to horror films is Machiavellianism. Machiavellianism has been thought of as the acceptance of a set of particular beliefs prescribed for success in a socially competitive and status-oriented society by Machiavelli in his 1513 treatise, *The Prince*. He advocated the use of power and force to achieve one's goals, and recommended behavior that was cruel, exploitive, and deceitful. According to Tamborini and Stiff (1987), one of the main attractions to horror lies in the audience's desire to see the type of power and force often contained in these films. In fact, this desire was found to be a stronger predictor of exposure to horror than was sensation seeking. Thus, to the extent that an individual accepts the type of values prescribed by Machiavelli, we might expect him or her to find horror films attractive. A wealth of evidence has been gathered relating aspects of social behavior to Machiavellianism (e.g., Cooper & Peterson, 1980; Harrell & Hartnagel, 1976). Hunter, Gerbing, and Boster (1982) have identified four unique dimensions of Machiavellianism: (a) flattery: telling people what they want to hear, (b) deceit: rejection of honesty, (c) immorality: rejection of the belief that people are moral, and (d) cynicism: the belief that people are vicious and untrustworthy. According to Hunter et al., because these are unique dimensions, we might expect to find different patterns in the relationships between each of these dimensions and attraction to horror films. This notion is supported in research by Tamborini et al. (1987) that demonstrates that although deceit, cynicism, and immorality were correlated with a preference for horror, regression analysis found only deceit to be a strong predictor. To the extent that deceit is representative of Machiavellianism in the general sense (i.e., belief in the use of power and force to achieve goals), this finding might be thought to support the belief that the enjoyment of this type of content is a prime motivator of exposure to horror films. However, because the deceit variable only measures a belief in the use of dishonesty to achieve goals, this provides indirect support at best.

Tamborini et al. (1987) also suggested that another possible explanation for the strength of deceit in predicting preference for graphic horror lies in the relationship of deceit with a desire to violate the norms of socially acceptable behavior, or to see them violated by others. In addition to portraying treachery and deceit, graphic horror films clearly violate many social norms (e.g., through scenes showing the suffering and pain of innocent adults and children, as well as scenes often found in recent horror films depicting casual sexual behavior between men and women). For this reason, it might be expected that individuals who enjoy seeing social taboos violated would show a preference for films of this genre. This explanation for the relationship between deceit and preference for graphic horror might seem implausible at first. However, inasmuch as deceit, cynicism, and immorality can be said to represent a desire to violate social norms, the moderate correlation of these variables with preference for graphic horror can be said to support the proposition that individuals with a desire to see social taboos violated would show a preference for graphic horror films to satisfy this need without fear of reprisal.

RESPONDING TO HORRIFIC CONTENT

Overall, personality characteristics have been only moderately successful in predicting graphic horror's appeal. In part, this might be due to the fact that the scales used in most research were designed to measure traits that should be only indirectly related to graphic horror's appeal. This points to the need for measures of traits more directly related to this appeal. In addition, this indicates the necessity to look elsewhere for a more complete understanding of horror's attraction. One area that has received some attention in this regard is the characteristic content often contained in graphic horror.

The Victimization of Women

The role of victim gender in horror films has become a topic of great concern with recent investigations of the relationship between exposure to films featuring female victimization and the desensitization toward real-life aggression against women. Although Weaver (1988) suggested that there is no evidence of a systematic bias toward the use of females as victims in graphic horror films, Donnerstein and Linz (1984) have suggested that exposure to films such as *Texas Chainsaw Massacre*, and *Tool Box Murders*, which feature brutality against women, makes viewers find this type of material not only less violent, but also less debasing and degrading toward women. In addition, they suggest that exposure can create change in real-life values. Their research demonstrates that subjects who are repeatedly exposed to these films and who are then asked to respond to information from a rape trial, are more likely to judge rape victims as more worthless and less injured.

Although the manner in which they interpret their findings has been challenged by Weaver (in press), the results of the research by Donnerstein and Linz (1984) are consistent with the concerns expressed by critics who object to the type of graphic horror films that contain "scene after scene of terrified, half-dressed women, screaming with pain and horror as they are raped, stabbed, chopped at, and strangled" (Logas, 1981, p. 21). These critics suggest that films of this genre appeal to a "mentally defective" audience that is predominantly male and aged 15 to 25, "who get rid of their aggression for $5.00" (Watkins, 1980, p. 33). Speculations of this kind project, in the face of an impressive body of research that challenges the implicit catharsis doctrine (cf. Geen & Quanty, 1977), that the victimization of women is a prime motivator for selective exposure to horror films. It suggests that men who harbor hostility toward women constitute the principal audience—as it is they who will most enjoy seeing women victimized.

The study by Tamborini et al. (1987) attempted to investigate the relationship between victim gender in graphic horror and selective exposure to these films. The results of this investigation demonstrated that women, when given a choice among violent drama, prefer material that features the *least* graphic depiction of female victimization, and that men, in contrast, prefer such drama that features the *most* graphic depiction of female victimization. In addition, a surprisingly strong relationship was found for males between the enjoyment of pornography and a preference for graphic horror featuring female victims—a relationship that does not exist in male subjects' preference for films featuring male victims, or in females subjects' preference for films featuring either male or female victims.

The findings have important implications. The data support the beliefs of critics like Logas (1981) and Watkins (1980) who claim that current horror films use the graphic portrayal of pain and suffering by female victims in appealing to men with hostile feelings toward women. Further, the fact that the preference for graphic horror featuring female victims is associated with the enjoyment of pornography might suggest that these feelings of hostility against women are related to sexuality or sexual frustration. The findings also pertain to Donnerstein and Linz's (1984) claims that exposure to graphic horror films featuring violence against women can create attitude changes in real life values concerning issues like rape. Although the data provide no evidence for such a causal contention, they are consistent with the claims of Donnerstein and Linz as well as with other potential interpretations, such as disposition theory of drama (Zillmann, 1980). For instance, they are consistent with the proposition that sexually frustrated men who harbor feelings of hostility against women will prefer female victimizing horror for the gratification derived from seeing the pain and suffering of those causing their frustrations. It might be that pornography offers a similar, transitory overcoming of these frustrations. If this were the case, it would explain observed relationships between enjoyment of pornography and preference for graphic horror featuring female victims.

The Resolution of Horror

One of the most plausible explanations for the appeal of horror suggests that pleasure is derived from the successful resolution of the threat presented by the antagonist responsible for the creation of horror. This proposition is consistent with dispositional explanations of reactions to several other forms of media entertainment. Zillmann (1980) suggested that an important element in deriving pleasure from suspenseful drama is the provision of a satisfying resolution. Typically, this type of resolution would be either a positive outcome for some liked protagonist, or a negative outcome for some disliked antagonist. In the absence of either of these, however, "the mere removal of the threat that produced empathic distress in the first place may be considered a minimal stimulus condition for the cognitive switch from dysphoria to euphoria" (Zillmann, 1980, p. 148). The concept is a simple one: We are aroused and upset by the threats of dire consequences presented during the course of the film. When a just ending is provided, or, when the dreadful threats are removed, we experience this arousal in a pleasurable form. Research by Tamborini and Stiff (1987) demonstrates that providing a just resolution is important in determining the like for frightening films among those individuals who view horror. Typically, the monster inflicts terrible suffering on its victims throughout a horror film and, in the end, there is a debt to be paid. When the good guy wins and the villain is destroyed, justice is served and the happy ending is provided. Curiously, the happy ending often includes more horror in the maiming and destruction of the monster than was contained in the monster's cruelty itself. In fact, such reciprocity seems to be the norm in tales of horror, and it may be that the appeal of many horror films depends on this.

According to Hallie (1969), this type of just ending has been a standard in tales of horror since their advent in 18th-century Gothic novels. Traditionally, the agent of horror is defeated in some manner as terrible as the horror the agent has inflicted. Similarly, this formula has been the rule in horror films since the 1930s when, for example, the mad scientist would realize his mistake and die in his successful effort to destroy the monster he had created (Sontag, 1966). Given this type of ending, a logical explanation of horror film's appeal would be that viewers enjoy seeing a successful resolution. Additionally, this might explain why so much graphic violence is tolerated and even enjoyed. Enjoyment in this situation is dependent on the provision of a negative outcome for the disliked antagonist. As the horrors inflicted by the antagonist increase, so does the intensity of dislike. Consequently, when the antagonist is destroyed in the end, the pleasure derived should be even greater.

Unfortunately, this explanation for selective exposure to horror has been challenged by movie critics who suggest that many horror films no longer provide satisfying resolutions (Rickey, 1982; Rosenbaum, 1979). Rosenbaum claimed that the basic format of horror films has changed to one in which the ending no longer brings about the elimination of the menacing force, but results, instead, in the triumph of evil over the forces of reason. Starting with the success of movies in the early 1970s like *Rosemary's Baby* and *The Exorcist*, horror films began to depart from the traditional happy-ever-after format to an unhappy-ever-after style. Instead, we now have films like *Night of the Living Dead, Halloween* and *Friday the 13th*, in which defenseless victims come across blood-crazed zombies and lunatics in terrifying no-win situations. The antagonist may vanish in the end, but is not destroyed. Beyond this, the protagonist is left badly injured or terrified; not heroic and happy. In light of the popularity of these movies it becomes difficult to maintain that audiences attend all horror films because they want a just ending and have learned to expect one. Yet, it may be that today enough horror films continue to provide the standard resolution in which the monster is destroyed and the survivors, including the audience members, live happily ever after. This should keep most viewers returning. In addition, even those horror films that do not fit this category may still contain the "minimal stimulus condition" necessary for a satisfying resolution. For example, a satisfying resolution in a horror film may be quite different from the ending of a typical adventure film or drama. In the setting created by the horror film, a successful resolution may be simply the termination of the threat. Maturin (1966) stated that "the drama of terror has the irresistible power of converting the audience into its victims" (p. 197). According to his reasoning, the viewers of horror films often mimic the pain and suffering of the victims on screen, and a successful ending may result not so much from the restoration of justice, but from getting the monster off the viewers' backs. By this logic, most horror films provide the type of endings that audience members consider satisfying.

The Graphic Portrayal of Destruction

In some horror films, however, even the "mere removal" of the threat is not provided. For example, the absence of such an ending leaves unexplained the appeal of movies like *The Omen* or *The Exorcist*. In films of this genre, the liked protagonist is killed, and the film ends with the disliked antagonist still alive and in control. Perhaps the appeal of these films lies, instead, in the type of destruction contained in them. Tamborini and Stiff (1987) demonstrated that the graphic portrayal of destruction is a good predictor of exposure to horror and suggest that it may be an important factor in determining horror's appeal. Although there are no data to support his explanation of this, Gothic horror novelist Stephen King (1981b) suggested that witnessing destruction and graphic violence provides a psychic relief by allowing emotions to run free; a release we rarely have in today's society. He suggested that destructive antisocial tendencies are a part of all of us, and these tendencies sometimes need to be let loose. The horror film "deliberately appeals to the worst in all of us. It is morbidity unchained, our most base instincts let free" (p. 246). This reasoning suggests that watching the graphic violence in horror films provides us with a type of catharsis, or at least allows us to experience taboo behaviors in the socially acceptable form of fictional horror.

Viewed in this way, horror films might be seen as performing a valuable service by appealing to tendencies found in each of us. Critics of this genre interpret the appeal of these films in a different manner, however. Watkins (1980) questioned the mental stability of individuals who like these films, stating that the audience and producers of horror films have begun to "accept demented revenge for violence as an artform" (p. 33). If indeed the graphic depiction of violence and destruction in these films appeals to individuals who are "sick," the effect of this exposure becomes the important issue. Because no evidence exists to support this claim, speculation on the impact of exposure to graphic horror may not be justified. It seems reasonable, however, to start looking for rationales concerning the effects of such films by investigating the characteristics of the individuals who like these films and the types of gratifications that they derive.

THE ROLE OF AROUSAL

Perhaps a better explanation of horror's appeal deals with the excitation that frightening films provide regardless of their resolution. It has been suggested that the jolt of horror is exhilarating, and that it leaves people feeling invigorated. Rickey (1982) claimed that "when we are afraid, adrenaline surges through our bloodstreams, accelerating our heartbeats and giving us a rush of energy. We're left feeling more alert, our senses operating at their peak" (p. 169).

Change in Arousal and Reactions in Horror

Rickey's reasoning is consistent with Berlyne's (1967) theories on arousal that state that "reinforcement, and in particular reward, can result in some circumstances from an increase in arousal" (p. 30). This reasoning can be used to suggest that increased arousal created by the fear that horror films induce can be experienced by some individuals as pleasure (cf. Tannenbaum, 1980), and that those who experience this type of arousal as rewarding would learn to seek out horror films for these gratifications.

Support for this rationale is found in research by Tamborini, Miller, Stiff, and Heidel (1988). In their research, they observed that some viewers demonstrated the dramatic swing in arousal projected by Berlyne during exposure to graphic horror. For high sensation seekers a trend showed that arousal started slowly and then increased dramatically. This sudden increase is the type of physiological rollercoaster consistent with revisions in Berlyne's (1967) arousal-jag explanation of the appeal of thrilling fears. Although the logic in the rationale presented for this model has been challenged (Zillmann, 1980), the pattern of arousal observed in high sensation seekers is consistent with the pattern that should be found rewarding. According to Berlyne, this rewarding experience should not only be enjoyable but, ultimately, should make this type of stimuli attractive and motivate high sensation seekers to expect these rewarding physiological reactions from viewing graphic horror. Thus, they should become heavy viewers of these materials. This rationale is consistent with several studies indicating that sensation seeking is associated with graphic horror exposure and appeal (Edwards, 1984; Sparks, 1984; Tamborini & Stiff, 1987; Zuckerman & Litle, 1986).

Intensifying Reactions to Horror

In addition to the manner in which arousal itself is experienced, arousal can also be an important factor in determining the strength of reactions to horror given direction by other mechanisms, particularly in highly empathic individuals (Tamborini, Stiff, & Heidel, 1990). Zillmann (this volume) suggests that an empathic response, like all affective responses, is associated with a notable increase in arousal. This increase in arousal is a response-energizing mechanism that intensifies affective reactions without determining the hedonic direction of resulting emotional experiences. Instead, dispositional considerations and an evaluation of the appropriateness of the affective reaction are thought to determine the direction of an individual's experience, whereas the excitatory component determines the strength of the response.

When taking into consideration the content of graphic horror, it quickly becomes apparent that the excitatory component of an empathic reaction to both a character's expressed emotion and the circumstances that produced the emotion have great potential. The audiovisual presentation of characters caught in life-threatening situations contain several components capable of increasing arousal. For example, in a scene showing a young woman being tortured by a deranged killer while trapped in the basement of a burning building, excitatory responses are likely to be induced by several different stimuli. The facial and bodily expressions of fear and pain exhibited by the young woman should, in and of themselves, elicit strong emotions in the viewer. At the same time, however, the viewer is likely to respond to the circumstances portrayed. The burning inferno, the dark entrapment, and the razor-sharp blade of the killer's knife each are capable of evoking heightened levels of arousal. Add to this the influence of stimulation from sound effects, music, and fast-paced editing techniques, and you have the potential for considerable excitation. Given most individuals' ineffectiveness in separating the different contributors to an excitatory state (cf. Zillmann, 1984), it is likely that a viewer's resulting emotional reaction will be intense, regardless of whether that reaction is one of fear, sorrow, distress, or even amusement.

The most common reaction to this type of situation is likely to be one of great emotional distress. This expectation is supported by research showing that over 80% of all subjects exposed to different horror films found graphic violence unappealing (Tamborini, 1987). In addition, the ability of this excitation to increase an individual's negative reaction to horror is supported by data showing a strong association between arousal and dislike of horror for individuals who found these films unappealing. An association stronger than that between arousal and like of the horror films for individuals who found horror appealing.

Arousal and Coping With Fear

One important aspect of arousal associated with exposure to graphic horror is its relationship to methods of coping with fear. Tamborini et al. (1990) asserted that physiological arousal follows directly from the different dimensions of empathy. They reasoned that typical responses to emotionally disturbing film events are unlike situations in which an individual is compelled to attend to another's emotional display. When watching a film it is easy to avoid upsetting stimuli by simply looking away, thinking of something else, or averting attention from the film. These activities can be considered coping behaviors. For individuals who are extremely sensitive and susceptible to the emotions of others, the events in graphic horror film might be too arousing to view. Realizing this from previous experience with horror, such individuals would be likely to employ these coping behaviors in an attempt to prevent the onset of negative affect. Indeed, many horror films provide clear cues to aid in this prevention process. For example, in the film *Jaws* there is the presence of the reoccurring musical theme to warn the audience of impending shark attacks. Given the expectation that coping would only be necessary for individuals who found the filmed material both highly arousing and unappealing, these behaviors can be expected to predict both arousal and dislike.

A much different approach to understanding the relationship between coping and arousal is suggested in the "activation-arousal" model of coping with stress (Sparks, 1989; Sparks & Spirek, 1988). According to this model, the innate origins of personality traits are seen as a cause of behavioral dispositions such as those associated with coping. Based on the work of Greene (1987), the model asserts a personality bias toward either an arousal system or an activation system. It suggests that individuals with a bias toward the arousal system are predisposed to higher levels of affective intensity. In contrast, those with a bias toward the activation system are predisposed to focus attention internally and are more likely to withdraw from their surrounding environment. This activation bias produces blunted emotional responses. In essence, the model speculates that blunters (those with an activation bias) prefer low amounts of information during stressful events. They engage in distraction and avoidance behaviors and typically have less intense responses due to this coping strategy. On the other hand, monitors (those with an arousal bias) prefer high amounts of information in the face of stress. They seek this information out and have more intense emotional reactions.

THE APPEAL OF GRAPHIC HORROR

The discussion in this chapter provides some insight on the appeal of graphic horror and the factors that lead to exposure. First, it specifies the type of individual who should *not* find these films appealing, and provides an explanation for *why* this individual should find graphic horror so distasteful. Second, it suggests situations and characteristics necessary for the viewing of horror to result in an enjoyable experience, and provides an explanation of why these enjoyable responses should be *so strong* when they do occur. In combination, these factors indicate that consideration of individual and social characteristics in relation to film content properties is important in predicting and explaining reactions to graphic horror.

Factors Prohibiting the Appeal of Horror

The evidence at hand indicates that the enjoyment of graphic horror is highly unlikely to occur in certain individuals and situations. For example, an adolescent male who has not learned to master his fear, or a young woman who is high on certain dimensions of empathy should find graphic horror films very unappealing. According to the reasoning set forth by Tamborini et al. (1990), individuals with a free-flowing imagination are more likely to sense and become involved with the emotions and actions of fictional characters. Thus, these individuals become susceptible to the feelings of pain and torment experienced by victims in horror films. Sparks and Spirek (1988) asserted that high monitors should have more intense emotional responses. These factors may result in a highly noxious affective reaction to graphic horror for these viewers. At first glance this might seem like a somewhat trivial consideration. It comes as no surprise that many individuals would find graphic horror so unappealing. However, understanding the conditions that create this unpleasant reaction to graphic horror can be helpful in specifying the conditions that must be absent in order for an individual to enjoy watching these films. Most research in this area has generally concentrated on factors thought to be responsible for the selective exposure and appeal of graphic horror without consideration of the specific reasons for avoidance. Perhaps this limited approach has been responsible for the failure of many investigations to find strong predictors of these behaviors.

Factors Permitting the Appeal of Horror

Implicit in the proposition that certain individuals and situations make the enjoyment of graphic horror highly unlikely to occur is the notion that other personality and social conditions can enhance this possibility. The young man who has finally conquered his fear, or the girl who is somewhat nonempathic may find reason to enjoy graphic horror.

One explanation for this can be based on the expected response, or lack of response, for nonempathic viewers. The nonempathic viewer is not likely to have the highly noxious reaction to the graphic portrayal of victimization that would be expected in empathic viewers. Individuals who are not involved in the feelings of the character being victimized should not suffer the distress that is experienced by viewers who imagine themselves in the terrifying situations that they observe. For individuals in whom this noxious experience does not occur, reactions to the film could be determined by a number of other factors. If the factors determining the viewer's experience result in a positive reaction, the elevated levels of arousal created by exposure to the film should result in that positive reaction being very strong. A similar process might be expected to occur in blunters. For individuals who avoid the most unpleasant parts of the film, other factors may result in a positive experience.

At first, it might be expected that the response strength of blunters or nonempathic individuals might be weak in comparison to that of a highly empathic viewer. Only monitors and highly empathic viewers should experience a strong response-energizing reaction to the facial expressions of pain and anguish exhibited by the film victim. However, this does not preclude blunters or nonempathic viewers from becoming highly aroused. As suggested earlier, when considering the excitatory component of reactions to graphic horror, one must not only take into account the victim's expressed emotions, but must also consider factors such as the film's music, the rapid editing techniques, the special visual and sound effects, and the situations presented in the film. Although we would not expect these viewers to respond to the victim's emotional expressions, we would expect them to experience excitatory reactions to the other arousing stimuli. The level of excitation might be expected to be somewhat less here than in monitors and empathic individuals; however, it should be much higher than normal.

If blunters and nonempathic viewers do not associate their arousal with the pain and suffering portrayed in a film, their reaction need not be a negative one. According to excitation transfer theory (cf. Zillmann, 1980), the manner in which individuals experience the arousal should be determined by their eventual appraisal of the circumstances they associate with the arousal reaction. Unfortunately, individuals often err in this appraisal and cognitively assess the cause of excitation based on their awareness of other circumstances at hand. Thus, when reacting to a horror film, the type of response that occurs may be determined by factors associated with the viewing experience other than those dealing with the pain and suffering of victims.

The literature reviewed here suggests several factors that can play a part in creating positive reactions to the arousal resulting from viewing horror. Included here are personality traits such as Machiavellianism and sensation seeking, horrific film content characteristics like the portrayal of destruction or the provision of a satisfying resolution, and social conditions corresponding to the opportunity to demonstrate mastery of fear. Clearly, this is not an exhaustive list. Many different social as well as psychological factors could result in a pleasurable reaction to the viewing experience; however, these provide a beginning for understanding why many individuals enjoy this genre of film. Throughout the film, the viewer's level of arousal is continuously elevated by the shocking events, the violent content, and the flashy film techniques. The more graphic the violence, the more elevated the arousal due to shock. The more uncertain the outcome, the greater the excitation created by suspense. Finally, when the hero destroys the evil menace and sends it to a fiery death, the viewer is left with a feeling of great joy. Justice is restored as good wins out over evil, and through it all safety was provided by the presence of a fearless protector. Still in a state of heightened arousal from the events in the story and the cinematic techniques, the viewer should enjoy the experience even more acutely and leave the theater with a feeling of great satisfaction. After several experiences of this kind, another fan of horror is created.

Looked at in this manner, the radical differences in individual responses to graphic horror film are more easily understood. For many individuals, assessment of the viewing experience is dominated by images of pain and suffering. It is no surprise that these individuals would develop a great dislike for films of this nature and even fear the thought of being exposed to them. On the other hand, the same type of reasoning can be used to explain the reactions of others who seek out these films and viewing situations for the rewarding experiences they provide. If their conscious experience of watching a horror film is not dominated by the recall of terrifying images, the feelings that they associate with exposure to horror can be determined by pleasurable features of the film or the viewing situation. It may be the just ending, it may be the thrill of excitation, or it may be one of several other social or psychological characteristics of exposure to horror. It is not necessarily the case that these individuals are sadistic creatures who enjoy the suffering of others. In fact, it seems much more likely that they are "normal" people who derive pleasure from the more positive aspects of the viewing situation while remaining somewhat unaffected by those characteristics that are less than pleasant.

Questions Concerning the Impact of Exposure

Although the perspective suggested here would consider seekers of graphic violence to be normal individuals, no discussion of horror would be complete without some mention of issues concerning the possible impact of viewing. The empirical work in this area remains controversial; however, critical speculation has historically warned of great evil that results from exposure. The questions about this impact cannot be answered here; however, concern over viewing such horror was put forth in St. Augustine's description of Alypius who was taken to the gladiator games against his will. According to St. Augustine, Alypius covered his eyes at first, but the shout of the crowd caused him to look.

> If only he had closed his ears as well! For an incident in the fight drew a great roar from the crowd, and this thrilled him so deeply that he could not contain his curiosity. Whatever had caused the uproar, he was confident that, if he saw it, he would find it repulsive and remain master of himself. So he opened his eyes, and his soul was stabbed with a wound more deadly than any which the gladiator, whom he was so anxious to see, had received in his body. He fell, and felt more pitifully than the man whose fall had drawn that roar of excitement from the crowd.
>
> When he saw the blood, it was as though he had drunk a deep draught of savage passion. Instead of turning away, he fixed his eyes upon the scene and drank in all its frenzy, unaware of what he was doing. He revelled in the wickedness of the fighting and he drunk with the fascination of bloodshed. He was no longer the man who had come to the arena, but simply one of the crowd which he had joined, a fit companion for the friends who had brought him.
>
> Need I say more? He watched and cheered and grew hot with excitement, and when he left the arena, he carried away with him a diseased mind which would leave him no peace until he came back again, no longer simply together with friends who had dragged him there, but at their head, leading new sheep to the slaughter. (Confessions, book 6, part 8, pp. 123-23)

Although St. Augustine seemed confident that only harm would come from watching this type of graphic horror, questions concerning this impact remain unchanged. What has changed, however, is the great accessibility of these spectacles in fictional form, and the difficulty of avoiding exposure to them. Indeed,

Twitchell (1989) suggested that there has been such an increase in the availability of preposterous horror that "For those who, like Ulysses, would muffle the ears of the young and keep their hands tied to the oars, the music of the sirens has never been noisier" (p. 6). With such a loud clamor, we might expect that in the future we will find even greater attention being paid to these horrific spectacles.

REFERENCES

Ansen, D., Kasindorf, M., & Ames, K. (1979, June 18). Hollywood's scary summer. *Newsweek*, pp. 54-59.

Augustine, St. (1961). *Confessions* (R. S. Pine-Coffin, Trans.). Baltimore, MD: Penguin.

Bem, S. L. (1976). Probing the promise of androgyny. In A. G. Kaplan & J. P. Bean (Eds.), *Beyond sex-role stereotypes: Readings toward a psychology of androgyny* (pp. 48-62). Boston: Little, Brown.

Bem, S. L. (1985). Androgyny and gender schema theory: A conceptual and empirical investigation. In T. B. Sonderegger (Ed.), *Nebraska symposium on motivation: Psychology and gender* (pp. 176-226). Lincoln: University of Nebraska Press.

Berlyne, D. E. (1960). *Conflict, arousal, and curiosity*. New York: McGraw-Hill.

Berlyne, D. E. (1967). *Arousal and reinforcement: In D. Levine (Ed.) Nebraska symposium on motivation* (pp. 1-111). Lincoln: University of Nebraska Press.

Brosnan, J. (1976). *The horror people*. New York: St. Martin's Press.

Campbell, M. (1984). Biological alchemy and the films of David Cronenberg. In B. K. Grant (Ed.), *Planks of reason: Essays on the horror film* (pp. 307-320).

Clarens, C. (1967). *An illustrated history of the horror film*. New York: G. P. Putnam's Sons.

Clark, J., & Motto, A. (1980). A bevy of negations invades the popular arts. *Studies in Popular Culture, 3*, 20-34.

Coke, J., Batson, C., & McDavis, K. (1978). Empathic mediation of helping: A two-stage model. *Journal of Personality and Social Psychology, 36*, 752-766.

Cooper, S., & Peterson, C. (1980). Machievellianism and spontaneous cheating in competition. *Journal of Research in Personality, 14*, 20-25.

Daniels, L. (1975). *Living in fear: A history of horror in the mass media*. New York: Charles Scribner.

Davis, M. (1980). A multidimensional approach to individual differences in empathy. *JSAS Catalog of Selected Documents in Psychology, 10*, 85.

Davis, M. H. (1983). Measuring individual differences in empathy: Evidence for a multidimensional approach. *Journal of Personality and Social Psychology, 44*, 113-126.

Dickstein, M. (1980, September). The aesthetics of fright. *American Film*, pp. 32-41.

Dillard, J. P. (1982). *Empathy in instrumental communication: Test of a theory*. Unpublished doctoral dissertation, Michigan State University, East Lansing, MI.

Donnerstein, E., & Linz, D. (1984, January). Sexual violence in the media: A warning. *Psychology Today*, pp. 14-15.

Douglas, D. (1966). *Horror*. New York: Macmillan.

Edwards, E. (1984). *The relationship between sensation-seeking and horror movie interest and attendance*. Unpublished doctoral dissertation, University of Tennessee, Knoxville, TN.

Freud, S. (1959). *Beyond the pleasure principle* (J. Strachey, Trans.). New York: Bantam Books.

Geen, R. G., & Quanty, M. B. (1977). The catharsis of aggression: An evaluation of a hypothesis. In L. Berkowitz (Ed.), *Advances in experimental social psychology* (Vol. 10, pp. 1-37). New York: Academic Press.

Goldsmith, W. (1975). Beloved monsters: A psychodynamic appraisal of horror. *Journal of Contemporary Psychotherapy, 7,* 17-22.

Greene, J. (1987). *The ecology of communication: An action-production approach to the process of person-situation interaction.* Paper presented at the annual conference of the International Communication Association, Montreal.

Hallie, P. P. (1969). *The paradox of cruelty.* Middletown, CT: Wesleyan University Press.

Harrell, W., & Hartnagel, T. (1976). The impact of Machiavellianism and the trustfulness of the victim on laboratory theft. *Sociometry, 39,* 157-165.

Hoffman, M. L. (1977). Empathy, its development and prosocial implications. In C. B. Keasey (Ed.), *Nebraska Symposium on Motivation* (Vol. 25, pp. 169-218). Lincoln: University of Nebraska Press.

Hunter, J. E., Gerbing, D. W., & Boster, F. J. (1982). Machiavellian beliefs and personality: Construct invalidity of the Machiavellian dimension. *Journal of Personality and Social Psychology, 43,* 1295-1305.

Johnson, J. A., Cheek, J. M., & Smither, R. (1983). The structure of empathy. *Journal of Personality and Social Psychology, 45*(6), 1299-1312.

King, S. (1979, December 27). A year in the dark: The horrors of '79. *Rolling Stone,* pp. 17-20.

King, S. (1981a). *Danse macabre.* New York: Everett House.

King, S. (1981b, January). Why we crave horror movies. *Playboy,* pp. 152-154; 237-246.

Logas, M. B. (1981, June). Chicago critics team up against film violence. *Ms.,* pp. 21.

Maturin, C. R. (1966). *Melmoth the wanderer.* Lincoln, NE: University of Nebraska Press.

Mehrabian, A., & Epstein, N. (1972). A measure of emotional empathy. *Journal of Personality, 40*(4), 525-543.

Mundorf, N., Weaver, J., & Zillmann, D. (1989). Effects of gender roles and self perceptions on affective reactions to horror films. *Sex roles, 20,* 655-673.

Rickey, C. (1982, November). Hooked on horror: Why we like scary movies. *Mademoiselle,* pp. 168-170.

Rosenbaum, R. (1979, September). Gooseflesh. *Harpers Magazine,* pp. 86-92.

Sharrett, C. (1984). The idea of apocalypse in *The Texas Chainsaw Massacre.* In B. K. Grant (Ed.), *Planks of reason: Essays on the horror film* (pp. 255-276). Metuchen, NJ: The Scarecrow Press.

Smith, A. (1971). *Theory of moral sentiments.* New York: Garland. (Original work published 1759)

Sontag, S. (1966). *Against interpretation.* New York: Farrar, Straus & Giroux.

Sparks, G. (1984). *The development of a scale to assess cognitive responses to frightening mass media.* Paper presented at the annual conference of the International Communication Association, San Francisco, CA.

Sparks, G. (1986). Developing a scale to assess cognitive responses to frightening films. *Journal of Broadcasting and Electronic Media, 30*(1), 65-73.

Sparks, G. (1989). *The relationship between delight and distress in males' and females' reactions to frightening films.* Paper presented at the annual conference of the Speech Communication Associaton, San Francisco, CA.

Sparks, G., & Spirek, M. (1988). Individual differences in coping with stressful mass media: An activation-arousal view. *Human Communication Research, 15,* 195-216.

Stotland, E. (1969). Exploratory investigations in empathy. In L. Berkowitz (Ed.), *Advances in experimental social psychology* (pp. 271-314). New York: Academic Press.

Stotland, E., Mathews, K. E., Jr., Sherman, S. E., Hansson, R. O., & Richardson, B. Z. (1978). *Empathy, fantasy and helping.* Beverly Hills, CA: Sage.

Tannenbaum, P. H. (1980). Entertainment as vicarious emotional experience. In P. H. Tannenbaum (Ed.), *The entertainment functions of television* (pp. 107-131). Hillsdale, NJ: Lawrence Erlbaum Associates.

Tamborini, R. (1987). [Emotional responses to horror: Appeal scores]. Unpublished raw data.

Tamborini, R., Miller, K., Stiff J., & Heidel, C. (1988). *Predictors of emotional reactions to audio and visual elements in graphic horror: A time series analysis.* Paper presented at the annual conference of the Speech Communication Association, New Orleans, LA.

Tamborini, R., & Stiff, J. (1987). Predictors of horror film attendance and appeal: An analysis of the audience for frightening films. *Communication Research, 14*, 415–436.

Tamborini, R., Stiff, J., & Heidel, C. (1990). Reacting to graphic horror: A model of empathy and emotional behavior. *Communication Research, 17*, 616–637.

Tamborini, R., Stiff, J., & Zillmann, D. (1987). Preference for graphic horror featuring male versus female victimization: Individual differences associated with personality characteristics and past film viewing experiences. *Human Communication Research, 13*, 529–552.

Twitchell, J. (1989). *Preposterous violence: Fables of aggression in modern culture.* New York: Oxford University Press.

Watkins, R. (1980, October 29). Demented revenge hits world films. *Variety*, pp. 3, 33.

Weaver, J. (1988). *A content analysis of ten commercially successful "teenage-slasher" horror films.* Paper presented at the annual conference of the Speech Communication Association, New Orleans, LA.

Weaver, J. (in press). The impact of exposure to horror film violence on perceptions of women: Is it the violence or an artifact? In B. A. Austin (Ed.), *Current Research in film* (Vol. 5). Norwood, NJ: Ablex

Werner, L. (1980, February). Why we love to scream in the dark. *Glamour*, pp. 126–129.

Zillmann, D. (1980). Anatomy of suspense. In P. H. Tannenbaum (Ed.), *The entertainment functions of television* (pp. 133–163). Hillsdale, NJ: Lawrence Erlbaum Associates.

Zillmann, D. (1984). Transfer of excitation in emotional behavior. In J. T. Cacioppo & R. E. Petty (Eds.), *Social psychology: A source book* (pp. 215–240). New York: Gilford.

Zillmann, D. (1990). *Three-factor theory of empathic delight and distress.* Unpublished manuscript.

Zillmann, D., Weaver, J., Mundorf, N., & Aust, C. (1986). Effects of an opposite-gender companion's affect to horror on distress, delight, and attraction. *Journal of Personality and Social Psychology, 51*, 586–594.

Zuckerman, M. (1979). *Sensation seeking: Beyond the optimal level of arousal.* Hillsdale, NJ: Lawrence Erlbaum Associates.

Zuckerman, M., & Little, P. (1986). Personality and curiosity about morbid and sexual events. *Personality and Individual Differences, 7*, 49–56.

CHAPTER
14

Responding to Erotica: Perceptual Processes and Dispositional Implications

James Weaver
Auburn University

The question of exactly which socially relevant messages are manifest in mass media depictions of human sexuality and what effects consumption of these messages has on individuals and society, especially consumption of messages that are extracted from entertainment presentations (i.e., erotica and pornography),[1] is examined in this chapter. First, the status of such materials in the modern entertainment marketplace is explored, their manifest content characteristics are delineated, and the crux of the controversy over these materials is articulated. Next, pertinent empirical investigations examining the perceptual and dispositional responses occasioned by exposure to contemporary erotica are summarized. Finally, several consistencies and contradictions evident from the growing volume of research are highlighted and their implications are discussed.

EROTICA IN THE ENTERTAINMENT MARKETPLACE

Public opinion about the availability and potential consequences of sexually explicit mass media portrayals (e.g., movies rated "X" by the Motion Picture Association of America) is quite diverse. Nationwide surveys for *Newsweek* (Press et al., 1985) and *Time* (Stengel, 1986), for example, reveal that many Americans view such materials as an important source of entertainment (61%) and sexual

---

[1] In this discussion, the terms *erotica*, *pornography*, and *sexually explicit materials* are used interchangeably.

information (52%) and believe that they can serve as "healthy" marital aids (47%) and as a useful outlet for sexual frustration (44%).[2] Apparent tolerance faded, however, when respondents were questioned about several specific consequences that might result from exposure to sexually explicit magazines, movies, and books. In particular, the majority of those interviewed thought that consumption of such materials leads some people to lose respect for women (76%), to consider women as sex objects (61%), to be more sexually promiscuous (65%), and to commit rape or other acts of sexual violence (73%). Similar evidence highlighting the diversity of public opinion over sexually explicit materials has been reported from other countries including Australia (Joint Select Committee on Video Material, 1988) and Canada (Peat, Marwick, & Partners, 1984).

Despite this apparent ambivalence, substantial evidence highlights the fact that a considerable proportion of the population is quite fascinated with modern sexually explicit materials. One measure of this fascination is the tremendous financial success enjoyed by the producers and distributors of such materials. Over the last two decades, for example, this enterprise has evolved from "a seedy and illicit cottage industry to a stable and well-refined, mass-production business employing the latest "know-how" and yielding annual worldwide sales revenues in excess of $5 billion (Hebditch & Anning, 1988, p. 3). A large portion of these revenues have resulted from an unparalleled consumer demand for sexually explicit materials in the home videotape and subscription cable television marketplaces of the United States.

Almost since the introduction of videotape technology for domestic use, graphic sexually explicit materials (i.e., hardcore pornography) have represented a very lucrative component for the videotape sales and rental industry. Indeed, because producers of pornography were among the earliest adopters of videotape technology for distribution of their software, many videotape retailers were "initially dependent on hard-core sex material for more than 50 per cent of their revenues" (Hebditch & Anning, 1988, p. 23). And, although the availability of other forms of video software has increased dramatically, the economic vitality of the sexually explicit videotape industry has continued to grow over the last decade. In 1988, for example, approximately 1,250 sexually explicit videotapes—about 500 of which were new, feature-length productions—were released for distribution in the United States with wholesale sales approaching $400 million ("Charting the adult video market," 1989). At the retail level, these materials accounted for approximately

---

[2]For the *Newsweek* poll (Press et al., 1985), the Gallup Organization conducted telephone interviews with a national sample of 1,020 adults on March 6 and 7, 1985. The poll reported in *Time* (Stengel, 1986) was conducted by Yankelovich Clancy Shulman and questioned 1,017 Americans by telephone July 7 to 9, 1986. The content and phrasing of the questions on the two surveys appear quite similar and, in fact, are the same in some instances. However, the distribution of responses reflect some differences. These differences seem due, at least to some extent, to the fact that the *Time* sample population reported a substantially higher level of familiarity with sexually explicit materials. In order to simplify presentation of these data, when essentially identical questions were presented by both surveys, the percentage reported here is the greater.

7% of all software and 9% of the revenues of a typical video rental outlet (Shaw, 1986).

Subscription television cable services that exhibit erotica have also enjoyed considerable success. For example, over 500,000 households or approximately 1% of the potential cable audience subscribe to one of three premium cable services (American Exxxtasy, The Playboy Channel, and Tuxxedo Channel). Additionally, almost 2 million subscribers have access to sexually explicit movies and special events via pay-per-view cable services ("Cable stats," 1989). Although specific data are not available, a conservative estimate suggests that fees paid by the subscribers of these various cable services may exceed $75 million annually. Taken together, these data accentuate the fact that, as a result of new communication technologies, the marketplace for contemporary sexually explicit materials has been transformed from one catering to a few elite and privileged consumers to one providing an affordable form of entertainment available to all (Zillmann & Bryant, 1989).

Although there exists considerable evidence of a growing demand for erotica in the entertainment marketplace, surprisingly little is known about the factors that underlie this consumer fascination (Bryant & Brown, 1989). One explanation can be derived from the repeatedly noted extreme curiosity about otherwise proscribed behaviors—essentially the "forbidden fruit" phenomenon. Specifically, given that the public exhibition of sexual behaviors has traditionally been strongly condemned in our society, it seems that the observed fascination with pornography can be explained, as least to some extent, as the result of consumer curiosity over the sexual activities of others.

Two aspects of contemporary erotica are particularly accommodating for the curiosity seeker and seem to bolster this explanation. First, these materials typically provide the user with a "bigger than life" view of sexual behaviors in a "you are there as it happens" documentary style (Hebditch & Anning, 1988; Rimmer, 1986). Second, and equally important, the broad diffusion of sexually explicit materials via videotape and cable outlets has exponentially increased their accessibility, enhanced their respectability, and permitted their consumption in safe, private circumstances. Together, these elements apparently have encouraged many individuals to sample otherwise socially proscribed explicit erotica (Zillmann & Bryant, 1989).

Although this curiosity-about-"forbidden-fruits"-explanation accommodates the initial surge of consumer demand for erotica, it must be recognized that this rationale cannot sufficiently explain the apparent continued popularity of these materials. In fact, research evidence suggests that curiosity about most sexually explicit materials quickly wains (Zillmann, 1989a). For instance, Zillmann and Bryant (1986) conducted a study that examined the impact of extensive consumption of common, nonviolent pornography on subsequent interest in such materials. They found that subjects with considerable prior exposure (1 hour sessions in 6 consecutive weeks) to common pornography showed little interest in such materials 2 weeks later in a private viewing situation. Instead, both male and female subjects elected to watch sexually explicit materials involving uncommon and unfamiliar sexual themes such as bondage, sadomasochism, and bestiality. Thus, the data suggest that the novelty of erotica commonly available in the modern entertainment marketplace is comparatively shortlived.

What other factors may underlie consumer fascination with erotica? Sustained interest in these materials appears to derive from their ability to satisfy perceived needs and serve particular functions for their audience (Glassman, 1977). Specifically, it must be recognized that explicit erotica are, like other "aesthetic commodities" (e.g., television programs), tailored to provide a sense-pleasing form of entertainment (Huer, 1987). Unlike other aesthetic commodities, however, the entertainment value of explicit erotica does not appear to be derived from the comic or dramatic content of the presentation. Indeed, attention to such basic theatrical considerations is typically extremely limited in, if not a completely ancillary component of, these materials (Abeel, 1987; Press et al., 1985; Rimmer, 1986). Instead, the entertainment value of contemporary erotica appears to arise from their utility as a prelude to, stimulant of, and/or source of information about sexual activities (e.g., Bryant & Brown, 1989; Kaplan, 1984; Lawrence & Herold, 1988).

As a form of entertainment, however, sexually explicit materials are not appreciated equally by male and female consumers (Bryant & Brown, 1989). Although some research evidence suggests that there are only minimal differences in the physiological arousal of men and women in response to graphic depictions of sexual activities (e.g., Kelley & Byrne, 1983), other data show that the genders are very different in their interest in, and perceptions of, such materials (Day, 1988; Hazen, 1983; Pickard, 1982). Males, for example, appear much more active in their search for, and use of, erotica and typically report considerable positive affect following exposure. Use of these materials by females, on the other hand, appears to be largely dependent on the initiative of others, especially a male partner, and negative affective reactions are typical (Lawrence & Herold, 1988). These gender differences are usually traced to cultural considerations, with the "social proscription of female interest in sexually explicit depictions" appearing particularly influential (Pickard, 1982, p. 114; also see Brownmiller, 1975). Equally important, however, is the fact that the bulk of contemporary pornography involves representations of human sexuality that are strongly biased toward the preferences of male consumers and entail images that many female viewers perceive as alien to their interests (Garry, 1978; Hazen, 1983; Lederer, 1980).

EXAMINING THE CONTENT CHARACTERISTICS OF EROTICA

Explication and categorization of the content characteristics of contemporary sexually explicit materials has benefited greatly from a wide breadth of both critical and empirical analyses (Brown & Bryant, 1989; Huer, 1987; Lederer, 1980). These examinations resulted in numerous typologies for the classification of erotica based on their manifest content (e.g., Attorney General's Commission on Pornography, 1986; Joint Select Committee on Video Material, 1988; Lawrence, 1936; Steinem, 1980). Common to all of these typologies are three categories that distinguish between presentations that feature (a) standard nonviolent themes, (b) coercive and/or violent themes, and (c) idealized sexual themes (cf. Zillmann, 1989a).

Standard Nonviolent Themes

The overwhelming majority of erotica available in the modern entertainment marketplace falls within this category. For example, Hebditch and Anning (1988) reported that the category of standard-fare or "mainstream" pornography accounts for "more than 90 per cent of the world production of still photographs and video/film sequences of heterosexual acts of intercourse where penile erection and penetration are the central feature" (p. 7). Furthermore, although most standard-fare presentations involve a range of content features, such productions typically adhere to highly stylized content conventions. Most appear to follow "a well-understood and thoroughly choreographed schema" (Hebditch & Anning, 1988, p. 23) of sexual behaviors that is "as strict and unvarying as the rules of the sonnet" (Abeel, 1987, p. 195; also see Hazen, 1983; Rimmer, 1986).

Although the specific origins of all the content conventions utilized in the production of standard erotic fare are not readily apparent, many clearly result from the fact that these materials have traditionally been produced and marketed for a predominantly male audience (Stauffer & Frost, 1976). Consequently, the bulk of the productions within this category strongly emphasize a distinctively "macho or masculinized orientation" toward sexual behaviors (Crabbe, 1988; Day, 1988), which entails several specific characteristics. Predominant among these is a complete "preoccupation with sexual activity to the exclusion of all other facets of human social behavior" (Hebditch & Anning, 1988, p. 15). Many analysts (e.g., Brown & Bryant, 1989; Palys, 1984, 1986; Prince, 1987; Slade, 1984; Winick, 1985) have noted, for instance, that typical standard erotic fare features all variants of heterosexual intercourse in innumerable circumstances and "as a matter of routine—lesbianism, group sex, anal intercourse, oral-genital contact and visible ejaculation" (Hebditch & Anning, 1988, p. 7) whereas, at the same time, depictions of other basic aspects of human sexuality—such as communication between sexual partners, expressions of affection or emotion (except for fear and lust), depictions of foreplay, afterplay, or friendly cuddling, and concern about sanitation or the consequences of sexual activities—are minimized (Prince, 1987; Rimmer, 1986). Furthermore, within this context, women are normally portrayed as eagerly soliciting participation in, and responding with hysterical euphoria to, any of a variety of sexual encounters (Abeel, 1987; Hazen, 1983; Palys, 1984; Rimmer, 1986). In short, standard-fare erotica present a "somewhat tasteless celebration of a 'sex is fun' mentality" (Palys, 1984, p. 61) that includes

demeaning or degrading portrayals of female sexuality and ignores the basic social and relational aspects of sexual activity.

Coercive and/or Violent Themes

Although considerable critical attention has been focused on this category of sexually explicit materials, the availability of productions involving coercive and/or
violent themes in the modern entertainment marketplace appears limited (Brown
& Bryant, 1989; Slade, 1984). Essentially, the materials included in this category
involve all of the content conventions evident in standard erotic fare with additional emphasis on coercion and/or violence as a precursor to, or integral part
of, sexual activities. A distinguishing content convention evident of materials in
this category is that, regardless of nature and severity of the actions that precipitate sexual activities, women are depicted as ultimately responding to such stimulation with great pleasure, and perpetrators (usually a single male) are shown
suffering no negative consequences as a result of their actions.

Research suggests that portrayals involving the use of rough or aggressive actions as a component of otherwise "normal" sexual behaviors (i.e., biting, hitting, spanking, verbal abuse) dominate this category. Palys (1984, 1986) found,
for instance, that most video-erotica that depicted some form of aggression or
sexual aggression entailed actions of this type. Relatively infrequent, yet clearly
evident in the entertainment marketplace, are erotica that portray coercion and/or
violence as a successful means of initiating sexual activities. Depictions of this
type involve numerous motifs ranging from circumstances where a woman is
coerced into sexual activities in exchange for material favors to instances where
women suffer overt physical aggression and rape. Of particular interest to many
theorists is a variant of the latter motif that is commonly referred to as the *rape-
myth* scenario. The basic rape-myth scenario begins with a rather realistic depiction of a woman being forced into an abusive rape that, despite her objections,
she is unable to prevent. The woman's initial expressions of disgust and trauma
are transitory, however, and she is ultimately portrayed as experiencing sexual
arousal and enjoyment as a result of the assault. In essence, the cultural myth
that women enjoy being raped (Burt, 1980) is graphically displayed.

Idealized Sexual Themes

A small proportion of commercially available erotica do not adhere to the content conventions detailed earlier. Instead, productions in this category, which are
sometimes contrasted with "pornography" (e.g., Steinem, 1980), present more
compassionate, egalitarian portrayals by focusing on the social and relational
aspects of heterosexual coital activities. Erotica depicting such idealized sexuality are typically targeted toward female consumers and, as a result, project a particularly "feminine orientation" toward sexual behaviors (Abeel, 1987; Hazen,

1983; Senn, 1985). Steele and Walker (1976) point out, for example, that a prototypic production within this category involves the following:

> The cast of the film would consist of one attractive male and one attractive female, displaying affection, "romance," and prolonged foreplay in a bedroom setting. The film would involve a *gradual* process leading to coitus involving a variety of positions, and the emotional tone of the film would emphasize the "total" relationship, and not merely genital sexual behavior. (p. 272)

Erotica depicting idealized sexuality contrast sharply with the sexuality portrayed in the other two erotica categories. Finally, although many analysts have predicted a significant increase in the number of productions within this category in response to the demands of female consumers (e.g., Rimmer, 1986), evidence of this trend is not readily apparent (Abeel, 1987).

THE CONTROVERSY OVER EROTICA

The prolific distribution of erotica, especially over the last two decades, has rejuvenated and substantially amplified the controversy over such materials. The basic issues involved in this debate – issues that have been the focus of considerable contention for some time (cf. Kendrick, 1987) – revolve around two distinct and yet inseparable concerns. One involves interpretation of the content characteristics of erotica. The other concern deals with the potential perceptual and dispositional implications of viewing such materials. Although a variety of theses have been advanced, three predominant theoretical perspectives have emerged. Common to all three viewpoints is the tenet that "merely observing a model engaging in sexual behavior (on film, in written material, or wherever) may affect our sexual beliefs, expectancies, and fantasies" and, consequently, our sexual behaviors (Fisher, 1986, p. 143). Projections of the nature and extent of the responses occasioned by exposure to contemporary erotica differ dramatically between the perspectives, however.

One viewpoint, which has been labeled the "sexual communication" model (Malamuth & Billings, 1986), maintains that erotica are simply entertaining communications that pertain to sexuality and have no discernible negative consequences. Advocates of this thesis (Gagnon, 1977; Kaplan, 1984; Stoller, 1976; Wilson, 1978) contend that such materials perform a positive function, serving as important educational and/or therapeutic tools that encourage "sexual pleasure and sexual abandon" and help eradicate "puritanical attitudes about sex that have long dominated our society" (Goldstein, 1984, p. 32). Wilson (1978) argued, for example, that pornographic presentations are "part of a latent mechanism by which our society provides opportunities for learning sex" – especially during adolescence – that "help to prevent sexual problems" such as guilt, anxiety, and inhibition regarding sex and the enactment of deviant sexual behaviors (pp. 160-161). Furthermore, according to this perspective, consumers readily recognize the various themes and portrayals of erotica as fictional representations (e.g., Gagnon, 1977) and, as a result, concern over such content characteristics is minimal (cf. Malamuth & Billings, 1986).

On the other hand, many analysts have rejected the idea that viewing pornography produces only beneficial effects. Indeed, advocates representing a wide variety of social and political orientations (e.g., feminists, family, and community organizations) have condemned such materials, charging that they foster detrimental perceptions of female sexuality, a misogynous cultural climate, and promote intergender violence (e.g., Attorney General's Commission on Pornography, 1986; Committee on Sexual Offenses Against Children and Youths, 1984; Joint Select Committee on Video Material; 1988; Lederer, 1980; Scott, 1985; Special Committee on Pornography and Prostitution, 1985).

Numerous variations of this "sexual callousness" model (Zillmann & Weaver, 1989) have been articulated (e.g., Attorney General's Commission on Pornography, 1986; Check & Malamuth, 1985; Kendrick, 1987). For example, the Commission on Obscenity and Pornography (1970) stated:

> It is often asserted that a distinguishing characteristic of sexually explicit materials is the degrading and demeaning portrayal of the role and status of the human female. It has been argued that erotic materials describe the female as a mere sexual object to be exploited and manipulated sexually.
>
> One presumed consequence of such portrayals is that erotica transmits an inaccurate and uninformed conception of sexuality, and that the viewer or user will (a) develop a calloused and manipulative orientation toward women and (b) engage in behavior in which affection and sexuality are not well integrated. (pp. 239-240)

Although the 1970 Commission concluded, based on sparse data, that such concerns were "probably unwarranted" (Commission on Obscenity and Pornography, 1970, p. 240), this basic proposition has remained a focal point of the continuing controversy.

Feminist analysts, for example, have been quite outspoken in their efforts to expand and refine this viewpoint (Snitow, 1985). Commentators have been especially critical of the depiction of women as promiscuous and sexually hyperactive, a portrayal that characterizes standard erotic fare and coercive and/or violent pornography. From their unique vantage point, these analysts maintain that such materials disparage and demean women by portraying them as "malleable, obsessed with sex, and willing to engage in any sexual act with any available partner" (Diamond, 1985, p. 42); that sexually explicit materials require "that women be subordinate to men and mere instruments for the fulfillment of male fantasies . . . that our pleasure consists of pleasing men, and not ourselves" (Longino, 1980, pp. 45-46); and that women are consistently depicted as "anonymous, panting playthings, adult toys, dehumanized objects to be used, abused, broken and discarded" (Brownmiller, 1975, p. 394).

The impact of exposure to this "dangerously distorted picture of female sexuality" (Brownmiller, 1984, p. 34), these writers argue, results in adverse perceptions of women—such as a general "loss-of-respect" for women as persons—and, ultimately, in asocial behavioral consequences ranging from sexual discrimination to rape (Brownmiller, 1975; Diamond, 1985; Garry, 1978; McCarthy, 1980). For example, Morgan (1980) proposed that exposure to contemporary erotica leads to "the erosion of the (traditional) virgin/whore stereotypes to a new 'all women are really whores' attitude, thus erasing the last vestige of (even corrupt) respect for women" (p. 138). Within this framework, Russell (1988) has developed an extensive rationalization for a causal connection between heightened sexual callousness toward women resulting from exposure to pornography and the enactment of rape, woman-battering, and other sexually violent crimes against women.

A third viewpoint, derived from a general "desensitization" model (e.g., Donnerstein, Linz, & Penrod, 1987), proposes that only particularly blatant portrayals of women as victims of coercion, aggression, and violence influence asocial attitudes and behaviors toward women. Specifically, advocates of this thesis (e.g., Donnerstein, 1984b; Donnerstein & Linz, 1986) maintain that concerns over negative consequences resulting from exposure to most contemporary sexually explicit materials (i.e., standard and idealized erotic fare) are ill-founded. It is proposed that the typical, sexually explicit presentation "does not foster negative attitudes or behaviors unless it is combined with images of violence" (Donnerstein et al., 1987, jacket). Thus, only innocuous effects are projected from exposure to erotica devoid of violent images.

Emphasizing the potential impact of images of the aggressive victimization of women on subsequent responses has led proponents of this perspective to argue for a broadening of the current debate to incorporate sexually suggestive media depictions (MPAA "R-rated" materials). To some extent, this shift of critical focus has been prompted by recognition of the fact that erotica depicting conspicuously violent themes are essentially unavailable in the entertainment marketplace (Brown & Bryant, 1989). Perhaps more important, however, has been the spectacular commercial success of "slasher" or "splatter" horror films over the last decade. One content convention common to many of these "slasher" films is the presentation of graphic, gory violence in otherwise erotic circumstances (Weaver, 1988). An illustrative example of this "eroticized violence," from a film entitled *The Toolbox Murders*, depicts a young woman bathing when a man forcefully enters her apartment. The nude woman is depicted as trying to escape. Failing in her attempt, she offers herself sexually. The attacker is sexually disinterested, however, and instead brutally murders the woman. Exposure to depictions of this sadistic type, it is argued, fosters and/or reinforces detrimental, malicious perceptions of women and encourages physically and sexually abusive treatment of women because, "while the sex is not explicit, but merely suggestive, the violence is graphically displayed and is overwhelmingly directed at women" (Donnerstein et al., 1987, p. 113).

PERTINENT RESEARCH FINDINGS

Over the last decade, a tremendous volume of data has been generated to address questions arising from the controversy over erotica. Although ethical considerations have imposed numerous restrictions, pertinent data have been collected using a broad range of research procedures and diverse samples (cf. Zillmann, 1989b). Unfortunately, considerable diversity is also evident in the way social scientists have conceptually and operationally defined sexually explicit materials; a fact that has led many to exclaim *caveat emptor* for consumers of this literature (e.g., Copp, 1983; Page, 1989; Zillmann & Bryant, 1988c). With this in mind, and in an effort to promote simplification and synthesis, the content characteristics of the stimuli employed in the studies summarized here have been carefully scrutinized and, whenever appropriate, organized within the framework of the three-category typology outlined earlier.

This summary concentrates on research findings illustrating the more immediate perceptual and dispositional responses resulting from exposure to erotica. In this light, particular attention is given several recent investigations offering comparisons of the perceptual impact of the three predominant content themes. Studies exploring the delayed, behavioral consequences of exposure to erotica have been examined in detail elsewhere (e.g., Zillmann, 1989a) and are excluded from this summary.

Perceptions Created by Exposure to Erotica

The most pervasive, consistently observed responses following exposure to erotica are perceptual and dispositional effects. Specifically, substantial research evidence illustrates that exposure to such materials can facilitate the formation and reinforcement of inappropriate or undesirable perceptions of women in nonsexual as well as sexual contexts (Donnerstein, 1983; Malamuth, 1984; McKenzie-Mohr & Zanna, 1990; Zillmann 1989a; Zillmann & Weaver, 1989). For example, in a series of investigations, Zillmann and Bryant (1982, 1984, 1988a, 1988b) have recorded a variety of persistent perceptual and dispositional changes concerning sexuality, and especially female sexuality, after prolonged exposure to erotica. In an initial study (Zillmann & Bryant, 1982, 1984) involving both male and female college students, prolonged exposure to standard erotica (six 1-hour weekly sessions) led to the trivialization of rape as a criminal offense, exaggerated perceptions of the prevalence of most sexual practices, and increased callousness toward female sexuality and concerns. Compared with the control groups, the prolonged exposure group recommended a far shorter term of incarceration for a convicted rapist. This was the case for both male and female respondents, although women prescribed much greater punishment for rape overall.

Based on these findings, Zillmann and Bryant (1982, 1984) speculated that, for many individuals, repeated viewing of commonly available sexually explicit materials might foster dissatisfaction with their existing sexual relationships and occasion diminished caring for and trust in their partners. A second investigation was conducted in order to test these considerations (Zillmann & Bryant, 1988a, 1988b). Men and women we recruited from both a college student body and the adult population of a city to view either standard pornographic videos or innocuous television fare during 1-hour sessions conducted over 6 consecutive weeks. One week later, in an ostensibly unrelated study, subjects completed a series of questionnaires designed to assess their perceptions of societal institutions and personal contentment with various aspects of their lives. The findings revealed that prolonged exposure to erotica adversely affected attitudes about sexual intimacy and the institution of marriage. Furthermore, such exposure induced dissatisfaction with numerous aspects of sexuality. Compared with their control group counterparts, subjects in the exposure group reported greater acceptance of pre- and extramarital sex, of nonexclusive sexual intimacy, and of sexual promiscuity as vital for emotional and physical health. Additionally, for both men and women, students and nonstudents, the exposure treatment facilitated acceptance of male dominance in intimate relationships, culminating in the "general abandonment of the notion that women are or ought to be equals in intimate relationships" (Zillmann, 1985, p. 10). Further, the findings showed that after prolonged consumption of sexually explicit materials, subjects reported less satisfaction with their intimate partners' affection, physical appearance, sexual curiosity, and sexual performance, and they attributed greater importance to sexual activities without emotional involvement. In contrast, the exposure treatment did not affect self-assessments of happiness and satisfaction in areas unrelated to sexuality (personal finances, professional/academic accomplishments, etc.).

A third investigation (Bryant, 1985) examined whether the greater acceptance of sexual promiscuity and infidelity and elevated sexual discontent and distrust instigated by prolonged consumption of contemporary erotica would generalize to everyday moral judgments. College students watched either standard erotica or television comedies for 3 hours per day over 5 consecutive days. Three days later, subjects were exposed to several vignettes, half of which featured nonsexual transgressions or crimes, whereas the others featured sexual indiscretions or improprieties. The findings revealed that prolonged exposure to the sexually explicit materials led subjects to report that the vignettes of sexual indiscretions were less objectionable, that the victims of the sexual improprieties were less wronged, and that the victims of the sexual transgressions suffered less. In contrast, judgments of vignettes involving nonsexual transgressions and crimes were not affected.

Evidence that exposure to sexually explicit materials can adversely impact perceptions of individuals who suffer sexual abuse has been recently extended to include child victims. Buchman (1988) recruited college men and women to view either sexually explicit videos, sexually suggestive videos, or nonsexual videos in four daily sessions. The sexual videos showed the behaviors of consenting adults only. On the fifth day, subjects were asked to respond to a series of case descriptions detailing a wide variety of criminal and noncriminal social transgressions. Included among these scenarios were incidents of sexual abuse (e.g., rape) experienced by both adult and child victims. The findings showed that exposure to pornography promoted callous attitudes about the degree of suffering endured by children victimized by sexual abuse. They also revealed that exposure to such materials significantly trivialized the sexual abuse of females whether adults or children.

Other research demonstrates that rather brief exposure to standard erotica can occasion adverse perceptions and dispositions. For example, the impact of prior exposure to sexually explicit materials on young mens' perceptions of their female sexual partners was examined in a study by Weaver, Masland, and Zillmann (1984). Subjects were exposed to slides and videotapes of either (a) nature scenes; (b) beautiful, nude females in provocative poses or engaged in precoital or coital behavior; or (c) rather unattractive females engaged in these activities. After a brief project interpolated to disguise the purpose of the study, subjects responded to a questionnaire assessing different aspects of their relationship with present girlfriends with whom they were sexually intimate. The findings showed that men exposed to materials featuring attractive women, compared with those who viewed unattractive women, reported a significant underappraisal of their mate's aesthetic sexual appeal. A similar pattern of findings observed in two experiments were also reported by Kenrick, Gutierres, and Goldberg (1989). Futhermore, these investigators found that both men and women reported that they loved their mates less following exposure to sexually explicit depictions involving highly attractive models. Thus, in a manner consistent with the effects of prolonged exposure (Zillmann & Bryant, 1988a, 1988b), even limited exposure to erotica appears sufficient to occasion dissatisfaction with one's intimate partner.

Research examining the perceptual and dispositional consequences of exposure to erotica involving coercive and/or violent themes reveals that exposure to unambiguous rape-myth scenarios consistently produces adverse effects on observers' perceptions of women, in general, and of rape victims, in particular. On the other hand, exposure to realistic rape depictions yields only inconsequential effects. This pattern is illustrated clearly in a series of experiments reported by Malamuth and others (Malamuth, 1984). For example, in two studies (Malamuth & Check, 1980; Malamuth, Haber, & Feshbach, 1980) that used the same protocol, male subjects were first presented with a brief, narrated story of a heterosexual couple engaged in either rape-myth, realistic rape, or idealized sex. All subjects were then exposed to a detailed depiction of a realistic rape and asked to indicate their perceptions of the victim's experience. Evidence from both studies shows that subjects first exposed to the rape-myth scenario reported significantly lower estimates of the victim's trauma than those in the other conditions.

Data from several other investigations (Check & Malamuth, 1983; Malamuth & Check, 1983, 1985) provide further documentation that exposure to rape-myth depictions adversely influences men's perceptions about the extent of enjoyment that women experience when forced to submit to unwanted sexual activities, including rape. Unfortunately, however, the generalizability of these findings is compromised by the absence of a neutral exposure control group.

Overcoming this limitation, an investigation reported by Malamuth and Check (1981) demonstrates that exposure to media portrayals of the rape-myth can produce prolonged adverse perceptual effects. Male and female college students were recruited to watch two commercially released, feature-length films on different evenings. Approximately half of the subjects viewed two sexually suggestive movies that—although devoid of the close-up, graphic depiction of sexual activities common to erotica—unambiguously portrayed women as responding positively to abusive sexual assaults. One film, in particular, conveyed very vivid images of female sexual promiscuity and marital disloyalty. A woman was first depicted as willing participant to a sexual assault and then as collaborating with her rapist to taunt her husband until he committed suicide. The remainder of the subjects watched two neutral films. A number of days later, all subjects completed several scales assessing their sexual perceptions. The results showed that, among male subjects, exposure to the rape-myth films significantly increased acceptance of interpersonal violence against women and tended to increase endorsement of rape-myth perceptions. The pattern of effects tended in the opposite direction for female subjects, however.

Comparing Responses to Sexual and/or Violent Content

One of the most disputed aspects in the debate over sexually explicit materials concerns the divergent projections of the sexual callousness and desensitization models. Considerable progress toward clarification of pivotal concerns has been provided by recent comparative analyses exploring the perceptual and dispositional effects resulting from consumption of both sexually explicit (X-rated) and suggestive (R-rated) materials portraying the standard-erotic theme, sexual coercion and/or violence, or idealized sexuality. Most notable among these are several studies utilizing quite elaborate designs (i.e., extended exposure treatments, delayed assessments) that have demonstrated strong negative shifts in dispositions toward rape and other sexual assaults and in perceptions of the victims of these crimes.

Findings reported from an investigation[3] conducted by Donnerstein (1984a)

---

[3]Some controversy has developed over this investigation (Christensen, 1987; Linz & Donnerstein, 1988; Zillmann & Bryant, 1987, 1988c). Specifically, procedural details and findings concerning the two conditions involving sexually explicit materials were reported in some forums (Donnerstein, 1984a; Donnerstein & Linz, 1984) but excluded from subsequent published accounts (Linz, 1985; Linz, Donnerstein, & Penrod, 1984). The results reported here are from an integration and reanalysis of these data conducted by Weaver (1987).

and his associates (Donnerstein & Linz, 1984; Linz, 1985; Linz, Donnerstein, & Penrod, 1984) illustrate these erotica-induced perceptual shifts. College men completed an extensive pretest and then were randomly assigned to one of three exposure conditions or a control group. Subjects in the exposure conditions viewed five films over 5 consecutive days. In two conditions, subjects viewed pornography that involved either standard sexual themes or coercive and/or violent themes. Subjects in the third exposure condition watched sexually suggestive "slasher" films. After viewing each film, the exposure condition subjects completed an extensive questionnaire that assessed their mood and asked them to evaluate the films on several dimensions (e.g., the number of violent, sexual, and sexually violent actions depicted; the simultaneous occurrence of sexual and violent content; and the extent that the film degraded women). A fourth group of men were assigned to a control condition without exposure to films.

On the fifth day, after viewing the last film and completing the mood assessment and film-evaluation questionnaires, the exposure condition subjects were joined by the men in the control group. All subjects then viewed a videotaped reenactment of a trial in which a man was accused of forcefully raping a women he had met briefly at a bar, and they reported various perceptions of both the defendant and victim. The findings revealed that dispositions toward the alleged rapist were not affected by the exposure treatments. However, prolonged consumption of the standard pornography increased evaluations of the victim's "worthlessness" to a level significantly above all other conditions. Approximately equal increases in judgments of victim "worthlessness" were also evident for the two conditions involving coercive and/or violent themes and proved significantly greater than those of the control group. Also, compared to the control, the men in all three exposure conditions perceived the rape victim as significantly less injured by her experience.

Linz, Donnerstein, and Penrod (1988; Linz, 1985) reported a second study, employing a protocol similar to that detailed earlier, from which substantially less distinctive results emerged. Specifically, male subjects completed an extensive pretest questionnaire, were recruited to view either standard pornographic films, "slasher" films, or "teen comedy" films in two or five sessions held every other day or for a no-exposure control group. As before, immediately after viewing each film, the exposure treatment subjects were queried concerning their mood and their perceptions of the number of violent and/or sexual acts depicted in each film and how degrading the film was to women. Two days after the final exposure treatment, all subjects completed a questionnaire involving numerous self-perceptions. They then viewed a videotape of a mock-jury trial involving the alleged rape of a woman by an acquaintance during a fraternity party. After watching the trial reenactment, subjects indicated their perceptions of the rapist and victim.

Using a complex and selective analytic procedure, the authors reported that men who displayed greater acceptance of rape-myth beliefs prior to the experimental manipulation were also less sympathetic toward the victim portrayed in the mock-jury rape case and less empathetic toward rape victims in general. Effects attributable to the exposure treatments were surprisingly weak, however. Specifically, the findings showed that men involved in the more extensive eroticized violence exposure condition tended to express less compassion for rape victims. Interestingly, although other analyses revealed that the men who consumed five eroticized violence films also appeared particularly anxious about their own personal vulnerability to criminal victimization (Ogles & Hoffner, 1987), no other significant effects emerged from this study.

A parallel pattern of findings resulted from a study reported by Linz, Donnerstein, and Adams (1989). This study utilized a substantially shorter exposure treatment. After completing an extensive pretest questionnaire, college males were randomly assigned to one of two exposure conditions. No control group was involved in the design. The exposure materials in both conditions consisted of a 90-minute montage of scenes taken from contemporary movies. The first montage consisted of several scenes of eroticized violence from slasher films that depicted nude women suffering brutal mutilation or murder. The second exposure condition involved a mixture of scenes from sexually suggestive depictions (e.g., full nudity and cloaked sexual activities) and nonsexual suspenseful drama (e.g., life-threatening mishaps and exciting sporting events). All scenes in this second condition were devoid of violence. Once again, immediately following the exposure treatment, the subjects were queried concerning their mood and their perceptions of the content characteristics of each montage. Next, the subjects viewed two scenes from contemporary movies in which men verbally and physically abused women and reported their perceptions of each victim and perpetrator on several scales (e.g., victim injury, sympathy for victim, responsibility of perpetrator and victim). Consistent with previous findings, the data revealed that men who reported greater acceptance of rape-myth beliefs prior to the exposure treatment also reported less victim sympathy, less perpetrator responsibility, and greater victim responsibility. However, effects attributable to the exposure treatments were again surprisingly weak and yielded a rather contradictory pattern. Specifically, the findings showed that, compared with those in the sexually suggestive condition, men who viewed eroticized violence perceived the victims as less injured. Further, those exposed to the sexually suggestive montage perceived the male perpetrators as less responsible for their actions and tended to attribute more responsibility to the female victims when compared with those who viewed the scenes of eroticized violence.

An investigation involving female respondents that incorporated many of the components of the previously described studies was conducted by Krafka (1985). After completing a pretest questionnaire, the women were randomly assigned to three different exposure conditions and viewed one film per day for 4 consecutive days. The films portrayed either standard sexually explicit fare, sexually explicit themes involving coercion and/or violence, or eroticized violence. Consistent with the Linz et al. studies, after watching each film the female subjects assessed their mood and indicated the number of violent and/or sexual acts depicted in each film and how degrading the film was to women. A fourth group served as a no-exposure control. On the fifth day, all subjects completed an extensive questionnaire that assessed a number of self-perceptions (self-esteem, body satisfaction, and concerns about potential criminal victimization). Responses to the Rape Myth Acceptance and Acceptance of Interpersonal Violence scales developed by Burt (1980) were also ascertained. Subjects then viewed and responded to a trial reenactment of a rape case. Using a series of nonorthogonal comparisons, Krafka (1985) found that, when compared individually to the control group, the sexually explicit and eroticized violence depictions each yielded a discrete pattern of effects. Specifically, repeated exposure to the sexually explicit materials increased rape-myth acceptance significantly above the level of the control.[4] Prolonged exposure to the coercive/violent sexually explicit materials had essentially no effect. On the other hand, women repeatedly exposed to depictions of eroticized violence reported elevated satisfaction with body build, a greater chance of resisting a nonsexual assault, and smaller likelihood of being the future victim of a violent or sexual assault. Exposure to eroticized violence had no effect on sexual perceptions, although the women in this group were more likely to exonerate the defendant than those in the other exposure conditions.

The findings of these comparative analyses provide insight into the relative impact of various sexually explicit and violent materials on rape-related perceptions and dispositions. Specifically, the range of findings indicates that exposure to standard erotica can yield substantial adverse consequences. These effects include significantly elevated callousness toward rape and rape victims in both male and female respondents. A similar pattern of perceptual shifts is apparent for the various sexually explicit and sexually suggestive materials involving themes of coercion and/or violence. These effects appear substantially weaker and much less consistent, however.

Unfortunately, shortcomings apparent in the designs and procedures of this group of investigations limit the generalizability and predictive utility of the findings. In particular, two aspects of the protocols employed in these studies are problematic.

The fact that the discussed investigations (Donnerstein et al., 1987) employed either a no-exposure control group, or no control group at all, severely undermines the confidence that can be accorded the findings. It must be recognized

---

[4]The significance of this effect was overlooked in the discussion presented by Krafka (1985). For example, Krafka reported that the nonorthogonal comparison of Rape Myth Acceptance scale means between the untreated control and the sexually explicit materials exposure group was not significant based on a two-tailed t test [$t(134) = 1.88, p > .06$]. However, given the findings of previous research with female subjects (e.g., Zillmann & Bryant, 1982, 1984), directional effects should have been anticipated and the one-tailed t test applied. When applied, it yields a significant effect ($p < .032$). The findings summarized here are based on this re-analysis.

that this design deficiency (the absence of a neutral-content control group with parallel experimental treatments), when combined with the repeated and complex nature of the interactions between the experimenters and subjects, leaves the data open to several alternative interpretations. For instance, one viable explanation is that the reported pattern of effects represents experimental artifact (Weaver, in press). Careful review of the protocols employed in these investigations suggests that experimenter demand characteristics—invited by the repeated administration of film-evaluation measures that cued constructs associated with the sexual abuse and degradation of women—offer a parsimonious account for the data at hand. Even a cursory examination of the film-evaluation questionnaires employed leaves little doubt that most subjects must have recognized the experimenters' interest in the sexually violent aspects of the materials. In short, it appears that the use of a no-exposure control group, or no control group at all, confounded the potential effect of the female-degradation cue with film exposure. This is to say that only those subjects seeing films could be influenced by the demands manifest in the cue-laden questions.

A second problematic aspect of these comparative analyses involves the manner in which the primary dependent measures were ascertained (Krafka, 1985; Linz, 1985; Linz, Donnerstein, & Penrod, 1984, 1988). Specifically, in those studies where dispositions toward sexual offenders were assessed, the various sexually explicit and/or violent materials failed to influence punitive recommendations against the rapists appreciably. This pattern of findings is surprising in light of the repeatedly demonstrated robustness of this effect in other research. As noted elsewhere (Zillmann, 1989a), one plausible explanation for these discrepant findings concerns the nature of the information provided in the mock jury scenarios. Unlike the scenarios used in previous studies, in which the vicious actions of rapists were unambiguously presented, the scenarios employed in these comparative analyses were highly ambiguous. Indeed, most of the scenarios entail extenuating circumstances (e.g., the rapist met his victim at a bar, the victim became intoxicated during a social gathering, or the victim was a prostitute) surrounding the assaults that could have served to mitigate the perpetrators actions.

The implications of these two considerations were explored in an investigation conducted by Weaver (in press) in which film content (neutral, eroticized violence) and female-degradation cues (cues present, cues absent) were systematically varied across subject gender. Subjects were randomly assigned to one of the film content conditions, where they viewed and evaluated three brief scenes from contemporary movies. Half of the subjects evaluated each scene by responding to questions designed to cue constructs associated with female degradation (e.g., "how degrading to women was this scene?"). The remaining subjects answered neutral questions (e.g., "how well produced was this scene?"). Subjects then participated in an ostensibly unrelated project where they read summaries of three legal proceedings in which men were said to have been convicted of physical and/or sexual assaults against women. The details of each case were varied so that the perpetrators' actions in two cases (incidences of domestic violence and rape) were unambiguous. The third case involved a guilt-ambiguous scenario in which the perpetrator of a sexual assault enjoys mitigating circumstance. After reading each summary, the subjects reported both punitive judgments for and perceptual dispositions toward the men and women involved in each case.

Consistent with the experimental artifact interpretation, the findings showed that, independent of both the exposure treatment and subject gender, the use of reactive film-evaluation measures resulted in subsequent judgments that reflected the disparagement of, and a loss of compassion for, female victims of physical and/or sexual assaults. Specifically, the data revealed that subjects in the female-degradation cue condition, when compared with those in the condition without such cues, reported significantly less concern for a female physical assault victim and more strongly endorsed the idea that a victim of rape is a "lesser woman." The findings also showed significant gender difference in the effect of the female-degradation cue manipulation on punitive judgments against the men who had assaulted women. Among females, for example, those exposed to the degradation cues prescribed significantly lower punitive judgments against the perpetrator who physically assaulted his female cohabitant. Although not significantly different, male subjects tended to respond in the opposite manner. A different pattern emerged for judgments of the convicted rapist. Among female subjects who viewed the eroticized violence, those also exposed to the degradation cues recommended a significantly longer period of incarceration for the rapist. Again, male subject's judgments, although not significant, tended in the opposite direction. Equally important, no significant effects emerged in the punitive judgments of the perpetrator in the guilt-ambiguous sexual assault scenario. This fact suggests that consideration of the degree of guilt-ambiguity incorporated into the assault scenarios offers a reasonable rationale for similar null effects obtained in the comparative analyses (e.g., Krafka, 1985; Linz, 1985; Linz, Donnerstein, & Penrod, 1984, 1988).

The findings reported by Weaver (in press), taken together, demonstrate that the basic design and procedural shortcomings evident in the studies reported by Donnerstein (1984a), Linz and his associates (Linz, Donnerstein, & Adams, 1989; Linz, Donnerstein, & Penrod, 1984, 1988), and Krafka (1985) are likely to have influenced the findings that have been reported. More importantly, these data highlight the necessity for prudence in the interpretation of these analyses.

In an investigation reported by Check and Guloien (1989), substantial differences in the impact of sexually explicit depictions of the rape (i.e., sexual violence not conforming with the rape-myth), standard erotica, and idealized sexual themes were evident. Male students and nonstudents participated in three exposure sessions over a 1- to 2-week period. During these sessions, subjects viewed a 30-minute videotape montage of excerpts from movies that exemplified one of the three themes and indicated, among other things, how exciting, boring, aggressive, and realistic they considered each montage. Approximately 5 days later, the exposure subjects and a no-exposure control group[5] completed a questionnaire tapping their sexually aggressive perceptions and dispositions, self-reported likelihood of (a) forcing a woman to engage in unwanted sexual activities and (b) committing rape, and sexual callousness toward women.

Compared with subjects in the control group, the likelihood of committing rape reported by those repeatedly exposed to either rape or standard erotic fare was significantly higher. Increases were also evident for those who viewed the idealized-sex materials, but were not reliable. Prolonged consumptions of standard erotica also elevated the reported likelihood of forced sexual acts above the control group level; whereas the other exposure groups did not differ significantly from the control. Further, among men who scored comparatively high on a pre-exposure measure of psychoticism — suggesting that they tend to be solitary and hostile and to prefer impersonal sex (Eysenck, 1978) — the impact of either rape or standard erotica was particularly strong. In contrast, negligible affects were evident for men scoring low on this measure.

Finally, a comparative analysis reported by Weaver (1987) provides one of the most detailed explications of the content characteristics of sexual and violent themes that adversely impact perceptions of women and attitudes toward rape. Both male and female volunteers were exposed to depictions of either neutral, sexual, or sexually coercive and/or violent themes in a study that was conducted in three phases. In the first phase, subjects reported their perceptual reactions to narrative descriptions of women and men. The females were, by design, described as assertive or permissive and sexually discriminating or sexually promiscuous. Thus, descriptions ranging from stereotypically nice, virtuous women to wild, promiscuous ones were created to provide reference points in determining the direction and magnitude of semantic shifts in the perception of women resulting from the exposure treatments.

In the study's second phase, approximately 1 week later, subjects were exposed to three brief scenes of similar content. The scenes were taken from contemporary television programs and movies. Five content conditions were distinguished. In a neutral condition, subjects viewed nonsexual and nonviolent intergender interactions. Portrayals of consenting sexual activities were divided into "consensual sex" and "female-instigated sex." The sexually coercive and/or violent themes were also subdivided. A condition labeled "male-coerced sex" presented scenes in which males employed verbal and/or physical coercion to gain sexual access to females. The other condition, labeled "eroticized violence," included scenes common to slasher films in which graphically violent acts were shown to occur within an erotic context. Subjects responded to a neutrally worded evaluative inventory after viewing each scene.

---

[5]The reader is cautioned that Check and Guloien (1989) also utilized a no-exposure control group. However, these researchers employed an essentially neutral post-exposure film evaluation questionnaire. Under these circumstances, although the potential for artifact must be recognized, the impact of demand characteristics on the observed results appears minimal.

Immediately following the exposure treatment (Phase 3), subjects participated in two ostensibly unrelated projects. The first project was a person-perception task in which subjects reported their perceptions of women and men presented via portrait slides. The women presented in this task were subdivided into peers and nonpeers (i.e., into women about the subjects' age or notably older). Based on pretest data, these groups were further divided into those women perceived as sexually discriminating and sexually promiscuous. Subjects rated each person using an extensive adjective inventory. In the second post-exposure project subjects responded to fictional summaries of two legal proceedings by providing punitive judgments for men convicted of assaulting women. The first case described the attack on a young woman by her intoxicated boy friend. The women was said to have sustained substantial physical injuries. Subjects were asked to recommend a monetary award against the male assailant. The second case described the knife-point rape of a woman. Subjects were asked to recommend the punitive incarceration period for the rapist whose guilt was not in doubt.

The findings revealed that exposure to depictions of both sexual and coercive and/or violent themes is capable of inducing shifts in the general perception of women and in dispositions about the punishment of a convicted rapist. The most striking finding was that exposure to sexual themes strongly influenced perceptions of the "sexual receptivity" of otherwise sexually discriminating peer females, without adversely impacting other personality assessments. Specifically, compared with men exposed to neutral materials, those who viewed the consensual and female-instigated sex perceived sexually discriminating peer women as substantially more permissive. This effect was not observed following exposure to either the male-coerced sex or eroticized violence conditions. Women responded quite differently. They did not perceive more permissiveness in these females after viewing the sexual themes. However, they did tend to perceive greater permissiveness after exposure to male-coerced sex. Judgments of innocence and pleasantness were also affected by the exposure treatments. For the most part, parallel effects were not observed for the perception of sexually promiscuous peer or nonpeer women.

Analyses of the semantic distance (Osgood, Suci, & Tannenbaum, 1957) between particular stereotypes ascertained in Phase 1 and the perceptions of women reported after the exposure treatment confirmed and expanded the discussed effects. Exposure to both the sexual and coercive themes shifted perceptions of sexually discriminating female peers significantly closer to both the sexually promiscuous and the sexually permissive prototypes.

The findings concerning dispositions toward rape as a criminal offense, as measured in the sentencing of a rapist, revealed that the exposure treatments trivialized the rape judgments of both genders. Exposure to consensual sex tended to reduce recommended incarceration terms, but not reliably so. Exposure to female-instigated sex produced the strongest overall reduction. The rape-trivializing effect of the two conditions involving coercion and/or violence was intermediate.

Finally, additional analyses revealed a close correspondence between perceptual shifts toward greater female sexual permissiveness and promiscuity and leniency towards the rapist. Specifically, the findings show that the more strongly the exposure treatments influenced perceptions of women in the indicated sexual terms, the greater the trivialization of rape as a criminal offense.

CONCLUSIONS

The fact that the most pervasive responses occasioned by exposure to contemporary erotica entail the establishment and/or facilitation of asocial perceptions and dispositions toward women is highlighted clearly by the research evidence. Enhanced sexual callousness toward women is most apparent following consumption of materials that unambiguously portray women as sexually promiscuous and indiscriminating—a depiction that dominates contemporary sexually explicit materials. Adverse perceptual consequences resulting from exposure to coercive and/or violent erotica—especially portrayals in which women are shown tolerating, if not enjoying, abusive treatment as part of otherwise "normal" sexual activities (e.g., the rape-myth scenario)—appear equally robust. Furthermore, the limited findings concerning idealized-sex depictions indicate that consumption of such materials can also elevate sexual callousness toward women, although this effect appears weaker than that produced by the other two content themes.

Given the available research evidence, the nature and extent of responses to contemporary erotica appears most consistent with the projections of the sexual callousness model (Zillmann & Weaver, 1989) while contradicting the expectations of the alternative viewpoints. For example, although it is evident that consumers can acquire information about sexuality from erotica as suggested by the sexual communication model, it is equally apparent that they typically fail to respond to the various content themes and portrayals as fictional representations "for enjoyment only." In fact, the findings show that many viewers extract callousness-promoting information from the most idealized and egalitarian erotica.

Similarly, the fact that exposure to sexually explicit materials that are devoid of violence (standard erotic and idealized sexuality fare) can produce significant asocial perceptual responses, presents a serious challenge to contentions derived from the desensitization model: "that violent images, rather than sexual ones, are most responsible for people's attitudes about women and rape" (Donnerstein & Linz, 1986, p. 59). Granted that some effects of eroticized violence are consistent with the often observed phenomenon that exposure to scenes of graphic violence influences the perceived likelihood of harm to self and others (e.g., Tamborini, Zillmann, & Bryant, 1984). In light of the volume of contradictory research, however, the "it is not sex, but violence" (Donnerstein & Linz, 1986, p. 56) proclamation espoused by advocates of the desensitization model emerges as an oddly myopic viewpoint constructed on a particularly weak evidential foundation.

REFERENCES

Abeel, E. (1987, October). Bedroom eyes: Erotic movies come home. *Mademoiselle*, pp. 194-195, 234, 238.

Attorney General's Commission on Pornography. (1986). *Attorney General's Commission on Pornography: Final Report.* Washington, DC: U.S. Government Printing Office.

Brown, D., & Bryant, J. (1989). The manifest content of pornography. In D. Zillmann & J. Bryant (Eds.), *Pornography: Research advances and policy considerations* (pp. 3-24). Hillsdale, NJ: Lawrence Erlbaum Associates.

Brownmiller, S. (1975). *Against our will: Men, women, and rape.* New York: Simon & Schuster.

Brownmiller, S. (1984, November). The place of pornography: Packaging eros for a violent age (Comments to a Forum held at the New School for Social Research in New York City moderated by L. H. Lapham). *Harper's*, pp. 31-39, 42-45.

Bryant, J. (1985, September). *Testimony on the effects of pornography: Research findings.* Presented to the U.S. Attorney General's Commission on Pornography in hearings at Houston, TX.

Bryant, J., & Brown, D. (1989). Uses of pornography. In D. Zillmann & J. Bryant (Eds.), *Pornography: Research advances and policy considerations* (pp. 25-55). Hillsdale, NJ: Lawrence Erlbaum Associates.

Buchman, J. G. (1988). *Effects of repeated exposure to nonviolent erotica on attitudes about sexual child abuse.* Unpublished doctoral dissertation, Indiana University, Bloomington, IN.

Burt, M. R. (1980). Cultural myths and supports for rape. *Journal of Personality and Social Psychology, 38,* 217-230.

Cable stats. (1989, May 8). *CableVision*, p. 73.

Charting the adult video market. (1989). *Adult Video News: 1989 Buyer's Guide*, pp. 6-7.

Check, J. V. P., & Guloien, T. H. (1989). Reported proclivity for coercive sex following repeated exposure to sexually violent pornography, nonviolent pornography, and erotica. In D. Zillmann & J. Bryant (Eds.), *Pornography: Research advances and policy considerations* (pp. 159-184). Hillsdale, NJ: Lawrence Erlbaum Associates.

Check, J. V. P., & Malamuth, N. M. (1983). Sex role stereotyping and reactions to depictions of stranger versus acquaintance rape. *Journal of Personality and Social Psychology, 45,* 344-356.

Check, J. V. P., & Malamuth, N. M. (1985). Pornography and sexual aggression: A social learning theory analysis. In M. L. McLaughlin (Ed.), *Communication yearbook 9* (pp. 181-213). Beverly Hills, CA: Sage.

Christensen, F. (1987). Effects of pornography: The debate continues. *Journal of Communication, 37*(1), 186-188.

Commission on Obscenity and Pornography. (1970). *Report of the Commission on Obscenity and Pornography.* Washington, DC: U.S. Government Printing Office.

Committee on Sexual Offences Against Children and Youths. (1984). *Sexual offences against children.* Ottawa, Canada: Canadian Government Publishing Centre.

Copp, D. (1983). Pornography and censorship: An introductory essay. In D. Copp & S. Wendell (Eds.), *Pornography and censorship* (pp. 15-41). Buffalo, NY: Prometheus Books.

Crabbe, A. (1988). Feature-length sex films. In G. Day & C. Bloom (Eds.), *Perspectives on Pornography: Sexuality in film and literature* (pp. 44-66). London: Macmillan.

Day, G. (1988). Looking at women: Notes toward a theory of porn. In G. Day & C. Bloom (Eds.), *Perspectives on Pornography: Sexuality in film and literature* (pp. 83-100). London: Macmillan.

Diamond, S. (1985). Pornography: Image and reality. In V. Burstyn (Ed.), *Women against censorship* (pp. 40-57). Vancouver, British Columbia: Douglas & McIntyre.

Donnerstein, E. (1983). Erotica and human aggression. In R. Geen & E. Donnerstein (Eds.), *Aggression: Theoretical and empirical reviews* (Vol. 2, pp. 127-154). New York: Academic Press.

Donnerstein, E. (1984a). Pornography: Its content, its effects, and its harm. In D. Scott (Ed.), *Proceedings of Symposium on Media Violence and Pornography* (pp. 78-94). Toronto, Ontario: Media Action Group.

Donnerstein, E. (1984b). Pornography: Its effect on violence against women. In N. M. Malamuth & E. Donnerstein (Eds.), *Pornography and sexual aggression* (pp. 53–81). Orlando, FL: Academic Press.

Donnerstein, E., & Linz, D. (1984, January). Sexual violence in the media: A warning. *Psychology Today*, pp. 14–15.

Donnerstein, E., & Linz, D. G. (1986, December). The question of pornography. *Psychology Today*, pp. 56–59.

Donnerstein, E., Linz, D., & Penrod, S. (1987). *The question of pornography.* New York: Macmillan.

Eysenck, H. J. (1978). *Sex and personality.* London: Shere Books.

Fisher, W. A. (1986). A psychological approach to human sexuality: The sexual behavior sequence. In D. Byrne & K. Kelley (Eds.), *Alternative approaches to the study of sexual behavior* (pp. 131–171). Hillsdale, NJ: Lawrence Erlbaum Associates.

Gagnon, J. H. (1977). *Human sexualities.* Glenview, IL: Scott, Foresman.

Garry, A. (1978). Pornography and respect for women. *Social Theory and Practice, 4,* 395–422.

Glassman, M. B. (1977). *A uses and gratifications approach to the study of sexual materials.* Unpublished doctoral dissertation, Columbia University, New York.

Goldstein, A. (1984, November). The place of pornography: Packaging eros for a violent age (Comments to a Forum held at the New School for Social Research in New York City moderated by L. H. Lapham). *Harper's,* pp. 31–39, 42–45.

Hazen, H. (1983). *Endless rapture: Rape, romance, and the female imagination.* New York: Charles Scribner's Sons.

Hebditch, D., & Anning, N. (1988). *Porn gold: Inside the pornography business.* London: Faber & Faber.

Huer, J. (1987). *Art, beauty, and pornography: A journey through American culture.* Buffalo, NY: Prometheus Books.

Joint Select Committee on Video Material. (1988). *Report of the Joint Select Committee on Video Material.* Canberra: Australian Government Publishing Service.

Kaplan, H. S. (1984, July). Have more fun making love. *Redbook,* pp. 88–89, 166.

Kelley, K., & Byrne, D. (1983). Assessment of sexual responding: Arousal, affect, and behavior. In J. Cacioppo & R. Petty (Eds.), *Social psychophysiology* (pp. 467–490). New York: Guilford.

Kendrick, W. (1987). *The secret museum: Pornography in modern culture.* New York: Viking.

Kenrick, D. T., Gutierres, S. E., & Goldberg, L. L. (1989). Influence of popular erotica on judgments of strangers and mates. *Journal of Experimental Social Psychology, 25,* 159–167.

Krafka, C. L. (1985). Sexually explicit, sexually violent, and violent media: Effects of multiple naturalistic exposures and debriefing on female viewers (Doctoral dissertation, University of Wisconsin, Madison). *Dissertation Abstracts International, 47,* 2672B.

Lawrence, D. H. (1936). Pornography and obscenity. In E. D. McDonald (Ed.), *Phoenix: The posthumous papers of D. H. Lawrence* (pp. 170–187). New York: Viking.

Lawrence, K., & Herold, E. S. (1988). Women's attitudes toward and experience with sexually explicit materials. *Journal of Sex Research, 24,* 161–169.

Lederer, L. (1980). *Take back the night: Women on pornography.* New York: William Morrow.

Linz, D. G. (1985). Sexual violence in the media: Effects on male viewers and implications for society (Doctoral dissertation, University of Wisconsin, Madison). *Dissertation Abstracts International, 46,* 4604B.

Linz, D., & Donnerstein, E. (1988). The methods and merits of pornography research. *Journal of Communication, 38*(2), 180–184.

Linz, D., Donnerstein, E., & Adams, S. M. (1989). Physiological desensitization and judgments about female victims of violence. *Human Communication Research, 15,* 509–522.

Linz, D., Donnerstein, E., & Penrod, S. (1984). The effects of multiple exposures to filmed violence against women. *Journal of Communication, 34*(3), 130–147.

Linz, D. G., Donnerstein, E., & Penrod, S. (1988). Effects of long-term exposure to violent and sexually degrading depictions of women. *Journal of Personality and Social Psychology, 55,* 758–768.

Longino, H. E. (1980). Pornography, oppression, and freedom: A closer look. In L. Lederer (Ed.), *Take back the night: Women on pornography* (pp. 40-54). New York: William Morrow.

McCarthy, S. J. (1980, September/October). Pornography, rape, and the cult of macho. *The Humanist*, pp. 11-20, 56.

Malamuth, N. M. (1984). Aggression against women: Cultural and individual causes. In N. M. Malamuth & E. Donnerstein (Eds.), *Pornography and sexual aggression* (pp. 17-52). Orlando, FL: Academic Press.

Malamuth, N. M., & Billings, V. (1986). The functions and effects of pornography: Sexual communications versus the feminist models in light of research findings. In J. Bryant & D. Zillmann (Eds.), *Perspectives on media effects* (pp. 83-108). Hillsdale, NJ: Lawrence Erlbaum Associates.

Malamuth, N. M., & Check, J. V. P. (1980). Penile tumescence and perceptual responses to rape as a function of victim's perceived reactions. *Journal of Applied Social Psychology, 10*, 528-547.

Malamuth, N. M., & Check, J. V. P. (1981). The effects of mass media exposure on acceptance of violence against women: A field experiment. *Journal of Research in Personality, 15*, 436-446.

Malamuth, N. M., & Check, J. V. P. (1983). Sexual arousal to rape depictions: Individual differences. *Journal of Abnormal Psychology, 92*, 55-67.

Malamuth, N. M., & Check, J. V. P. (1985). The effects of aggressive pornography on beliefs in rape myths: Individual differences. *Journal of Research in Personality, 19*, 299-320.

Malamuth, N. M., Haber, S., & Feshbach, S. (1980). Testing hypotheses regarding rape: Exposure to sexual violence, sex differences, and the "normality" of rapists. *Journal of Research in Personality, 14*, 121-137.

McKenzie-Mohr, D., & Zanna, M. P. (1990) Treating women as sexual objects: Look to the (gender schematic) male who has viewed pornography. *Personality and Social Psychology Bulletin, 16*, 296-308.

Morgan, R. (1980) Theory and practice of pornography and rape. In L. Lederer (Ed.), *Take back the night: Women on pornography* (pp. 134-140). New York: William Morrow.

Ogles, R. M., & Hoffner, C. (1987). Film violence and perceptions of crime: The cultivation effect. In M. L. McLaughlin (Ed.), *Communication yearbook 10* (pp. 384-394). Newbury Park, CA: Sage.

Osgood, C. E., Suci, G. J., & Tannenbaum, P. H. (1957). *The measurement of meaning.* Urbana, IL: University of Illinois Press.

Page, S. (1989). Misrepresentation of pornography research: Psychology's role. *American Psychologist, 44*, 578-580.

Palys, T. S. (1984). A content analysis of sexually explicit videos in British Columbia. *Working Papers on Pornography and Prostitution* (Research Report #15). Ottawa, Canada: Department of Justice.

Palys, T. S. (1986). Testing the common wisdom: The social content of video pornography. *Canadian Psychology, 27*(1), 22-35.

Peat, Marwick, & Partners. (1984, October 22). Working papers on pornography and prostitution, Report #6. *A National Population Study of Prostitution and Pornography.* Ottawa, Canada: Department of Justice.

Pickard, C. (1982). A perspective on female responses to sexual material. In M. Yaffe & E. C. Nelson (Eds.), *The influence of pornography on behavior* (pp. 91-117). London: Academic Press.

Press, A., Namuth, T., Agrest, S., Gander, M., Lubenow, G. C., Reese, M., Friendly, D. T., & McDaniel, A. (1985, March 18). The war against pornography. *Newsweek*, pp. 58-66.

Prince, S. R. (1987). *Power, pain, and pleasure in pornography: A content analysis of pornographic feature films, 1972-1985.* Unpublished doctoral dissertation, University of Pennsylvania, Philadelphia, PA.

Rimmer, R. H. (1986). *The X-rated videotape guide.* New York: Harmony.

Russell, D. E. H. (1988). Pornography and rape. A causal model. *Political Psychology, 9*, 41-73.

Scott, D. A. (1985). *Pornography: Its effects on the family, community and culture.* Washington, DC: The Child and Family Protection Institute.

Senn, C. Y. (1985). *A comparison of women's reactions to non-violent pornography, violent pornography, and erotica.* Unpublished master's thesis, University of Calgary, Canada.

Shaw, D. A. (1986, August). New kid on the block: Video stores brought pornography uptown. Will communities stand for it? *Video Store*, pp. 40-42.

Slade, J. W. (1984). Violence in the hard-core pornographic film: A historical survey. *Journal of Communication, 34*(3), 148-163.

Snitow, A. (1985). Retrenchment versus transformation: The politics of the antipornography movement. In V. Burstyn (Ed.), *Women against censorship* (pp. 107-120). Vancouver, British Columbia: Douglas & McIntyre.

Special Committee on Pornography and Prostitution. (1985). *Report of the Special Committee on Pornography and Prostitution.* Ottawa, Canada: Canadian Government Publishing Centre.

Stauffer, J., & Frost, R. (1976). Explicit sex: Liberation or exploitation? Male and female interest in sexually-oriented magazines. *Journal of Communication, 26*(1), 25-30.

Steele, D. G., & Walker, C. E. (1976). Female responsiveness to erotic films and the "ideal" erotic film from a feminine perspective. *Journal of Nervous and Mental Disease, 162*, 266-273.

Steinem, G. (1980). Erotica and pornography: A clear and present difference. In L. Lederer (Ed.), *Take back the night: Women on pornography* (pp. 35-39). New York: William Morrow.

Stengel, R. (1986, July 21). Sex busters: A Meese commission and the Supreme Court echo a new moral militancy. *Time*, pp. 12-22.

Stoller, R. (1976). Sexual excitement. *Archives of General Psychiatry, 33*, 899-909.

Tamborini, R., Zillmann, D., & Bryant, J. (1984). Fear and victimization: Exposure to television and perceptions of crime and fear. In R. N. Bostrom (Ed.), *Communication yearbook 8* (pp. 492-513). Beverly Hills, CA: Sage.

Weaver, J. B. (1987). Effects of portrayals of female sexuality and violence against women on perceptions of women (Doctoral dissertation, Indiana University). *Dissertation Abstracts International, 48*(10), 2482-A. (University Microfilms No. DA8727475).

Weaver, J. B. (1988, November). *A content analysis of ten commercially successful "teenage slasher" horror films.* Paper presented at the Speech Communication Association annual meeting, New Orleans, LA.

Weaver, J. B. (in press). The impact of exposure to horror film violence on perceptions of women: Is it the violence or an artifact? In B. Austin (Ed.), *Current research in film* (Vol. 5). Norwood, NJ: Ablex.

Weaver, J. B., Masland, J. L., & Zillmann, D. (1984). Effect of erotica on young men's aesthetic perception of their female sexual partners. *Perceptual and Motor Skills, 58*, 929-930.

Wilson, W. C. (1978). Can pornography contribute to the prevention of sexual problems? In C. B. Qualls, J. P. Wincze, & D. H. Barlow (Eds.), *The prevention of sexual disorders: Issues and approaches* (pp. 159-179). New York: Plenum.

Winick, C. (1985). A content analysis of sexually explicit magazines sold in an adult bookstore. *Journal of Sex Research, 21*, 206-210.

Zillmann, D. (1985, September). *Effects of repeated exposure to nonviolent pornography.* Presented to the U.S. Attorney General's Commission on Pornography in hearings at Houston, TX.

Zillmann, D. (1989a). Effects of prolonged consumption of pornography. In D. Zillmann & J. Bryant (Eds.), *Pornography: Research advances and policy considerations* (pp. 127-157). Hillsdale, NJ: Lawrence Erlbaum Associates.

Zillmann, D. (1989b). Pornography research and public policy. In D. Zillmann & J. Bryant (Eds.), *Pornography: Research advances and policy considerations* (pp. 387-403). Hillsdale, NJ: Lawrence Erlbaum Associates.

Zillmann, D., & Bryant, J. (1982). Pornography, sexual callousness, and the trivialization of rape. *Journal of Communication, 32*(4), 10-21.

Zillmann, D., & Bryant, J. (1984). Effects of massive exposure to pornography. In N. M. Malamuth & E. Donnerstein (Eds.), *Pornography and sexual aggression* (pp. 115-138). Orlando, FL: Academic Press.

Zillmann, D., & Bryant, J. (1986). Shifting preferences in pornography consumption. *Communication Research, 13,* 560-578.

Zillmann, D., & Bryant, J. (1987). Pornography and behavior: Alternative explanations. A reply. *Journal of Communication, 37*(3), 189-192.

Zillmann, D., & Bryant, J. (1988a). Effects of prolonged consumption of pornography on family values. *Journal of Family Issues, 9,* 518-544.

Zillmann, D., & Bryant, J. (1988b). Pornography's impact on sexual satisfaction. *Journal of Applied Social Psychology, 18,* 438-453.

Zillmann, D., & Bryant, J. (1988c). The methods and merits of pornography research: A response. *Journal of Communication, 38*(2), 185-192.

Zillmann, D., & Bryant, J. (Eds.). (1989). *Pornography: Research advances and policy considerations.* Hillsdale, NJ: Lawrence Erlbaum Associates.

Zillmann, D., & Weaver, J. B. (1989). Pornography and men's sexual callousness toward women. In D. Zillmann & J. Bryant (Eds.), *Pornography: Research advances and policy considerations* (pp. 95-125). Hillsdale, NJ: Lawrence Erlbaum Associates.

CHAPTER

15

The Social Psychology of Watching Sports: From Ilium to Living Room

Peter B. Crabb
West Chester University
Jeffrey H. Goldstein
University of Utrecht and Temple University

The division of labor in Western sports has usually, but not always, fallen loosely into two roles, player-contestants and spectators. The historical course of spectator roles and changes (if any) in the behavior of spectators indicates that sports spectatorship appeared about 5,000 years ago in the cosmopolitan cultures of the Mediterranean and Middle East. In this chapter, we explore the development of spectatorship through the ages, report on recent empirical investigations into the social psychology of watching sports, and make some speculations about the function of sports in everyday life, especially as sports enters interpersonal transactions and conversation.

HISTORICAL OVERVIEW OF SPORTS SPECTATORSHIP

What little is known of sports in Western cultures prior to the high civilizations of Greece and Rome comes from pictorial representations of sports-like activities in Egyptian tombs, Cretian frescoes, Etrurian graves, and painted pottery from Sumeria and Assyria. These activities were generally combative or martial, like boxing, wrestling, fencing, and archery in Old Kingdom Egypt. Or they were demonstrations of agility and courage, like the bull-leaping and bull-fighting of the Minoan culture of Crete.

Just who participated in early sports is not certain. A Minoan fresco, however, shows what appears to be a spectators' box in which well-dressed, presumably aristocratic women watch events. It is not known where such events were held and how spectators behaved, but it has been speculated that the functions of sports events was to consolidate the power of leaders, thus serving political, religious, and military ends (Mandell, 1984). This integrative function of sports apparently flourished well into Homeric Greece (ca. 900-700 B.C.).

Greece and Rome

In *The Iliad* (1950), Homer described games held during the seige of Troy around 1000 B.C. In honor of the spirit of Patroclus, the Achaen chieftain killed by Hector, the Trojan prince, an arena was constructed around a stone circle and monument. The artistocratic Greek warriors took turns competing while their colleagues and armies looked on—all men except for captured Trojan women who were offered as prizes. The contests included chariot racing, boxing, wrestling, running, spear fighting, discus throwing, archery, and javelin throwing.

Homer described betting and heated arguments among spectators about the outcomes of contests, as well as intervention in one game to prevent the contestants from killing one another. As for an aesthetic appreciation of the strength and skill of the contestants, Homer wrote that "the spectators were lost in admiration" (pp. 435-436). As with the earlier Egyptians and early Celts in Britain, the spectacle of sport served to amplify status and consolidate alliances (Baker, 1982).

The Olympic games were first held around the 8th century B.C. The first stadium was built at Olympia two centuries later. Participants in the games were probably all males, as were the spectators because the games were an expression of the Hellenic value of male athleticism. Indeed, the sexual segregation of Greek society excluded women from any opportunity to observe sacred athletic festivals, except for games in honor of Hera, which were played and observed by women (although officiated by men).

Evidence for the behavior of spectators at these events indicates that they may have been as unruly as sports fans of any era. There was a prohibition against bringing wine into the arena at Delphi, and "bouncers" with whips and truncheons were employed to control the crowds (Guttmann, 1986).

A central function of athletic events appears to have been to bolster community pride and identity. Unruly Greek spectators were once goaded by a "hometown" boxer named Clitomachus in mid-fight when they cheered for his Egyptian opponent. Taken with Clitomachus's eloquent speech about community pride, the crowd adjusted its sentiments and cheered the native son on to defeat the Egyptian (Guttmann, 1986).

Games during the early Roman era were held in wooden stadia, which tended to collapse under the weight of the spectators. The burgeoning wealth of the Empire and a steadfast dedication to spectator sports eventually enabled the construction of stone stadia, the most famous of which is the Flavian amphitheater or "Colosseum," completed in 80 A.D. and seating 50,000. Entrance to these stadia was by admission charge, and seating was arranged by social status and communal membership.

Gladiators were usually slaves, criminals, or prisoners of war, and the norm for Roman sports was for free men and women to enjoy the performance of slaves, the reverse of the arrangement in Hellenic Greece. Women were well represented in the arena crowds. In fact, the remains of at least one woman was found in the gladiator quarters in ash-covered Pompeii (Guttmann, 1986).

Violence among spectators was relatively absent in the Roman arena, but instances of disorder at the games in Pompeii led to the prohibition of further games there. Following a game at Antioch in 507 A.D., one faction of spectators, the "Greens," rampaged through the town and burned down a synagogue in the fracas. But the worst riot on record was at Constantinople in 532 A.D., when supporters of the "Blues" and "Greens," usually at odds, joined forces and rioted for nearly a week. They liberated prisoners from jail, called for reappointment of government officials, and even named themselves a new emperor. The riot was put down by Legionnaires in a blood bath that claimed an estimated 30,000 lives (Guttmann, 1986). Interestingly, the extent to which the games were violent appears to be negatively correlated with spectator violence. The most violent spectator riots were in response to chariot races and not to the bloody combative games.

In contrast to the functions of Greek games, the early Roman arena sports were primarily religious. The symbolic "death" of defeat in the Greek games was replaced in Roman society by actual death in the name of the gods. This characteristic of Roman sports resembled the Aztec and Mayan ball games in the Americas, where to win was often to be sacrificed (Baker, 1982; Guttmann, 1986).

Medieval Europe

Following the dissolution of the Roman Empire there is little evidence of spectator sports in Europe until the 12th century. Several types of ball games were popular, including stick-and-ball games called *la soule* or *choule* in France, *pall mall* in Scotland, and *cambuca* and *bandy* in England and Wales. Medieval football was also common, called *calcio* in its Italian version, and *knappan* in Wales.

Ball games were generally associated with religious holidays, and were sponsored by (and played by) local clerics. Football games were sometimes played between entire communities, so that there were no spectators: everyone was a player. In Italy, *calcio* was played in city piazzas between well-dressed teams comprised of 27 aristocratic young men and observed by noblemen and noblewomen.

Some exclusively aristocratic games comprise what we know as the tournament, combative events originally held in open fields and "played" by often large numbers of knights. What spectators there were on the skirts of these mock battlefields were not distinct from the aristocratic participants because they were likely to join in and become participants on impulse. By the 16th century, the tournament had assumed the format made familiar to us by Sir Walter Scott. As the tournament became less deadly and more civilized, spectators increased in number and were often seated on wooden stands built especially for the occasion. Spectators were seated by aristocratic rank, and women were in wide attendance. In fact, as the popular image of the days of chivalry suggests, women were often the *raison d'etre* for the competition, and it was of great value for aristocratic ladies to be "seen" socially at these events.

Spectator violence was not unknown at tournaments. A riot at Boston Fair, England, in 1288 resulted in the partial burning of the town. In Basel in 1376, spectators were accidentally trampled by mounted noblemen, setting off a rampage that left several knights dead (Guttmann, 1986).

Pre-Modern Developments

Except for a brief period of Puritan censorship in 17th-century England, spectator sports flourished in Europe through the 19th century. In addition to ball games and combative sports, spectator-centered animal sports were quite popular, both at the race track and in the pit. These "blood sports" included cockfighting, dogfighting, bearbaiting, and bullbaiting, and they were held in pits or "gardens" surrounded by stands. The events were frequented by males of all social strata, and gambling was routine. Outcry against the brutality of these events and the effects they allegedly had on young people eventually led to their prohibition in the 1840s.

By contrast, horse racing emerged as the biggest business spectator sport since the Roman games. Originally an occupation of upper class men in England and North America, the races came to express the growing democratization of sports in the 19th century. Race tracks were enclosed around 1875, turnstiles were installed, and admission charged. Crowds of up to 100,000 were recorded at large tracks like Epsom and Ascot. Although the ale flowed freely and fistfights sometimes erupted, the staid scene satirized in *My Fair Lady* seems to have been the norm.

Racetracks were the settings for other events, including boxing. Boxers were both men and women, and the sport was popular among the lower classes and some aristocrats, but deplored by the reformist middle class in England. Spectators sometimes broke into fights among themselves, and were known to attack the opponents in the ring.

Although spectators at cricket matches were originally quite unruly, by the 19th century the bucolic image of entire communities turned out for gentlemanly competition was realized. Matches on the village green in both England and the United States sometimes went on for 2 or 3 days. Everyone in the community played or watched, including women. Eligibility to play cut across class boundaries, the only real discrimination made being age. Indeed, one's first cricket game was a sort of rite of passage, especially for adolescent males.

Just as baseball has been indicted as American "internationalism" (Voigt, 1976), cricket became emblematic of British imperialism into the 20th century. Spectators in such far-flung colonies as India and the British West Indies were segregated by race and class, with the Governor and other dignitaries seated in a position of dominance in the grandstands, above "the native rabble." In Australia, lower class spectators often caused ruckuses at matches as demonstrations of their contempt for the rigid class system.

Even by the 19th century, spectator sports had achieved complete secularization, codification of rules, and explicit roles for players and spectators, both written and unwritten. Sports came to be institutionalized: Clubs, leagues, and associations embraced almost all sports events. English public schools adopted sports as part of the curriculum. Sportsmanship and fair play became dominant themes in schools and in juvenile literature. American universities instituted collegiate sports, including track and field, football, and basketball. (Baseball, a derivative of the English game of rounders, never became especially popular among colleges and universities, but remained a people's sport.)

The alliance between sports and commercial interests that is the hallmark of contemporary professional sports was established by the early 20th century. Stadia were erected in major cities as well as at universities, and admission was regulated by ticket charges and turnstiles. Yet probably the most significant development in the shaping of modern sports has been the absorption of sports by the mass media.

Contemporary Mediated Sports

The rise of sports journalism began with the appearance of sports pages in newspapers. Hundreds of single-sport magazines and newspapers came to be published in Europe and the Americas. Publishers often sponsored events, upon which they then reported to their readership. Unruliness at sporting events was publicly condemned in the papers, and sterling sportsmanlike behavior was acclaimed. Increased news coverage of disorder at sporting events aroused fear of being victimized by spectator violence, and thus "raised" the collective consciousness about proper conduct at the track or stadium.

In contrast to this "civilizing process" (Elias, 1978), the emerging mass media also unwittingly contributed to spectator violence. The first media-influenced debacle was on July 4, 1910, when the notorious Black boxer Jack Johnson took on the aging "great White hope," James J. Jeffries, in Reno, Nevada. The fight was tainted with racial vindictiveness, and as news of Johnson's easy victory on a 15th-round knockout was wired around the country to telegraph offices and newspaper desks, racial conflicts broke out in at least 50 cities. Eight deaths were reported, and the showing of the motion pictures of the fight was banned by Congress (Baker, 1982).

Although the print media could publicize events in advance, which fostered anticipation of the big fight, race, or game, the outcome could not be reported until the next day at the earliest. The new telecommunications eliminated the time lag in spectatorship and changed a number of other structural features of viewing sports as well.

The advent of network sports broadcasting over radio in 1921 signalled two major developments: expansion of audience size and geographical and social distribution, and simultaneity of experience. By 1927, an estimated 50 million listeners were tuned in to the second Dempsey–Carpentier fight, most presumably in the privacy of their own homes. Guttmann (1986) observed that radio permitted immediate celebration in the event of a home team victory, and an attendant increase in identification with city and university teams. McPhail and Miller (1973) have shown how the immediacy of radio coverage contributed to the eruption of violence following a home team's arrival back in town after a victorious away game.

Especially in the United States, broadcast sports found a ready bedfellow in big business. Ford Motor Company, for example, bought the broadcast rights to the 1934 World Series for $100,000 (Guttmann, 1986). By the end of World War II, all major league baseball clubs were associated with broadcast sponsors, with the Gillette Safety Razor Company taking the lead, while brewers and other male-directed commercial interests followed closely behind. The radio listener's role as sports enthusiast became interwoven with the role of consumer.

In Europe, state-controlled broadcast interests began experimenting with television on a large scale in the mid-1930s. The first televised sports event was the 1936 Berlin Olympics, which were transmitted to "TV locales" throughout the city of Berlin itself. In the United States, sports television premiered on May 17, 1939, with the broadcast of a Columbia–Princeton baseball game by an NBC station in New York City. About 200 television sets were operating in the New York area at the time (Rader, 1984).

Televised sports events must have been satisfying because actual attendance at events plummeted. A glut of televised boxing matches during the 1940s and 1950s contributed to a drop by as much as 80% in attendance at Madison Square Garden, and attendance at British football matches dropped from 41 million in 1948-1949 to less than 19 million in 1982-1983 (Guttmann, 1986). Television nearly destroyed baseball's minor leagues, local boxing clubs, and small college football. Even the major leagues were not immune. The Cleveland Indians, an outstanding team that televised most of their home games, lost 67% in home attendance between 1948 and 1956 (Calhoun, 1981). To combat this trend, Los Angeles Rams owner Dan Reeves invented the infamous "local blackout" (Baker, 1982). Home games were not broadcast locally in order to coax area fans out of their living rooms and neighborhood taverns and back to the stadium—as paying ticket-holders.

On the other hand, television created a nationwide, and later worldwide, market for major and minor sports. The Polish sociologist Wohl noted that "it is precisely television which in an unbelievably short time managed to transform people, who so far had been most indifferent in regard to sport, completely unaware of its role and significance, into its ardent adherents" (cited in Calhoun, 1981, p. 112).

Operating on the assumption that sports are intrinsically interesting to viewers, and that they attract large audiences, television networks began buying exclusive broadcast rights. The commercial success of the venture is told in very round figures: in 1964, NBC purchased the rights to the Tokyo Olympics for $600,000, whereas in 1984 ABC bought the rights to the Los Angeles Olympic Games for $225 million. Sponsors of the 1984 broadcasts paid up to $520,000 per minute for advertising time. In 1982 the NFL sold 5 years' of Super Bowl rights to all three major networks for a stultifying $2 billion (Guttmann, 1986).

Professional teams came to be associated with favorable market sectors, and sports gradually began to lose their community characteristics. The first clear intrusion of the television marketplace in professional sports came when the Dodgers moved from Brooklyn to the lucrative and untapped Los Angeles market. Eventually, teams even took the names of market sectors rather than local communities: Minnesota Vikings, California Angels, New England Patriots. The spectator market was expanded and divided among sports interests by the late 1960s. An agreement between collegiate and professional football standardized the scheduling of college games on Saturdays, while NFL and AFL games were played on Sundays, and professional leagues eventually pushed out into "Monday Night Football."

Rules for football, baseball, and basketball were changed in the 1970s to favor dramatic offensive action, thus enhancing spectator appeal and fitting more efficiently into the requirements of television programming. Rules and schedule changes have continued through the 1980s. Baseball includes more night games and World Series play begins on a weekend. The pitcher's mound was lowered from 15 to 10 inches, thus making the curve and slider effective pitches. In 1973, the designated hitter was instituted. Less substantial changes include the addition of color to uniforms and the building of more symmetrical ball parks. In basketball, rule changes were designed to facilitate scoring, as with the 24-second clock. National Football League goal posts were moved back to the endline, kickoffs begin at the 35-yard line rather than at the 40, and the penalty for offensive holding was reduced from 15 yards to 10 yards. Sudden death overtimes were instituted and schedules were arranged so that the better teams (and, broadcasters hope, those in the more lucrative New York and California markets) play one another most often. Television also begat "synthetic sports," such as ABC's "Battle of the Superstars."

Guttmann (1986) wrote that, although teams, leagues, and sponsors are packaging sports for the video age, "ballpark spectators have become the equivalent of studio guests; at worst they are background, mere television prompts" (p. 141). But, as throughout the history of sports, televised sports spectators continue to be predominantly male. In a 1978 poll of Americans (Kowett, 1978), 90% of the males surveyed stated that they watch sports, compared with 75% of the women surveyed. A similar pattern holds for European viewers (Guttmann, 1986). The average age of stadium-goers has apparently decreased, whereas older enthusiasts shun the hassles of jammed highways, parking, or mass transit in favor of the comforts of home. Class distribution of televised sports viewers seems to be similar to the pre-television pattern in both the United States and Europe. Baseball continues to be "the game of the people," as does European football. American football continues to attract a more elite viewership, presumably as a vestige of its collegiate beginnings. Tennis and golf on both continents similarly appeal to more elite viewers (Guttmann, 1986).

A broad nationwide audience of eligible voters may be too attractive for politicians to dismiss. Although in some respects contemporary sports are much less politicized than those preceding the 20th century, one still finds politicians throwing out the first ball at a World Series, calling the locker rooms of winning teams, and hosting champion athletes at the White House. Indeed, the nominally nonpolitical Olympic games have been loaded with political posturing, boycotts, and terrorism (Keefer, Goldstein, & Kasiarz, 1983). Coincident with such blatant political use of sports is the conservative ideological message that often unwittingly is transmitted by sports broadcasters (Goldstein & Bredemeier, 1977; Prisuta, 1979).

On the underside of politically symbolic gestures, sociologists of sport have postulated covert social-structural functions of sports for players and spectators alike. Whether sports are viewed as positive, constructive activities, as in a functionalist perspective (Luschen & Sage, 1981), or as deceptive and oppressive, as in the neo-Marxist view (Brohm, 1978), sports are a rich confluence of political and social values.

SYSTEMATIC STUDIES OF SPORTS AND MASS MEDIA

Social scientists have examined the ways in which sports are presented in the mass media, particularly on television, from the interrelated yet conceptually distinct perspectives of reception processes on the one hand, and cognitive and behavioral effects on the other. The most systematic work in both areas is that conducted by Bryant and Zillmann and their colleagues.

Reception Factors

The question raised here concerns factors that determine or facilitate a person's attraction to sports in the first place. And further, given the ubiquity of sports — and now of 24-hour sports programming on pay-TV — what biosocial conditions influence a person's choice to watch sports at a given time? Such questions are addressed in research into a priori dispositions of viewers, including gender, attitudes, affective states, and personality factors. Accounting for such reception factors is consistent with the "uses-and-gratifications" model of communication proposed by Katz, Blumler, and Gurevitch (1974). This model assumes that humans are active agents who selectively expose themselves to, perceive, and attend to the informational stimuli, based on individual needs and dispositions. One hypothesized predisposition that has received much attention by researchers is the alleged appetite for violence in sports.

In a study by Bryant, Comisky, and Zillmann (1981) it was found that male spectators tended to enjoy NFL football telecasts more if they contained high levels of violence and roughness. The relationship between enjoyment and violence for female spectators was in the same direction as for males but was not statistically significant.

The importance of attitudes on the effects of witnessing sports violence is demonstrated in a study by Harrell (1981). Active hockey fans who were tolerant of aggression (measured in response to the question, "In your opinion should fighting be allowed to go unpenalized because it is an important part of the game?" About half the fans said "yes") were more hostile after the first and second periods of a professional hockey game than fans who were intolerant of player aggression. If spectators believe that opponents in a game despise one another, they tend to enjoy the game more, but also believe that the players' actions themselves are more hostile and competitive than if they believe the opponents are friends (Zillmann, Bryant, & Sapolsky, 1979). Not surprisingly, the evidence indicates that the predispositions and beliefs that sports fans bring with them to the event determine what effects, if any, the event itself will have on them.

Likewise, broader social norms also play a role. When sports events or sports fans have a reputation for rowdiness, as is the case with the fans of some British soccer teams, those attracted or prone to violence are more apt to attend. Hence, there is a perpetuating and self-fulfilling nature to sports violence. One reason there has been less violence by fans at American than at British football games may be because Americans tend to define a football game as a social occasion, fit for adults, children, and family tailgate picnics. This crowd heterogeneity has a dampening effect on aggression, whereas the much more homogeneous youthful male crowd at British soccer matches minimizes the informal social control that the presence of older and much younger fans would have. Further, if witnessing violence in sports were truly cathartic for observers, we might expect them to be attracted to violent events, because the consequences would be beneficial. However, a study by Russell (1986) found that attendance immediately following especially violent and nonviolent hockey matches were not significantly different.

Unlike many other students of sports, Bryant and Zillmann (1983) hold a relatively benign view of sports spectators and their apparent lust for violence. They propose that violence in sports serves neither cathartic nor self-aggrandizing functions, but instead heightens the drama of sport and acts as a cue to observers that athletes are so highly motivated to win that they are often willing to take life-threatening risks. "Vigor and aggression serve to prove that the players 'mean business.' Therefore aggression has utility not for its own sake, but because it is the ultimate proof that the athletes are giving their all to the contest" (p. 199). Conflict is one of the proven elements in the creation of high drama, and therefore, conflict and aggression intensify the sense of drama in sport. Thus, fans may be attracted to sports where death or serious injury are immanent possibilities "not for the lust of blood per se, but because the contestants' willingness to risk serious injury and death creates the type of intensity necessary for the maximal enjoyment of the dramatic event" (p. 200). Gunter (1979, 1985) corroborated the notion that suspense and drama are more potent in attracting individuals to viewing violent programming than the violence per se.

Cognitive and Behavioral Effects

The second focus of research has been on a rather different set of questions than that of reception processes. What are of interest from this perspective are the cognitive and behavioral effects of viewing sports. One central question in this area is whether viewing sports promotes aggressiveness in spectators.

Of course, it is not the actual degree of violence in a game but the viewers' perceptions of violence that are apt to influence their enjoyment of a contest. Comisky, Bryant, and Zillmann (1977) found that broadcast commentary is capable of altering the observer's perception of roughness. They selected videotaped examples of extremely rough and of normal play in professional ice hockey games and presented them to subjects with or without broadcast commentary. The subjects rated the degree of roughness in each segment. Comisky et al. found that in the normal action condition, commentary stressing roughness of play made the plan seem even rougher than the depicted rough play. In the rough action condition, the commentary ignoring roughness made rough play appear less rough and more normal. Thus, commentary can alter perceptions of violence in play. Finally, in their study, Comisky et al. reported that the entertainment value followed the degree to which play was perceived to be rough.

Although sportscasters may emphasize or de-emphasize rough play in their comments, it happens that other remarks about the participants may also influence the spectators' level of enjoyment of broadcast sports. Bryant, Brown, Comisky, and Zillmann (1982) examined enjoyment of a televised tennis match as a function of commentary about the relationship between the two players involved. The commentary was altered so that it appeared the players either liked, hated, or had no particular feelings toward each other. Compared with presenting the players as the best of friends or not specifying their affective relationship, the commentary stressing enmity between them made the match appear to be more hostile and intense. Spectators who thought the opponents hated one another reported significantly greater enjoyment from watching the match than did viewers believing the players to be good friends. A study by Berkowitz and Alioto (1973) exposed college students, who had first been angered, to a football or boxing film. Some subjects were informed by the experimenter that the athletes were seeking revenge for previous insults or that they were professionals simply doing their jobs. Students who believed that the athletes were seeking revenge were subsequently more aggressive than others.

Russell (1983) noted that studies of exposure to actual violent incidents in sports find the same effects as laboratory experiments using film or videotape instances of sports violence. That is, the mass media effects mirror "real-world" effects. Neither the mass-mediated nor the real-life situation provides evidence of aggression catharsis. However, we know from the studies reviewed earlier that sportscasters' commentary and other features of mass media may influence the perception, and subsequently the effects of broadcast sports. If sportscasters speak favorably of violence, as they often do (Bryant & Zillmann, 1983), then observers are more apt to learn and perhaps perform violent behaviors than if the same violence is witnessed without commentary or with remarks that condemn violence. So there is reason to suspect that the aggressive effects of watching televised sports violence may exceed those of witnessing such events in person. On the other hand, because television viewing often takes place in relative social isolation, the milling and arousal associated with large crowds at sporting events are absent in the case of mass-mediated spectatorship.

There are some benign interpretations of spectator violence. Much group violence at sporting events follows what fans perceive to be unfair or inequitable action on the playing field: a referee makes a bad call, a player unnecessarily injures an opponent, or a winning horse is disqualified from a race. Mark, Bryant, and Lehman (1983) suggested that in such cases, fan violence may be seen as a response to injustice. In this interpretation, fan violence stems from a sense of fair play and not from any thirst for blood. Because sports fans have few or no acceptable channels for expressing grievances or disapproval, violence becomes a form of communication. Furthermore, the catharsis-like feelings reported by some fans may result from the restoration of justice or equity following the demonstration of their disapproval. Likewise, fighting among athletes may be interpreted in terms of restoring equity, and in some instances may even have a ritual or stereotypic quality that permits athletes to consider themselves nonviolent (Colburn, 1985).

Much of the mythology of sports violence is based on folk wisdom concerning emotions, particularly negative emotions such as anger and hostility. The beliefs that body-contact sports produce healthier and less violent individuals, and that these sports are also beneficial to society, are based on the notion that direct expression is an effective means of dealing with anger and hostility. Evidence well known to social scientists suggests that this is not the case.

Social Darwinism and the Folklore of Emotion

Part of the cultural baggage we "inherit" in the Western world is a set of beliefs about emotion. This includes the beliefs that emotions are uncontrollable, internally generated determinants of actions, and that many emotions, particularly negative ones such as anger, anxiety, and hostility, are more "primitive" than positive emotions, like love and joy. This belief system views negative emotions as inherited from our ancient forebears, and in this sense their display is often regarded as less than human. We have not tried here to trace the origins of such beliefs, but can speculate that they stem from theological debate about the essential nature of humankind in relation to other species. This bolstered the belief in a hierarchy of species and subspecies, such that those who display negative emotions must, by definition, be closer to our more primitive ancestors.

Social science research is consistent in finding that witnessing or participating in sports violence teaches and stimulates further violence (Goldstein, 1988; Russell, 1983). There is little doubt among social scientists that engaging in and observing violence in sports teaches violence. They do not purge the individual athlete or spectator of any aggressive "impulses." In fact, athletes in aggressive sports have four times the rate of hypertension as other athletes, engage in more violence off the field than athletes in other sports and nonathletes, and, among college athletes, visit college mental health clinics more frequently than nonathletes (Yeager, 1979). Furthermore, there is no evidence indicating that sports violence is particularly efficacious. Volkamer (1972) reported that soccer teams with lower league standings engaged in the most aggression. Russell and Drewery (1976) found that members of soccer teams near, but not in, first place, tended to use the most aggression. These two studies find that the lowest incidence of aggression occurs among teams in first place (Cox, 1986).

It is noteworthy that in the face of highly consistent evidence to the contrary, so many people, athletes and sports fans alike, persist in the belief that body-contact sports are healthy outlets for pent-up hostility. A journalist writing a story on violence among sports fans asked us to name a reputable psychologist or sociologist who believed that violence in sports was cathartic for athletes or fans. We could not think of a single active researcher who holds such an opinion (Goleman, 1985). Yet there are countless individuals who adhere to the folk belief that sports violence is cathartic.

A central belief underlying the popular view that sports can be cathartic is the notion that aggression is a universal drive that everyone possesses. Aggression is frequently spoken of as a finite entity, like money, whose expenditure reduces its residual quantity. "Letting off steam," "getting it out of your system," and considering sports as "safety valves" are popular expressions reflecting this belief. If an individual has 10 units of aggression and expresses 3 units at a hockey game, this position assumes that the person has 7 units left. But there is little evidence to suggest that aggression operates in anything like this fashion. Rather than conceiving of aggression as a finite quantity, a better analogy is to compare aggression with the expression of love. No one believes that if a man has 10 units of love for his wife, the expression of 3 units leaves him with a balance of 7. Indeed, the expression of emotional behavior is frequently paradoxical in that it is not diminished through expression. It is likely that a man will have more than 10 units of love if he expresses 3 units toward his wife. And try as he might, he will be unable to rid himself of his love for his wife by expressing it. Likewise, the expression of aggression does not diminish the capacity of the aggressor for subsequent aggression (except to the extent that temporary fatigue sets in following rigorous activity).

The Social Construction of Sports Talk

Much of the focus of contemporary sports studies has been on the mass media and sports. Relatively little attention has been devoted to the role of interpersonal communication concerning sports (cf. Fine, 1987). Because the literature concerning sports focuses on newspaper, radio, and television journalism, that has been a principal focus of this chapter. Despite a virtual absence of the study of interpersonal sports talk, sports are primary topics of conversation in much of the world. Therefore, we present some speculations and preliminary analyses of sports talk in the hope that this ubiquitous form of communication is explored systematically.

Sports are frequently considered safe topics of conversation, particularly among American males. Introducing the topic into conversation produces, if it does not already exist, a "nonserious" or mock-serious tone to social interaction. There is a tacit agreement not to discuss politics, the economy, or personal matters that might lead to serious conflict. Within this nonthreatening context, however, heated argument and debate may occur. Perhaps one function of such discourse is to learn and rehearse conflict-resolution strategies.

It is possible for two people to discuss sports only if they share some assumptions, experiences, or beliefs about the subject. They may disagree on particulars, but they must share a common frame of reference and a common set of experiences and concepts in order even to disagree. This implicitly agreed upon perspective provides the background against which argument may take place. Not that argument and disagreement are inevitable, but one of the functions of sports talk may be to produce a mock conflict in which argument and disagreement occur.

Sports talk itself may be interpreted as a loosely structured game, that is, a form of nonutilitarian play that produces a status hierarchy, something akin to a "winner" and a "loser." One may play a variety of roles in "sports talk," including the expert/intellectual, or aesthete, which may be played passively or assertively, and the loyalist, defender of home teams who displays unswerving allegience, tested during a losing streak or season. The noble sports fan roots always for the underdog. Discourse about sports-related violence also enables one to display the hypermasculine characteristics of adventurousness, fearlessness, and assertiveness, or the less stereotypical but (in some circles) more socially desirable traits of emotional sensitivity, intense emotional expression, and a sense of fair play.

Talk about violence generally serves to highlight and reinforce traditional values concerning violence. For example, when we condemn violent crime or the individuals who commit it, we are also proclaiming the cultural values of honesty, tranquility, and individual responsibility. If there were no important cultural beliefs involved, we would not speak of violent crime at all, indeed, we would not consider it offensive in the first place. Likewise, violent incidents in sports generate conversation precisely because cultural values enter into play. Our cultural beliefs do not merely enable us to speak of violence, they are in part what such talk is about. In sports talk we acquire, maintain, and perpetuate a belief system about aggression, justice, and fair play.

Surprisingly little has been written about the contents, frequency, or functions of sports talk of any sort, and much of that sparse literature focuses on radio and television sports commentary (Bryant, Comisky, & Zillmann, 1977; Ferguson, 1983; Prisuta, 1979; Rainville & McCormick, 1977) and on newspaper sports pages (Tannenbaum & Noah, 1959; Trujillo & Ekdom, 1985). If we begin by noting that talking about sports is primarily an activity of sports fans, then we can examine the larger literature on the psychology of sports fans for clues about the functions of sports talk.

Sloan (1979) has noted six functions that sports may serve for fans:

1. *Belonging* needs, filled by identifying with a (usually local) team.
2. A *diversion* from daily routines of work and family life.
3. Sports serve as a source of *stimulation* and excitement.
4. It has been proposed that *tension* and *aggression* may be relieved vicariously through sports.
5. Sports are a source of *entertainment.*
6. Individuals may vicariously gain a sense of *achievement* or accomplishment through the victories of their team.

Of these six, conversation centering on sports may serve identification, belonging, and achievement needs, and may provide diversion, stimulation, and entertainment. Research, however, suggests that talking about sports is unlikely to serve as any sort of aggression catharsis.

In addition to these functions, we might add, as we have already suggested, that sports provide us with an opportunity to *perpetuate cultural norms* and beliefs, and also to help *mark time.* A study by Trujillo and Ekdom (1985) suggests that normative themes that surface in sports writing include winning and losing, tradition and change, teamwork and individuality, work and play, youth and experience, and logic and luck. Issues of fair play and adjudication of disputes (Novak, 1985) also emerge in sports talk.

Sports events serve both to establish the continuity of time and to divide time into discrete units. The sports calendar is predictable from year to year, thus lending continuity to time, and specific events divide time into meaningful intervals: the World Series is played every fall, the SuperBowl in mid-winter, the Olympic Games are held quadrennially, and so forth. When winter comes can spring training be far behind?

Being a sports fan is a way of defining oneself to others. A person who presents him or herself as a yachting or squash fan defines him or herself differently from one who is a boxing or hockey fan. Although some have argued that these differences are associated with social class, it is perhaps more accurate to say that they reflect the sports fans' social reference groups.

Stone (1981) has noted that sports spectacles "are conversation-pieces, and conversations about them, before, during, and after the event bring people together in an emotional rapport" (p. 222). He noted that community studies, such as the Lynds' study of Middletown,

> confirm the assertion that sport is a collective representation passionately (if at times irrationally and irresponsibly) embraced by community members. Moreover, it is a salient part of their awareness, quite probably due to the fact that it is a focus of conversation, publicity, and in more recent times, the mass media. Finally, it is a unifying force for those communities it represents, and this is at once a consequence of the inter-community conflict it engenders and the intra-community communication network it establishes. (p. 230)

Talk about sports may thus provide individuals with practice in conflict and conflict resolution. Even two fans of the same team often reach a point of conflict over within-team issues such as the most valuable player or most interesting game. At the same time, allegiances are forged and strengthened by common support of a team.

CONCLUSION

The role of sports spectator has changed since the Classical era, having become more clearly defined. At one time, sports fans were not clearly distinguishable from athletes. They then became distinct from participants in games and later served as a prime reason for holding athletic contests. This process led to spectators being a passive audience. Eventually sports fans began to be perceived merely as consumers. The mass media both facilitated and reflected this transition. Yet being a sports fan also serves a variety of personal, interpersonal, and societal functions. Despite the occurrence of violent outbursts at or surrounding sports,

370   CRABB AND GOLDSTEIN

nonetheless, the larger and more persistent effect of the widespread existence of spectator sports is as a means of social control. Social norms are reflected in the games we play and in what we say and hear about them.

REFERENCES

Baker, W. J. (1982). *Sports in the Western world.* Totowa, NJ: Rowman & Littlefield.
Berkowitz, L., & Alioto, J. T. (1973). The meaning of an observed event as a determinant of its aggressive consequences. *Journal of Personality and Social Psychology, 28,* 206-217.
Brohm, J. M. (1978). *Sport: A prison of measured time.* London: Ink Links.
Bryant, J., Brown, D., Comisky, P. W., & Zillmann, D. (1982). Sports and spectators: Commentary and appreciation. *Journal of Communication, 32,* 109-119.
Bryant, J., Comisky, P., & Zillmann, D. (1977). Drama in sports commentary. *Journal of Communication, 27,* 140-149.
Bryant, J., Comisky, P., & Zillmann, D. (1981). The appeal of rough-and-tumble play in televised professional football. *Communication Quarterly, 29,* 256-262.
Bryant, J., & Zillmann, D. (1983). Sports violence and the media. In J. H. Goldstein (Ed.), *Sports violence* (pp. 195-211). New York: Springer-Verlag.
Calhoun, D. (1981). *Sports, culture and personality.* West Point, NY: Leisure Press.
Colburn, K., Jr. (1985). Honor, ritual and violence in ice hockey. *Canadian Journal of Sociology, 10,* 153-170.
Comisky, P., Bryant, J., & Zillmann, D. (1977). Commentary as a substitute for action. *Journal of Communication, 27* 150-152.
Cox, R. H. (1986). *Sport psychology.* Dubuque, IA: W. C. Brown.
Elias, N. (1978). *The civilizing process: The history of manners.* New York: Urizen.
Fine, G. A. (1987). *With the boys.* Chicago: University of Chicago Press.
Ferguson, C. A. (1983). Sports announcer talk: Syntactic aspects of register variation. *Language and Society, 12,* 153-172.
Goldstein, J. H. (1988). The social construction of sports violence. In J. H. Goldstein (Ed.), *Sports, games, and play* (2nd ed., pp. 319-339). Hillsdale, NJ: Lawrence Erlbaum Associates.
Goldstein, J. H., & Bredemeier, B. J. (1977). Sport and socialization: Some basic issues. *Journal of Communication, 27,* 154-159.
Goleman, D. (1985, August 13). Brutal sports and brutal fans. *The New York Times,* pp. C1, C3.
Gunter, B. (1979). Television violence and entertainment value. *Bulletin of the British Psychological Society, 32,* 100-102.
Gunter, B. (1985). Determinants of television viewing preferences. In D. Zillmann & J. Bryant (Eds.), *Selective exposure to communication* (pp. 93-112). Hillsdale, NJ: Lawrence Erlbaum Associates.
Guttmann, A. (1986). *Sports spectators.* New York: Columbia University Press.
Harrell, W. A. (1981). Verbal aggressiveness in spectators at professional hockey games: The effects of tolerance of violence and amount of exposure to hockey. *Human Relations, 34,* 643-655.
Homer (1950). *The Iliad* (E. V. Rieu, Trans.). Harmondsworth: Penguin Books.
Katz, E., Blumler, J., & Gurevitch, M. (1974). Utilization of mass communication by the individual. In J. Blumler & E. Katz (Eds.), *The uses of mass communications: Current perspectives on gratifications research* (pp. 19-32). Beverly Hills, CA: Sage.
Keefer, R., Goldstein, J. H., & Kasiarz, D. (1983). Olympic Games and warfare. In J. H. Goldstein (Ed.), *Sports violence* (pp. 183-193). New York: Springer-Verlag.
Kowett, D. (1978, August 19). TV sports. *TV Guide,* pp. 2-8.
Luschen, G., & Sage, G. H. (1981). Sport in sociological perspective. In G. Luschen & G. H. Sage (Eds.), *Handbook of social science of sport* (pp. 3-21). Champagne, IL: Stipes.
Mandell, R. D. (1984). *Sport: A cultural history.* New York: Columbia University Press.

Mark, M. M., Bryant, F. B., & Lehman, D. R. (1983). Perceived injustice and sports violence. In J. H. Goldstein (Ed.), *Sports violence* (pp. 83-109). New York: Springer-Verlag.

McPhail, C., & Miller, D. (1973). The assembling process. *American Sociological Review, 38,* 721-735.

Novak, M. (1985). American sports, American virtues. In W. L. Umphlett (Ed.), *American sport culture* (pp.). Lewisburg, PA: Bucknell University Press.

Prisuta, R. H. (1979). Televised sports and political values. *Journal of communication, 29*(1), 94-101.

Rader, B. G. (1984). *In its own image: How television has transformed sports.* New York: Macmillan.

Rainville, R. E., & McCormick, E. (1977). Extent of covert racial prejudice in pro football announcers' speech. *Journalism Quarterly, 54,* 20-26.

Russell, G. W. (1983). Psychological issues in sports aggression. In J. H. Goldstein (Ed.), *Sports violence* (pp. 157-181). New York: Springer-Verlag.

Russell, G. W. (1986). Does sports violence increase box office receipts? *International Journal of Sports Psychology, 17,* 173-182.

Russell, G. W., & Drewery, B. R. (1976). Crowd size and competitive aspects of aggression in ice hockey: An archival study. *Human Relations, 29,* 723-735.

Sloan, L. R. (1979). The function and impact of sports for fans. In J. H. Goldstein (Ed.), *Sports, games, and play* (pp. 219-262). Hillsdale, NJ: Lawrence Erlbaum Associates.

Stone, G. P. (1981). Sport as a community representation. In G. Luschen & G. Sage (Eds.), *Handbook of social science of sport* (pp. 214-245). Champagne, IL: Stipes.

Tannenbaum, P. H., & Noah, J. E. (1959). Sportuguese: A study of sports page communication. *Journalism Quarterly, 36,* 163-170.

Trujillo, N., & Ekdom, L. R. (1985). Sportswriting and American cultural values: The 1984 Chicago Cubs. *Critical Studies in Mass Communication, 2,* 262-281.

Voigt, D. Q. (1976). *America through baseball.* Chicago: Nelson-Hall.

Volkamer, N. (1972). Investigations into the aggressiveness in competitive social systems. *Sportwissenschaft, 1,* 33-64.

Yeager, R. C. (1979). *Seasons of shame.* New York: McGraw-Hill.

Zillmann, D., Bryant, J., & Sapolsky, B. S. (1979). The enjoyment of watching sport contests. In J. H. Goldstein (Ed.), *Sports, games, and play* (pp. 297-335). Hillsdale, NJ: Lawrence Erlbaum Associates, pp. 297-335.

CHAPTER

16

Perceiving and Processing Music Television

Barry L. Sherman
University of Georgia
Laurence W. Etling
University of North Carolina, Greensboro

THE EVOLUTION OF MUSIC VIDEOS

Since the advent of Music Television (MTV) on August 1, 1981, the phenomenon of rock videos has been the subject of considerable analysis and criticism. Much of the attention has focused on the visual aspect of the genre, and it has been claimed that the genealogical line of such videos could be traced through "live drama, opera, and theatre to ancient times" (Burns & Thompson, 1987, p. 10).

To fully understand the appeal of MTV to youth, however, one must look back not only to the visual arts, but also to radio and records. Rock videos are the most current manifestation of a youth culture that has developed over the past 30 years, whose emergence "has been one of the most dramatic aspects of a cultural change in American society since the adoption of motorized travel" (Snow, 1987, p. 326). It developed in the 1950s and, according to Snow:

> By the end of the next decade, youth culture was setting major fashion and music trends, but not just for itself. . . . The real story was in the aristocratic autonomy and the leisure ethic that youth culture had developed. (p. 326)

Influences Shaping Youth Culture ‹

Two distinct influences helped shape the youth culture which is manifest today in music videos generally and MTV in particular. These were rock music and radio.

Rock Music.   Rock is more than just music for teenagers; it has been referred to as "the lever by which teens came to move the world" (Fornatale & Mills, 1980, p. 37). Primarily, the rock music of the 1950s was symbolic of a clash of the values held by teens and those held by their parents because "the youth culture reflected antiadult characteristics such as hedonism and irresponsibility" (Kotarba & Wells, 1987, p. 398). Rock was the product of a union of rhythm and blues and country music, and has been described as "primitive" and reflecting "cultural needs" (Frith, 1981, p. 27). One of the earliest hits of the genre, *Rock Around the Clock,* resulted in, among other things, a mob scene on the campus of Princeton University, where it had apparently incited students' "baser passions" (Ward, Stokes, & Tucker, 1986, p. 107).

Concomitant with the development of rock music was the introduction of the 45 rpm record. This served as an efficient marketing tool for record companies, being cheaper to distribute to disc jockeys and higher in fidelity than the 78 rpm discs. It also gave teenagers control over their listening environment through the use of cheap portable phonographs. The 45 rpm records were more affordable than long-play records, which had been introduced in 1948. Teenagers looked upon the 45 as "a cachet of their generation" (Fornatale & Mills, 1980, p. 41).

Radio.   Without radio, the development of a youth culture might not have been possible, for "radio was the driving force behind the early success of rock music in middle class society" (Snow, 1987, p. 328). It was the "tribal drum," which provided a "tight tribal bond" (McLuhan, 1964, p. 264). Specifically, the radio disc jockey became the leader of the new wave, a co-conspirator in a "secret society" of young listeners (Ward et al., 1986, p. 68). Announcers such as Alan Freed and Dick Clark helped create what has been called a "mystic screen of sound," which gave teenagers privacy and "immunity" from the demands of parents (McLuhan, 1964, p. 264).

Marketing to the Youth Culture

The development of a distinct youth culture was not lost on those who wished to sell products and services to a new target market. The 45 rpm record was popularized, in large part, as a marketing tool by which record companies could effectively reach this market segment. And, of course, radio and music have been inextricably intertwined since radio's early years. Pioneer disc jockeys such as Al Jarvis could ensure a record's popularity by playing it on the air (Dexter, 1969). Fifty years after radio first demonstrated its power to sell records, the broadcast medium was found to act more in the interests of the recording industry than in the interests of the listeners it purportedly served (Rothenbuhler, 1985).

In order to reach particular demographic blocks of listeners, radio stations developed formats, or specific guidelines on the content of their broadcasts. According to Fornatale and Mills (1980):

The purpose of these formats is to enable radio stations to deliver to advertisers a measured and defined group of consumers, known as a segment. To a certain extent, then, the history of radio formats in linked loosely to the history of marketing research. (p. 61)

Specific formats, known generally as "Top 40," and "Contemporary Hit Radio" were designed to appeal to the youth culture and its subgroups. The youth market was particularly appealing to advertisers both because of its size (the postwar "baby boom") and its spending power. In 1956, for example, there were about 13 million American teenagers, with an income exceeding $7 billion a year; the sale of 45 rpm records alone was valued in 1960 at $75 million (Ward et al., 1986). Teenagers were also targeted by advertisers because "they constituted the largest and most easily co-opted part of the audience" (Peterson & Davis, 1978, p. 171).

Radio has been nothing if not adept at catering to the tastes of America's youth. The 1960s brought the advent of progressive rock, made possible by the expansion of the FM band. The primacy of the 45 rpm record gave way to the 12-inch, 33⅓ rpm long-playing record, or LP. In the 1970s, disco formats were constructed to cater to afficionados of that short-lived phenomenon. By the end of the 1970s, the length of songs released for radio airplay increased and punk and new wave music began "recharging the voltage for a bored, restless youth in a more expansive economy" (Mooney, 1980, p. 190).

The Emergence of MTV

MTV was developed out of radio formatting to appeal to specific audience groups.

Run on the same format and "clock" as a radio station, MTV is always in the air . . . Like a radio station, it plays a selection of songs and has a small roster of personalities who introduce the songs. Like a radio station, it gets its songs free from record companies, who hope that the exposure will sell records. (Levy, 1983, p. 30)

Although MTV added the dimension of video, it was not intended (at least initially) to be consumed as *television*. According to one MTV executive, the service was not designed "on the premise that audiences will turn on the channel and watch it for hours at a time," but rather it was expected that it would be used "as if it were a radio station" (Wolfe, 1983, p. 42). This may not seem surprising as Robert Pittman, one of the prime movers behind MTV, was a former radio program director. In fact, the staff that put MTV on the air in 1981 was composed mostly of people with radio or record industry backgrounds, not television executives ("MTV latest," 1981).

Just as radio serves the interests of the music and recording industries by providing an effective means of exposing new product, so MTV acts largely as a marketing tool for musical artists and record companies. In addition, it has proven to be extremely effective for delivering the youth audience for advertisers of almost any product. According to the innovators behind MTV, the channel was designed to reach the 12- to 34-age group that was not being tapped by other media, especially print (Gardner, 1983). Some media buyers, those who make decisions as to where advertising should be placed to reach specific audiences, have described the music channel as the "ideal broadcast medium for reaching teens and young adults" (Paskowski, 1985, p. 67).

According to Pittman, however, the music industry was more eager to embrace MTV at the start than were cable operators or advertisers because they could see its potential as a marketing tool (Poskowski, 1985). In the same manner that radio stations effectively serve as conduits to the public for the recording industry, so MTV was seen as an ideal vehicle for record and recording artist promotion. As the 45 rpm record became the standard means of new product release to radio stations, so the music video proved to be a primary method of reaching an important segment of the youth culture.

MTV Segmentation Strategies

MTV was designed to appeal to a somewhat broader demographic audience than is usually targeted by radio stations. According to Marshall Cohen, the man responsible for gathering research data upon which MTV's programming was based, the original concept study explored the viewing habits of 12- to 40-year-olds (Denisoff, 1987). Cohen has referred to MTV's programming not as "narrowcasting" to a tightly defined audience, but rather as "coalition programming."

> What we tried to do was to figure out what music we could play, what people would like, and what music we could not play, or they would switch the dial . . . I call that sort of coalition programming. You can build up the coalition, but don't violate what they expect from you, because you'll lose them. (Denisoff, 1987, p. 30)

Because MTV was available only on cable, the demographic profile of its viewers was necessarily skewed toward the more upscale cable subscribers. Cohen described the MTV viewer as being essentially "the 23, 24 years old educated, affluent, suburban viewer" (Denisoff, 1987, p. 31). Subsequent research by MTV indicated that this audience was, in fact, being reached effectively, with 83% of the MTV audience being between 12 and 34 years of age, and with a median household income of $30,000 thousand (Gardner, 1983). MTV has been found to be the cable channel most watched by college students, an average of 2.5 hours per week ("BA, BS," 1988). Those who watch MTV do so, on average, more than 4 days per week, and "are the most frequent viewers of music video programming" (Shalett, 1988, p. 44). In addition, MTV viewers watch their channel more than do viewers of VH-1, a second music video channel aimed at an older demo,

"Video Soul" on Black Entertainment Television, or country music videos aired on the Nashville Network (Shalett, 1988).

Criticism of MTV Programming

Critics of MTV have been numerous. Some of the sharpest attacks have come from those who believe that because of its marketing roots, the channel has "sold out" to the record companies who supply the videos, or to the advertisers who use the channel to reach the youth market. Hartman (1987), for example, has referred to MTV as "AD-TV." Levy (1983), charged that

> Profit-making television creates an unreal environment to get people into what is called a "consumer mode"; MTV, as its executives boast, is pure environment. . . . It is the ultimate junk-culture triumph. (p. 33)

Gehr (1983) claimed that its essential role as a marketing tool means that MTV is "changing the way in which we hear records and radio" because it is a "self-reflecting medium for narcissists of a limited age bracket" (p. 37).

Others have stated that the commercially oriented nature of MTV means that musical artists may have to adapt their styles in order to ensure acceptance by the music channel (Levine, 1983). Homogenization of rock music is feared because MTV is unlikely to play videos that would not be appealing to the upscale audience who views it. Indeed, much early criticism of MTV focused on a perceived lack of exposure of Black performers, although additional airplay was later given to Black artists due to a widely policized backlash led by jazz performer Herbie Hancock (Levine, 1983). In general, music critics in the print media have been most critical of MTV, possibly because they were uncomfortable dealing with a new idiom (Denisoff, 1985).

THE NEW VIEWERS AND THE NEW MUSIC

It has been said that "recording is a cultural artifact that is an analogue for a symbolic communication" (Kealy, 1982, p. 100). If so, we may then study the nature of the communication by examining the analogue, and an examination of the phenomenon of music television may reveal much about not only the nature of the communication but also the receivers of the message.

The New Generation of TV Viewers

As has been noted, MTV was designed to reach the under-40 television viewer. These people differ from older viewers because they are the first members of the TV generation, or "TV babies" who grew up with television in their home

(Pittman, 1985, p. 34). According to Pittman, the TV generation processes information differently than did their parents, members of the rock-and-roll radio generation. The older viewers processed information sequentially, moving from one idea to the next in a logical manner.

> Conversely—drastically conversely—the TV generation processes information in a nonlinear manner. . . . They readily respond to more elusive *sense impressions* transferred by way of feelings, mood and emotion. (Pittman, 1985, p. 34)

One reason for the fast-paced, nonlinear look of rock videos is that the MTV generation uses time differently than did their immediate forebears.

> People are increasingly pressed for time and more assaulted with demands for their time. Now, instead of finding a *use* of leisure time, we search for the ways to *maximize* our use of limited leisure time. That means we get rid of the transitions and connections. We're looking for the meat of the information. We want what we want *immediately.* (Pittman, 1985, p. 34)

The elimination of transitions and connectors, in an effort to time-compress leisure activities, means that many rock videos take on a surrealistic appearance, one of discontinuity and disjunction (in which) "gestures, actions, and intentions are nearly always divorced from a systematic context" (Gehr, 1983, p. 39). Kaplan (1987) referred to "an excited state of expectation" that MTV generates by presenting videos that are no longer than four minutes. This "decentering experience" means that viewers are "trapped by the constant hope that the next video will finally satisfy and, lured by the seductive promise of immediate plenitude, we keep endlessly consuming short texts" (Kaplan, 1987, p. 4).

Since the "TV babies" think in a non-linear or non-sequential fashion, the task of the rock video producer is to keep their attention. As events do not generally follow each other in a logical way, there is little reason for attending to the video continuously. Thus, one producer of rock videos can observe that the first rule of making videos is to keep interest, an "obsession" that measures videos in IPMs, or ideas per minute, and compels the producer to create "movement where there isn't any (and) eliminate any visual slack" (Levy, 1983, p. 76).

MTV may have been merely the first crest of a new wave of television production techniques designed to appeal to the television-weaned generation. The head of the television productions division of Universal Television, which produced, among other programs, "Miami Vice," referred to the new audience as the "MTV" or "Sesame Street" generation. These viewers "are used to getting visually stimulated very quickly" (Dorfman, 1986, p. 8). In fact, "Miami Vice," a show popular with the MTV cohort, was referred to as "MTV cops" at its conception by Brandon Tartikoff (Waters, 1985).

Thus, as rock radio provided the "tribal drum" of the preceding generation, the rock video may supply the beat for the new "secret society"—the MTV generation. This beat, both aural and visual, catches and holds the attention with techniques borrowed from advertising and commercial production and leads to new definitions of both listening to music and watching television.

The New Music: Aural and Visual

The presentation of music both aurally and visually encounters certain physiological barriers. The eyes can receive and transmit to the brain millions of separate pieces of information simultaneously via the rods and cones of the retina. The ears, however, transmit information sequentially, as a "constantly varying series of impulses" (Masters, 1987, p. 32). This presents a challenge to the producer of a music video—the matching of aural and visual signals so that the result is identifiable at least as an artistic endeavor and at most, a coherent communication event. Ironically, music video may also point to the development of a new musical form in which, for the first time, the writer of the music does not have artistic control over the product. Although viewers may not be aware of this shift of control, the true creative force behind a video may frequently be the producer-director, not the performer or writer (Levy, 1983).

The demands of the visual medium may, in fact, detract from the music by which the creators of a song present their ideas or emotions. An artist may be forced to generate imagery that may have little to do with the actual meaning of the song (Gehr, 1983). Hirsch (1971) noted that the lyrics of pop songs are often obscure and not easily understood. According to Hirsch:

> Lyrics, generally, are treated by performers as but one of several components of the total sound. Consequently, they must be abstracted from accompanying complex and instrumental arrangements . . . by a special effort on the part of the listener. Once the lyrics are deciphered, their meanings may appear ambiguous or confusing. (p. 377)

Hirsch found that teenage rock music listeners often do not understand what the song writer or performer is trying to say, and that most teens are attracted to rock more by the overall sound than by the content of a song's lyrics. Another step removed, then, is the rock video, which imposes onto the music a visual overlay that may or may not have any direct relation to the content of the song.

Kaplan (1987) classified MTV videos into five main types—romantic, socially conscious, nihilist, classical, and postmodernist—dealing with three predominant themes—authority, love/sex, and style. According to this categorization, socially conscious videos were prevalent on the music channel during its early years, but have generally been supplanted by the postmodern video. These postmodern productions are seen as using "more pastiche, less self-reflexivity" (pp. 55-57), are ambiguous in meaning and have an increasingly nonlinear style. Although many of the videos seen on MTV certainly are clear as to meaning and visual construction, the postmodernist influence that is now dominating tends to leave the viewer insecure as to the rationality of the universe—the viewer is "decentered, perhaps confused, perhaps fixated on one particular image or image-series, but most likely unsatisfied and eager for the next video where perhaps closure will take place" (Kaplan, 1987, p. 63).

Rock Video Production Techniques

Television content is largely the creation of middle-aged adults and tends to reflect traditional American values; rock music, however, is usually the creation of younger people "who stand apart and may be at odds with adult society" (Larson & Kubey, 1983, p. 14). The rock video, then, is a unique amalgam of artistic expression and commercial endeavor—it must appeal to and hold the attention of the demographically desirable youth cohort so that viewers will attend to the commercial messages interspersed throughout the videos. At the same time, it must satisfy the viewers' expectations for meaning or artistic satisfaction. Combining aural and visual stimulation "may produce an even more involving context of media use" than music listening or television viewing alone (Rubin et al., 1986, p. 355).

Kealy (1982) noted that although millions of people enjoy listening to music, few do so in a situation of direct interpersonal contact with the musicians. The music is produced by means of a complex technological process which involves numerous people, not only in the actual production of sounds but also in distributing and promoting the product to the public. This task of personalization is more difficult in the production of music videos than in disc-recorded music because of the problem of combining the visual and aural components into a unified artistic whole.

Given the nature of the task facing them, it is perhaps not surprising that rock video producers turned to production techniques often used in television commercials. Much could be learned by music video producers from studying the techniques of commercial production. Commercials and rock videos have much in common. They are both short in length; while videos are longer than commercials, they are both significantly shorter than conventional television programs. Both forms of production also need to catch the viewer's attention quickly. According to Pittman (1985), this need to gain attention has led to the development of a "non-narrative mode" of TV advertising in which commercials "move very quickly, with quick cuts, no transitions" and which "feature music at the foreground—not the background—to create the all-important mood, a *sense impression*" (p. 34). In fact, Pittman referred to the new commercials as "non-narrative mood videos" designed to sell products (Stein, 1986, p. 16). This type of TV advertising has been called the "new wave commercial," and is closely related to the rock video.

The New Wave commercial in fact resembles silent film, with synchronous, non-diegetic background music. Actors perform in a strange matrix of nonnaturalistic place and threatening character. Impossible things happen. . . . Ostensibly unrelated images are edited together to create surprising associations. (Burns & Thompson, 1987, p. 15)

In fact, at about the time that MTV debuted, new wave television production techniques began to appear in American TV commercials, following their use in Europe several years earlier. These surrealistic productions featured "quick cuts, bands of light, optical illusion" ("New wave," 1982, p. 75).

Some commercial production techniques that have been adapted for rock videos include macro close ups, double and triple images, slow motion, "various dextrous camera moves and hallucinatory special effects" (Levine, 1983, p. 55).

Fry and Fry (1987) compared the number of different shots per minute in MTV videos with those in TV commercials and in dramatic programs. TV commercials averaged 28.33 shots per minute; conceptual rock videos (those with visual images unrelated to the lyrics) averaged 20.38 shots per minute. Although concert videos had a somewhat lower average, 19.94, commercials and videos averaged far more shots per minute than did dramas, which had a mean of only 9.95. The authors noted that the function of television drama is to engage the audience over an extended period of time and that this can be done effectively by using longer scenes. The short-form videos and commercials, on the other hand, do not have the luxury of using the extended scene format. Indeed, if Pittman's analysis of the viewing patterns of "TV babies" is correct, longer scenes would not hold the attention of the nonlinear processes of the MTV viewer and are therefore, avoided.

Burns and Thompson (1987) analyzed the conventions of rock video production and found them rife with techniques that promote fragmentation and dehumanization of the body (through extreme close-ups of body parts, especially the eyes); separation of space and time (removal from time or location of contemporary life, resulting in "strong mythic resonance"); impossible imagery (slow or fast motion, repeated sequences, animation, time-lapse photography, chromakey and matte effects, freeze frames, multiple images); shots into the bright lights (drawing viewers "toward a twilight, never-nether world of mystery, instinct, and totality").

Kaplan (1987) has noted that music video production styles vary according to the content of the music, so that nihilist videos differ from romantic ones "in their aggressive use of camera and editing; wide angle lenses, zoom shots, rapid montage typify devices used" (p. 60).

Not everyone is enamored of the techniques of rock video production. The need to grab and keep the viewer's attention "leads producers into an endless search for offbeat themes and startling images" (Levy, 1983, p. 76). Many shots have managed to become miserably tired clichés that are imitated by other rock video producers. Gehr (1983) claimed that any emotional sympathy the listener might experience from hearing the music over the radio is dissipated by the spurious imagery that is made to represent the song's meaning. Because many videos have no narrative line "there is no narrative as such within which the viewer can 'find' himself (Gehr, 1983, p. 40)."

AUDIENCE RESPONSE

Interestingly, little research has been done to investigate viewer reactions to production techniques in music video. Hall, Miller, and Hanson (1986) studied perceptions of high school and college students to various styles of videos and found some evidence of preference for those in which the visuals enhanced a portrayed storyline rather than those in which either the storyline did not match the lyrics or was totally unrelated to the lyrics.

Rubin et al. (1986) examined responses of college students to both audio and audiovisual productions of music. Music videos were seen as "more creative, rough, loud, dynamic, hot, and bold" than audio-only versions of the songs (p. 357). The researchers concluded that the combining of audio and visual may result in more complete images of the content being formed than by the audio alone. Unknown, however, is whether these more "complete" images are different from and perhaps opposed those of the audio-only condition.

Most of today's youth grow up in an electronic environment and have been said to be "located at the virtual center of an emerging technological revolution" (Ellis, 1983, p. 4). The question which has arisen with the emergence of the electronic environment is: What is the impact of the technological revolution upon those who are surrounded by it? Certainly, a concern over the effects of entertainment content is not new, and can be traced back to 16th-century England (Powell, 1985). Neither has interest in the impact of television been expressed only since the advent of rock videos. For example, Lake (1981) listed more than 500 books and articles dealing with the impact of TV on children and adolescents in the period 1976–1980 alone. However, as rock videos have become one of the principal forms of entertainment for adolescents and young adults, increasing concern has been voiced about the content of the videos and the effects of that content. This concern may be categorized into two broad areas—behavioral effects and enculturation or socialization effects.

Behavioral Effects of Music Videos

In examining the effects of music video viewing, many critics have noted a high degree of sexual and violent content, and frequent depiction of drug use. This perhaps should not be surprising if one considers that the main purpose of a video is to sell a product, either the music of the artist or the products whose commercials appear between the videos.

One explanation for the extensive use of sex and violence in videos may be the need to quickly attract the attention of the nonlinear thinking "TV babies." From this perspective, "the surest shortcut to memorable videos seems to be a liberal dose of sex, violence, or both" (Levy, 1983, p. 76). That the use of such themes is controversial is beyond doubt.

Sherman and Dominick (1986), in conducting a content analysis of more than 40 hours of music videos on three networks, found that "music videos are violent, male-oriented and laden with sexual content" (p. 92). Violence and sex were also found to be frequently linked, with more than 80% of those videos containing violence also containing sexual imagery. Perhaps more disturbing was the discovery that many videos have a strong male orientation, in that half of the women who appeared in the videos were dressed "provocatively." In another video content analysis, Brown and Campbell (1986) concluded that those videos they studied contributed to stereotyping of women "as less active, less goal-directed, and less worthy of attention" (p. 101). Vincent, Davis, and Boruszkowski (1987) found the majority of videos they studied showed women portrayed as subservient, in a condescending manner, or kept in "her place." More than half of the videos suggested female nudity or used highly seductive clothing or undergarments. McKenna (1983) said that MTV videos portray women as, among other things, "vampiric dominatrixes," "the Punk Lolita," and "Amazonian beauties." Men were also noted as frequently being portrayed one-dimensionally, often as "misunderstood toughs" (p. 66–67). Gehr (1983) suggested that many of the females in the videos are merely portrayed as "the comic-book fantasies of adolescent males" which "play to, and play with, his isolation, frustration, and loneliness" (p. 40).

In a detailed analysis of female images in rock videos, Kaplan (1987) noted that, due to the commercial nature of MTV,

> Only those female representations considered the most marketable are frequently cycled: and what is most marketable is obviously connected to dominant idealogy . . . and to the organization of symbolic order around the phallus as signifier. (p. 115)

Numerous critics contend that the depiction of sex, violence, and drug use in rock videos leads to an increasingly violent and sexist society. The National Council of Churches has warned against heavy viewing of music videos due to their frequent violent and erotic content (Powell, 1985). The American Academy of Pediatricians urged parents to restrict their children's viewing time of music videos because of "an excess of sexism, violence, substance abuse, suicides and sexual behavior" ("Concerned pediatricians," 1988, p. 4H). The press periodically contains stories regarding youths who injure themselves and others while imitating the behavior of artists featured in music videos (see "Boy burns," 1988). These stories are often cited as evidence of a negative impact on young people's behavior (Powell, 1985).

The portrayal of women in music videos is disturbing to some because of the implication that in order to have power, women must rely on their sexuality (Powell, 1985). A Beverly Hills school psychologist believes that many videos glamorize the drug culture by creating role models of rock stars, some of whom are admitted drug users (Lansky, 1984).

However, critical analysis of music videos does not necessarily lead to the conclusion that there is a direct casual link to attitude or behavioral change. For example, Sherman and Dominick (1986) found that "sex in music television was more implied than overt" (p. 88), was generally portrayed in a traditional heterosexual context, and that "the rank of physical/sexual activities in music videos was exactly the same as in conventional TV" (p. 91). Walker (1987) noted that content analyses of MTV videos have not demonstrated a positive correlation between MTV viewership and harmful effects. He postulated that this is because music video violence does not occur in a "media vacuum"; violence is typical program content in many other forms of television besides music videos. Some psychologists and psychiatrists interviewed by Lansky (1984) expressed little concern about possible negative influences of music video viewing, seeing the content as "attention-getting" and "fantasies" that are interpreted differently by young viewers than by the adults who are critical of video content.

In examining the relationship between rock music and behavior, Leming (1987) concluded that any such link has not been clearly established. Thornton and Voigt (1984) reviewed several studies of television viewing by adolescents and their behavior, and found little evidence to support a strong casual relationship between TV viewing and subsequent negative behavioral patterns. After studying juvenile delinquency in three public schools the authors suggested that "the impact of select family, school, and peer factors exerts a strong or stronger influence on delinquency than key media variables" (p. 460). Greenfield et al. (1987) reviewed the literature regarding rock lyrics and behavior and pointed out that many studies have indicated low understanding of rock lyrics by listeners. They also noted some evidence that music videos may result in less involvement with music than when listening to the aural component alone, and that the visual aspect may, in fact, detract from the aural message. Hall et al. (1986) found confusion as to music video content, particularly when the visual did not match the lyrics, and that, among the adolescents studied, there was a preference for videos in which the visual content matched the lyrical storyline or content.

Thus, a review of the literature indicates that the evidence linking behavioral change to television or music video viewing is tenuous at best, and concern about negative behavioral outcomes resulting from rock video viewing may be misplaced.

Enculturation Effects of Music Videos

As stated by Gerbner (1973), the pervasiveness of television in most people's lives means that the medium plays a disproportionate role in the cultivation of social concepts. The premises we draw about the world and the "rules of the game of life" are a function of the medium by which our social concepts are communicated.

> A culture cultivates the images of a society. The dominant communication agencies produce the message systems that cultivate the dominant image patterns. They structure the public agenda of existence, priorities, values, and relationships. (Gerbner, 1973, p. 569)

According to Gross and Morgan (1985), television helps establish common cultural norms. It is this power of the visual medium that has aroused concern over some content of music videos. If we accept that television has at least some influence as a shaper of our culture, then we should be aware of how cultural norms are being changed, especially among youth. As noted by Leming (1987), "the very stability and existence of any society depends in large measure on the degree to which that society is able to instill in youth the shared norms and values of existing adult society" (p. 363). If the images of society presented in rock videos are at variance with societal norms, then these images may be seen as a threat to the existing norms to the extent that they might change the societal expectations or even the character of those who view the videos. The power to affect attitudes, assumptions, values, and even personality has been referred to as epistemic socialization (Bennett & Ferrell, 1987).

> The steady, ongoing cultivation of images, assumptions, and beliefs about life and society may be a more important and widespread consequence of exposure than are discrete instances of short-term change . . . The substance of the consciousness cultivated by television is not so much comprised of specific attitudes and outlooks as it is by broad, underlying assumptions about the facts of life. (Gross & Morgan, 1985, p. 222)

Whether music videos actually act as an agent of socialization is not yet clear, partly because of a paucity of research on the subject. Bennett and Ferrell (1987), in analyzing music video content, found that many videos presented images of social instability, and uncertain and ambiguous messages concerning interpersonal and social relationships. This ambiguity may result in young viewers simply becoming confused about the messages they are receiving. In a study of grade-school children, Leming (1987) discovered that, although music influenced many youngsters' way of thinking about an important topic, there was confusion regarding the content of the songs, including those seen on videos. The author concluded that for music to have a "socially significant influence on the value socialization of youth" a shared understanding of the content would be needed. In addition,

> Simply recognizing the value content of a song is no guarantee among adolescents of acceptance of that value content; youth bring to the experience of music a value framework that influences their reaction to that music. Music is filtered through

this perceptual screen and the individual's reaction results from this existing value framework. (p. 379)

From this perspective, music videos do not influence the viewer's values, but rather these values affect the viewer's perceptions of the videos. As rock videos gain an ever-increasing share of youth's attention, however, some influence might be expected and, in fact, the impact of MTV on the lifestyles of both viewers and nonviewers may be emerging.

Unlike any television phenomenon past, present and perhaps future, the 24-hour cable music channel has had a profound impact on music, television, and pop culture in America. (Thomas, 1988, p. 18)

This impact includes, among other things, changes in fashion, influences on the music played on radio stations, and the content and production techniques of movies and television programs (Thomas, 1988). Caplan (1985) referred to the violence present in many videos as typifying "the Punk and Post-Punk subculture" (p. 146).

Thus, as the 45 rpm rock 'n' roll record supplied the musical pulse for their parents' generation, so the rock video is generating the beat for today's youth. And, as the impact of rock music on the earlier generation provoked a storm of controversy, so the evolution of music video seems certain to continue to generate debate into the new decade.

REFERENCES

BA, BS, MBA and MTV. (1988, October). *Marketing and Media Decisions*, p. 144.

Bennett, H. S., & Ferrell, J. (1987). Music videos and epistemic socialization. *Youth & Society, 18*, 344-362.

Boy burns himself imitating Motley Crue video. (1988, February). *Atlanta Journal & Constitution*, p. 2A.

Brown, J. D., & Campbell, K. (1986). Race and gender in music videos: The same beat but a different drummer. *Journal of Communication, 36*(1), 94-106.

Burns, G., & Thompson, R. (1987). Music, television, and video: Historical and aesthetic considerations. *Popular Music & Society, 11*(3), 11-25.

Caplan, R. E. (1985). Violent program content in music video. *Journalism Quarterly, 62*, 144-147.

Concerned pediatricians group no fan of rock 'n' roll videos. (1988, November). *Atlanta Journal & Constitution*, p. 4H.

Denisoff, R. S. (1985). Music videos and the rock press. *Popular Music & Society, 10*(1), 59-61.

Dexter, D., Jr. (1969, December). Origin of the species. *Billboard*, pp. 56-58.

Dorfman, R. (1986, January). Never a dull moment on *West 57th*. *Quill*, pp. 8-9.

Ellis, G. J. (1983). Youth in the electronic environment: An introduction. *Youth & Society, 15*, 3-12.

Fornatale, P., & Mills, J. G. (1980). *Radio in the television age*. Woodstock, NY: Overlook.

Frith, S. (1981). *Sound effects*. New York: Pantheon.

Fry, D. L., & Fry, V. H. (1987). Some structural characteristics of music television videos. *The Southern Speech Communication Journal, 52*, 151-164.

Gardner, F. (1983, August). MTV rocks cable. *Marketing and Media Decisions*, pp. 66-68, 113.

Gehr, R. (1983). The MTV aesthetic. *Film Comment, 19*(4), 37, 39, 40.

Gerbner, G. (1973). Cultural indicators: The third voice. In G. Gerbner, L. P. Gross, & M. H. Williams. *Communication technology and social policy—Understanding the new cultural revolution* (pp. 555-573). New York: Wiley.

Greenfield, P. M., Bruzzone, L., Koyamatsu, K., Satuloff, W., Nixon, K., Brodie, M. A., & Kingsdale, D. (1987). What is rock music doing to the minds of our youth? A first experimental look at the effects of rock music lyrics and music videos. *Journal of Early Adolescence, 7*, 315-329.

Gross, L., & Morgan, M. (1985). Television and enculturation. In J. R. Dominick & J. E. Fletcher (Eds.), *Broadcasting research methods* (pp. 221-234). Boston: Allyn & Bacon.

Hall, J. L., Miller, C., & Hanson, J. (1986). Music television: A perceptual study of two age groups. *Popular Music & Society, 10*(4), 17-28.

Hartman, J. K. (1987). I want my AD-TV. *Popular Music & Society, 11*(2), 17-23.

Hirsch, P. (1971). Sociological approaches to the pop music phenomenon. *American Behavioral Scientist, 14*, 371-388.

Kaplan, E. A. (1987). *Rocking around the clock*. New York: Methuen.

Kotarba, J. A., & Wells, L. (1987). Styles of adolescent participation in an all-ages, rock 'n' roll nightclub. *Youth & Society, 18*, 398-417.

Kealy, E. R. (1982). Conventions and the production of the popular music aesthetic. *Journal of Popular Culture, 16*(2), 100-115.

Lake, S. (1981). *Television's impact on children and adolescents: A special interest resource guide in education*. Phoenix: Onyx.

Lansky, K. (1984, July). Psyching out MTV. *Los Angeles Times Calendar*, p. 4.

Larson, R., & Kubey, R. (1983). Television and music: Contrasting media in adolescent life. *Youth & Society, 15*, 13-31.

Leming, J.S. (1987). Rock music and the socialization of moral values in early adolescence. *Youth & Society, 18*, 363-383.

Levine, E. (1983, May). TV rocks with music. *The New York Times Magazine*, pp. 42, 55, 56, 59, 60, 61.

Levy, S. (1983, December). How MTV sells out rock & roll. *Rolling Stone*, pp. 30, 33, 34, 37, 74, 76, 78, 79.

Masters, I. (1987, January). Scanning the picture. *Sound & Vision*, pp. 32-33.

McKenna, K. (1983, August). Videos—Low in art, high in sex & sell. *Los Angeles Times Calendar*, p. 66.

McLuhan, M. (1964). *Understanding media*. New York: McGraw-Hill.

Mooney, H. (1980). Twilight of the age of aquarius? Popular music in the 1970s. *Popular Music & Society, 7*(3), 182-198.

MTV latest to emerge from WASEC's bag of programming tricks. (1981, July 27). *Broadcasting*, p. 105.

New wave television commercials: Agencies go with the flow. (1982, April 19). *Broadcasting*, p. 75.

Paskowski, M. (1985, Spring). Everybody wants their MTV: *Marketing and Media Decisions*, p. 61.

Peterson, R. A., & Davis, R. B. Jr. (1978). The contemporary American radio audience. *Popular Music & Society, 6*(2), 169-183.

Pittman, R. (1985, May). MTV's lesson: We want what we want when we want immediately. *Adweek*, pp. 34, 36.

Powell, S. (1985, October). What entertainers are doing to your kids. *U.S. News & World Report*, p. 46.

Rothenbuhler, E. E. (1985). Programming decision making in popular music radio. *Communication Research, 12*, 209-232.

Rubin, R. B., Rubin, A. M., Perse, E. M., Armstrong, C., McHugh, M., & Faix, N. (1986). Media use and meaning of music video. *Journalism Quarterly, 63*, 353-359.

Shalett, M. (1988, July). Do music videos make dollars and sense? *Radio & Records*, p. 44.

Sherman, B. L., & Dominick, J. R. (1986). Violence and sex in music videos: TV and rock 'n' roll. *Journal of Communication, 36*(1), 79-93.

Snow, R. P. (1987). Youth, rock 'n' roll, and electronic media. *Youth & Society, 18,* 326-343.

Stein, M. L. (1986, May). The MTV generation. *Editor & Publisher,* p. 16.

Thomas, K. L. (1988, December). In tune with the times. *Atlanta Journal,* pp. 1B, 4B.

Thornton, W., & Voigt, L. (1984). Television and delinquency: A neglected dimension of social control. *Youth & Society, 15,* 445-468.

Vincent, R. C., Davis, D. K., & Boruszkowski, L. A. (1987). Sexism on MTV: The portrayal of women in rock videos. *Journalism Quarterly, 64,* 750-755.

Walker, J. R. (1987). How viewing of MTV relates to exposure to other media violence. *Journalism Quarterly, 64,* 756-762.

Ward, E., Stokes, G., & Tucker, K. (1986). *Rock of ages.* New York: Summit.

Waters, H. (1985, October). Being there. *Gentlemen's Quarterly,* pp. 239, 240, 241, 322, 325, 326.

Wolfe, A. S. (1983). Rock on cable: On MTV: Music television, the first video music channel. *Popular Music & Society, 9*(1), 41-50.

Author Index

Page numbers in *italics* indicate complete bibliographic entries.

A

389

Subject Index